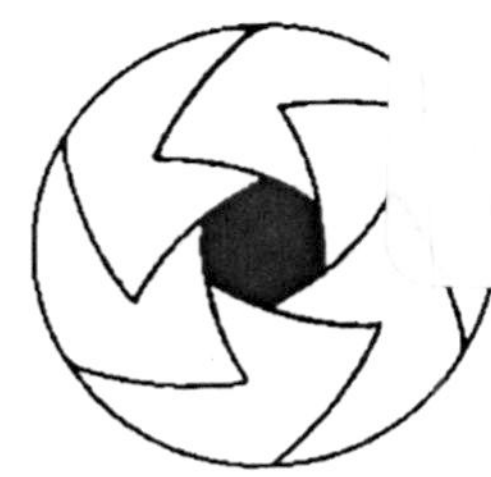

AMERICAN CINEMATOGRAPHER MANUAL

NINTH
EDITION

Volume II

EDITED BY
Stephen H. Burum, ASC

THE ASC PRESS
HOLLYWOOD, CALIFORNIA

American Cinematographer Manual
Ninth Edition — Volume II

Hollywood, California, USA

ISBN 0-935578-32-3

Cover and Book Design by Martha Winterhalter

Production layout by Andrea Stodulski, Mary Lee and Tim Humphrey

Foreword

We must look back over seventy years to find the beginnings of this manual. The great grandfather was called *The Cinematographers Annual.* Two volumes were published before the Great Depression of the 1930s took its toll. These books were a collection of articles and charts written by ASC members and other experts in Hollywood.

In 1935 with the economy becoming better, Jackson J. Rose, ASC continued what had been started by completely reformatting and adding to the basic concept. Calling it *American Cinematographer Hand Book and Reference Guide,* he edited and wrote nine editions published by the American Society of Cinematographers. With his passing, the ASC took over the task, calling it The *American Cinematographer Manual.* The newest format is a cross between the first Annual and The Rose. Invited experts, associate members, and members donate their time to write, edit, and calculate the information in this manual. Hundreds of years of experience and expertise is between the covers of this book. With so many hands in the pie, there are some slip ups. That's why we always ask that our readers forward any questions or comments to us at the ASC, so we can make any corrections for the next edition. Your help over these many years has been an excellent resource.

Information in this manual is accurate to the best of our knowledge. Including or omitting does not signify endorsement or disapproval by the ASC. The ASC is not responsible for mistakes.

Information is based, and/or reviewed by manufacturers or distributors. If you have any questions, a test is always advisable.

A debt of gratitude goes to the authors of the many chapters that make-up this volume. They are: Jim Branch, Richard Crudo, ASC, Dan Curry, Richard Edlund, ASC, Robert L. Eicholz, Jonathan Erland, Jon Fauer, ASC, Bill Feightner, Tom Fraser, William Hansard, Bill Hogan, Michael Hofstein, John Hora, ASC, Rob Hummel, Steve Irwin, Dave Kenig, Jon Kranhouse, Lou Levinson, Dennis Muren, ASC, Iain Neil, Marty Ollstein, Allan Peach, Steven Poster, ASC, Pete Romano, Andy Romanoff, Dr. Rod Ryan, Garrett Smith, Bill Taylor, ASC, Ira Tiffen, Don Ver Ploeg, Petro Vlahos, Evans Wetmore, Michael Whitney and Irwin W. Young. The late Edmund, M. DiGuilio, Linwood G. Dunn, ASC and George E. Turner.

A special thanks to the companies and individuals who provided and checked the information in this edition of the manual. They are:John Gresh at Arri, Denny Clairmont at Clairmont Cameras, Mitch Bagdonowiz, Judy Doherty and Don Henderson at Eastman Kodak, Joe Matza at Efilm, Mark Murphy and Mike Mimaki at Fuji, Steve Altman at Formatt Filters, Joe Tawil at GAM, Frieder Hochhiem at Kino Flo, Sean Hise and Kristin Vitali at Lee Filters, Larry Mole Parker at Mole-Richardson, Otto Nemenz at Otto Nemenz International, Tak Miyagishima and Phil Radin at Panavision, David Pringle at Soft Sun and Stan Miller at Rosco. As well as the diligent proofing team of Russell Alsobrook, ASC, Richard Edlund, ASC, Michael Goi, ASC, David Mullen, ASC, Daryn Okada ASC and Woody Omens, ASC.

Many hard-working staff members have put in many long and frustrating hours. Their dedication goes far beyond the pale. The love and care they lavish on the ninth edition shines through. They are: Douglas Bankston, Rachael Bosley, Delphine Figueras, Marion Gore, Jay Holben, Tim Humphrey, Mary Lee, Sanja Pearce, Stephen Pizzello, Christopher Probst, Andrea Stodulski and Martha Winterhalter.

Stephen H. Burum, ASC is a member of the ASC Board of Governors and chairman of the Publications Committee. Among his credits are the feature films Rumblefish, The Untouchables, Mission Impossible, Mission to Mars *and* Hoffa, *for which he recieved an Academy Award nomination in 1993.*

Note: This 2007 paperback edition of the 9th American Cinematographer Manual has been revised and updated.

Table of Contents

CAMERA SECTION

compiled by Jon Fauer ASC

Information in this section is correct to the best of our knowledge. Including or omitting products does not signify endorsement or disapproval by the ASC. The ASC is not responsible for mistakes.

Listings are based on information supplied by manufacturers or distributors. As always, confirm doubts with film tests. Where possible, we tried to keep categories consistent, and tried to describe each camera with the following specifications:

Notes, Models: Facts, tidbits, iterations and modifications

Weight: English and Metric

Movement: Film transport—single or double pull-down claw, registration pins, adjustable pitch, 4-perforation, 3-perforation

FPS: Frame rate—fwd, reverse, speeds, sync.

Aperture: The "gate" in which each frame of film is exposed. The opening may be fixed or removable. Masks may define additional sizes and cropping. Information here includes format size and position, format masks, in-gate filters and gel slots. Among the aperture sizes are:

Full Silent Aperture (variously called Full Aperture, Super 35, Full Frame, Full Frame Centered for TV, ANSI, Big TV) is .980"x.735" (24.89mm x 18.67mm).

European Silent Aperture is 24mm x 18mm (.945" x .709")

Academy Aperture (sometimes called Standard or Normal 35) is 22mm x 16mm (.868" x .630").

3-Perf Panaflex Camera Aperture is .981" x .546" (style D) per SMPTE 59-1998.

dB: Operating Noise Level as measured by manufacturer, for sound cameras only.

Displays: Indicators/Readout

Lens: Lens Mount—things like PL, Panavision, BNC or bayonet. Also, how the mount is centered: Academy (Standard) or Full Frame Centered for TV (Super35).

Shutter: fixed, variable (change while camera is running) or adjustable (change when camera is stopped). Mirror (reflex) shutter or beamsplitter.

Viewfinder: Eyepieces, finder extenders, levelers

Video: Video Assist

Viewing Screen: Ground glasses, fiber optic viewing screens, rangefinders. In addition to the ones offered by manufacturers, there are many permutations supplied by rental houses and custom suppliers. Note that there are two different SMPTE accepted Super35 sizes: Panavision's is .945" wide x .394" height and ARRI/Clairmont/etc is .925" wide x .394" height.

Mags or Loads: Magazines and/or internal film loading. Core or daylight spools.

Accessories: Mechanical, mounting, matteboxes, rods, lens controls, follow focus, wireless, barneys, covers, and after-market add-ons.

Connections: Electrical and electronic accessories, inputs, outputs and connectors; timecode.

Motors and Power: Power Pin-out, Operating Voltage, Camera Motors, Batteries

Misc: More information

Thanks to the following for additions, suggestions and proofing: Peter Abel, Bill Bennett, Denny Clairmont, Ron Dexter, Dave Kenig, Oli Laperal, Al Mayer, Jr., Tak Miyagishima, Nolan Murdock, George Schmidt, Juergen Schwinzer, Douglas Underdahl.

Credit really should go to all the people who have compiled past editions, upon which this is based.

Aaton 35-3P, 35-III, 35-II

Models: 35-3P (newest, optimized for quiet operation in 3-perf.); 35-III, 35-II (original)

Weight: 16 lbs / 7 kg with 400' (122m) load and 12V DC onboard battery.

Movement: Single pull-down claw which is also the registration pin (steady to 1/2000th of image height). Spring-loaded side pressure guides. Adjustable pitch. 3 or 4 perf.

FPS: 35-3P: Sync speeds: 24, 25, 29.97, 30 fps. Built-in var crystal control to 2 to 40 fps in 0.001 increments.

35-III: 3-32 fps crystal-controlled adjustable in .001 fps increments via mini-jog wheel. 24, 25, 29.97, 30 fps sync speeds. Internal phase shift control for TV bar elimination

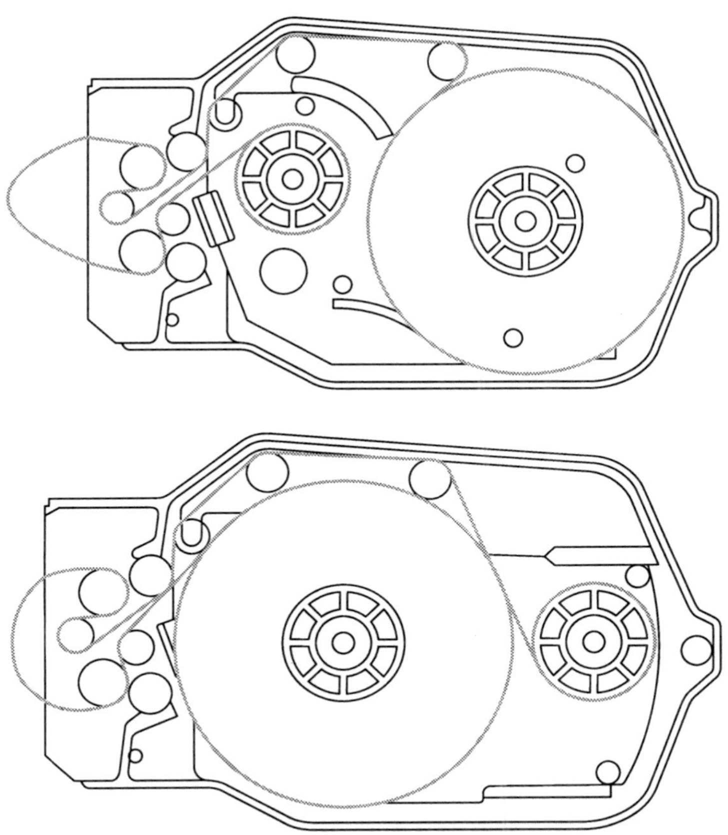

Aaton Magazine Diagrams

Top: Position of film before exposure form 24-25 hole loop by placing a 2" core between front of magazine and film while lacing and make equal top and bottom loops. Bottom: Position of film after exposure. Film takes up emulsion side in.

35-II: 24, 25, and 29.97 or 30 fps. Variable speeds 6-32 fps. Maximum speed with external speed control is 32 fps, with 180° shutter only.

Aperture: 732"x.980" (18.59mm x 24.89mm).

dB: 4-perf 30 dB. 3-perf 30 dB. 26 dB with barney. 35-3P: 3-Perf: 26 dB. 4-Perf: 30/33 dB

Displays: LCD Display, speed selection, remaining footage, ISO selection, battery voltage, time and date, full AatonCode readout via a single rotating jog wheel. Warning for speed discrepancy, misloading and low battery. Camera shut-off is automatic at end of roll.

Lens: Interchangeable Lens Mounts: Arri PL, Panavision, Nikon. User adjustable for Standard or Super 35.

Shutter: Mechanically adjustable mirror using shutter tool: 180°; 172.8°; 150°; 144°.

Viewfinder: Reflex Viewfinder. Eyepiece heater. Optional anamorphic viewing system.

Video: Integrated CCD Color Video Assist: NTSC or PAL; flicker-free at all camera speeds. Also black-and-white model with manual iris. Film camera time code, footage, on/off camera status are inserted in both windows and VITC lines. Built-in frameline generator.

Viewing Screen: Over 16 stock groundglasses; custom markings available. Aatonlite illuminated markings.

Mags: 400' (122m) active displacement mag (core spindles shift left to right) with LCD counter in feet or meters. Mag attaches by clipping onto rear of camera. Uses 2" plastic film cores.

Accessories: 15mm screw-in front rods below lens. 15mm and 19mm bridgeplate compatible. Chrosziel and Arri 4x5 matteboxes and follow focus.

Connections: Inputs: Amph9 (video sync), Lemo6 (power zoom), Lemo8 (phase controllers), Lemo5 (SMPTE and ASCII time code). Time recording with AatonCode II: Man-readable figures and SMPTE time code embedded in rugged dot matrices. 1/2 frame accuracy over 8 hours. Compatible with Film-Video synchronizer and precision speed control.

Power: 12 V DC (operates from 10-15v).

Motor: brushless, draws 1.4A with film at 25°C (77°F) Batteries: on-board 3.0 Ah NiMH and 2.5 Ah NiCd.

ARRICAM Lite

Weight: Body: 8.8 lbs/4 kg. Body+Finder: 11.7 lbs/5.3 kg. Body+Finder+400' (122m) Shoulder Mag: 17.5 lbs/7.95 kg.

Movement: Dual pin registration and dual pull down claws, 4 or 3-Perf, low maintainance 5 link movement with pitch adjustment for optimizing camera quietness.

FPS: Forward 1–40 fps. Reverse 1–32 fps. All speeds crystal and can be set wtih 1/1000th precision

Aperture: Full frame with exchangeable format masks in gate. Gel holder in gate, very close to film plane. Aperture plate and spacer plate removable for cleaning.

dB: Less than 24 dB(A). 3-Perf slightly noisier than 4.

Displays: (on camera left side) Main Display with adjustable brightness red LEDs for FPS, shutter angle, footage exposed, or remaining raw stock. Run/Not Ready LED. Extra display camera left & right (Studio Readout) with Studio viewfinders.

Push-button controls for setting fps, shutter angle, display brightness, electronic inching, phase, footage counter reset.

Lens: 54mm stainless steel PL mount, switchable for Standard or Super 35, with two sets of Lens Data System (LDS) contacts. LDS, when used with Lens Data Box, provides lens data readout as text on video assist or shown on dedicated Lens Data Display. Also simplifies ramps and wired and wireless lens control.

Shutter: 180° mirror shutter, electronically adjustable from 0°–180° in 0.1° increments. Closes fully (0°) for in-camera slating. Tiny motor in shaft controls shutter opening. Ramps range is 11.2°-180°.

Viewfinder: 4 reflex viewfinders fit both cameras: Lite, Universal Lite, Studio, and Universal Studio. Universal Finders can switch between spherical and anamorphic viewing. All swing to either side of camera and have contrast viewing filter, automatic or manual image orientation. Also available are Frameglows, various eyepiece extenders (with optical magnifier for critical focusing), 100 percent video tops, heated eyecup.

Video: ARRICAM Integrated Video System (IVS), color, flicker-free at all camera speeds, mechanical iris and electronic gain for exposure control, with frameline, camera status and lens (LDS) status inserter, image freeze and compare, color balance settings (auto, standard presets or manual), composite or S-VHS outputs. Video capture rate can be synchronized to film shutter for motion blur preview. Studio IVS fits on Studio viewfinders, Lite IVS fits on Lite viewfinders. 2" and 6" flat-panel on-board mini-monitors.

Viewing Screen: Over 60 stock Regular and Super 35 ground glasses. Custom rush ground glass design service via web.

Mags: 400' (122m) Lite Steadicam mag. 400' (122m) Lite shoulder magazine. Both mags are active displacement: they are smaller than standard displacement mags because the feed and take-up cores move left and right to stay out of the way of the film. The mags use torque motors, have mechanical and LCD footage counters, and. ARRICAM 400'(122m) and 1000'(300m) Studio magazines can also be used on the Lite camera with the Studio Mag to Lite Camera Adapter. All mags attach to the rear of the ARRICAM Lite. Accept standard Kodak cores. Wind emulsion IN.

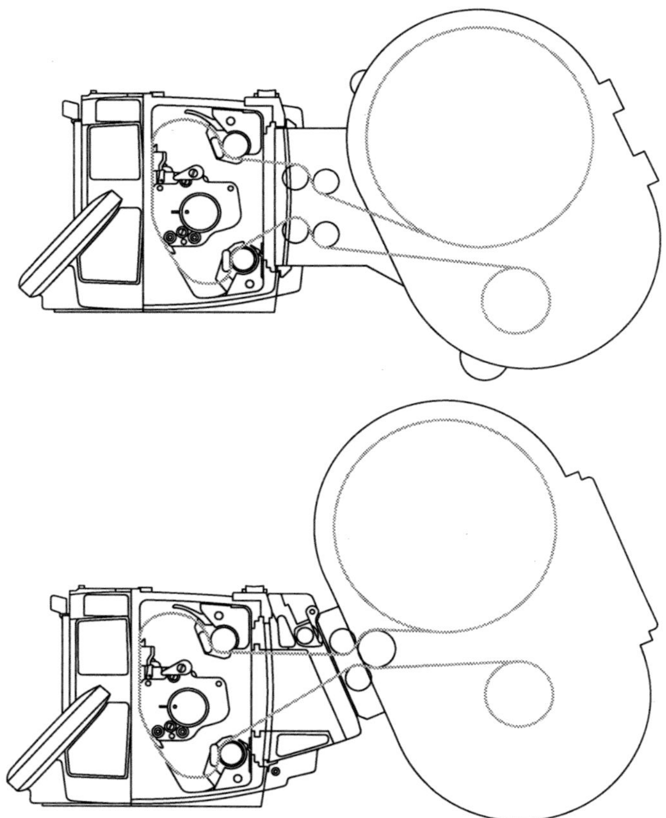

Arricam Lite Threading and Magazine Diagrams
Top: LT shoulder. Bottom: LT/ST magazine. Film takes up emulsion side in.

Accessories: Accepts the whole range of Arriflex matte boxes, 15mm or 19mm rod systems. Steadicam low-mode bracket, Shoulder Set, lens light and power bridge plate. Wired and wireless lens & camera control system, wired and wireless speed/shutter/iris ramping controls. Electronic accessories (see below) attached to Lite via cable or Remote Control Station, LDS Ultra and Variable Primes.

Connections: Speed control box(with built-in sync functions to shoot monitors, displays, rear-projection, etc. and master/slave function for phase accurate multiple camera shoots), Manual Control Box, Lens Data Box, Lens Data Display, In-Camera Slate Box, Timing Shift Box, Accessory Power Box, Remote Control Station.

Power: 24V DC. (operates from 21 to 35 V DC). Two motors for movement and shutter; linked electronically.

ARRICAM Studio

Weight: Body: 12.3 lbs/5.6 kg. Body+Finder: 17.8 lbs /8.1 kg. Body+Finder+400' (122m) Studio Mag: 25.1 lbs / 11.4 kg.

Movement: Low maintainance 5 link movement with dual pin registration and dual pull down claws, 4- or 3-perf, pitch adjustment for optimizing camera quietness.

Fps: 1–40 fps forward, 1-32 fps reverse, all speeds crystal and can be set with 1⁄1000th precision.

Aperture: Full frame with exchangeable format masks in gate. Gel holder in gate, very close to film plane. Aperture plate and spacer plate removable for cleaning.

dB: Less than 20 dB(A).

Displays: (on camera left side) Main Display with adjustable brightness red LEDs for FPS, shutter angle, footage exposed, or remaining raw stock. Run/Not Ready LED. Extra display camera left & right (Studio Readout) with Studio viewfinders.

Push-button controls for setting fps, shutter angle, display brightness, electronic inching, phase, footage counter reset.

Lens: 54mm stainless steel PL mount, switchable for Standard or Super 35, with two sets of Lens Data System (LDS) contacts. LDS, when used with Lens Data Box, provides lens data readout as text on video assist or shown on dedicated Lens Data Display. Also simplifies ramps and wired and wireless lens control.

Shutter: 180° miror shutter, electronically adjustable from 0°-180° in 0.1° increments. Closes fully (0°) for In-Camera Slating. For ramps, range is 11.2°-180°.

Viewfinder: 4 reflex viewfinders fit both cameras: Lite, Universal Lite, Studio, and Universal Studio. Universal finders can switch between spherical and anamorphic viewing. All swing to either side of camera and have a contrast viewing filter, automatic or manual image orientation. Also available are Frameglows, various eyepiece extenders (with an optical magnifier for critical focusing), 100 percent video tops, heated eyecup.

Video: ARRICAM Integrated Video System (IVS), color, flicker-free at all camera speeds, mechanical iris and electronic gain for exposure control, with frameline, camera status and lens (LDS)

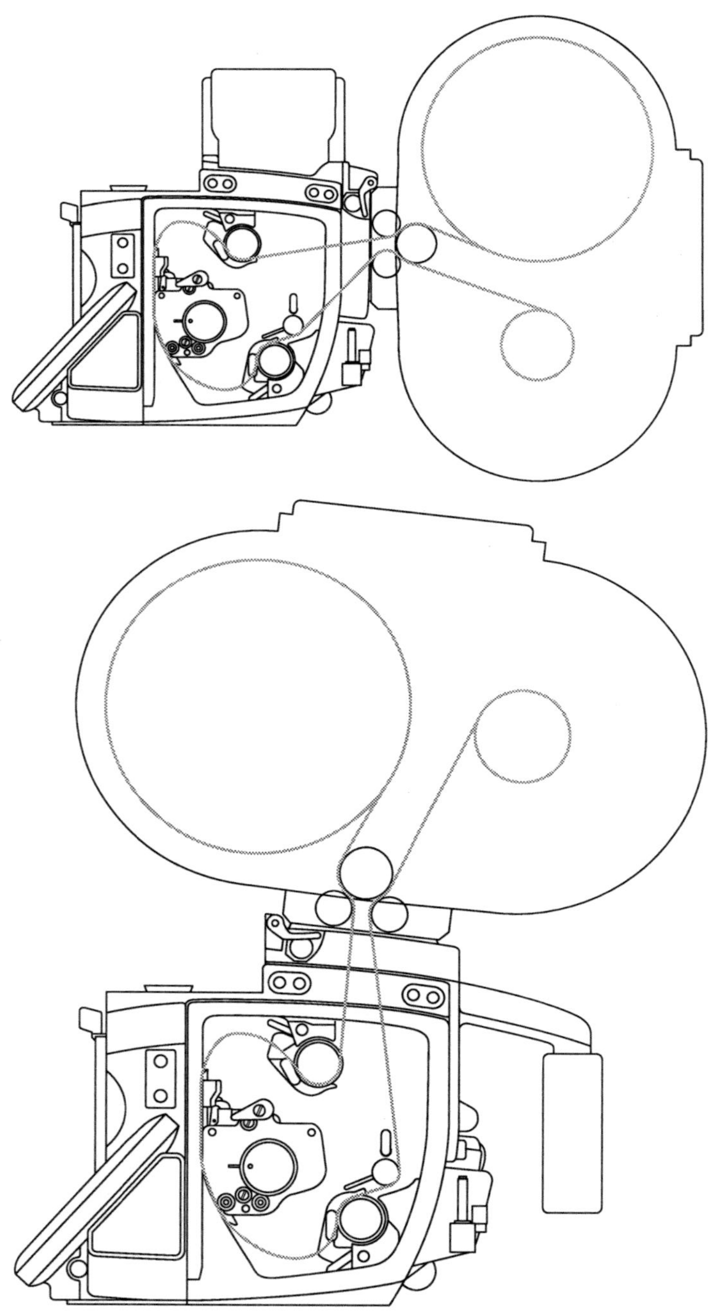

Arricam Studio Threading and Magazine Diagrams
Top: ST back load. Bottom: ST top load. Film takes up emulsion side in.

ARRICAM Cameras Compared		
	Studio	**Light**
Physical	Door hinges at rear Longer, higher 3 accessory covers	Door hinges at front 2 accessory covers
fps	1-60 fps fwd 1-32 fps rev	1-40 fps fwd 1-32 fps rev
Noise Level	Less than 20 dB(A)	Less than 24 dB(A)
Weight	**Body:** 12.3 lbs/ 5.6 kg **Body + Finder:** 17.8 lbs/ 8.1 kg **Body + Finder + 400'(122m) Studio Mag:** 25.1 lbs/ 11.4 kg	**Body:** 8.8 lbs/ 4 kg **Body + Finder:** 11.7 lbs/ 5.3 kg **Body + Finder + 400'(122m) Studio Mag:** 17.5 lbs/ 7.95 kg
Mags	Studio 400' (122m) and Studio 1,000' (300m). Requires Mag Adapter for top, angled or rear mount Accepts Lite mags with Mag Adapter	Lite 400' (122m) Steadicam and Lite400' (122m) Shoulder Accepts Studio mags with Mag adapter

status inserter, image freeze and compare, color balance settings (auto, standard presets or manual), composite or S-VHS outputs. Video capture rate can be synchronized to film shutter for motion blur preview. Studio IVS fits on Studio viewfinders, Lite IVS fits on Lite viewfinders. 2" and 6" flat-panel on-board mini-monitors.

Viewing Screen: Over 60 stock Regular and Super 35 ground glasses. Custom rush ground glass design service via web.

Mags: 400' (122m) and 1,000' (300m) Studio displacement magazines. Both mags use torque motors, have mechanical and LCD footage counters, and are standard displacement.

Lite 400' (122m) Steadicam and Lite 400' (122m) Shoulder Mags can be used with a Lite Mag to Studio Camera Adapter.

Studio Mags attach to the top or rear of the camera with one of three mounts: Top Load Adapter, Dual Port Adapter, or Back Load Adapter. Accept standard Kodak cores. Wind emulsion IN.

Accessories: Accepts the whole range of Arriflex matte boxes, 15mm or 19mm rod systems. Steadicam low-mode bracket, Shoulder Set, lens light and power bridge plate. Wired and wireless lens & camera control system, wired and wireless speed/shutter/iris ramping controls. Electronic accessories (see below) can attached to Studio directly, via cable or Remote Control Station. LDS Ultra and Variable Primes.

Connections: Speed Control Box(with built-in sync functions to shoot monitors, displays, rear-projection, etc. and master/slave function for phase accurate multiple camera shoots), Manual Control Box, Lens Data Box, Lens Data Display, In-Camera Slate Box, Timing Shift Box, Accessory Power Box, Remote Control Station.

Power: 24V DC. (operates from 21 to 35 V DC). Two motors for movement and shutter; linked electronically.

Arriflex 35-2C

Models: Over 17,000 were made, in various iterations; many still in use with numerous modifications—especially conversions from original 3 lens turret to PL mount and updated motors. The 35-2C/B has a three-lens turret, and an interchangeable motor drive system.

Weight: 5.3 lbs/2.5 kg (body only, no motor, PL mount) 12 lbs./5.5 kg (camera w/ 200' (61m)mag, without film and lens.)

Movement: Single pulldown claw with extended dwell-time to ensure accurate film positioning during exposure. Academy aperture is standard, with other formats available.

FPS: The most widely-used motor is the Cinematography Electronics Crystal Base: 1-80 fps in 1 frame increments via push-buttons (1-36 fps with 12 V battery; 1-80 with 2x 12 V batteries). It puts camera at standard lens height for rods.

With ARRI handgrip motors:

20–80 fps with ARRI 32V DC high-speed handgrip motor (over 60 fps may be unsteady or may jam)
24/25 fps with 16V DC governor motor
20–64 fps with 24-28V DC variable speed motor
8–32 fps with 16V DC variable speed motor
Arri Sync Motors (120V)(240V) for Blimps.
(120S, 1000)(50/60 Hz)

Aperture: .866" x .630" (22mm x 16mm).

Displays: Dial tachometer on camera shows fps; footage indicated by analog gauge on magazines.

Lens: Originally made with three-lens turret with three Arri standard mounts (squeeze the tabs, push lens straight in). Later followed by turret with 2 standard mounts and one Arri bayonet mount (insert and twist). Hard-front PL mount modifications widely available.

Shutter: This is the camera that introduced the spinning mirror shutter with reflex viewing. Two segment (butterfly) mirror shutter, mechanically adjustable in 15° increments from 0°-165° when camera not running. Model 2C-BV fixed shutter of 165°. Exposure is 1⁄52nd of a second at 24 fps with a 165-degree shutter.

Viewfinder: 6.5x wide-angle eyepiece. Various camera doors with fixed, video, anamorphic and pivoting finders available.

Viewing Screen: Interchangeable for all aspect ratios.

Video: Aftermarket video assist with Jurgens Video Door among other companies.

Mags: Mags attach on top of camera. Accepts gear-driven, friction take-up, 2C, 35-3 and 435 magazines. 200' (61m) forward operation only, 400' (122m) forward or reverse, 1,000' (300m) not recommended. Mags are displacement and wind emulsion in. Some have collapsible cores. Others use 2" plastic cores .

Accessories: Matte Boxes, Bellows, clip-on, and lightweight versions. periscope finder; finder extender; and flat motor bases to mount on flat surface or inside blimp housing. Sound Blimp: Model 120S for 400' (122m) magazines and model 1000 for 1,000' (300m) magazines. Aftermarket rain covers, splash housings, rain deflectors and underwater housings.

Connections: Cinematography Electronics 2C Crystal Motor Base. Norris intervalometer.

Power: 12, 16, 24, 32 V DC depending on motor.

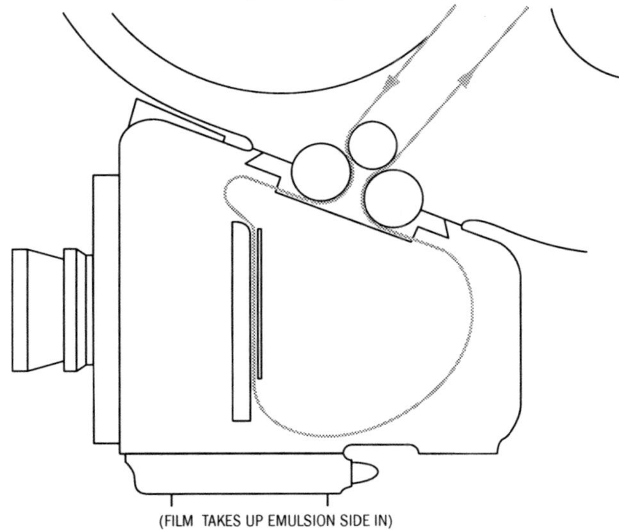

Arriflex 35-2C Threading Diagram

Arriflex 35 II Models

Arriflex 35 II: 1946.

Arriflex 35 IIA: 1953. 180° shutter

Arriflex 35 IIB: 1960. New claw design, fixed 180° shutter

Arriflex 35 II BV: 1960. Variable shutter 0°-165°

Arriflex 35 II HS: 1960 high speed version (to 80fps)

Arriflex 35 II C: 1964. Improved viewing system; larger viewfinder optics to view full frame (anamorphic). Introduction of interchangeable ground glass system. Viewfinder door with de-anamorphoser. Interchangeable eyepieces.

Arriflex 35 II C/B: Three port lens turret with one stainless steel Bayonet mount and two ARRI Standard mounts.

Arriflex 35 II CGS/B: Pilotone output and start marking

Arriflex 35 II CHS/B: High speed model, 80fps maximum, specially prepared movement and 80fps tachometer. Uses 32VDC motor.

Arriflex 35 II CT/B: Techniscope™ format model. Uses 2-perf pulldown and half-height gate for wide-screen aspect ratio of 2.35:1 with normal (not anamorphic) lenses, reducing film use by half.

ARRI 35IIC Medical Camera: 1964. Medical version of the 35-II used to shoot black & white 35mm film of moving X-Ray images (used to diagnose heart problems, for example). Medical cameras are usually gray, beige or light green. No lens turret; no viewfinder system. Sometimes equipped with ARRI standard lens mounts.

ARRITECHNO: 1970. Medical camera mounts to X-Ray. No viewfinder or lens mount. Quick-change magazines snap on like a 16SR. These cameras require major modification to use for cinematography.

(courtesy of Jorge Diaz-Amador, Cinetechnic; Larry Barton, Cinematography Electronics)

Arriflex / SL-35 Mark III

Notes: A super lightweight camera for Steadicam, remote mounting, underwater and sports. Uses an Arri Medical 2C modified in a lightweight magnesium and delrin plastic body with custom camera electronics for Steadicam, handheld and rigging. Uses Arri 2C doors; 35-3 groundglasses; Super35 gate. Stops with mirror in viewing position

Weight: 5.7 lbs/2.6kg without magazine.

Movement: Re-manufactured Medical 2C high speed

FPS: 1–80 fps, forward and reverse; extra 50Hz speeds 33.333 and 16.666.

Aperture: Full aperture. Aperture Plate: Non-removable.

Power: Quartz-controlled DC motor, 24V; 5 pin #0 Lemo connector; camera on/off toggle and remote.

Displays: Red LED digital tach; red LED feet/meters igital footage/meters; red LED with reset and memory.

Lens: PL mount Standard or Super35, Panavision and Panavision Super 35.

Shutter: 165º reflex mirror shutter.

Viewfinder: Works with Arri eyepiece and extender; also works with Jurgens door.

Video: Video only doors and finder/video doors

Viewing Screen: uses 35-3 groundglasses. Super35 holder for Super35 groundglass.

Mags: Accepts Arri 2-C and 35-3 style magazines. SL Cine makes lightweight magnesium low-profile (extended horizontal) and Steadicam (vertical) mags in 200' (61m)and 400' (122m) loads—to fit Arriflex 435, III series (35-3), II series (2-C) and SL-35 cameras.

Accessories: Low mode mount for Steadicam. Uses many existing 2C type accessories such as external speed controls, Arri- or Jurgens-2C doors and, with SL Cine lightweight riser, standard matte boxes and focus iris controls.

Connections: Two 11-pin Fisher connectors on back: 8.5 amp output at 12V DC. 2- 24V Lemo connectors on front. Fischer 3-pin combi video and 12V power out; 5-pin Fischer remote on/off 12V.

Dimensions of body: 6"L x 5.5"H x 6"W

Arriflex 35-3C

Notes: A single PL mount evolution of the 2C design. About two dozen made.

Weight: 5.8 lbs. / 2.6 kg. (body only) 11.7 lbs. / 5.3 kg. (body, handgrip, 200' (61m) mag; no lens or film) 13.5 lbs./ 6.1 kg (body, handgrip, 400' (122m) mag, no lens or film.)

Movement: Same as 2C: single pin pulldown claw with extended dwell-time to ensure accurate film positioning during exposure.

FPS: 24/25 fps crystal; 5–50 fps variable.

Aperture: .862" x .630" (22mm x 16mm).

Lens: 54mm diameter PL mount. Arri bayonet and standard mount lenses (41mm diameter) can be used with PL adapter. Flange focal distance of 52mm stays the same.) All zoom and telephoto lenses should be used with a special 3-C bridge plate support system.

Shutter: Like the 2C, spinning reflex mirror shutter, adjustable from 0°–165° in 15-degree increments while camera is stopped. Exposure is 1⁄52nd of a second at 24 fps with a 165-degree shutter.

Viewfinder: Three doors: fixed viewfinder, offset for handheld, pivoting finder. Three choices for fixed viewfinder door: regular, anamorphic and video tap. 6.5x super-wide-angle eyepiece.

Viewing Screen: 2C groundglasses.

Video: On fixed door.

Mags: Uses 2C, 35-3 and 435 mags. Some have collapsible cores. Others use 2" plastic cores .

Accessories: 2C, 35-3 and 435 accessories.

Power: Power input through a 4-pin connector. Pin 1 is negative; Pin 4 is +12 V DC.

Arriflex / SL 35 Mark II

Notes: Earlier lightweight model, uses 2C groundglasses

Weight: 5.3 lbs/2.4kg without magazine.

Movement: Re-manufactured Arriflex Medical 2C

FPS: 1–80 fps, forward and reverse; extra 50Hz speeds 33.333 and 16.666.

Aperture: .862" x .630" (22mm x 16mm). Full aperture. Aperture Plate: Non-removable.

Power: Quartz-controlled DC motor, 24V; 3 pin #1 Lemo B connector; camera on/off toggle and remote.

Displays: Digital footage/meters; red LED with reset and memory.

Arriflex 35-3

Models: 3 generations of 35-3

Weight: 14.8 lbs./ 6.71 kg camera with 400' (122m) magazine (without film and lens).

Movement: One registration pin and dual-pin pulldown claw. Film channel incorporates a pressure pad at the back of aperture area. 3-perf available. Camera can run in reverse.

FPS: Quartz-controlled sync at 24/25/30 fps, 50/60Hz. An onboard variable-speed dial may be used to adjust camera speed from 4–50 fps at 12V DC. The camera is continuously variable from 4–100 fps (130 fps on the 35-3 130 fps camera) at 24V DC with a variable speed unit.

Aperture: .862 " x .630" (22mm x 16mm) full aperture, custom sizes available. Aperture Plate Removable for cleaning.

Motors, Power: 12/24V DC motor. Operating temperature range is -13°F to +122°F (-25°C to +50°C).

Displays: An electronic tachometer and footage counter. An external red LED located below the counter indicates when a low memory battery condition exists. A red LED to indicate an out-of-sync condition and a green LED to indicate variable speed mode are visible in the viewfinder.

Lens: 54mm diameter PL mount. Flange focal distance is 52mm. Super Speed and Standard lenses with PL mount, those with Arri Bayonet (41mm diameter) and Arri Standard lens mounts with PL adapter may be used. After-market Nikon mounts.

Shutter: Rotating mirror shutter—three generations: 1st generation: 180° fixed shutter; 2nd generation: 180°, 172.8°, 144° and 135°; 3rd generation: 15°-135° in 15° increments, 144°, 172.8°, 180°

2nd and 3rd generations are mechanically adjustable with 2mm hex driver.

Viewfinder: Reflex Viewfinder: Four interchangeable doors with viewfinders are available: standard door with fixed viewfinder and mount for video tap; offset finder door for use with 400' (122m) coaxial shoulder magazine; pivoting finder door, pivots 210°; new pivoting finder door with optical adapter to attach video camera. All have adjustable super-wide-angle eyepiece with manual iris closure. Finder extenders available are 9" standard, 9" anamorphic, and 12.2" standard with ND.6 contrast viewing glass.

Video: Arri pivoting video door, Jurgens, Denz, P&S, JC&C, Boltersdorf, and other aftermarket video doors as well as CEI, Phillips and Sony taps.

Viewing Screen: Ground glasses for all aspect ratios are easily interchangeable.

Mags: Displacement type. 2C, 3C and 435 400' (122m) mags will fit. Top-mounted 200' (61m), 400' (122m), and 1,000' (300m) mags; 400' (122m) low profile, coaxial shoulder magazine for

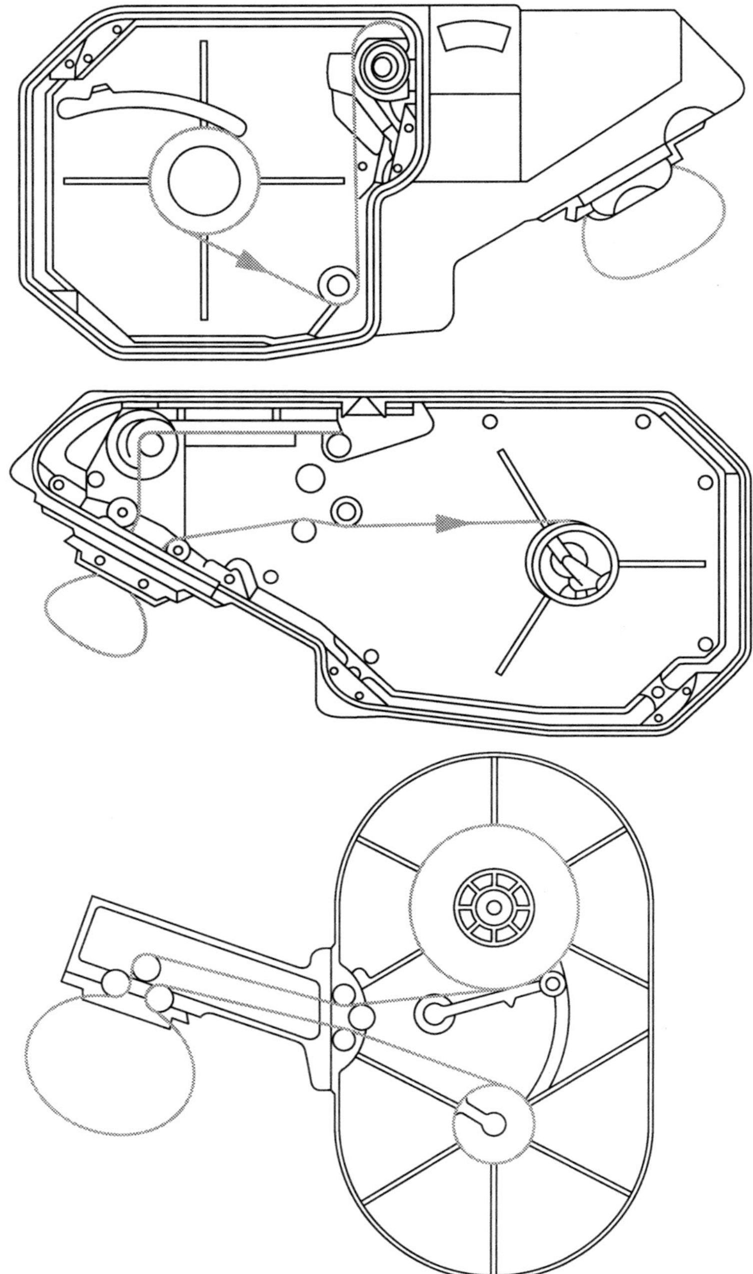

Arriflex 35-3 Shoulder and Steadicam Magazines
Top: Shoulder magazine, feed side. Center: Shoulder magazine, take-up side.
Bottom: Steadicam magazine. Film takes up emulsion side in.

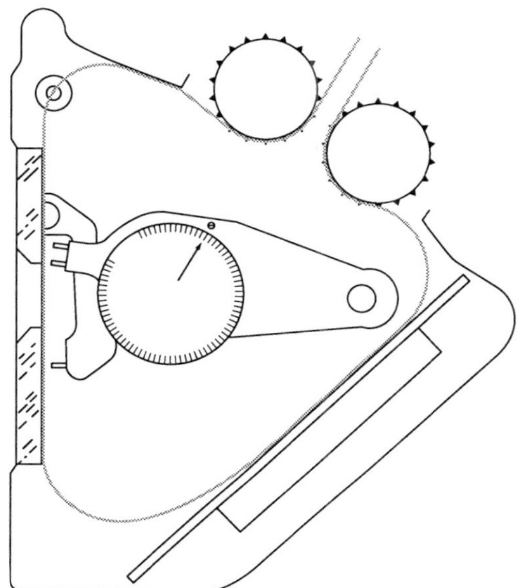

Arriflex 35-3 High Speed MOS Threading Diagram
Film takes up emulsion side in.

handholding. Aftermarket Steadicam mags available.

Cores: Collapsible cores on some. May require a 2" plastic core on other mags.

Accessories: external speed control

Connections: The 50/60Hz EXB-2 External Sync Control may be used to interlock the 35-3 with a video source, projector or another camera. A 4-pin power connector is located in the rear of the electronics housing. Pin 1 is (-); Pin 4 is 12V (+). Cinematography Electronics Precision Speed Control I and II, accessory block w/lens light, film/video synchronizing control, and 35-3 crystal high-speed control, intervalometer. Norris intervalometer, Preston's Speed Aperture Computer.

Power: 12V DC. Two batteries for high speed.

Arriflex 235

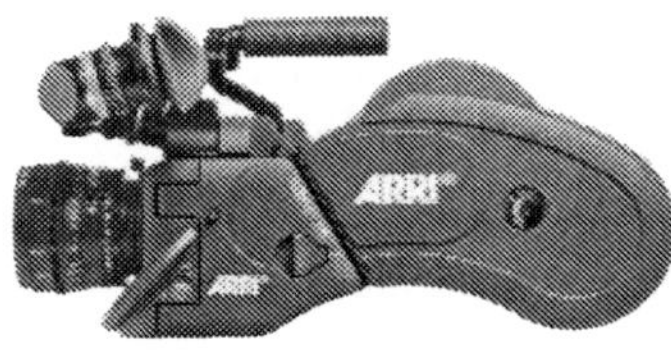

Notes: Small, lightweight MOS camera for handheld, rigs, underwater and crash housings. About half the weight and size of a 435.

Weight: 3.5 kg/7.7 lbs. (body, viewfinder and eyepiece, without magazine)

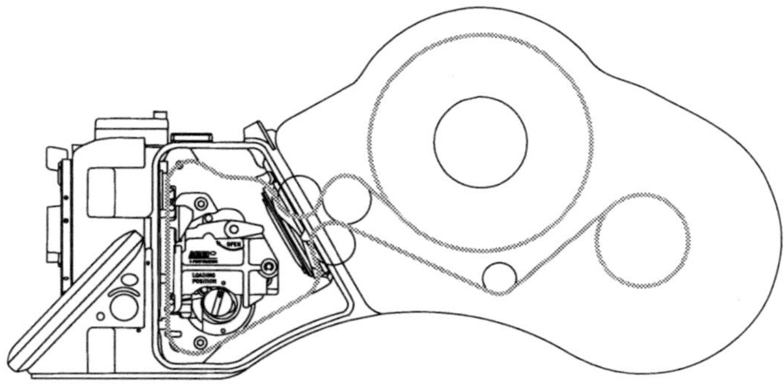

Arriflex 235 Threading Diagram
Film takes up emulsion side in.

Movement: Single pull down claw with two prongs; single registration pin. Registration pin in optical printer position (like 435). Camera available with 3- or 4-perf movements.

Frame Rate: 1–60 fps forward. 23.976, 24, 25, 29.97, 30 fps reverse (quartz accurate to .001 fps.).

Aperture: Super 35 (24.9 x 18.7 mm) 0.98" x 0.74", same as ARRICAM ANSI S35 Silent 1.33 format mask). Fixed gap film gate.

Display: Operating buttons with an adjustable backlight

Lens: 54mm PL mount, adjustable for Normal or Super 35. Flange focal depth 51.98mm -0.01.

Shutter: Spinning, manually-adjustable reflex mirror shutter. Mechanically adjustable with a 2mm hex driver at: 11.2°, 22.5°, 30°, 45°, 60°, 75°, 90°, 105°, 120°, 135°, 144°, 150°, 172.8° and 180°.

Viewfinder: Reflex viewfinder, can be rotated and extended like the 435. Automatic or manual image orientation in the viewfinder. Viewfinder and video assist are independent of each other, so switching to Steadicam or remote operation is done by simply removing the finder, leaving video assist on board. No need for a 100% video top. Optional medium finder extender.

Video: IVS color Integrated Video System

Viewing Screen: Interchangeable, uses 435 groundglasses.

Mags: New 200' (60m) shoulder magazine. Uses all existing 200' (60m) and 400' (122m) 2C, 3C, 35-3 and 435 displacement mags. Winds emulsion in. Cannot use 1000' (300m) magazines.

Connections: Power, mini monitor, remote accessory, 2x RS Remote Start. Uses most ARRI electronic accessories: RCU, WRC, ICU, ESU

Power: 24V DC (runs from 21 to 35 V DC)

Misc.: Extra attachment points for rigging, reversible camera handle, extra low mode handle.

Arriflex 435, 435 ES, 435 Advanced, 435 Extreme

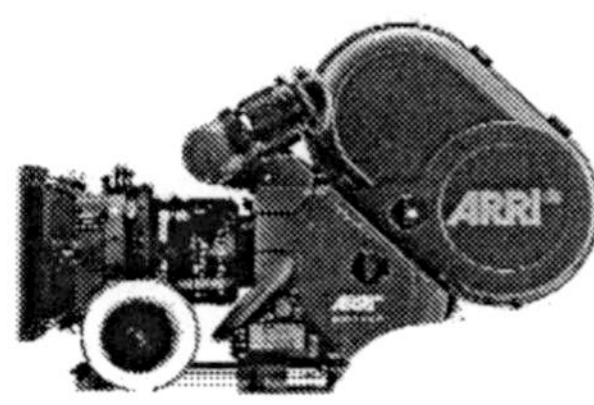

Weight: 14.3 lbs/6.5kg without magazine.

Models: Usually called 435, it is probably the 435 ES model, (ES=Electronic Shutter). The basic 435 uses a mechanically adjustable shutter, but only a handful have been made. The newest model is the 435 Advanced, which has a more powerful shutter motor to enable shutter ramps 2.5 times faster. The Advanced does time lapse, motion control, the LCD is easier to read, LDS lens data contacts are built in. Extreme has many updated electronics.

Movement: Dual-pin registration conforming to optical printer standards, and dual pulldown claws. Can be replaced with a 3-perforation movement. Adjustable pitch control.

Frame Rate: 1–150 fps, forward or reverse (quartz accurate to .001 fps.).

435 Advanced Model: 0.1-150fps (1/10 fps-150 fps)

Aperture: Interchangeable masks with full range of aspect ratios. Aperture Plate removable for cleaning.

Power: Quartz-controlled DC motors.

Display: Fps, forward and reverse run, film counter in feet and meters, shutter angle, time code (user bit and TC sensitivity). Warnings include incorrect movement position, asynchronous film speed, low battery voltage and film end.

Lens: 54mm PL mount, adjustable for Normal or Super 35.

Shutter: Spinning, adjustable reflex mirror shutter. The 435ES (Electronic Shutter) can be adjusted continuously from 11.2°–180° while camera is running. The plain 435 (non-ES) reflex mirror shutter is mechanically adjustable with a 2mm hex driver at: 11.2°, 15°, 22.5°, 30°, 45°, 60°, 75°, 90°, 105°, 120°, 135°, 144°, 172.8° and 180°. Both 435ES and 435 Advanced have these mechanical shutter angles as well; be sure not to activate electronic shutter at same time.

Viewfinder: Reflex Viewfinder, the standard finder, which covers full aperture (Super 35), pivots to either side of the camera, with an adjustment knob to orient the image upright in any position. Adjustable in-out for left- or right-eyed viewing. ND.6 contrast

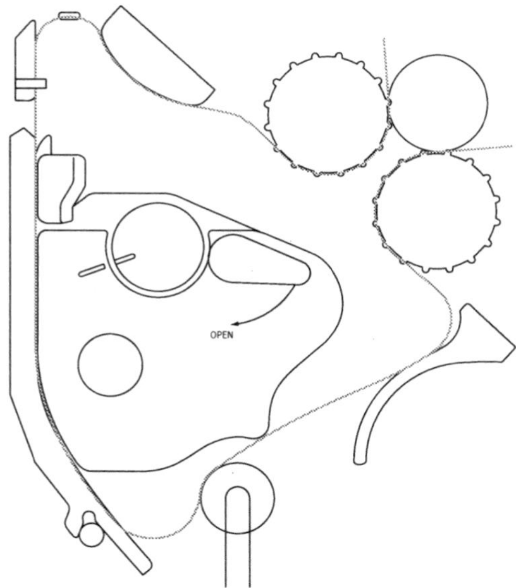

Arriflex 435 Threading Diagram
Film takes up emulsion side in.

filter flips in. The 435 uses 535 extension finders, eyepieces, ground glasses, field lenses and gate masks. An optional anamorphic viewfinder is also available for de-squeezing anamorphic lenses.

An optical tap with interchangeable beamsplitter ratio is integrated into the standard viewfinder, enabling the adaptation of the ½" video camera CCD-2. The entire viewfinder module can be removed and replaced with a lightweight 100 percent video tap for Steadicam or remote filming.

Video: 435 Integrated Video System (IVS), color, flicker-free at all camera speeds, mechanical iris and electronic gain for exposure control, with frameline and camera status inserter, image freeze and compare, color balance settings (auto & standard presets), composite or S-VHS outputs. Video capture rate can by synchronized to film shutter for motion blur preview. IVS2 has additional features: ablility to turn flicker free off, manual color balancing, enhanced data display, etc.

Very early 435 cameras had a C mount for ½" CCD camera.

Viewing Screen: Interchangeable. ARRIGLOW.

Mags: Displacement, winds emulsion in. Uses all 2C, 3C, 35-3, as well as 435 magazines. Top-mounted 400' (122m) and 1000' (300m) magazine (435) 1000' (300m) mag torque motor driven). Also, a 400'(122m) Steadicam mag. Arri 35-3 and older magazines can be used but without time code.

Accessories: Accepts the whole range of Arriflex matte boxes, 15mm or 19mm rod systems. Steadicam low-mode bracket, Shoulder Set, lens light. Wired and wireless lens & camera control system, wired and wireless speed/shutter/iris ramping controls. Single frame system, motion control interfaces. For 435 Advanced: LDS Ultra and Variable Primes.

Connections: 24V DC, 3/5 amps and 12V, 3/5 amps. Most camera functions can be controlled via the remote control unit (RCU-1) or Wireless Remote Control (WRC-1).

Electronic Sync Unit (ESU) provides synchronization with an external PAL or NTSC video signal (50/60Hz), another camera or a projector, or computer or video monitor via a monitor pick-up. It also contains a phase shifter, pilt tone generator, and selectable division ratio between an external source and the camera's frame rate.

Power: 28 to 30V "nominal" V DC . The camera will start and run at speeds up to 129 fps as long as the battery voltage does not drop below 20.6 volts, high speed running at speeds of 130 fps through 150 fps requires that the camera voltage remain above 24 volts during camera startup. 35V is the absolute maximum, above which, the camera will not start.

Arriflex 535

Notes: The 535 came first, followed by the lighter 535B. There is no 535A—just the 535. Main difference is the viewfinder: the 535B is simpler and lighter. 535 has electronically controlled mirror shutter; 535B shutter is manual. 535 has 3-position beam-splitter.

Weight: Body only 21.6 lbs / 9.82 kg.. body+finder 29.4 lbs/14.19 kg., body+finder+mag (no film or lens) 36.4 lbs /16.55 kg.

Movement: dual-pin registration conforming to optical printer standards, and dual pulldown claws. Can be replaced with a 3-perforation movement. Adjustable pitch control.

FPS: Quartz controlled 24/25/29.97/30 fps onboard; and 3-50 fps with external control such as Remote Unit (RU) or Variable Speed Unit (VSU). With external control, does speed changes while camera is running, and runs at 24/25 fps in reverse. Pushing the Phase Button runs camera at 1 fps — but precise exposure not ensured at 1 fps.

Aperture: Universal aperture plate with interchangeable format masks provides full range of aspect ratios. Has a behind-the-lens gel filter holder. Gels are positioned very close to image plane, so they must be scrupulously clean and free of dust. Gate is easily removed for cleaning.

dB: 19 dB.

Displays: In-finder displays use LEDs to allow the operator to monitor various camera functions, battery status, and programmable film-end warning. Digital LCD Tachometer and Footage Displays: camera left/right; audible and visible out-of-sync warning; visible film jam; film end; error codes; improper movement position; improper magazine mounting; disengaged rear film guide indicators.

Lens: PL lens mount, 54mm diameter, with relocatable optical center for easy conversion to Super 35. Flange focal distance is 52mm.

Shutter: Microprocessor-controlled variable mirror shutter (535 only; the B is manual). Continuously adjustable from 11°–180° while running, in .01° increments, at any camera speed. The Arriflex 535 permits shutter angle changes while running at the camera or remotely. The 535's program also permits simultaneous frame rate/shutter angle effects, such as programmed speed changes with precise exposure compensation.

Viewfinder: Swing-over viewfinder enables viewing from either camera left or camera right, with constant image correction side to side and upright. A selectable Beam Splitter provides 80% viewfinder-20% video; 50-50 or video only. Programmable Arriglow for low-light filming. Nine pre-programmed illuminated formats, an optional customized format module, and fiber-optic focus screens. Switchable ND.3 and ND.6 contrast viewing glasses, a variety of in-finder information LEDs, and a 12"-15" variable finder.

Viewing Screen: Ground glasses and fiber-optic focus screens for all aspect ratios.

Video: Video Optics Module (VOM): provides flicker reduction and iris control.

Mags: Rear-mounted 400' (122m) and 1,000' (300m) coaxial, each with two microprocessor-controlled torque motors. Feed and take-up tension and all other functions are continuously adjusted by microprocessors. Mechanical and digital LCD footage counters built in.

Accessories: Variable Speed Unit (VSU) can attach to the 535 and permits camera speed changes between 3 and 50 fps, non-crystal.

Shutter Control Unit (SCU): mounts directly to the camera and permits camera shutter angle changes between 11° and 180° (535 only).

Remote Unit (RU): operational remotely from up to 60', provides a VSU/SCU (variable shutter/variable speed) combination. The RU links the SCU and VSU to permit manual adjustment of the frame rate while the 535's microprocessor varies the shutter angle — all to ensure a constant depth of field and exposure.

SMPTE time code module plugs in to utilize onboard time code generator, and provides full SMPTE 80-bit time code capability.

Electronic Sync Unit (ESU): Operational remotely from up to 60'; provides synchronization with an external PAL or NTSC video signal (50/60Hz), another camera or a projector, or computer or video monitor via a monitor pick-up. It also contains a phase shifter, pilotone generator, and selectable division ratio between an external source and the camera's frame rate.

Camera Control Unit (CCU): provides integrated control over all electronic functions. External Sync Unit is designed for multi-camera, video or projector interlock.

Laptop Camera Controller is software to control the camera via a serial cable.

Power: 24VDC. 3-pin XLR connector: Pin 1 is (-), and Pin 2 is +24V.

Arriflex 535 B

Notes: 535B is lighter than the 535.

Fps: same as 535—runs at crystal-controlled speeds from 3–60 fps. Has a manually adjustable mirror shutter, variable from 11° to 180° in 15-degree steps, and 144° and 172.8°. The 535B has a lightweight swing-over viewfinder. The entire finder is easily removed without tools and accepts a 100 percent video module for Steadicam use.

Weight: Body only 17 lbs / 7.7 kg.; body+finder 22 lbs/10 kg.; body+finder+lightweight 400' (122m) mag; (no film or lens) 27.8 lbs /12.6 kg.

Movement: Same as 535. Same adjustable pitch control.

FPS: Crystal controlled onboard 24/25/29.97/30 fps forward and reverse ; and 3-60 fps with external control such as remote unit

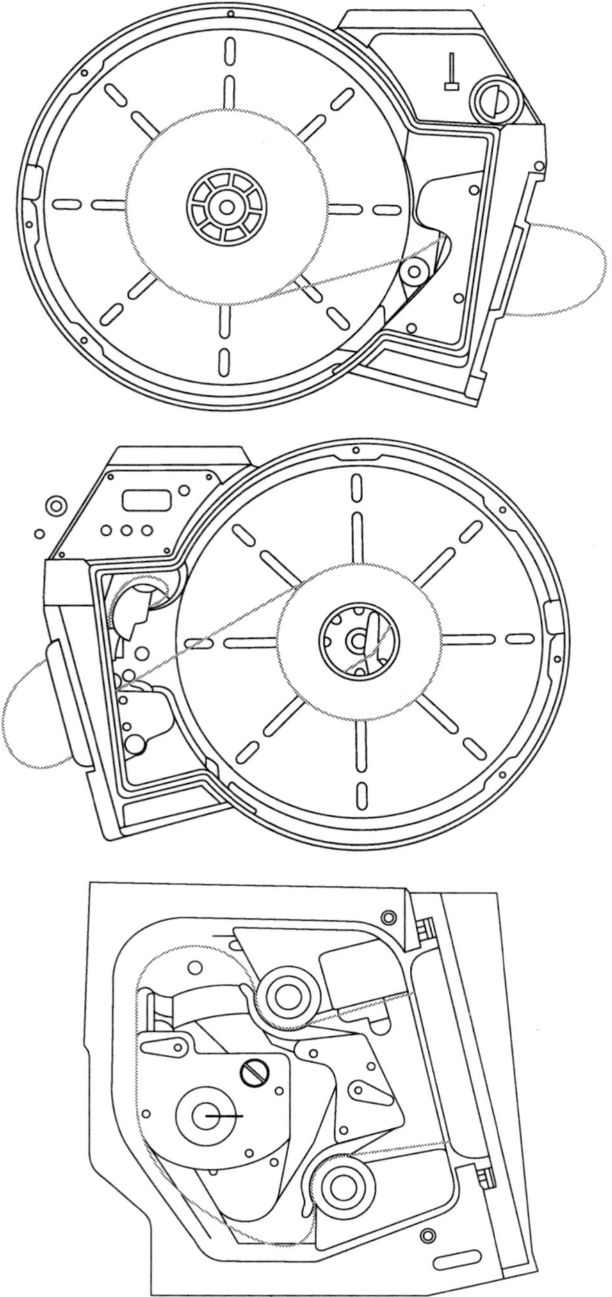

Arriflex 535 and 535B Magazine and Threading Diagrams
Top: Magazine supply side. Center Magazine take-up side.
Bottom: Threading diagram. Film takes up emulsion side in.

(RU) or Variable Speed Unit (VSU).

Aperture: Same as 535—Universal aperture plate with interchangeable format masks. Behind-the-lens gel filter holder.

dB: 19 dB.

Displays: LEDs in viewfinder displays ASY (out of sync), BAT (low battery), END (out of film). Digital LCD Tachometer and Footage Displays: camera left/right; audible and visible out-of-sync warning; visible film jam; film end; error codes; improper movement position; improper magazine mounting; disengaged rear film guide indicators.

Lens: PL lens mount, 54mm diameter, converts from Standard to Super35.

Shutter: Mechanically adjustable from 15° -180° in 15° increments, along with 144° and 172.8° while camera is stopped

Viewfinder: Finder block with swing-over viewfinder enables viewing from either camera left or camera right, with constant image correction side to side and upright. Choice of Beam Splitters: 80% viewfinder-20% video or 50-50. Programmable Arriglow for low-light filming. Nine pre-programmed illuminated formats, an optional customized format module, and fiber-optic focus screens. ND.6 contrast viewing glass, a variety of in-finder information LEDs, and a 12"-15" variable finder. 535B finder block fits on 535. variously called a 535 A/B, 535B+ or 535A-.

Viewing Screens: Same as 535

Video: Video Optics Module (VOM): provides flicker reduction and iris control. Video only top or video only.

Mags: Same as 535. A lightweight displacement 400' (122m) mag was made for the 535B—it will fit the 535 as well.

Power and Accessories are same as 535.

535B threads the same as 535.

Arriflex 35BL

Notes: The Arriflex 35BL was conceived in 1966 as the first portable, dual pin registered, hand-held, silent reflex motion picture camera. Its first significant production use was at the 1972 Olympic Games, where it was employed for sync-sound, cinéma vérité and slow motion filming at speeds to 100 fps. At the same time, its theatrical and television use began, especially for location work.

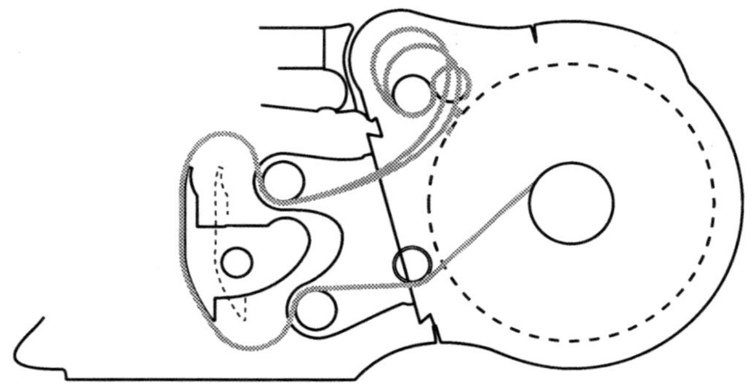

Arriflex BL-4s Threading and Magzine Diagram
Film takes up emulsion side in.

The camera evolved. The analog footage and frame rate indicators of the 35BL-1 were replaced by a digital read-out on the 35BL-2. With the 35BL-3, the lens blimp was eliminated. The Arri 41mm bayonet mount was soon replaced by the larger 54mm diameter PL lens mount.

The 35BL-4 introduced a brighter eyepiece and illuminated groundglass. The 35BL-4s came out with a new, quieter, adjustable-pitch multi-link compensating movement, new footage/meters counter, redesigned internal construction, and magazines with an external timing adjustment.

Movement: Industry standard dual pin registration. Two double pronged pull-down claws on early 35BL-1 cameras for high speed to 100 fps with special magazine roller arms. Two single prong pull-down claws on all other 35BL cameras.

35BL-4s movement has an adjustable pitch control.

Aperture: .862" x .630" (22mm x 16mm), custom sizes available. Aperture Plate is removable for cleaning.

35BL-3, 4 and 4s gates will fit 35BL-1 and 2 cameras, but not vice versa.

Displays: LED digital fps and footage readout on camera left. Audible out-of-sync warning. A red LED near the footage counter indicates low footage, memory, battery. BL-1 has mechanical readout.

Lens: 54mm diameter PL mount. Newer cameras switch from Normal to Super35.

Early 35BL cameras had Arri bayonet mount. Some cameras were converted to BNC mount.

35BL-2 and BL-1 cameras require lens blimps for silent operation.

Shutter: Rotating mirror shutter. See table.

Arriflex 35BL Camera Models				
Camera	**Shutter Angles**	**Frame Rate**	**dB**	**Weight***
35BL-4s	180° 172.8° 144°	24, 25, 30 6 - 40	20	14.5 kg (31.9 lbs)
35BL-4	180°, 172.8°, 144°	24, 25 6 - 40	22	14 kg (30.9 lbs)
35BL-3	180°, 172.8° 144°	24, 35 6 - 42	22	13 kg (28 lbs)
35BL-2	180°	24, 25 5 - 50	26	12.5 kg (28 lbs)
35BL-1	180°	24, 25 5 - 100	26	12.5 kg (28 lbs)
*Weight with 400' mag, no lens, no film				

Dimensions of 35BL-4s, and 35BL4			
with 400' (120m) mag	**L** 17.3" **L** 440mm	**W** 12" **W** 305mm	**H** 9.1" **H** 230mm
with 100' (300m) mag	**L** 21.5" **L** 546mm	**W** 12" **W** 305mm	**H** 12.5" **H** 317mm
Dimensions of 35BL-1, 2, and 3: same length and height. Width is 11" (280mm).			

Viewfinder: Reflex Viewfinder. 35BL-4s and BL-4 viewfinders are a stop brighter than earlier 35BL cameras and feature a larger exit pupil. The finder rotates 90° above and 90° below level with the image upright. Super Wide Angle eyepiece with manual leaf closure and 6.5x magnification standard on 35BL-4s and BL-4 cameras. Adjustable eyecup allows the operator to select the optimum eye-to-exit pupil distance. Finder extenders available for the 35BL-4s and 35BL-4 include a 12.5" standard with switchable contrast viewing filter, and variable magnification up to 2x. For the 35BL-3, 35BL-2 and 35BL-1: 9" standard and 9" anamorphic finder extenders.

Video: Video elbow with Arri and aftermarket video taps from CEI, Jurgens, Denz, Philips, Sony and many others.

Viewing Screens: pullout with Hirschmann forceps to clean and interchange. ArriGlow illuminated frame lines.

Mags: 400' (122m) and 1,000' (300m) coaxial. The 35BL can be handheld with either magazine. Mechanical footage counters are integral.

Accessories: Sound Barney and heated barney.

Connections: Electronic Accessories: Multi-camera interlock is achieved with the EXS-2 50/60Hz External Sync Unit. SMPTE time code available for later models.

Motors, Power: 12V DC. Power input through a 4-pin XLR connector on camera. Pin 1 is (-); Pin 4 is +12V. Although most of the industry settled on 4 pin connectors on both ends, some cables have 5-pin XLR male connectors on the battery end.

Arri Accessories

Arri accessories common to most cameras with flat bases—(many 2C cameras still have with handgrip motors, not flat bottoms):

Rods: There are two diameters of lens support/accessory rods in use: 15mm and 19mm. The 19mm rods are centered below the lens; 15mm rods are off-center.

Environmental Protection Equipment: Aftermarket rain covers, splash housings, rain deflectors and underwater housings available.

Camera Support Equipment: arrihead; arrihead 2 (newer, lighter, smaller). arrimotion (small & lightweight moco).

Lens Controls: Arri FF2 or FF3 follow focus. Preston Microforce or Arri LCS/wireless lens control. Lens Control: Arri FF3 follow focus. Preston Microforce zoom control. Iris gears available for remote iris.

Arri Matte Boxes

Matte Boxes :

MB-16 (4 x 4 Studio): two 4" x 4" filters and one 4½" round filter (maximum of four 4" x 4" and one 4½" round). Swing-away mechanism for fast lens changes. Can be equipped with top and side eyebrows.

MB-17B (4 x 4 LW): A lightweight matte box holding two 4" x 4" filters and one 4½" round filter. Swing-away mechanism; can easily be adapted to 15mm or 19mm support rods via the BA bracket adapters. It can also be used on the SR lightweight rods. It can be equipped with a top eyebrow.

MB-16A (4 x 5.6 Studio): A studio matte box holding two 4" x 5.650" filters and one 4½" round filter (maximum of four 4" x 5.6" and one 4½" round). Swing-away mechanism. Can be equipped with top and side eyebrows.

MB-18 (4 x 5.6 Studio): A studio matte box holding three 4" x 5.650" filters and one 138mm filter (maximum of four 4" x 5.650"

Arri Accessories		
Accessory	**19mm Rod Size**	**15mm Rod Size**
Camera Baseplate	BP-8	BP-9
Lens support	LS-7, LS-9	LS-8, LS-10
FF-4 Follow Focus	BA-2	BA-3
Mattebox	mounting adapters	mounting adapters
Baseplates for a new generation of Arriflex cameras		
Camera	**19mm Rods**	**15mm Rods**
235, 435	BP-8	BP-9
535, 535B	BP-5	BP-3
16 SR3	BP6	BP-7
New Baseplates for new accessories on old cameras If you want to use new style matteboxes. lens supports, and accessories with older cameras.		
Camera	**19mm Rods**	**15mm Rods**
35 BL1, 2, 3, 4, 4s	BP-5	BP-3
35-3	BP-5	BP-3
16SR1, 16SR2	BP-6	BP-7
Old Baseplates for old accessories on old cameras If you want to use older style accessories with older cameras.		
Camera	**Baseplate**	
35 BL1, 2, 3, 4, 4s	BP-3	
35-3	BP-3	
16SR1, 16SR2	SR1	

and one 138mm). Swing-away mechanism for fast lens changes. Can be equipped with top and side eyebrows. Covers Super 16mm.

MB-19 (4 x 5.6 LW): A lightweight matte box holding two 4" x 5.650" filters and one 138mm or 4½" round filter (maximum of three 4" x 5.650" and one 138mm or 4½" round). Swing away mechanism for fast lens changes and can easily be adapted to 15mm or 19mm support rods via the BA bracket adapters. Can also be used on SR lightweight rods. Can be equipped with top and side eyebrows. Covers Super 16mm.

MB-15 (5 x 6 Studio): A studio matte box holding two 5" x 6" filters and one 6", 138mm or 4½" round filter. A rotating stage can be attached, adding two 4" x 4" filters. Swing-away mechanism for fast lens changes. Can be equipped with top and side eyebrows. Covers fixed lenses 14mm and up, as well as most zooms. Geared filter frame.

MB-14 (6.6x6.6 Studio): A studio matte box holding four 6.6" x 6.6" filters and one 6", 138mm or 4½" round filter (maximum of six 6.6"

Arri Fuses (electronics/motor)	
Camera	**Fuse**
35-2B/C	4 A 5 x 20mm motor circut
35-3C	¾ A pico / 10 A pico
35-3 1st, 2nd gen	¾ A pico / 15 A pico
35-3 3rd gen	¾ A pico / 15 A pico
35-3 BNC Mount	¾ A pico / 15 A pico
235, 435, ES, Adv	Polyfuse
35 BL-1, 2	¾ A radial micro / 15 A pico
35 BL-3, 4, 4s	1 A pico / 15 A pico 3 A pico accessories (4s only) ½ A pico Arriglow (4, 4s only)
35 BL BNC Mount	¾ A pico / 15 A pico
535 A, 535 B	2.5 pico / 15 A pico
Arricam ST, LT	Polyfuse
765	2 A blade type - electronics 15 A blade type - movement 20 A blade type - shutter 2 A blade type - accessories

Part numbers for Arri Fuses					
Pico		**Pico**		**Micro Fuse**	
1/4A	05.07953.0	3A	05.07956.0	3/4A	05.07962.0
1/2A	05.07954.0	5A	05.07957.0	**5 x 20mm**	
3/4A	05.07955.0	7A	05.07985.0	4A	05.07984.0
1A	ZELE-MISC-14	10A	05.07958.0		
2.5A	ZELE-MISC-34	15A	05.07959.0		

x 6.6" and one 6", 138mm or 4½" round). The four 6.6" x 6.6" filter trays are grouped in two stages with two filter trays each. The two stages can be rotated independently of each other, and each stage contains one filter tray with a geared moving mechanism allowing for very precise setting of grad filters. Swing-away mechanism. Can be equipped with top and side eyebrows.

6.6 x 6.6 Production Matte Box: Covers lenses 12mm and up, as well as most zooms. Interchangeable two, four or six filter stages, rotatable 360°, swing-away for changing lenses. Geared filter frames.

MB-14W: same as MB-14, but with a wider front piece for 9.8mm lenses or longer.

MB-14C: same as MB-14, but with a shorter front piece for close-up lenses.

Arriflex Cameras: Flange Focal Distance Chart		
Camera Lens	**Mount to Filmgate (mm)**	**Lens Mount to Groundglass (mm)**
35-2B/C	51.970 to 51.980	52.000
35.3C	51.970 to 51.980	52.000
35-3 1st, 2nd gen.	51.990 to 52.000	52.000
35-3 3rd gen	51.980 to 51.990	52.000
35-3 BNC Mount	61.450 to 61.460	61.470
235	51.98 to 0.01	52.000
435, ES, Adv., Extm.	51.970 to 51.980	52.000
35 BL-1, 2	51.970 to 51.980	52.000
35 BL3, 4, 4s	51.970 to 51.980	52.000
35 BL BNC-Mount	61.450 to 61.460	61.470
535A, 535B	51.970 to 51.980	52.000
Arricam ST, LT	51.970 to 51.980	52.000
765	73.500 to 73.500	73.500

LMB-3 (4x4 clip-on): A very lightweight matte box that clips to the front of 87mm or 80mm lenses, holding two 4"x4" filters. When using prime lenses with a 80mm front diameter (most Arri/Zeiss prime lenses), a Series 9 filter can be added with an adapter ring. Shade part can be easily removed from the filter stages if only the filter stages are needed. Can be used for 16mm prime lenses 8mm–180mm and 35mm prime lenses 16mm–180mm. It also attaches to the 16mm Vario-Sonar 10–100mm or 11–110mm zoom lens.

LMB-5 (4 x 5.650 clip-on): A matte box that clips onto the front of the lens, holding two 4"x5.6" filters. Can be attached to lens front using clamp adapters of the following diameters: 80mm, 87mm, 95mm and 114mm. Can be equipped with a top eyebrow.

LMB-4 (6.6 x 6.6 clip-on): A matte box that clips onto the front of the lens, holding two 6.6"x6.6" filters. Can be used on 156mm front diameter lenses (like the Zeiss T2.1/10mm) or, with an adapter, on 144mm front diameter lenses (like the Zeiss T2.1/12mm).

Additional Accessories: Bridge plate support system for CG balance and mount for matte box, follow focus, servo zoom drive, and heavy lenses; handheld rig for shoulder operation of the camera.

Many good aftermarket matteboxes and accessories from Chrosziel, Cinetech and many others.

Bell & Howell 35mm Eyemo Model 71

Eyemo K

Eyemo Q

Notes, Models: "Beats the Other Fellow to the Pictures" (from original 1926 ad)

71 M—Compact 3 lens turret
71 Q—wide " Spider" three-lens turret.
71 K—single Eyemo mount.

Weight: 11 lbs/ 4.9 Kg, size: 4" x 6" x 8"

Movement: No registration pins. Pulldown claw on soundtrack side only. Cam-operated single claw. Spring loaded edge guide and pressure plate.

FPS: 8, 12, 16, 24, 32, 48 fps. Governor controlled

Aperture: Full, Academy centered or full centered. Filter slot behind lens

Displays: Read out/indicators dial on side for 100' body. Veeder root counter, for Q with magazines.

Lens: Eyemo Bell & Howell Mount, many conversions to Nikon, PL, Panavison and Canon.

Shutter: 160°. Replacement shutters of different degrees available.

Viewfinder: Non Reflex Viewfinder: External with parallex correction and matching objective lenses. Reflex shift over plate for Q model only with full frame viewing and focusing. Taking lens rotate 180° to reflex eye piece.

Loads: 100' (30.5m) daylight spools.

Motors, Power: Spring wind-up, 55' (16.8M) per wind. 6V DC, 12V DC, 24V DC, 110V AC.

Mags: 200' (61m) 400' (122m) Some models don't except magazines.

Misc: Reprinted Instructions Manuals at www.photobooks online.com/books/manual23.html

Bell & Howell 35mm
Steve's Cine Service Conversion

Movement: No registration pins. Pulldown claw on soundtrack side only.

FPS: 4–50 fps.

Aperture: Full: optically centered or full centered

Displays: LED footage and fps.

Lens: Nikon, PL, Panavison and Canon mounts. Since this is often used as a "crash" camera, be sure your lenses are expendable. That's why Nikon or Canon still lenses are often used. Some of Steve's conversions have a neutral mount, with adapters for various mounts.

Shutter: 160°. Replacement shutters of different degrees available.

Viewfinder: Reflex Viewfinder: Cube beamsplitter reflex system (-½ stop loss due to cube beamsplitter and 160° shutter). Viewing optics use Arriflex eyepieces. Other models have parallax finders (not reflex).

Video: Black-and-white CCD.

Viewing Screen: Arri III type. All Academy and Super 35 formats.

Loads: Uses 100' (30.5m) daylight spools in camera body.

Accessories: Remote start cables, Crash housing, underwater housings and Clairmont Camera fire housings.

Motors, Power: 12V DC only

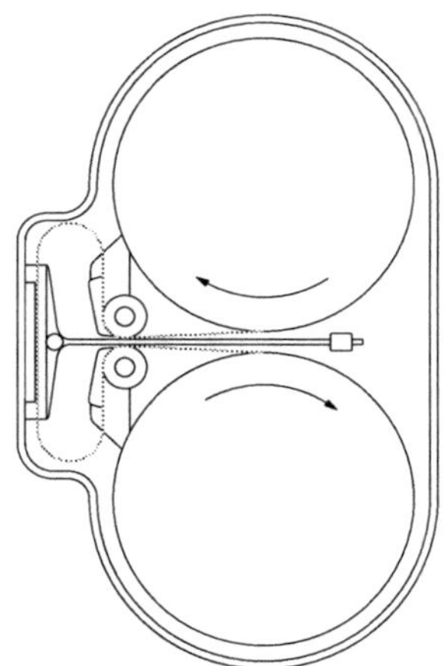

Bell & Howell 35mm Eyemo Threading Diagram
Film takes up emulsion side in. (Daylight load only.)

Cinema Products FX 35

Weight: 28.5 lbs./12.9 kg with 400' (122m) mag, no film.

Movement: Dual-pin pulldown, dual-pin registration in Mitchell position. Adjustable stroke length and entry position. Exit and entry buckle trips. Forward and reverse operation.

FPS: Crystal controlled 1–120 fps in 0.01 fps steps. (Requires 24 to 32V over 64 fps).

Aperture: .980" x .735" (24.89mm x 18.67mm) standard aperture with provision for hard mattes.

Displays: Digital footage counter to two decimal points. Audible/visible out-of-sync indicator. Display module over viewfinder swivels for operator or assistant -- showing speed, footage, frame, camera mode, battery voltage, current and low-battery alarm.

Lens: BNCR standard, PL optional; anamorphic locating pin. Optional adapter for Arri standard or bayonet-mounted lenses.

Shutter: Butterfly reflex with focal plane cup. Adjustable 180°, 172.8°, 144°, 90°, 45°, 0°. Stops in viewing position. Internal phasing control to sync with video monitors.

Viewfinder: Reflex, erect, orientable image. Precision register pins for matte alignment. Three viewing filters. 360-degree adjustable

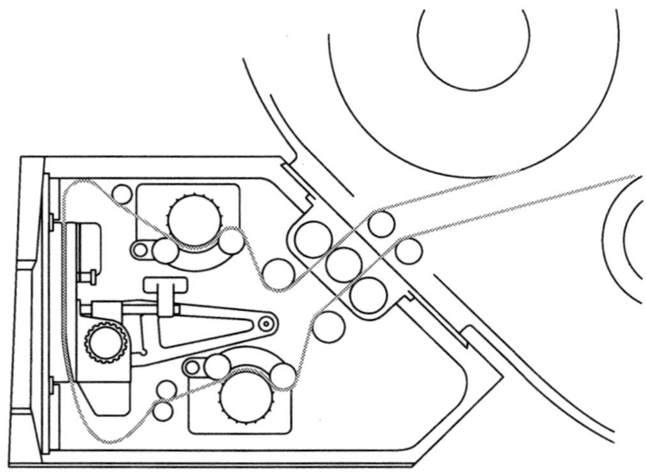

Cinema Products FX 35 Threading Diagram
Film takes up emulsion side in.

eye piece. Viewfinder exposure meter. Eyepiece extender.

Video: Video Assist available.

Viewing Screen: Interchangeable viewing screens.

Mags: FX 35 QUAD (quick acting displacement) 400' (122m) forward/reverse, 1,000' (300m) forward only. Single latch cover, footage indicator, anti-spill brake, easily cleaned light trap. Adapter for Mitchell magazines. Magazine Loading: Double chamber.

Power: 12V to 32V DC. 24V DC to 64 fps. 32V DC to 120 fps.

Accessories: Time code, computer interface module. Can be run from personal computer. Feedback: status information, alarms. Shutter and digital shaft coder quadrature and all control functions.

Cinema Products XR35 Lightweight Studio Camera

Weight: 93 lbs./42kg body only.

Movement: Standard Mitchell pin-registered; Cinema Products independent adjustment of stroke length and entry position. Timing marks for reassembly after cleaning. Inching knob.

FPS: Crystal-controlled motor continuously variable 4–32 fps. Pushbutton for sync speed, selector switch for 24 or 25 fps.

Aperture: 35mm full .980" x .735" (24.89mm x 18.67mm). Removable aperture plate with built-in matte slide for various formats.

dB: 26 dB 3' in front of lens.

Displays: FPS indicator and control knob. Visible/audible out-of-sync warning. Circuit breaker, power indicator, running indicator lights. Illuminated level, lens light and interior threading lights. LED footage counter in feet or meters.

Lens: BNCR with anamorphic locating pin.

Shutter: focal plane, continuously variable 5°–180°. Control and lock on rear panel.

Viewfinder: Reflex, rotating mirror stops in viewing position. Standard or de-anamorphic optics. High-low magnification relay lens. Large eyepiece with diopter adjustment lock. Contrast viewing filter.

Video: Optional.

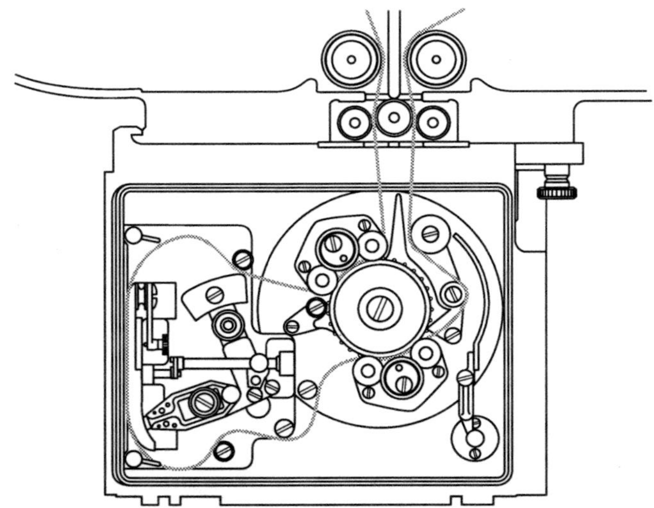

Cinema Products XR 35 Threading Diagram
Film takes up emulsion side out.

Viewing Screen: Interchangeable screens.

Mags: 1,000' (300m) QUAD (quick acting displacement), steel toe plate, velvet rollers, snap latch mounting, single latch cover. Footage indicator, anti-spill brake. Magazines are installed on the camera through a "clamshell" opening in the blimp housing, which provides maximum access without requiring side or headroom clearance.

Film Cores: 2" plastic.

Accessories: Six-station filter wheels accepting standard gelatin filters. Built-in carrying handles. Viewfinder mattes available.

Built-in focus control system with right and left side knobs, magnetic calibration discs, brake, auxiliary drive mounted on front housing.

Power: 30V DC.

Eclair CM-3 16/35mm

Notes: Darling camera of the new wave.

Movement: Easily converts from 35mm to 16mm with two sets of ratchet-type pulldown claws: one on each side for 35mm and a single, smaller claw for 16mm. Adjusting the claw stroke adapts camera to either normal 4-perf pulldown or 2-perf pulldown for Techniscope, or single-perf pulldown for 16mm operation.

Pulldown claws mounted on sliding cam-driven plate, which is reached through opening in aperture plate. No disassembly or special tools required. Registration and steadiness achieved by double rear pressure plate and very long side rails. Top plate keeps film flat in focal plane, bottom plate holds film at edges only to keep it properly aligned for pulldown claws.

FPS: 50 fps maximum.

Aperture: Optically centered and Academy centered on some models. Aperture plate made of one piece of steel, hand-polished and undercut to prevent scratching. Aperture plate is part of camera body proper, pressure plates are built into magazine. Raised area in center of aperture portion of pressure plate eliminates breathing. Sliding mattes for film aperture and viewfinder for 16mm. Techniscope or other widescreen ratios. Gel filter behind the lens.

Displays: Built-in tachometer.

Lens: Three-lens divergent cam-lock turret with Camerette CA-1 lens mounts. CA-1 lens mount is large-diameter brass bayonet-type. Divergent turret permits mounting 5.7mm focal length and longest telephoto lenses without optical or physical interference.

Shutter: 200° variable front-surfaced mirror reflex shutter; may be varied to 35° by turning knob on left side of camera body.

Viewfinder: Reflex, 360° rotating eyepiece for right or left eye. Adjustable mattes for various aspect ratios.

Viewing Screen: Fixed. Various markings available.

Mags: Quick change (snap-on) 200' (61m) and 400' (122m) displacement type mags. Fixed loop (which may be set from outside at any time). Automatic footage counter. Removal of magazine allows inspection and cleaning of aperture plate and film channel. For Techniscope operation, T-Type magazine operates at either 45' per minute or 90' per minute by merely changing gears. Plastic film cores.

Accessories: Dovetail adapter to mount to tripod has twin matte box rods. Mattebox with two 3" x 3" filter stages, one rotatable and removable, for use with extra-wide-angle lenses.

Sound Blimp has one door to allow sliding camera out on rails for instant magazine change and automatically connects follow focus, lens diaphragm and external eyepiece. Camera may be used with all anamorphic and zoom lenses, in or out of blimp. Full instrumentation capabilities available with single-frame pulse and intervalometer operation.

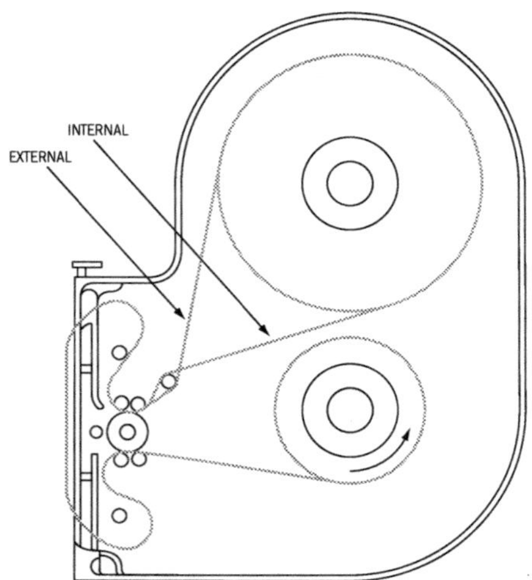

Eclair CM3 400ft Magazine
Film takes up emulsion side out

Aquaflex underwater housing for 35mm Techniscope and 16mm.

Lightweight magnesium tripod. Entire tripod bowl and movements can be lifted from legs and clamped to table edges, doors, ladders, etc.

Motors, Power: Motors mounted on side of camera can be changed in a few seconds.

Basic motor: 6-8V DC rheostat-controlled variable-speed type (also available for 24V power).

Other motors: 6, 12 and 24V DC transistor-controlled regulated motors with variable-speed or constant-speed operation with 50 or 60Hz sync pulse outputs, crystal plus variable also. Stops in viewing position. 115V 60Hz and 220V three-phase, 60 Hz AC motors for synchronous sound shooting.

Hand-crank drive also available for 1, 8 or 16 pictures per turn.

Fries 435

Weight: 26 lbs./11.8 kg body only.

Movement: Mitchell movement

FPS: 2–150 fps. in one-frame increments, crystal controlled.

Aperture: .980" x .735" (24.89mm x 18.67mm), removable aperture plate: Displays: Panel

Lens: BNCR, Panavision, Arri PL mounts

Shutter: Spinning mirror reflex with 170° shutter.

Viewfinder: A light valve allows the operator to direct all the light to the viewfinder, the video-assist, or combo which splits between the two.

Mags: 400' (122m) and 1,000' (300m) displacement

Motors, Power: 30V DC. Equipped with take-up and supply torque motors.

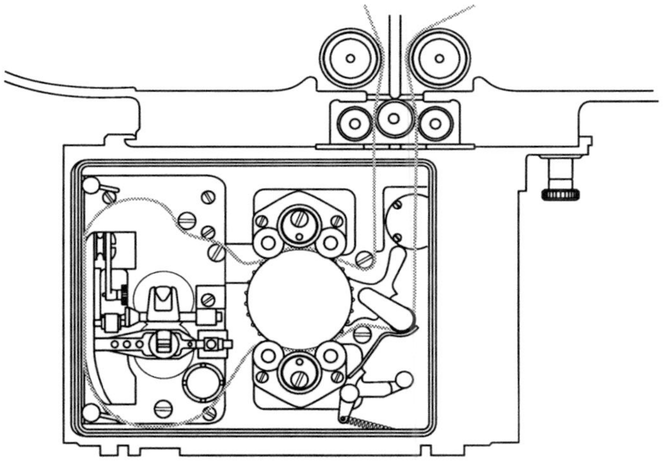

Fries 435 Threading Diagram
Film takes up emulsion side out.

IMAGE 300 35mm

Movement: 6 pulldown claws; 2 register pins in Mitchell position. Frame-to-frame register 0.0005" (0.01270mm) or better.

FPS: 10 pushbutton actuated speeds, 24-300 fps.

Aperture: Full (silent) aperture.

Displays: Sync pulse for strobe light, sync at all operating speeds. Footage counter with memory.

Lens: BNCR mount.

Shutter: Beryllium rotating two-blade 120° mirror.

Viewfinder: upright image, interchangeable ground glasses, variable magnification, light trap prevents accidental fogging.

Video: Video tap available

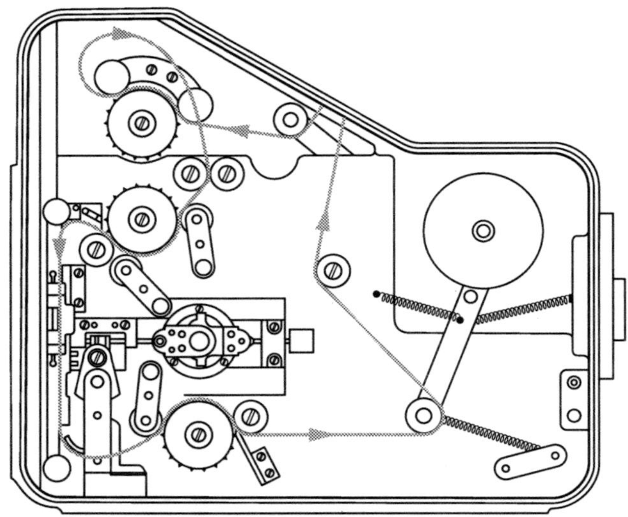

Image 300 Threading Diagram
Film takes up emulsion side in.

Mags: Coaxial, displacement. 1,000' (300m) feed and take-up magazines are identical and separately mounted; take-up can be removed without removing the feed magazine. Gear driven, differentially controlled. Automatic drive engagement and supply overrun brake. Footage-used counter for acetate or polyester base. 2" plastic film cores.

Accessories: Matte box iris rods compatible with Arriflex.

Connections: Remote-control input jack.

Motors, Power: Built-in motor and circuitry; maximum speed in three seconds. Self-braking; will stop in five feet from 300 fps. Requires 115V AC, 50/60Hz, 30A starting, 18A running.

Mitchell NC, NCR, BNC, BNCR

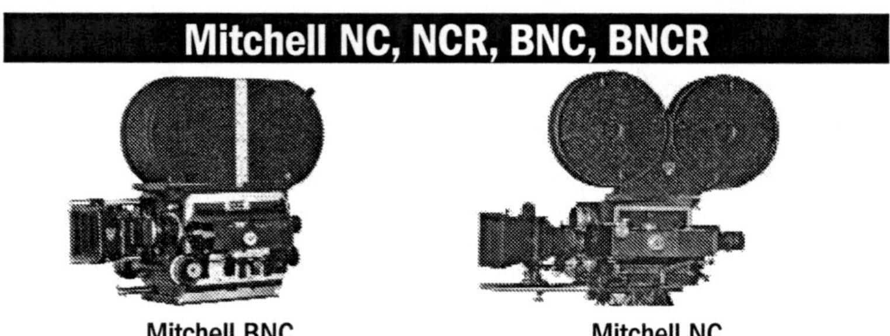

Mitchell BNC

Mitchell NC

Weight: BNC 122 lbs/55.4 Kg; NC 70.5 lbs/32.1 Kg

Notes, Models: The NC camera differs from the "standard" model in that it uses a mechanically different and quieter movement. NC,

BNC are rack-over models. NCR, BNCR are reflex models. NC model has a four-lens turret, the others a single lens mount. B models are blimped versions. Numerous modifications and after-market conversions.

Movement: Dual register pins, four-prong pulldown; adjustable stroke. Timing marks on shutter and movement facilitate removal and reassembly.

FPS: Single frame to 32 fps.

Aperture: 35mm full .980"x.735" (24.89mm x 18.67mm) aperture. Removable aperture plate with built-in matte slot. Slot for dual gel filters.

Displays: Mechanical. Footage, frame, shutter position.

Lens: Four-lens turret, NC only; flange depth 1.695" (43.05mm). Single mount all others: 35mm flange depth 2.420" (61.47mm). Lenses can be centered on full or Academy aperture. Mitchell lens control system.

Shutter: Focal plane 175° maximum, variable to 0° in 10-degree increments. Phase and opening indicator on back of camera. Some models have automatic 4' fade in or out.

Viewfinder: NCR & BNCR. Rotating mirror, beam splitter prism or pellicle. Viewing tube same on rackover and reflex, variable magnification, film clip/matte slot, contrast viewing filters. Adjustable focusing eyepiece.

On non-reflex models — external large screen erecting finder with parallax correction coupled by camera-to-lens focus knob, reducing and enlarging adapter lenses.

Viewing Screen: Interchangeable.

Mags: 400' (122m), 1,000' (300m), 1,200' (366m) double compartment sound insulated. NC magazines will not fit standard camera, but standard magazines may be used on NC models with adapter; not recommended for sound shooting. Plastic film cores (that come with film) on feed side, collapsible and removable on take-up side.

Accessories: Film matte punch, Director's finder which takes camera lenses, Norris intervalometer for the BNC. Wide angle and normal matte boxes with rotating and slide diffusion, filters, and matte stages (2" x 2") (3" x 3") and 4" x 4" on wide angle matte box only.

Motors, Power: Detachable motors. Synchronous motors are sound insulated. Crystal sync 30V DC with 50/60Hz signal, mirror

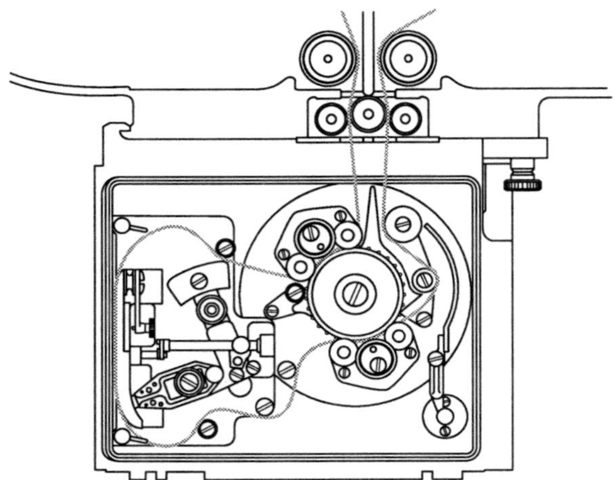

Mitchell NC, NCR, BNC, BNCR 35mm (FC, BFC 65mm) Threading Diagram
Film takes up emulsion side out.

positioning circuit and audible offspeed indicator. Power requirements vary with motor.

220V AC-3 phase interlocking (sync).
96V DC/220V AC 3 phase multi duty.
110V AC/DC variable speed 8-24 fps.
110V AC single phase sync.

Misc: these cameras have been heavily modified over the years from "basic" models. Some BNCs were turned into process projectors.

Mitchell 35 Standard & High-Speed Cameras

Notes: Cameras are similar except for clearances and silencing. Lens board and base contain tracks and pinion on which camera body racks over for focusing and critical lineup. There are several versions of modifications available from sources other than Mitchell for special applications.

Movement: High-Speed movements has dual registration pins, dual forked pulldown claws engaging four perforations simultaneously. Standard movement cannot be used for high-speed work. Not possible to convert standard to high-speed camera by interchanging movements.

FPS: Single frame to 120 fps (160 fps can be achieved but is not recommended).

Aperture: Full Aperture: .980" x .735" (24.89mm x 18.67mm). Academy aperture mask: 868"x631" (22.04mm x 16.02mm). Removable aperture plate with built-in matte. Behind the lens gel filter slot

Displays: Mechanical. Footage, frames, speed.

Lens: Four-lens turret. Positive index type, with rising and falling front. Mitchell-designed, heavy-duty, rotary-type lens mounts. Flange depth: 1.695" (43.05mm). Mitchell Lens Control System. Internal 4-way mattes, matte wheel, and floating iris.

Shutter: 170° maximum. Variable in 10-degree calibrated segments to 0° manually, forward or reverse. Automatic fade in and fade out 2', 4', 8'. Other length by special order.

Viewfinder: Large erect viewfinder (not reflex) calibrated for different focal length lenses. Available with dual calibrations for any two aspect ratios. Parallax-free follow focus attachment available. Variable magnification erect image focusing telescope built into the camera. Through-the-lens ground glass critical focus and viewing when camera is racked over. Built-in contrast viewing filters for color and monochrome emulsions. Interchangeable ground glasses. Any aspect ratio outline available. Camera focus tube has built-in matte slot and permits the making of perfect match dissolves.

Video: After market video tap can be added to conversion.

Viewing Screen: Changeable.

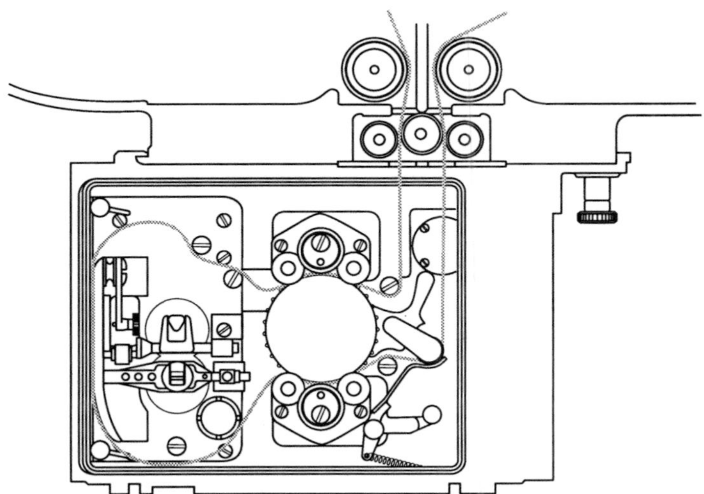

Mitchell 35mm Standard and High Speed Threading Diagram
Film takes up emulsion side out.

Mags: 400' (122m), 1,000' (300m) and 1,200' (366m). Double chamber. Plastic film cores on feed side, collapsible and removable on take-up.

Accessories: Norris makes an intervalometer.

Motors, Power: Variable (wild) motors: 12V DC (8–24 fps), 110V AC or DC (8–24 fps), High Speed. 110V AC or DC rheostat controlled (24–128 fps). Synchronous (sound) motors: 110V, 60-cycle, one phase AC; 220V, 60-cycle, three-phase AC; 220V, three-phase interlocking AC; 220V, three-phase AC/96V DC multi-duty (synchronous at 220V AC only) 50-cycle motors available on request. Animation motor: Stop-motion, 110V AC.

Misc: Fries Conversion

Fries Engineeering completely reworks and modifies this camera. PL and Panavision lens mounts. The rackover is removed and a new base is added. The lens turret is replaced with a hard front available in Arri, BNCR, Panavision, or Nikon mount. The camera is refitted with a spinning mirror and an orientable viewfinder. Crystal motors are available from Fries and Lynx Robotics with speeds from single frame to 120 fps. Stepper motors can be installed, with capping shutter system made by Dan Norris. Many custom (one of a kind) models.

Mitchell MK II S35R (RB/RC) 35mm

Movement: Dual register pins, four-prong pulldown. Removable movement; sync marks for replacement.

FPS: Single frame to 128 fps.

Aperture: 35mm full .980"x.735" (24.89mm x 18.67mm) aperture. Removable Aperture Plate for cleaning. Filter slot for two gels.

Displays: Mechanical footage, frame counter, tachometer. Electronic on RC model.

Lens: BNCR, Panavision, MK II mounts, and Arri PL (but not wider than 50mm—lens elements hit mirror or pellicle).

Shutter: Focal plane, variable 0°–170° in five-degree increments. Capable of manual fades, forward or reverse.

Viewfinder: Spinning mirror, reflex viewfinder. External Mitchell sidefinder, except RB/RC models.

Video: Available.

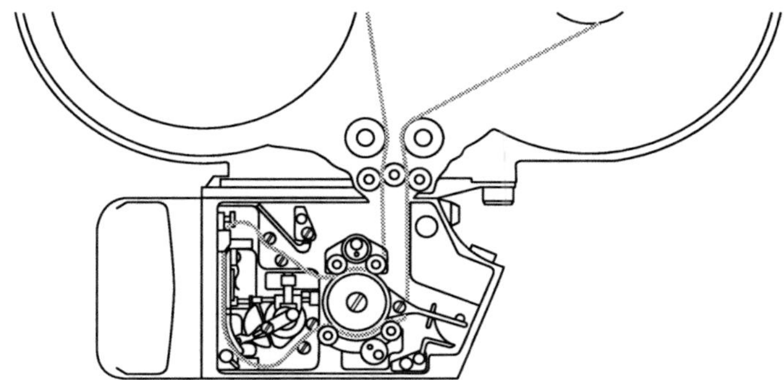

Mitchell S35RB and S35RC Threading Diagram
Film takes up emulsion side out.

Viewing Screen: Interchangeable.

Mags: Mitchell and other compatible magazines. Mounting depends on model and modifications.

Accessories: Sound Blimp--two versions made by Mitchell. Norris intervalometer.

Motors, Power: Various motors are available (variable, DC, sync, crystal, high-speed, Lynx Robotics, etc.).

Misc: Fries Conversion

Fries Engineeering reworks and modifies this camera. PL and Panavision lens mounts. The rackover is removed and a new base is added. The lens turret is replaced with a hard front available in Arri, BNCR, Panavision, Nikon. The camera is refitted with a spinning mirror and an orientable viewfinder. A video tap is added.

35R: Has a beamsplitter.

35R3: Has a spinning mirror.

35R-AF: For motion control, Fries makes an auto-focus version with bellows on rails. The lens stays fixed and the camera moves to maintain focus.

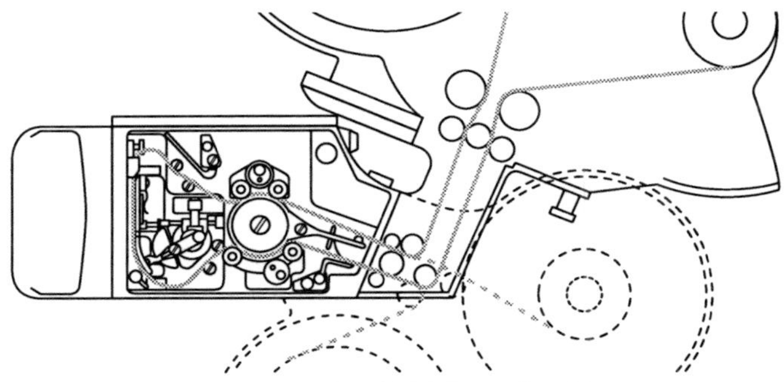

Mitchell MK II S35R Threading Diagram
Film takes up emulsion side out.

Mitchell-Fries Low Profile

Movement: Dual-register pin/dual pulldown claw Mitchell GC movement.

FPS: 12–120 fps forward only.

Aperture: 35mm full .980"x.735" (24.89mm x 18.67mm) aperture. Aperture Plate Removable for cleaning.

Displays: LED footage display and fps display, out of sync warning light.

Lens: Arri PL mount only, full aperture or Academy center.

Shutter: 175° spinning mirror shutter, not adjustable.

Viewfinder: Spinning mirror reflex. Integral long reflex finder with focusing eyepiece.

Video: Black-and-white CCD or flicker-free color video assist.

Viewing Screen: Interchangeable. All 35mm formats.

Mags: 200' (61m) custom "low profile" magazines.

Accessories: Uses Arri style matte boxes, but clamp-on filter holders are recommended to preserve low profile height.

Connections: Remote start cables, electronic remote lens control, Preston FIZ system.

Motors, Power: Fries crystal motor with Cinematography Electronics crystal speed control. 30V DC.

Misc: Limited production—Clairmont has 2, Jacques Cousteau had 1.

Moviecam Compact

Weight: 13 lbs 10 oz/6.3kg.

Movement: Dual pin registration and double pulldown pins. The movement slides back for easy threading. Loop adjustment.

FPS: 12–32 fps forward or reverse. 2-50 fps forward with moviespeed control. Frame rate speed preset buttons.

Aperture: .980" x .735" (24.89mm x 18.67mm). Aperture plates available in all 35mm aspect ratios and easily interchanged. Mattes and masks only at Clairmont by special order.

dB: Under 20 dBA.

Displays: Footage and frame rate. Digital counters for frame rate.

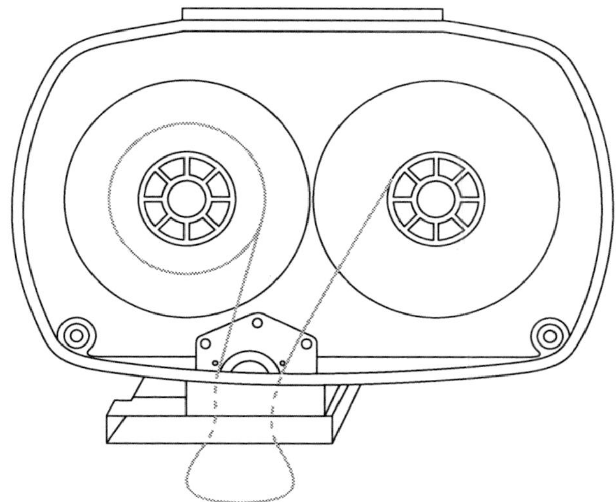

Moviecam Compact Magazine Diagram
Moviecam standard type magazine. Film takes up emulsion side in.

Flashing control display which indicates incorrect operation or buckle trips. Digital display for forward and reverse. Shutter angles are displayed only on the shutter.

Lens: BNCR and PL mounts. Regular and Super 35mm. Iris gears are available and necessary for speed/iris ramps. Electronic dust check (gate check) button.

Shutter: 180° variable to 45°. Calibrated in segments with positive locks at 45°, 90°, 120°, 144° and 172.8°. Mirror stops automatically in viewing position. 22.5° available on newer cameras.

Viewfinder: Reflex 6.1x magnification viewfinder. 3-position filter wheel (clear, blocked and ND.6). Reflex viewfinder is rotatable 360° while maintaining an erect image. 12" viewfinder extension with built-in 2.4x magnification zoom. 9.22mm eyepiece exit pupil has heated rear element to prevent condensation. The eyepiece diopter is adjustable. Anamorphic viewing system available.

Video: Several flicker-reduced CCD video pick-ups may be attached. 100 percent color or black-and-white, 80/20 optical black-and-white video, 80/20 optical/color video. On board 1.5" monitor and 6.5" color LCD monitors available. All video-assist cameras have built-in iris controls.

Viewing Screen: Interchangeable, available in all aspect ratios. Movielite projects the aspect ratio of the ground glass in selectable combinations of all standard formats. Custom Movielite module for Super 35mm and HDTV formats.

Mags: Top- or rear-mounted 500' (152m) and 1,000' (300m). Lightweight composite 400'(122m) and 1,000'(300m) mags. Lightweight 400' (122m) Steadicam mags. All mags have built-in heaters and torque motors. No gear or belt connection to the camera. Each mag has its own mechanical and electronic footage counter with digital display of raw stock with memory. Displacement type mag loading. 2" plastic film cores.

Accessories: Uses Moviecam and Arri baseplates, rods and matte boxes. Arriflex, Chrosziel or Willie Tec follow focus.

Electronic Accessories: Moviespeed attachment plugs into camera right side, and allows speeds to be changed during the shot at programmed rates from 1–50 fps forward and 12–32 fps reverse over user-defined time intervals (set with push-button switches). Fully automatic exposure corrections are made with the iris control

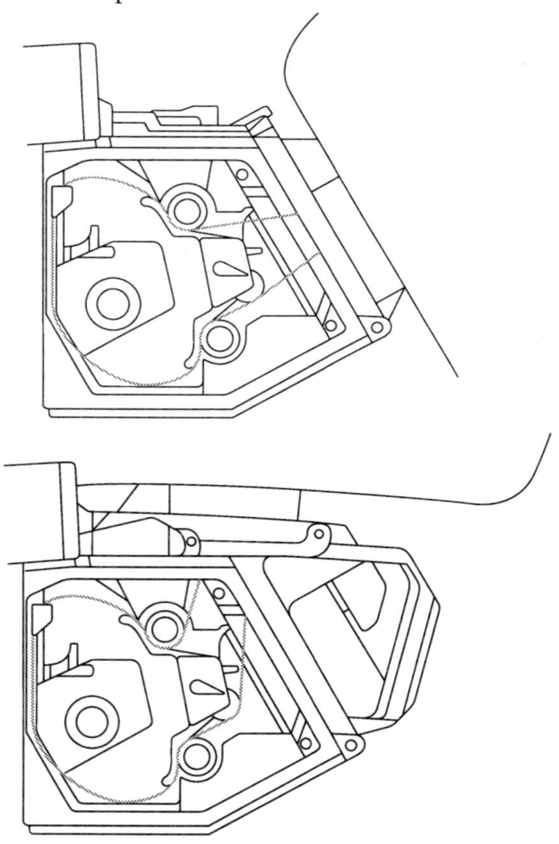

Moviecam Compact Threading Diagrams
Top: Slant loading. Bottom: Top Loading.
Film takes up emulsion side in.

servo motor coupled to the lens iris ring.

Running speed can be preset in three-digit accuracy for filming computer screens.

Connections: Synchronization attachment slaves the camera motor to an external pulse for flicker-free generator-powered HMI shooting, filming monitors, or process photography.

Time code plug-in TC-Module for recording AatonCode on specially equipped cameras.

Illuminated on/off switch. TV line phase shifter for synchronizing film with any TV monitor. Sync in and sync out. Cinematography Electronics makes the Compact Precision Speed Plus for the Moviecam Compact. Allows Arri accessory ports. Expands frame rate range from 2-50.999 fps. Also single frame feature.

Motors, Power: Microprocessor-controlled (quartz crystal accuracy) motor with variable speed from 12–32 fps in one-frame increments. 24V DC.

Moviecam SL

Weight: 8.25 lbs/3.7kg.

Movement: Dual pin registration and double pulldown pins. The movement slides back for easy threading. Loop adjustment.

FPS: Variable speed from 12–40 fps in one-frame increments. All speeds operate with quartz crystal accuracy. Setting camera to 43 fps causes camera to run 23 fps. Setting camera to run at 49 fps causes camera to run at 29 fps.

Aperture: Full aperture .980"x.735" (24.89mm x 18.67mm).

Aperture Plates available in all 35mm aspect ratios and easily interchangeable. PL lens mount can be oriented for Academy center or full aperture center. Mattes and masks available by special order at Clairmont Cameras.

Displays: Illuminated on/off switch. Frame speed preset buttons. Digital counters for frame rate. Sync in and sync out. Dust check knob. Footage counters on magazines. Shutter angles indicated on shutter.

Lens: PL mount. Regular and Super 35mm.

Shutter: 180°, variable to 22.5°. Calibrated in segments with positive locks at 45°, 90°, 120°, 144° and 172.8°. Mirror stops automatically in viewing position.

Viewfinder: Reflex Viewfinder, 6.1x magnification. 3-position filter wheel (clear, blocked and ND.6). Reflex viewfinder rotates 360° while maintaining an upright image. A 12" viewfinder extension with built-in 2.4x magnification zoom available only at Clairmont. 9.22mm exit pupil has heated rear element to prevent condensation. Eyepiece diopter is adjustable. Anamorphic viewing system also available only at Clairmont.

Video: Flicker-free CCD video pick-ups. 100 percent color or black-and-white, 80/20 optical black-and-white video. CEI color video.

Viewing Screen: Interchangeable ground glasses in all aspect ratios.

Mags: 400' (122m) lightweight. Rear mounted. All magazines have

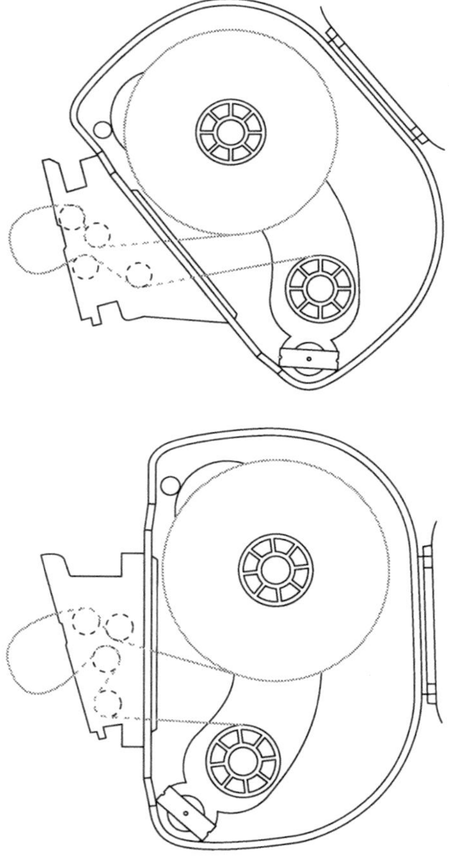

Moviecam SL MagazineDiagrams
Active displacement magazines in shoulder-hold and Steadicam configurations. Film takes up emulsion side in.

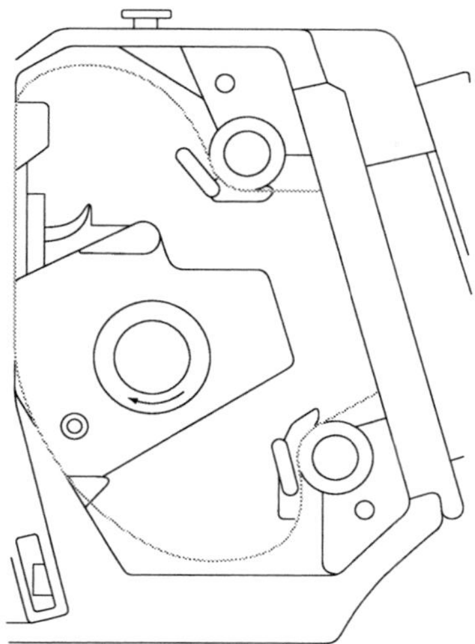

Moviecam SL Threading Diagram
Film takes ep emulsion side in.

built-in heaters and torque motors. Electronic footage counter. 400' (122m) lightweight Steadimag with vertical displacement to maintain center of gravity. Moviecam SL is designed to accept magazines from the Moviecam Compact with a special adapter. Specialized magazines for Steadicam.

Magazine Loading: Displacement type. : 2" plastic film cores.

Accessories: Uses Moviecam Compact and Arri bridge plates and follow focus units.

Optical Accessories: With of a special adapter plate, all viewfinder systems of the Moviecam Compact may be used with the Moviecam SL, including video systems and the Movielite system.

Motors, Power: Camera is powered by a microprocessor-controlled motor. 24V DC.

Moviecam Super America Mk 2

Weight: 29 lbs./13.2 kg with 500' (152 m) of film and 50mm lens.

Movement: Same as Moviecam SL.

FPS: Variable speed from 12–32 fps in one-frame increments. All speeds operate with quartz crystal accuracy.

Aperture: .980"x.735" (24.89mm x 18.67mm). Aperture Plate adjustable for full aperture or Academy centered. Easily interchangeable. Mattes and masks available at Clairmont by special order.

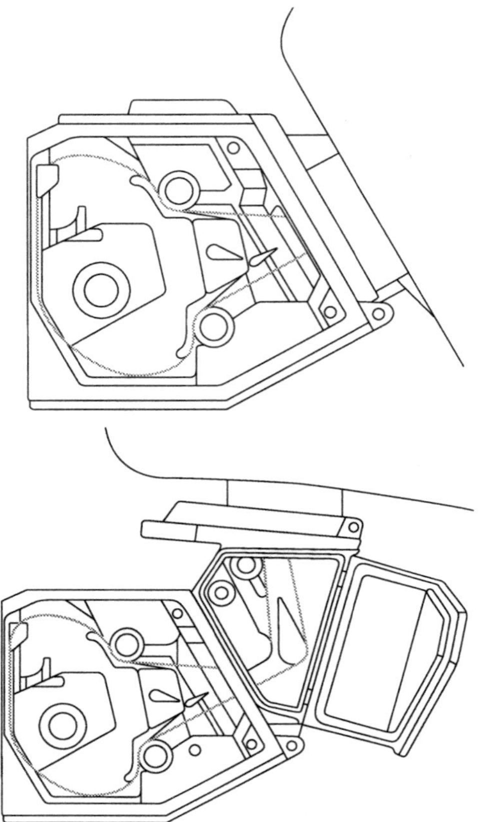

Moviecam Super America MK2 Threading Diagrams
Top: Slant loading loop adjustment. Bottom: Top loading.
Film takes up emulsion side in.

dB: 20 dB(A).

Displays: Footage and frame rate digital display forward and reverse. Illuminated on/off switch. Frame speed preset buttons. Digital counters for frame rate. Flashing control display indicates incorrect operation or buckle trips. Digital display for forward and reverse. Shutter angle is displayed directly on the shutter via engraved marks. TV line phase shifter for synchronizing film with any TV monitor. Sync in and sync out. Dust check button.

Lens: BNCR and PL mounts.

Shutter: 180°, variable to 45°. Calibrated in segments with positive locks at 45°, 90°, 120°, 144° and 172.8 °. Mirror stops automatically in viewing position.

Viewfinder: Reflex viewfinder (same as SL.)

Video: CCD black-and-white or color video pickups, flicker reduced at 24/25 fps, which can easily be plugged into the camera. 1.5" black-and-white onboard monitor or 6.50" CCD color onboard monitor. Iris control for the video system.

Viewing Screen: Interchangeable ground glasses available in all aspect ratios.

Mags: Displacement, rear mounted 500' (152m) and 1,000' (300m) feet. Can be top mounted by using an adapter. All magazines have built-in heaters and torque motors for FWD and REV operation. Each magazine has its own mechanical and electronic footage counter with digital display of raw stock with memory. Additional manual take-up controls. 2" plastic cores.

Accessories: Uses Arriflex bridge plates and follow focus units. Right and left hand grips. Carry handles.

Electronic Accessories: Moviespeed and Synchronization attachments—see Movicam Compact.

Connections: Computer diagnosis digitally displays by number any malfunctioning circuit boards. Plug-in boards easily interchangeable in the field. Digiclapper: Built-in automatic slate optically prints dialed scene and take number onto the film.

Power: 24V DC.

Panavision GII Golden Panaflex (PFX-GII)

Notes: Very similar to the Platinum Panaflex. Incorporates most of the features and operates with most of the accessories listed for that camera.

Weight: 24.4 lbs / 11.08 kg (body with short eyepiece).

Movement: Dual pin registration, double pulldown claws. Pitch and stroke controls for optimizing camera quietness. 4-perf movement standard, 3-perf available. Movement may be removed for servicing.

FPS: 4–34 fps (forward only), crystal controlled at 24, 25, 29.97, and 30 fps.

Aperture: .980" x .735" (24.89mm x 18.67mm) Style C (SMPTE 59-1998). Aperture Plate removable for cleaning. Full-frame aperture is standard, aperture mattes used for all other frame sizes. A special perforation-locating pin above the aperture ensures trouble-free and rapid film threading. Interchangeable aperture mattes are available for academy, anamorphic, Super 35mm, 1.85:1, 1.66:1, and any other.

dB: Under 24 dB with film and lens, measured 3' from the image plane.

Displays: Camera-left LED display readout with footage, film speed and low battery.

Lens: Panavision mount. All lenses are pinned to ensure proper rotational orientation. (Note: This is particularly important with anamorphic lenses.) Super 35mm conversion upon request.

Behind-the-lens gel filter holder.

Iris-rod support on camera right side. A lightweight modular follow focus control works on either side of the camera; optional electronic remote focus and aperture controls.

Shutter: Reflex rotating mirror standard--independent of the focal-pane shutter. Interchangeable, semi-silvered, fixed (not spinning) reflex mirror (pellicle) for flicker-free viewing upon request. Focal-plane shutter, infinitely variable and adjustable in-shot. Maximum opening 200°, minimum 50°, with adjustable maximum and minimum opening stops. Adjustable for synchronization with monitors, etc. Manual and electronic remote-control units.

Viewfinder: High-magnification, orientable viewfinder tube gives a constantly upright image through 360°. Short, intermediate and long viewfinder tubes available. Optical magnifier for critical focusing, de-anamorphoser, contrast viewing filter and lightproof shutter. Ocular adjustment with marker bezel to note individual settings. A built-in "Panaclear" eyepiece heater ensures mist-free viewing. Entire optical viewfinder system may be removed and replaced with a video viewfinder display for lightweight camera configuration (e.g., for Steadicam, crane, and remote camera usage). An eyepiece diopter to suit the operator's eyesight can be provided on request.

Video: CCD video systems available in black-and-white or color.

Viewing Screen: Interchangeable ground glasses with any marking or combination of markings. "Panaglow" illuminated reticle system with brightness control is standard. Ground glasses with finer or coarser texture available on request. Provision for a cut frame to be placed in the viewfinder system for optical image matching. Frame cutters available to suit negative or positive perforations.

Mags: Top or rear mounted displacement magazines. 250' (76.2m), 500' (152m), 1,000' (300m), and 2,000' (610m) magazines all available. All can be used on the top of the camera or at the rear (for good balance when handholding). 2,000' (610mm) magazines can be used in the top position only. 3" plastic core required. All others 2".

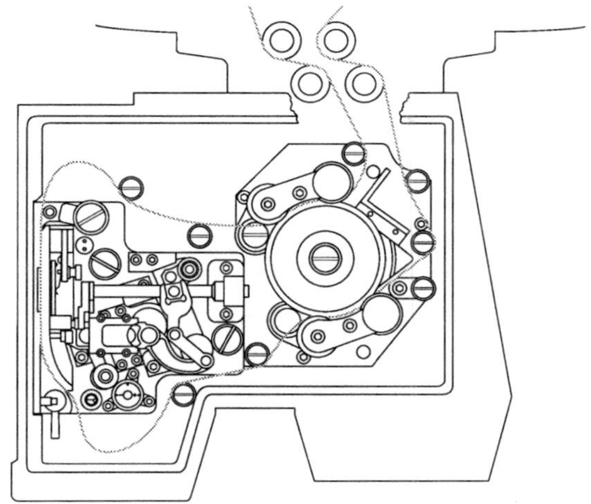

Panavision GII Golden Panaflex Threading Diagram
Film takes up emulsion side out.

Electronic Accessories: Special sync boxes available to synchronize the camera with computers, video signals and process projectors in shutter phase synchronization.

Connections: AatonCode time code system (on request) encodes every frame with a SMPTE time code, which is readable by both computer and human. Camera will accept external drive signals via the 10-pin accessory connector.

Motors, Power: Camera, magazines, heaters and accessories all operate off a single 24V DC battery. A crystal-controlled motor drives the system.

Misc: Hand-Holdability: Handles and a shoulder rest provided. When handheld, the camera is best used with a 500' (152m) or 250' (76.2m) magazine fitted at the rear.

Panavision Millennium XL (PFXMXL), XL2

Weight: 11.8 lbs/5.36kg. (body only)

23.6 lbs/10.76 kg (Steadicam configuration: body, 400' (122m) mag w/film, Steadicam plates, 4x5 matte box, lightweight zoom lens).

27.8 lbs/12.6 kg (handheld configuration, all of above plus handheld viewfinder, shoulder pad and right handgrip).

Movement: Dual pin registration, double pulldown claws. Pitch and stroke controls for optimizing camera quietness. 4-perf movement standard, 3-perf available. Movement may be removed for servicing. Special coatings allow for less frequent lubrication.

FPS: XL: 3–40 fps. . Forward only Crystal speeds selected in 1⁄1000th of a frame increments

XL2: 3-50 fps. Forward only. Crystal speeds selected in 1⁄1000th of a frame increments.

Aperture: .980" x .735" (24.89mm x 18.67mm) Style C (SMPTE 59-1998).

Aperture Plate removable for cleaning. Full-frame aperture standard, aperture mattes used for all other frame sizes. A special perforation-locating pin above the aperture ensures trouble-free and rapid film threading.

dB: Under 23 dB(A) with film and lens, measured 3' from the image plane.

Displays: Pivoting and removable dual-sided LED digital display showing speed, film footage, shutter angle. Rear control panel for speed and shutter setting with full display and connector for included remote speed/shutter controller.

Lens: Panavision titanium positive clamp lens mount. Super 35mm conversion upon request. Camera right iris-rod support supplied.

Behind-the-lens gel filter holder.

Shutter: Reflex spinning mirror. Focal plane shutter, infinitely variable and adjustable in-shot, 11.2° – 180°; with adjustable maximum and minimum opening stops. Digital display confirms adjustments in 1⁄10th-degree increments. System is adjustable for synchronization with monitors, etc. Manual and electronic remote control units.

Viewfinder: Reflex viewfinder detaches for quick conversion to handheld, Steadicam or studio mode. A 5" LCD video monitor can replace the optical viewfinder, often used for handheld. Left- or right-eyed handheld eyepiece. Utilizes Millennium studio viewfinder system, including the telescoping extension eyepiece. Panaglow.

Viewfinder tube is orientable and gives a constantly upright image through 360°. Short and modular-length viewfinder tubes are available. Modular tube can telescope over 3" for optimum viewing position. System incorporates an optical magnifier for critical focusing, a de-anamorphoser, a contrast viewing filter and a lightproof shutter. Wide-range ocular adjustment with marker bezel to note individual settings. A built-in "Panaclear" eyepiece heater ensures mist-free viewing. Entire optical viewfinder system may be easily removed without tools for video viewfinder display for lightweight camera configuration (e.g., for Panaglide, Steadicam, Louma or remote camera usage). An eyepiece diopter to suit the operator's eyesight can be provided on request.

Video: Integrated Color Video Assist, flicker-free at all camera speeds. Internal iris for exposure control. Selectable neutral density filter. Freeze and compare picture modes. Auto color balance or two preset color temperatures. Multiple gain settings. Frameline and character generator. Film camera speed and footage display output in video display.

Viewing Screen: Interchangeable ground glasses available with any marking or combination of markings. "Panaglow" illuminated reticle system with brightness control is standard. Ground glasses with finer or coarser texture available on request. Provision for a cut frame to be placed in the viewfinder system for optical image matching. Frame cutters available to suit negative or positive perforations. Clear format screen can replace ground glass in first viewing plane for better video image.

Mags: Top or rear mounted displacement magazines. Brushless motor driven 200' (76.2m), 400' (122m) and 1,000' (300m) magazines. Traditional 250' (83m), 500' (152m), 1,000' (300m), 2,000' (610m) magazines available. All can be used on the top of the

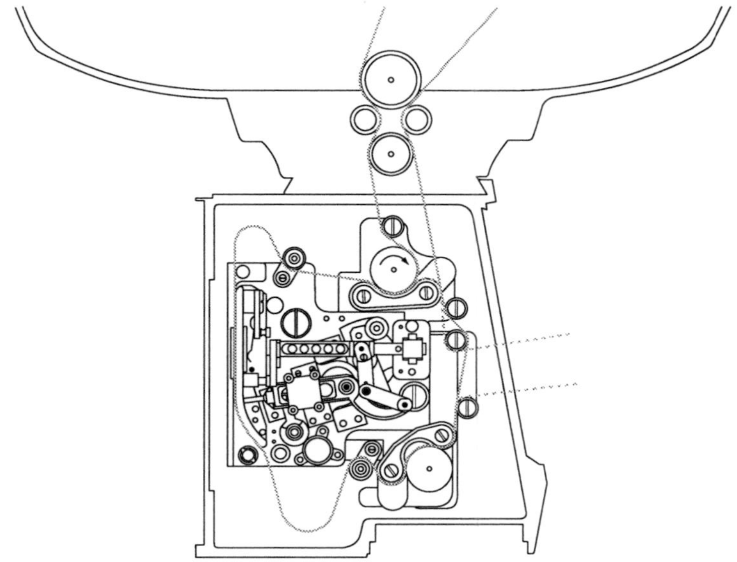

Panavision Millenium XL Threading Diagram
Film takes up emulsion side out.

camera,or at the rear for minimum camera height and for good balance when handholding (2,000' magazines can be used in the top position only). 2" plastic cores required, 3" for 2,000' (610m).

Accessories: Internal servo motor controls electronics for focus, T-stop and zoom. Wired or wireless remote control. Iris rod bracket with 24V DC power connectors. Separate remote control for timed speed shutter compensated shots. Digital Link Smart Shutter controller for speed-iris and/or shutter ramps, also depth of field shift. Sync box to synchronize the camera with computers, video signals and projectors for shutter phase synchronization.

Environmental Protection Equipment: Same as Panavision GII.

Camera Support Equipment: Same as Panavision GII.

Hand-Holdability: Handles and a shoulder rest provided for handholding the camera. In this configuration, camera is best used with a 200', 250', 400' or 500' magazine fitted at the rear.

Motors, Power: Camera, magazines, heaters and accessories all operate off a single 24V battery. Separate (dual) brushless drive motors for shutter and movement, easily re-timed for effects. Single variable shutter motor for ramp functions.

Panavision Millenium (PFX-M)

Weight: 17.5 lbs/7.95 kg. (body only).

29.12 lbs/13.23 kg (Steadicam configuration: body, 400' (122m) mag w/film, Steadicam plates, 4" x 5.650" clip on matte box, lightweight zoom lens).

34.2 lbs/15.5 kg (hand-held configuration, all of above plus: focus tube, short eyepiece).

Movement: Same as Millenimium XL.

FPS: 3–50 fps (forward and reverse), crystal controlled at all speeds in 1⁄1000th of a second increments.

Aperture: .980" x .735" (24.89mm x 18.67mm) Style C (SMPTE 59-1998).

Aperture Plate removable for cleaning. Full-frame aperture is standard; aperture mattes used for all other frame sizes. A special perforation-locating pin above the aperture ensures trouble-free and rapid film threading.

dB: Under 19 dB(A) with film and lens, measured 3' from the image plane.

Displays: Pivoting and removable dual-sided LED digital display showing speed, film footage, shutter angle. Additional status indicator and speed/footage display on operator side. Rear control panel for speed and shutter setting with full display and connector for included remote speed/shutter controller.

Lens: Panavision positive clamp lens mount.

Super 35mm conversion upon request. Iris-rod support supplied. Lens Controls same as Millenium XL.

Behind-the-lens gel filter holder.

Shutter: Same as Millennium XL.

Viewfinder: Same as Millennium XL.

Video: Color video, flicker-free at all camera speeds. Internal iris for exposure control. Clear format replaces the traditional ground glass. Approximately 2000 ASA. Freeze and compare picture modes. Electronic de-anamorphoser. RGB output for on-set compositing. Auto color balance or two preset color temperatures. Multiple gain settings. Frameline and character generator. Film camera speed and footage display. Outputs to video display. Two composite video outputs, one RGB output.

Viewing Screen: Same as Millennium XL.

Mags: Same as Millennium XL.

Accessories: Same as Millennium XL. Matte Boxes same as GII.

Electronic Accessories: Special sync boxes available to synchronize the camera with computers, video signals and process projectors in shutter phase synchronization.

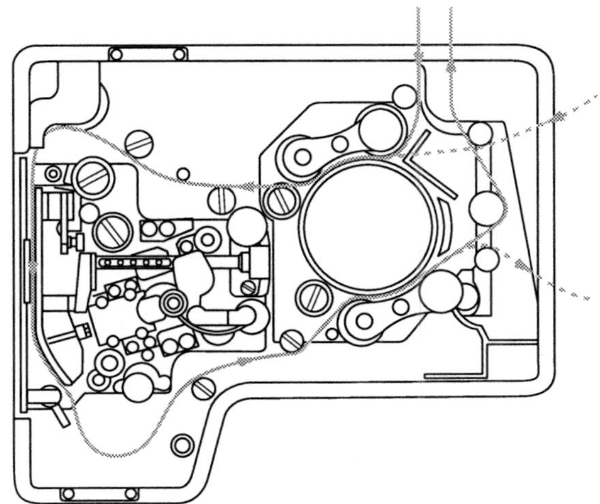

Panavision Millenium Threading Diagram
Film takes up emulsion side out.

Additional Accessories: A shutter/speed compensation box comes standard.

Environmental Protection Equipment: Same as GII.

Camera Support Equipment: Same as GII.

Hand-Holdability: Handles and a shoulder-rest are provided for hand-holding the camera. In this configuration camera is best used with a 250' (76.2m), 400',(122m) or 500' (152m) magazine fitted at the rear.

Power: Brushless crystal motor drive. 24V DC.

Panavision Panaflex-X (PFX-X)

Notes: Similar to the GII Golden Panaflex but has a fixed viewfinder system and is not hand-holdable.

Weight: 20.5 lbs / 9.31 kg (body only).

Movement: same as GII

FPS: Same as GII: 4–34 fps (forward only), xtal 24, 25, and 29.97.

Aperture: same as GII

dB: Under 24 dB(A) with film and lens, measured 3' from the image plane.

Displays: Single-sided LED display readout with footage and film speed. Same as GII

Lens: Same as GII. Same behind-the-lens gel filter holder.

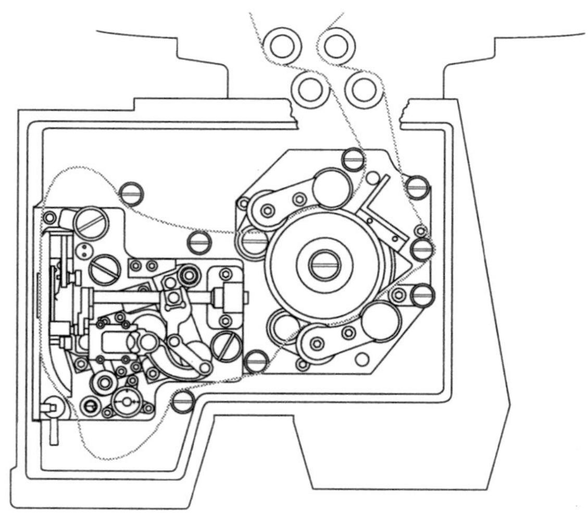

Panavision Panaflex-X Threading Diagram
Film takes up emulsion side out.

Shutter: Same as GII. 200°–50°

Viewfinder: Non-orientable.

Video: CCD video systems in black-and-white or color.

Viewing Screen: Interchangeable, same as GII

Mags: Same as GII

Accessories: Matte Boxes: Same as GII.

Electronic Accessories: Same as GII.

Optical Accessories: Same as GII.

Environmental Protection Equipment: Same as GII.

Camera Support Equipment: Same as GII.

Motors, Power: same as GII (24V DC) and Millenium.

Misc: Camera cannot be handheld.

Panavision Panaflex Panastar II High-Speed

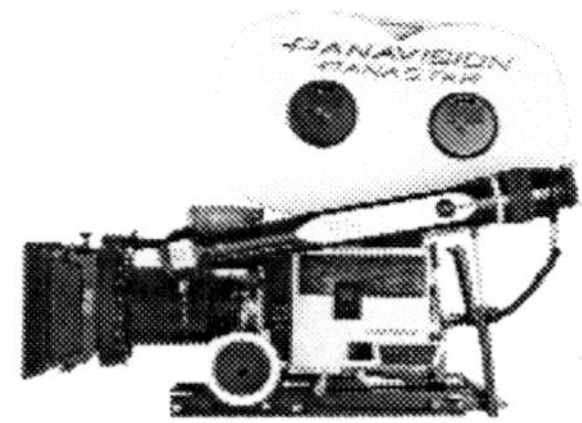

Weight: 24.4 lbs/11.08 kg (body with short eyepiece).

Movement: Dual pin registration. Four pulldown claws. Entire movement may be removed for servicing.

FPS: Camera runs at any speed from 4–120 fps, crystal-controlled at all speeds, and may be adjusted in 1 fps increments. Fwd and rev.

Aperture: .980" x .735" (24.89mm x 18.67mm) Style C (SMPTE 59-1998). Aperture Plate same as Platinum Panaflex.

Displays: Dual-sided LCD display readout with footage, film speed, shutter angle, and time code bits. LED indicators for low battery / film jam/ film out/ MVMT SW/Mag/RVS.

Lens: Lens mount and lens control information the same as Panavision GII. Behind the lens filter holder.

Shutter: Focal plane shutter with infinitely variable opening and adjustable in-shot. Maximum opening 180°, minimum 45°, with adjustable maximum and minimum opening stops. Digital display allows adjustments in 1⁄10th-degree increments. Adjustable for synchronization with monitors, etc. Manual and electronic remote-control units available.

Viewfinder: Reflex. Same as Platinum Panaflex.

Video: Same as Platinum Panaflex.

Viewing Screen: Same as Platinum Panaflex.

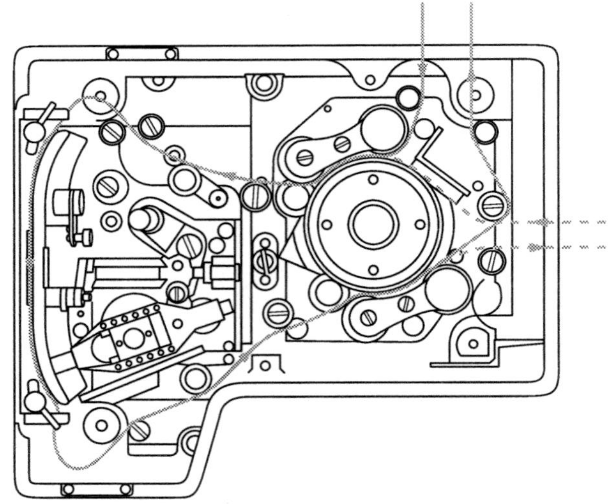

Panavision Panaflex Panastar II High-Speed Threading Diagram
Film takes up emulsion side out.

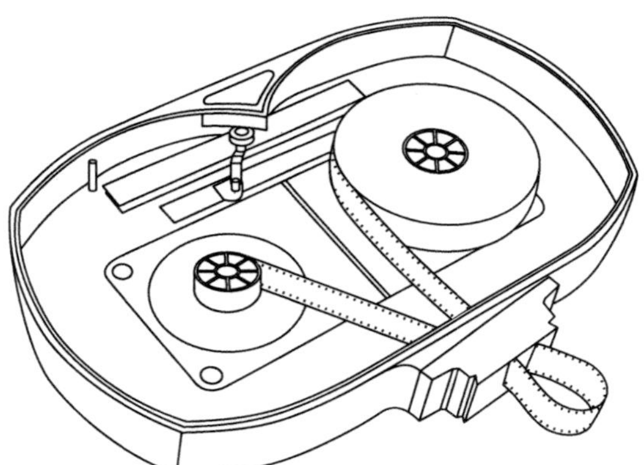

Panastar reverse running type magazine threading
Film takes up emulsion side in.

Mags: 250'(76.2m) *(Note: 250' mag up to 34fps only)*, 500' (152m) and 1,000' (300m) magazines. Either can be used on the top of the camera or at the rear. 1,000'(300m) reverse-running magazines—film takes up emulsion side IN.

Film Cores: 2" plastic core required. Note Panastar reverse running-type magazine threading.

Accessories Matte Boxes: Same as Platinum Panaflex.

Optical Accessories: Same as Platinum Panaflex.

Camera Support Equipment: Same as Platinum Panaflex. Handles and a shoulder rest provided.

Connections: The camera will accept external drive signals via the 10-pin accessory connector.

Motors, Power: 24V DC. Batteries same as Platinum Panaflex.

Panavision Platinum Panaflex 35mm (PFX-P)

Weight: 24 lbs / 10.9 kg (body with short eyepiece).

Movement: Dual pin registration; Double pulldown claws. Pitch and stroke controls for optimizing camera quietness. 4-perf movement standard, 3-perf available. Movement may be removed for servicing.

FPS: 4–36 fps (forward and reverse), crystal-controlled at all speeds and adjusted in 1⁄10th fps increments.

Aperture: .980" x .735" (24.89mm x 18.67mm) Style C (SMPTE 59-1998).

Aperture Plate: Removable for cleaning. Full-frame aperture is standard, aperture mattes are used for all other frame sizes. A special perforation-locating pin above the aperture ensures trouble-free and rapid film threading.

dB: Under 22 dB with film and lens, measured 3' from the image plane.

Displays: Dual-sided LCD display readout with footage, film speed, shutter angle, and time code bits. LED indicators for low battery / low film / film jam/ illegal speed.

Lens: same as Panavision GII. Behind-the-lens gel filter holder.

Shutter: Reflex mirror. Focal plane shutter, infinitely variable and adjustable in-shot. Maximum opening 200°, minimum 50°, with adjustable maximum and minimum opening stops. Digital display allows adjustments in 1⁄10th-degree increments. Adjustable for synchronization with monitors. Manual and electronic remote-control units.

Viewfinder: Reflex Viewfinder. Same as GII.

Video: Same as GII.

Viewing Screen: Same as GII.

Mags: Same as GII.

Accessories: Matte Boxes same as GII.

Electronic Accessories: Same as GII.

Optical Accessories: Same as GII.

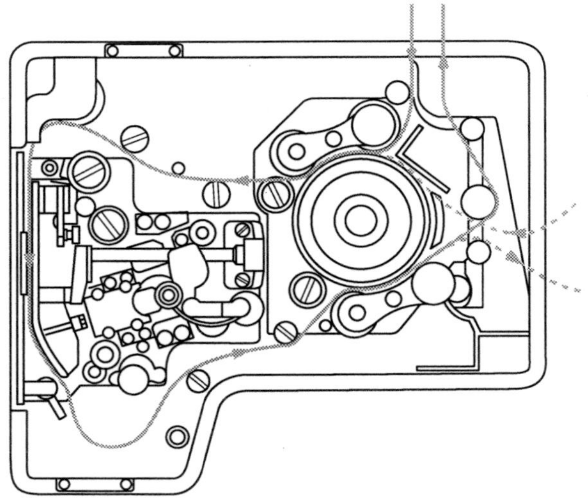

Panavision Platinum Panaflex Threading Diagram
Film takes up emulsion side out.

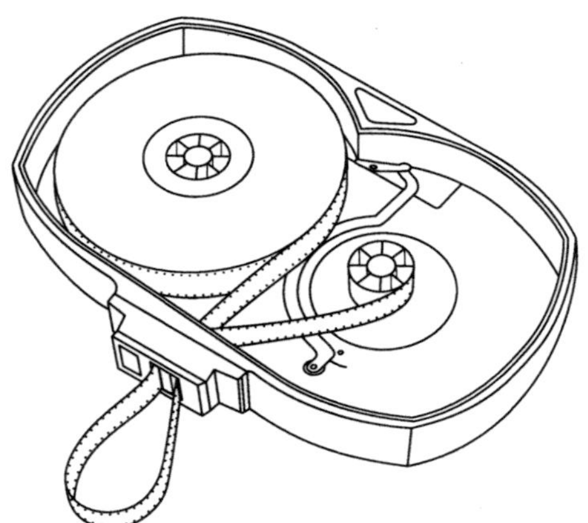

Panavision film magazine.
Film takes up emulsion side out.

Environmental Protection Equipment: Same as GII.

Camera Support Equipment: Same as GII. Handles and shoulder rest provided for handheld use.

Connections: The camera will accept external drive signals via the 10-pin accessory connector. AatonCode can be provided on request.

Motors, Power: 24V DC. A crystal-controlled brushless motor drives the system. Batteries: Same as Millennium.

Panavision 35mm Camera Models
Panavision Notes and Accessories

Most cameras in the Panavision system share the following accessories and attributes.

Movement: Dual Pilot pins register in the same perforation holes (immediately below the bottom frameline) as optical printers. This ensures process-plate image steadiness. Entire movement may be removed for servicing.

Lenses: All lenses are pinned to ensure proper rotational orientation. *(Note: This is particularly important with anamorphic lenses.)*

Panavision supplies a wide range of spherical, anamorphic and specialty lenses, all checked and calibrated by MTF. Primo lenses are all color matched and range from a distortion-free 10mm to 150mm. Primo zoom lenses are equal to Primo lenses in image look and optical performance. All Primo lenses have widely spaced lens focus calibrations and have been especially designed for low veiling glare. Physically long lenses are supplied with adequate-length iris rods for matte box and filter support, ultra-wide-angle lenses are supplied with a suitable sunshade and matte box.

Zoom lenses are supplied with a motor-driven zoom control unit as standard. Iris gears are incorporated into most prime and zoom lenses.

Physically long lenses are supplied with adequate-length iris rods for matte box and filter support, ultra-wide-angle lenses are supplied with a suitable sunshade and matte box.

Lens Control: A lightweight modular follow focus control which can be used from either side of the camera is standard; optional electronic remote focus and aperture controls also available. Zoom lenses supplied with a motordriven zoom control unit as standard. Iris gears incorporated into most prime and zoom lenses.

An eyepiece leveler is supplied with every Panahead to keep the eyepiece position constant while tilting the camera.

Optical Accessories: Front-of-lens optical accessories include an exceptionally wide range of color-control filters, diffusion filters, fog filters, low-contrast filters, black, white and colored nets, full-cover and split diopters, low/high angle inclining prisms.

Matte Boxes: Standard matte box incorporates a sunshade and two 4" x 5.650" filters which can be individually slid up and down.

Optional matte box incorporates a sunshade, and two 4" x 5.650" filters which can be individually slid up and down.

Panavision 35mm Camera Models				
Camera	**Shutter Angles**	**Frame Rate**	**dB**	**Weight**
GII Gold	50°-200°	4-34 fps (fwd only) crystal controlled at 24, 25 29.97	Under 24 dB	24.4 lbs/11.08 kg (body with short eyepiece)
Millennium XL	11.2°-180°	3-40 fps (fwd only) crystal controlled at sync speeds	Under 23 dB(A)	11.8 lbs/5.36 kg (body only)
XL2	Same as XL	3-50 fps (fwd only) crystal controlled at sync speeds	Same as XL	Same as XL
Millennium	11.2°-180°	3-50 fps (fwd & reverse) crysal controlled at sync speeds	Under 19 dB(A)	17.5 lbs/7.95 kg (body only)
Panaflex-X	50°-200°	4-34 fps (fwd only) crystal controlled at 24, 25 29.97	Under 24 dB(A)	20.5 lbs/9.31 kg (body only)
Panastar II	45°-180°	4-120 fps (fwd & reverse) in 1 fps increments		12.5 kg (28 lbs)
Platinum	50°-200°	4-36 fps (fwd & reverse) crystal controlled at sync speeds	Under 22 dB	24 lbs/10.9 kg (body with short eyepiece)

Special matte boxes incorporating more filter stages, with provision for sliding (motorized if required), rotating and/or tilting and for taking 6.6" square filters optional. Panavision can also supply special sliding diffusers, diopters and image-control filters, to use in matte boxes.

Image Contrast Control: "Panaflasher" light overlay unit is an optional accessory.

Environmental Protection Equipment: All Panaflex cameras and magazines have built-in heaters. Heated covers available to give additional protection to lenses, especially zoom lenses, to keep their operation smooth in intensely cold conditions. Other covers available to protect camera, magazines and lenses from heat, dust, rain and water. Spinning-glass rain deflectors available for use in storm conditions. Autobase available to secure the camera in conditions of vibration, high "g-forces" and other stressful and dangerous conditions. Water-box available to protect the camera in shallow water conditions, a hazard box to protect the camera from explosions, collisions and other dangerous situations.

Camera Support Equipment: "Panahead" geared head incorporates a 60° tilt range with a built-in wedge system to allow the operator to select where that range is, anywhere between the camera pointing directly up or directly down, and three gear ratios in both the pan and tilt movements. A sliding base unit enables camera to be attached and detached and to be slid backwards and forwards on the head for optimum balance. "Panatate" turn-over mount allows 360° camera rotation about the lens axis while permitting nodal pan and tilt movements. Nodal adapter available to mount a Panaflex on a Panahead. The normal battery complement is two cased units with built-in chargers. Belt batteries and a newly designed onboard battery for handholding optional.

Photo-Sonics 35mm 4CR

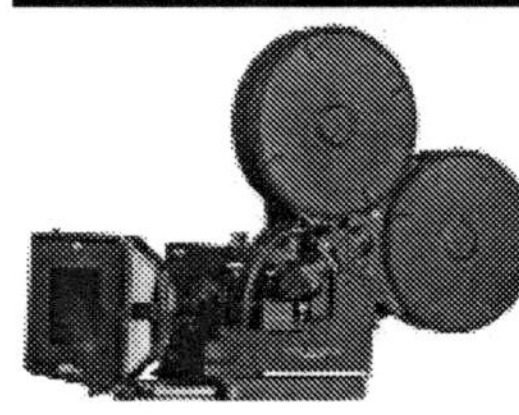

Notes: Reflex rotary prism camera 125–2,500 fps. This is a rotary prism camera and is not pin-registered.

Film Specifications: 35mm B&H perforation .1866" pitch. 1,000' (300m) loads preferable.

Weight: 125 lbs./56.81 kg. with loaded 1,000' (300m) mag, without lens.

Movement: Rotary prism. Continuous film transport. Rotary imaging prism.

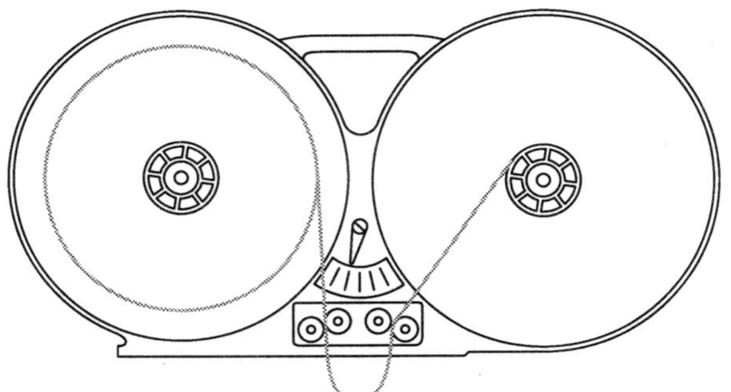

Photo-Sonics 35mm 35-4B/4C magazine.
Film takes up emulsion side in.

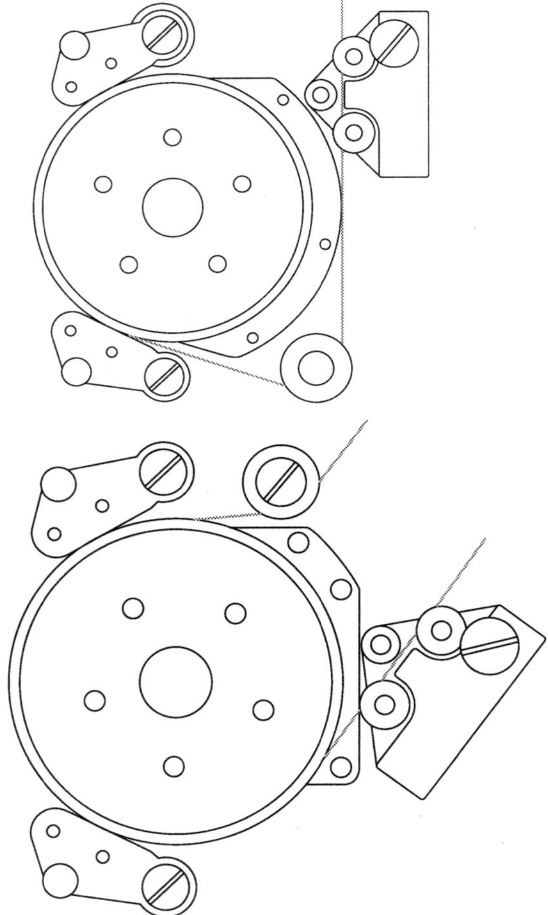

Photo-Sonics 35mm 4CR Diagrams
Top: 35 4B. Bottom: 35 4C.

FPS: High-speed system: 500–2500 fps in 500-frame intervals. Low-speed system: 250–1,250 fps in 250-frame increments. Special low-speed motor, 125–625 fps available on request.

Aperture: Full-frame 35mm.

Displays: Mechanical footage indicator. Camera ready and power indicators.

Lens: Pentax 6x7 lens mount. 17mm through 165mm Pentax lenses, in addition to zooms and Probe II lenses.

Shutter: Rotary disc, 4C has 72-degree fixed shutter. 36°, 18° or 9° available upon request.

Viewfinder: The 4C utilizes a Jurgens orientable reflex viewfinder system with a behind-the-lens beamsplitter to achieve flickerless reflex viewing. Extension eyepiece with leveling rod.

Video: CEI Color V or III available in NTSC version only.

Viewing Screen: Standard ground glass formats available. Specify when ordering camera package to ensure availability.

Mags: 1000' (300m). Double chamber. 35mm B&H perforation .1866" pitch. Film must be rewound onto dynamically balanced aluminum cores. Twelve cores with each 4CR rental package.

Accessories: Follow Focus: Arri follow focus.

Matte Boxes: 6.6.x6.6 Arri matte box. Heavy-duty tilt plate, high and low hat, flicker meter, 90° angle plate. Raincovers are included with camera package.

Motors, Power: High-speed 208V AC, three phase, 60Hz, Y-connected synchronous speed motor. Surge at maximum frame rate 60 amps (each phase); running 30 amps (each phase). Low-speed 115V AC, single phase, 60Hz, synchronous speed motor. Surge at maximum frame rate: 40 amps; running 20 amps. Power: 208V AC, three phase, Y-connected.

Misc: Standard 3⁄8-16 thread fits most large tripods and heads and may require extension plates on some remote heads.

Photo-Sonics 35mm 4ER

Notes: The 4ER pin registered camera produces solid registration at frame rates from 6–360 fps. Camera is compatible with Unilux strobes (mid-shutter pulse).

Film Specifications: Standard 35mm B&H perforation with .1866" (4.74mm) pitch. 1,000' (300m) loads preferable).

Weight: 125 lbs./56.81 kg with loaded 1,000' (300m) magazine, without lens.

Movement: Intermittent, pin registered. Intermittent with four registration pins, 12 pulldown arms and a vacuum pressure plate to hold the film absolutely stationary and registered during exposure.

FPS: 6–360 fps.

Aperture: Full-frame 35mm. Removable aperture plate.

Displays: Mechanical footage indicator.

Lens: BNCR or Panavision. (Academy centered.)

Shutter: 5° to 120°, adjustable with mechanical indicator.

Viewfinder: The 4ER utilizes a Jurgens/Arriflex reflex, orientable viewfinder system with a behind-the-lens beamsplitter to achieve flickerless reflex viewing. Optional external boresight tool available.

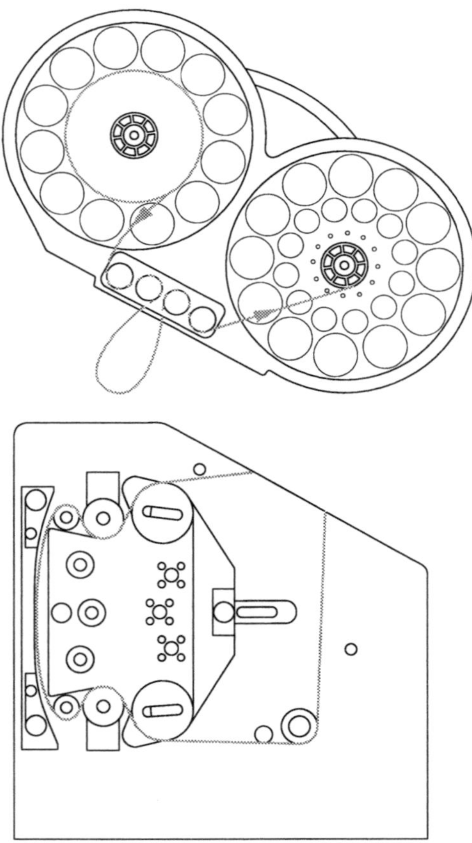

Photo-Sonics 35mm 4E and 4ER Diagrams
Film takes-up emulsion side out.

Video: CEI Color V or III availabe in NTSC version only.

Viewing Screen: Most standard ground glasses are available. Specify when ordering camera package to ensure availability.

Mags: 1,000' (300m). Double chamber. Standard plastic 35mm 2" film cores. 35mm B&H perforation .1866" pitch.

Accessories: Environmental Protection Equipment: Same as 4C.

Camera Support Equipment: Same as 4C. Arri follow focus unit with right-hand knob. Zoom Control and Iris Gears available on request.

Electronic Accessories: Optional remote cables (75' (23m) and 150' (45.7m)), remote speed indicator.

Additional Accessories: Extension eyepiece with leveling rod, heavy duty tilt plate, high and low hat, flicker meter, 90-degree angle plate, Panavision lens mount and "L" bracket support adapter with ⅝" support rods, extension eyepiece, follow focus.

Optical Accessories: Various Zeiss T1.3and Nikkor primes, in addition to macro and zoom and Probe II lenses.

Motors, Power: 208V AC, single phase (200 to 250V AC is acceptable). 35 amps surge at 360 fps and 20 amps running. Cannot use batteries. Requires AC power 208V AC single phase.

Photo-Sonics 35mm 4ML (Reflex and Non-reflex)

Notes: The 4ML reflex is a compact, rugged, pin registered, high-speed camera capable of crystal-controlled filming speeds from 10-200 fps. The 4ML reflex can be configured at only 9" total height with prime lenses and a 400' (122m) magazine. Only 51⁄2" with a 200' (61m) magazine. Compatible with Unilux strobe lighting (mid-shutter pulse).

Standard B&H perforation .1866" (4.74mm) pitch.

Weight: 28lbs./12.72kg with loaded 400' (122m) mag, without lens.

Movement: Intermittent with two registrations pins and four pull-down arms.

FPS: 10–200 fps.

Aperture: .745" x .995" (18.92mm x 25.27mm). Academy centered.

Displays: Digital readout plate w/accessory port.

Lens: Lens Mount: BNCR, Panavision, Nikon, PL (Warning: Depth restriction with certain lenses—restricted to certain zooms and

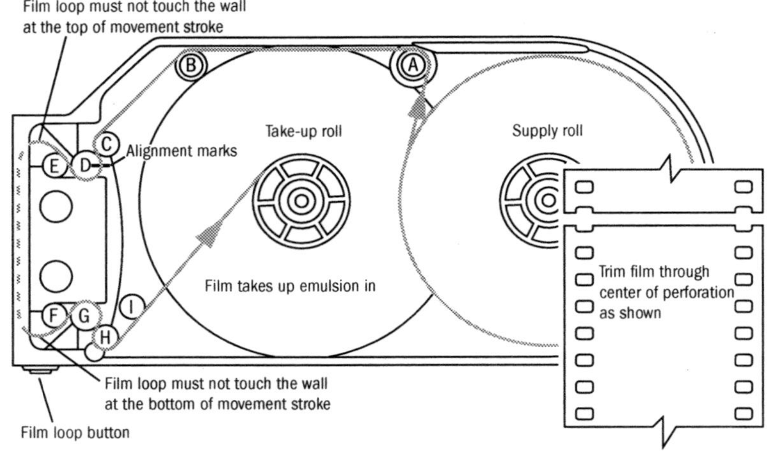

Photo-Sonics 35mm 4ML Magazine Diagram
Film takes-up emulsion side in.

longer primes.) Various Nikkor lenses (extension tube set for close-focus available), Probe II lens

Shutter: 144° maximum, adjustable to 72°, 36°, 18°, and 9°.

Viewfinder: A behind-the-lens beamsplitter block provides flickerless reflex viewing. Extension eyepiece. External Viewfinder: Non-reflex model utilizes a boresight tool.

Video: CEI Color V or III available in NTSC version only.

Viewing Screen: TV/Academy/1:1.85 combo standard. Specify ahead for different ground glass.

Mags: 200' (61m) and 400' (122m) displacement, snap-on magazines for quick reloading. Single chamber with daylight cover. 2" film cores.

Accessories: Clamp-on 4x4 two-stage Arri Studio matte box.

Follow Focus: Arri follow focus unit with right-hand knob.

Electronic Accessories: Digital readout plate with accessory port, crystal-controlled filming speeds from 10–200 fps, Unilux strobe lighting (mid-shutter pulse).

Additional Accessories: Compatible with Panavision and Arri lens accessories.

Environmental Protection Equipment: Splash housings depth-rated 12' (3.6m)-15' (4.6m), rain covers.

Power: 28V DC. 12 amps surge, 7 amps running.

Ultracam

Weight: 31 lbs./14.06 kg with 400' (122m) of film and 50mm lens.

Movement: Single claw, dual registration pin. Automatic film location by spring-loaded pin. Pitch adjustment compensated for 3x more change in stroke length at end of stroke than at start. Entire movement can be removed for cleaning; coupling is keyed for correct alignment on replacement.

FPS: 8, 12, 16, 18, 20, 24, 25, 30 and 32 fps and by a 10V P-P external pulse of 60x frame rate.

Aperture: Full aperture .985" x .736" (25.02mm x 18.69mm). Aperture plate removes easily for cleaning and lubrication.

dB: Sound level 20 +1 dB at 3' with film and 50mm lens.

Displays: Built-in follow focus. LED counter feet/meters may be preset to any reading; battery-operated memory.

Lens: Lens Mount: SBNCR.

Shutter: Focal plane 175° on same shaft with mirror. Rotating, two-blade, half-speed mirror. 41°30' to permit short back-focus lenses.

Viewfinder: Reflex finder, eyepiece rotates 360° using prism to provide upright image. Exit pupil 10mm. 6x to 9x true zoom magnification. Anamorphic correction available. Internal diopter

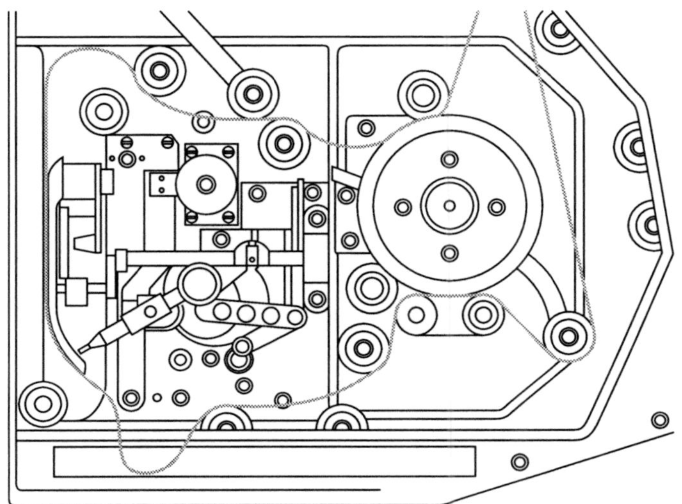

Ultracam Magazine and Threading Diagrams
Film takes up emulsion side in.

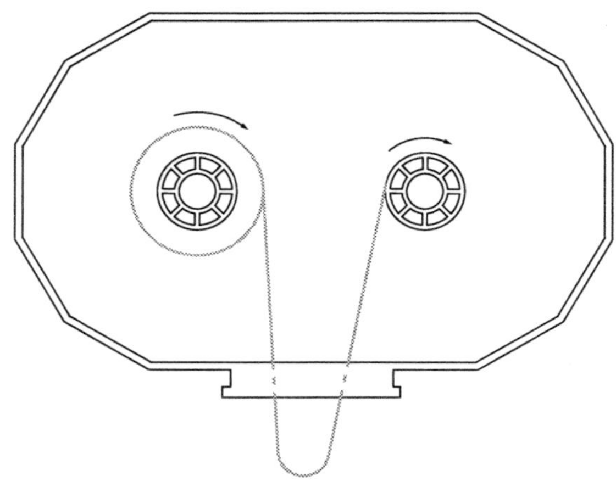

Ultracam Magazine and Threading Diagrams
Film takes up emulsion side in.

accommodation. Right- or left-eye operation. Video assist on bayonet mount.

Viewing Screen: Interchangeable.

Mags: 500' (152m) and 1,000' (300m) displacement. Built-in torque motor and electric brake. Either size mounts on camera top or rear.

Accessories: Quick-release balance plate. Swing-away matte box; rotating feature accepts various size filters with two stationary stages and two rotating stages.

Motors, Power: Internal 28V DC optically encoded. Crystal sync +15 ppm over 0° to 130° F. range 50/60Hz and frame rate output pulse.

Wilcam 12

Weight: Body and mags 77 lbs./34.93 kg.

Movement: Eight pulldown pins, two register pins.

FPS: 4-300 fps crystal control to two decimal places.

Aperture: .735" x .980" (18.67mm x 24.89mm). Optically centered and Academy centered. Vacuum back register plate.

dB: MOS camera.

Displays: Digital readout. Footage and frame rate.

Lens: PL Mount.

Shutter: 120° fixed Berylium mirror.

Viewfinder: Reflex finder, 120° rotatable. Image stays upright.

Normal and 10x magnifier modes.

Video: External CEI flicker-free color video assist.

Viewing Screen: Interchangeable. All Academy and Super formats.

Mags: 1000' (300m), Single-chamber magazine, supply or take-up interchangeable. 2" plastic cores. 35mm B&H .1866" (4.74mm) perfs (normal stock).

Accessories: Standard Arri Follow Focus, Microforce Zoom Control. Standard Arri Matte Boxes.

Connections: Accessory connection via the 19-pin Galloway Group Interface. Line Sync Box for interlock with other cameras and rear projection. Strobe output on camera body with settings for one or two pulses for each pulldown/exposure cycle. Quartz-locked remote control.

Motors, Power: Integrated. Batteries: 48V DC. Can yoke two 24V batteries.

16mm

Aaton A Minima (Super 16 only)

Weight: 5 lbs./2kg with onboard battery and film.

Movement: single co-planar claw movement and lateral pressure plate ensure vertical and lateral steadiness to 1⁄2000th of image dimensions. Hair-free gate.

FPS: 1–32 fps crystal speed control, on internal lithium batteries. Runs 50 fps with external NiMH or NiCd battery.

Aperture: 1.66 (7.44mm x 12.4mm).

Aperture Plate: Super 16 only. Super 16-centered lens port and viewfinder.

dB: 29 dB +/-½ dB.

Displays: Illuminated readout displays speed, footage (in feet and meters), ASA, time code, video sync speed, intervalometer setting program.

Lens: Nikon and PL, mount

Shutter: 172.8° spinning reflex mirror shutter.

Viewfinder: DistantEye viewfinder. Removing eye from eyecup doesn't fog the running film.

Video: Black-and-white LCD video-assist.

Viewing Screen: Fiber optic 9x magnification (fixed). Aspect ratio markings: 1.66:1 Super16/1.78:1 16x9 (HDTV) 14x9/1.85:1 and 4:3/1.33:1 (Standard 16 frame indicator). Standard 16 (1.33:1) extraction possible at telecine or printing, centered on Super or Standard frame.

Mags: 200' (61m) coaxial quick-change magazines, "B" wound rolls in Aaton's "flexible" daylight spools. Requires Kodak A-Minima spools. Magazine can be loaded in subdued light without edge fogging using custom Kodak film loads. Requires Kodak A-Minima spools. Cannot use standard metallic 200' (61m) spools or 400' (122m) rolls.

Accessories: Time recording by XTRprod compatible AatonCode-II matrices, accurate to ¼ of a frame. The camera can be used as a master clock to other Aaton/ASCII devices. Uses 15mm mini rods. Chrosziel sunshades and matte boxes.

Sound Blimp: Leather sound barney.

Connections: Lemo6 (accessories), Lemo6 (in base to accept powerbase), Lemo5 (time code). Powerbase provides film/video sync, two Lemo6 connectors, one Lemo2 and one XLR 4.

Motors, Power: Batteries, on-board lithium battery. Four disposable 3V cells (CR17345). Also accepts 10-14V NiMH or NiCd batteries, or any 12V power source with cable.

Tri-phase brushless motor. 400mA with film, 550mA with film and video assist. Built-in intervalometer.

Misc: Built-In Incident Lightmeter: via rear dome (not TTL) T-stop and speed differential T-stop. Works with DV-size tripods, Steadicam mini.

Aaton XTRprod

***Weight:** 13 lbs./6kg with 400' (122m) load, 18 lbs/ 8.5 Kg with 800' (244m) load, and 12V onboard battery.

Movement: Co-planar single claw movement with lateral pressure plate that ensures vertical and lateral steadiness to 1/2000th of image dimensions. Hair-free gate.

FPS: 18 sync speeds including 23.98, 24, 29.97, 30, 48 and 75 fps and crystal-controlled adjustable speeds from 3–75 fps in 0.001 increments via a mini-jog. Internal phase shift control for TV bar elimination.

Aperture: 1.66. Optical center is switchable for Super 16 and standard 16mm operation.

dB: 20 dB -1/+2.

Displays: Illuminated LCD display, speed selection, elapsed footage, remaining footage, ISO selection, battery voltage timer and date. Pre-end and end of film warning, mag ID, full time code readout. Memo-mag allows magnetic recognition by the camera body of seven different magazines. Counter provides LCD display of remaining footage for short-end load or multi-emulsion shoot.

Lens: Interchangeable hard fronts: Arri PL as standard, Aaton, Panavision. Quick centering of lens axis for 16mm to Super 16 conversion formats. Field-convertible quick centering of lens axis, viewfinder and CCD target between formats.

Shutter: Reflex mirror shutter is user adjustable: 180°, 172.8°, 150° for 25 fps under 60 Hz lighting, 144°, 135°, 90°, 60°, 45°, 30°, 15°.

Viewfinder: Reflex from shutter. Fiber-optic imaging finder field is 120 percent of standard 16mm frame. Swiveling auto-erect image eyepiece with 10x magnification. 20cm or 40cm extensions and left-eye extender available. Field interchangeable standard 16mm/Super16 ground glass with Aatonite markings available. Built-in light meter display in viewfinder, also indicates low battery, out of sync and pre-end and end of film warnings.

Video: Integrated high-definition CCD color video assist. NTSC flicker-free at all camera speeds. Black-and-white video tap available. Film camera time code, footage, camera run status are inserted in both windows and VITC lines. Built-in frameline generator.

Viewing Screen: Quick-release, interchangeable fiber-optic screen available in 1.37, 1.66, 1.78 (16:9) and 1.85 aspect ratios and

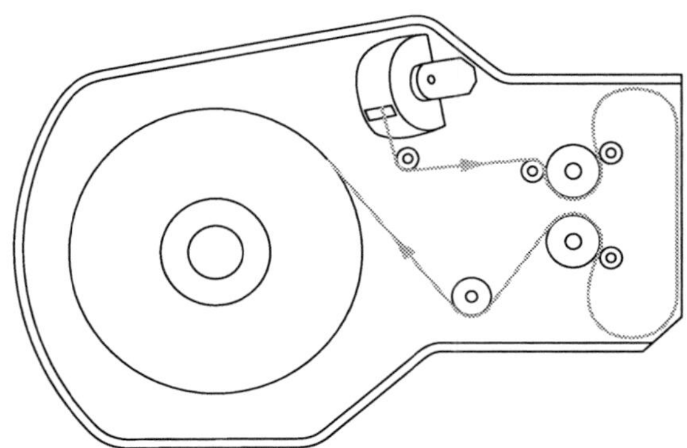

Aaton XTRprod Magazine Diagram
Film takes up emulsion side in.

combinations thereof. Aatonite illuminated markings.

Mags: 400' (122m) and 800' (244m) Coaxial instant preloaded magazine, magnetic drive, feed chamber loaded in dark and loop threaded in daylight. 14- to 15-perf loop length. Twistless film threading and hair-free gate eliminates pressure marks and emulsion pile-up. No time code-related parts to clean. Reads in feet and meters. Magnetically driven take-up with electronic and mechanical counters. Memo-mag indices for magazine ID recognition. Standard 2" plastic core for 400' (122m) mag, 3" plastic core required for 800' (244m) mag.

Accessories: Chrosziel follow focus and matteboxes. Leather sound barney. 15mm screw-in front rods. 15mm and 19mm bridgeplate compatible. Lightweight wide-format, swing-away matte box: two 4" x 5.6" and one 138mm rotating stages. Also accommodates Panavision mattes. Lightweight follow-focus system.

HydroFlex deepwater housing, ScubaCam splashbag.

Eshot intervalometer, CE F/V synchronizer and speed control, and Preston speed aperture computer.

Connections: Electronic Accessories: Inputs; Amph9 (video sync), Lemo6 (power zoom), Lemo8 (phase controllers), Lemo5 (SMPTE and ASCII time code). Time recording with AatonCode: Man-readable figures and SMPTE time code imbedded in rugged dot matrixes ½ frame accuracy over eight hours. Key-code compatible.

Motors, Power: Batteries: 10-14V DC. 12V DC NiMH onboard or external source via cable.

Tri-phase brushless motor. 600 mA, with film at 25°C/ 77°F under standard 12V power supply (10-12V). Temperature range: -20°C / +4°F to +40°C / +10°F.

Models: XTRplus (BiPhase)

24, 25, 30 fps plus 6–54 fps in 12 steps, no built-in TV bar eliminator on XTRplus. No backlight or elapsed time on XTRplus display. Memo-mag allows magnetic recognition by camera of three different magazines. Bottom of camera to lens optical axis distance is 109.2mm to make XTRplus compatible with 35mm camera accessories.

Shutter: True 180-degree front surface mirror essential for 60Hz HMI and video-monitor roll-bar elimination. Stops in viewing position. May be inched for aperture inspection.

LTR Model

Superceded by the XTRs, LTRs are differentiated by the magazine mechanical drive, no LCD counter and no CCD video-assist compatibility.

Ikonoskop A-Cam SP-16

Notes: Possibly the smallest, lightest MOS Super 16 camera, for the price of a DV camera: About the size of the old GSAP, much lighter, and uses readily-available 100' daylight spools.

Weight: 3.3 lbs./1.5kg with lens, internal battery and film.

Movement: Single transport claw

FPS: 6, 10, 12.5, 18, 20, 24, 25, 30, 36, 37, 37.5; timelapse from 1 fps to 1 frame in 24 hours.

Aperture: Super 16

Aperture Plate: Super 16 only. Super 16-centered lens port and viewfinder.

Displays: Backlit LCD main readout with 3 control buttons shows battery status, film exposed, frame rate and time-lapse mode.

Lens: C mount. Comes with Kinoptik 9mm f/1.5.

Shutter: 160°

Viewfinder: Non-reflex, magnetically-attached, parallel-mounted ocular.

Loads: 100' (30.5 m) daylight spools.

Accessories: ¼" x 20 and ⅜" x 16 tripod mounting threads.

Connections: Main power switch. Start/stop button. Connector for charger and external 12 V DC power (runs on 10.8-15 V DC). Requires external power for speeds of 30 and 37.5 fps. Remote on/off connector.

Power: Batteries: Camera comes with single-use Lithium Battery pack. 1400 mAh, 70 g. Runs 25 rolls at 25 fps at 20°C. A charger or an external power supply must NEVER be connected to the camera

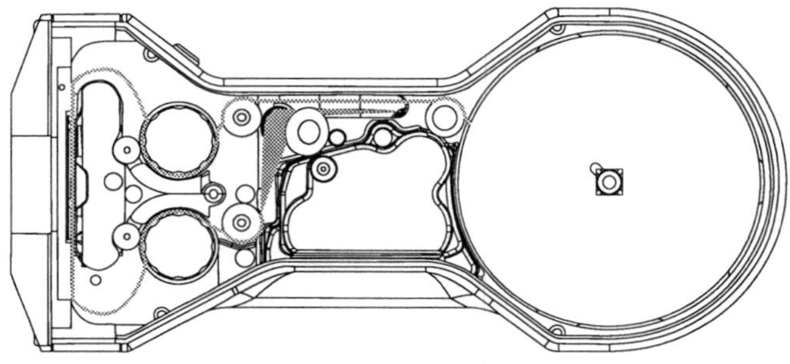

A-Cam SP-16 Magazine Diagram
Film takes up emulsion side in.

when using a single-use lithium battery pack.

Optional internal rechargeable Li-Ion battery, 480 mAh, 46 g, Runs 25 rolls at 25 fps at 20°C. Battery is located under the Battery Compartment Cover on the left side of the camera.

Arriflex 16 BL

Weight: 16.3 lbs./7.39 kg, camera, 400' (122m) magazine and lens

Movement: Pin registered.

FPS: 5-50 fps, forward or reverse, when used with appropriate motor and speed controls.

Aperture: .405" x.295" (10.3mm x 7.5mm). Standard 16mm.

dB: 30 dB.

Displays: Tachometer and footage counter.

Lens: Lens Mount: Steel Arri Bayonet mount (lens housings required to maintain minimal camera operating sound levels). All Arriflex Standard or Bayonet mount lenses that cover the 16mm format can be used with lens housings. Standard zoom and telephoto lenses should be used with the bridgeplate support system. Lenses: Fixed focal length Standard and Zeiss Superspeed lenses. Zeiss, Angenieux and Cooke zoom lenses. Some wide-angle lenses may hit shutter.

Shutter: Rotating mirror-shutter system with fixed 180-degree opening (1⁄48th of a second at 24 fps).

Viewfinder: Reflex Viewfinder: High-aperture/parallax-free viewing, 10x magnification at the eyepiece. Offset finder accessory available for handheld camera applications for additional operator comfort. Finder extender also available. APEC (Arri Precision Exposure Control): Exposure control system meters behind the lens and displays continuous exposure information (match-needle mode) in the viewfinder.

Video: May be attached to eyepeiece.

Viewing Screen: Non-interchangeable ground glass. Requires trained tech to change, using special tools.

Mags: 200' (61m), 400' (122m) forward and reverse, and 1200' (366m) forward-only magazines. Magazine loading: displacement.

Film Cores: 2" plastic cores. Film core adapter removable to adapt 100' (30.5m) daylight spools.

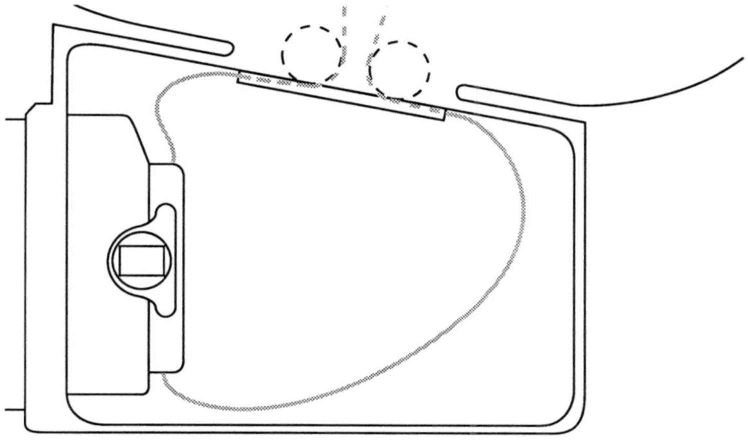

Arriflex 16BL Single System Threading Diagram
Film takes up emulsion side in.

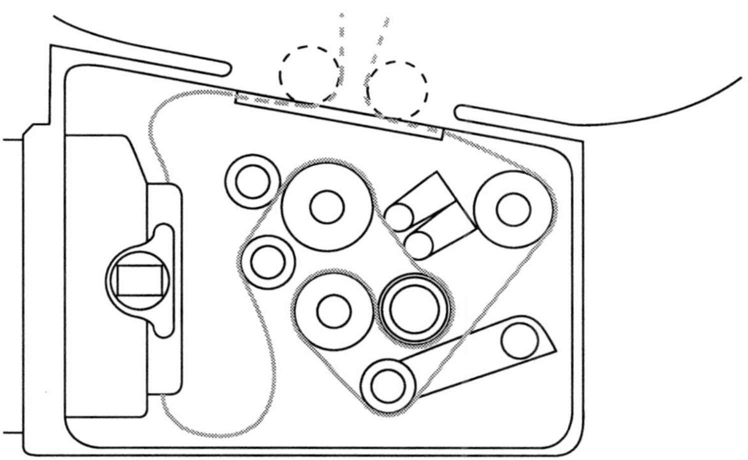

Arriflex 16BL Double System Threading Diagram
Film takes up emulsion side in.

Accessories: Universal Lens Housing for use with fixed focal-length lenses when minimal camera operating sound level is required (accepts 3" x 3" or a 94mm diameter filter).

Electronic Accessories: Variable Speed Controls. Jensen, CPT, Tobin.

Additional Accessories: Plug-in Single-System Sound Module and Single-System Record Amplifier. Hand-holdable.

Optical Accessories: Periscope finder orients image.

Batteries: 12V DC. Accepts blocks and belts.

Camera Support Equipment: Offset finder, assorted lens blimps, speed control, bellows matte box, sound module.

Matte Boxes: Bellows type available for all 16BL lens housings.

Motors, Power: Two motor drive systems available. The 12V DC quartz-controlled motor provides cordless sync-control and automatically stops shutter in viewing position. Speed range is 6, 12, 24 (quartz-controlled) and 48 fps. The Universal motor is transistorized and governor-controlled. A Variable Speed Control accessory will drive the Universal motor from 10 fps to 40 fps.

Arriflex 16S; 16M

Arriflex M

Arriflex S

Models: About 20,000 (for Standard) S cameras made, and 1500 M (for Magazine) cameras. 16S/B; 16S/B-GS; 16M/B. Main difference—you can use 100' daylight spools in the Arri S body without magazines; Arri M only uses magazines.

Arriflex 16S/B: accepts 100' (30.5m) daylight spools in body as well as top-mounting torque-motor driven 200' (61m) and 400' (122m) magazines.

Arriflex 16 S/B-GS: (Generator-Start) Pilotone sync generator with built-in start-mark light.

Arriflex 16M/B: no internal daylight film spool load capacity, takes gear-driven mags--200' (61m), 400' (122m) and 1,200' (366m) coaxial. Accepts all of the accessories in the 16S system except the magazines and power cables.

Weight: 5.8 lbs./2.63 kg

Movement: Pin registered. 16S, 16M and 16BL movements are identical.

FPS: Variable speed range to 75 fps with appropriate motor, forward or reverse.

Aperture: .405" x .295" (10.3mm x 7.5mm). Standard 16mm.

Displays: Tachometer, footage and frame counter.

Lens: divergent three-lens mount turret with two standard and one steel bayonet-lock. Any Arriflex Standard or Bayonet mount lens that covers the full 16mm format may be used. Zoom and telephoto

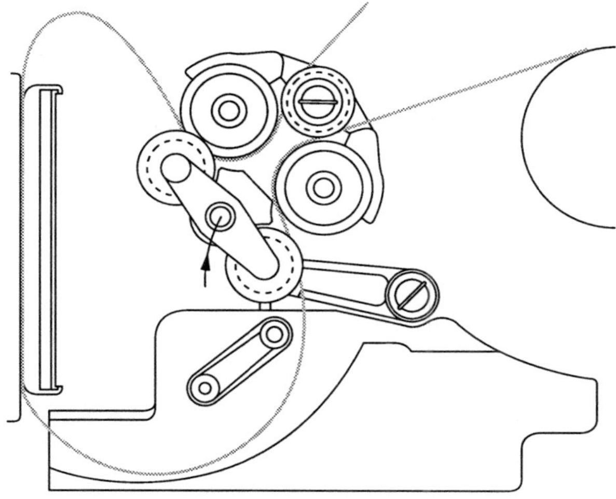

Arriflex 16 S/B Series Threading Diagram
Film takes up emulsion side in.

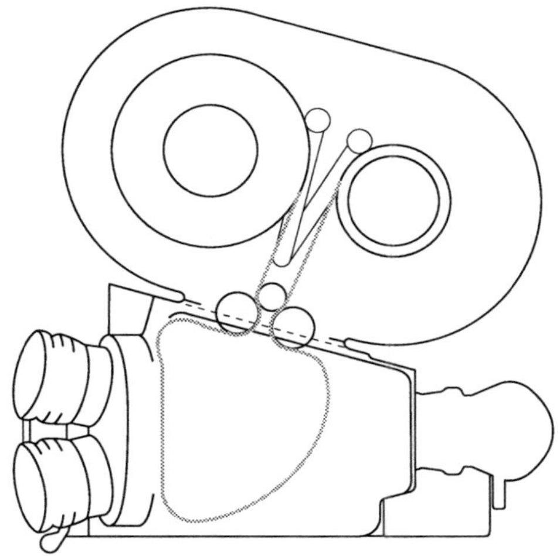

Arriflex 16M Magazine and Threading Diagram
Film takes up emulsion side in.

lenses require use of the bridgeplate support system.

Shutter: Rotating 180° mirror-shutter.

Viewfinder: Reflex, parallax-free viewing, 10x image magnification at the eyepiece. An interchangeable ground glass or fiber-optic screen, and an optional APEC exposure control indicator are located within the viewfinder system. APEC: Exposure control system meters behind the lens and displays continuous exposure information (match-needle mode in viewfinder, 16S only).

Viewing Screen: Interchangeable.

Mags: 16S: Accepts 100' (30.5m) daylight spools in body or in mags (core adapter releases from spindle). 200' (61m) and 400' (122m) torque motor-driven magazines. The torque motor drive is essential with 16S magazines and is interchangeable with all 16S magazines of the same film capacity. Lever for forward or reverse.

16M: 200' (61m), 400' (122m) and 1,200' (366m). Magazines are gear-driven and do not use torque motor drives. The 1,200' (366m) magazine operates in forward only.

Accessories: Bridgeplate support system, Adapter for microscope stand and microscope optical link. Fiber-optic screen, periscope viewfinder, finder extender. Norris intervalometer. Sound barney and blimp housings. Standard Matte-box (16 S/M) with adjustable bellows, a rotary and stationary filter stage. Accepts 2" x 2" glass or gelatin filters, and 60mm x 100mm glass filters. Universal matte-box (16 S/M) with adjustable bellows, a rotary and stationary filter stage. Accepts 3" x 3", 3" x 4", and 4" x 4" glass filters. A 94mm round Pola screen can also be used. Lightweight sunshade and filter holder (Rubber) for 16 S/M accepts 3" x 3" filters. Bridge plate support system. Adapter for microscope stand and microscope connector.

Motors, Power: Quartz-regulated, governor-controlled, synchronous and variable-speed motors.

12V DC quartz-motor for 24/25 fps 50/60Hz, variable speeds 5–75 fps, and single-frame forward and reverse capability and pilotone output.

8V and 12V DC governor motor for 24 fps forward operation only.

8V or 12V DC variable motor for 5–40 fps forward or reverse operation.

110V AC/60Hz synchronous motor and inline power supply for 12V DC, 24 fps operation.

Arriflex 16SR-1, 16SR2

Notes: Over 6,000 still in use. Many conversions and after-market adaptations.

Weight: 11–12 lbs. / 5–5.5 kg, body and magazine, without film and lens.

Movement: Single pull-down claw; single registration pin, with fixed-gap film channel.

FPS: 16SR-1 and 16SR-2 from 5–75 fps with external variable speed control. 16HSR-1 and 2 High-Speed from 10–150 fps with external variable speed control.

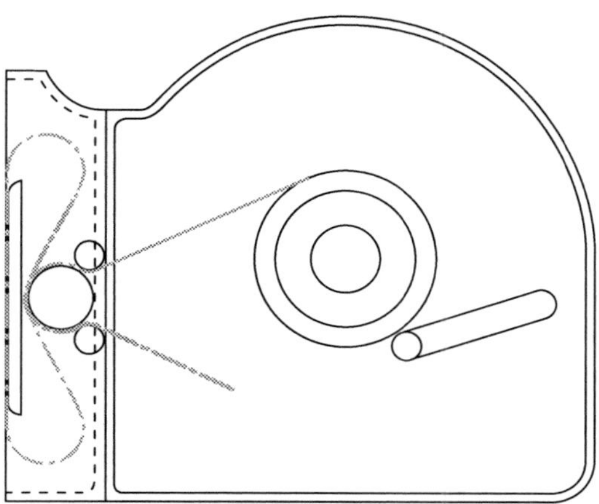

Arriflex 16 SR 1, 2 and 3 Magazine Diagram
Film takes up emulsion side in.

Switches located in the camera base of early versions lock in crystal speeds of 24 and 25 fps, 50 and 60 Hz and, in later SR cameras, 30 fps. All 16SRs can be modified with a 30 fps kit.

Aperture: Aperture plate is fixed. Standard cameras can be modified to Super 16. Aperture of regular 16SR camera is .295" x .405" (7.5mm x 10.3 mm); aperture of Super16 camera is .295" x .484" (7.5mm x 12.3mm).

Super16 conversion cannot be done in the field--requires repositioning of the optical center axis of lens mount, viewfinder, tripod thread and accessory holder by 1mm to the left. Height of Super 16 aperture is identical to Standard 16, but the aperture is 2mm wider, pushing into the left perf area on the negative—which is why you use single-perforation film stock.

dB: 22 dB - 28 dB (+/- 2 dB)

Displays: Footage remaining on back of magazine, and footage shot on take-up side of magazine (dial settable).

Lens: Bayonet on earlier models and PL on later models and conversions.

Lens Control: Arri Follow Focus 2 or FF3. Preston Microforce or Arri LCS/wireless zoom control.

Shutter: Rotating mirror-shutter.

Viewfinder: Reflex, swing-over viewfinder with parallax-free viewing and 10x magnification at the eyepiece. Swings 190° to either side of the camera for left- and right-side operation. The finder also rotates 360° parallel to camera on either side and swings out 25°. Red out-of-sync LED, and APEC exposure indicator. APEC through-the-lens system provides continuous exposure information (match-needle mode) on four-stop indicator displayed in viewfinder. For film speeds ASA 16-1000. Optional servo-operated automatic exposure control system (with manual override) for complete automatic exposure control with auto-iris lenses available. Super 16 SRs have same exposure meter system in regular 16SRs, but automatic exposure control feature cannot be installed.

Video: OEM removable video "T-bar" viewfinder assembly. optional and necessary for video assist.Aftermarket video assists from Denz, P&S, CEI, others.

Viewing Screen: Interchangeable fiber-optic viewing screen.

Mags: Rear mounted coaxial snap-on 400' (122m) mags. Black mags are for the regular speed cameras (up to 75 fps). Gray and black (marked HIGHSPEED) are for the Highspeed Cameras (up to 150 fps.) You should not interchange them.

Loop formed during loading for quick magazine change. White loop index line on bottom of mag.

2" plastic and collapsible cores, removable to accept 100' (30.5m) and 200' (61m) daylight loads. NASA used 400' (122m) daylight spools by milling off 1⁄8" of spool's edge.

Accessories: External speed control for operation of Standard 16SRs up to 75 fps or 16HSR High-Speed up to 150 fps. 16SR-2 Super 16 cameras time code compatible. Cinematography Electronics 16SR

Arriflex 16SR-1, 16SR-2

Camera	Xtal fps; Variable	dB	Weight Body+Mag	Shutter	Mags
16SR-1	24/25; 5-75	28	12 lbs/ 5.5 kg	180°	Black
16SR-1 Highspeed	24/25; 10-150	N/A	12 lbs/ 5.5 kg	180° (optional 144°)	Gray & Black
16SR-2	24/25, 24/30; 5-75	22	11 lbs/ 5 kg	180° (optional 144°)	Black Black
16HSR-2 Highspeed	24/25, 24/30 10-150	28	11 lbs/ 5 kg	180° (optional 144°)	Gray & Black
16SR-2 S16	24/25, 24/30; 5-75	22	11 lbs/ 5 kg	172.8° (optional 144°)	Black
16HSR-2 S16	24/25, 24/30;	28	11 lbs/ 5 kg	172.8° (optional 144°)	Gray & Black

Notes: Over 6,000 still in use. Many conversions and after-market adaptations.

Frameline Glow and Speed Control and intervalometer. Norris Intervalometer.

Bridgeplate, lightweight support rods, left and right grips for handheld operation, finder extender, lightweight follow focus, shoulder set.

Connections: Variable speed control, precision speed controls, external monitor synchronizer, multi-camera interlock achieved with FSZ-II sync control accessory. Modular plug-in electronics boards contain circuitry controlling all electronic functions, including a built-in start-marking system, out-of-sync light, Pilotone output and pre-wiring for SMPTE 80-bit time code.

Motors, Power: 12V DC . Four-pin connector. Pin 1 is (-); pin 4 is +12V. 12V on-board batteries with on-board battery adapter. Many after-market on-board batteries, including adapters for power-tool batteries. Accepts blocks and belts with power cable.

Arriflex 16SR3, 16HSR3, 16SR Advanced, 16HSR3 Advanced

Models: 16SR3 (5-75 fps)
16HSR3 High-Speed (5-150 fps)
16SR3 Advanced and HSR-3 Advanced (updated electronics, brighter finder, no APEC exposure meter)

All models thread the same as 16SR-1 and 16SR-2.

Weight: 13.5 lbs/6.1kg. (body+mag). 15.4 lbs/7kg. (body+loaded 400' mag+on-board battery)

Movement: Single pull-down claw; single registration pin, with fixed-gap film channel. 16SR-3 Advanced: Film guide has sapphire-rollers on one side, for reduced film dust and improved image steadiness.

FPS: 5-75 fps Standard; 5-150 fps High-Speed. Onboard programmable speeds of 24, 25, 29.97 and 30 fps, and variable crystal speeds from 5-75 fps in the Standard camera, or 5-150 fps in the High-Speed 16SR-3, variable in 0.001 increments at crystal accuracy. Speeds continuously variable when the Remote Unit (RU-1), Remote Control Unit (RCU-1), or Wireless Remote Control Unit (WRC-1) is used. Speeds can be programmed from the 16SR-3's onboard LCD with the RU-1 or with the Camera Control Unit (CCU), Arri's standard off-camera programming unit.

Aperture: .405" x .295" (10.3mm x 7.5mm). Easily converts from normal 16mm to Super 16. 16SR-3 Super 16 aperture can be masked for standard 16mm frame. No additional aperture is needed. Universal film gate needs only slight adjustment on Advanced models.

dB: Standard 20 dB(A) + 2 dB(A).

Displays: LCD Display—set/display frame rates, set/display film counter, display mirror shutter opening (during electronic inching mode), set/display time code and user bits, display TC sensitivity readout, battery voltage and low-battery warning, film end and asynchronous camera speed.

Lens: Standard Arri PL mount will take most 16mm and 35mm format PL mount lenses. Adapters available for 41mm diameter bayonet and standard mount lenses.

Shutter: rotating mirror shutter; manually adjustable when camera is switched. Shutter openings of 90°, 135°, 144°, 172.8°, 180°. Shutter opening indicated on LCD display during electronic inching mode. SR-3 Advanced: Variable (manually) rotating mirror shutter with shutter openings of 45°, 90°, 135°, 144°, 172.8°, 180°.

Viewfinder: Reflex Viewfinder: Reflex viewfinder swings 190° to camera left or camera right, with fully upright image in any position. Finder rotates 360° parallel to the body and can be swung away by 25°. Viewfinder provides automatic upright images at all times. Image can also be manually oriented.

With CCD video assist and flicker-reduction electronics attached, viewfinder swings in a 120° arc. Finder equipped with Arriglow continuously adjustable illuminated framelines for standard 16mm and Super 16. Finder also has warning indications for asynchronous camera speed, film end and low battery.

Finder center can be adjusted to either normal 16mm or Super 16. Switchable magnification built into viewfinder extension. With integrated video system attached, viewfinder can pivot from left to right camera side.

SR3 Advanced: Leaving out the exposure meter and utilizing a specifically designed mirror for the Arriglow results in gain in viewfinder brightness of ¾ of an f-stop.

Video: Takes Arri ½" black-and-white or color CCD video assist, and Arri AFP-2 flicker reduction electronics for bright, flicker-reduced images. Adjustable for standard 16mm and Super 16, with full image of either format on monitor. Changing beam-splitter ratio for color or black-and-white is easy and requires no adjustment. LCD display.

SR-3 Advanced: Video-assist system, IVS-Integrated Video System (can be used on 16SR-3). High-speed, high-resolution and flicker-free from 5 frames on. The IVS has two components: a video electronic module and a CCD module available in PAL and NTSC. Equipped with interchangeable optics with Super and normal 16mm formats. Effective ASA is 4000. Format markings can be electronically inserted into video image for low lighting conditions. Area outside format marking can be darkened electronically to better emphasize viewing area. Time code and camera status indicators such as "Standby/Run" can be directly inserted into video image.

Viewing Screen: Interchangeable fiber optic viewing screens. ArriGlow.

Mags: Rear mounted coaxial snap-on 400' (122m) and 800' (244m) mags. Loop formed during loading for quick magazine change. 2" plastic and collapsible cores, removable to accept 100' (30.5m) and 200' (61m) daylight loads. Standard 80-bit SMPTE time code module built in. Existing 16SR-2 magazines can be used. 16SR-3 magazines without time code available. Black 16SR mags work on regular speed 16SR-3 cameras. Gray and black 16HSR (marked HIGHSPEED) work on 16HSR-3 Highspeed Cameras.

Do not use regular mags on highspeed cameras; do not use highspeed mags on regular cameras.

Arriflex Cameras: Flange Focal Distance Chart

Camera Lens	Mount to Filmgate (mm)	Lens Mount to Groundglass (mm)
16S	51.970 to 51.980	52.000
16BL	51.970 to 51.980	52.000
16BLEQ	51.970 to 51.980	52.000
16M	51.970 to 51.980	52.000
16 SR-1, 2, 3 Adv.	51.990 to 52.000	52.000
16 SR-1, 2 ,3 Adv. HS	51.960 to 51.970	52.000

Arri Fuses (electronics/motor)

Camera	Fuse
16 S	None
16BL	1 A pico - slanting system 15 pico - protect wiring harness soldered inline below drive motor
16BLEQ	1/2 A & spare / 15 A & spare Access via coin slot
16M	None
16 SR-1, 2, 3, Adv.	3/4 A pico / 10 A pico
16 SR-1, 2, 3, Adv. HS	3/4 A pico / 10 A pico

For fuse part numbers, see chart on page 464.

Accessories: camera handgrip, finder extender, heated eyecup, lightweight support rods, lightweight follow focus, shoulder set, low-mode support, handgrips, matte boxes.

The 16SR-3 uses Arri 19mm rod Camera Support System. Bridgeplates and lens supports. 15mm rod adapters. Handheld accessories. A wide variety of Arriflex 35mm accessories can be used with the 16SR3.

Matte Boxes: 4x4 Production Matte Box ideal for 16SR-3. Its swing-away design covers lenses 16mm and up, has interchangeable two- and four-frame geared filter stages, is fully rotatable and accepts most support system accessories. Support system includes a full range of matte boxes in 6.6x6.6, 5x5, and a variety of 4x4. See pages 462–65 for a complete list.

Connections: Many 435 and 535 accessories can be used--External Synchronizing Unit(ESU), Remote Unit(RU-1), Remote Switch(RS). RCU, ICU, CCU and Laptop Computer Controller to control or set most functions (speed, footage counters, shutter angles, etc.) 24V to 12V power converter, multi-accessory connector. Integral 80-bit SMPTE time code. Recording module built into 16SR-3 magazines. Fully complies with SMPTE RP 114 standard.

Motors, Power: 24V DC. Onboard batteries. Accepts blocks and belts. Built-in crystal-controlled 24V DC motor.

Bell & Howell 16mm Filmo 70

Note: For threading diagram see Bell & Howell Eyemo 35mm.

Movement: Cam-operated single claw. Spring-loaded edge guide and pressure plate. Relieved aperture plate.

FPS: Models DA, DL and DR 8, 12, 16, 24, 32, 48, 64 fps. Model 70SR HR8-128 fps, 70J (rack over)

Aperture: Standard 16mm. Aperture plate optically centered.

Displays: Standard dial footage indicator, optional Veeder, root counter for motorized models.

Lens: Three-lens turret, geared to finder lens turret. C mount (DR), four-lens turret C mount (70J).

Shutter: 204° (models before SN 154,601 are 216°). Replacement shutter for less than 204°.

Viewfinder: External Viewfinder: Outside finder tube, three-lens turret, parallax-correcting eyepiece with matching objectives lenses. 70J Mitchell type side finder.

Focusing: Magnified central image on ground glass when objective lens turret is rotated 180°. Safety latch prevents camera running when in focusing mode. 70J rack over base

Mags: Rear mounted. Specialized double chamber magazine. Model 70SR HR and 70J use optional 400' (122m) compartment-type magazines (electric motor should be used for magazine operation). Light trap locking release adapter needed for loading. 100' (30.5m) internal daylight spools.

Motors: Spring-driven, governor-controlled. 22' (6.7m) per wind. AC and DC motors. 6V DC, 12V DC, 24V DC, 110V AC. Hand back wind for dissolves. Single frame drive.

Accessories: Filter slot modification. DA, DL and DR can be modified for 400' (122m) mags and electric motors. Ingate focusing and framing prism.

Bell & Howell Minicam 16mm (GSAP)

Notes: lightweight, almost expendable, "Point-of-View" camera often used for skiing, auto racing, sky diving.

Weight: 2.5 lbs/1.13kg.

Movement: Intermittent, single pulldown claw, cam actuated.

FPS: Adjusted for 24 or 48 fps.

Aperture: Standard 16mm. Optically centered.

Displays: Mechanical footage.

Lens: C mount or Arriflex mount configuration.

Shutter: 133° fixed.

Viewfinder: External Viewfinder: Boresight alignment tool available as optional accessory.

Mags: 50' (15m) rear mounted, displacement. Uses preloaded Alan Gordon Enterprises magazines, 16mm x 50', in all popular emulsions.

Motors, Power: 24V DC.

Bolex H16mm

Movement: Single-claw pulldown. No registration pin. Gate has automatic threading device that loops film and inserts it into gate and around sprockets. Rear pressure plate can be removed for cleaning gate. Automatic loop former prevents loss of loop.

FPS: single frame, 8-64 fps

Aperture: Standard. Super 16 on certain models. Fixed aperture plate.

Displays: Footage and frame counters add and subtract. Audible scene-length signal clicks every 28 frames. Single-frame exposure button for instantaneous or time exposures.

Lens: H-16 Rex 5 has three-lens turret for C-mount lenses, other models have large Bolex bayonet mount suitable for heavy zoom and telephoto lenses. Adapter for C-mount lenses and accessories available. Full line of Switar, Vario Switar and Angenieux zoom and standard lenses, matte box, extension tubes. Aspheron wide-angle adapters.

Shutter: Bolex spring-driven cameras (H-16 Rex 5 and H-16 SBM) have 135° variable shutter (some earlier models do not have this feature), which can be opened or closed while camera is running. It can be locked at ¼, ½ and can be opened and closed automatically with Rexofader accessory. Bolex electrically driven cameras (H-16 EBM and H-16 EL) have fixed 170-degree shutter. Shutter speeds electronically controlled 10-50 fps.

Viewfinder: Flickerless and parallax-free reflex viewfinder via prism reflex finder. Image magnified 14x in eye-level finder and may be continuously viewed in filming or stopped position. H-l6 EL has built-in, through-the-lens silicon light meter with shockproof LED indicators in the VF. All cameras have filter slot behind the lens.

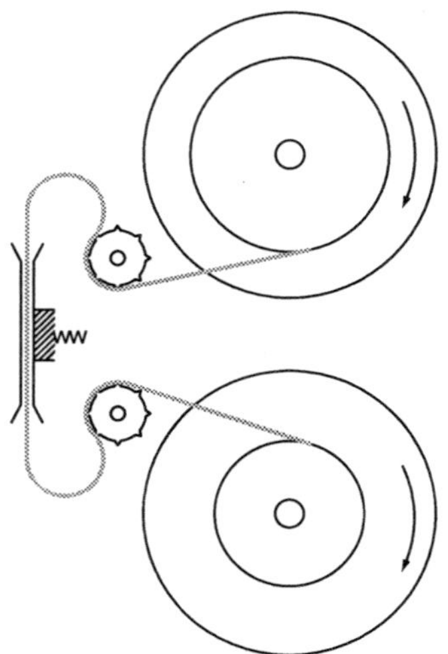

Bolex 16mm Threading Diagram
Film takes up emulsion side in (daylight spool load only)

Bolex H16 Models	
1933	H-16
1956	H-16 reflex H-16 R
1959	H-16 rex-1 (var. shutter 145°)
1963	H-16 rex-2 (var shutter 130°)
1963	H-16 rex-3 built-in flat base
1964	H-16 m-3 built-in flat base
1965	H-16 s
1965	H-16 rex-4 1:1 ratio shaft
1965	H-16 m-4 1:1 ratio shaft
1967	H-16 rex-5 400' magazine saddle, clapper
1967	H-16 m-5 400' magazine saddle
1971	H-16 rex-5 new vf, magnification 13x
1971	H-16 sbm bayonet mount, 400' magazine saddle
1971	H-16 sb bayonet mount, 100' capacity
1971	H-16 ebm built-in electric motor
1975	H-16 el built-in elec. motor, exp. meter
1978	H-16 el/tv (serries ii) tv mask, x-sync
1978	H-16 sbm/tv tv mask in vf, 13x magnification
1980	H-16 el/tv (series iii) 1600 asa exp meter
2000	Super 16 conversions

External Viewfinder: External sidefinder on some models.

Film, Mags: All cameras accept 100' (30.5m) daylight loading spools, which can be ejected with built-in lever device.

Optional 400' (122m) magazine with self-contained take-up motor available.

Accessories: Automatic Rexofader device for H-16 REX and SBM available for 40-frame fades. Camera grip, extension tubes for macrocinematography. Cable releases, shoulder brace. NOTE: Many other accessories, such as animation motors, microscope attachments and time-lapse units, are available from other firms. Norris makes intervalometer for REX 4 and 5, EBM, SBM. Sound Blimp. Underwater housing for EL and EB.

Motors, Power: Spring-driven cameras will expose 16 ½' of film on one winding. Variable-speed motor and electronically stabilized motor suitable for sync pulse, and crystal sync available for spring-driven cameras. H-16 EBM and H-16 EL have 10-50 fps electronically regulated motors built in. H-l6 EL has single frame and electric rewind, instant start and stop. All models accept 400' (122m) magazine with take-up motor. Spring motor may be disengaged. Full 100' (30.5m) film rewind.

Canon Scoopic 16, 16M, 16MS

Notes: Point-and-shoot 16mm camera from 1972.

Weight: 7.5 lbs./3.2kg.

Movement: Single claw pulldown; uses single or double perf on 100' (30.5m) spools.

FPS: Single frame, 16, 24, 32, 48 fps..

Aperture: Standard 16mm.

Displays: Self-resetting analog footage counter to 100' in 5' settings; frame speed indicator..

Lens: Fixed 13–76mm f/1.6 Canon zoom; 16M has 12.5–75mm f/1.8 zoom; 16MS has 12.5–75mm f/1.8 macro zoom; manual zoom controls.

Shutter: 135° fixed.

Viewfinder: Reflex Viewfinder, adjustable eyepiece.

Exposure Control: Cross coupled Cds cell located above the lens can be programmed for ASA film speeds 10–320 and automatically controls diaphram setting (f/1.6 to 22) in relation to camera's running speeds. Also instant manual override.

Motors, Power: 12V DC. 12V DC onboard block; external battery by cable.

Cinema Products CP-16, A, R, RA

Weight: 17.4lbs/7.9kg with 10-150mm zoom, 400' (122m) film, battery.

Movement: Single-claw film pulldown. Film guided over a series of stainless-steel balls for scratch-free pictures (with no emulsion pickup).

FPS: Standard speeds 12, 16, 20, 24, 28, 32 and 36 fps. Pulley change 24 to 25 makes range 12.5, 16.5, 21, 25, 29, 33.5 and 37.5 fps.

Aperture: Standard 16mm. Stainless-steel pressure plate, ground lapped with recessed center area, easily removable for cleaning. After market Super 16 conversions.

dB: 24-28 dB.

Displays: Viewfinder indicator LED for battery, out of sync, film runout, sound VU. Battery test.

Lens: Thread-locking bayonet. Adapters for Arri or Nikon mounts.

Shutter: Focal plane 170° (optional 144°).

Viewfinder: Reflex Viewfinder, Rotating mirror integral with focal-plane shutter. Stops in viewing position. Fiber-optics screen marked with TV safe action, projection, and 35mm blow-up lines. Adjustable focusing eyepiece 12x magnification, 90-degree click stop rotation; optional 360-degree rotatable right or left eyepiece upright image. 7" Finder extension.

Video: Cinevid-16 video assist, bayonet mounted.

Viewing Screen: Fiber-optic plate. Interchangeable.

Mags: 400' (122m). Adapter for Mitchell 400' (122m) and 1,200' (366m) magazines.

Accessories: Automatic or semi-automatic exposure system with viewfinder display. Behind the lens filter slot. Shoulder mounts.

Sound Recording System: CP-16R and CP-16R/A cameras accept Crystasound 3XL-type magnetic record/playback heads. The CP-16R/A features Crystasound built-in amplifier system, a self-contained recording system complete with two low-impedance dynamic microphone inputs, one 600 ohm line input, VU meter, headphone monitoring, switchable AGC and auxiliary mixer input. Provision for wireless receiving also available. Auxiliary mixer, model 6C, provides six channels of microphone input. Auxiliary mixer is complete with VU meter, switchable AGC and headphone monitoring. Mixer, built-in amplifier and wireless units are powered from the camera's NiCd battery (model NC-4).

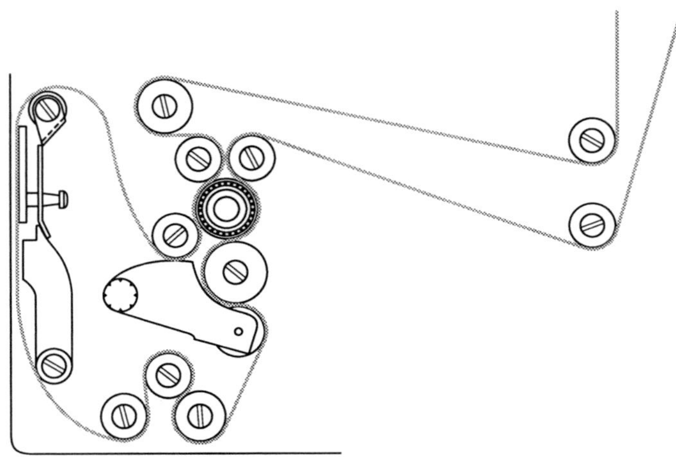

Cinema Products CP-16 Threading Diagram
Film takes up emulsion side out.

CP-16, CP-16A: Non-reflex, 180-degree fixed shutter. C-type lens mount.

CP-16R, CP-16R/A: 156-degree shutter. 170° on later models. CP(miniature BNCR mount). Com-mag, Integral Com-mag, and Sep-mag capability (also on model 16R/ADS).

Motors, Power: 20V plug-in battery drives crystal controlled motor 24 or 25 fps sync speed. On-board battery adapter and cable to run camera with 16.8 v battery belts. Power supply/charger. Batteries: 20V DC onboard block.

Cinema Products GSMO 16mm

Weight: 12.44lbs/5.65kg with 400' (122m) load and 17.5-70mm zoom lens.

Movement: single-claw, sinusoidal registration movement with a curved film gate for minimum pulldown time. Interchangeable film gate assembly with floating pressure plate and hard-chrome edge film guides located in cassette-type coaxial magazine.

FPS: Remote speed control with continuously variable speed from 12-64 fps. Crystal-controlled motor speeds of 12, 16, 24, 25, 32, 48 and 64 fps or alternate speeds of 12, 20, 24, 25, 30, 48 and 64 fps.

Aperture: Full 16mm frame. Optically centered.

dB: 25-30 dB 3' from front lens.

Displays: Illuminated digital film counter (feet or meters) with memory. Full-frame auto slating. External battery test. LED out of sync and low-battery indicator in viewfinder.

Lens: Single-thread locking bayonet with locating pin. Optional adapters for Arri- and Nikon-mounted lenses.

Shutter: Rotating mirror 180°, stops in viewing position.

Viewfinder: Reflex Viewfinder, fiber-optic viewing screen marked with TV safe action, 16mm projection and 35mm blow-up lines. Two viewfinder options have 12x magnification, high-efficiency optics, focusing eyepieces. Dual-purpose viewfinder provides 32 adjustable viewing positions; may be extended 7" for tripod operation. Optional viewfinder pivots for left or right eye and provides 360-degree rotation. Upright image. Optional 7" extender.

Video: Available.

Viewing Screen: Fiber-optic plate, interchangeable.

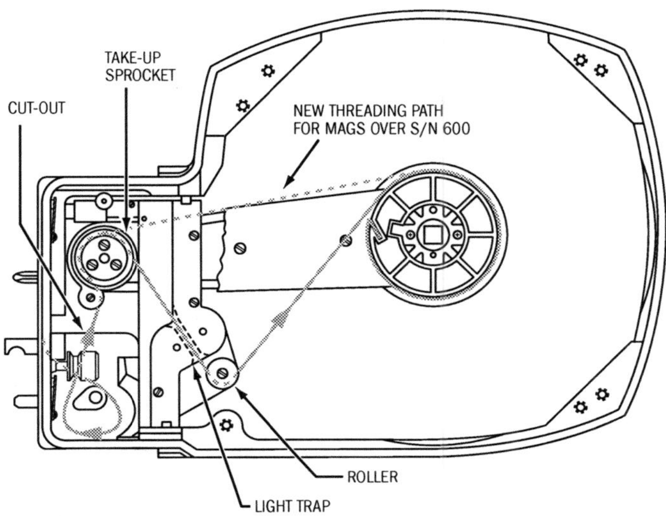

Cinema Products GSMO 16mm Magazine Diagram
Film takes up emulsion side in.

Mags: Quick-change, coaxial double chamber, rugged, cassette-type coaxial magazine contains interchangeable film gate assembly. (Preloaded magazines can be changed instantly without touching film.) 100' (30.5m) and 400' (122m) capacities. 400' (122m) magazine features "film remaining" manual indicator.

Accessories: Exposure control system with display in viewfinder. Quick-release shoulder and tripod mounts.

Motors, Power: 20V DC. AC power supply, battery charger.

Éclair ACL 16mm

Weight: 7.7lbs/3.5kg.

Movement: Claw movement is wedge-shaped claw controlled by eccentric and fixed cam and rendered positive by use of counter cam. Steadiness of image is excellent, with tolerance of less than 1⁄1000th of frame height. Lateral steadiness is ensured in gate by fixed side bar and spring-loaded guide. Image sharpness ensured by spring-loaded pressure plate which forms part of the front of ACL magazine and maintains film perfectly against aperture during exposure.

FPS: Crystal-controlled motor at 24 or 25 fps directly on shutter shaft. Variable-speed capability 12–40 fps. Optional 115V sync motor.

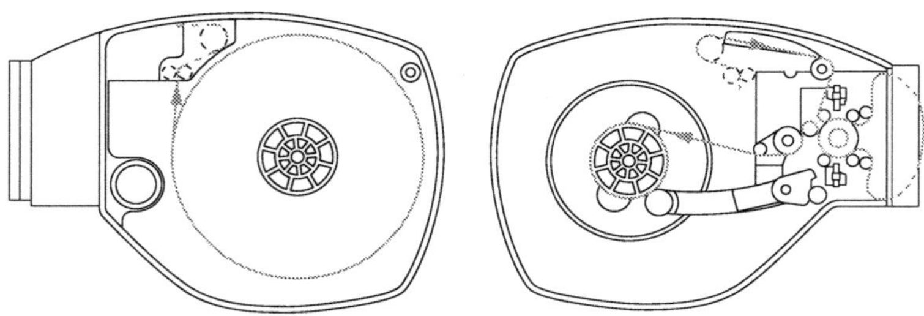

Éclair ACL 16mm Magazine Diagram
400' magazine. Left: supply side Right: Take-up side
Film takes-up emulsion side in.

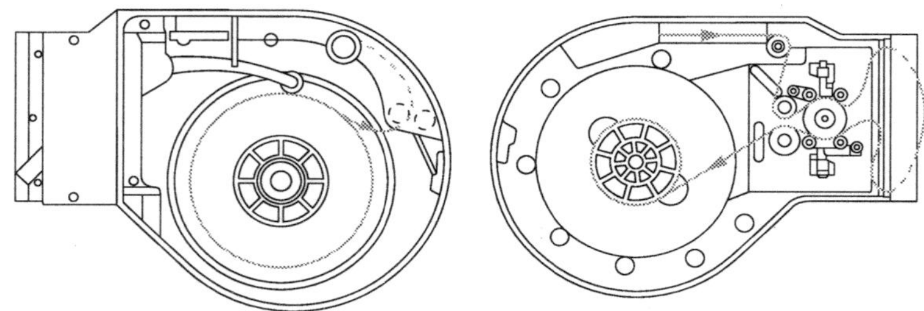

Éclair ACL 16mm Magazine Diagram
200' magazine. Left: supply side Right: Take-up side
Film takes-up emulsion side in.

Aperture: Fixed, Standard 16. Super16 aftermarket conversions.

Displays: Counter on magazine.

Lens: Lens Mount: Universal Type C. Outside thread for various adapters. Behind the lens filter slot. Must be in to avoid light leaks.

Shutter: Focal plane 175°.

Viewfinder: Reflex Viewfinder: Oscillating mirror, low-loss optical system, fine-grain ground glass. Image magnification 12x. Focusing eyepiece will rotate through 360° parallel to the camera. Later cameras have orientable (auto-erect) finders.

Mags: Snap-on 200' (61m), Coaxial. Pre-threaded for quick change. Core-load film or daylight spools. Film remainder dial. 400' (122m) mags available in two versions - both require more powerful aftermarket motors. Later cameras have stronger magazine locks.

Accessories: Electronic Accessories: Automatic start mark. Pilotone output 50 or 60 Hz. Norris makes intervalometer.

Motors, Power: 12V DC.

Éclair NPR 16mm

Movement: Film advanced by cam movement. Quiet movement achieved by wedge-shaped claw which slides into perforation with a wedging motion. Film is pulled down and registered upon bench-type registration pin which begins moving into position before film has stopped.

FPS: See camera motor.

Aperture: Raised areas in center of aperture portion of pressure plate eliminates possibility of breathing or focal shift. Extra-long rear pressure plates and side guide rails steady film.

dB: 29.5 dB at 3'. Standard 16mm. Super16 after market conversions.

Displays: Footage on magazine.

Lens: Standard two-position turret has one Camerette CA-l lens mount and one C mount. Turrets available with two CA-1 mounts, or with two C mounts. Any lens from 5.7mm focal length may be used without affecting sound level of camera. CA-1 is bayonet mount without springs or other loose-fitting adjustments. Lenses by Angenieux, Kinoptik, Taylor Hobson Cooke and some Berthiot optics can be supplied in CA-l mount.

Shutter: 180° mirror reflex shutter, centered on motor shaft below aperture, variable 5 -180° in 5° increments while camera is stopped.

Viewfinder: Reflex Viewfinder, Double 360° swiveling viewfinder shows more area than film aperture. Inner rectangle outlines full aperture. Inaccuracies in alignment of viewfinder do not affect accuracy of ground glass positioning. Eyepiece adjusts for either

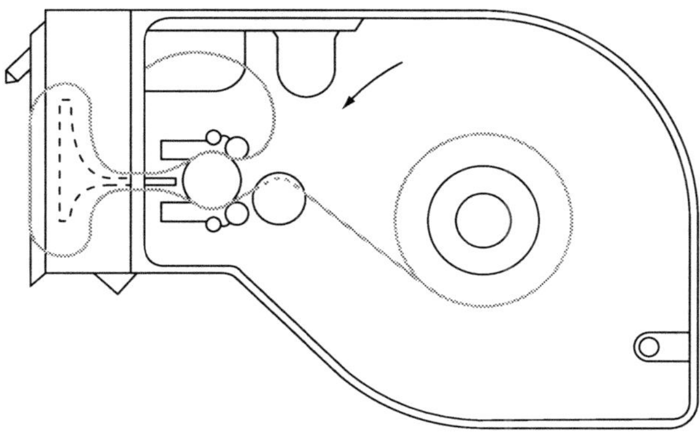

Éclair NPR Take-up Side of Magazine Threading Diagram
Film takes up emulsion side out.

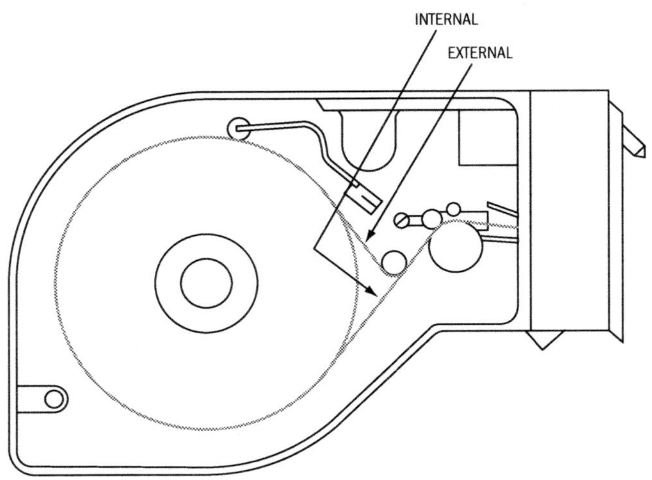

Éclair NPR Feed Side of Magazine Threading Diagram
External: Film wound emulsion side out. Internal: Film wound emulsion side in.

left- or right-eye operation and has full diopter compensation with automatic opening and closing light trap. Image magnified 12x. Critical focusing possible even at low light levels or with stopped down lens because of extremely fine-grain ground glass, high-gain mirror and low-loss optical system. Parallax-free, through-the-lens focusing and viewing.

Mags: 400' (122m) instant-changing coaxial magazine has pre-threaded loop and may be snapped on and off instantly. Entire film aperture and film channel may be inspected and cleaned when magazine is removed. No torque motors required for take-up. Each magazine takes either core loads or daylight spools of 100' (30.5m), 200' (61m) or 400' (122m) capacity. Separate footage counters provided for core and daylight spool loads. As soon as core load film is engaged in sprocket wheel of magazine feed chamber, remainder of threading operation may be carried on in daylight. Magazine has noisemaking clutches and loop guards to disengage drive and warn of malfunction.

Accessories: Built-in automatic clapper for start marks with bloop modification for use with Nagra ¼" magnetic tape recorder and other oscillator markers.

Matte box with adjustable bellows and two-stage filter (2" x 2") holder with rod and long-lens supports.

Motors, Power: Standard motor is 12V DC transistor-controlled regulated 24 fps type. Motor generates 60-cycle sync pulse when operating exactly at 24 fps and maintains speed accuracy within .2

percent (indicated by running light). Motor has high torque and operates at 1,440 rpm to turn shutter shaft directly, so that no noise is caused by gearing down. Also available: variable speed (wild) 12V DC motor (0-40 fps); synchronous (sound) 110V AC, 220V AC single or three-phase motors for operation from mains or from crystal-controlled power packs for cordless synchronous operation. All sync motors are available for 25 fps 50 cycle (European TV) operation. Motors are interchangeable without tools. Several aftermarket motors—recently from Tobin Cinema Systems.

Frezzolini FR-16

*__Notes:__ See Cinema Products CP-16R (Reflex). Same movement and threading. Same magazines, lens mounts, eyepiece mounts.

Power: Frezzi is 12 v DC (CP-16 is 20 v DC).

Frezzolini LW-16

*__Notes:__ See Cinema Products CP-16A (non-reflex). Same movement and threading. Same magazines, lens mounts, eyepiece mounts.

Power: Frezzi is 12 v DC (CP-16 is 20 v DC).

Mitchell 16mm Professional, HS, & HSC

Movement: Dual pilot pins. Dual-claw pulldown. Removable aperture plate has built-in filter slot. Pressure plate removable. Timing marks on shutter and movement permit easy removal of entire mechanism for cleaning, eliminating danger of improper insertion.

FPS: Professional model single frame to 128 fps. HS and HSC single frame to 400 fps. All models will run 1200' (366m) roll of film at maximum frame rates. Standard 16mm aperture.

Displays: Professional and HS: Veeder footage and frame counters. Camera base has incorporated spirit level. Calibrated tachometer built into back of camera. Built-in buckle trip operates if film fails to take-up. HS and HSC: End-of-run switch.

Lens: Professional and HS: Four-lens turret, positive index type. Flange depth 0.900N, Mitchell-designed, heavy-duty, precision rotary-type lens mounts with built-in follow-focus gear ring. C-type Mitchell adapter available, permits use of C-mounted lenses on 16 Mitchell turret. HSC has single-hole lens board on camera body.

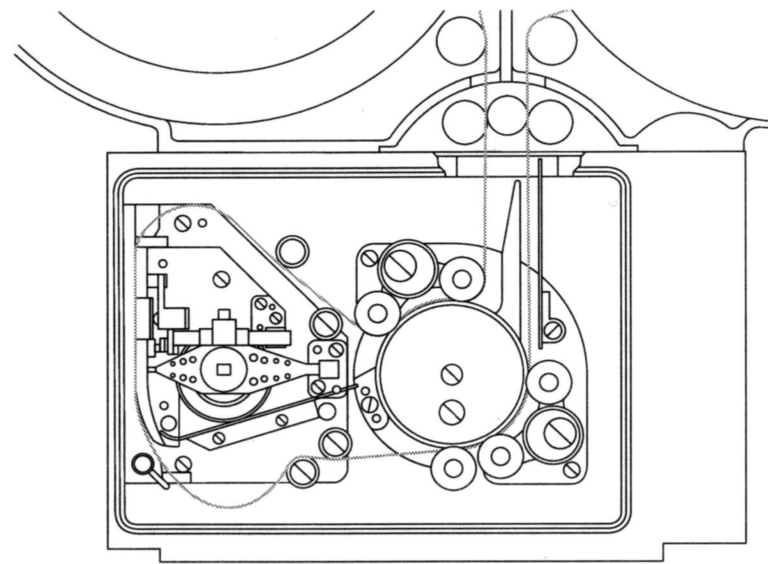

Mitchell 16mm Professional HS and HSC Threading Diagram
Film takes up emulsion side out.

Uses lenses in Mitchell mounts. Mitchell C-mount adapter for lenses in standard C mounts available. Gel filter slot in aperture plate.

Shutter: Professional Model: 0°–235°. HS and HSC: 0°–140°. Both adjustable while running (not recommended above 150 fps on HS and HSC models).

Viewfinder: External Viewfinder. Professional, HS: Large, erect viewfinder calibrated for different focal-length lenses provides sharp, bright image and accurate field for ease of composition. Parallax-free follow-focus attachment available. Special tracking and monocular finders available for sports and instrumentation filming. HSC: 10x prismatic boresight.

Focusing: Professional and HS: Variable magnification, upright image focusing telescope built into camera door. Through-the-lens ground glass critical focus and viewing when camera is racked over. Built-in contrast viewing filters for color and monochrome film. Interchangeable ground glasses with different aspect ratios available. HSC: uses 10x prismatic boresight looking through aperture plate opening in register plate.

Mags: Double compartment-type units. Professional, HS & HSC: 400' (122m) and 1,200' (366m). Magazines accept 100' (30.5m) or 200' (61m) daylight spools or 400' (122m) or 1,200' (366m) lab loads. Brake recommended on feed side when running high-speed.

Accessories: Complete line of accessories. Intervalometer. Sportsfinder. Sound Blimp:

Motors, Power: Professional, HS and HSC models: up to 128 fps. Variable (wild) motors: 12V DC, 110V AC or DC. High-Speed motors: 110V AC or DC (48–128 fps), 24V DC (16–64 fps). Synchronous (sound) motors: 110V, 60-cycle, 1-phase AC; 220V, 60-cycle, 3-phase AC; 220V AC/96V DC multi-duty (synchronous at 220V only). 50-cycle motors available on request. Animation motor: Stop-motion 110V AC. HS and HSC: 115V, 60-cycle AC (12–400 fps). Has solid-state variable speed control.

Mitchell 16mm Reflex, SSR-16 Single System, DSR-16 Double-System Sound Cameras

Movement: Single claw, single (or double for double-system sound) registration pin. Adjustable stroke. Three sprockets. Removable aperture plate has built-in filter slot. Movement removable without losing timing. Alternate non-metallic and steel gears for quietness. Guides and locks interlocked with compartment door.

FPS: 16–64 fps. Standard 16mm aperture.

dB: 36 dB at 3'.

Displays: Footage counter and tachometer dials. Electrical panel has lighted switch. Buckle trip will turn out light.

Lens: Three-lens divergent turret. Flange depth 2.047" (52mm).

Lens Control: External follow focus and zoom knobs on both sides, viewing windows for lens scales. Flat front door with removable sunshade for use with fixed focal-length lenses is easily exchanged for extension housing when using zoom lens.

Shutter: Focal plane 170° separate from mirror.

Viewfinder: Reflex Viewfinder, rotating mirror. Ground glass tinted outside film-aperture area. Interchangeable ground glasses. Dovetail on camera for outside finder.

Mags: 400' (122m) and 1,200' (366m). Double compartment. Five internal lights at strategic points. Threading knob for motor.

Accessories: Norris intervalometer, sound Blimp (through-the-lens reflex viewing is extended through the blimp door-- Same as S35R blimp.)

Sound Recording Features: SSR-16 contains sound head for

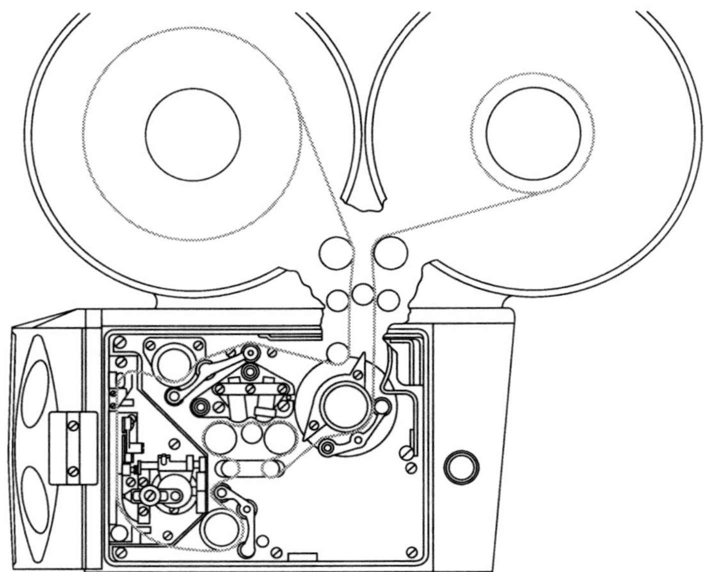

Mitchell 16mm Reflex Magazine and Threading Diagram
SSR-16 Single-System
Filmtakes up emulsion side out.

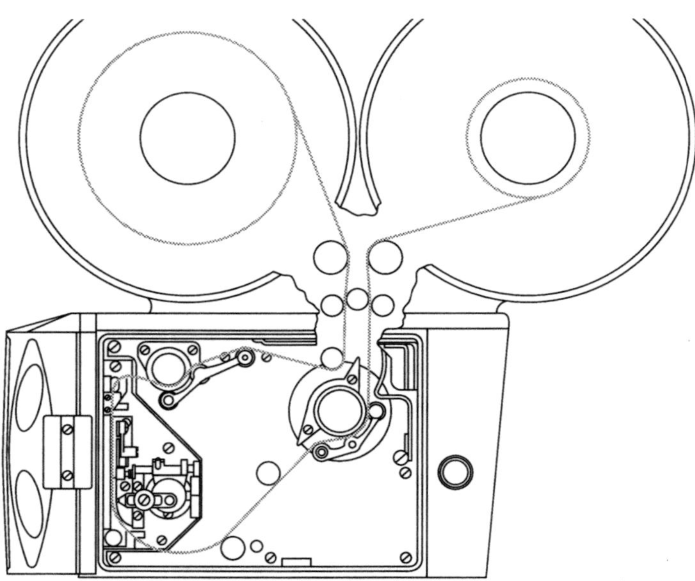

Mitchell 16mm Reflex Magazine and Threading Diagram
DSR-16 Double-System
Filmtakes up emulsion side out.

magnetic recording on pre-striped film. Record and playback head contained internally in camera box behind the movement. Extremely high quality of recording system and camera allows wow and flutter characteristics of less than 0.3 percent and 0.4 percent, respectively. Mixer amplifier allows use of two low-impedance microphones. System is all solid-state, contains VU meter, bias adjustment, individual and master monitoring control for microphones; power supply is self-contained, using alkaline nickel cadmium batteries with built-in charger. Produces 30 volts DC and charger operates on 115V AC 50/60 Hz. Recording heads and mixer-amplifier made by RCA. The SSR-16 also contains pic-sync generator for recording double-system lip-sync sound. DSR 16 is for double-system lip-sync sound work. Has same features as SSR-16 except RCA recording system is deleted and pic-sync generator is used. Both models available for use on 50 Hz power.

Motors, Power: Variety of de-mountable motors, no tools required.

Panaflex 16mm - "Elaine"

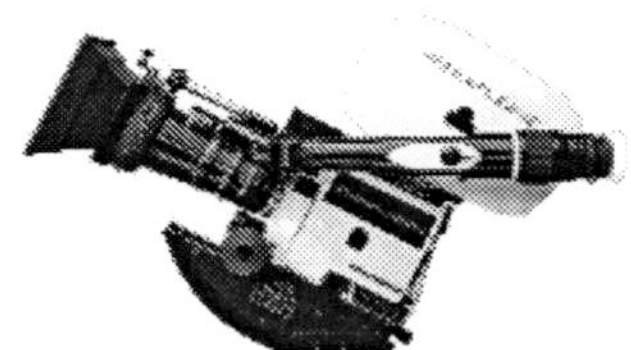

Notes: Named after a lady who works at Panavision (still does).

Weight: 16.6 lbs / 7.54 Kg (body with short eyepiece)

Movement: Dual pilot pin registration. Entire movement may be removed for servicing.

FPS: 4-50 fps, crystal-controlled at all speeds; may be adjusted in 1⁄10 fps increments.

Aperture: .486" x .295" (12.34mm x 7.49mm) SMPTE 201M – 1996. Aperture Plate removable for checking and cleaning. Super 16 aperture plate is standard.

dB: Less than 20 dB with film and lens, measured 3' from the image plane.

Displays: Camera speed and footage, LED indicators for low battery / low film / film jam/ illegal speed.

Lens: Panavision 16 positive clamp lens mount with index pin. Super 16 lens mount is standard, regular 16 upon request.

Lenses: Panavision/Zeiss Superspeeds and other 16mm image format lenses. 6mm to 135mm (see separate lens list). Wide range of Panavision-engineered zoom lenses by other manufacturers also available. All lenses have widely spaced lens focus calibrations and T-stop marks. Most prime and zoom lenses will cover Super 16.

Lens Control: Lightweight modular follow-focus control which can be used from either side of the camera is standard; optional electronic remote focus and aperture controls also available. Zoom lenses supplied with a motor-driven zoom control unit as standard. Iris gears are incorporated into most prime and zoom lenses.

Shutter: Focal plane shutter with infinitely variable opening, adjustable in-shot. Maximum opening 200°, minimum 50°, with adjustable maximum and minimum opening stops; adjustable for critical synchronization with computers, TV monitors and HMI lighting at unusual frame rates. Manual and electronic remote control units available.

Viewfinder: Reflex Viewfinder, reflex rotating mirror is standard and independent of camera shutter. Viewfinder tube is orientable and gives a constantly upright image through 360°. Short viewfinder provided for handheld operation. Viewfinders may be swung out to suit left- or right-eye viewing. System incorporates optical magnifier for critical focusing and picture composition, contrast viewing filter and lightproof shutter. Wide-range ocular adjustment with marker bezel to note individual settings. Built-in "Panaclear" eyepiece heater ensures mist-free viewing. Eyepiece leveler supplied to keep eyepiece position constant while tilting the camera up or down. Eyepiece diopter to suit operator's eyesight can be provided on request.

Video: Flicker-free at 24 fps and 30 fps. Auto color balance, normal and boost gain, ND filter, wide sensitivity range.

Viewing Screen: "Panaglow" illuminated reticle system with brightness control is standard.

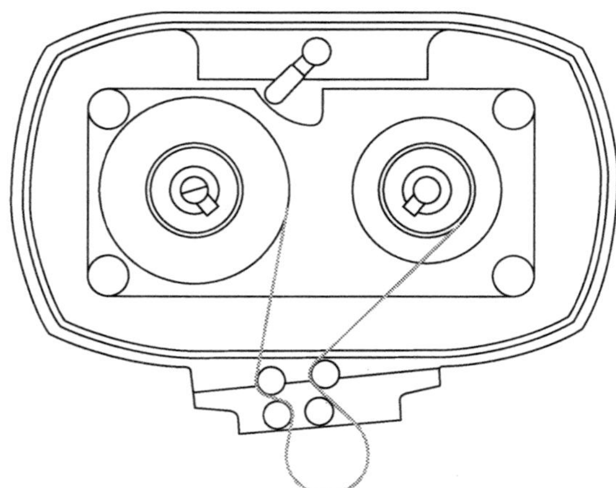

Panavision 16mm film magazine.
Film takes up emulsion side out.

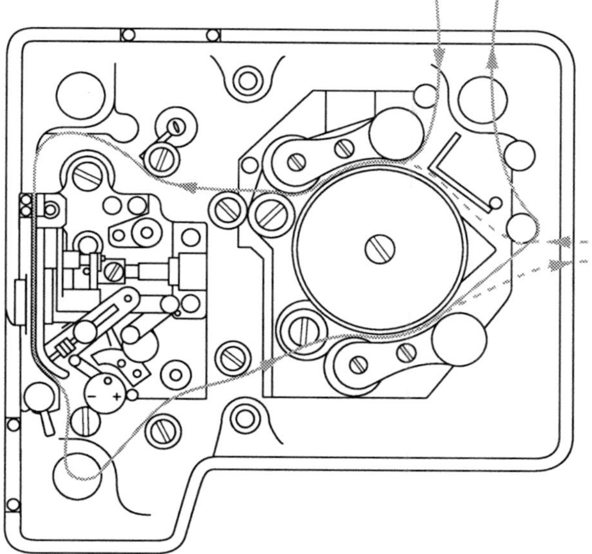

Panaflex 16mm Camera System (The Elaine) Threading Diagram
Film takes up emulsion side out.

Mags: 400' (122m) and 1,200' (366m) film magazines available. The 400' (122m) can be rear mounted for good balance when handholding. Magazine Loading: Displacement, top or rear mount. 2" plastic core required for 400' (122m), 3" for 1,200' (366m) magazine.

Accessories: Heated covers available to give additional protection to lenses, especially zoom lenses, for smooth operation in intensely cold conditions. Other covers available to protect the camera, magazines and lenses from heat, dust, rain and water. Spinning-glass rain deflectors available for use in storm conditions. Autobase available to secure camera in conditions of vibration, high "g" forces and other stressful and dangerous forces. Water-box available to protect camera in shallow water conditions, and hazard box can be used to protect camera from explosions, collisions and other dangerous situations.

Camera Support Equipment: Standard Panahead. Sliding base unit enables camera to be quickly attached and detached and to be slid backwards and forwards on the head for optimum balance. "Panatate" turn-over mount allows 360° camera rotation about the lens axis while permitting nodal pan-and-tilt movements.

Handheld handles and shoulder rest for handholding the camera. In this configuration, camera is best used with 400' (122m) magazine fitted on the rear.

Standard matte box incorporating a sunshade, provision for two 4" x 5.650" filters. Special matte boxes incorporating more filter stages, with provision for sliding (motorized if required), rotating and tilting to take 6.6" square filters optional.

Connections: Sync box to synchronize the camera with computers, video signals and projectors for shutter phase synchronization. Camera will accept external drive signals via the 10-pin accessory connector.

Motors, Power: 24V DC. Crystal-controlled brushed motor drives system. Camera, magazines, heaters and accessories operate off a single 24V battery. Belt batteries for handholding optional.

Misc: All Panaflex-16 cameras and magazines have built-in heaters.

Photo-Sonics 16mm 1PL

Weight: 14 lbs./6.36 kg. with 400' (122m) loaded magazine, no lens.

Movement: Intermittent with two registration pins and two pulldown arms.

Film specifications: Standard 16mm 400' (122m) double-perf. (2R) .2994" (7.6mm) pitch.

FPS: 24–500 fps.

Aperture: .296" x .410" (7.52mm x 10.41mm). Standard 16. Aperture plate non-removable.

Displays: Edge-of-film time code to the millisecond (optional).

Lens: Lens Mount: C mount. Non-reflex. Full set of primes available from Photo-Sonics, from 3.5mm.

Shutter: 160° adjustable to 120°, 90°, 60°, 45°, 22.5°, 7.5°.

Viewfinder: External Viewfinder: Viewing through lens for line-up purposes is accomplished using boresight device that attaches to camera in place of magazine. Once camera is locked into position, magazine is attached. There is no provision for viewing while camera is running.

Video: Sony XC 999 lipstick video camera can be mounted to the 1PL to provide a parallax video assist.

Viewing Screen: Standard ground glass formats available.

Mags: 200' (61m) or 400' (122m) cartridge-style coaxial magazines for quick reloading.

Preloaded daylight spools or 2" plastic cores to be used in conjunction with supplied daylight split reels.

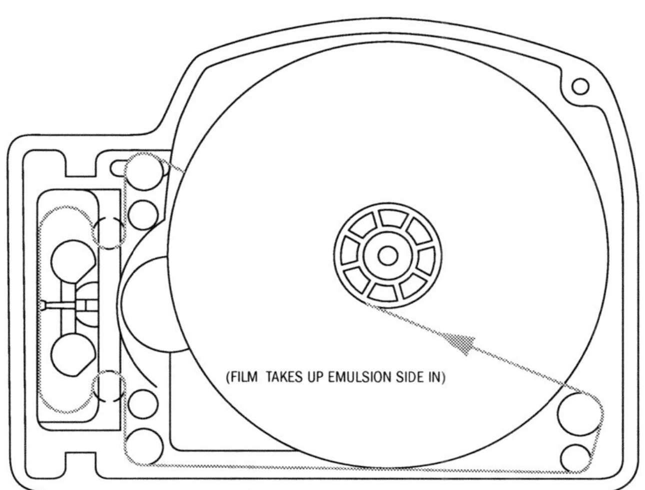

Photo-Sonics 16mm 1PL Magazine Diagram
Film takes-up emulsion side in. Take-up spool not shown.

Accessories: Film data recording system, power on/off box, 50' (15m) remote cable.

Motors, Power: 115V AC or 28V DC.

Photo-Sonics 1VN Standard 16mm and Super 16

Notes: Extremely compact high speed camera

Weight: 3.75 lbs./1.7 kg. with body, loaded 100' daylight spool, no lens.

Movement: Standard: Intermittent with two registration pins and two pulldown arms. Super 16: Intermittent with single registration pin and single pulldown arm.

Film specifications: Standard: 100' (30.5m) double perf (2R) .2994" (7.6mm) pitch; Super 16: 100' (30.5m) single-perf (1R) .2994" pitch on daylight load camera spools.

FPS: Standard: 24, 48, 64, 100, 150, 200 fps. Super 16: 24, 48, 72, 96, 144, 168.

Aperture: .295" x .410" (7.49mm x 10.41mm) Standard. .295" x .490" (7.49mm x 12.45mm) Super 16. Aperture plate non-removable.

Displays: Mechanical footage indicator.

Lens: C mount. Primes available from Photo-Sonics. Lens Control: Boresight tool for aligning shot. Optional side-mounted, parallax-type lipstick camera.

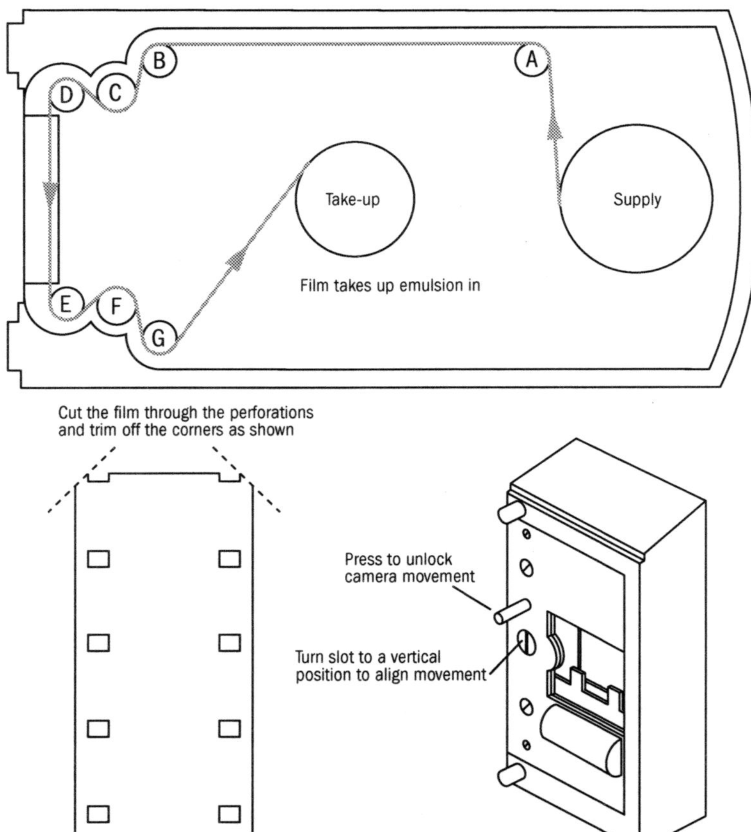

Photo-Sonics 1VN Standard 16mm and Super 16 Magazine Diagram
Film takes-up emulsion side in.

Shutter: Standard is 120° fixed, Super 16 is 92° fixed.

Viewfinder: 1VN is a non-reflex camera. Viewing through lens for line-up purposes is accomplished using a boresight device that attaches in place of magazine. Once camera is locked in position, boresight is removed and magazine is attached. There is no provision for viewing through lens while camera is running.

Video: Lipstick-type video camera can be mounted to 1VN to provide a parallax-type video assist.

Viewing Screen: Standard ground glass formats available.

Mags: 100' (30.5m) cartridge-type magazines. Daylight load in subdued light. Also: 65' (19.8m) darkroom load, 100' (30.5m) darkroom load, 100' (30.5m) daylight load, 200' (61m) darkroom load, 200' (61m) coaxial load.

Accessories: Splash housings, handheld and remote-controlled splash housings for both standard and Super 16 1VN cameras. Depth rated 12' (3.6m) to 15' (4.6m). tripod mounting adapter, mounting kit and bike mount.

Motors, Power: 28V DC. 30 volt DC batteries can be used.

Photo-Sonics Actionmaster 500 Series 3000, Standard 16mm and Super 16

Notes: rugged high-speed cameras for sports, table-top, commercial, documentary and wildlife cinematography.

Weight: 20 lbs./9.09 kg. with 400' (122m) mag, handheld mode, no lens.

Movement: Intermittent with two registration pins and two pull-down arms.

Film specifications: Standard requires 400' (122m) double-perf (2R) .2994" (7.6mm) pitch; Super 16 requires 400' (122m) single-perf (1R) .2994" pitch.

FPS: 24–500 fps in standard and 24–360 fps in Super 16. Crystal speed control available in Series 3000 model.

Aperture: .296" x .410" (7.52mm x 10.41mm) Standard; .296" x .490" (7.52mm x 12.45mm) Super 16. Aperture Plate non-removable.

Displays: Camera ready, 28V DC camera power, 12V DC video power and crystal speed indicator lights. Digital speed read-out riser plate with accessory port. Mechanical footage and shutter angle indicator.

Lens: PL mount (with depth restrictions).

Shutter: Standard adjustable with mechanical indicator from 160° to 7.5° (marked at 144°, 120°, 90°, 45°, 22.5°, 7.5°); Super 16 adjustable with mechanical indicator from 144° to 9° (marked at 144°, 72°, 36°, 18°, 9°).

Viewfinder: Reflexed by means of a partial mirror prism. Orientable Angenieux or Cinema Products reflex viewfinder.

Video: CEI Color V or III.

Viewing Screen: Most standard ground glasses available. Specify when ordering camera package.

Mags: 400' (122m) coaxial cartridge-type magazines for quick reloading. Rear-mounting with positive lock mechanism. 200' (61m) magazines also available.

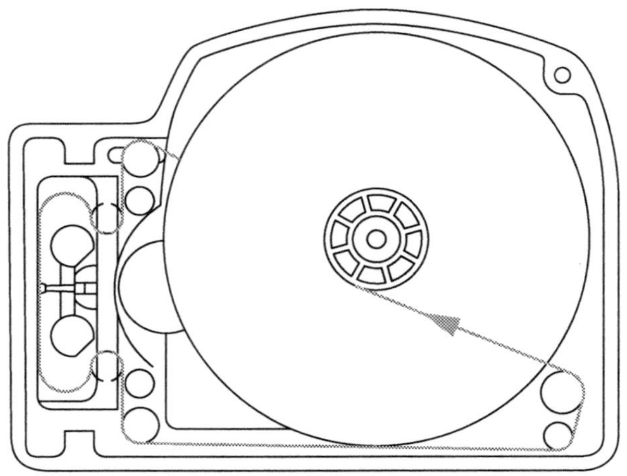

Photo-Sonics Actionmaster Magazine Diagram
Film takes-up emulsion side in.

Preloaded daylight spools or 2" plastic cores to be used in conjunction with supplied daylight split reels.

Accessories: Arri balance plate with 15mm rods, additional magazines. Studio (on Arri 15mm rods) or lightweight handheld follow focus.

Environmental Protection Equipment: Splash bag and raincovers available.

Camera Support Equipment: Handholdable, pistol grip with shoulder mount and dual speed switch. Camera can also be mounted on most camera heads and tripods.

Connections: Electronic Accessories: Unilux strobe output shutter pulse, AC power supply and optional 50' (15m) remote cable. Power zoom control powered through 11-pin Fischer connector.

Motors, Power: 28V DC.

16mm Photo-Sonics Nac E-10 and Nac HD 16

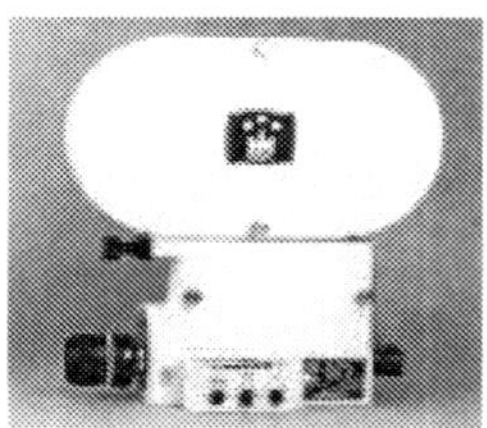

Weight: 42 lbs./19.09 kg. with film and no lens.

Movement: Rotary prism imaging. Continuous film transport.

FPS: 300–10,000 fps for Nac E-10 and 100–8,000 fps for Nac HD-16.

Aperture: .295" x .410" (7.49mm x 10.41mm). Standard 16.

Displays: LED speed indicator (Nac E-10 only).

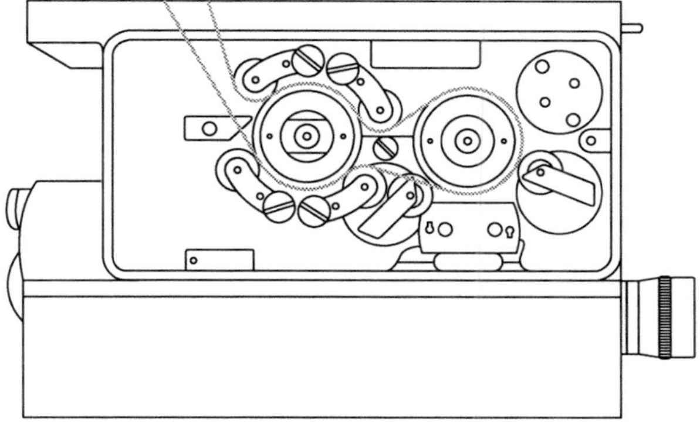

Photo-Sonics NAC E-10 Threading Diagram
Film takes-up emulsion side in.

Film specifications: 16mm 400' (122m) double-perf (2R) .2994" (7.6mm) pitch. Film must be wound onto special balanced film spools.

Lens: Lens Mount: C mount. Lenses available (set: 5.9mm, 10mm, 16mm, 25mm, 50mm and 75mm Macro Switar.)

Shutter: 72° fixed.

Viewfinder: Reflex Viewfinder, beamsplitter behind lens permits reflex viewing while camera is running.

Mags: 400' (122m). Single chamber on daylight spools. Frame rates above 7,000 require film to be wound on dynamically balanced film cores included in camera order.

Accessories: Control box, 15' (4.6m) remote switch. TTL exposure indicator, lighting packages, flicker meter. C-mount to Nikon adapter.

Motors, Power: 200-240V AC single phase. 100 amp surge/35 amps running at 10,000 fps on Nac E-10 and 8,000 fps on Nac HD-16. 115V AC 300-5,000 fps.

Super 8mm

Beaulieu 4008

FPS: 2–70 fps (speed select for either 18, 24 or 25 fps). Mechanical single frame.

Aperture: .166"x .224" (4.22mm x 5.69mm).

Displays: Footage.

Lens: C mount with power lens contacts. Power Zoom Lenses available are Schneider 6–66mm or 16–70mm and Angenieux 8–64mm or 6–8mm. Macrocinematography mode

Focusing ring. Built-in electric zoom control. On-lens variable speed. Iris gears on lens governed by camera meter.

Built-in 85 filter, through-the-lens internal meter ISO 12–400 ASA.

Shutter: Guillotine 1/90th second at 24 fps and 1/60th at 24 fps variable with frame rate closed lock position.

Viewfinder: Reflex viewfinder.

Viewing Screen: Focusing-screen. Retractable.

Mags: 50' (15m) silent Super 8 or Pro8mm cartridges.

Accessories: Remote cable release.

Power: Onboard 250Ma. 7.2V/3.6V combined.

Weight: 2 lbs. 3 oz./1kg. body only.

Beaulieu 6008 Pro

FPS: 4, 9, 18, 24/25, 36 and 80 fps. Electronic single frame and three time-lapse speeds. Optional crystal control at 24 or 25 fps.

Aperture: .166" x .224" (4.22mm x 5.69mm).

Displays: Some with footage, others with frames.

Lens: Schneider 6-70mm f/1.4 zoom or Beaulieu 7mm-56mm f/1.4 power zoom lens.

Center-weighted TTL metering. ISO 12-400.

Zoom Control: Electric or manual. Iris Gears: Electric.

Shutter: Guillotine, two-position; 1/90th at 24 and 1/60th at 24 variable with frame rate speed in closed position.

Viewfinder: Reflex viewfinder

Viewing Screen: Matte focusing screen.

Mags: 50' (15m) sound or silent Super 8 and Pro8mm cartridges, 200' (61m) sound. (Sound ctg. no longer available.)

Accessories: Electromagnetic trigger, remote control, external power supply.

Power: 7.2V AA battery pack.

Beaulieu 7008 Pro

Weight: 2.82 lbs/1.28kg, body only.

Movement: Forward and limited reverse.

FPS: 4, 9, 18, 24/25 (optional 24 or 25 fps crystal), 36, 80 fps. Single-frame capabilities and three time-lapse filming speeds.

Aperture: .166" x .224" (4.22mm x 5.69mm).

Displays: Digital readouts for frames and centimeters.

Lens: C mount and Beaulieu power mounts. Automatic control sets lens to minimum depth of field. Zoom Control: Electric or manual.

Shutter: Guillotine, two-position; 1⁄90th at 24 and 1⁄60th at 24 variable with frame rate speed in closed position.

Viewfinder: Reflex viewfinder

Viewing Screen: Fine-grain focusing screen.

Mags: 50' (15m) sound or silent Super 8 and Pro8mm cartridges. 200' (61m) sound ctg. (sound ctg. no longer available).

Accessories: Center-weighted TTL metering. ISO 12-400. Output sockets, flash synchronization, electromagnetic trigger, remote control. Remote cable release. Fader (in and out.)

Power: Six 1.2VC-Cell NiCd battery packs. Power Cable Adapter. Quick Charger.

Canon 814XL-S, 1014 XL-S

FPS: 9, 18, 24 and 36 fps.

Aperture: .228" x .165" (5.8mm x 4.2mm).

Displays: Battery check, film end, film transport, sound recording levels, correct exposure, manual aperture indicator, footage indicator.

Lens: 814XL-S has 7–56mm (8:1) f/1.4 with built-in wide angle and telephoto macro mechanisms. 1014XL-S has 6.5–65mm (10:1) f/1.4 with wide angle and telephoto macro mechanisms. Zoom control: two-speed electric or manual. 85 filter switch, filter rings, 4.3mm wide-angle attachment for 1014XL-S and 4.5mm wide-angle attachment for the 814XL-S, 1.4x 67 teleconverter, close-up lens attachment,

Shutter: Semi-disc rotating, automatic or manual 150° and 250°.

Viewfinder: Single-lens reflex viewfinder with split image rangefinder.

Mags: 50' (15m) sound or silent Super 8 and Pro8mm cartridges.

Accessories: Film Mode Dial allows lap-dissolves (1014XL-S only), fade-in/fade-out, timed interval filming, single-frame filming, light meter, microphones, earphones, intervalometer, self-timer, remote control, flash socket. Chest Pod II, extension cord.

Power: Six AA-size 1.5V alkaline manganese, carbon zinc, or NiCd. 9V power pack available.

Nautica

Notes: Underwater camera, no housing required. Watertight to 30' (9.1m).

FPS: Single frame and 18 fps.

Displays: Depth indicator, footage counter.

Lens: Fixed 9-30mm Panorama-Viennon f/1.9 zoom. Exposure is automatic. Aspheric wide-angle attachment needed for underwater. Focus is automatic. Zoom lever.

Mags: 50' (15m) sound or silent Super 8 and Pro8mm cartridges.

Accessories: Cable release.

Power: Two AA batteries.

Nikon R8, R10

FPS: 18, 24, 54 fps. Single frame.

Displays: F-numbers, exposure warning, film end, shutter opening, footage, battery.

Lens: Fixed Cine-Nikkor zoom lens. 7-70mm (10:1) f/1.4 macro. 67mm front attachment size. Two-speed power zoom with manual override.

Shutter: Variable shutter from 160° to 0°.

Viewfinder: Reflex viewfinder, SLR with split-image rangefinder.

Mags: 50' (15m) sound or silent Super 8 and Pro8mm cartridges.

Accessories: Exposure meter, 100 frame rewind, automatic fade-in/fade-out with manual override, double exposure, reverse filming, remote control, flash sync.

Power: Six AA 1.5V.

Pro8mm Pro II

FPS: 23.97, 24, 25, 29.97 and 30 fps crystal controlled. 4, 9, 18, 24, 36 and 80 fps non-crystal. New crystal also features built-in phase control so TV monitors can be shot without video bar. Single frame function with variable shutter rate for animation effects. Intervalometer for timed exposures.

Aperture: .166" x .224" (4.22mm x 5.69mm). Optional mask for 1.85 Academy.

Displays: Visual display in viewfinder indicating an absolute crystal lock. Liquid crystal display frame and centimeter counters keep track of exact footage transported in forward and reverse. Two-stage LED informs user when camera service is required.

Lens: C mount and custom Beaulieu power mount. Lenses: Angenieux 6-90mm T1.6. Schneider 6-70mm. 3mm super-wide prime. Super-wide elements can be removed from lens to obtain 6mm focal length. Nikon compatible 60-300mm telephoto. Anamorphic Lens System. Aspect ratio is 2.35:1 (1.75x squeeze) and lens is mounted with custom brackets. Same lens can also be used with any standard projector to permit widescreen projection. C-mount adapters allow various non-C-mount lenses to be used.

Lens Control Unit for variable power zoom and aperture control. These features include manual override.

Viewfinder: Reflex viewfinder

Viewing Screen: Focusing screen.

Mags: 50' (15m) sound or silent Super 8 and Pro8mm cartridges. 200' (61m) sound ctg. (Sound ctg. no longer available.)

Accessories: Additional Accessories: Motor-driven rewind is included to perform dissolves and double exposures. Hard-shell sound blimp made from industrial-grade aluminum and sound-absorbing foam (-22 dB effective). Rental only.

Motors, Power: 12V DC input. Regulated and fused for 12-volt DC battery belt. Microprocessor crystal-controlled 1.5 amp motor.

65mm

Arriflex 765

Movement: Microprocessor control technology to link two quartz-controlled DC motors in a direct drive configuration to control shutter and film transport. No belts or mechanical couplings used in drive system. Dual registration pins, triple-pin pulldown claws and user-adjustable pitch control to optical printer standards.

FPS: Quartz-accurate sync at 15/24/25/29.97/30/60/75 fps onboard; 2-100 fps with the CCU; 24 fps reverse; and 1 fps with the 765's Remote Control Unit. Run-up time is less than 1 second at 24 fps.

Aperture: 2.17" x 1.004" (55mm x 25.5mm).

dB: 25 dB at 24 fps; 28.5 dB(A) at 30 fps.

Displays: LCD Tachometer and Footage Displays: Digital camera left/right; audible and visible out-of-sync; low battery; feet/meters footage display.

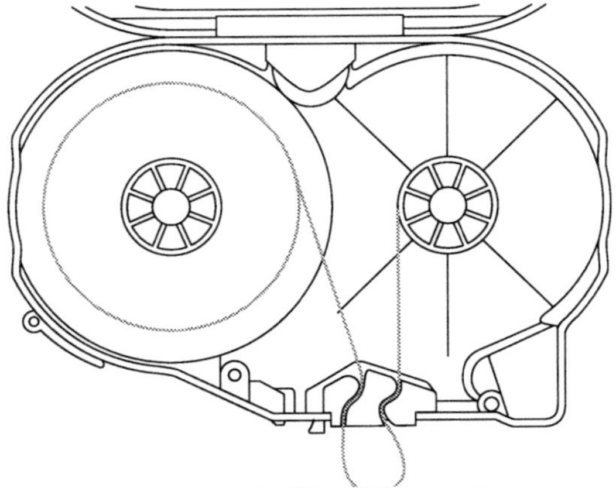

Arriflex 765 magazine.
Film takes up emulsion side in.

Lens: 64mm diameter Maxi-PL lens mount; flange focal distance of 63.5mm; designed for Arri Maxi-PL prime and RTH Cooke zoom, wide-angle and telephoto lenses. Lenses: Arri/Zeiss 65mm format lenses include 30mm, 40mm, 50mm, 60mm, 80mm, 100mm, 110mm, 120mm, 150mm, 250mm, 350mm, 2x Mutar Extender, and a 38-210mm zoom.

Shutter: Rotating, microprocessor-controlled silicon mirror shutter, mechanically variable from 15° to 165°, including 144°, 172.8°, and 180°.

Viewfinder: Reflex viewfinder has built-in optical turret that permits on-the-fly selection of either 80:20 or 100:0 video/viewing ratios, and has switchable ND.6 contrast viewing glass, ArriGlow illuminated frame lines, and finder extender with built-in 2x image magnification. Short finder (for portable operation) and video finder are also available. Wide-angle eyepiece with manual iris closure, 8x magnification, and +2 diopter adjustment standard. In-finder displays: out-of-sync and film-end.

Video: Video Optics Module: Color and black-and-white CCD video tap cameras with flicker reduction and iris control.

Viewing Screen: Interchangeable with full range of aspect ratios.

Mags: 400' (122m) and 1,000' (300m) displacement with microprocessor-controlled torque motors. Microprocessor samples and adjusts feed/take-up tension and all other functions continuously. Automatic connection and data transfer to camera via multi-plug pin plug. Mechanical and digital LCD counters.

Accessories: 6.6"x6.6" swing-away production matte box covers all 65mm format lenses. Has two fully rotatable two-filter stages.

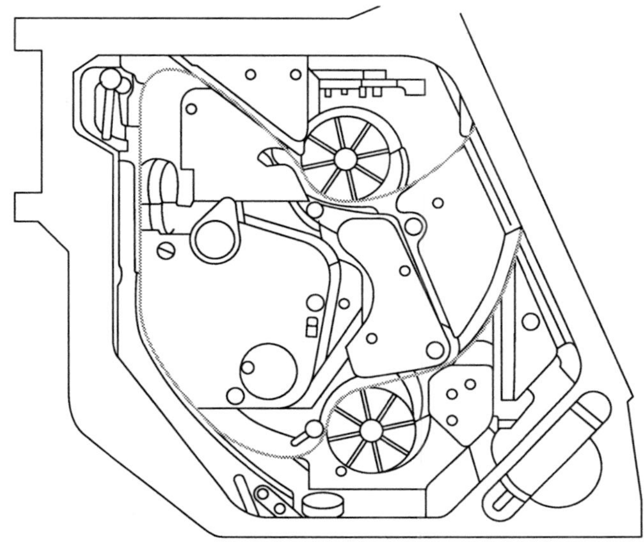

Arriflex 765 Threading Diagram

Geared filter frames. Bridgeplate support system for balance and mount for matte box, follow focus, servo zoom drive and heavy lenses. Finder extender and leveling rod.

Camera Control Unit (CCU) remotely turns 765 on and off, and activates speed change from up to 100' (30.5m) away.

Variable Speed and Sync Unit: VSSU module allows remote speed changes between 6 and 100 fps non-crystal; provides synchronization with external PAL or NTSC video signal (50/60 Hz) via up to 100' BNC cable.

Barney and heated barney.

Motors, Power: Power input via a three-pin connector: pin 1 is (-), pin 2 is + 24V.

Cinema Products CP-65

Notes: This camera, designed in conjunction with Wilcam, is intended to meet the exacting needs of Showscan cinematography (60 fps).

Movement: Dual registration pins and four pulldown claws. Retractable register pins and two-axis stroke adjustment permits tuning movement for most silent operation.

FPS: 1–72 fps. forward or reverse. four-decade digital dial that is

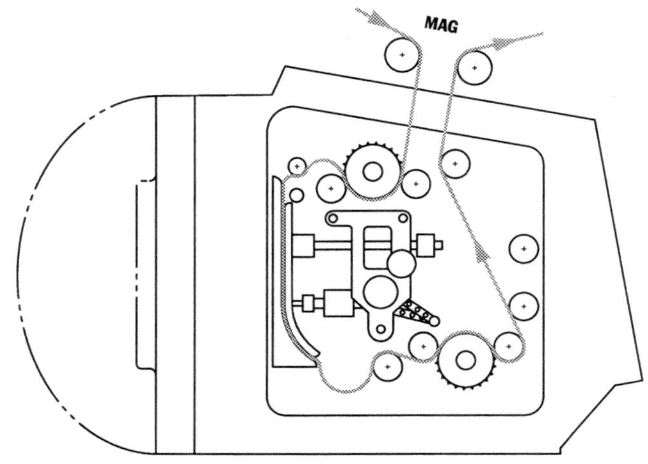

Cinema Products CP-65 Threading Diagram
Film takes up emulsion side in.

crystal accurate at all selected speeds up to two decimal digits.

Aperture: Photographed aperture is standard 5-perf 65mm, 2.072" x 0.906" (52.63mm x 23.01mm). Removable aperture and pressure plates for ease of cleaning.

dB: 32dB at 60 fps with 1000' (300m) magazines and blimp.

Displays: Footage.

Lens: Quick-acting bayonet lock for specially mounted CP-65 lenses. Lenses: Complete series of specially mounted prime lenses varying from 24mm to 1200mm, and high-quality zoom lenses are available.

Shutter: 170° fixed-opening focal plane shutter.

Viewfinder: Reflex viewfinder, rotating mirror reflex image through ground glass, with provision for film clip insertion, to a 360-degree upright image orientable viewfinder. Eyepiece extender with automatic leveler.

Video: Built-in video tap with CCD chip camera.

Viewing Screen: Interchangeable.

Mags: Two-chamber, 1000' (300m) magazines and 2500' (762m) individual supply and take-up cassettes available. Magazine blimps for both sizes also available.

Accessories: Single-frame operation with external intervalometer. 3-D rig available. Camera's self-blimped design permits sync-sound shooting at 24 fps. At Showscan speed of 60 fps, a lightweight composite material sound blimp is provided.

Camera can be externally controlled for phase locking as required by process photography and 3-D filming.

Fries Model 865 65mm/8-perf.

Notes: A large-format 65mm 8-perf camera for special venue productions.

Weight: Camera body 45 lbs./20.45kg., 1000' (300m) mag 13.5 lbs/6.13kg.

Movement: Dual registration pins and six pulldown claws. A cam and eccentric mounted on a single shaft actuate pulldown and operate register pins.

Film specifications: 65mm KS-1866.

FPS: 2-72 fps forward or 2-30 fps reverse. All speeds crystal-controlled.

Aperture: Photographed aperture is 2.072" x 1.450" (52.63mm x 36.83mm). Removable aperture and pressure plates for ease of cleaning. Aperture Plate: Optically centered.

Displays: Footage counters.

Lens: Universal bayonet type with large port diameter. Special mounts available. Complete series of Hasselblad lenses available.

Shutter: 170-degree fixed opening blanking shutter.

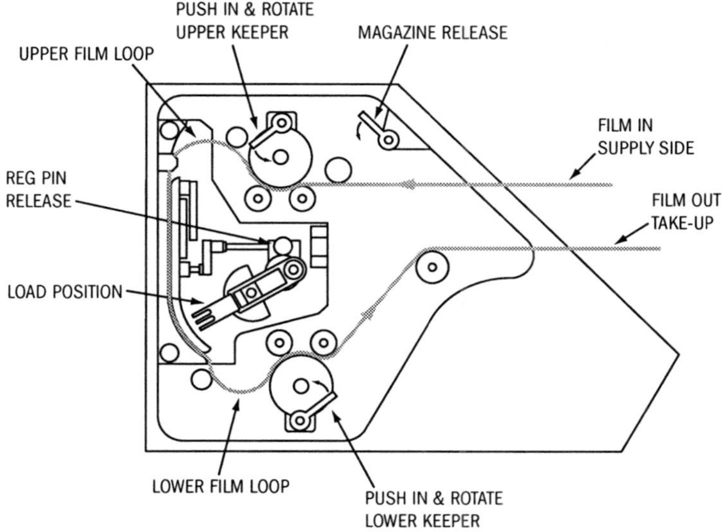

Fries 865 65mm/8-perf. Threading Diagram
Film takes up emulsion side out.

Viewfinder: Reflex viewfinder, rotating mirror reflex image. Viewfinder is orientable through a full 360° and self-corrected through approximately 180°. Lightvalve allows operator to direct to viewing system, to video assist, or to combo, which splits light between both viewing and video assist.

Video: Video tap with ½" CCD chip camera, color or black-and-white.

Mags: Displacement magazines with torque motor take-up and hold-back. Standard 65mm 3" plastic cores.

Accessories: Remote on/off. Standard Arri matte box.

Motors, Power: 30V DC. Internal 30V DC crystal-controlled motor.

Mitchell FC, BFC (65mm)

Notes, Models: Scaled up design of 35mm rackover Mitchell NC and BNC. B models are blimped.

Movement: Dual register pins, four-prong pulldown; adjustable stroke. Timing marks on shutter and movement facilitate removal and reassembly.

FPS: Single frame to 32 fps.

Aperture: Removable aperture plate with built-in matte slot. Slot for dual gel filters.

Displays: Mechanical. Footage and frames.

Shutter: Focal plane 175° maximum, variable to 0° in 10-degree increments. Phase and opening indicator on back of camera. Some models have automatic 4' fade in or out.

Viewfinder: Non-reflex models-external large screen erecting finder with parallax correction coupled by camera-to-lens focus knob

Viewing Screen: Interchangeable.

Mags: 400' (122m), 1,000' (300m), 1,200' (366m) double compartment sound insulated. Plastic film cores (that come with film) on feed side, collapsible and removable on take-up side.

See Mitchell 35mm for threading diagram

Accessories: Film matte punch

Motors, Power: Detachable motors. Synchronous motors are sound insulated. Crystal sync 30V DC with 50/60Hz signal, mirror positioning circuit and audible offspeed indicator. Power requirements vary with motor.

Mitchell 65mm Reflex Todd-AO

Weight: 27 lbs./12.27kg with 350' (107m) of film.

Movement: Dual registration pins. Four pull-down claws. Adjustable pulldown stroke.

FPS: 12, 18, 20, 22, 24, 28 and 32 fps.

Aperture: 2.072" x .9055" (52.63mm x 23mm). Removable aperture plate with built-in matte slot. Dual gelatin filter slot in front of film aperture.

Displays: Film runout indicator.

Lens: Single mount with quick-release flange T-stop calibration allows for mirror absorption. Accepts all Todd-AO fixed focal-length and zoom lenses: 60–150mm, 100–300mm and 65–390mm.

Follow Focus: All lenses geared for manual follow-focus control.

Shutter: Focal plane 175°.

Viewfinder: Reflex viewfinder, Pellicle beam splitter (shock mounted) views more than full aperture area. High magnification for critical focusing; contrast viewing filters. Built-in exposure meter.

External Viewfinder: Large upright image viewfinder calibrated for different focal length lenses. Calibrated for any two aspect ratios. Parallax correcting cams for all focal length lenses.

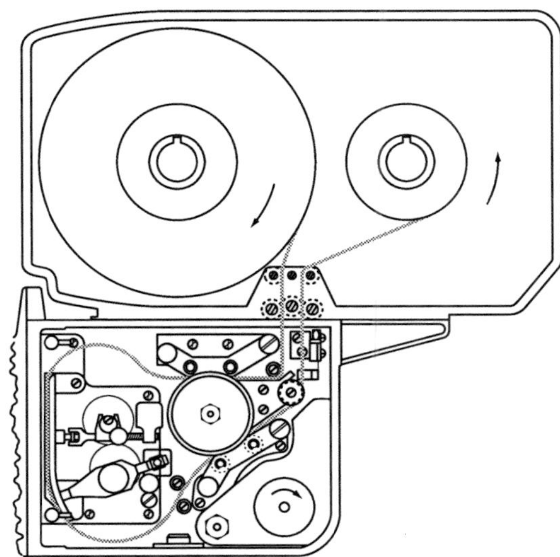

Mitchell 65mm Reflex Todd-AO Magazine and Threading Diagram
Film takes up emulsion side out.

Mags: 350' (107m) lightweight magnesium and 1,000' (300m). Remaining footage indicator. Positive clutch drive. Displacement type.

Accessories: Remote control. Underwater housing with internal battery and externally controlled film speed, stops and focus. Designed for 50' (15m) depth or less.

Motors, Power: Internal 28V DC motor, solid-state speed control. Rectifier unit 110V AC-28V DC. Camera will also accept externally mounted motors for special purposes.

MSM Model 8870 65mm/8-perf

Movement: MSM Monoblock high-speed, dual register pins, claw engages six perfs. Shrinkage adjustment changes stroke and entry position. Indexable loop-setting sprockets have independent locking keeper rollers. Vacuum backplate ensures filmplane accuracy, removes without tools for cleaning. Removable for cleaning and lubrication.

FPS: From time-lapse to 60 fps forward, also to 30 fps reverse. Crystal sync from 5–60 fps in .001 increments.

Aperture: 2.072" x 1.485" (52.63mm x 37.72mm). Aperture plate removable for cleaning and lubrication.

Displays: Status LEDs for power, heat, low battery, mag ready, buckle and speed sync. Two illuminated LCD footage counters. Digital battery volt/amp meter. Circuit breakers for camera, mag, heat and accessories. Control port allows operation from handheld remote or interface with computers and external accessories.

Lens: MSM 75mm diameter x 80mm flange depth. BNC-style lens mount is vertically adjustable 7mm for flat or dome screen composition. Mount accepts modified Zeiss (Hasselblad), Pentax, Mamiya and other large-format lenses.

Shutter: Focal plane shutter, manually variable from 172.8° to 55° with stops at 144° and 108°.

Viewfinder: Reflex viewfinder, spinning mirror reflex. Finder rotates 360° with upright image, which can be manually rotated for unusual setups. Finder shows 105 percent of frame, magnifier allows critical focusing at center of interest. Single lever controls internal filter and douser. Heated eyepiece has large exit pupil and long eye relief. High resolution black-and-white or optional color CCD video tap is built into camera door with swing-away 50/50 beamsplitter. Viewfinder removes completely for aerial or underwater housing use.

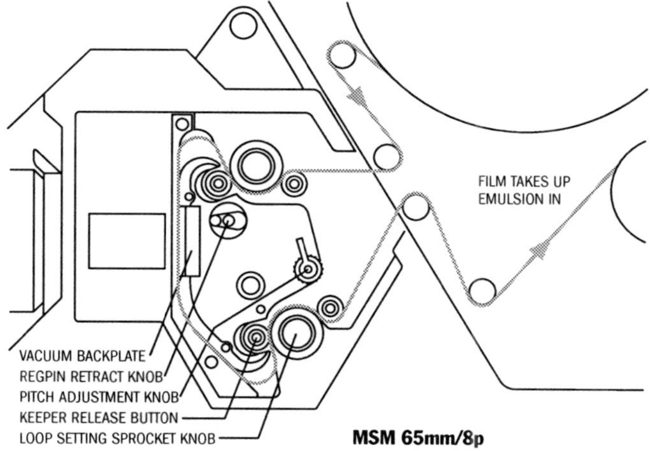

MSM 8870 65mm/8 perf. Threading Diagram

Viewing Screen: Interchangeable ground glasses with register pins for film clips.

Mags: 1,000' (300m) displacement magazines use MSM TiltLock mount. Magazines lock to camera with pair of 8mm hardened pins and can tilt away from operator to allow easier camera threading. Optional minimum profile 1,000' (300m) coaxial magazines use same mount without tilt feature. Both magazines operate bi-directionally at all camera speeds. Positive camlock secures mag in running position and switches power to motor and heater contacts in mag foot. Expanding core hubs have integral DC servo motors controlled by film tension in both directions, with soft startup to eliminate slack. Tightwind rollers guide film winding for smooth solid rolls at any camera angle. Non-contact light traps feature infrared end-of-film sensors.

Accessories: 15mm matte rods are on Arri BL centers for accessory compatibility and use standard Arri accessories.

Motors, Power: Integrated.

Panavision System-65 65mm

Movement: Four pulldown claws. Pitch adjustment to optimize camera quietness. Entire movement may be removed for servicing. Dual pilot pin registration ensures FPS: 4-30 fps.

Aperture: .906" x 2.072" (23.01mm x 52.63mm).

Aperture Plate removable for checking and cleaning. Full-frame aperture is standard, aperture mattes used for all other frame sizes. A special perforation-locating pin above aperture ensures trouble-free and rapid film threading.

Interchangeable aperture mattes available. Anamorphic, Super 35, 1.85:1, 1.66:1 and any other as required. Special hard mattes available on request.

Behind-the-lens gel filter holder.

dB: 24 Db(a)

Lens: Panavision positive clamp lens mount for maintaining critical flange focal depth setting. All lenses pinned to ensure proper rotational orientation. (Note: This is particularly important with anamorphic lenses.) Iris-rod support supplied. Lenses: Exceptionally wide range of spherical, anamorphic, speciality, and primo lenses available.

Shutter: Focal plane shutter with infinitely variable opening and adjustable in-shot. Maximum opening: 180°; minimum: 40° with adjustable maximum and minimum opening stops. Digital display allows adjustments in 1⁄10° increments. Micrometer adjustment allows critical synchronization with computers, TV monitors and HMI lighting at unusual frame rates. Manual and electronic remote-control units available.

Viewfinder: Reflex viewfinder, reflex rotating mirror standard and independent of light shutter system. Interchangeable semi-silvered fixed reflex mirror for flicker-free viewing optional.

Viewfinder tube is orientable and gives a constantly upright image through 360°. Short, intermediate and long viewfinder tubes available. System incorporates an optical magnifier for critical focusing and picture composition, a de-anamorphoser, a contrast viewing filter and a lightproof shutter. Wide range ocular adjustment with marker bezel to note individual settings. Built-in "Panaclear" eyepiece heater ensures mist-free viewing. Adjustable eyepiece leveling link-arm. Entire optical viewfinder system may be removed and replaced with video viewfinder display for lightweight camera configuration. An eyepiece diopter to suit operator's eyesight can be provided.

Video: State-of-the-art CCD video systems available in black-and-white or color.

Viewing Screen: Interchangeable ground glasses available with any marking or combination of markings. "Panaglow" illuminated reticle system with brightness control standard. Ground glasses with finer or coarser texture available. Provision for a cut frame to be placed in viewfinder system for optical image matching. Frame

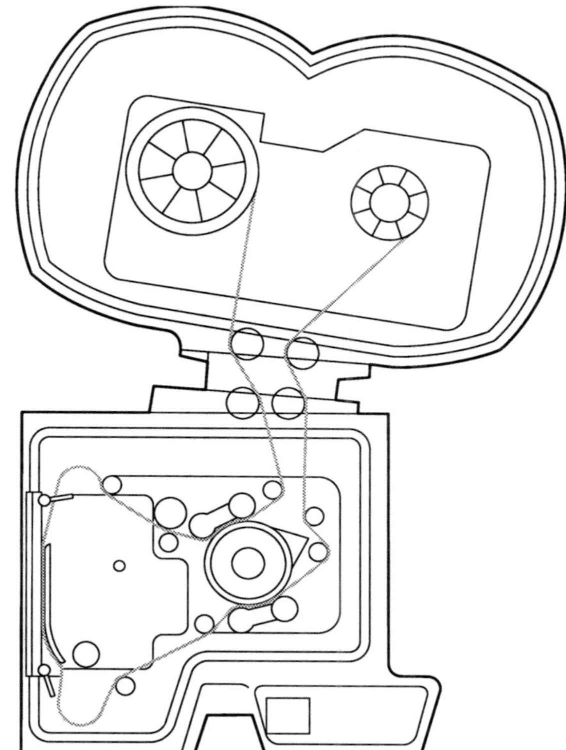

Panavision 65mm AC/SPC Magazine and Threading Diagram
Film takes up emulsion side out.

cutters available to suit negative or positive perforations.

Mags: 500' (152m) and 1000' (300m) magazines available. Both can be used on top of the camera for minimum camera length, or at rear for minimum camera height.

Accessories: Almost all Panaflex 35mm front-of-lens optical accessories and filters can be used on System-65 cameras.

All System-65 cameras and magazines have built-in heaters for operation in any temperature. Heated covers available to give additional protection to lenses, especially zoom lenses. Other covers available to protect camera, magazines and lenses. Spinning-glass rain deflectors available. Autobase available to secure the camera in conditions of vibration, high "g" forces and other stressful and dangerous conditions. Water-box available to protect camera in shallow water conditions, a hazard box to protect camera from explosions, collisions and other dangerous situations.

Camera Support Equipment: "Super Panahead" geared head incorporates a 60° tilt range with a built-in wedge system to allow operator to select where that range is, anywhere between the camera pointing directly up or directly down, and three gear ratios in both the pan and tilt movements. A sliding base unit enables camera to be quickly attached and detached and to be slid backwards and forwards on the head for optimum balance. "Panapod" tripods with carbon fiber legs are available in a range of sizes.

Power: Camera, magazines, heaters and accessories operate off a single 24V DC battery.

Panavision System 65mm Hand-Holdable

Weight: 35 lbs./15.88kg with 500' (152m) magazine and film

Movement: Dual pilot pin registration ensures process-plate image steadiness. Pilot pins register in same perforation holes (immediately below the bottom frame line) as optical printers. Four pull-down claws. Entire movement may be removed for servicing.

FPS: Camera runs at any speed from 4–72 fps. Motor is crystal-controlled at all speeds and may be adjusted in 1-fps increments.

Aperture: .906" x 2.072" (23.01mm x 52.63mm). Aperture Plate optically centered. Removable for checking and cleaning.

Displays: Single-sided display fps/footage/ low battery.

Lens: Panavision positive clamp lens mount for maintaining critical flange focal depth setting. All lenses pinned to ensure proper rotational orientation. Lenses are interchangeable with the System-65 Studio Camera.

Shutter: 172.8° fixed-opening focal plane shutter.

Viewfinder: Reflex viewfinder. Two models available; one has rotating mirror, the other a semi-silvered fixed reflex mirror for flicker-free viewing and is especially suitable for Panaglide, Steadicam, Louma and remote camera operation.

Viewfinder tube is orientatable and gives a constantly upright image through 180°. Short and long viewfinder tubes available for handheld and tripod usage. System incorporates optical magnifier for critical focusing and picture composition, contrast viewing filter and lightproof shutter. Wide-range ocular adjustment with marker bezel to note individual settings. A built-in "Panaclear" eyepiece heater ensures mist-free viewing. Adjustable leveler link arm supplied with every Panahead to keep eyepiece position constant while tilting camera up or down. An eyepiece diopter to

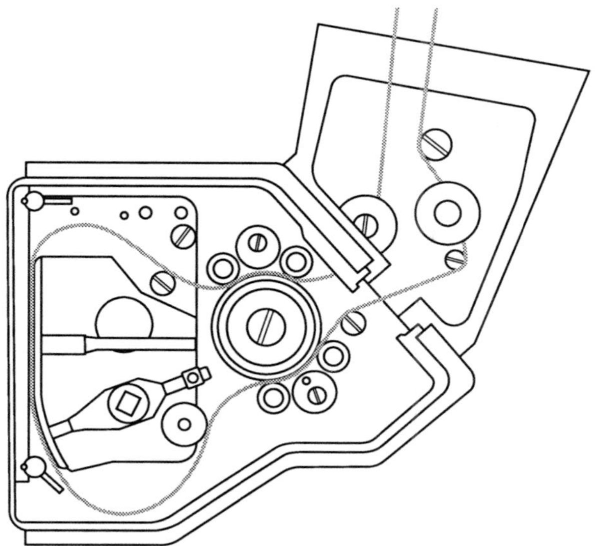

Panavision 65mm HH Threading Diagram
Note: The extension unit is used only for top-magazine configuration. Film takes up emulsion side out.

suit operator's eyesight can be provided on request.

Video: State-of-the-art CCD video systems available in black-and-white or color. Flicker-free images possible with the pellicle reflex system.

Viewing Screen: Interchangeable ground glasses available with any marking or combination of markings. "Panaglow" illuminated reticle system with brightness control standard. Ground glasses with finer or coarser texture available.

Mags: 250' (76m), 500' (152m), and 1000' (300m) magazines are available. 1000' (300m) reverse-running magazines available on request.

Same as Panavision PSR 200°.

Accessories: Interchangeable with System-65 Studio camera. Focus control can be used from either side of the camera. Zoom lenses are supplied with an electronic zoom control unit as standard.

Standard matte box incorporating a sunshade, provision for two 4" x 5.650" filters which can be individually slid up and down. Special matte boxes incorporating more filter stages with provision for sliding (motorized if required), rotating and/or tilting and for taking 6.6" square filters optional. Panavision can also supply special sliding diffusers, diopters and image-control filters, etc., to use in matte boxes.

Lightweight System-65 hand-holdable cameras are ideal for use with Panaglide and Steadicam floating camera rigs and on remotely controlled camera cranes. They can also be used with "Panatate" 360° turn-over rig.

Connections: Special sync boxes available to synchronize the camera with a main power supply, computers, video signals and process projectors in shutter phase synchronization. Internal heaters.

Motors, Power: 24-volt DC. Camera, heaters and accessories operate off a single 24v Ni-Cad battery. Belt batteries available for handholding.

VistaVision 35mm

MSM Model 8812 35mm/8-perf VistaVision

Movement: MSM Monoblock high-speed, triple register pins, claw engages four perfs. Shrinkage adjustment changes stroke and entry position. Indexable loop-setting sprockets have independent locking keeper rollers. Movement removes easily for cleaning and lubrication. Vacuum backplate ensures film plane accuracy, removes without tools for cleaning.

FPS: Frame rates from time-lapse to 72 fps forward, to 30 fps reverse. Crystal sync from 5–72 fps in .001 increments.

Aperture: 1.485" x .992" (37.72mm x 25.2mm). Aperture removes easily for cleaning and lubrication.

Displays: Status LEDs for power, heat, low battery, mag ready, buckle and speed sync. Two illuminated LCD footage counters. Digital battery volt/amp meter. Circuit breakers for camera, mag, heat and accessories. Control port allows operation from handheld remote or interface with computers and external accessories.

Lens: BNC lens mount. 15mm matte rods are on Arri BL centers for accessory compatibility.

Shutter: Focal plane shutter, manually variable from 172.8° to 55° with stops at 144° and 108°.

Viewfinder: Reflex viewfinder, spinning mirror reflex. Inter-changeable ground glasses with register pins for film clips. Finder rotates 360° with upright image, image can be manually rotated for unusual setups. Finder shows 105 percent of frame, magnifier allows critical

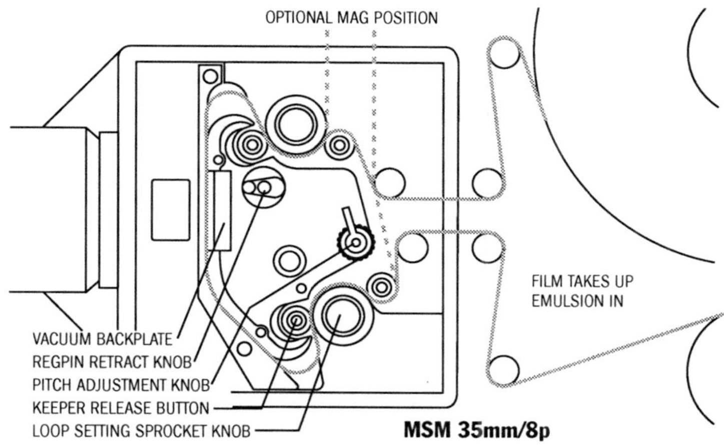

MSM 8812 Threading Diagram

focusing at center of interest. Single lever controls internal filter and douser. Heated eyepiece has large exit pupil and long eye relief. High-resolution black-and-white CCD videotap built into camera door with swing-away 50/50 beamsplitter. Viewfinder removes completely for aerial or underwater housing use.

Mags: 400' (122m) and 1,000' (300m) displacement magazines operate bi-directionally at all camera speeds. Positive camlock secures the mag in running position and switches power to motor and heater contacts in mag foot. Expanding core hubs have integral DC servo motors controlled by film tension in both directions, with soft startup to eliminate slack. Tightwind rollers guide film winding for smooth solid rolls at any camera angle. Non-contact light traps feature infrared end-of-film sensors.

Wilcam W-7 VistaVision High Speed

Notes: VistaVision 35mm/8-perf. Designed for operation at 200 fps.

Weight: 110 lbs./50kg. with 50mm lens and film.

Movement: Three dual-register pins. Two claw pins. Transport claws never enter registration pin perforations.

FPS: 200 fps.

Aperture: VistaVision. Aperture Plate optically centered full.

Lens: BNCR. Lenses: 14mm f/2.8 Canon, 19mm f/2.8 Leitz, 25mm T2.8 Zeiss, 28mm T1.8 Zeiss, 35mm T1.4 Zeiss, 50mm T1.4 Zeiss,

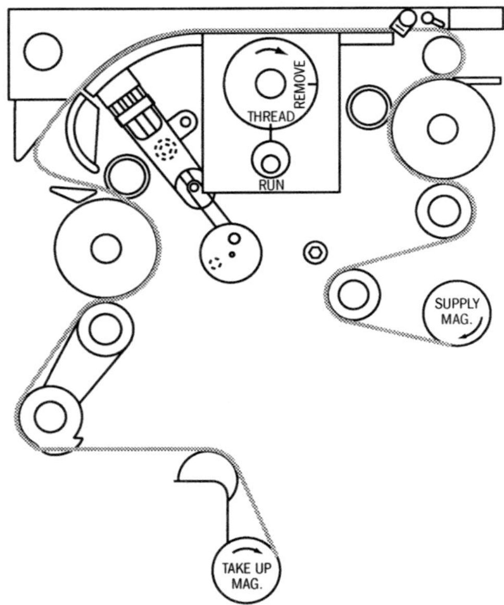

Wilcam W-7 Threading Diagram
Film takes up emulsion side in.

85mm T1.4 Zeiss, 135mm T1.8 Zeiss, 35-140mm f/1.4 Vivitar zoom. Also 200mm, 400mm and 600mm.

Shutter: Beryllium mirror with tungsten counterweights.

Viewfinder: Reflex viewfinder, Rotating mirror. Uses servo motors for constant upright image while eyepiece is rotated.

Mags: 1,000' (300m). Coaxial. 2" plastic cores. Magazine drive gear-driven through torque motors permanently mounted on camera body.

Accessories: Wilcam 4" x 5.65", also standard Arriflex 6.6" x 6.6" Matte Boxes

Power: 48V DC required.

Wilcam W-9 VistaVision Lightweight

Notes: VistaVision 35mm/8 perf. Designed for general-purpose use. Maximum speed 100 fps.

Weight: 37 lbs./16.81 kg. with 50mm lens and film.

Movement: Three dual-register pins. Two claw pins. Transport claws never enter registration pin perforations

FPS: 100 fps.

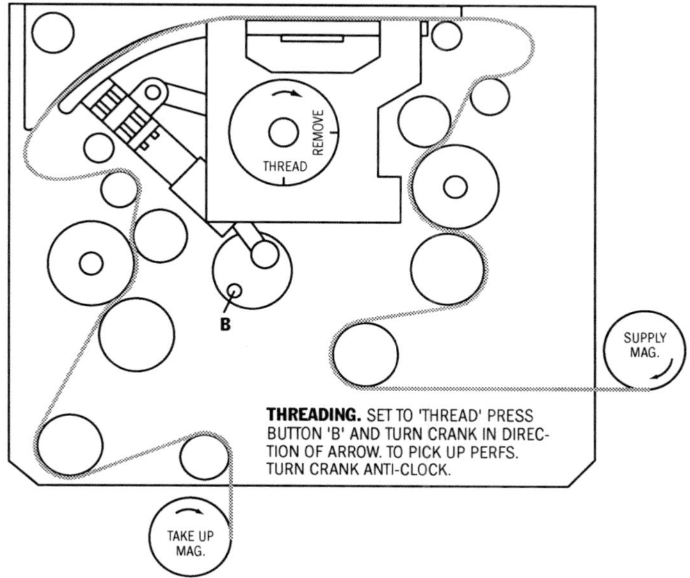

Wilcam W-9 Threading Diagram
Film takes up emulsion side in.

Aperture: VistaVision.

Lens: BNCR Lenses: 14mm f/2.8 Canon, 19mm f/2.8 Leitz, 25mm T2.8 Zeiss, 28mm T1.8 Zeiss, 35mm T1.4 Zeiss, 50mm T1.4 Zeiss, 85mm T1.4 Zeiss, 135mm T1.8 Zeiss, 35-140mm f/1.4 Vivitar zoom. Also 200mm, 400mm and 600mm.

Shutter: 180-degree Beryllium mirror with tungsten counter-weights.

Viewfinder: Reflex viewfinder, Rotating mirror. Uses servo motors for constant upright image while eyepiece is rotated.

Mags: 1,000' (300m). Coaxial. 2" plastic cores. Magazine drive torque motors mounted on each magazine.

Accessories: Wilcam 4" x 5.65", also standard Arriflex 6.6" x 6.6" Matte Boxes

Wilcam W-11 VistaVision Sound Camera

Notes: VistaVision 35mm 8-perf. Designed for soundstage shooting.

Weight: 60lbs./27.27kg. with 50mm lens and 1,000' (300m) of film.

Movement: Three dual-register pins. Two pairs in conventional location, one pair .050-wide perforations trailing. Two claw pins.

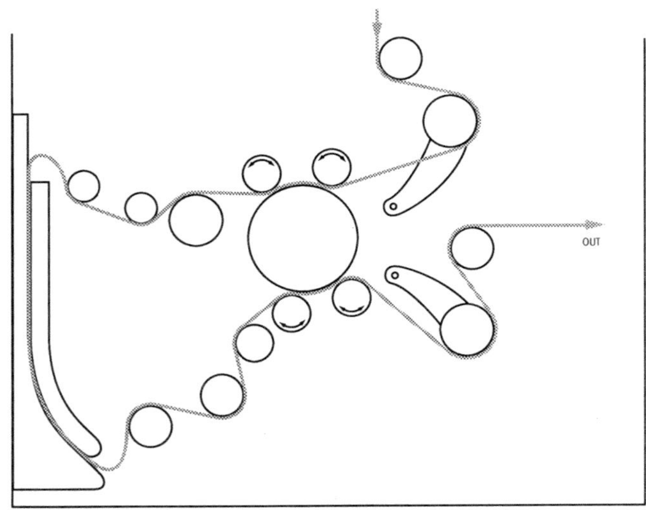

Wilcam W-11 Threading Diagram
Film takes up emulsion side out.

Transport claws never enter registration pin perforations.

FPS: Crystal sync at 24, 25 and 30 fps.

Aperture: VistaVision. Aperture Plate optically centered and full centered.

dB: Noise level in operating condition with a prime lens is 25 dB(A) at 3' in front of camera.

Lens: BNCR lenses: 14mm f/2.8 Canon, 19mm f/2.8, Leitz, 25mm T2.8 Zeiss, 28mm T1.8 Zeiss, 35mm T1.4 Zeiss, 50mm T1.4 Zeiss, 85mm T1.4 Zeiss, 135mm T1.8 Zeiss, 35-140mm f/1.4 Vivitar zoom. Also 200 mm, 400mm and 600mm.

Lens Control: Follow focus on left side of camera. Detachable.

Shutter: Half-speed, 144°. Beryllium mirror driven by second motor, phase-locked to camera motor.

Viewfinder: Reflex viewfinder, automatic image erection with manual override for odd angle viewing. 10x magnifier for critical focusing.

Video: Built-in Sony CCD video camera.

Viewing Screen: Ground glass with locating pins for film clip.

Mags: 1,000' (300m). Coaxial. 2" plastic cores. Supply on right side of camera, take-up on rear. Magazine Drive: Hysteresis clutch with sensing arms in camera body for correct film tension.

Accessories: Wilcam 4" x 5.65", also standard Arriflex 6.6" x 6.6" Matte Boxes

Motors, Power: 36V. Current: 3 Amperes.

IMAX

IMAX 3-D

Notes: Dual-strip camera comprised of two separate movements and film-handling systems all contained in single camera body. To properly record 3-D images, lenses are separated by the same interocular as the average human eye interocular of 2.85". Behind each of the taking lenses are beamsplitter mirrors that reflect right eye image up to right eye movement, and left eye image is reflected down to left eye movement. The beamsplitter mirrors also allow some light to pass through to provide for through-the-lens viewing.

Weight: 215 lbs./97.52 kg (camera, lens and 1,000' (300m) magazine); 329 lbs./149.23 kg (camera, lens and 2,500' (762m) magazine)

Movement: Two separate movements, with pulldown driven by counterbalanced crankshaft; has six claw pins and six register pins. Uses a vacuum backplate in the aperture to hold film flat for steadier images and more uniform focus.

FPS: Variable crystal speed from 1–36 fps. Camera speed can be synchronized to external reference signal. Draws 9 amps at 36V DC running at 24 fps.

Aperture: Shoots two images simultaneously on separate film strips where each negative is 15 perf x 65mm — film travels horizontally.

Lens: Custom-design IMAX lens carriage that holds pair of lenses mounted in single-lens block.

Lens Control: Remote focus and iris controller, wireless remote focus and iris controller, clip-on 3.3"x6.6" filters.

Lenses: Lens pairs mounted in single-lens block with optics supplied by Zeiss, except where noted. Include integrated iris drive and convergence motors where applicable. Fixed interocular at 2.85": 30mm T3.1 (Hughes Leitz), 40mm T4.3, 60mm T3.8, 80mm T3.1. Adjustable convergence: 50mm f/4, 60mm T3.8, 80mm T3.1, 105mm f/4 macro (Rodenstock), 250mm f/5.6.

Shutter: Focal plane shutter, manually variable from 172.8° to 55° with stops at 144° and 108°.

Viewfinder: Beamsplitter reflex viewfinding (70/30 split) with Imax 3-D and Imax 3-D dome reticle markings on ground glass.

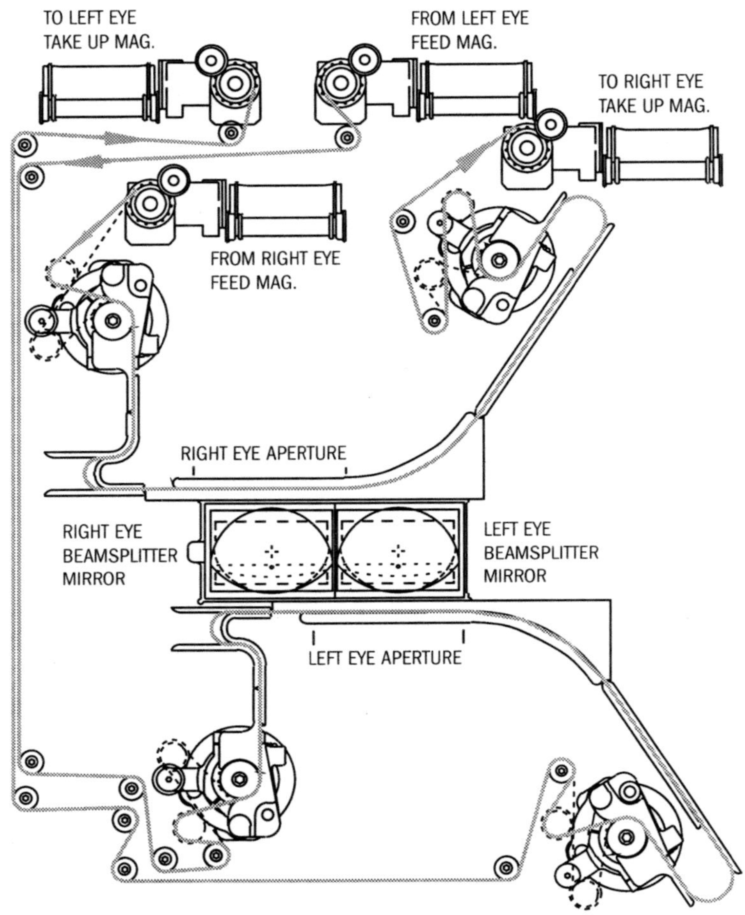

Imax 3-D Threading Diagram
Film takes up emulsion side out.

Viewfinder is orientable and has 10x magnifier.

Mags: Normally equipped with (four) 1,000' (300m) single-chamber magazines (3 minutes at 24 fps). Or (four) 2,500' (762m) magazines (7.5 minutes at 24 fps).

Accessories: 3-D underwater housing (depth rated to 120' (36.6m)), weather barney, matte box (with one 14" x 14" filter stage), sunshade (with mattes), 3-D microscope, viewfinder monitors, environmental box, motorized remote head, Vinten fluid head, Cartoni fluid head, parallax-corrected video assist (mounted above taking lenses).

IW5, IW5A

Notes: IW5 and IW5A are general-purpose mirrored-shutter reflex cameras. The quietest of all IMAX cameras, although not suitable for sync sound without a blimp. Very durable and robust cameras, ideal for rough environments.

IW5A is a slightly later version of IW5. IW5A uses many aluminum, parts in place of magnesium making for a more robust camera body but at the expense of a little more weight (10 lbs. difference). IW5A uses an upgraded set of electronics, but the camera operational features remain the same.

Weight: IW5 88 lbs./39.91 kg (camera plus lens and 1,000' (300m) magazine with film). IW5A, 98 lbs./ 44.45 kg (camera plus lens and 1,000' (300m) magazine with film). IW5A, 155 lbs./ 70.3 kg (camera plus lens and 2,500' (762m) magazine with film).

Movement: Pulldown is a combination cam and pin-driven system. Has four register pins and four claws with adjustable pitch control. Movement is removable for easy cleaning and lubrication. Uses vacuum backplate in aperture to hold film flat for steadier images and more uniform focus.

FPS: Variable frame rate from 1–36 fps, crystal speed at 24 and 25 fps. Camera speed can be synchronized to an external reference signal. Current draw is 9 amps at 30V DC running at 24 fps.

Aperture: Negative is 15 perf x 65mm, film travels horizontally.

Lens: Custom design IMAX bayonet lens mount.

BNC lens mount. 15mm matte rods on Arri BL centers for accessory compatibility.

Lenses: Custom-packaged for the IW5/IW5A camera with optics supplied by Zeiss (except where noted): Wide-angle 30mm f/3.5 (fisheye), 40mm f/4; medium 50mm f/2.8, 60mm f/3.5, 80mm f/2.8; long 110mm f/2, 120mm f/4, 150mm f/2.8, 250mm f/4, 350mm f/5.6, 500mm f/8, 800mm f/4 (Pentax), 1000mm f/8 catadioptic (Pentax); zoom 75–150mm f/4.5 (Schneider), 300 – 1200mm f/11 (Canon/Century).

Shutter: Focal plane shutter with fixed 155° opening. Wings can be added to close down to 10° opening for intervalometer shooting.

Viewfinder: Spinning mirror reflex viewfinding with Imax and Imax Dome reticle markings on ground glass. Finder rotates 360° with manual upright image correction. Footage and camera speed displayed in viewfinder.

Video: Video tap is modular in design, using color CCD camera.

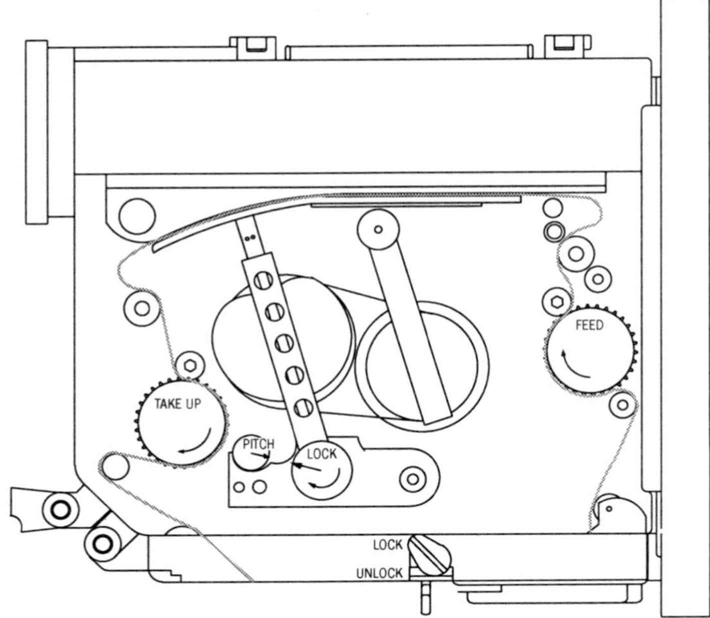

IW5 Threading Diagram
Film takes up emulsion side out.

Mags: Normally equipped with (two) 1000' (300m) dual coaxially stacked magazines (3 minutes at 24 fps). IW5A also uses 2500' (762m) magazine (7.5 minutes at 24 fps).

Accessories: Norris intervalometer, spinning disc, video assist, video lid and extension eyepiece.

Follow focus with Arri whip extension. Pentax director's finder (shoots still photos using camera lenses listed below), Preston FIZ controller and Microforce zoom controller, Preston Radio transmitter, 2x Pentax extender (for 800mm and 1000mm Pentax lenses only), extension tubes (10mm, 20mm and 40mm lengths), diopter lenses 0.5, 1 and 2.

Arri 6.6" x 6.6" three stage mattebox. Sound Blimp. HydroFlex underwater housing (depth rating 150' (45.7m), rain barney and heater barney.

MKII L/W and H/S

Notes: MKII-L/W and MKII-H/S are based on same MKII camera design and are identical in appearance and features, with one optimized for weight and the other for higher speeds.

MKII-L/W and MKII-H/S are beamsplitter reflex cameras intended for special applications where a light or high-speed camera is required in very rough or remote environments. MKII-H/S contains beryllium movement parts, and camera body was allowed to remain slightly heavier than MKII-L/W for improved image resolution when running at higher speeds.

Weight: MKII-L/W 59 lbs./ 26.8 kg (camera plus lens and 1,000' (300m) magazine with film), 46 lbs/20.9 kg. (camera plus lens and 500' (152m) magazine with film). MKII-H/S 68 lbs./30.84 kg (camera plus lens and 1,000' (300m) magazine with film), 55 lbs./24.95 kg (camera plus lens and 500' (152m) magazine with film).

Movement: Pulldown is a cam-driven claw arm. Four register pins and four claw pins. Uses vacuum backplate in aperture to hold film flat for steadier images and more uniform focus.

FPS: MKII-L/W has variable frame rate from 1–36 fps, crystal speed at 24 and 25 fps. MKII-H/S has variable frame rate from 1–4 fps, crystal speed at 24 and 25 fps. Camera speed can be synchronized to external reference signal. Both cameras draw 9 amps at 30V DC running at 24 fps.

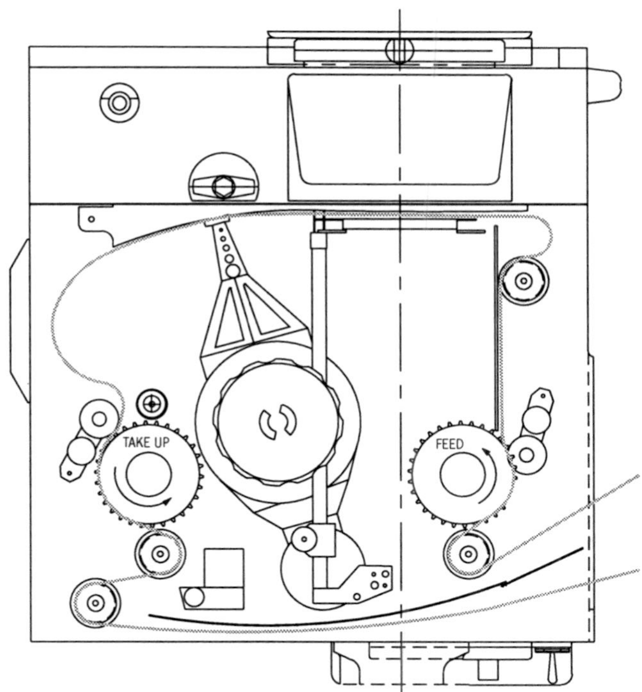

MKII L/W and H/S Threading Diagram
Film takes up emulsion side out.

Aperture: Negative is 15 perf x 65mm, film travels horizontally.

Lens: Custom-design IMAX bayonet lens mount.

Lenses: Custom-packaged for MKII-L/W and MKII-H/S with optics supplied by Zeiss (except where noted). Uses same lenses as IW5 and IW5A.

Shutter: Flat blade shutter with fixed 155° opening interchangeable with shutters with smaller openings for intervalometer use or shooting with HMIs.

Viewfinder: Beamsplitter reflex viewfinding (50/50 split) with IMAX and IMAX Dome reticle markings on ground glass. Finder is fixed straight to back of camera with 8x magnifier.

Video: No video tap due to beamsplitter light levels, but has video lid for 100-percent video in remote environments.

Mags: Normally equipped with 1,000' (300m) Mitchell dual-chamber magazine (3 minutes at 24 fps) or Mitchell 500' (152m)magazine (1.5 minutes at 24 fps).

Accessories: Norris intervalometer, spinning disc and video assist.

Pentax director's finder (shoots still photos using camera lenses listed below), Preston FIZ controller and Microforce zoom controller, Preston Radio transmitter, 2x Pentax extender (for 800mm and 1000mm Pentax lenses only), extension tubes (10mm, 20mm and 40mm lengths), diopter lenses 0.5, 1 and 2.

Arri 6.6" x 6.6" three stage mattebox. Sound Blimp. MKII underwater housing (depth rating 120') (36.6m), rain barney and heater barney.

MSM 9801

Notes: Latest addition to IMAX inventory with all the features of a normal 435 production camera. Designed and built by MSM Design of Hayden Lake, Idaho, lightweight camera can be configured for handheld, Steadicam or powered-head applications. Special adapter allows it to fly in Spacecam gyrostabilized aerial mount.

Weight: 56 lbs./ 25.4 kg (camera, lens and 1,000' (300m) magazine with film). 38 lbs./17.24 kg Steadicam configuration (camera without viewfinder, lens and 500' (152m) (displaced magazine with film).

Movement: MSM five-bar link, four register pins and eight claws with adjustable pitch control. Movement is removable for easy cleaning and lubrication. Uses vacuum backplate in aperture to hold film flat for steadier images and more uniform focus.

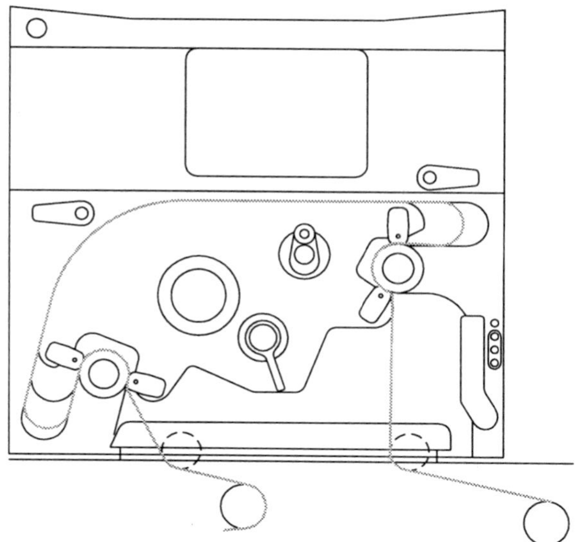

MSM 9801 Threading Diagram
On 1000' magazine film takes up emulsion side in.
500' magazine takes up emulsion side out.

FPS: Crystal speed from 1–36 fps. Camera speed can be synchronized to external reference signal. Draws 6 amps at 30V DC running 24 fps.

Aperture: Negative is 15 perf x 65mm, film travels horizontally.

Lens: Custom-designed MSM rectangular lens mount. Makes for quick lens changes with very positive lens locating.

Lenses: Custom-packaged for MSM 9801 with optics supplied by Zeiss (except where noted): Wide-angle 30mm f/3.5 (fisheye), 40mm f/4; medium 50mm f/2.8, 60mm f/3.5, 80mm f/2.8; long 110mm f/2, 120mm f/4, 150mm f/2.8, 250mm f/4, 350mm f/4, 500mm f/8, 800mm f/6.7 (Pentax); zoom 75–150mm f/4.5 (Schneider), 300–1200mm f/11 (Canon/Century); macro 120mm slant focus (Nikon).

Shutter: Focal plane shutter with fixed 180-degree opening.

Viewfinder: Spinning mirror reflex viewfinding. IMAX and IMA Dome reticle markings on ground glass with register pins for film clips. Finder rotates 360° with constant upright image.

Video: Integrated color CCD video tap. Viewfinder is detachable to reduce weight for aerial shoooting or Steadicam applications.

Mags: Normally equipped with 1,000' (300m) dual-chamber, coaxially stacked magazine (3 minutes at 24 fps). Also uses 500' (152m) displacement magazine (1.5 minutes at 24 fps) with automatic compensation for center of gravity shift of film roll.

Accessories: Norris intervalometer, Hi-G plate, Spacecam adapter.

Built-in follow focus. Preston FIZ controller (focus, iris, zoom), Preston radio transmitter, 1.4x Pentax extender (for 800mm Pentax only).

Arri 6.6" x 6.6" three stage mattebox. Sound Blimp. MKII underwater housing (depth rating 120') (36.6m), rain barney and heater barney. HydroFlex shallow water housing (depth rated to 15' (4.6m)), weather barney.

Jon Fauer, ASC is an award-winning director of photography and director who often writes and lectures about cameras, equipment, techniques, technology, film history and the future of film. He is the author of eight best-selling books on cinematography and digital imaging. These publications are available at www.theasc.com.

Photos by Steven Gainer, ASC.

Using the same movement (and factory) as the Lumiere, the Pathé Studio camera of 1905 became the industry standard. Used by such notables as Arthur Miller, ASC and Billy Bitzer, this camera was eventually replaced by the Bell & Howell 2709 in 1912. *(From the ASC collection donated by Arthur Miller, ASC.)*

Reference Tables

Mired Shift Values

Light Source

Color Balancing

SunPath

Film Stocks

Incident Light

EI Reduction

T-Stop Compensation

Shutter Compensation

Shutter Speeds

Footage Tables

16mm/35mm Frame Totalizers

Panning Speeds

Time/Speed Effects

Projection/Process

Lighting Fixture Intensity

CINE LENS LIST + NEAR FOCUS

The Cine Lens List includes most of the current lenses available for rental or purchase. Many of these lenses are no longer made, but are available used or remounted. Many "House" brands exist that are reworked versions of still camera lenses and older cine-lenses. For complete data, see your local rental house or lens manufacturer.

ANGENIEUX
35mm Prime Lenses
14.5mm f/3.5 1'
18.5mm f/2.2
24mm f/2.2
28mm f/1.8
32mm f/1.8
40mm f/1.8
50mm f/.95
75mm f/1.8
100mm f/2

35mm Zoom Lenses
17-102mm T2.9 HR 2'6"
20-120mm T2.9 3'
24-290mm T2.8 Optimo 4'
25-250mm T3.5 HR 5'7"
25-250mm T3.7 HP 5'7"
25-250mm T4.2 5'6"
25-625mm T8 4'4"
35-140mm f/3.5

16mm Prime Lenses
5.9mm T1.9
Fixed @ 4'- inf.
10mm f/1.8 f.f.
14.5mm T3.9 f.f.
15mm f/1.3 10"
25mm f/.95 18"
25mm f/1.4 20"
25mm f/1.8 20"
28mm f/1.2 20"
50mm f/1.5 2'
75mm f/2.5 3'
100mm f/2.5 3'
150mm f/2.7 5'

16mm Zoom Lenses
9.5-57mm T1.9 2'
9.5-95mm T2.8 2'6"
10-150mm T2.3 5'
12-120mm T2.5 5'
12-240mm T4.2 5'
12.5-75mm T2.5 4'
16-44mm T1.3 5'
17-68mm f/2.2 4'
17.5-70mm T2.5 4'

Super 16 Zoom Lenses
7-81mm T2.4 HR 2'
11-66mm T2.6 2'
11.5-138mm T2.3 HR 5'
15-300mm T5 5'

ARRIFLEX VARIABLE PRIMES
(See Zeiss 35mm Zoom Arri Variable Primes)

BAUSCH & LOMB
35mm Prime Lenses
Super Baltar Series Lenses
20mm T2.3
25mm T2.3
35mm T2.3 1'6"
50mm T2.3 1'6"
75mm T2.3 1'10"
100mm T2.3 4'
150mm T3 6'

Baltar Series Lenses
25mm T2.5 2'
30mm T2.5 2'
35mm T2.5 2'
40mm T2.5 2'
50mm T2.5 2'
75mm T2.5 3'
100mm T2.5 4'
152mm T2.8 9'
225mm T4

16mm Prime Lenses
Baltars Series Lenses
15mm T2.5 2'
17.5mm T2.5 2'
20mm T2.5 2'
25mm T2.5 2'
30mm T2.5 2'
35mm T2.5 2'
40mm T2.5 2'
50mm T2.5 2'
75mm T2.5 3'
100mm T2.5 4'
152mm T2.8 9'

B&L CINEMASCOPE
35mm Anamorphic Prime Lenses
40mm f/2.3
50mm f/2.3
75mm f/2.8
100mm f/2.8
150mm f/3.5

BERTHIOT
16mm Prime Lenses
Cinor Series Lenses
10mm f/1.9
25mm f/1.4
75mm f/2.5
100mm f/3.5
145mm f/4.5

Lytar Series Lenses
25mm f/1.8

16mm Zoom Lenses
Pan Cinor Lenses
17.5-85mm T2.6
17.5-85mm f/3.8
25-100mm f/3.4 7'
28-154mm T4.7
Monital Series Lenses
12-120mm T3.8

CANON
(Also see Century Precision & OpTex)
16mm Zoom Lenses
7-63mm T2.6 2'
8-64mm T2.4 2'

Super 16 Zoom Lenses
11.5-138mm T2.4 3'6"
11-165mm T2.5 3'6"

CENTURY PRECISION
35mm Prime Lenses
6mm T2.8
(Century/Nikkor Fisheye) 1'

7.5mm T5 (Century) 3'
8mm T2.8
(Century/Nikkor Fisheye) 1'1"
9.8mm T2.3
(Century/Kinoptic) 8.5"
14mm T2.8 (Canon) 10"

Cooke/Century Speed Panchro (Close Focus) Lenses
18mm T2.2 5.5"
25mm T2.2 5.5"
32mm T2.3 6.5"
40mm T2.3 7"
50mm T2.3 8"
75mm T2.3 1'3"
100mm T2.8 1'5"

Cooke/Century Speed Panchro Lenses
18mm T2.2 1'
25mm T2.2 1'
32mm T2.3 1'
40mm T2.3 1'
50mm T2.3 1'6"
75mm T2.3 2'
100mm T2.8 3'
152mm T3.2 (Macro 1:2) 2'3"

Century/Canon Telephoto Lenses
200mm T2 10'
200mm T2 Mark II 8'
300mm T2.8 9'9"
300mm T3 Mark II 15'
400mm T2.8 15'
400mm T3 Mark II 15'
400mm T4.5 13'
500mm T4.5 15'3"
600mm T4.5 27'
800mm T5.6 45'

Century/Canon Telephoto Lenses (EOS & FD)
200mm f/2 (EOS MK II)
300mm f/3 (EOS MK II)
300mm f/2.8 (FD MK I)
400mm f/3 (EOS MK II)
400mm f/2.8 (FD MK I)

Century/Nikkor Telephoto Lenses
200mm T2 9'
200mm T4 (Micro-Nikkor 1:2)
300mm T2.4 13'
300mm T2.8 13'
400mm T2.8 13'2"
500mm T4 15'6"
600mm T4 25'
800mm T5.6 27'
1000mm T6.1 25'

35mm Zoom Lenses
17-35mm T3
(Century/Canon-Compact) 1'4"
23-460mm T8
(Century/Angenieux) 5'
28-70mm T3
(Century/Minolta-Compact) 3'
50-300mm f/4.5 (Canon)
50-300mm f/4.5 (Nikkor)
150-600mm T6.7
(Century/Canon) 9'9"

16mm Prime Lenses
1.9mm T2.8 (extreme fisheye) f.f.
3.5mm T2 (fisheye) 2'
5.9mm f/1.8 f.f.
10mm f/1.8

Super 16 Prime Lenses
6mm Series 2000 T1.9 (4.5 w/Wide Angle Adapter) 1'

Super 16 Zoom Lenses
11.5-215mm T2.6 -T3.5(Century/Fujinon) 4'

Special Purpose Lenses
Century/Canon Tilt Focus Lenses
24mm T4 1'
45mm T2.8 1'4"
90mm T2.8 1'8"

Clairmont/Century Swing/Shift Lens System
14mm T2.8 (Canon) 0
18mm T3.8 (Nikkor) 0
20mm T3.2 (Nikkor) 0
24mm T3.8 (Olympus) 0
28mm T3.8 (Pentax) 0
35mm T3.2 (Canon) approx. 6" (1/2")
45mm T2.8 (Canon)
55mm T2.8 (Mamiya)
75mm T2.8 (Pentax)
90mm T2.8 (Canon)
105mm T2.4 (Nikkor) 2'6"
135mm T4 (Pentax)
150mm T2.8 (Zeiss) 5'
150mm T3.5 (Pentax)

Swing/Shift Macro Lenses
120mm T4
(Zeiss/Clairmont 1:1) 1'8"
135mm T5.6
(Zeiss/Clairmont 1:1) 1'8"

Optical Accessories
Double Asphere Wide-Angle Adapter
35mm Format (Converts: 16mm=12mm, 18mm=16)
16mm Format (Converts: 8=6mm, 9.5=7mm, 12=9mm, 10-100mm=7mm, 11-110=7.3)
Super 16 Format (6mm=4.5)

Optical Extenders:
1.4x (PL to PL) (1 1/2-stop loss)
2x (PL to PL) (2-stop loss)

Fish Eye Adapter:
35mm Format (Zeiss lens examples: 16mmCF=10.5mm, 18mm=11.5mm)
16mm Format (Zeiss lens examples: 8mm=5mm,9.5mm=6mm, 12=7mm, 10-100 zoom=5.5mm, 11-110 zoom=5.7)

2/3" Video-to-Super 16mm Mount Transformer

Low Angle Prism
(1/2-stop loss)

Periscope T3.8
(1-stop loss)

Series 2000 Mark II Periscope T4
(w/ a fixed T2.8 lens setting)

CINEMA PRODUCTS
35mm Prime Lenses
K-35 High Speed Aspheric (CP/Canon) Lenses
18mm T1.4
24mm T1.4
35mm T1.4
55mm T1.4
85mm T1.4

16mm Prime Lenses
Ultra T (CP/Canon) Lenses
9.5mm T1.2
12.5mm T1.2
16mm T1.2
25mm T1.2

CINE MAGIC
35mm Special Purpose Lenses
Cinewand Probe Lens

System T5.6
10mm
12mm
16mm
24mm
32mm
40mm
60mm

Revolution Dual-swivel Snorkel/Probe T7.5 Lens System
Mini-PL mount Lenses: (Standard PL-mount adapter also available)
9.5mm
12mm
16mm
20mm
24mm
32mm
40mm
60mm

CLAIRMONT
35mm Prime Lenses
14mm T2.8 (Clairmont/Canon) 10"
20mm T2.8 (Clairmont/Canon) 10"
1000mm T4.5 70'

35mm Zoom Lenses
140-420mm T2.7 (Clairmont/Isco)
150-600mm T8 (Clairmont/Canon) 10'

35mm Anamorphic Prime Lenses
Clairmont Anamorphic Prime Lenses
22mm T2.4
32mm T2.3 2'6"
40mm T2.3 3'
50mm T2.3 3'
75mm T2.8 3'
100mm T3.4 5'

Anamorphic Telephoto Lenses
360mm T4.5 (Zeiss) 5'
400mm T4 (Nikkor) 9'
400mm T6 (Nikkor Macro 1:2) 1'7"
600mm T4 (Nikkor) 13'
600mm T4.5 (Canon) 9'9"
800mm T5.6 (Nikkor) 13'2"
800mm T5.6 (Canon) 12'3"
1000mm T6.3 (Nikkor) 15'6"
1000mm T8 (Canon) 15'3"
1200mm T6.3 (Nikkor) 25'
1200mm T6.3 (Canon) 25'
1600mm T9 (Nikkor) 25'
1600mm T9 (Canon) 45'
2000mm T8 (Clairmont/Canon) 70'

35mm Anamorphic Zoom Lenses
28-140 T4.5 (Cooke) 2'4"
34-204 T4.5 (Angenieux) 2'6"
36-200 T4.5 (Cooke) 2'4"
40-200 T4.5 (Cooke) 2'4"
50-500mm T5.6 (Cooke MK II) 5'6"
50-500mm T5.6 (Cooke MK III) 5'6"
50-500mm T5.6 (Angenieux HR) 5'7"
300-1200mm T11 (Clairmont) 10'

Special Purpose Lenses
Blurtar Lenses (single element vignette-focus lenses)
28mm T2.3
40mm T2.6
50mm T3
75mm T3.8

Clairmont/Century Swing/Shift Lens System
14mm T2.8 (Canon) 0
18mm T3.8 (Nikkor) 0
20mm T3.2 (Nikkor) 0
24mm T3.8 (Olympus) 0
28mm T3.8 (Pentax) 0
35mm T3.2 (Canon) approx. 6" (1/2")
50mm T4 (Zeiss) approx. 1' (4")
60mm T3.5 (Zeiss) approx. 1' (4")
80mm T2.8 (Zeiss) approx. 1'4" (9")
105mm T2.4 (Nikkor) 2'6"
110mm T2.4 (Zeiss) approx. 3'
150mm T2.8 (Zeiss) 5'

Swing/Shift Macro Lenses
120mm T4 (Zeiss/Clairmont 1:1) 1'8"
135mm T5.6 (Zeiss/Clairmont 1:1) 1'8"

InfinFX K2 T22 Long Distance Macro Lens System
#1 Objective Lens (1.3x Magnification) 1'5"
#2 Objective Lens (1.6x Magnification) 1'4"
#3 Objective Lens (2.1x Magnification) 1'
#4 Objective Lens (3.9x Magnification) 6"
#5 Objective Lens (5.3x Magnification) 4"
#6 Objective Lens (10x Magnification) 1.9"

Microscope T51-T60 (PL mount) Lens System
4x Objective Lens
10x Objective Lens
40x Objective Lens

Pinhole Lens f48-f143 (50mm equivalent)

Optical Accessories
Baby Periscope T5.6
Image Shaker
Rifle Scope
Spy EFX (Night vision front attachment)
Squishy Lens

COOKE
35mm Prime Lenses
S4 & S4/i (information) Lenses
(S4/i lenses are compatible with Arri's LDS system)
14mm T2 9"
16mm T2 9"
18mm T2 9"
21mm T2 9"
25mm T2 9"
27mm T2 10"
32mm T2 1'
35mm T2 1'2"
40mm T2 1'4"
50mm T2 1'8"
65mm T2 2'3"
75mm T2 2'6"
100mm T2 3'
135mm T2 5' (2'6" at T4)

S2 & S3 Speed Panchro Lenses
18mm T2.2 1'
25mm T2.2 1'
32mm T2.3 1'
40mm T2.3 1'
50mm T2.3 1'6"

75mm T2.3 2'
100mm T2.8 (Deep Field) 3'
152mm T3.2 (Macro 1:2) 2'3"

S3 Speed Panchros (Close Focus) Lenses
18mm T2.2 5.5"
25mm T2.2 5.5"
32mm T2.3 6.5"
40mm T2.3 7"
50mm T2.3 8"
75mm T2.3 1'3"
100mm T2.8 1'5"

Double Speed Panchro
28mm T2.5 2'

35mm Zoom Lenses
14-70mm T3.1 (Wide Angle Varotal) 2'4"
18-100mm T3 (Varotal) 2'4"
20-60mm T3.1 (Varopanchro) 2'4"
20-100mm T3.1 (Varotal) 2'4"
25-250mm f/2.8 (MK I Super Cine Varotal) 5'6"
25-250mm T3.9 (MK II Cine Varotal) 5'6"
25-250mm T3.7 (MK III Cinetal) 5'6"

16mm Zoom Lenses
9-50mm T2.5 (Varokinetal) 1'6"

Super 16 Zoom Lenses
10-30mm T1.6 (Veropanchro)
10.4-52mm T2.8 (Varokinetal) 1'6"

EASTMAN KODAK
16mm Prime Lenses
Cine-Ektar Series Lenses
15mm f/2.5 6"
20mm f/3.5
25mm f/1.4
25mm f/1.9
50mm f/1.9
63mm f/2 2'

Anastigmat Series Lenses
50mm f/1.6 2'
63mm f/2.7 1'6"
102mm f/2.7 4'6"
153mm f/4

ELGEET
35mm Prime Lenses
Cine-Navitar Series Lenses
13mm f/1.5 1'
25.4mm f/2.0 1'
50mm f/2.0 2'
75mm f/1.9 3'
150mm f/3.8 6'

Cine-Tel Series
75mm f/2.9 3'
100mm f/2.7 2'6"

ELITE
35mm Prime Lenses
9.6mm T2.1 10"
10mm T2.4 (Lightweight) 10"
12mm T1.9 10"
14mm T1.9 10"
16mm T1.6 10"
18mm T1.3 10"
20mm T1.3 10"
22mm T1.3 10"
24mm T1.3 10"
28mm T1.3 10"
35mm T1.3 1'8"
40mm T1.3 1'8"
50mm T1.3 2'4"
60mm T1.3 2'4"
75mm T1.3 3'4"
100mm T1.6 3'4"
135mm T1.9 5'
180mm T2.8 6'6"
200mm T2.8 6'6"

35mm Zoom Lenses
25-80mm T3.2 (Lightweight) 3'
120-520mm T3 11'

35mm Anamorphic Prime Lenses
21mm T2.8 2'6"
24.5mm T2.1 3'
32mm T2.1 3'
40mm T2.1 3'
50mm T2.1 3'
75mm T2.1 3'
100mm T2.1 3'
135mm T2.5 5'
180mm T2.8 5'
250mm T3 5'

35mm Anamorphic Zoom Lenses
40-160mm T4 (Lightweight) 3'
240-1040mm T4 11'

16mm Prime Lenses
4mm T2.2 f.f.

Super 16 Prime Lenses
4.5mm T2.2 (Fisheye) 4"
6.6mm T1.3 8"
7mm T1.3 8"
8mm T1.3 10"
9.5mm T1.3 10"
12mm T1.3 10"
16mm T1.3 10"
20mm T1.3 10'
25mm T1.3 10"
35mm T1.3 10"
50mm T1.3 1'8"

Super 16 Zoom Lenses
10-100 T2.5 1'6"

Special Purpose Lenses
200mm T1.3 (Reverse Perspective) focuses 4' to 6' only

EYEMO
35mm Prime Lenses
Canon Lenses
14mm T2.8 10"
17mm T4 10"
20mm T2.8 10"
24mm T2.8 1'3"
35mm T2.8 1'

Nikkor Lenses
8mm T2.8 (Fisheye) 1'1"
15mm T3.5 1'
18mm T2.8 10"
20mm T2.8 10"
24mm T2 1'
28mm T1.4 1'3"
28mm T2
35mm T1.4 1'
35mm T2
50mm T1.4 2'
55mm T2.8
105mm T2.8

HAWK
(See Vantage Film Lenses)

INNOVISION
16mm & 35mm Special Purpose Lenses
Probe II+ - T6.3 (35mmFormat), T4 (16mm/Video Formats)
9mm (35mm format), 5mm (16mm format)
12mm (35mm format), 7mm (16mm format)
16mm (35mm format), 9.5mm (16mm format)
20mm (35mm format), 12.5mm (16mm format)

32mm (35mm format),
18mm (16mm format)
40mm (35mm format),
24mm (16mm format)

Probe II - T5.6 (35mm Format), T2.8 (16mm/Video Formats)
9mm (35mm format),
5mm (16mm format)
12mm (35mm format),
7mm (16mm format)
16mm (35mm format),
9.5mm (16mm format)
20mm (35mm format),
12.5mm (16mm format)
32mm (35mm format),
18mm (16mm format)
40mm (35mm format),
24mm (16mm format)

High Resolution Probe II & Probe II+ Prime Lenses
12mm
20mm
28mm
40mm
55mm

Probe I - T16 (35mm Format), T8 (16mm/Video Formats)*
*(1-Stop loss w/90° Attachment)
10mm (35mm format),
5mm (16mm format)
14mm (35mm format),
6.5mm (16mm format)
16mm (35mm format),
9mm (16mm format)
24mm (35mm format),
12.5mm (16mm format)
32mm (35mm format),
18mm (16mm format)
50mm (35mm format),
28mm (16mm format)
75mm (35mm format),
40mm (16mm format)
100mm (35mm format),
60mm (16mm format)

6000 Series
35mm Format: 30mm T45
16mm Format: 20mm T30

KENWORTHY/NETTMAN SNORKEL
The lens on the camera will be 4.1 times net focal length of the combined optical system with the periscope included. For 35mm, Kenworthy/Nettman can supply a T/3 18mm,combined focal length, (Pentax 75mm, PL or BNC mount) or a T/4.5 Zoom 19.5-39mm, combined focal length, (Pentax 80-160mm, PL or BNC mount). The customer may supply Zeiss in 85-180mm range. For Arri 16mm SR the client supplies these primes: 35mm, 40mm, 50mm, 60mm. Divide by 4.1 for combined focal length. For Panavision use these Panaflex Spherical Primes: SP type 75mm, 100, & 150mm, which net at 18mm, 24.4mm and 36.6mm. When ordering SP 75mm, specify late model design with serial # approx SP75-94. Earlier designs may cause vignetting. Panavision zooms are too large. Use the modified Pentax 80-160mm with the Panavision mount. For Panavision Anamorphic there are no zooms available. Use primes T/3.5 Series C Panatar 150mm which will look like an anamorphic 37mm. Longer focal length Panatar primes may work. Anamorphic alternative: Super 35 with spherical lenses using Arriflex or Panavision cameras.

KERN-PAILLARD
16mm Prime Lenses
Switar Series Lenses
10mm f/1.6 8"
16mm f/1.8 8"
25mm f/1.4 1'6"
50mm f/1.4 3'
75mm f/1.9 5'

Pizar Series Lenses
26mm f/1.9 1'6"
50mm f/1.8

Yvar/Macro-Yvar Series Lenses
16mm f/2.8 1'
75mm f/2.8 5'
100mm f/3.3 8'
150mm f/4 13'

Macro-Switar Series Lenses
50mm f/1.4

16mm Zoom Lenses
16-86mm f/2.5

KILFITT
35mm Prime Lenses
Tele-Kilar Series Lenses
150mm f/3.5 5'
300mm f/4 5'6"
300mm f/5.6 10'

Fern-Kilar Serise Lenses
400mm f/4
600mm f/5.6

Macro-Kilar Series Lenses
40mm f/2.8
(Macro 1:1) 4"
90mm f/2.8
(Macro 1:1) 6"

KINOPTICS
35mm Prime Lenses
9.8mm f/1.8 (Tegea) 8.5"
18mm f/1.8 (Apochromat)
28mm f/2 (Apochromat) 9"
32mm f/1.9
32mm f/2.8
35mm f/2 (Apochromat)
40mm f/2 (Apochromat)
50mm f/2 (Apochromat)
75mm f/2 (Apochromat)
100mm f/2 (Apochromat) 3'
150mm f/2.5 (Apochromat)
210mm f/2.8 (Special-Cine)
300mm f/3.5 (Special-Cine)
500mm f/5.6 (Aplanat)
1000mm f/8 (Kinoptar)

16mm & Super 16 Prime Lenses
1.9mm f/1.9 (Super Tegea)
5.7mm f/1.8 (Tegea)
9mm f/1.5 (Apochromat)
12.5mm f/2.5 (Apochromat)
18mm f/1.8 (Apochromat)
25mm f/2 (Apochromat)
28mm f/2 (Apochromat)
32mm f/1.9
32mm f/2.8
35mm f/1.3 (Fulgior Apochromat)
35mm f/2 (Apochromat)
40mm f/2 (Apochromat)
50mm f/2 (Apochromat)
75mm f/2 (Apochromat)
100mm f/2 (Apochromat)
150mm f/2.5 (Apochromat)
210mm f/2.8 (Special-Cine)
300mm f/3.5 (Special-Cine)

500mm f/5.6 (Aplanat)
1000mm f/8 (Kinoptar)

16mm, Super 16 & 35mm Macro Lenses
50mm T2.5 (Macro-Apochromat 1:1) 8"
75mm T2.5 (Macro-Apochromat 1:1) 2'6"
100mm T2.5 (Macro-Apochromat 1:1) 4'
150mm T3 (Macro-Apochromat 1:1) 2'

KINETAL
16mm Prime Lenses
9mm T2
12.5mm T2
17.5mm T2
25mm T2
37.5mm T2
50mm T2
75mm T2
100mm T2.8
150mm T4

KISH OPTICS
Optical Accessories
Rear Anamorphic Attachment (PL)
Mesmerizer
Mini-Mesmerizer (35mm format: 50mm widest angle, 16mm format: 25mm)
Rear Zoom-Mesmerizer (PL or Panavision Mount) (1 1/3-stop loss)
Kaleida-Lens (PL or Panavision Mount) T2.8 Maximum aperture.

KOWA
35mm Prime Lenses
Prominar Series Lenses
15mm T4 1'
18mm T2.6 1'
25mm T2.3 1'6"
32mm T2.3 1'6"
40mm T2.3 2'6"
50mm T2.3 2'6"
75mm T2.3 2'8"
100mm T2.6 5'

LOMO
35mm Anamorphic Prime Lenses
22mm T3.6 3'
30mm T3.2 3'
35mm T2.4 3'
50mm T2.4 3'
75mm T2.4 3'
100mm T3.2 5'
150mm T4.5 7'
300mm T5.6 11'
500mm T8 11'

65mm Prime Lenses
28mm T3.8
40mm T3.4
56mm T2.9
75mm T2.9
100mm T2.9
150mm T3

OPPENHEIMER-NIKKOR
35mm Prime Lenses
8mm T3.2

OPTAR
35mm Prime Lenses
Zome Series Lenses
25-80mm T3.3 3'

OPTEX
35mm Prime Lenses
10mm f/2.8 (OpTex/Canon)
10.5mm T2.1 (OpTex/Zeiss) 6"
14mm f/2.8 (OpTex/Canon)
20mm f/2.8 (OpTex/Canon)

Optex/Nikkor (Close Focus) Lenses
15mm T3.5 7"
20mm T2.8 6"
24mm T2.8 6"
28mm T2.8 6.5"
35mm T2.8 8"

Telephoto Lenses
100mm T2 (Optex/Canon) 3'6"
135mm T2 (Optex/Canon) 5'
150mm T3 (OpTex)
180mm f/2 (OpTex/Nikon)
200mm f/2.8 (OpTex/Canon)
200mm f/1.8 (OpTex/Canon) 9'
200mm f/2 (OpTex/Nikon)
200mm f/4 (OpTex/Pentax-Macro)
300mm f/2 (OpTex/Canon)
300mm f/2.8 (OpTex/Canon)
300mm T2.1 (Nikon)
300mm f/3.2 (OpTex/Canon Mk-IIIB)
400mm f/2.8 (OpTex/Canon)
800mm f/5.6 (OpTex/Canon)
1000mm f/11 (OpTex/Nikon)

Macro Lenses
50mm f/3.5 (OpTex/Canon)
60mm f/2.8 (OpTex/Leica) 10.63"
100mm T5.6 (Auto Compensating Iris) (OpTex) 1'2"
200mm f/4 (OpTex/Pentax)

35mm Zoom Lenses
150-600mm f5.6 (OpTex/Canon) 10'

Macro Zoom Lenses
7.8-164mm T2-T2.8

16mm & Super 16 Prime Lenses
4mm T1.9 (OpTex) fixed focus @ 4'- inf.
5.5mm T1.9 (OpTex) 8"
8mm T1.9 (OpTex) 1'3"
150mm T3

16mm Zoom Lenses
5-30mm f3.5 (OpTex/Canon)

Super 16 Zoom Lenses
6-60mm T2.4 (OpTex/Canon)
7-63mm T2.4 (OpTex/Canon) 2'
10.3-216mm T3.3 (OpTex/Canon) 4'
10.5-158mm T2.4
10.5-210mm T2.4-T4 4'
10.8-60mm T3 (OpTex/RTH Cooke)
12-120mm T2.4 (OpTex/Zeiss) 5'
14.5-480mm T3-T5 (OpTex/Canon) 9'

Special Purpose Lenses
Excellence Periscope/Probe System T2.8 (Super 16), T5.6 (35mm), T8 Anamorphic
60° (14mm - Super 16, 28mm - 35mm, 56mm - Anamorphic)
79° (10mm - Super 16, 20mm - 35mm, 40mm - Anamorphic)
100° (7mm - Super 16, 14mm - 35mm, 28mm - Anamorphic)
120° (5mm - Super 16, 10mm - 35mm, 20mm - Anamorphic)

Optical Accessories
2X Extenders: For 16mm, S16 and 35mm Format Lenses.
1.4X Extender

OTTO NEMENZ
35mm Prime Lenses
Eyemo Lenses
14mm T2.8 (Canon) 10"
15mm T3.5 (Nikkor) 1'
17mm T4 (Canon) 10"
18mm T2.8 (Nikkor) 10"
20mm T2.8 (Canon) 10"
20mm T2.8 (Nikkor) 10"
24mm T2.8 (Canon) 1'3"
24mm T2 (Nikkor) 1'
28mm T1.4 (Nikkor) 1'3"
35mm T1.4 (Nikkor) 1'
35mm T2.8 (Canon) 1'
50mm T1.4 (Nikkor) 2'

P+S TECHNIK
35mm Special Purpose Lenses
T-Rex Superscope System
T7.1 (PL, BNC, Panavision mounts)

PANAVISION LENSES
35mm Prime Lenses
Primo Series Lenses
10mm T1.9 2'
14.5mm T1.9 2'
17.5mm T1.9 2'
21mm T1.9 2'
27mm T1.9 2'
35mm T1.9 2'
40mm T1.9 2'
50mm T1.9 2'
75mm T1.9 3'
100mm T1.9 3'
150mm T1.9 5'9"
210mm T2.8 5'10"
(150mm w/ 1.4x Primo Extender)

Primo Classic Series (Close Focus) Lenses
21mm T1.9 (1:5) 9.5"
24mm T1.7 (1:4)
w/ soft effect 10"
27mm T1.9 (1:2.5) 9.5"
30mm T1.7 (1:3.5)
w/ soft effect 10"
35mm T1.9 (1:3) 11"
50mm T1.9 (1:1.25) 11"
65mm T1.7 (1:1.8)
w/soft effect 13.5"
85mm T1.7 (1:3)
w/ soft effect 16.5"
100mm T1.9 (1:2) 16"
125mm T1.8 (1:2.5)
w/ soft effect 25.5"

Primo Close Focus Lenses
11.5mm T1.9
(14.5mm w/ low distortion Wide Angle Adapter)
14.5mm T1.9 (1:6.5) 8.25"
17.5mm T1.9 (1:4.5) 7.5"
21mm T1.9 (1:5) 9.5"
27mm T1.9 (1:3) 9.5"
35mm T1.9 (1:3) 11"

Macro Lenses
50mm T1.4 (1:2) 9"
90mm T2 (1:0.7) 13.5"
180mm T4 (1:0.35) 14.25"
(90mm w/ 2x Primo Extender)
100mm T2 (1:2.5) 18"
140mm T2.8 (1:1.8) 19"
(100mm w/ 1.4x Primo Extender)
200mm T4 (1:2) 27"
280mm T5.6 (1:1.4) 28"
(200mm w/ 1.4x Primo Extender)
Slant Focus Lenses
24mm T3.5 12"
34mm T4.9 13"
(24mm w/ 1.4x Primo Extender)
45mm T2.8 16"
63mm T4 17"
(45mm w/ 1.4x Primo Extender)

Ultra Speed "Z" Series MKII Lenses
14mm T1.9 2'
24mm T1.3 2'
29mm T1.3 2'
35mm T1.4 2'
50mm T1.4 2'
85mm T1.4 2'
100mm T2 3'
135mm T2 5'
180mm T2.8 5'
252mm T4 5'1"
(180mm w/ 1.4x Primo Extender)

Super Speed "Z" Series MKII Lenses
14mm T1.9 2'
24mm T1.9 2'
29mm T1.9 2'
35mm T1.9 2'
50mm T1.9 2'
85mm T1.9 2'6"
100mm T2 3'
135mm T2 5'
180mm T2 5'
252mm T2.8 5'1"
(180mm w/ 1.4x Primo Extender)

Ultra Speed MKII Lenses
14mm T1.9 2'
17mm T1.9 2'
20mm T1.9 2'6"
24mm T1.3 2'
29mm T1.3 2'3"
35mm T1.3 2'
40mm T1.3 2'
50mm T1 2'
75mm T1.6 2'
100mm T1.6 4'
125mm T1.6 3'6"
150mm T1.5 5'

Super Speed MKII Lenses
24mm T2 2'
28mm T2 2'
35mm T1.6 2'
50mm T1.4 2' - 2'3"
55mm T1.1 2'6"

Normal Speed MKII Lenses
8mm T2.8 (Nikon Fisheye) 1'
8mm T2.8 (Distortion Lens) 14"
9.8mm T2.8 2'
16mm T2.8 1'9"
20mm T3 or T4 2'6"
24mm T2.8 2'3"
28mm T2.8 2'
32mm T2.8 2'
35mm T2 1'9" - 2'
40mm T2 2'
50mm T2 2'3" - 2'6"
75mm T2 2'6" - 2'9"
100mm T2.4 3'6"
150mm T2.8 5'

Close Focus/Macro Lenses
17mm T1.9 10"
20mm T4 8"
24mm T2.8 8"
28mm T2.8 8"
35mm T2 8"
40mm T2.8 (1:2)
60mm T2.8 (1:2)
90mm T2.8 (1:2)
100mm T2.8 (1:2)

Telephoto Lenses (Panavised)
200mm T2 (Canon) 8'
200mm T2 (Nikon) 9'
200mm T2 (Ultra Speed) 6'
280mm T2.8 (Canon) 8'1"
(Canon 200mm w/ 1.4x Primo Extender)
280mm T2.8 (Nikon) 9'1"
(Nikon 200mm w/ 1.4x Primo Extender)
300mm T2.8 (Ultra Speed) 15'
300mm T2.8 (Canon) 10'
300mm T2 (Nikon) 11'
420mm T2.8 (Nikon) 11'
(Nikon 300mm w/ 1.4x Primo Extender)

400mm T4 (Panavision)	15'
400mm T2.8 (Nikon)	15'
400mm T2.8 (Canon)	15'
560mm T4 (Canon) (Canon 400mm w/1.4x Primo Extender)	15'
500mm T4 (Panavision)	23'
600mm T4 (Nikon)	25'
600mm T4.5 (Canon)	27'
840mm T6.3 (Canon) (Canon 600mm w/ 1.4x Primo Extender)	27'
800mm T5.6 (Canon)	45'
1120mm T8 (Canon) (Canon 800mm w/1.4x Primo Extender)	45'
1000mm T6 (Nikon)	25'

35mm Zoom Lenses

14.5-50mm T2.2 (Primo Macro)	2'6"
17.5-75mm T2.3 (Primo 4:1)	2'9"
24-275mm T2.8 (Primo11:1)	4'
135-420mm T2.8 (Primo 3:1)	8'6"
27-68mm T2.8 Lightweight I	3'
17.5-34mm T2.8 Lightweight II	1'6"
85-200mm T4 Lightweight III	4'
17-102mm T2.9 (Angenieux/Panavision)	2'6"
20-120mm T3 (Angenieux/Panavision)	3'6"
20-60mm T3 (Cooke/Panavision)	2'6"
20-100mm T3.1 (Cooke/Panavision)	2'6"
25-250mm T4 Super Panazoom (Cooke)	5'6"
150-600mm T6.3 (Canon/Panavision)	10'

35mm Special Purpose Lenses

6mm T2.9 (Fisheye)	**1'6"**
6mm T3.5 (Nikon Fisheye)	10'6"

Frazier T7.1 Lens System

14mm (gives 9.9mm)
17mm (gives 12mm)
20mm (gives 14mm)
24mm (gives 17mm)
28mm (gives 20mm)
35mm (gives 25mm)
45mm (gives 32mm)
50mm (gives 35mm)
85mm (gives 60mm)
105mm (gives 75mm)
135mm (gives 95mm)
15mm (Sigma Fisheye)

Portrait Lenses

14mm T1.9	2'
16mm T2.8	1'9"
20mm T3	2'
24mm T2.8	2'3"
28mm T1.9	2'
35mm T1.4 (Zeiss)	2'
35mm T1.6	2'
35mm T2	2'
50mm T1.4	2'3"
50mm T2	2'6"
75mm T2	2'6"

Macro Lenses

50mm T1 (1:2)	9"
90mm T2 (1:0.7)	14.75"
180mm T4 (1:0.35) (90mm w/ 2x Primo Extender)	15.5"
100mm T2 (1:2.5)	18"
140mm T2.8 (1:1.8) (100mm w/ 1.4x Primo Extender)	19"
200mm T4 (1:2)	27"
280mm T5.6 (1:1.4) (200mm w/ 1.4x Primo Extender)	28"

Slant Focus Lenses (Bellowless)

24mm T3.5 (Close Focus)	12"
34mm T4.9 (Close Focus) (24mm w/ 1.4x Primo Extender)	13"
45mm T2.8 (Close Focus)	16"
63mm T4 (Close Focus) (45mm w/ 1.4x Primo Extender)	17"

35mm Anamorphic Prime Lenses

Primo Series Anamorphic Lenses

35mm T2	3'6"
40mm T2	3'6"
50mm T2	3'6"
75mm T2	4'6"
100mm T2	4'6"

Mark II Primo (Close Focus) Series Anamorphic Lenses

35mm T2	2'9"
40mm T2	2'9"
50mm T2	2'9"
75mm T2	2'6"
100mm T2	2'6"

"E" Series Anamorphic Lenses

28mm T2.3	5'
35mm T2	5'
40mm T2	5'
50mm T2	5'
75mm T2	5'
85mm T2	5'
100mm T2.3	5'
135mm T2.8	3'9"
180mm T2.8	4'6"
252mm T4 (180mm w/ 1.4x Primo Extender)	4'7"

"C" Series Anamorphic Lenses

30mm T3	4'
35mm T2.3	2'9"
40mm T2.8	2'6"
50mm T2.3	2'6"
60mm T2.8	3'6"
75mm T2.5	4'6"
100mm T2.8	4'6"
150mm T3.5	5'
180mm T2.8	7'
252mm T4 (180mm w/ 1.4x Primo Extender)	7'1"

Super High Speed Anamorphic Lenses

24mm T1.6	6'
35mm T1.4	4'6"
50mm T1.1	4'
50mm T1.4	4'
55mm T1.4	4'
75mm T1.8	4'6"
100mm T1.8	4'6" - 5'

35mm Anamorphic Telephoto Lenses

360mm T4	5'6"
400mm T3.5 (Nikon)	9'
400mm T3 (Canon)	8'
600mm T4 (Nikon)	13'
600mm T4.5 (Canon)	27'
800mm T5.6 (Canon)	15'
1000mm T5.6	22'
1200mm T8 (Canon)	27'
2000mm T9	30'

35mm Anamorphic Zoom Lenses

38-85mm T2.8	2'
48-550mm T4.5 (Primo 11:1)	4'1"
270-840mm T4.5 (Primo 3:1)	8'7"
40-200mm T4.5 (Super Panazoom/Cooke)	2'6"
50-500mm T5.6 (Super Panazoom/Cooke)	5'6"

Special Purpose 35mm Anamorphic Lenses
25mm T2.5 (Wide Angle Distortion) 5'
55mm T2.5 (Close Focus) 10"
90mm T4.3 (Slant Focus w/ Close Focus) 17"
100mm T2.8 (Insert or Process) 4'6"
150mm T3.2 (Macro Panatar 1:1.5) 17"
200mm T3.2 (Macro Panatar 1:2) 18"
250mm T3.2 (Macro Panatar 1:2) 29"

16mm Prime Lenses
8mm T2.3 (Zeiss/Panavision) 2'
9.5mm T1.3 (Zeiss Super Speed/Panavision) 1'6"

Super 16 Prime Lenses
12mm T1.3 (Zeiss Super Speed/Panavision) 2'
16mm T1.3 (Zeiss Super Speed/Panavision) 2'
25mm T1.3 (Zeiss Super Speed/Panavision) 1'9"
35mm T2 2'
50mm T2 (Zeiss/Panavision) 2'
85mm T2 (Panavision) 4'
100mm T2 (Zeiss/Panavision) 4'
135mm T2 (Zeiss/Panavision) 4'6"

16mm Zoom Lenses
9-50mm T2.5 (Cooke/Panavision) 1'6"
10-30mm T1.6 (Cooke/Panavision) 2'4"
10-100mm T2 (Zeiss/Panavision) 5'

Super 16 Zoom Lenses
8-64mm T2.4 (Canon/Panavision) 2'
10.4-52mm T2.8 (Cooke/Panavision) 1'6"
11-165mm T2.5 (Canon/Panavision) 3'6"
11.5-138mm T2.5 (Canon/Panavision) 2'6"
11.5-138mm T2.3 (Angenieux/Panavision) 5'

65mm Panavision Prime Lenses
21mm T3 1'6"
24mm T3.5 1'6"
28mm T3 3'
35mm T2.8 1'6"
35mm T2.8 1'9"
40mm T2.8 1'6"
50mm T2 2'
50mm T2 2'6"
55mm T2.8 3'6"
75mm T2 2'3"
75mm T2.3 2'9"
100mm T2 2'
100mm T2.5 3'6"
150mm T2 4'
180mm T2 5'6"
200mm T2 8'
300mm T2.8 (Zeiss) 8'
300mm T2.8 (Canon) 10'
400mm T2.8 (Canon) 12'
800mm T5.6 (Canon) 40'

Primo Series Lenses
75mm T1.9 3'
100mm T1.9 3'
150mm T1.9 5'9"

65mm Zoom Lenses
35-68mm T2.8 (Lightweight) 3'
50-150mm T4.5 7'
60-360mm T6.3 8'
150-600mm T6.3 (Canon/Panavision) 10'

65mm Special Purpose Lenses
19mm T4.5 (Fisheye) 1'6"
24mm T3.5 (Fisheye) **1'**
35mm T2.8 (Slant Focus with Close Focus) 1'

45mm T2.8 (Slant Focus with Close Focus) 1'4"
55mm T4 (Macro) 11"

Optical Accessories
Optex Periscope (Panavision Mount)
Century Precision Periscope (Panavision Mount)
2x Extender
1.4x Extender

RANK-TAYLOR-HOBSON
35mm Prime Lenses
Speed Panchro Series Lenses
18mm f/1.7
25mm f/1.8
32mm f/2
40mm f/2
50mm f/2
75mm f/2
100mm f/2

16mm Prime Lenses
Kinetal Series Lenses
9mm f/1.9
12.5mm f/1.8
17.5mm f/1.8
25mm f/1.8
37.5mm f/1.8
50mm f/1.4 3'
75mm f/2.6
100mm f/2.6
150mm f/3.8

REVOLUTION
(See Cine Magic)

ROESSEL-CPT
CPT Superscope Prime Lenses
10mm T5.7
15mm T5.7
25mm T5.7
40mm T5.7
60mm T5.7

Special Purpose Lenses
Supersnorkel T8
T-Rex T7.1

SCHNEIDER
35mm Prime Lenses
Cinegon Series Lenses
18mm f/2

Cine-Xenon Series Lenses
24mm T1.4 1'1"
28mm T2.2 1'8"
35mm T2.2 2'
40mm T2.2 2'6"
50mm T2.2 3'6"
75mm T2.2 5'
100mm T2.2 5'
300mm T2.2

35mm Zoom Lenses
Televariogon Series Lenses
80-240mm f/4

16mm Prime Lenses
Cinegon Series Lenses
10mm f/1.8 8"
11.5 f/1.8
16mm T2 10"
18mm T2
25mm T1.4 1'1"
28mm f/1.8

Cine-Xenon Series Lenses
16mm f/2
25mm T2 1'1"
28mm T2.2 1'8"
35mm T2.2 2'

40mm T2.2 2'6"
50mm T2.2 3'6"
75mm T2.2 5'
100mm T2.2 5'
300mm T2.2

Tele-Xenar Series Lenses
100mm f2.8

16mm Zoom Lenses
10-100mm T2.2
16-60mm T2.2
16-80mm

TECHNOVISION
35mm Prime Lenses
9mm T2.8 10"
9.5 mm T2.8
12 mm T2.1 (Technovision-Zeiss)
12mm T2.1 8"
15 mm T3.5 (Technovision-Leitz)
18mm T1.6
18 mm T1.4 (Technovision-Zeiss)
24mm T1.4 (Technovision)
50mm T1.6 (Technovision-Leitz)
80mm T1.4 (Technovision-Leitz)

High Speed Lenses
18mm T1.4
25mm T1.4
35mm T1.4
50mm T1.4
85mm T1.4

Technovision-Leitz Lenses
15mm T2.3
19mm T2.3
24mm T2.3
35mm T2.3
50mm T2.3
60mm T2.3
80mm T2.3
100mm T2.3
135mm T2.3
180mm T2.3

Macro Lenses
50mm T1.6
60mm T1.4
80mm T1.4
85mm T1.4
100mm T1.4
135mm T1.4
180mm T1.4

40mm T1.8 (Technovision)
50mm T1.4 (Technovision)
60mm T2.3 (Technovision-Leitz)
80mm T2.3 (Technovision-Leitz)
85mm T1.4 (Technovision)
100mm T2.3 (Technovision-Leitz)
135mm T2.3 (Technovision-Leitz)
180mm T2.3 (Technovision-Leitz)

Technovision/Cooke (Close Focus) Lenses
18mm T2.3
25mm T2.3
32mm T2.3
40mm T2.3
50mm T2.3
75mm T2.3
100mm T2.3

35mm Zoom Lenses Technovision/Cooke Lenses
14-42mm T3.1
18.5-55.5mm T2.3 2'4"
15-75mm T3.1
18-90mm T2.3 2'7"
25-250mm T2.3

35mm Anamorphic Prime Lenses
High Speed Anamorphic Lenses
20mm Tl.4 3'6"
35mm Tl.4 3'
40mm Tl.4 3'
50mm Tl.4 3'
85mm Tl.6 3'

Anamorphic Prime Lenses
25mm T2 3'6"
32mm T2.1 4'
40mm T2.1 3'6"
50mm T2.1 3'
85mm T2.1 4'
100mm T2 3'6"
135mm T2.3 4'
270mm T3.5 5'

Anamorphic Prime Lenses
32mm T2.8 3'5"
40mm T2.5 3'
50mm T2.5 3'
75mm T2.8 3'
100mm T2.8 3'
150mm T3.5 3'
152mm T3 3'5"
200mm T4 2'

Anamorphic Prime Lenses
40mm T2.3 3'
50mm T2.3 3'
75mm T2.5 3'
100mm T2.8 3'

Compact Anamorphic Lenses
40mm T2.3 3'
50mm T2.3 3'
75mm T2.8 3'
100mm T3.4 5'
150mm T3.5 3'

Telephoto Anamorphic Lenses
200mm T3.5 (Techno/Nikon)
200mm T3.2 (Techno/Canon)
400mm T3.6 (Techno/Nikon) 9'
500mm T3 (Techno/Olympus)
600mm T4.5 (Techno/Canon) 10'
800mm T4.5 (Techno/Canon) 15'
1000mm T6.3 (Techno/Canon) 20'
1200mm T6.3 (Techno/Canon) 27'
1600mm T11 (Techno/Canon) 45'
2000mm T11 (Techno/Pentax) 30'

Macro Anamorphic Lenses
50mm Tl.4
200mm T4

35mm Anamorphic Zoom Lenses
28-84mm T4.5 (Techno/Cooke)
28-140mm T4.5 (Techno/Cooke) 2'4"
30-150mm T4.5 (Techno/Cooke)
40-120mm T4.5 (Techno/Cooke) 2'4"

40-200mm T4.5 (Techno/Cooke) 2'6"
50-500mm T4 (Techno/Cooke) 5'6"
50-500mm T5.6 (Techno/Cooke) 5'6"
300-1200mm T8 (Techno/Canon) 10'

TODD-AO
35mm Anamorphic Prime Lenses
28mm T3.9 5'
35mm T1.4 2'6"
55mm T1.4 1'6"
75mm T2.5 3'
100mm T3.4 3'
200mm T4 (Macro 1:1) 1'6"

65mm Prime Lenses
28mm f/3.2
40mm f/2.8
50mm f/2
60mm f/2

75mm f/2.8
100mm f/2.8
150mm f/2.8

65mm Zoom Lenses
60-150mm f/2.8
100-300mm f/4

VAN-DIEMEN
35mm Prime Lenses
Leica Motion Picture Lenses
15mm T3.7 (Super Elmarit)
19mm T3 (Elmarit)
35mm T3 (Elmarit)
50mm T2.1 (Summicron)

Leica Compact Macro Prime Lenses
24mm T3 (Elmarit)
28mm T3 (Elmarit)
35mm T1.5 (Summilux)
50mm T1.5 (Summilux)
60mm T3 (Elmarit)
75mm T1.5 (Summilux)
80mm T1.5 (Summilux)

Leica Variable Pitch Full Macro Lenses
60mm T3 (Elmarit)
80mm T1.5 (Summilux)
90mm T3 (Elmarit)
90mm T2.1 (Summicron)
100mm T3 (Elmarit)
135mm T3 (Elmarit)
180mm T3 (Elmarit)

Leica APO Telephoto Modular Lenses (Head Units & Focus
Modules)
Head A= 280mm T3
Head A + Focus Module Factor 1 = 280mm T3
Head A + Focus Module Factor 1.4 = 400mm T4.2
Head A + Focus Module Factor 2 = 560mm T5.8
Head B= 400mm T3
Head B + Focus Module Factor 1 = 400mm T3
Head B + Focus Module Factor 1.4 = 560mm T4.2
Head B + Focus Module Factor 2 = 800mm T5.8

VANTAGE FILM LENSES
35mm Zoom Lenses
150-450 T2.8 (Hawk) 9'9"
17-35mm T2.8 (Vantage Lightweight) 11"

35mm Macro Lenses
Vantage Macro Lenses (Leica)
19mm T2.8
21mm T2.8
24mm T2.8
28mm T2.8
35mm T2.8
60mm T2.8
90mm T2.8
135mm T2.8
180mm T2.8

35mm Anamorphic Prime Lenses
Hawk V-Series Lenses
25mm T2.2 3'6" (2'9" w/ matched Diopter #1, 2'1" w/Diopter #2)
30mm T2.2 2'9"
35mm T2.2 2'6"
40mm T2.2 2'6"
50mm T2.2 (close focus) 2'
60mm T2.2 (close focus) 2'
75mm T2.2 (close focus) 2'
100mm T2.2 3'6"
135mm T3 3'6"
120mm T3 1'6"
180mm T3 6'6"
250mm T3 6'6"

Hawk C-Series Lenses
40mm T2.2 3'6"
50mm T2.2 3'6"
60mm T2.2 3'6"
75mmT2.2 3'6"
100mmT3 3'6"

35mm Anamorphic Zoom Lenses
Hawk V-Series Lenses
46-230mm T4 1'6"
300-900mm T4 9'9"

Hawk C-Series Lenses
55-165mm T4 3'6"

Optical Accessories
Hawk Anamorphic Rear Attachment (1-stop loss)
Hawk V 350mm 1.4x Extender (extends a 250mm to 350mm)
Vantage 6mm Fisheye Attachment for Nikon 8mm
Vantage 0.7x Reducer (1-stop gain)

WILCAM/VISTAVISION LENSES
35mm Prime Lenses
19mm T2.8 (BNC) 9"
24mm T1.4 (BNC) 9"
28mm T1.4 (BNC) 10"
35mm T1.4 (BNC) 12"
50mm T1.4 (BNC) 18"
85mm T1.4 (BNC) 2'
100mm T2 (Macro Schneider)
135mm T1.8 (BNC) 3'

Zeiss BNC Wilcam Lenses
25mm T2.8 1'
35mm T1.4 1'
50mm T1.4 1'3"
85mm T1.4 1'

35mm Zoom Lenses
35-140mm T3.5 (BNC) 5'5"
50-300mm T4.5 (BNC) 8'

WOLLENSAK
35mm Prime Lenses
Fastair Pro Raptar Series Lenses
13mm f/2.3 1'2"
17mm f/2.3 1'4"
25mm f/2.3 1'1"
50mm f/2.3 2'3"
76mm f/2.5 2'4"
101mm f/2.5 3'9"
152mm f/3.8 6'9"

Fastax Raptar Series Lenses
25mm f/2.5 1'6"
35mm f/2.5 2'4"
50mm f/2.5 2'
75mm f/2.5 8'
101mm f/3.5 20'
152mm f/4.5 25'
254mm f/4.5
305mm f/4.5
356mm f/4.5
380mm f/4.5
406mm f/5.6
457mm f/5.6

Velostigmat Series Lenses
35mm f/2 2'6"
50mm f/3.5 1'6"
105mm f/3.5 8'

Mirrotel Series Lenses
508mm f/5.6
610mm f/5.6
1016mm f/8
2032mm f/14

16mm Prime Lenses
Cine Raptar Series Lenses
12.7mm f/1.5 1'6"
13mm f/1.2 1'
17mm f/2
f.f. (15-inf. @ f/2.7)

17mm f/2.5 10"
17mm f/2.7 10"
25mm f/1.5 2'
25mm f/1.9 2'
40mm f/1.5 2'
50mm f/1.5 2'
50mm f/1.9 1'6"
50mm f/3.5 2'6"
75mm f/2.5 3'
75mm f/2.8 3'
75mm f/4 3'
100mm f/4.5 4'6"
150mm f/4.5 9'

ZEISS
35mm Prime Lenses
Ultra Prime & Ultra Prime LDS (Lens Data System) Lenses
8mm (R) T2.8 1'
10mm T2.1 (Distagon) 1'3"
12mm T1.9 (Distagon) 1'
14mm T1.9 (Distagon) 9"
16mm T1.9 (Distagon) 9"
20mm T1.9 (Distagon) 1'
24mm T1.9 (Distagon) 1'
28mm T1.9 (Distagon) 1'3"
32mm T1.9 (Distagon) 1'3"
40mm T1.9 (Distagon) 1'6"
50mm T1.9 (Planar) 2'
65mm T1.9 (Planar) 2'3"
85mm T1.9 (Planar) 3'
100mm T1.9 (Sonnar) 3'3"
135mm T1.9 (Sonnar) 5'
180mm T1.9 (Sonnar) 8'6"

Super Speed Prime Lenses
18mm T1.3 (Distagon) 10"
25mm T1.3 (Distagon) 10"
35mm T1.3 (Distagon) 14"
50mm T1.3 (Planar) 2'4"
65mm T1.3 (Planar) 2'4"
85mm T1.3 (Planar) 3'

Standard Prime Lenses
10mm T2.1 (Distagon) 14"
12mm T2.1 (Distagon) 10"
14mm T2 (Distagon) 9"
16mm T2.1 (Distagon) 10"
20mm T2.1 (Distagon) 8"
24mm T2.1 (Distagon) 1'2"
28mm T2.1 (Distagon) 11"
32mm T2.1 (Planar) 2'
40mm T2.1 (Planar) 1'4"
50mm T2.1 (Planar) 1'5"
60mm T3
(Planar/Macro 1:2) 11" (4")
85mm T2.1 (Planar) 3'
100mm T2.1 (Planar) 3'4"
135mm T2.1 (Planar) 5'
180mm T3 (Sonnar) 5'

300mm T4 (Sonnar) 10'
Master Prime Lenses
14mm T1.3
16mm T1.3 1'2"
18mm T1.3 1'2"
21mm T1.3 1'2"
25mm T1.3 1'2"
40mm T1.3 1'4"
50mm T1.3 1'8"
65mm T1.3 2'1"
75mm T1.3 2'7"
100mm T1.3 3'4"
150mm T1.3

Close Focus Standard Prime Lenses
16mm T2.1 (Distagon) 6"
18mm T1.3 (Super Speeds) 9"
24mm T2.1 (Distagon) 6"
25mm T1.3 (Super Speeds) 9"
32mm T2.1 (Planar) 9"

Arri Macro Prime Lenses
(*) = distance from front of lens
16mm T2.1 (1:4)
5.5" (1.5")*
24mm T2.1 (1:4)
6.5" (2.5")*
32mm T2.1 (1:4)
7.5" (3.5")*
40mm T2.1 (1:4) 9" (5")*
50mm T3 (1:1) 7.5" (2")*
100mm T3 (1:1)1' 2" (6")*
200mm T4.3 (1:2) 1'11"

Telephoto Lenses
300mm T3 11'6"

35mm Zoom Lenses
Arri Variable Prime Lenses
(Vario-Sonnar)
16-30mm T2.2 VP1 2'
29-60mm T2.2 VP2 2'9"
55-105mm T2.2 VP3 2'9"

35mm Anamorphic Prime Lenses
Arriscope Prime Anamorphic Lenses
40mm T2.3 3'3"
50mm T2.3 3'3"
75mm T2.3 3'9"
100mm T3.5 4'
135mm T3 4'6"

35mm Special Purpose Lenses
Arriflex Shift & Tilt System
18mm T3.8
20mm T2.8
28mm T2.8
35mm T2.8
60mm T2.8
80mm T1.9
110mm T3.2
150mm T2.8

Slant Focus Lenses
Bellowless)
24mm T4
45mm T2.8
90mm T2.8

16mm Prime Lenses
8mm T2.1 (Distagon) 8"
9.5mm T1.3 (Distagon) 10"

Super 16 Prime Lenses
Super Speed Prime Lenses
12mm T1.3 (Distagon) 8"
16mm T1.3 (Distagon) 8"
25mm T1.3 (Distagon) 10"
50mm T1.4 (Planar) 1'3"
85mm T1.3 3'

Super 16 Ultra Prime Lenses
6mm T1.3 (Distagon t*xp) 8"
8mm T1.3 (Distagon t*xp) 1'
9.5mm T1.3 (Distagon t*xp) 1'
12mm T1.3 (Distagon t*xp) 1'
14mm T1.3 (Distagon t*xp) 1'

Standard Speed Prime Lenses
16mm T2.1 (Distagon) 10"
20mm T2.1 (Distagon) 8"
24mm T2.1 (Distagon) 1'1"
28mm T2.1 (Distagon) 11"
32mm T2.1 (Planar) 2'
40mm T2.1 (Planar) 1'4"
50mm T2.1 (Planar) 1'6"
100mm T2.1 3'4"
135mm T2 5'
180mm T2.1 (Planar) 5'

16mm Zoom Lenses
10-100mm T2 (Macro II) 5'
10-100mm T3 (Macro)

Super 16 Zoom Lenses
11-110mm T2.2
(Vario-Sonnar) 5'
15.5-45mm T2.6
(Vario-Sonnar T*xp) 18"

Optical Accessories
Mutar: Attachment for 10-100mm
Aspheron: 9.5=5.6mm, 12=6.6mm
Panspheron (Cooke 9-50mm=6-30, Zeiss 18mm=14mm)

Special Purpose Lenses

Swing Shift Lens

The Clairmont Swing Shift Lens System consists of a multi axis moveable lens board receiver attached to a Arriflex style PL lens mount by a rubber bellows. Specially modified lenses are attached to the receiver board by two captive screws. The assembly is able to move the entire lens in the following directions: tilt up and down, swing side to side, shift position and focus right to left, or up and down. Tilting/swinging the lens plane alters the focus; tilting/swinging the film plane alters the shape. By combining the various parameters of movement, different and unusual effects can be accomplished such as increased or decreased depth of field, selective planes of focus, repositioning of image without changing placement of the camera, correction or addition of image distortion. The focal lengths available are, 20mm, 24mm, 28mm, 35mm, 50mm, 60mm, and 80mm.

Panavision 24mm T3.5 or 45mm T2.8 Slant Focus Lens

The plane of focus of this lens can be tilted in any direction (including vertical and diagonal) as well as horizontal by adjusting the rear lens rotating mount.

If the lens focus is set on an object near the center of the field of view, the plane of focus can be tilted so that objects (left side of frame and/or right side of frame) located along this tilted plane of focus will also be sharp.

If there is not an object near the center of the field of view, measure the distance to the near and far object and set the focus at an average between the two distances. The plane of focus can now be tilted so that the two objects will be brought into focus. In all situations, an object near the center of the field of view should still be in focus after tilting the lens.

Due to the tilting nature of this lens, it cannot be used with a Panaflex follow focus. For the initial focus and any change in focus, eye focusing is necessary. This lens accepts a 1.4 X Primo extender with negligible change in performance and no change in operation. The focal length becomes 63mm with a maximum aperture of T4.0. If filters are used with this lens they should (when ever possible) be glass filters in front of the lens. If needed, the lens does accept a 40.5mm rear filter.

Continental Camera Systems Remotely-Controlled "Pitching Lens" f/3.9 Optical Relay

Concept: A system to remotely control a prime lens that is mounted at the end of an optical relay tube. In normal configuration the 18" tube extends downward from the camera. The prime lens is mounted at right angles to the tube and can tilt 15° up to 90° down. The entire system rotates 380°. This allows lenses such as Nikkor or Arriflex to get into very small areas. Use of an anamorphic element between the end of relay tube and camera allows a spherical lens to produce an anamorphic image on film. Because focus is controlled in the relay tube, it is possible to continuously follow focus from ½ inch to infinity thus greatly extending the normal focus range of most prime lenses. The system may also be mounted vertically (as in a submarine)or extended straight out in a horizontal position.

Clear length of relay: 18" Maximum diameter: 3"

Control of Lens: Control console with built-in video monitor. Pressure sensitive joystick for pan and tilt operation. System power requirements 110V, 220V or 24V DC.

Cameras: Arriflex IIC, Norelco PCP90 (video), Mitchell R35, Lightweight Technicolor VistaVision equipped with Nikon mount.

Focus: Remotely controlled from hand-held unit. Focus speed is proportional to focus command.

Taking Formats: 16mm, 35mm anamorphic, VistaVision.

Optics: Nikon mount through adapter rings can use a wide assortment of Nikkor and Arriflex lenses from 7.2 mm to 100mm. Speed of system is f/3.9 to f/32. Prime lens is set wide open and aperture controlled in the relay system. Suspension: Standard dolly with small jib arm and C.C.S. balanced cross arm at camera end of jib. Large telescopic billboard cranes and Chapman "Titan" cranes can be used.

Kenworthy Snorkel Camera Systems

A remote image taking system with operator and camera components removed from shooting area. The camera looks into a periscope-like optical relay tube that extends downward below the camera and ends with a small front-surfaced mirror. Since the mass of the camera with operator is removed from the shooting area ,considerations of scene staging are concerned only with the small end (1¼"x 1¼" at the mirror) of the tube. The tilting mirror is remotely controlled, as are other functions such as pan, focus, roll, zoom and iris. The mirror system permits more intimate shooting (due to its small size) than do add-on right-angled lens periscopes. It also permits tilting up in constricted situations because the mirror, rather than the tube/camera combination, does the tilting. The system allows viewpoints in tight quarters reachable from overhead, or from very low viewpoints or in miniature sets. Pans and tilts are on system nodal point. An added waterproof tube permits underwater or transition shots.

There are two systems available:

The Kenworthy Nettman Snorkel features fast optics and lightweight, interchangeable formats, and carries a shorter tube for use on light weight dollies. The cameras are butterfly VistaVision, 65mm, and 16mm film and ⅔" video cameras. Camera lenses are used.

Type B Kenworthy Snorkel is designed for shooting actors with dialogue at moderate lighting levels. It carries a longer tube (48" or 66") which permits more overhead clearance for deeper penetration into four-walled sets or water tanks. This system uses 35mm only: Arriflex, Mitchell Mark II, Panaflex or other similar cameras. The Panacam is used for video. System lenses are used on the Type B; 28 mm & 50mm T8 for film 13mm T5.6 for video. Both systems can use anamorphic lenses. Type B requires a camera crane.

With both systems a console is used with a video monitor and pan, tilt and lens controls.

Dynalens

An optical stabilizing device mounted on the camera optical axis for compensating for image motion due to vibration of the camera.

A pair of gyro sensors detect rapid motion and drive two gimbal-mounted glass plates, between which is a liquid filled cell. One plate moves around a vertical axis and the other around a horizontal axis in a manner which deviates the light path opposite to the vibratory movement, causing the image to stay still relative to the image receptor (film or video).

A low-frequency-response manually operated potentiometer on the control module adjusts the frequency sensitivity of the unit so controlled panning or tilting may be done.

The Dynalens is available in 2.3" diameter for 16mm film or small video cameras and 3.8" and 8" for larger format cameras. The maximum useful angular deviation is + 6°.

Extreme Close-up Cinematography

There are two basic methods for focusing a lens on very close objects: (1) by adding extension tubes or extension bellows and (2) by employing plus diopter supplementary lenses in front of the normal lens.

Extension Tubes or Bellows

Generally speaking, extension tubes or bellows produce the best overall results since the lens itself is not altered- it is simply placed further away from the film plane so that it can produce a sharp image of an object at very close distances.

Extension tubes should not be employed with wide-angle or zoom lenses. They work best with normal or semi-telephoto lenses. For practical purposes the diaphragm of a normal focal length lens may be considered the point at which the light rays cross (the rear nodal point). For simplicity the close-up tables on page 746–747 show measurements from the diaphragm (not necessarily the diaphragm actuating the ring.) to the object being filmed and from the diaphragm to the film plane.

Conventional lenses of moderate focal length usually will develop a better quality image if reversed in their mounts when the distance from the lens to the film plane is greater than the distance from the lens to the object. Specially designed close working lenses should be used if a great deal of ultra-close filming is required.

Since depth of field is shallow at close distances, even when the lens is stopped down, try to keep the object or the area being filmed in as compact as a space, from front to back, as possible. Camera, lens tube, or bellows, and object must be held as rigid and vibrationless as possible during filming.

When a lens is focused closer than ten times its focal length its *effective* aperture, rather than its marked aperture, must be taken into consideration. Long extension tubes decrease lens speed considerably since the farther the lens is moved from the film plane the more its speed is proportionately reduced.

Image to Object manifestation, or reduction, ratios are based on the size of the actual film frame compared to the size of the object being photographed. Close-up tables can thus be used with either 16mm or 35mm cameras because comparisons are "area for area" since similar focal length lenses with similar extension will deliver the same ratio- with a smaller portion of the object being filmed on 16mm than on 35mm. The first number of the ratio is the film image- the second is the object. Thus 1:1 means that the size of the image on the film equals the size of the object being filmed. (Note: Any lens at *twice* its normal focal length will be an equal distance from the object being photographed, and shoot its actual size. Thus a 2 inch lens at 4 inches from the film will also be 4 inches from the object and record an object area the same size as the film area. A 3 inch lens will perform the same way at 6 inches from the film and the object. A 4 inch lens at 8 inches, etc.)

1 to 1 is a good starting point to compute ratios, exposures, etc. With a 16mm camera an object area the size of the full frame (.404" x .295") can thus be filmed with any lens at twice its focal length. The same holds true for a 35mm camera except that a larger object area (.866" x .630" say 1 to 5 (film area is ⅕ the size of object area), would require much less extension. Greater magnification, say 5 to 1 (film area is 5 times the size of the object area) would require much longer extension.

Depth of field is identical at the same *magnification* (not lens extension!) and same f/stop for any focal length lens. Nothing is gained as far as depth of field is concerned by using a shorter focal length lens for the same size image. Since the f/stop is the only factor to consider any convenient focal length lens may be used.

The simplest method for finding the exposure factor is to add "1" to the scale of reproduction and multiply the result by itself. Thus for a scale of 1:2 (film area is ½ the size of object area), ½ + 1 or 1.5 x 1.5 equals 2.25. Similarly, for same-size reproduction or 1:1, 1+1 equals 2. 2 x 2 equals 4 (or 2 stops increase). 3:1 would be 3+ 1 equals 4. 4 x 4 equals 16 (or 4 stops increase).

Exposure for extreme close-ups can best be determined by an incident light meter. The effective aperture should be used for determining the light.

Diopter Lenses

Extreme close-ups may be filmed by employing positive supplementary lenses, generally of a weak meniscus form, called diopter lenses, in front of the normal lens.

The power of these positive supplementary lenses is commonly expressed in diopters. The power in diopters is the reciprocal of the focal length in meters. The plus sign indicates a positive, or converging lens. Thus, a +3 diopter lens has a focal length of ⅓ meter, or 39.3 inches divided by 3 or approximately 13 inches. A +2 diopter lens would have a focal length of approximately 20 inches. A +1 would be one meter or roughly 40 inches. In other words, the positive diopter lens *alone* will form an image of a distant object when held at its respective focal length. When two such lenses are used together, their combined power is practically equal to the sum of both powers. A +2 and a +3, for instance, would equal a +5 and possess a focal length of approximately 8 inches (39.3 divided by 5 equals approximately 8).

When two diopter lenses are combined, the highest power should be closest to the prime lens. Plus diopters should be placed in front of the prime lens with their convex (outward curve) side toward the subject. If an *arrow* is engraved on the rim of the diopter lens mount, it should point *toward the subject.*

High power plus diopter lenses, such as +8 or +10, are not practical to manufacture for large diameter prime lenses because their optical performance would be inferior. Best screen quality results with lower power diopters. It is better to use a longer focal length lens and a less powerful plus diopter lens, then to employ a high power diopter on a short focal length lens.

A plus diopter lens placed in front of a conventional lens set at infinity all form a sharp image at its particular focal length. Thus a cine lens may be focused for extreme close-ups, without the necessity of racking it out with the extension tubes or bellows, simply by placing a plus diopter lens, of the required focal length, in front of it. The distance at which a diopter lens can be focused is *decreased,* however, by racking the normal lens out to its nearest focusing distance. Cine lens may be focused much closer, therefore, with the same power diopter lens, by simply utilizing closer focus settings on the lens.

Diopter lenses may be focused at the same distance with any focal length lens, since their power remains the same. The magnification will vary, however, depending on the focal length of the actual camera lens employed.

The longer the focal length of the prime lens, the smaller the area covered by the same power diopter lens. The shorter the focal length of the prime lens, the closer the camera will have to be positioned to the subject and the more powerful the diopter lens required- to cover the same area as a longer focal length lens. There are several advantages in employing longer focal length lenses; a less powerful plus diopter lens is required and results are better; more space is available between camera and subject for lighting; the same area may be panned with a shorter arc so the subject is not distorted.

Diopter lenses alter the basic lens design and therefore require stopping the lens down for reasonable sharpness. Since illuminating a small area generally presents no problem (except heat) it is a simple matter to close down to f/8 or f/11. Diopter lenses on the order of +½, +1, +2 or +3 will give satisfactorily sharp results with normal focal length or semi-telephoto lenses.

Plus diopter lenses shorten the focal length of the prime lens. *(See: Plus Diopter Lenses Focal Length Conversion Table page 747.)* A 100mm prime lens with a +3 diopter lens, for instance, becomes 76.91mm in focal length. The indicated f/number, therefore, should be divided by approximately 1.4 to get its true value. In practice, however, the use of close-up diopter lenses does not require any change in exposure setting; because the change in effective f/number exactly compensates for the exposure change caused by increased image size.

Split-Field Diopter Lenses

Split-field diopter lenses are *partial* lenses, cut so that they cover only a *portion* of the prime lens. They are generally cut in half, although they may be positioned in front of the prime lens so that more or less than half is covered. They may be compared with bi-focals for human vision, in which the eye may focus near and far. They have an advantage over bi-focals, however, in that they may be *focused sharply on both near and far subjects simultaneously.*

The depth of field of the prime lens is not extended. The split-field diopter lens simply permits focusing on a very close subject on one side of the frame, while a distant subject is photographed normally through the uncovered portion of the prime lens. Generally, the area in between will *not* be in focus. There are instances, such as using a zoom lens with a small aperture at the wide-angle position, when sharpness may extend all the way from the ultra-close-up to the distant subject. The split-diopter equipped lens possesses *two* distinct *depths of field:* one for the close subject (which may be very shallow or possess no depth whatsoever) and another for the distant subject (which will be the normal depth of field for the particular focal length lens and f/stop in use). It is important, therefore, to exclude subject matter from the middle distance because it will create a situation where the foreground is sharp, the middle distance out of focus and the distant subject sharp!

Split-field diopter lenses require ground glass focusing to precisely line-up both foreground and background subjects and visually check focus on each. This is particularly important with zoom lenses, which may require camera movement during the zoom.

Very unusual effects are possible, which would otherwise require two separate shots, which would be later combined in an optical printer via a matting process. Making such split shots in the camera permits viewing the scene as it will appear, rather than waiting for both shots to be optically printed onto one film.

The proper power split-field diopter lens is positioned in front of the taking lens on the same side as the near object- so that it is sharply focused on one side of the frame. The uncovered portion of the conventional or zoom lens is focused in the usual manner on the distant subject. (Note: Use the *Plus Diopter Lenses Focus Conversion Table on page 752* to find near and far focusing distances with various power diopter lenses.)

The edge of the split-diopter lens should be positioned, if possible, so that it lines up with a straight edge in the background- such as the corner of a room, the edge of a column or a bookcase. Eliminating the edge may prove difficult under certain conditions, particularly with a zoom lens because the edge will shift across the frame slightly when the lens is zoomed. It is wise to leave space between the foreground and background subjects so that they do not overlap and each is removed from the lens edge. This will minimize "blending". The split-diopter need not be lined up vertically- it may be used horizontally or at any angle to cover a foreground subject on top, bottom, either side or at an angle across the frame.

The split may sometimes be "covered" by filming both foreground and background against a distant neutral background- for a "limbo" effect. The can of wax, for instance, may be placed on a table so that it appears against the same distant neutral background as the housewife.

Lighting may be employed to lighten or darken the background area where the split occurs, to make it less noticeable. Lighting should generally be balanced so that both near and far subjects may be varied, of course, for pictorial effects. Either foreground or background may be filmed in silhouette, or kept in darkness so that one or the other may be fully illuminated during the scene. Since the diopter lens requires no increase in exposure, balancing the lights is a simple matter.

OPTICAL LENS EXTENDER EXPOSURE FACTORS

1.4X = Factor of 2 – 1 Stop increase
1.6X = Factor of 2.5 – 1 ⅓ Stop Increase
2X = Factor of 4 – 2 Stop Increase
Magnification squared = Factor
Example: 1.4 x 1.4 = 1.96 closest factor 2

Non-Optical Extension Tube or Bellows Exposure Factors

Distance of lens from film plane squared, divided by the focal length squared = factor.

Example:
50mm lens + 50mm extension = factor of 4 – 2 stop increase.

$$\frac{(50+50)^2}{50^2} = \frac{10,000}{2500} = 4$$

Comparison of lens "depths" for collimatation of lens (not for setting flange depth of camera)					
Arri (2.04")	52.00mm	**Nikon** (1.831")	46.5mm	**Lecia R** (1.85")	47.00mm
Panavision (2.2500")	57.15mm	**Canon** (1.659")	42.14mm	**Leica M** (1.10")	27.95mm
BNCR (2.42")	61.47mm				

This chart is for reference only; note there are different standards for collimation or setup, often set by rental house.

Formulas

By R. Evans Wetmore. P. E. ASC Associate Member

1 Lens Formulas

The formulas given in this section are sufficiently accurate to solve most practical problems encountered in cinematography. Many of the equations, however, are approximations or simplifications of very complex optical relationships. Therefore, shooting tests should always be considered when using these formulas, especially in critical situations.

1.1 Hyperfocal Distance

The hyperfocal distance (H) is the focus distance setting of a lens where all objects from half the focus distance setting through infinity are in acceptable focus. Acceptable focus is characterized by a parameter called the circle of confusion (C_C). The lens aperture setting and the circle of confusion affect the hyperfocal distance. The formula for hyperfocal distance is:

$$H = \frac{F^2}{fC_C} \qquad (1)$$

where F = focal length of lens
f = f-stop of lens
C_C = circle of confusion

All values in this and the following equations must be in the same units, e.g., millimeters, inches, etc. For instance, when using a circle of confusion value measured in inches, the lens focal length must be in inches, and the resulting answer will be in inches. (Note: f-stop has no dimensions and so is not affected by the type of units used.)

As mentioned above, the circle of confusion characterizes the degree of acceptable focus. The smaller the circle of confusion is the higher the resulting image sharpness. For practical purposes the following values have been used in computing depth of field and hyperfocal distances in this manual:

35mm photography = 0.001 inch ($\frac{1}{1000}$ inch) or 0.025mm

16mm photography = 0.0005 inch ($\frac{5}{10,000}$ inch) or 0.013mm

TAK'S TIPS

Multiplication Constants for Calculating Hyperfocal Distance for Circle of Confusions in Feet

CC (in Inches)	Decimal of CC	Constant
1/500	0.002	0.06458
1/707	0.0014	0.09226
1/1000	0.001	0.12917
1/1414	0.0007	0.18452
1/1666	0.0006	0.21528
1/2500	0.0005	0.32292

Example: For CC = .0005

F = 35mm $f/4$

$$H = \frac{.32292 \times 35^2}{4} = 98.89'$$

Courtesy of Panavision's Tak Miyagishima.

1.2 Depth of Field

For a discussion on the concept of depth of field, please see the introduction to the Depth of Field Tables. It should be understood that the detemination of depth of field involves a subjective judgement that requires taking into account the conditions under which the final projected image will be viewed.

The following two formulas are for calculating the depth of field. To use these equations one must first calculate the hyperfocal distance from Equation 1.

$$D_n = \frac{HS}{H + (S - F)} \tag{2}$$

$$D_f = \frac{HS}{H - (S - F)} \tag{3}$$

where D_n = Camera to Near Limit
D_f = Camera to Far Limit
H = Hyperfocal Distance
S = Distance from Camera to Subject
F = Focal Length of Lens

The total depth of field is equal to $D_f - D_n$.

The following shows how the above equations can be used to make hyperfocal and depth of field calculations:

Example: A 35mm camera lens of 50mm focal length is focused at 20 feet and is set to f/2.8. Over what range of distances will objects be in acceptable focus?

First convert all the units to the same system. In this example inches will be used. Therefore, the 50mm focal length will be converted to 2 inches. (This is an approximation as 50mm is exactly 1.969 inches, but 2 inches is close enough for normal work.) Also the 20 feet converts to 240 inches (20 × 12). The circle of confusion is 0.001 inches for 35mm photography.

Using Equation 1 and filling in the converted values yields:

$$H = \frac{2^2}{2.8 \times 0.001} = \frac{4}{0.0028} = 1429 \text{ inches} = 119 \text{ feet}$$

Using the hyperfocal distance just calculated and equations 2 and 3, we can now calculate the near and far distances that will be in acceptable focus.

$$D_n = \frac{1429 \times 240}{1429 + (240 - 2)} = 205.7 \text{ inches} = 17.1 \text{ feet}$$

$$D_f = \frac{1429 \times 240}{1429 - (240 - 2)} = 288 \text{ inches} = 24.0 \text{ feet}$$

Therefore, when a 50 mm lens at f/2.8 is focused at 20 feet, everything from 17.1 feet to 24.0 feet will be in acceptable focus. The total depth of field for this example is:

$$D_{total} = D_f - D_n = 24.0 - 17.1 = 6.9 \text{ feet}$$

If a more approximate answer is all that is needed, equations 2 and 3 may be simplified to

$$D_n = \frac{HS}{H + S} \qquad (4)$$

$$D_f = \frac{HS}{H - S} \qquad (5)$$

Using these equations, D_n and D_f are:

$$D_n = \frac{119 \times 20}{119 + 20} \approx 17 \text{ feet}$$

$$D_f = \frac{119 \times 20}{119 - 20} \approx 24 \text{ feet}$$

Therefore, $D_{total} = 24 - 17 = 7$ feet

TAK'S TIPS

SIMPLIFIED DEPTH OF FIELD

$$\frac{1}{D_n} = \frac{1}{S} + \frac{1}{H}$$

$$\frac{1}{D_f} = \frac{1}{S} - \frac{1}{H}$$

D_n = Camera to Near Limit
D_f = Camera to Far Limit
H = Hyperfocal Distance
S = Distance from Camera to Subject

Courtesy of Panavision's Tak Miyagishima.

1.2.1 Finding Lens Settings When D_n and D_f are Known

When the near and far focus requirements are known, equations 4, 5 and 1 can be rearranged as follows:

$$L_s = \frac{2D_n D_f}{D_n + D_f} \tag{6}$$

$$H = \frac{2D_n D_f}{D_f - D_n} \tag{7}$$

$$f = \frac{F^2}{HC_c} \tag{8}$$

where D_n = Camera to Near Limit
D_f = Camera to Far Limit
H = Hyperfocal Distance
L_s = Lens Focus Distance Setting
F = Focal Length of Lens
f = f-stop Setting of Lens
C_c = circle of confusion

Example: A scene is being photographed on 35mm using a 75 mm lens. Everything in the scene from 15 to 27 feet must be in acceptable focus. How must the lens f-stop and focus be set?

First convert all distances and focal lengths to inches. Focal length is 2.953 inches (75 ÷ 25.40). D_n is 180 inches (15 × 12), and D_f is 324 inches (27 × 12).

$$L_S = \textit{focus distance setting} = \frac{2 \times 180 \times 324}{180 + 324} = 231 \textit{ inches} = 19.3 \text{ feet}$$

$$H = \textit{hyperfocal distance} = \frac{2 \times 180 \times 324}{324 - 180} = 810 \textit{ inches} = 67.5 \text{ feet}$$

$$\text{f-stop} = \frac{2.953^2}{0.001 \times 810} = \text{f}/10.77 \approx \text{f}/11$$

Therefore, focus the lens to 19.3 feet, and set the f-stop to f/11.

1.3 Depth of Focus

Depth of Focus should not be confused with Depth of Field as they are very different and do *not* refer to the same thing.

Depth of Focus is the range of distance between the lens and the film plane where acceptable focus is maintained. This range is quite small and is measured usually in very small units such as thousands of an inch.

For an image to be in sharp focus, the distance from the lens to the film must be held to very tight tolerances, hence the design of motion-picture cameras which holds the film very securely during exposure. Any buckling of the film or anything that shifts the film's postition in the aperture can cause a deterioration of focus.

The following equation provides a good approximation of the depth of focus of a lens:

$$\text{Depth of Focus} \approx \frac{Ff}{1000} \tag{9}$$

where F = focal length of lens (in mm)
f = f-stop of lens

Example: A 50mm f/2.8 lens has the following depth of focus:

$$\frac{50 \times 2.8}{1000} = 0.14 \text{ mm} = 0.0055 \text{ inch}$$

As this is the *total* depth of focus, the film must stay within plus or minus half that value which is about ±0.00275 inch or ±0.07 mm. This dimension is equal to the approximate value of a single strand of human hair. This is a very small value indeed which further amplifies the statement above about the need for precision in the gate and aperture area of the camera.

1.4 Lens Viewing Angles

The angle, either horizonal or vertical, that a lens images onto the film frame may be calculated using the following equation:

$$\Theta = 2\,atan\left(\frac{AR_S}{2F}\right) \qquad (10)$$

where F = focal length of lens
A = camera aperture height or width
R_S = squeeze ratio (use 1.0 for spherical lenses and Scope vertical and use 2.0 for Scope horizontal)
Θ = viewing angle

The inverse tangent (written as *atan, arctan,* or tan^{-1}) can be found with many pocket calculators. Alternately Table 1 relates *atan* to Θ

Example: What are horizontal and vertical viewing angles for a 75mm Scope lens?

Inverse Tangent Function

Angle	atan	Angle	atan	Angle	atan	Angle	atan
1°	.018	12°	.213	23°	.424	34°	.675
2°	.035	13°	.231	24°	.445	35°	.700
3°	.052	14°	.249	25°	.466	36°	.727
4°	.070	15°	.268	26°	.488	37°	.754
5°	.088	16°	.287	27°	.510	38°	.781
6°	.105	17°	.306	28°	.532	39°	.810
7°	.123	18°	.325	29°	.554	40°	.839
8°	.141	19°	.344	30°	.577	41°	.869
9°	.158	20°	.364	31°	.601	42°	.900
10°	.176	21°	.384	32°	.625	43°	.933
11°	.194	22°	.404	33°	.649	44°	.966
						45°	1.000

Table 1: *atan* Table

A typical Scope camera aperture is 0.868" wide by 0.735" high. Converting 75 mm to inches yields 2.953 inches (75÷25.4 = 2.953)

$$\textit{Horizontal Angle} = 2\ atan\ \frac{0.868 \times 2.0}{2 \times 2.953} = 32.8°$$

$$2\ atan\ \frac{1.736}{5.906} = .2939$$

$$atan\ of\ .2939 = 16.4°$$
$$2\ atan = 32.8°$$

$$\textit{Vertical Angle} = 2\ atan\ \frac{0.735 \times 1.0}{2 \times 2.953} = 14.2°$$

$$2\ atan\ \frac{0.735}{5.906} = .1244$$

$$atan\ of\ .1244 = 7.1°$$
$$2\ atan = 14.2°$$

1.5 Lens, Subject, Distance, and Image Size Relationships

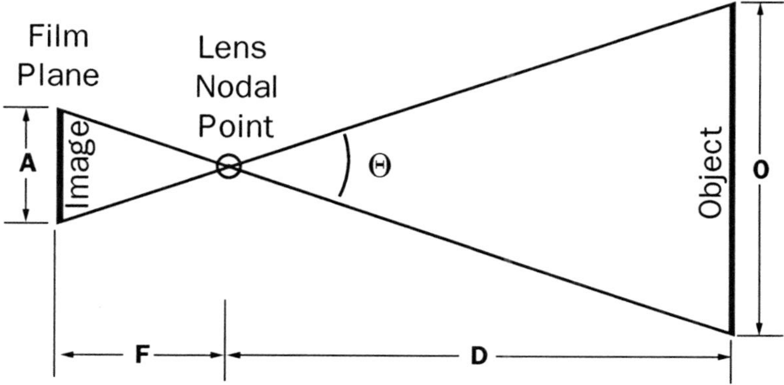

Using the above simple drawing, the relationships between camera distance, object size, image size, and lens focal length for spherical lenses may easily be calculated in the following equation:

$$\frac{O}{A} = \frac{D}{F} \tag{11}$$

where F = focal length of lens
D = distance to object being photographed
O = size of object being photographed
A = aperture size
Θ = viewing angle

Equation 11 may be rewritten in any of the following ways depending on the problem being solved:

$$D = \frac{OF}{A} \tag{12}$$

$$O = \frac{AD}{F} \tag{13}$$

$$F = \frac{AD}{O} \tag{14}$$

$$A = \frac{OF}{D} \tag{15}$$

1.6 Lens Apertures - T versus f-Stops

The f number of a lens is its focal length divided by the diameter of its lens pupil. Stated mathematically

$$f = \frac{F}{D_a} \tag{16}$$

where F = focal length of lens
D_a = diameter of aperture
f = f-stop value of lens

The T-stop of a lens controls the transmission of light through a lens. The same logarithmic progression of numbers is used for T-stops as for f-stops. If a lens lost no light passing through it, the f and T-stops would be equal, but as no lens passes light through it without loss, the f and T-stops for lenses are not the same. (See ANSI PH22.90 for more information.)

The rule is: Use f-stops for computing depth of field, and use T-stops for setting exposure.

When setting the f/T-stop on a lens, first always open the lens to its widest aperture, and then set the desired f/T-stop value. This practice removes the effects of backlash in the lens mechanism and insures repeatable results.

1.7 Lens Displacement for Focusing

When a lens is focused at infinity, the distance from the film plane to the lens nodal point is nominally equal to the focal length of the lens. For instance, a 50mm lens, when focused at infinity, has 50mm between the film plane and the nodal point of the lens. However, when a lens is focused closer than infinity, the lens must be moved away from the film plane to maintain focus. The following equation computes the amount of displacement from the infinity position needed to focus on an object not at infinity.

$$d = \frac{F^2}{a - F} \tag{17}$$

where F = focal length of lens
a = distance to object being photographed
d = lens displacement from infinity position

Example: The displacement from the infinity position of a 50 mm (2 inch) lens focused at 10 feet is as follows:

Converting all distances to inches and applying Equation 17 yields

$$d = \frac{2^2}{120 - 2} = \frac{4}{118} = 0.031 \text{ inches}$$

2 Shooting Practices

2.1 Running Times, Feet, and Frames

The Table 2 shows the linear sound speed of common theatrical film gages and the number of frames per foot.

Table 2: Speed and Frame Information for Common Film Gages

Film Gage (in mm)	Linear Speed (ft/min)	Frames per Foot
16	36	40
35	90	16
65/70	112.5	12.8

2.1.1 Footage versus Time Relationship

$$T_F = St \tag{18}$$

where T_F = total footage
S = speed of film (in ft/min)
t = time (in minutes)

Example: How many feet of 35 mm film run through a sound camera in 4 and a half minutes?

$$T_F = 90 \times 4.5 = 405 \text{ feet}$$

2.1.2 Footage in Feet and Frames

$$F_T = \frac{t\,F_S}{F_F} \tag{19}$$

where F_T = total footage
F_S = frames per second
t = time (in seconds)
F_F = frames per foot

Example: How much film goes through a 16 mm sound camera in 8 seconds?

$$F_T = \frac{8 \times 24}{40} = 4.8 \text{ feet}$$

To convert the decimal to frames, multiply the decimal part by number of frames per foot:

$$.8 \times 40 = 32$$

Therefore, the answer is 4 feet 32 frames.

HIGH SPEED FORMULAS

Times Normal Speed = frame rate ÷ normal frame rate (24 or 30 fps)
  Example: 360 ÷ 24 = 15 times normal speed
Frames Exposed = frame rate x event duration
  Example: 360 x .5 second = 180 frames exposed
Screen Time = frame rate x event duration ÷ normal frame rate (24 or 30 fps)
  Example: 360 x .5 ÷ 24 = 7.5 seconds screen time
Frame Rate Required = screen time ÷ event duration x transfer rate
  Example: 7.5 seconds ÷ .5 x 24 = 360 fps required
Running Time = frames per foot x footage ÷ frame rate
  Example: 16 x 1000' ÷ 360 = 44.4 seconds running time
Screen Time for Moving Objects = field of view ÷ 20' per second x 360 fps ÷24 = 1.5 seconds screen time
  Example: 2' field of view ÷ 20' per second x 360 fps ÷ 24 = 1.5 seconds screen time

Notes: Field of view and object velocity must be in same type measurement (inches, feet)
Falling objects will increase in velocity (use velocity charts to determine event time)

2.2 Computing Exposure Times

The following equations relates frame rate, shutter angle, and exposure time:

$$T_e = \frac{1}{\frac{S\,360}{\alpha}} \quad (20) \qquad \text{and} \qquad \alpha = 360ST_e \quad (21)$$

where α = shutter angle (in degrees)
S = frames per second
T_e = exposure time (in seconds)

Example: What is the exposure time when shooting at 24 frames per second with a 180° shutter?

$$T_e = \frac{1}{\frac{24 \times 360}{180}} = \frac{1}{48} \text{ second}$$

2.3 Frame Rates for Miniatures

To make the action in minatures look convincing, it is often necessary to shoot at frame rates faster than 24 fps. The exact frame rate for a given miniature shot must be determined by shooting test footage. Even skilled minature cinematographers will shoot tests to confirm proper effect on film.

Shooting frame rate depends on, among other things, subject matter, direction of movement in relation to the camera position, and minature scale. Generally, however, the smaller the minature, the faster the required frame rate. Also as magnification decreases, the necessary frame rate drops.

The following may be used as a guide and a starting point:

$$R_f = 24\sqrt{\frac{1}{S}} \tag{22}$$

where R_f = frame rate
S = scale of miniature

Example: What frame rate should be used to shoot a 1:4 (quarter scale) miniature?

$$R_f = 24\sqrt{\frac{1}{0.25}} = 24\sqrt{4} = 24 \times 2 = 48 \text{ fps}$$

2.4 Image Blur

When shooting high speed photography, the question often comes up: what frame rate is needed to reduce the image blur to an acceptable amount. This question is especially important to cinematographers shooting fast moving subject such as missile tests, horse races, airplanes, etc.

The following equations may be used to calculate the blur of an image caused by the movment of an object during exposure:

$$m = \frac{F}{D} \tag{23}$$

$$d = vtm \tag{24}$$

$$v = \frac{d}{tm} \tag{25}$$

where D = object to lens distance
F = taking focal length
m = magnification
d = image movement during exposure
v = object speed
t = exposure

Example: What is the image blur of a thin vertical line painted on the side of a racing car moving at 153 miles per hour when shot from 33.3 feet away with a 2 inch lens at 48 fps with a shuter angle of 180°?

First, all of the units have to be brought to common units; in this case inches and seconds are a good choice. Therefore, D is 400 inches (12 × 33.3) and v is 2693 in/sec (153 × 5280 × 12 ÷ 3600)

$$m = \frac{F}{D} = \frac{2}{400} = \frac{1}{200}$$

$$d = 2693 \times \frac{1}{96} \times \frac{1}{200} = 0.14 \text{ inch}$$

3 Light and Exposure

3.1 Units for Measuring Light

The terms used to measure light can often be confusing. The three main measures of light are intensity, illumination, and brightness. Each refers to a very different characteristic.

3.2 Intensity (I)

The unit of intensity is the candle or candela. The name, not surprisingly, comes from the fact that a standard wax candle was used for many years as the standard source of light. The luminous inensity from one candle was, therefore, one candle power.

Another unit which is also encountered in discussions about luminous intensity is the lumen. One candle power emits one lumen in a standard three dimensional cone called a steradian.

3.3 Illumination (E)

The unit of illumination is the foot candle which is one lumen falling onto one square foot. (In the SI system, the unit is the lux which is 1 $lumen/m^2$.) In simple terms the foot candle measures the amount of light falling on a surface, hence the term illumination.

3.4 Brightness (B)

When light falls upon a surface some of that light is reflected. The unit of brightness is the foot-lambert which is $1/\pi$ candles being relfected from a one square foot area. The reflected light give the surface a "bright" appearance, hence the term brightness.

3.5 Exposure Using Incident Light

The following equation may be used to find the required number of foot candles required for a given film speed, f-stop, and exposure time:

$$E = \frac{25f^2}{St} \tag{26}$$

where E = Illumination in foot candles
f = T-stop of taking lens (use f-stop if lens does not have T-stop markings)
t = exposure time (in seconds)
S = film speed (in ASA)

Example: How many foot candles are required to expose an ASA 100 film for 1/50 second at f/2.0?

$$E = \frac{25 \times 2.0^2}{100 \times \frac{1}{50}} = \frac{100}{2} = 50 \textit{ foot candles}$$

Equation 26 may be simplified for shooting at 24 fps with a shutter angle of 172.8° which gives an effective exposure of 1/50 second.

$$E = \frac{1250f^2}{S} \tag{27}$$

Example: How many foot candles are required to expose an ASA 200 film shooting at 24 fps at f/4.0?

$$E = \frac{1250 \times 4.0^2}{200} = \frac{20000}{200} = 100 \textit{ foot candles}$$

3.6 Exposure Using Extention Tubes or Bellows

When using a bellows or extension tube to move the lens further than normal from the film plane, use the following formula to calculate the required increase in exposure:

$$\Delta = \frac{(d + F)^2}{F^2} \qquad (28)$$

where Δ = Exposure Multiplier
d = length of extension tube or bellows
F = lens focal length

Example: A 3 inch lens is moved 150 mm further from the film plane by a bellows. The exposure time before the lens was moved was 1/48 of a second. What is the new exposure time?

First the units must be made the same. A 3 inch lens has a focal length of 76.2 mm (3 x 25.4). Then using the above equation

$$\Delta = \frac{(150 + 76.2)^2}{76.2^2} = 8.812$$

Then multiply the old exposure time of 1/48 by Δ to get the new exposure time of

$$\frac{1}{48} \times 8.812 = 0.184 \text{ seconds}$$

0.184 seconds is approximately 1/5 second which is the new, corrected exposure time. Alternately, if depth of field is not an issue, the exposure could also be corrected by a three stop increase in aperture. (Remember that each stop doubles the exposure, so for a roughly nine-fold increase, 3+ stops are needed.) Also, the esposure could be corrected by increasing the illumination approximately nine-fold.

It should also be noted that vignetting may occur when using extention tubes or bellows. It is good practice, therefore, to check the corners of the image for proper exposure prior to production shooting when using extension tubes or bellows.

3.7 Shooting Close-Ups with Diopters

Often in shooting extreme close-ups supplemental lens called "diopters"[1] are affixed to the front of a prime lens. These "diopters" allow very close focusing.

Diopters for all practical purposes do not affect many of the characteristics of the prime lens. For instance, the f-stop of lens is not affected by a positive diopter.[2] Also the depth of field calculations are unaffected. Principally, the diopter allows for much closer than normal focusing by the prime lens.

When using diopters it is a good idea to stop the prime lens down to at least f/8 as diopters do add lens abberations which degrade the image quality. By stopping down, these degradations may be minimized.

---

[1]A diopter is actually a unit that measures the focal length of a lens. A diopter is 1/focal length where the focal length is expressed in meters. For example, a lens with a focal length of 500 mm(0.5 meters) has a strength of 2 diopters (1/0.5 = 2.0).

[2]Negative diopters are rarely, if ever, used in motion picture work.

Feet Per Second	to Miles Per Hour *	Feet Per Second	to Miles Per Hour *
1 ¼	1	44	30
3	2	51	35
7	5	59	40
9	6	66	45
10 ½	7	73	50
12	8	80	55
13	9	88	60
14 ½	10	110	75
15	11	147	100
17 ½	12	183	125
22	15	220	150
29	20	257	200
37	25		** rounded off*

1.4667 x MPH = feet per second
88 x MPH = Feet per minute

1 Nautical mile = 6080 feet
1 Land or Statute mile = 5280 feet
1 Kilometer = 3280 feet

DISTANCE AND VELOCITY OF FREE FALLING BODY

Distance	Velocity	Time
0	0	0
16	32	1
64	64	2
144	96	3
256	128	4
400	160 (max)	5
Feet	**Feet Per Seconds**	**Seconds**

CONVERSION TABLES

Feet to Meters

ft		m
3	=	.91
4	=	1.22
5	=	1.52
6	=	1.83
7	=	2.13
8	=	2.44
9	=	2.74
10	=	3.05
12	=	3.66
15	=	4.57
20	=	6.10
25	=	7.62
30	=	9.14
40	=	12.19
50	=	15.24
75	=	22.86
100	=	30.48
150	=	45.72
200	=	60.96
300	=	91.44
400	=	121.92
500	=	152.40
1000	=	304.80

Meters to Feet

m		ft	in
1	=	3	3
1 ¼	=	4	1
1 ½	=	4	11
2	=	6	7
2 ½	=	8	2
3	=	9	10
4	=	13	1
5	=	16	5
6	=	19	8
7	=	23	
8	=	26	3
9	=	29	6
10	=	32	10
15	=	49	3
20	=	65	7
30	=	98	5
50	=	164	
55	=	180	
60	=	196	9
70	=	229	7
80	=	262	6
90	=	295	3
100	=	328	

Inches to Millimeters

in		mm
1/16	=	1.6
1/8	=	3.2
3/16	=	4.8
1/4	=	6.4
5/16	=	7.9
3/8	=	9.5
7/16	=	11.1
1/2	=	12.7
9/16	=	14.3
5/8	=	15.9
11/16	=	17.5
3/4	=	19.1
13/16	=	20.7
7/8	=	22.2
15/16	=	23.8
1	=	25.4
2	=	50.8
3	=	76.2
4	=	101.6
5	=	127.0
6	=	152.4
7	=	177.8
8	=	203.2
9	=	228.6
10	=	254.0

Millimeters to Inches

mm		in
1	=	.04
2	=	.08
3	=	.12
4	=	.16
5	=	.20
6	=	.24
7	=	.28
8	=	.32
9	=	.36
10	=	.39
12	=	.47
14	=	.55
16	=	.63
18	=	.71
20	=	.79
22	=	.87
24	=	.94
25	=	.98
25.4	=	1.00
26	=	1.02
27	=	1.06
28	=	1.1
29	=	1.14
30	=	1.18
35	=	1.37
40	=	1.57

Inches to Centimeters

in		cm
1	=	2.54
2	=	5.08
3	=	7.62
4	=	10.16
5	=	12.70
6	=	15.24
7	=	17.78
8	=	20.32
9	=	22.86
10	=	25.40
11	=	27.94
12	=	30.48
13	=	33.02
14	=	35.56
15	=	38.10
16	=	40.64
17	=	43.18
18	=	45.72
19	=	48.26
20	=	50.80
21	=	53.34
22	=	55.88
23	=	58.42
24	=	60.96
25	=	63.50
30	=	76.20

Centimeters to Inches

cm		in
1	=	00.4
2	=	00.8
3	=	01.2
4	=	01.6
5	=	02.0
6	=	02.4
7	=	02.8
8	=	03.1
9	=	03.5
10	=	03.9
11	=	04.3
12	=	04.7
13	=	05.1
14	=	05.5
15	=	05.9
16	=	06.3
17	=	06.7
18	=	07.1
19	=	07.5
20	=	07.9
21	=	08.3
22	=	08.7
23	=	09.0
24	=	09.4
25	=	09.8
25.4	=	10.0

LENS FOCAL LENGTH
Converted from Millimeters into Inches

mm		in	mm		in	mm		in
12 ½	=	½	140	=	5 ⅗	290	=	11 ⅗
15	=	⅗	150	=	6	295	=	11 ⅘
20	=	⅘	155	=	6 ⅕	300	=	12
25	=	1	160	=	6 ⅖	305	=	12 ⅕
28	=	1 ⅛	165	=	6 ⅗	310	=	12 ⅖
30	=	1 ⅕	170	=	6 ⅘	315	=	12 ⅗
32	=	1 ¼	175	=	7	320	=	12 ⅘
35	=	1 ⅖	180	=	7 ⅕	325	=	13
38	=	1 ½	185	=	7 ⅖	330	=	13 ⅕
40	=	1 ⅝	190	=	7 ⅗	335	=	13 ⅖
45	=	1 ⅘	195	=	7 ⅘	340	=	13 ⅗
50	=	2	200	=	8	350	=	14
55	=	2 ⅕	205	=	8 ⅕	355	=	14 ⅕
60	=	2 ⅖	210	=	8 ⅖	360	=	14 ⅖
65	=	2 ⅗	215	=	8 ⅗	365	=	14 ⅗
70	=	2 ⅘	220	=	8 ⅘	370	=	14 ⅘
75	=	3	225	=	9	375	=	15
80	=	3 ⅕	230	=	9 ⅕	385	=	15 ⅖
85	=	3 ⅖	235	=	9 ⅖	400	=	16
90	=	3 ⅗	240	=	9 ⅗	415	=	16 ⅗
95	=	3 ⅘	245	=	9 ⅘	425	=	17
100	=	4	250	=	10	435	=	17 ⅖
105	=	4 ⅕	255	=	10 ⅕	450	=	18
110	=	4 ⅖	260	=	10 ⅖	465	=	18 ⅗
115	=	4 ⅗	265	=	10 ⅗	475	=	19
120	=	4 ⅘	270	=	10 ⅘	485	=	19 ⅖
125	=	5	275	=	11	495	=	19 ⅘
130	=	5 ⅕	280	=	11 ⅕	500	=	20
135	=	5 ⅖	285	=	11 ⅖			

The table is rounded off for practical purposes. Actually 25.4mm equals 1 inch.

Decimal Equivalents of Fractions and Equivalents of Fractions of an Inch in mm.

1/8	1/10	1/32	1/64	1/128	mm.	Decim. of an Inch	1/8	1/10	1/32	1/64	1/128	mm.	Decim. of an Inch
				1	.198	.0078125					65	12.898	.5078125
			1	2	.397	.0156250				33	66	13.097	.515625
				3	.595	.0234375					67	13.295	.5234375
		1	2	4	.794	.031250			17	34	68	13.494	.531250
				5	.992	.0390625					69	13.692	.5390625
			3	6	1.191	.046875				35	70	13.891	.546875
				7	1.389	.0546875					71	14.089	.5546875
	1	2	4	8	1.588	.062500		9	18	36	72	14.288	.562500
				9	1.786	.0703125					73	14.486	.5703125
			5	10	1.984	.078125				37	74	14.684	.578125
				11	2.183	.0859375					75	14.883	.5859375
		3	6	12	2.381	.093750			19	38	76	15.081	.593750
				13	2.580	.1015625					77	15.280	.6015625
			7	14	2.778	.109375				39	78	15.478	.609375
				15	2.977	.1171875					79	15.677	.6171875
1	2	4	8	16	3.175	.125000	5	10	20	40	80	15.875	.625000
				17	3.373	.1328125					81	16.073	.6328125
			9	18	3.572	.140625				41	82	16.272	.640625
				19	3.770	.1484375					83	16.470	.6484375
		5	10	20	3.969	.156250			21	42	84	16.669	.656250
				21	4.167	.1640625					85	16.867	.6640625
			11	22	4.366	.171875				43	86	17.066	.671875
				23	4.564	.1796875					87	17.264	.6796875
	3	6	12	24	4.763	.187500		11	22	44	88	17.463	.687500
				25	4.961	.1953125					89	17.661	.6953125
			13	26	5.159	.203125				45	90	17.859	.703125
				27	5.358	.2109375					91	18.058	.7109375
		7	14	28	5.556	.218750			23	46	92	18.256	.718750
				29	5.755	.2265625					93	18.455	.7265625
			15	30	5.953	.234375				47	94	18.653	.734375
				31	6.152	.2421875					95	18.852	.7421875
2	4	8	16	32	6.350	.250000	6	12	24	48	96	19.050	.750000
				33	6.548	.2578125					97	19.248	.7578125
			17	34	6.747	.265625				49	98	19.447	.765625
				35	6.945	.2734375					99	19.645	.7734375
		9	18	36	7.144	.281250			25	50	100	19.844	.781250
				37	7.342	.2890625					101	20.042	.7890625
			19	38	7.541	.296875				51	102	20.241	.796875
				39	7.739	.3046875					103	20.439	.8046875
	5	10	20	40	7.938	.312500		13	26	52	104	20.638	.812500
				41	8.136	.3203125					105	20.836	.8203125
			21	42	8.334	.328125				53	106	21.034	.828125
				43	8.533	.3359375					107	21.233	.8359375
		11	22	44	8.731	.343750			27	54	108	21.431	.843750
				45	8.930	.3515625					109	21.630	.8515625
			23	46	9.128	.359375				55	110	21.828	.859375
				47	9.327	.3671875					111	22.027	.8671875
3	6	12	24	48	9.525	.375000	7	14	28	56	112	22.225	.875000
				49	9.723	.3828125					113	22.423	.8828125
			25	50	9.922	.390625				57	114	22.622	.890625
				51	10.120	.3984375					115	22.820	.8984375
		13	26	52	10.319	.406250			29	58	116	23.019	.906250
				53	10.517	.4140625					117	23.217	.9140625
			27	54	10.716	.421875				59	118	23.416	.921875
				55	10.914	.4296875					119	23.614	.9296875
	7	14	28	56	11.113	.437500		15	30	60	120	23.813	.937500
				57	11.311	.4453125					121	24.011	.9453125
			29	58	11.509	.453125				61	122	24.209	.953125
				59	11.708	.4609375					123	24.408	.9609375
		15	30	60	11.906	.46875			31	62	124	24.606	.96875
				61	12.105	.4765625					125	24.805	.9765625
			31	62	12.303	.484375				63	126	25.003	.984375
				63	12.502	.4921875					127	25.202	.9921875
4	8	16	32	64	12.700	.500000	8	16	32	64	128	25.400	1.0000000

OHM's Law Formulas

(D.C. or 100% P_f A.C. Circuits)

To find:			
W = (Watts)	$E \times I$	$I^2 R$	$\frac{E^2}{R}$
E = (Volts)	$I \times R$	$\sqrt{W \times R}$	$\frac{W}{I}$
I = (Amperes)	$\frac{E}{R}$	$\sqrt{\frac{W}{R}}$	$\frac{W}{E}$
R = (Ohms)	$\frac{E}{I}$	$\frac{E^2}{W}$	$\frac{W}{I^2}$

1ø A.C. Power: $W = I \times E \times P_f$

3ø A.C. Power: $W = 1.73 \times I \times E \times P_f$

Watts = Power

Ohms = Resistance

Amperes = Current

E = Electromotive Force

P_f = Power Factor

1 Kilo-Watt = 1,000 Watts

1 Kilo-Watt = 1.344 Input H.P.

1 Horse Power = 746 Watts

1 Ampere = 1,000 Milli-Amperes

1 Meg Ohm = 1,000,000 Ohms

Ohm's Law

The formulas for D.C. and A.C. differ when inductance (L.) and capacity (C.) are involved in A.C. circuits. When L and/or C are used in A.C. circuits, these reactances (X) cause leading or lagging currents vs. voltage. The subsequent apparent and true powers differ by the ratio known as the Power Factor (P_f). More complex formulas, or lab measurements are used to determine the Power Factor involved. Usually Ohms Law can be applied to line loss with reasonable accuracy in A.C. motor circuits, by using the equipment name-plate data. It is highly recommended to use larger instead of smaller conductors when in doubt of the actual load conditions.

VOLTAGE DROP OF COPPERWIRE

(D.C. or 100% Power Factor A.C. Circuits)

Single Phase (1ø)

$$\text{Voltage Drop} = \frac{\text{Amperes} \times \text{Feet} \times 21.6}{\text{Circular Mills}}$$

Three Phase (3ø)

$$\text{Voltage Drop} = \frac{\text{Amperes} \times \text{Feet} \times 18.7}{\text{Circular Mills}}$$

Amperes = Amperes of Load Current (Amps)

Feet = Length of Conductors One Way

Circular Mills = Cross Sectional Area of Conductor in Circular Mills (C.M.)

Example: 100 feet #14 Ga. Cable
1000 Watt (1 K.W.) Lamp
117 Volt Source
(1000W @ 117V = 8.5 Amps)

$$\frac{8.5\text{A} \times 100 \text{ Feet} \times 21.6}{4107 \text{ (C.M.)}} = 4.5 \text{ Volts Drop (V.D.)}$$

Voltage Available at Load = 117 - 4.5 = 112.5 Volts

Note: Increasing conductor length increases the voltage drop. The V.D. is subtracted from the source voltage and the difference is the voltage available at the load. This indicates that undersize, or overly long conductors result in too low a voltage at the load. Low voltage reduces light output and lowers color temperature of lamps. It also decreases the efficiency of motors, with subsequent increased heat losses. Generally a 5% V.D. can be tolerated (or, 5.85V on a 117 volt line). Voltage regulation varies from power houses, and a range of 105V to 135V is not uncommon over a few hours of time. The 117 volt mean should be used in calculations, and care exercised to measure the source and load voltage when more precise control is desired.

To find amps (load) divide watts by volts.
Example: 1000 watts ÷ by 120 volts = 8.3 amps.

How to Use the Following Tables

1) Know the total amount power at your supply point.
2) Be sure your supply has ample fusing.
3) Compute the amperage load (Table 1) for the maximum units of lighting equipment you expect to use and be sure it does not exceed your total supply. The quantity of and variety of lights should be sufficient to provide flexibility in all photographic situations and since all will not be used at one time, only the maximum number of lights to be used at one time will form the basis for computing amperage load.
4) Relate your available power to the current carrying capacities in Table 2 and decide on adequate cables.
5) See Table 3 for Cable Voltage Drop at different distances.

TABLE 1

INCANDESCENT LAMPS	
Globe Wattage	**Globe Amperage**
200	1.7
500	4.2
650	5.4
750	6.3
1,000	8.3
1,500	12.5
2,000	16.7
5,000	41.6
10,000	83.3
20,000/208	86.0A @ 208V
20,000/220	99.2 @ 240V
HMI	
Globe Wattage	**Globe Amperage**
200	5
575	7
1,200	15
2,500	25
4,000	38
6,000	65
12,000	70A @ 240V
18,000	75A @ 240V 105A @ 208V

Courtesy of Mole-Richardson.

TABLE 1 – CONTINUED

ARC LAMPS AT 115-120 VOLTS

Type Number	Amperage
40	40
90	120
170	150
450, 4591, 4581	225
4601, 4611, 4691	225

TABLE 2

COPPER CABLE TYPE SC ENTERTAINMENT 90°C

Type SC Entertainment 90°C		
AWG Size of Conductors	Ampacity* **	
	Numbers of Conductors	
	1	2†
8	80	74
6	105	99
4	140	130
2	190	174
2/0	300	-
4/0	405	-

* Based on 2002 NEC.
** Additional capacity can be obtained by paralleling cables.
† Number of conductors carrying current in a single jacket.

TABLE 3

CABLE VOLTAGE DROP

Cable Size	Amp @120V	100 ft	200 ft	300 ft	400 ft	500 ft	600 ft
4Ø	300A	116.6	112.8	109.5	105.6	102	98.4
2Ø	225A	115.9	111.9	107.7	102.8	99.6	-
#2	140A	114.7	109.3	104.8	98.3	-	-
#4	105A	113.6	107.1	100.7	-	-	-
#6	80A	112.2	106	96.5	-	-	-
#8	60A	110.6	101.1	-	-	-	-

Courtesy of Mole-Richardson.

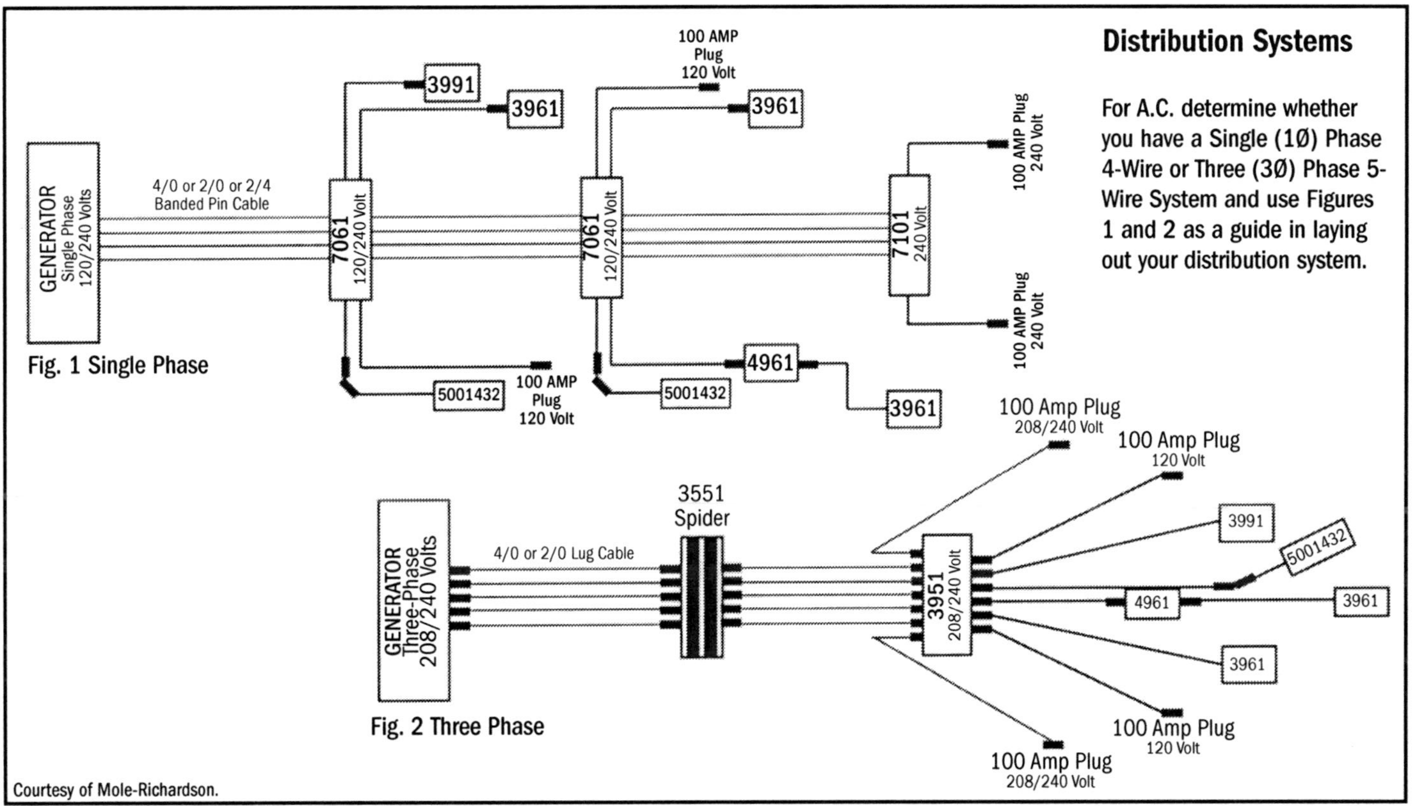

Fig. 1 Single Phase

Fig. 2 Three Phase

Courtesy of Mole-Richardson.

Distribution Systems – Continued

For D.C. determine whether you have a Two or Three-Wire System and use either Figure 3 or 4 as a guide in laying out your distribution system.

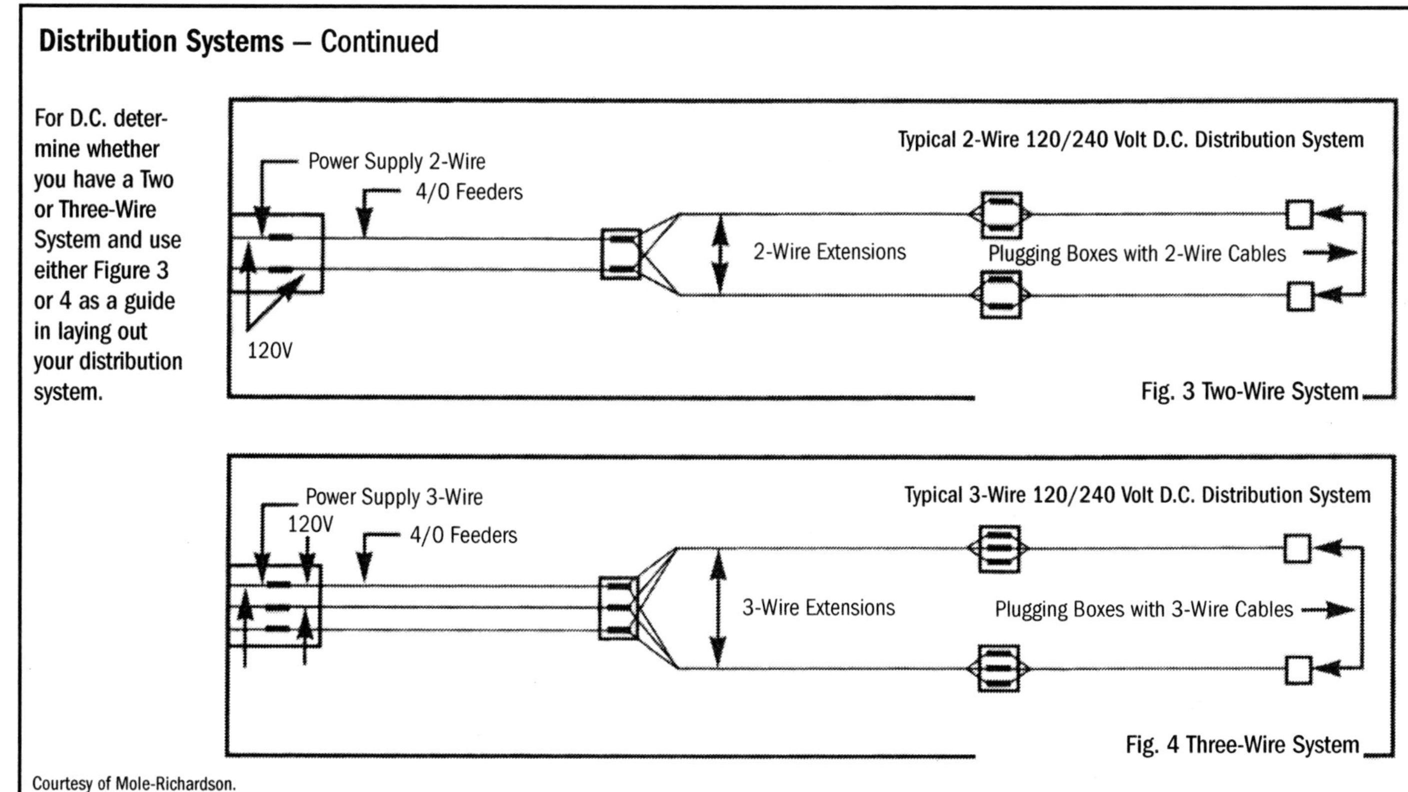

Fig. 3 Two-Wire System

Fig. 4 Three-Wire System

Courtesy of Mole-Richardson.

Bell & Howell 2709 (1912). It's shuttle intermittent movement is the steadiest ever devised. Still used in optical printers today. (ASC collection.)

Measurement Conversion Factors

Use multiplying factor to convert from one system to the other.
Example: 6 feet x .3048 = 1.8288 meters.

English to Metric Factors	
Yards to meters (m)	.914
Feet to meters (m)	.3048
Inches to millimeters (mm)	25.4
Miles to kilometers (km)	1.61
Pounds to kilograms (kg)	.454
Ounces to grams (g)	28.4
Gallons to liters (l)	3.79
Quarts to liters (l)	.946
Fluid ounces to milliliters (ml)	29.6

Metric to English Factors	
Meters to yards (yd)	1.09
Meters to feet (ft)	3.28
Centimeters to feet (ft)	.03281
Centimeters to inches (in)	.3937
Millimeters to inches (in)	.0394
Kilometers to miles (mi)	.621
Kilograms to pounds (lb)	2.21
Grams to ounces (oz)	.0353
Liters to gallons (gal)	.264
Liters to quarts (qt)	1.06
Milliliters to fluid ounces (fl oz)	.0338

1 inch = 25.4mm = 2.54cm =.0254m
1 foot = 304.8mm = 30.48cm = .3048m
1yard = .9144m

Depth of Field Tables Introduction

These comprehensive "All Formats Depth of Field Tables" will provide you with depth of field information for virtually all of the currently used 16, 35, and 65mm lenses. You will also find tables for Super 8mm and additional 16mm tables beginning on page 734.

Please see the chapter on lenses for a more thorough discussion of this subject.

These tables are computed mathematically, and should be used as a guide only. Depth of field is a useful concept within limits. The near and far distances indicated in the tables do not mean the image suddenly falls out of focus at those precise points.

Technically speaking, an object is only in focus at one precise point in space. Depth of field determines the range in front of and behind a designated focusing distance, where an object still appears to be acceptably in focus. A low resolving film stock or lens may appear to have greater depth of field, because the "in focus" image is already so soft, it is more difficult to determine when it goes further out of focus. Conversely, a very sharp, high contrast lens may appear to have shallow depth of field, because the "in focus" image has such clarity, it is much easier to notice when it slips out of a range of acceptable focus.

These tables can be nothing other than generic in their information. They will give you a very close approximation of any given focal length's depth of field characteristics. Truly precise Depth of Field calculations cannot be performed without knowing the size of a specific lens' entrance pupil.

That being said, these charts should be very helpful, unless you are trying to measure down to an accuracy of less than a couple of inches. If you are demanding that level of precision, then you must shoot a test of the lens in question, because no calculation can provide the empirical data a visual evaluation can.

These tables are calculated based on a circle of confusion of 0.001" (1⁄1000"). To calculate a depth of field based upon a more critical circle of confusion of half that size (0.0005" or 5⁄10,000"), find your chosen f-stop at the distance desired, then read the depth of field data two columns to the left. The 0.0005" circle of confusion can be used for lenses of greater sharpness or contrast, or for a more traditional method of determining 16mm depth of field.

One more note: you will see some lenses at certain distances that indicate a depth of field of effectively nothing (e.g.: 10' 0" to 10' 0"). This means the depth of field is less than an inch, and we recommend that a test is shot to determine such a critical depth of field. Charts should never be relied upon when exploring such narrow fields of focus.

For further discussion on this subject see pages 170 and 176.

These tables were compiled with the invaluable help of Evans Wetmore, P.E. Evans is Vice-President of Advanced Engineering in the News Technology Group, of Fox NewsCorp. A fellow of SMPTE; his feature film credits include the special effects engineering for Star Trek, the Motion Picture, Blade Runner, *and* Brainstorm.

5.9mm ALL FORMATS DEPTH OF FIELD TABLE CIRCLE OF CONFUSION=0.0010 inches

	f/1.4	f/2	f/2.8	f/4	f/5.6	f/8	f/11	f/16	f/22
Hyper. Dist.	3' 3"	2' 3"	1' 7"	1' 1"	0' 10"	0' 7"	0' 5"	0' 3"	0' 2"
FOCUS (feet)	NEAR FAR	NEAR FAR	NEAR FAR	NEAR FAR	NEAR FAR	NEAR FAR	NEAR FAR	NEAR FAR	NEAR FAR
2	1' 3" 5' 3"	1' 1" INF	0' 11" INF	0' 9" INF	0' 7" INF	0' 5" INF	0' 4" INF	0' 3" INF	0' 2" INF
2 1/2	1' 5" 11' 0"	1' 2" INF	1' 0" INF	0' 9" INF	0' 7" INF	0' 6" INF	0' 4" INF	0' 3" INF	0' 2" INF
3	1' 7" INF	1' 3" INF	1' 1" INF	0' 10" INF	0' 8" INF	0' 6" INF	0' 4" INF	0' 3" INF	0' 2" INF
3 1/2	1' 8" INF	1' 4" INF	1' 1" INF	0' 10" INF	0' 8" INF	0' 6" INF	0' 4" INF	0' 3" INF	0' 2" INF
4	1' 9" INF	1' 5" INF	1' 2" INF	0' 11" INF	0' 8" INF	0' 6" INF	0' 4" INF	0' 3" INF	0' 2" INF
4 1/2	1' 11" INF	1' 6" INF	1' 2" INF	0' 11" INF	0' 8" INF	0' 6" INF	0' 5" INF	0' 3" INF	0' 2" INF
5	2' 0" INF	1' 7" INF	1' 3" INF	0' 11" INF	0' 8" INF	0' 6" INF	0' 5" INF	0' 3" INF	0' 2" INF
5 1/2	2' 0" INF	1' 7" INF	1' 3" INF	0' 11" INF	0' 8" INF	0' 6" INF	0' 5" INF	0' 3" INF	0' 2" INF
6	2' 1" INF	1' 8" INF	1' 3" INF	0' 11" INF	0' 9" INF	0' 6" INF	0' 5" INF	0' 3" INF	0' 2" INF

6 1/2	2' 2" INF	1' 8" INF	1' 3" INF	1' 0" INF	0' 9" INF	0' 6" INF	0' 5" INF	0' 3" INF	0' 2" INF
7	2' 2" INF	1' 8" INF	1' 4" INF	1' 0" INF	0' 9" INF	0' 6" INF	0' 5" INF	0' 3" INF	0' 2" INF
8	2' 4" INF	1' 9" INF	1' 4" INF	1' 0" INF	0' 9" INF	0' 6" INF	0' 5" INF	0' 3" INF	0' 2" INF
9	2' 4" INF	1' 10" INF	1' 4" INF	1' 0" INF	0' 9" INF	0' 6" INF	0' 5" INF	0' 3" INF	0' 2" INF
10	2' 5" INF	1' 10" INF	1' 5" INF	1' 0" INF	0' 9" INF	0' 6" INF	0' 5" INF	0' 3" INF	0' 2" INF
12	2' 6" INF	1' 11" INF	1' 5" INF	1' 0" INF	0' 9" INF	0' 6" INF	0' 5" INF	0' 3" INF	0' 2" INF
14	2' 7" INF	1' 11" INF	1' 5" INF	1' 1" INF	0' 9" INF	0' 6" INF	0' 5" INF	0' 3" INF	0' 2" IN
16	2' 8" INF	2' 0" INF	1' 6" INF	1' 1" INF	0' 9" INF	0' 7" INF	0' 5" INF	0' 3" INF	0' 2" INF
18	2' 9" INF	2' 0" INF	1' 6" INF	1' 1" INF	0' 9" INF	0' 7" INF	0' 5" INF	0' 3" INF	0' 2" INF
20	2' 9" INF	2' 0" INF	1' 6" INF	1' 1" INF	0' 9" INF	0' 7" INF	0' 5" INF	0' 3" INF	0' 2" INF
25	2' 10" INF	2' 1" INF	1' 6" INF	1' 1" INF	0' 9" INF	0' 7" INF	0' 5""" INF	0' 3" INF	0' 2" INF
50	3' 0" INF	2' 2" INF	1' 7" INF	1' 1" INF	0' 9" INF	0' 7" INF	0' 5" INF	0' 3" INF	0' 2" INF

For circle of confusion = .0005 use depth data two columns left of chosen F-Stop.

8mm ALL FORMATS DEPTH OF FIELD TABLE CIRCLE OF CONFUSION=0.0010 inches

	f/1.4	f/2	f/2.8	f/4	f/5.6	f/8	f/11	f/16	f/22
Hyper. Dist.	5' 11"	4' 2"	2' 11"	2' 1"	1' 6"	1' 0"	0' 9"	0' 6"	0' 5"
FOCUS (feet)	NEAR FAR	NEAR FAR	NEAR FAR	NEAR FAR	NEAR FAR	NEAR FAR	NEAR FAR	NEAR FAR	NEAR FAR
2	1' 6" 3' 0"	1' 4" 3' 10"	1' 2" 6' 0"	1' 0" INF	0' 10" INF	0' 8" INF	0' 7" INF	0' 5" INF	0' 4" INF
2 1/2	1' 9" 4' 4"	1' 7" 6' 3"	1' 4" 15' 5"	1' 2" INF	0' 11" INF	0' 9" INF	0' 7" INF	0' 5" INF	0' 4" INF
3	2' 0" 6' 1"	1' 9" 10' 8"	1' 6" INF	1' 3" INF	1' 0" INF	0' 9" INF	0' 7" INF	0' 5" INF	0' 4" INF
3 1/2	2' 2" 8' 6"	1' 11" 21' 11"	1' 7" INF	1' 4" INF	1' 1" INF	0' 10" INF	0' 7" INF	0' 5" INF	0' 4" INF
4	2' 5" 12' 3"	2' 0" INF	1' 8" INF	1' 4" INF	1' 1" INF	0' 10" INF	0' 8" INF	0' 6" INF	0' 4" INF
4 1/2	2' 7" 18' 7"	2' 2" INF	1' 9" INF	1' 5" INF	1' 1" INF	0' 10" INF	0' 8" INF	0' 6" INF	0' 4" INF
5	2' 9" 31' 9"	2' 3" INF	1' 10" INF	1' 6" INF	1' 2" INF	0' 10" INF	0' 8" INF	0' 6" INF	0' 4" INF
5 1/2	2' 10" INF	2' 4" INF	1' 11" INF	1' 6" INF	1' 2" INF	0' 10" INF	0' 8" INF	0' 6" INF	0' 4" INF
6	3' 0" INF	2' 5" INF	2' 0" INF	1' 7" INF	1' 2" INF	0' 11" INF	0' 8" INF	0' 6" INF	0' 4" INF

6 1/2	3' 1" INF	2' 6" INF	2' 0" INF	1' 7" INF	1' 2" INF	0' 11" INF	0' 8" INF	0' 6" INF	0' 4" INF
7	3' 3" INF	2' 7" INF	2' 1" INF	1' 7" INF	1' 3" INF	0' 11" INF	0' 8" INF	0' 6" INF	0' 4" INF
7 1/2	3' 5" INF	2' 9" INF	2' 2" INF	1' 8" INF	1' 3" INF	0' 11" INF	0' 8" INF	0' 6" INF	0' 4" INF
9	3' 7" INF	2' 10" INF	2' 3" INF	1' 8" INF	1' 3" INF	0' 11" INF	0' 8" INF	0' 6" INF	0' 4" INF
10	3' 9" INF	2' 11" INF	2' 3" INF	1' 9" INF	1' 3" INF	0' 11" INF	0' 8" INF	0' 6" INF	0' 4" INF
12	4' 0" INF	3' 1" INF	2' 4" INF	1' 9" INF	1' 4" INF	0' 11" INF	0' 9" INF	0' 6" INF	0' 4" INF
14	4' 2" INF	3' 2" INF	2' 5" INF	1' 10" INF	1' 4" INF	1' 0" INF	0' 9" INF	0' 6" INF	0' 4" INF
16	4' 4" INF	3' 3" INF	2' 6" INF	1' 10" INF	1' 4" INF	1' 0" INF	0' 9" INF	0' 6" INF	0' 4" INF
18	4' 5" INF	3' 4" INF	2' 6" INF	1' 10" INF	1' 4" INF	1' 0" INF	0' 9" INF	0' 6" INF	0' 4" INF
20	4' 7" INF	3' 5" INF	2' 7" INF	1' 11" INF	1' 5" INF	1' 0" INF	0' 9" INF	0' 6" INF	0' 4" INF
25	4' 9" INF	3' 7" INF	2' 8" INF	1' 11" INF	1' 5" INF	1' 0" INF	0' 9" INF	0' 6" INF	0' 4" INF
50	5' 3" INF	3' 10" INF	2' 9" INF	2' 0" INF	1' 5" INF	1' 0" INF	0' 9" INF	0' 6" INF	0' 4" INF

For circle of confusion = .0005 use depth data two columns left of chosen F-Stop.

9.8mm

ALL FORMATS DEPTH OF FIELD TABLE — CIRCLE OF CONFUSION=0.0010 inches

	f/1.4	f/2	f/2.8	f/4	f/5.6	f/8	f/11	f/16	f/22
Hyper. Dist.	8' 10"	6' 2	4' 5"	3' 1"	2' 3"	1' 7"	1' 2"	0' 9"	0' 7"
FOCUS (feet)	NEAR FAR	NEAR FAR	NEAR FAR	NEAR FAR	NEAR FAR	NEAR FAR	NEAR FAR	NEAR FAR	NEAR FAR
2	1' 8" 2' 7"	1' 6" 2' 11"	1' 5" 3' 7"	1' 3" 5' 6"	1' 1" INF	0' 11" INF	0' 9" INF	0' 7" INF	0' 5" INF
2 1/2	1' 11" 3' 6"	1' 9" 4' 2"	1' 7" 5' 8"	1' 5" 12' 3"	1' 2" INF	1' 0" INF	0' 9" INF	0' 7" INF	0' 6" INF
3	2' 3" 4' 6"	2' 0" 5' 9"	1' 10" 9' 1"	1' 6" INF	1' 3" INF	1' 0" INF	0' 10" INF	0' 7" INF	0' 6" INF
3 1/2	2' 6" 5' 9"	2' 3" 7' 11"	2' 0" 16' 1"	1' 8" INF	1' 4" INF	1' 1" INF	0' 10" INF	0' 8" INF	0' 6" INF
4	2' 9" 7' 3"	2' 5" 11' 1"	2' 1" INF	1' 9" INF	1' 5" INF	1' 1" INF	0' 11" INF	0' 8" INF	0' 6" INF
4 1/2	3' 0" 9' 1"	2' 7" 16' 1"	2' 3" INF	1' 10" INF	1' 6" INF	1' 2" INF	0' 11" INF	0' 8" INF	0' 6" INF
5	3' 2" 1' 5"	2' 9" 25' 1"	2' 4" INF	1' 11" INF	1' 7" INF	1' 2" INF	0' 11" INF	0' 8" INF	0' 6" INF
5 1/2	3' 5" 4' 4"	2' 11" INF	2' 6" INF	2' 0" INF	1' 7" INF	1' 3" INF	0' 11" INF	0' 8" INF	0' 6" INF
6	3' 7" 8' 5"	3' 1" INF	2' 7" INF	2' 1" INF	1' 7" INF	1' 3" INF	0' 11" INF	0' 8" INF	0' 6" INF

6 1/2	3' 9" 4' 1"	3' 2" INF	2' 8" INF	2' 1" INF	1' 8" INF	1' 3" INF	1' 0" INF	0' 8" INF	0' 6" INF
7	3' 11" 2' 9"	3' 4" INF	2' 9" INF	2' 2" INF	1' 8" INF	1' 3" INF	1' 0" INF	0' 8" INF	0' 6" INF
8	4' 3" INF	3' 6" INF	2' 10" INF	2' 3" INF	1' 9" INF	1' 4" INF	1' 0" INF	0' 9" INF	0' 6" INF
9	4' 6" INF	3' 8" INF	3' 0" INF	2' 4" INF	1' 9" INF	1' 4" INF	1' 0" INF	0' 9" INF	0' 6" INF
10	4' 8" INF	3' 10" INF	3' 1" INF	2' 4" INF	1' 10" INF	1' 4" INF	1' 0" INF	0' 9" INF	0' 6" INF
12	5' 1" INF	4' 1" INF	3' 3" INF	2' 6" INF	1' 10" INF	1' 5" INF	1' 0" INF	0' 9" INF	0' 6" INF
14	5' 5" INF	4' 4" INF	3' 4" INF	2' 7" INF	1' 11" INF	1' 5" INF	1' 1" INF	0' 9" INF	0' 7" INF
16	5' 9" INF	4' 6" INF	3' 6" INF	2' 7" INF	1' 11" INF	1' 5" INF	1' 1" INF	0' 9" INF	0' 7" INF
18	5' 11" INF	4' 7" INF	3' 7" INF	2' 8" INF	2' 0" INF	1' 5" INF	1' 1" INF	0' 9" INF	0' 7" INF
20	6' 2" INF	4' 9" INF	3' 8" INF	2' 8" INF	2' 0" INF	1' 5" INF	1' 1" INF	0' 9" INF	0' 7" INF
25	6' 7" INF	5' 0" INF	3' 9" INF	2' 9" INF	2' 0" INF	1' 6" INF	1' 1" INF	0' 9" INF	0' 7" INF
50	7' 6" INF	5' 6" INF	4' 1" INF	2' 11" INF	2' 1" INF	1' 6" INF	1' 1" INF	0' 9" INF	0' 7" INF

For circle of confusion = .0005 use depth data two columns left of chosen F-Stop.

10mm

ALL FORMATS DEPTH OF FIELD TABLE **CIRCLE OF CONFUSION=0.0010 inches**

	f/1.4	f/2	f/2.8	f/4	f/5.6	f/8	f/11	f/16	f/22
Hyper. Dist.	9' 3"	6' 6"	4' 7"	3' 3"	2' 4"	1' 7"	1' 2"	0' 10"	0' 7"
FOCUS (feet)	NEAR FAR	NEAR FAR	NEAR FAR	NEAR FAR	NEAR FAR	NEAR FAR	NEAR FAR	NEAR FAR	NEAR FAR
2	1' 8" 2' 7"	1' 6" 2' 11"	1' 5" 3' 6"	1' 3" 5' 1"	1' 1" 13' 7"	0' 11" INF	0' 9" INF	0' 7" INF	0' 6" INF
2 ½	2' 0" 3' 5"	1' 10" 4' 1"	1' 8" 5' 4"	1' 5" 10' 7"	1' 2" INF	1' 0" INF	0' 10" INF	0' 7" INF	0' 6" INF
3	2' 3" 4' 5"	2' 1" 5' 7"	1' 10" 8' 5"	1' 7" INF	1' 4" INF	1' 1" INF	0' 10" INF	0' 8" INF	0' 6" INF
3 ½	2' 7" 5' 7"	2' 3" 7' 7"	2' 0" 14' 1"	1' 8" INF	1' 5" INF	1' 1" INF	0' 11" INF	0' 8" INF	0' 6" INF
4	2' 10" 7' 0"	2' 6" 10' 4"	2' 2" 28' 7"	1' 10" INF	1' 6" INF	1' 2" INF	0' 11" INF	0' 8" INF	0' 6" INF
4 ½	3' 0" 8' 9"	2' 8" 14' 7"	2' 3" INF	1' 11" INF	1' 6" INF	1' 2" INF	0' 11" INF	0' 8" INF	0' 6" INF
5	3' 3" 10' 10"	2' 10" 21' 8"	2' 5" INF	2' 0" INF	1' 7" INF	1' 3" INF	0' 11" INF	0' 8" INF	0' 6" INF
5 ½	3' 5" 13' 6"	3' 0" 35' 10"	2' 6" INF	2' 1" INF	1' 8" INF	1' 3" INF	1' 0" INF	0' 8" INF	0' 6" INF
6	3' 8" 17' 0"	3' 1" INF	2' 7" INF	2' 1" INF	1' 8" INF	1' 3" INF	1' 0" INF	0' 9" INF	0' 6" INF

6 1/2	3' 10" 21' 9"	3' 3" INF	2' 8" INF	2' 2" INF	1' 9" INF	1' 4" INF	1' 0" INF	0' 9" INF	0' 6" INF
7	4' 0" 28' 7"	3' 4" INF	2' 9" INF	2' 3" INF	1' 9" INF	1' 4" INF	1' 0" INF	0' 9" INF	0' 7" INF
8	4' 4" 58' 7"	3' 7" INF	2' 11" INF	2' 4" INF	1' 10" INF	1' 4" INF	1' 0" INF	0' 9" INF	0' 7" INF
9	4' 7" INF	3' 9" INF	3' 1" INF	2' 5" INF	1' 10" INF	1' 4" INF	1' 1" INF	0' 9" INF	0' 7" INF
10	4' 10" INF	3' 11" INF	3' 2" INF	2' 5" INF	1' 11" INF	1' 5" INF	1' 1" INF	0' 9" INF	0' 7" INF
12	5' 3" INF	4' 2" INF	3' 4" INF	2' 7" INF	1' 11" INF	1' 5" INF	1' 1" INF	0' 9" INF	0' 7" INF
14	5' 7" INF	4' 5" INF	3' 6" INF	2' 8" INF	2' 0" INF	1' 5" IN	1' 1" INF	0' 9" INF	0' 7" INF
16	5' 10" INF	4' 7" INF	3' 7" INF	2' 8" INF	2' 0" INF	1' 6" INF	1' 1" INF	0' 9" INF	0' 7" INF
18	6' 1" INF	4' 9" INF	3' 8" INF	2' 9" INF	2' 1" INF	1' 6" INF	1' 1" INF	0' 9" INF	0' 7" INF
20	6' 4" INF	4' 11" INF	3' 9" INF	2' 9" INF	2' 1" INF	1' 6" INF	1' 1" INF	0' 9" INF	0' 7" INF
25	6' 9" INF	5' 2" INF	3' 11" INF	2' 10" INF	2' 1" INF	1' 6" INF	1' 1" INF	0' 9" INF	0' 7" INF
50	7' 10" INF	5' 9" INF	4' 3" INF	3' 0" INF	2' 2" INF	1' 7" INF	1' 2" INF	0' 10" INF	0' 7" INF

For circle of confusion = .0005 use depth data two columns left of chosen F-Stop.

12mm ALL FORMATS DEPTH OF FIELD TABLE CIRCLE OF CONFUSION=0.0010 inches

	f/1.4	f/2	f/2.8	f/4	f/5.6	f/8	f/11	f/16	f/22
Hyper. Dist.	13' 3"	9' 4"	6' 8"	4' 8"	3' 4"	2' 4"	1' 8"	1' 2"	0' 10"
FOCUS (feet)	NEAR FAR	NEAR FAR	NEAR FAR	NEAR FAR	NEAR FAR	NEAR FAR	NEAR FAR	NEAR FAR	NEAR FAR
2	1' 9" 2' 4"	1' 8" 2' 6"	1' 7" 2' 10"	1' 5" 3' 5"	1' 3" 4' 11"	1' 1" 12' 9"	0' 11" INF	0' 9" INF	0' 7" INF
2 1/2	2' 1" 3' 1"	2' 0" 3' 5"	1' 10" 4' 0"	1' 8" 5' 4"	1' 5" 9' 8"	1' 3" INF	1' 0" INF	0' 10" INF	0' 8" INF
3	2' 5" 3' 10"	2' 3" 4' 5"	2' 1" 5' 5"	1' 10" 8' 3"	1' 7" INF	1' 4" INF	1' 1" INF	0' 10" INF	0' 8" INF
3 1/2	2' 9" 4' 9"	2' 7" 5' 7"	2' 4" 7' 4"	2' 0" 13' 8"	1' 9" INF	1' 5" INF	1' 2" INF	0' 11" INF	0' 8" INF
4	3' 1" 5' 8"	2' 10" 7' 0"	2' 6" 9' 11"	2' 2" 27' 0"	1' 10" INF	1' 6" INF	1' 2" INF	0' 11" INF	0' 8" INF
4 1/2	3' 4" 6' 9"	3' 0" 8' 8"	2' 8" 13' 8"	2' 4" INF	1' 11" INF	1' 7" INF	1' 3" INF	0' 11" INF	0' 9" INF
5	3' 8" 8' 0"	3' 3" 10' 9"	2' 10" 19' 9"	2' 5" INF	2' 0" INF	1' 7" INF	1' 3" INF	0' 11" INF	0' 9" INF
5 1/2	3' 11" 9' 4"	3' 6" 13' 4"	3' 0" 30' 11"	2' 6" INF	2' 1" INF	1' 8" INF	1' 4" INF	1' 0" INF	0' 9" INF
6	4' 2" 10' 11"	3' 8" 16' 9"	3' 2" INF	2' 8" INF	2' 2" INF	1' 8" INF	1' 4" INF	1' 0" INF	0' 9" INF

6 ½	4' 4" 12' 8"	3' 10" 21' 3"	3' 4" INF	2' 9" INF	2' 2" INF	1' 9" INF	1' 4" INF	1' 0" INF	0' 9" INF
7	4' 7" 14' 8"	4' 0" 27' 10"	3' 5" INF	2' 10" INF	2' 3" INF	1' 9" INF	1' 4" INF	1' 0" INF	0' 9" INF
8	5' 0" 20' 0"	4' 4" 55' 7"	3' 8" INF	2' 11" INF	2' 4" INF	1' 10" INF	1' 5" INF	1' 0" INF	0' 9" INF
9	5' 4" 27' 8"	4' 7" INF	3' 10" INF	3' 1" INF	2' 5" INF	1' 10" INF	1' 5" INF	1' 0" INF	0' 9" INF
10	5' 9" 39' 11"	4' 10" INF	4' 0" INF	3' 2" INF	2' 6" INF	1' 11" INF	1' 5" INF	1' 1" INF	0' 9" INF
12	6' 4" INF	5' 3" INF	4' 3" INF	3' 4" INF	2' 7" INF	1' 11" INF	1' 6" INF	1' 1" INF	0' 10" INF
14	6' 10" INF	5' 7" INF	4' 6" INF	3' 6" INF	2' 8" INF	2' 0" INF	1' 6" INF	1' 1" INF	0' 10" INF
16	7' 3" INF	5' 11" INF	4' 8" INF	3' 7" INF	2' 9" INF	2' 0" INF	1' 6" INF	1' 1" INF	0' 10" INF
18	7' 8" INF	6' 2" INF	4' 10" INF	3' 8" INF	2' 10" INF	2' 1" INF	1' 7" INF	1' 1" INF	0' 10" INF
20	8' 0" INF	6' 4" INF	5' 0" INF	3' 9" INF	2' 10" INF	2' 1" INF	1' 7" INF	1' 1" INF	0' 10" INF
25	8' 8" INF	6' 9" INF	5' 3" INF	3' 11" INF	2' 11" INF	2' 2" INF	1' 7" INF	1' 1" INF	0' 10" INF
50	10' 6" INF	7' 10" INF	5' 10" INF	4' 3" INF	3' 1" INF	2' 3" INF	1' 8" INF	1' 2" INF	0' 10" INF

For circle of confusion = .0005 use depth data two columns left of chosen F-Stop.

14mm — ALL FORMATS DEPTH OF FIELD TABLE — CIRCLE OF CONFUSION=0.0010 inches

	f/1.4	f/2	f/2.8	f/4	f/5.6	f/8	f/11	f/16	f/22
Hyper. Dist.	18' 1"	12' 8"	9' 1"	6' 4"	4' 6"	3' 2"	2' 4"	1' 7"	1' 2"
FOCUS (feet)	NEAR FAR	NEAR FAR	NEAR FAR	NEAR FAR	NEAR FAR	NEAR FAR	NEAR FAR	NEAR FAR	NEAR FAR
2	1' 10" 2' 3"	1' 9" 2' 4"	1' 8" 2' 7"	1' 6" 2' 11"	1' 5" 3' 6"	1' 3" 5' 3"	1' 1" 13' 3"	0' 11" INF	0' 9" INF
2 1/2	2' 2" 2' 11"	2' 1" 3' 1"	2' 0" 3' 5"	1' 10" 4' 1"	1' 7" 5' 6"	1' 5" 11' 2"	1' 3" INF	1' 0" INF	0' 10" INF
3	2' 7" 3' 7"	2' 5" 3' 11"	2' 3" 4' 5"	2' 1" 5' 8"	1' 10" 8' 8"	1' 7" INF	1' 4" INF	1' 1" INF	0' 10" INF
3 1/2	2' 11" 4' 4"	2' 9" 4' 10"	2' 6" 5' 8"	2' 3" 7' 8"	2' 0" 14' 10"	1' 8" INF	1' 5" INF	1' 1" INF	0' 10" INF
4	3' 3" 5' 1"	3' 1" 5' 10"	2' 9" 7' 1"	2' 6" 10' 8"	2' 2" INF	1' 9" INF	1' 6" INF	1' 2" INF	0' 11" INF
4 1/2	3' 7" 6' 0"	3' 4" 6' 11"	3' 0" 8' 10"	2' 8" 15' 2"	2' 3" INF	1' 10" INF	1' 6" INF	1' 2" INF	0' 11" INF
5	3' 11" 6' 11"	3' 7" 8' 3"	3' 3" 11' 1"	2' 10" 23' 0"	2' 5" INF	1' 11" INF	1' 7" INF	1' 3" INF	0' 11" INF
5 1/2	4' 3" 7' 11"	3' 10" 9' 8"	3' 5" 13' 10"	2' 11" 39' 9"	2' 6" INF	2' 0" INF	1' 8" INF	1' 3" INF	0' 11" INF
6	4' 6" 8' 11"	4' 1" 11' 4"	3' 7" 17' 7"	3' 1" INF	2' 7" INF	2' 1" INF	1' 8" INF	1' 3" INF	1' 0" INF

6 ½	4' 9" 10' 1"	4' 4" 13' 3"	3' 10" 22' 9"	3' 3" INF	2' 8" INF	2' 2" INF	1' 9" INF	1' 3" INF	1' 0" INF
7	5' 1" 11' 4"	4' 6" 15' 6"	3' 11" 30' 4"	3' 4" INF	2' 9" INF	2' 2" INF	1' 9" INF	1' 4" INF	1' 0" INF
8	5' 7" 14' 3"	4' 11" 21' 6"	4' 3" INF	3' 7" INF	2' 11" INF	2' 3" INF	1' 10" INF	1' 4" INF	1' 0" INF
9	6' 0" 17' 10"	5' 3" 30' 9"	4' 6" INF	3' 9" INF	3' 0" INF	2' 4" INF	1' 10" INF	1' 4" INF	1' 0" INF
10	6' 5" 22' 3"	5' 7" 46' 10"	4' 9" INF	3' 11" INF	3' 1" INF	2' 5" INF	1' 11" INF	1' 4" INF	1' 0" INF
12	7' 3" 35' 5"	6' 2" INF	5' 2" INF	4' 2" INF	3' 4" INF	2' 6" INF	1' 11" INF	1' 5" INF	1' 1" INF
14	7' 11" 61' 4"	6' 8" INF	5' 6" INF	4' 4" INF	3' 5" INF	2' 7" INF	2' 0" INF	1' 5" INF	1' 1" INF
16	8' 6" INF	7' 1" INF	5' 9" INF	4' 7" INF	3' 6" INF	2' 8" INF	2' 0" INF	1' 5" INF	1' 1" INF
18	9' 0" INF	7' 5" INF	6' 0" INF	4' 8" INF	3' 7" INF	2' 8" INF	2' 1" INF	1' 5" INF	1' 1" INF
20	9' 6" INF	7' 9" INF	6' 3" INF	4' 10" INF	3' 8" INF	2' 9" INF	2' 1" INF	1' 6" INF	1' 1" INF
25	10' 6" INF	8' 5" INF	6' 8" INF	5' 1" INF	3' 10" INF	2' 10" INF	2' 1" INF	1' 6" INF	1' 1" INF
50	13' 3" INF	10' 1" INF	7' 8" INF	5' 7" INF	4' 2" INF	3' 0" INF	2' 2" INF	1' 6" INF	1' 2" INF

For circle of confusion = .0005 use depth data two columns left of chosen F-Stop.

16mm

ALL FORMATS DEPTH OF FIELD TABLE — CIRCLE OF CONFUSION=0.0010 inches

	f/1.4	f/2	f/2.8	f/4	f/5.6	f/8	f/11	f/16	f/22
Hyperf. Dist.	23' 7"	16' 6"	11' 10"	8' 3"	5' 11"	4' 2"	3' 0"	2' 1"	1' 6"
FOCUS (focus)	NEAR FAR	NEAR FAR	NEAR FAR	NEAR FAR	NEAR FAR	NEAR FAR	NEAR FAR	NEAR FAR	NEAR FAR
2	1' 10" 2' 2"	1' 9" 2' 3"	1' 9" 2' 5"	1' 7" 2' 7"	1' 6" 3' 0"	1' 4" 3' 9"	1' 3" 5' 8"	1' 0" INF	0' 10" INF
2 1/2	2' 3" 2' 9"	2' 2" 2' 11"	2' 1" 3' 2"	1' 11" 3' 7"	1' 9" 4' 3"	1' 7" 6' 2"	1' 5" 13' 5"	1' 2" INF	0' 11" INF
3	2' 8" 3' 5"	2' 7" 3' 8"	2' 5" 4' 0"	2' 3" 4' 8"	2' 0" 6' 0"	1' 9" 10' 5"	1' 6" INF	1' 3" INF	1' 0" INF
3 1/2	3' 1" 4' 1"	2' 11" 4' 5"	2' 9" 4' 11"	2' 6" 6' 0"	2' 3" 8' 5"	1' 11" 21' 1"	1' 8" INF	1' 4" INF	1' 1" INF
4	3' 5" 4' 10"	3' 3" 5' 3"	3' 0" 6' 0"	2' 8" 7' 8"	2' 5" 12' 1"	2' 1" INF	1' 9" INF	1' 4" INF	1' 1" INF
4 1/2	3' 9" 5' 7"	3' 7" 6' 2"	3' 3" 7' 3"	2' 11" 9' 9"	2' 7" 18' 3"	2' 2" INF	1' 10" INF	1' 5" INF	1' 2" INF
5	4' 2" 6' 4"	3' 10" 7' 2"	3' 6" 8' 7"	3' 2" 12' 5"	2' 9" 30' 10"	2' 3" INF	1' 11" INF	1' 6" INF	1' 2" INF
5 1/2	4' 6" 7' 2"	4' 2" 8' 2"	3' 9" 10' 3"	3' 4" 16' 2"	2' 10" INF	2' 4" INF	1' 11" INF	1' 6" INF	1' 2" INF
6	4' 10" 8' 0"	4' 5" 9' 4"	4' 0" 12' 1"	3' 6" 21' 5"	3' 0" INF	2' 6" INF	2' 0" INF	1' 7" INF	1' 3" INF

6 1/2	5' 1" 8' 11"	4' 8" 10' 8"	4' 2" 14' 4"	3' 8" 29' 6"	3' 1" INF	2' 6" INF	2' 1" INF	1' 7" INF	1' 3" INF
7	5' 5" 9' 11"	4' 11" 12' 1"	4' 5" 17' 0"	3' 10" 43' 10"	3' 3" INF	2' 7" INF	2' 1" INF	1' 7" INF	1' 3" INF
8	6' 0" 12' 1"	5' 5" 15' 5"	4' 9" 24' 6"	4' 1" INF	3' 5" INF	2' 9" INF	2' 2" INF	1' 8" INF	1' 3" INF
9	6' 6" 14' 6"	5' 10" 19' 7"	5' 1" 37' 2"	4' 4" INF	3' 7" INF	2' 10" INF	2' 3" INF	1' 8" INF	1' 4" INF
10	7' 0" 17' 3"	6' 3" 25' 1"	5' 5" 63' 5"	4' 6" INF	3' 9" INF	2' 11" INF	2' 4" INF	1' 9" INF	1' 4" INF
12	8' 0" 24' 3"	7' 0" 43' 3"	6' 0" INF	4' 11" INF	4' 0" INF	3' 1" INF	2' 5" INF	1' 9" INF	1' 4" INF
14	8' 10" 34' 2"	7' 7" 89' 6"	6' 5" INF	5' 3" INF	4' 2" INF	3' 2" INF	2' 6" INF	1' 10" INF	1' 4" INF
16	9' 7" 49' 3"	8' 2" INF	6' 10" INF	5' 6" INF	4' 4" INF	3' 4" INF	2' 6" INF	1' 10" INF	1' 5" INF
18	10' 3" 75' 0"	8' 8" INF	7' 2" INF	5' 8" INF	4' 5" INF	3' 4" INF	2' 7" INF	1' 10" INF	1' 5" INF
20	10' 10" 128' 8"	9' 1" INF	7' 5" INF	5' 10" INF	4' 7" INF	3' 5" INF	2' 7" INF	1' 11" INF	1' 5" INF
25	12' 2" INF	10' 0" INF	8' 0" INF	6' 3" INF	4' 9" INF	3' 7" INF	2' 8" INF	1' 11" INF	1' 5" INF
50	16 1" INF	12' 5" INF	9' 7" INF	7' 1" INF	5' 3" INF	3' 10" INF	2' 10" INF	2' 0" INF	1' 6" INF

For circle of confusion = .0005 use depth data two columns left of chosen F-Stop.

18mm — ALL FORMATS DEPTH OF FIELD TABLE — CIRCLE OF CONFUSION=0.0010 inches

	f/1.4	f/2	f/2.8	f/4	f/5.6	f/8	f/11	f/16	f/22
Hyper. Dist.	29' 11"	20' 11"	14' 11"	10' 6"	7' 6"	5' 3"	3' 10"	2' 7"	1' 11"
FOCUS (feet)	NEAR FAR	NEAR FAR	NEAR FAR	NEAR FAR	NEAR FAR	NEAR FAR	NEAR FAR	NEAR FAR	NEAR FAR
2	1' 11" 2' 2"	1' 10" 2' 2"	1' 9" 2' 4"	1' 8" 2' 5"	1' 7" 2' 8"	1' 6" 3' 2"	1' 4" 4' 1"	1' 2" 7' 9"	1' 0" INF
2 1/2	2' 4" 2' 9"	2' 3" 2' 10"	2' 2" 3' 0"	2' 0" 3' 3"	1' 11" 3' 9"	1' 8" 4' 8"	1' 6" 7' 0"	1' 4" INF	1' 1" INF
3	2' 9" 3' 4"	2' 8" 3' 6"	2' 6" 3' 9"	2' 4" 4' 2"	2' 2" 4' 11"	1' 11" 6' 10"	1' 8" 13' 3"	1' 5" INF	1' 2" INF
3 1/2	3' 2" 3' 11"	3' 0" 4' 2"	2' 10" 4' 7"	2' 8" 5' 3"	2' 5" 6' 6"	2' 1" 10' 3"	1' 10" INF	1' 6" INF	1' 3" INF
4	3' 6" 4' 7"	3' 4" 4' 11"	3' 2" 5' 5"	2' 11" 6' 5"	2' 7" 8' 6"	2' 3" 16' 3"	2' 0" INF	1' 7" INF	1' 4" INF
4 1/2	3' 11" 5' 3"	3' 9" 5' 9"	3' 6" 6' 5"	3' 2" 7' 10"	2' 10" 11' 1"	2' 5" 29' 9"	2' 1" INF	1' 8" INF	1' 4" INF
5	4' 3" 6' 0"	4' 1" 6' 7"	3' 9" 7' 6"	3' 5" 9' 6"	3' 0" 14' 9"	2' 7" INF	2' 2" INF	1' 9" INF	1' 5" INF
5 1/2	4' 8" 6' 9"	4' 4" 7' 5"	4' 0" 8' 8"	3' 7" 11' 6"	3' 2" 20' 3"	2' 8" INF	2' 3" INF	1' 9" INF	1' 5" INF
6	5' 0" 7' 6"	4' 8" 8' 5"	4' 4" 9' 11"	3' 10" 13' 11"	3' 4" 29' 3"	2' 10" INF	2' 4" INF	1' 10" INF	1' 5" INF

6½	5' 4" 8' 3"	5' 0" 9' 5"	4' 7" 11' 5"	4' 0" 16' 11"	3' 6" INF	2' 11" INF	2' 5" INF	1' 11" INF	1' 6" INF
7	5' 8" 9' 1"	5' 3" 10' 6"	4' 9" 13' 1"	4' 2" 20' 10"	3' 8" INF	3' 0" INF	2' 6" INF	1' 11" INF	1' 6" INF
8	6' 4" 10' 11"	5' 10" 12' 11"	5' 3" 17' 1"	4' 7" 33' 2"	3' 11" INF	3' 2" INF	2' 7" INF	2' 0" INF	1' 7" INF
9	6' 11" 12' 10"	6' 4" 15' 9"	5' 8" 22' 5"	4' 10" 61' 11"	4' 1" INF	3' 4" INF	2' 8" INF	2' 0" INF	1' 7" INF
10	7' 6" 15' 0"	6' 9" 19' 1"	6' 0" 29' 10"	5' 2" INF	4' 3" INF	3' 5" INF	2' 9" INF	2' 1" INF	1' 7" INF
12	8' 7" 20' 0"	7' 8" 27' 11"	6' 8" 59' 8"	5' 7" INF	4' 7" INF	3' 8" INF	2' 11" INF	2' 2" INF	1' 8" INF
14	9' 7" 26' 3"	8' 5" 41' 11"	7' 3" INF	6' 0" INF	4' 11" INF	3' 10" INF	3' 0" INF	2' 3" INF	1' 8" INF
16	10' 5" 34' 3"	9' 1" 67' 2"	7' 9" INF	6' 4" INF	5' 1" INF	3' 11" INF	3' 1" INF	2' 3" INF	1' 8" INF
18	11' 3" 45' 0"	9' 8" 126' 3"	8' 2" INF	6' 8" INF	5' 4" INF	4' 1" INF	3' 2" INF	2' 3" INF	1' 9" INF
20	12' 0" 60' 1"	10' 3" INF	8' 7" INF	6' 11" INF	5' 5" INF	4' 2" INF	3' 2" INF	2' 4" INF	1' 9" INF
25	13' 8" 150' 11"	11' 5" INF	9' 4" INF	7' 5" INF	5' 9" INF	4' 4" INF	3' 4" INF	2' 4" INF	1' 9" INF
50	18' 9" INF	14' 9" INF	11' 6" INF	8' 8" INF	6' 6" INF	4' 9" INF	3' 6" INF	2' 6" INF	1' 10" INF

For circle of confusion = .0005 use depth data two columns left of chosen F-Stop.

20mm

ALL FORMATS DEPTH OF FIELD TABLE — CIRCLE OF CONFUSION=0.0010 inches

	f/1.4	f/2	f/2.8	f/4	f/5.6	f/8	f/11	f/16	f/22
Hyper. Dist.	36' 11"	25' 10"	18' 5"	12' 11"	9' 3"	6' 6"	4' 8"	3' 3"	2' 4"
FOCUS (feet)	NEAR FAR	NEAR FAR	NEAR FAR	NEAR FAR	NEAR FAR	NEAR FAR	NEAR FAR	NEAR FAR	NEAR FAR
2	1' 11" 2' 1"	1' 10" 2' 2"	1' 10" 2' 3"	1' 9" 2' 4"	1' 8" 2' 6"	1' 6" 2' 10"	1' 5" 3' 5"	1' 3" 5' 0"	1' 1" 11' 4"
2 1/2	2' 4" 2' 8"	2' 3" 2' 9"	2' 3" 2' 11"	2' 1" 3' 1"	2' 0" 3' 5"	1' 10" 4' 0"	1' 8" 5' 2"	1' 5" 10' 2"	1' 3" INF
3	2' 9" 3' 3"	2' 8" 3' 5"	2' 7" 3' 7"	2' 5" 3' 11"	2' 3" 4' 5"	2' 1" 5' 6"	1' 10" 8' 0"	1' 7" INF	1' 4" INF
3 1/2	3' 2" 3' 10"	3' 1" 4' 0"	2' 11" 4' 4"	2' 9" 4' 9"	2' 7" 5' 7"	2' 3" 7' 6"	2' 0" 13' 0"	1' 8" INF	1' 5" INF
4	3' 7" 4' 6"	3' 6" 4' 9"	3' 4" 5' 1"	3' 1" 5' 9"	2' 10" 7' 0"	2' 6" 10' 3"	2' 2" 24' 8"	1' 10" INF	1' 6" INF
4 1/2	4' 0" 5' 1"	3' 10" 5' 5"	3' 8" 5' 11"	3' 4" 6' 10"	3' 0" 8' 8"	2' 8" 14' 4"	2' 4" INF	1' 11" INF	1' 7" INF
5	4' 5" 5' 9"	4' 2" 6' 2"	3' 11" 6' 10"	3' 7" 8' 1"	3' 3" 10' 9"	2' 10" 21' 2"	2' 5" INF	2' 0" INF	1' 7" INF
5 1/2	4' 10" 6' 5"	4' 7" 7' 0"	4' 3" 7' 10"	3' 10" 9' 6"	3' 6" 13' 5"	3' 0" 34' 8"	2' 7" INF	2' 1" INF	1' 8" INF
6	5' 2" 7' 2"	4' 11" 7' 9"	4' 6" 8' 10"	4' 1" 11' 1"	3' 8" 16' 10"	3' 2" INF	2' 8" INF	2' 1" INF	1' 8" INF

6 1/2	5' 6" 7' 10"	5' 2" 8' 8"	4' 10" 10' 0"	4' 4" 12' 11"	3' 10" 21' 6"	3' 3" INF	2' 9" INF	2' 2" INF	1' 9" INF
7	5' 11" 8' 7"	5' 6" 9' 7"	5' 1" 11' 3"	4' 7" 15' 1"	4' 0" 28' 2"	3' 5" INF	2' 10" INF	2' 3" INF	1' 9" INF
8	6' 7" 10' 2"	6' 1" 11' 7"	5' 7" 14' 0"	4' 11" 20' 9"	4' 4" 57' 2"	3' 7" INF	3' 0" INF	2' 4" INF	1' 10" INF
9	7' 3" 11' 10"	6' 8" 13' 9"	6' 1" 17' 5"	5' 4" 29' 2"	4' 7" INF	3' 9" INF	3' 1" INF	2' 5" INF	1' 10" INF
10	7' 11" 13' 8"	7' 3" 16' 3"	6' 6" 21' 8"	5' 8" 43' 4"	4' 10" INF	3' 11" INF	3' 3" INF	2' 5" INF	1' 11" INF
12	9' 1" 17' 9"	8' 2" 22' 4"	7' 3" 34' 0"	6' 3" INF	5' 3" INF	4' 3" INF	3' 5" INF	2' 7" INF	2' 0" INF
14	10' 2" 22' 6"	9' 1" 30' 5"	8' 0" 57' 2"	6' 9" INF	5' 7" INF	4' 5" INF	3' 6" INF	2' 8" INF	2' 0" INF
16	11' 2" 28' 2"	9' 11" 41' 9"	8' 7" 117' 3"	7' 2" INF	5' 10" INF	4' 7" INF	3' 8" INF	2' 8" INF	2' 1" INF
18	12' 1" 35' 0"	10' 7" 58' 10"	9' 2" INF	7' 6" INF	6' 1" INF	4' 9" INF	3' 9" INF	2' 9" INF	2' 1" INF
20	13' 0" 43' 6"	11' 3" 87' 7"	9' 7" INF	7' 10" INF	6' 4" INF	4' 11" INF	3' 10" INF	2' 9" INF	2' 1" INF
25	14' 11" 77' 1"	12' 9" INF	10' 8" INF	8' 6" INF	6' 9" INF	5' 2" INF	4' 0" INF	2' 10" INF	2' 2" INF
50	21' 3" INF	17' 1" INF	13' 6" INF	10' 3" INF	7' 10" INF	5' 9" INF	4' 4" INF	3' 0" INF	2' 3" INF

For circle of confusion = .0005 use depth data two columns left of chosen F-Stop.

24mm — ALL FORMATS DEPTH OF FIELD TABLE — CIRCLE OF CONFUSION=0.0010 inches

	f/1.4	f/2	f/2.8	f/4	f/5.6	f/8	f/11	f/16	f/22
Hyper. Dist.	53' 2"	37' 2"	26' 7"	18' 7"	13' 3"	9' 4"	6' 9"	4' 8"	3' 5"
FOCUS (feet)	NEAR FAR	NEAR FAR	NEAR FAR	NEAR FAR	NEAR FAR	NEAR FAR	NEAR FAR	NEAR FAR	NEAR FAR
2	1' 11" 2' 1"	1' 11" 2' 1"	1' 10" 2' 2"	1' 10" 2' 3"	1' 9" 2' 4"	1' 8" 2' 6"	1' 7" 2' 10"	1' 5" 3' 5"	1' 3" 4' 8"
2 1/2	2' 5" 2' 7"	2' 4" 2' 8"	2' 3" 2' 9"	2' 3" 2' 10"	2' 1" 3' 1"	2' 0" 3' 5"	1' 10" 3' 11"	1' 8" 5' 3"	1' 5" 8' 10"
3	2' 10" 3' 2"	2' 9" 3' 3"	2' 8" 3' 4"	2' 7" 3' 7"	2' 6" 3' 10"	2' 3" 4' 4"	2' 1" 5' 3"	1' 10" 8' 1"	1' 7" INF
3 1/2	3' 3" 3' 9"	3' 2" 3' 10"	3' 1" 4' 0"	2' 11" 4' 3"	2' 9" 4' 9"	2' 7" 5' 6"	2' 4" 7' 1"	2' 0" 13' 3"	1' 9" INF
4	3' 9" 4' 4"	3' 7" 4' 6"	3' 6" 4' 8"	3' 4" 5' 1"	3' 1" 5' 8"	2' 10" 6' 11"	2' 6" 9' 6"	2' 2" 25' 6"	1' 10" INF
4 1/2	4' 2" 4' 11"	4' 0" 5' 1"	3' 10" 5' 5"	3' 8" 5' 11"	3' 5" 6' 9"	3' 1" 8' 7"	2' 9" 13' 0"	2' 4" INF	1' 11" INF
5	4' 7" 5' 6"	4' 5" 5' 9"	4' 3" 6' 2"	3' 11" 6' 10"	3' 8" 7' 11"	3' 3" 10' 7"	2' 11" 18' 4"	2' 5" INF	2' 0" INF
5 1/2	5' 0" 6' 1"	4' 10" 6' 5"	4' 7" 6' 11"	4' 3" 7' 9"	3' 11" 9' 3"	3' 6" 13' 2"	3' 1" 27' 9"	2' 6" INF	2' 1" INF
6	5' 5" 6' 9"	5' 2" 7' 2"	4' 11" 7' 9"	4' 7" 8' 10"	4' 2" 10' 10"	3' 8" 16' 6"	3' 2" INF	2' 8" INF	2' 2" INF

6 1/2	5' 10" 7' 5"	5' 7" 7' 10"	5' 3" 8' 7"	4' 10" 9' 11"	4' 5" 12' 7"	3' 10" 21' 0"	3' 4" INF	2' 9" INF	2' 3" INF
7	6' 2" 8' 1"	5' 11" 8' 7"	5' 7" 9' 6"	5' 1" 11' 2"	4' 7" 14' 7"	4' 0" 27' 4"	3' 6" INF	2' 10" INF	2' 4" INF
8	7' 0" 9' 5"	6' 7" 10' 2"	6' 2" 11' 5"	5' 7" 13' 11"	5' 0" 19' 10"	4' 4" 54' 0"	3' 8" INF	3' 0" INF	2' 5" INF
9	7' 8" 10' 10"	7' 3" 11' 10"	6' 9" 13' 7"	6' 1" 17' 4"	5' 5" 27' 5"	4' 7" INF	3' 11" INF	3' 1" INF	2' 6" INF
10	8' 5" 12' 4"	7' 11" 13' 8"	7' 3" 16' 0"	6' 6" 21' 5"	5' 9" 39' 6"	4' 10" INF	4' 1" INF	3' 2" INF	2' 7" INF
12	9' 10" 15' 6"	9' 1" 17' 8"	8' 3" 21' 9"	7' 4" 33' 5"	6' 4" INF	5' 3" INF	4' 4" INF	3' 4" INF	2' 8" INF
14	11' 1" 19' 0"	10' 2" 22' 4"	9' 2" 29' 5"	8' 0" 55' 8"	6' 10" INF	5' 7" INF	4' 7" INF	3' 6" INF	2' 9" INF
16	12' 4" 22' 10"	11' 2" 28' 0"	10' 0" 39' 11"	8' 7" 111' 1"	7' 3" INF	5' 11" INF	4' 9" INF	3' 7" INF	2' 10" INF
18	13' 6" 27' 2"	12' 2" 34' 9"	10' 9" 55' 4"	9' 2" INF	7' 8" INF	6' 2" INF	4' 11" INF	3' 8" INF	2' 10" INF
20	14' 7" 32' 0"	13' 0" 43' 1"	11' 5" 79' 11"	9' 8" INF	8' 0" INF	6' 4" INF	5' 1" INF	3' 9" INF	2' 11" INF
25	17' 0" 47' 1"	15' 0" 75' 9"	12' 11" INF	10' 8" INF	8' 8" INF	6' 10" INF	5' 4" INF	3' 11" INF	3' 0" INF
50	25' 9" INF	21' 4" INF	17' 4" INF	13' 7" INF	10' 6" INF	7' 10" INF	6' 0" INF	4' 3" INF	3' 2" INF

For circle of confusion = .0005 use depth data two columns left of chosen F-Stop.

25mm

ALL FORMATS DEPTH OF FIELD TABLE — CIRCLE OF CONFUSION=0.0010 inches

	f/1.4	f/2	f/2.8	f/4	f/5.6	f/8	f/11	f/16	f/22
Hyper. Dist.	57' 8"	40' 4"	28' 10"	20' 2"	14' 5"	10' 1"	7' 4"	5' 1"	3' 8"
FOCUS (feet)	NEAR FAR	NEAR FAR	NEAR FAR	NEAR FAR	NEAR FAR	NEAR FAR	NEAR FAR	NEAR FAR	NEAR FAR
2	1' 11" 2' 1"	1' 11" 2' 1"	1' 11" 2' 2"	1' 10" 2' 3"	1' 9" 2' 4"	1' 8" 2' 6"	1' 7" 2' 8"	1' 5" 3' 3"	1' 4" 4' 2"
2 1/2	2' 5" 2' 7"	2' 4" 2' 8"	2' 4" 2' 9"	2' 3" 2' 10"	2' 2" 3' 0"	2' 0" 3' 3"	1' 11" 3' 9"	1' 8" 4' 10"	1' 6" 7' 4"
3	2' 10" 3' 2"	2' 10" 3' 3"	2' 9" 3' 4"	2' 7" 3' 6"	2' 6" 3' 9"	2' 4" 4' 3"	2' 2" 5' 0"	1' 11" 7' 1"	1' 8" 14' 8"
3 1/2	3' 4" 3' 9"	3' 3" 3' 10"	3' 2" 4' 0"	3' 0" 4' 3"	2' 10" 4' 7"	2' 7" 5' 4"	2' 5" 6' 7"	2' 1" 10' 10"	1' 10" INF
4	3' 9" 4' 3"	3' 8" 4' 5"	3' 6" 4' 8"	3' 4" 5' 0"	3' 2" 5' 6"	2' 11" 6' 6"	2' 7" 8' 7"	2' 3" 17' 11"	1' 11" INF
4 1/2	4' 2" 4' 10"	4' 1" 5' 1"	3' 11" 5' 4"	3' 8" 5' 9"	3' 5" 6' 6"	3' 2" 8' 0"	2' 10" 11' 4"	2' 5" INF	2' 1" INF
5	4' 7" 5' 6"	4' 5" 5' 8"	4' 3" 6' 0"	4' 0" 6' 7"	3' 9" 7' 7"	3' 4" 9' 9"	3' 0" 15' 2"	2' 6" INF	2' 2" INF
5 1/2	5' 0" 6' 1"	4' 10" 6' 4"	4' 8" 6' 9"	4' 4" 7' 6"	4' 0" 8' 10"	3' 7" 11' 11"	3' 2" 21' 0"	2' 8" INF	2' 3" INF
6	5' 5" 6' 8"	5' 3" 7' 0"	5' 0" 7' 7"	4' 8" 8' 6"	4' 3" 10' 2"	3' 9" 14' 6"	3' 4" 31' 0"	2' 9" INF	2' 4" INF

6 ½	5' 10" 7' 4"	5' 7" 7' 9"	5' 4" 8' 4"	4' 11" 9' 6"	4' 6" 11' 9"	4' 0" 17' 10"	3' 6" INF	2' 10" INF	2' 4" INF
7	6' 3" 7' 11"	6' 0" 8' 5"	5' 8" 9' 3"	5' 3" 10' 8"	4' 9" 13' 6"	4' 2" 22' 3"	3' 7" INF	2' 11" INF	2' 5" INF
8	7' 0" 9' 3"	6' 8" 9' 11"	6' 3" 11' 0"	5' 9" 13' 2"	5' 2" 17' 9"	4' 6" 37' 2"	3' 10" INF	3' 1" INF	2' 6" INF
9	7' 10" 10' 8"	7' 4" 11' 7"	6' 10" 13' 0"	6' 3" 16' 2"	5' 7" 23' 7"	4' 9" INF	4' 1" INF	3' 3" INF	2' 7" INF
10	8' 6" 12' 1"	8' 0" 13' 3"	7' 5" 15' 3"	6' 8" 19' 8"	5' 11" 32' 1"	5' 1" INF	4' 3" INF	3' 4" INF	2' 8" INF
12	9' 11" 15' 2"	9' 3" 17' 0"	8' 6" 20' 5"	7' 7" 29' 4"	6' 7" 69' 3"	5' 6" INF	4' 7" INF	3' 7" INF	2' 10" INF
14	11' 3" 18' 5"	10' 5" 21' 4"	9' 5" 27' 1"	8' 3" 45' 1"	7' 1" INF	5' 11" INF	4' 10" INF	3' 9" INF	2' 11" INF
16	12' 6" 22' 1"	11' 6" 26' 5"	10' 4" 35' 9"	8' 11" 75' 9"	7' 7" INF	6' 2" INF	5' 1" INF	3' 10" INF	3' 0" INF
18	13' 9" 26' 1"	12' 6" 32' 4"	11' 1" 47' 7"	9' 6" INF	8' 0" INF	6' 6" INF	5' 3" INF	3' 11" INF	3' 1" INF
20	14' 10" 30' 7"	13' 5" 39' 6"	11' 10" 64' 8"	10' 1" INF	8' 5" INF	6' 9" INF	5' 5" INF	4' 1" INF	3' 1" INF
25	17' 5" 44' 0"	15' 5" 65' 4"	13' 5" 184' 2"	11' 2" INF	9' 2" INF	7' 2" INF	5' 8" INF	4' 3" INF	3' 3" INF
50	26' 10" 372' 3"	22' 4" INF	18' 4" INF	14' 5" INF	11' 2" INF	8' 5" INF	6' 5" INF	4' 7" INF	3' 5" INF

For circle of confusion = .0005 use depth data two columns left of chosen F-Stop.

28mm — ALL FORMATS DEPTH OF FIELD TABLE — CIRCLE OF CONFUSION=0.0010 inches

	f/1.4	f/2	f/2.8	f/4	f/5.6	f/8	f/11	f/16	f/22
Hyper. Dist	72' 4"	50' 8"	36' 2"	25' 4"	18' 1"	12' 8"	9' 2"	6' 4"	4' 7"
FOCUS (feet)	NEAR FAR	NEAR FAR	NEAR FAR	NEAR FAR	NEAR FAR	NEAR FAR	NEAR FAR	NEAR FAR	NEAR FAR
2	1' 11" 2' 1"	1' 11" 2' 1"	1' 11" 2' 1"	1' 10" 2' 2"	1' 10" 2' 3"	1' 9" 2' 4"	1' 8" 2' 6"	1' 6" 2' 10"	1' 5" 3' 5"
2 1/2	2' 5" 2' 7"	2' 5" 2' 7"	2' 4" 2' 8"	2' 3" 2' 9"	2' 2" 2' 11"	2' 1" 3' 1"	2' 0" 3' 5"	1' 10" 4' 0"	1' 8" 5' 3"
3	2' 11" 3' 2"	2' 10" 3' 2"	2' 9" 3' 3"	2' 8" 3' 5"	2' 7" 3' 7"	2' 5" 3' 11"	2' 3" 4' 5"	2' 1" 5' 7"	1' 10" 8' 2"
3 1/2	3' 4" 3' 8"	3' 3" 3' 9"	3' 2" 3' 10"	3' 1" 4' 1"	2' 11" 4' 4"	2' 9" 4' 9"	2' 7" 5' 7"	2' 3" 7' 7"	2' 0" 13' 6"
4	3' 10" 4' 3"	3' 9" 4' 4"	3' 7" 4' 6"	3' 6" 4' 9"	3' 3" 5' 1"	3' 1" 5' 9"	2' 10" 6' 11"	2' 6" 10' 5"	2' 2" 26' 6"
4 1/2	4' 3" 4' 10"	4' 2" 4' 11"	4' 0" 5' 1"	3' 10" 5' 5"	3' 7" 5' 11"	3' 4" 6' 11"	3' 1" 8' 8"	2' 8" 14' 10"	2' 4" INF
5	4' 8" 5' 4"	4' 7" 5' 6"	4' 5" 5' 9"	4' 2" 6' 2"	3' 11" 6' 10"	3' 7" 8' 2"	3' 3" 10' 9"	2' 10" 22' 3"	2' 5" INF
5 1/2	5' 1" 5' 11"	5' 0" 6' 2"	4' 9" 6' 6"	4' 6" 7' 0"	4' 3" 7' 10"	3' 10" 9' 7"	3' 6" 13' 4"	3' 0" 37' 10"	2' 6" INF
6	5' 7" 6' 6"	5' 4" 6' 10"	5' 2" 7' 2"	4' 10" 7' 10"	4' 6" 8' 11"	4' 1" 11' 3"	3' 8" 16' 9"	3' 1" INF	2' 8" INF

6 1/2	6' 0" 7' 2"	5' 9" 7' 5"	5' 6" 7' 11"	5' 2" 8' 8"	4' 10" 10' 1"	4' 4" 13' 2"	3' 10" 21' 5"	3' 3" INF	2' 9" INF
7	6' 5" 7' 9"	6' 2" 8' 1"	5' 11" 8' 8"	5' 6" 9' 8"	5' 1" 11' 4"	4' 6" 15' 5"	4' 0" 28' 1"	3' 4" INF	2' 10" INF
8	7' 3" 9' 0"	6' 11" 9' 6"	6' 7" 10' 3"	6' 1" 11' 8"	5' 7" 14' 3"	4' 11" 21' 4"	4' 4" 56' 9"	3' 7" INF	2' 11" INF
9	8' 0" 10' 3"	7' 8" 10' 11"	7' 3" 11' 11"	6' 8" 13' 11"	6' 0" 17' 9"	5' 3" 30' 5"	4' 7" INF	3' 9" INF	3' 1" INF
10	8' 10" 11' 7"	8' 4" 12' 5"	7' 10" 13' 9"	7' 2" 16' 5"	6' 6" 22' 1"	5' 7" 46' 0"	4' 10" INF	3' 11" INF	3' 2" INF
12	10' 4" 14' 4"	9' 9" 15' 8"	9' 0" 17' 11"	8' 2" 22' 8"	7' 3" 35' 2"	6' 2" INF	5' 3" INF	4' 2" INF	3' 4" INF
14	11' 9" 17' 4"	11' 0" 19' 4"	10' 1" 22' 9"	9' 0" 31' 1"	7' 11" 60' 8"	6' 8" INF	5' 7" INF	4' 5" INF	3' 6" INF
16	13' 1" 20' 6"	12' 2" 23' 4"	11' 1" 28' 7"	9' 10" 43' 1"	8' 6" INF	7' 1" INF	5' 10" INF	4' 7" INF	3' 7" INF
18	14' 5" 23' 11"	13' 4" 27' 10"	12' 0" 35' 8"	10' 7" 61' 6"	9' 1" INF	7' 5" INF	6' 1" INF	4' 8" INF	3' 8" INF
20	15' 8" 27' 7"	14' 4" 33' 0"	12' 11" 44' 6"	11' 2" 93' 7"	9' 6" INF	7' 9" INF	6' 4" INF	4' 10" INF	3' 9" INF
25	18' 7" 38' 2"	16' 9" 49' 2"	14' 10" 80' 4"	12' 7" INF	10' 6" INF	8' 5" INF	6' 9" INF	5' 1" INF	3' 11" INF
50	29' 7" 161' 3"	25' 2" INF	21' 0" INF	16' 10" INF	13' 4" INF	10' 1" INF	7' 9" INF	5' 8" INF	4' 3" INF

For circle of confusion = .0005 use depth data two columns left of chosen F-Stop.

32mm — ALL FORMATS DEPTH OF FIELD TABLE — CIRCLE OF CONFUSION=0.0010 inches

	f/1.4	f/2	f/2.8	f/4	f/5.6	f/8	f/11	f/16	f/22
Hyper. Dist.	94' 6"	66' 2"	47' 3"	33' 1"	23' 7"	16' 6"	12' 0"	8' 3"	6' 0"
FOCUS (feet)	NEAR FAR	NEAR FAR	NEAR FAR	NEAR FAR	NEAR FAR	NEAR FAR	NEAR FAR	NEAR FAR	NEAR FAR
2	2' 0" 2' 0"	1' 11" 2' 1"	1' 11" 2' 1"	1' 11" 2' 1"	1' 10" 2' 2"	1' 10" 2' 3"	1' 9" 2' 4"	1' 8" 2' 7"	1' 6" 2' 11"
2 1/2	2' 5" 2' 7"	2' 5" 2' 7"	2' 5" 2' 8"	2' 4" 2' 8"	2' 3" 2' 9"	2' 2" 2' 11"	2' 1" 3' 1"	1' 11" 3' 6"	1' 9" 4' 2"
3	2' 11" 3' 1"	2' 10" 3' 2"	2' 10" 3' 2"	2' 9" 3' 3"	2' 8" 3' 5"	2' 7" 3' 8"	2' 5" 3' 11"	2' 3" 4' 7"	2' 0" 5' 9"
3 1/2	3' 5" 3' 8"	3' 4" 3' 8"	3' 3" 3' 9"	3' 2" 3' 11"	3' 1" 4' 1"	2' 11" 4' 5"	2' 9" 4' 11"	2' 6" 5' 11"	2' 3" 8' 0"
4	3' 10" 4' 2"	3' 9" 4' 3"	3' 8" 4' 4"	3' 7" 4' 6"	3' 5" 4' 9"	3' 3" 5' 3"	3' 0" 5' 11"	2' 9" 7' 7"	2' 5" 11' 4"
4 1/2	4' 4" 4' 9"	4' 3" 4' 10"	4' 1" 5' 0"	4' 0" 5' 2"	3' 10" 5' 6"	3' 7" 6' 2"	3' 4" 7' 1"	2' 11" 9' 7"	2' 7" 16' 9"
5	4' 9" 5' 3"	4' 8" 5' 5"	4' 6" 5' 7"	4' 4" 5' 10"	4' 2" 6' 4"	3' 10" 7' 1"	3' 7" 8' 5"	3' 2" 12' 3"	2' 9" 26' 11"
5 1/2	5' 2" 5' 10"	5' 1" 6' 0"	4' 11" 6' 3"	4' 9" 6' 7"	4' 6" 7' 2"	4' 2" 8' 2"	3' 10" 10' 0"	3' 4" 15' 10"	2' 11" INF
6	5' 8" 6' 5"	5' 6" 6' 7"	5' 4" 6' 10"	5' 1" 7' 4"	4' 10" 8' 0"	4' 5" 9' 4"	4' 0" 11' 9"	3' 6" 20' 11"	3' 0" INF

6 ½	6' 1" 7' 0"	5' 11" 7' 2"	5' 9" 7' 6"	5' 5" 8' 1"	5' 1" 8' 11"	4' 8" 10' 7"	4' 3" 13' 11"	3' 8" 28' 9"	3' 2" INF
7	6' 6" 7' 7"	6' 4" 7' 10"	6' 1" 8' 2"	5' 10" 8' 10"	5' 5" 9' 11"	4' 11" 12' 0"	4' 5" 16' 5"	3' 10" 42' 2"	3' 3" INF
8	7' 5" 8' 9"	7' 2" 9' 1"	6' 10" 9' 7"	6' 5" 10' 6"	6' 0" 12' 0"	5' 5" 15' 4"	4' 10" 23' 4"	4' 1" INF	3' 6" INF
9	8' 3" 9' 11"	7' 11" 10' 5"	7' 7" 11' 1"	7' 1" 12' 4"	6' 6" 14' 5"	5' 10" 19' 6"	5' 2" 34' 7"	4' 4" INF	3' 8" INF
10	9' 1" 11' 2"	8' 8" 11' 9"	8' 3" 12' 8"	7' 8" 14' 3"	7' 1" 17' 3"	6' 3" 24' 11"	5' 6" 56' 6"	4' 7" INF	3' 9" INF
12	10' 8" 13' 9"	10' 2" 14' 8"	9' 7" 16' 0"	8' 10" 18' 9"	8' 0" 24' 2"	7' 0" 42' 9"	6' 0" INF	4' 11" INF	4' 0" INF
14	12' 2" 16' 5"	11' 7" 17' 9"	10' 10" 19' 10"	9' 10" 24' 2"	8' 10" 34' 0"	7' 7" 87' 9"	6' 6" INF	5' 3" INF	4' 3" INF
16	13' 8" 19' 3"	12' 11" 21' 1"	12' 0" 24' 1"	10' 10" 30' 10"	9' 7" 48' 11"	8' 2" INF	6' 11" INF	5' 6" INF	4' 5" INF
18	15' 2" 22' 2"	14' 2" 24' 8"	13' 1" 29' 0"	11' 8" 39' 3"	10' 3" 74' 3"	8' 8" INF	7' 3" INF	5' 8" INF	4' 6" INF
20	16' 6" 25' 4"	15' 4" 28' 7"	14' 1" 34' 7"	12' 6" 50' 3"	10' 10" 126' 10"	9' 1" INF	7' 6" INF	5' 10" INF	4' 8" INF
25	19' 9" 33' 11"	18' 2" 40' 1"	16' 4" 52' 10"	14' 3" 101' 2"	12' 2" INF	10' 0" INF	8' 2" INF	6' 3" INF	4' 10" INF
50	32' 9" 106' 0"	28' 6" 203' 8"	24' 4" INF	19' 11" INF	16' 1" INF	12' 5" INF	9' 9" INF	7' 1" INF	5' 5" INF

For circle of confusion = .0005 use depth data two columns left of chosen F-Stop.

35mm

ALL FORMATS DEPTH OF FIELD TABLE — CIRCLE OF CONFUSION=0.0010 inches

	f/1.4	f/2	f/2.8	f/4	f/5.6	f/8	f/11	f/16	f/22
Hyper. Dist.	113' 0"	79' 1"	56' 6"	39' 7"	28' 3"	19' 9"	14' 5"	9' 11"	7' 2"
FOCUS (feet)	NEAR FAR	NEAR FAR	NEAR FAR	NEAR FAR	NEAR FAR	NEAR FAR	NEAR FAR	NEAR FAR	NEAR FAR
2	2' 0" 2' 0"	1' 11" 2' 1"	1' 11" 2' 1"	1' 11" 2' 1"	1' 10" 2' 2"	1' 10" 2' 3"	1' 9" 2' 4"	1' 8" 2' 6"	1' 7" 2' 9"
2 ½	2' 5" 2' 7"	2' 5" 2' 7"	2' 5" 2' 7"	2' 4" 2' 8"	2' 4" 2' 9"	2' 3" 2' 10"	2' 2" 3' 0"	2' 0" 3' 4"	1' 11" 3' 9"
3	2' 11" 3' 1"	2' 11" 3' 1"	2' 10" 3' 2"	2' 10" 3' 3"	2' 9" 3' 4"	2' 7" 3' 6"	2' 6" 3' 9"	2' 4" 4' 3"	2' 2" 5' 0"
3 ½	3' 5" 3' 7"	3' 4" 3' 8"	3' 4" 3' 9"	3' 3" 3' 10"	3' 2" 4' 0"	3' 0" 4' 3"	2' 10" 4' 7"	2' 7" 5' 4"	2' 5" 6' 7"
4	3' 10" 4' 2"	3' 10" 4' 2"	3' 9" 4' 4"	3' 8" 4' 5"	3' 6" 4' 8"	3' 4" 5' 0"	3' 2" 5' 6"	2' 10" 6' 7"	2' 7" 8' 8"
4 ½	4' 4" 4' 8"	4' 3" 4' 9"	4' 2" 4' 11"	4' 1" 5' 1"	3' 11" 5' 4"	3' 8" 5' 9"	3' 5" 6' 6"	3' 1" 8' 1"	2' 10" 11' 6"
5	4' 10" 5' 3"	4' 9" 5' 4"	4' 7" 5' 6"	4' 5" 5' 8"	4' 3" 6' 1"	4' 0" 6' 8"	3' 9" 7' 7"	3' 4" 9' 11"	3' 0" 15' 7"
5 ½	5' 3" 5' 9"	5' 2" 5' 11"	5' 0" 6' 1"	4' 10" 6' 4"	4' 7" 6' 10"	4' 4" 7' 7"	4' 0" 8' 9"	3' 7" 12' 1"	3' 2" 21' 11"
6	5' 8" 6' 4"	5' 7" 6' 6"	5' 5" 6' 8"	5' 3" 7' 1"	5' 0" 7' 7"	4' 7" 8' 6"	4' 3" 10' 2"	3' 9" 14' 10"	3' 4" 33' 0"

6 ½	6' 2" 6' 11"	6' 0" 7' 1"	5' 10" 7' 4"	5' 7" 7' 9"	5' 4" 8' 5"	4' 11" 9' 7"	4' 6" 11' 8"	3' 11" 18' 4"	3' 5" INF
7	6' 7" 7' 5"	6' 5" 7' 8"	6' 3" 8' 0"	6' 0" 8' 6"	5' 8" 9' 3"	5' 2" 10' 9"	4' 9" 13' 5"	4' 2" 23' 1"	3' 7" INF
8	7' 6" 8' 7"	7' 3" 8' 11"	7' 0" 9' 4"	6' 8" 10' 0"	6' 3" 11' 1"	5' 9" 13' 4"	5' 2" 17' 8"	4' 5" 39' 6"	3' 10" INF
9	8' 4" 9' 9"	8' 1" 10' 2"	7' 9" 10' 8"	7' 4" 11' 7"	6' 10" 13' 2"	6' 3" 16' 4"	5' 7" 23' 6"	4' 9" INF	4' 0" INF
10	9' 2" 11' 0"	8' 11" 11' 5"	8' 6" 12' 1"	8' 0" 13' 4"	7' 5" 15' 5"	6' 8" 20' 0"	5' 11" 32' 0"	5' 0" INF	4' 3" INF
12	10' 10" 13' 5"	10' 5" 14' 1"	9' 11" 15' 2"	9' 3" 17' 2"	8' 5" 20' 9"	7' 6" 30' 1"	6' 7" 69' 1"	5' 5" INF	4' 6" INF
14	12' 6" 16' 0"	11' 11" 17' 0"	11' 3" 18' 7"	10' 4" 21' 7"	9' 5" 27' 6"	8' 3" 47' 0"	7' 1" INF	5' 10" INF	4' 9" INF
16	14' 0" 18' 7"	13' 4" 20' 0"	12' 6" 22' 3"	11' 5" 26' 9"	10' 3" 36' 7"	8' 10" 81' 3"	7' 7" INF	6' 2" INF	5' 0" INF
18	15' 6" 21' 5"	14' 8" 23' 3"	13' 8" 26' 4"	12' 5" 32' 10"	11' 0" 49' 1"	9' 5" INF	8' 0" INF	6' 5" INF	5' 2" INF
20	17' 0" 24' 3"	16' 0" 26' 9"	14' 10" 30' 10"	13' 4" 40' 3"	11' 9" 67' 6"	10' 0" INF	8' 5" INF	6' 8" INF	5' 4" INF
25	20' 6" 32' 1"	19' 0" 36' 6"	17' 4" 44' 8"	15' 4" 67' 5"	13' 4" INF	11' 1" INF	9' 2" INF	7' 1" INF	5' 7" INF
50	34' 8" 89' 6"	30' 8" 135' 4"	26' 7" INF	22' 1" INF	18' 1" INF	14' 2" INF	11' 2" INF	8' 3" INF	6' 4" INF

For circle of confusion = .0005 use depth data two columns left of chosen F-Stop.

37.5mm ALL FORMATS DEPTH OF FIELD TABLE CIRCLE OF CONFUSION=0.0010 inches

	f/1.4	f/2	f/2.8	f/4	f/5.6	f/8	f/11	f/16	f/22
Hyper. Dist.	129' 9"	90' 10"	64' 10"	45' 5"	32' 5"	22' 8"	16' 6"	11' 4"	8' 3"
FOCUS (feet)	NEAR FAR	NEAR FAR	NEAR FAR	NEAR FAR	NEAR FAR	NEAR FAR	NEAR FAR	NEAR FAR	NEAR FAR
2	2' 0" 2' 0"	2' 0" 2' 1"	1' 11" 2' 1"	1' 11" 2' 1"	1' 11" 2' 1"	1' 10" 2' 2"	1' 10" 2' 3"	1' 9" 2' 5"	1' 8" 2' 7"
2 1/2	2' 5" 2' 7"	2' 5" 2' 7"	2' 5" 2' 7"	2' 5" 2' 8"	2' 4" 2' 8"	2' 3" 2' 10"	2' 2" 2' 11"	2' 1" 3' 2"	1' 11" 3' 6"
3	2' 11" 3' 1"	2' 11" 3' 1"	2' 10" 3' 2"	2' 10" 3' 2"	2' 9" 3' 4"	2' 8" 3' 5"	2' 7" 3' 8"	2' 5" 4' 0"	2' 3" 4' 7"
3 1/2	3' 5" 3' 7"	3' 4" 3' 8"	3' 4" 3' 8"	3' 3" 3' 9"	3' 2" 3' 11"	3' 1" 4' 1"	2' 11" 4' 5"	2' 8" 5' 0"	2' 6" 5' 11"
4	3' 11" 4' 1"	3' 10" 4' 2"	3' 9" 4' 3"	3' 8" 4' 4"	3' 7" 4' 7"	3' 5" 4' 10"	3' 3" 5' 3"	3' 0" 6' 1"	2' 9" 7' 6"
4 1/2	4' 4" 4' 8"	4' 4" 4' 9"	4' 3" 4' 10"	4' 1" 5' 0"	4' 0" 5' 2"	3' 9" 5' 7"	3' 7" 6' 1"	3' 3" 7' 4"	2' 11" 9' 7"
5	4' 10" 5' 2"	4' 9" 5' 3"	4' 8" 5' 5"	4' 6" 5' 7"	4' 4" 5' 11"	4' 1" 6' 4"	3' 10" 7' 1"	3' 6" 8' 9"	3' 2" 12' 3"
5 1/2	5' 3" 5' 9"	5' 2" 5' 10"	5' 1" 6' 0"	4' 11" 6' 3"	4' 9" 6' 7"	4' 5" 7' 2"	4' 2" 8' 2"	3' 9" 10' 5"	3' 4" 15' 9"
6	5' 9" 6' 3"	5' 8" 6' 5"	5' 6" 6' 7"	5' 4" 6' 11"	5' 1" 7' 4"	4' 9" 8' 1"	4' 5" 9' 4"	3' 11" 12' 5"	3' 6" 20' 10"

6 1/2	6' 2" 6' 10"	6' 1" 7' 0"	5' 11" 7' 3"	5' 8" 7' 7"	5' 5" 8' 1"	5' 1" 9' 0"	4' 8" 10' 7"	4' 2" 14' 10"	3' 8" 28' 7"
7	6' 8" 7' 5"	6' 6" 7' 7"	6' 4" 7' 10"	6' 1" 8' 3"	5' 9" 8' 11"	5' 4" 10' 0"	4' 11" 12' 0"	4' 4" 17' 9"	3' 10" 41' 11"
8	7' 7" 8' 6"	7' 4" 8' 9"	7' 2" 9' 1"	6' 10" 9' 8"	6' 5" 10' 7"	5' 11" 12' 3"	5' 5" 15' 4"	4' 9" 26' 2"	4' 1" INF
9	8' 5" 9' 8"	8' 2" 10' 0"	7' 11" 10' 5"	7' 6" 11' 2"	7' 1" 12' 5"	6' 6" 14' 9"	5' 10" 19' 6"	5' 1" 41' 3"	4' 4" INF
10	9' 4" 10' 10"	9' 0" 11' 3"	8' 8" 11' 10"	8' 3" 12' 9"	7' 8" 14' 5"	7' 0" 17' 8"	6' 3" 24' 11"	5' 4" INF	4' 7" INF
12	11' 0" 13' 3"	10' 7" 13' 10"	10' 2" 14' 8"	9' 6" 16' 3"	8' 9" 18' 11"	7' 11" 25' 2"	7' 0" 42' 9"	5' 10" INF	4' 11" INF
14	12' 8" 15' 8"	12' 2" 16' 6"	11' 6" 17' 10"	10' 9" 20' 2"	9' 10" 24' 6"	8' 8" 36' 0"	7' 7" 87' 8"	6' 4" INF	5' 3" INF
16	14' 3" 18' 3"	13' 7" 19' 5"	12' 10" 21' 2"	11' 10" 24' 7"	10' 9" 31' 4"	9' 5" 53' 2"	8' 2" INF	6' 8" INF	5' 6" INF
18	15' 10" 20' 11"	15' 0" 22' 5"	14' 1" 24' 10"	12' 11" 29' 8"	11' 7" 40' 1"	10' 1" 84' 8"	8' 8" INF	7' 0" INF	5' 8" INF
20	17' 4" 23' 7"	16' 5" 25' 7"	15' 4" 28' 10"	13' 11" 35' 7"	12' 5" 51' 8"	10' 8" INF	9' 1" INF	7' 3" INF	5' 10" INF
25	21' 0" 30' 11"	19' 7" 34' 5"	18' 1" 40' 7"	16' 2" 55' 3"	14' 2" 107' 3"	11' 11" INF	10' 0" INF	7' 10" INF	6' 3" INF
50	36' 1" 81' 3"	32' 3" 110' 11"	28' 3" 216' 4"	23' 10" INF	19' 8" INF	15' 8" INF	12' 5" INF	9' 3" INF	7' 1" INF

For circle of confusion = .0005 use depth data two columns left of chosen F-Stop.

40mm ALL FORMATS DEPTH OF FIELD TABLE CIRCLE OF CONFUSION=0.0010 inches

	f/1.4	f/2	f/2.8	f/4	f/5.6	f/8	f/11	f/16	f/22
Hyper. Dist.	147' 7"	103' 4"	73' 10"	51' 8"	36' 11"	25' 10"	18' 9"	12' 11"	9' 5"
FOCUS (feet)	NEAR FAR	NEAR FAR	NEAR FAR	NEAR FAR	NEAR FAR	NEAR FAR	NEAR FAR	NEAR FAR	NEAR FAR
2	2' 0" 2' 0"	2' 0" 2' 0"	1' 11" 2' 1"	1' 11" 2' 1"	1' 11" 2' 1"	1' 10" 2' 2"	1' 10" 2' 3"	1' 9" 2' 4"	1' 8" 2' 6"
2 1/2	2' 6" 2' 6"	2' 5" 2' 7"	2' 5" 2' 7"	2' 5" 2' 7"	2' 4" 2' 8"	2' 3" 2' 9"	2' 3" 2' 10"	2' 1" 3' 1"	2' 0" 3' 4"
3	2' 11" 3' 1"	2' 11" 3' 1"	2' 11" 3' 1"	2' 10" 3' 2"	2' 9" 3' 3"	2' 8" 3' 4"	2' 7" 3' 6"	2' 5" 3' 10"	2' 4" 4' 4"
3 1/2	3' 5" 3' 7"	3' 5" 3' 7"	3' 4" 3' 8"	3' 3" 3' 9"	3' 2" 3' 10"	3' 1" 4' 0"	3' 0" 4' 3"	2' 9" 4' 9"	2' 7" 5' 5"
4	3' 11" 4' 1"	3' 10" 4' 2"	3' 10" 4' 3"	3' 9" 4' 4"	3' 7" 4' 6"	3' 6" 4' 8"	3' 4" 5' 0"	3' 1" 5' 9"	2' 10" 6' 10"
4 1/2	4' 4" 4' 8"	4' 4" 4' 8"	4' 3" 4' 9"	4' 2" 4' 11"	4' 0" 5' 1"	3' 10" 5' 5"	3' 8" 5' 10"	3' 4" 6' 10"	3' 1" 8' 5"
5	4' 10" 5' 2"	4' 9" 5' 3"	4' 8" 5' 4"	4' 7" 5' 6"	4' 5" 5' 9"	4' 2" 6' 2"	4' 0" 6' 9"	3' 8" 8' 0"	3' 4" 10' 5"
5 1/2	5' 4" 5' 8"	5' 3" 5' 10"	5' 2" 5' 11"	5' 0" 6' 2"	4' 10" 6' 5"	4' 7" 6' 11"	4' 3" 7' 8"	3' 11" 9' 5"	3' 6" 12' 10"
6	5' 9" 6' 3"	5' 8" 6' 4"	5' 7" 6' 6"	5' 5" 6' 9"	5' 2" 7' 2"	4' 11" 7' 9"	4' 7" 8' 9"	4' 2" 11' 0"	3' 8" 16' 0"

6 1/2	6' 3" 6' 10"	6' 1" 6' 11"	6' 0" 7' 1"	5' 9" 7' 5"	5' 7" 7' 10"	5' 3" 8' 8"	4' 10" 9' 10"	4' 4" 12' 10"	3' 10" 20' 2"
7	6' 8" 7' 4"	6' 7" 7' 6"	6' 5" 7' 9"	6' 2" 8' 1"	5' 11" 8' 7"	5' 6" 9' 6"	5' 2" 11' 0"	4' 7" 14' 11"	4' 1" 26' 0"
8	7' 7" 8' 5"	7' 5" 8' 8"	7' 3" 8' 11"	6' 11" 9' 5"	6' 7" 10' 2"	6' 2" 11' 6"	5' 8" 13' 9"	5' 0" 20' 6"	4' 4" 49' 3"
9	8' 6" 9' 7"	8' 3" 9' 10"	8' 0" 10' 3"	7' 8" 10' 10"	7' 3" 11' 10"	6' 8" 13' 8"	6' 1" 17' 1"	5' 4" 28' 9"	4' 8" INF
10	9' 4" 10' 9"	9' 2" 11' 1"	8' 10" 11' 7"	8' 5" 12' 4"	7' 11" 13' 8"	7' 3" 16' 2"	6' 7" 21' 1"	5' 8" 42' 5"	4' 11" INF
12	11' 1" 13' 1"	10' 9" 13' 7"	10' 4" 14' 4"	9' 9" 15' 7"	9' 1" 17' 8"	8' 3" 22' 2"	7' 4" 32' 7"	6' 3" INF	5' 4" INF
14	12' 10" 15' 5"	12' 4" 16' 2"	11' 9" 17' 3"	11' 0" 19' 2"	10' 2" 22' 5"	9' 1" 30' 3"	8' 1" 53' 6"	6' 9" INF	5' 8" INF
16	14' 5" 17' 11"	13' 10" 18' 11"	13' 2" 20' 5"	12' 3" 23' 1"	11' 2" 28' 1"	9' 11" 41' 6"	8' 8" 103' 0"	7' 2" INF	5' 11" INF
18	16' 1" 20' 6"	15' 4" 21' 9"	14' 6" 23' 9"	13' 4" 27' 6"	12' 2" 34' 11"	10' 8" 58' 5"	9' 3" INF	7' 7" INF	6' 2" INF
20	17' 8" 23' 1"	16' 9" 24' 9"	15' 9" 27' 4"	14' 5" 32' 6"	13' 0" 43' 4"	11' 4" 86' 7"	9' 9" INF	7' 11" INF	6' 5" INF
25	21' 5" 30' 1"	20' 2" 32' 11"	18' 8" 37' 8"	16' 11" 48' 2"	14' 11" 76' 8"	12' 9" INF	10' 9" INF	8' 7" INF	6' 10" INF
50	37' 4" 75' 6"	33' 9" 96' 8"	29' 10" 154' 2"	25' 5" INF	21' 3" INF	17' 1" INF	13' 8" INF	10' 3" INF	7' 11" INF

For circle of confusion = .0005 use depth data two columns left of chosen F-Stop.

50mm

ALL FORMATS DEPTH OF FIELD TABLE — CIRCLE OF CONFUSION=0.0010 inches

	f/1.4	f/2	f/2.8	f/4	f/5.6	f/8	f/11	f/16	f/22
Hyper. Dist.	230' 8"	161' 6"	115' 4"	80' 9"	57' 8"	40' 4"	29' 4"	20' 2"	14' 8"
FOCUS (feet)	NEAR FAR	NEAR FAR	NEAR FAR	NEAR FAR	NEAR FAR	NEAR FAR	NEAR FAR	NEAR FAR	NEAR FAR
2	2' 0" 2' 0"	2' 0" 2' 0"	2' 0" 2' 0"	1' 11" 2' 1"	1' 11" 2' 1"	1' 11" 2' 1"	1' 11" 2' 2"	1' 10" 2' 2"	1' 9" 2' 3"
2 1/2	2' 6" 2' 6"	2' 6" 2' 6"	2' 5" 2' 7"	2' 5" 2' 7"	2' 5" 2' 7"	2' 4" 2' 8"	2' 4" 2' 9"	2' 3" 2' 10"	2' 2" 3' 0"
3	3' 0" 3' 0"	2' 11" 3' 1"	2' 11" 3' 1"	2' 11" 3' 1"	2' 10" 3' 2"	2' 10" 3' 3"	2' 9" 3' 4"	2' 8" 3' 6"	2' 6" 3' 9"
3 1/2	3' 5" 3' 7"	3' 5" 3' 7"	3' 5" 3' 7"	3' 4" 3' 8"	3' 4" 3' 9"	3' 3" 3' 10"	3' 2" 3' 11"	3' 0" 4' 2"	2' 10" 4' 6"
4	3' 11" 4' 1"	3' 11" 4' 1"	3' 10" 4' 2"	3' 10" 4' 2"	3' 9" 4' 3"	3' 8" 4' 5"	3' 6" 4' 7"	3' 4" 4' 11"	3' 2" 5' 5"
4 1/2	4' 5" 4' 7"	4' 5" 4' 7"	4' 4" 4' 8"	4' 3" 4' 9"	4' 2" 4' 10"	4' 1" 5' 0"	3' 11" 5' 3"	3' 8" 5' 9"	3' 6" 6' 5"
5	4' 11" 5' 1"	4' 10" 5' 2"	4' 10" 5' 3"	4' 9" 5' 4"	4' 7" 5' 5"	4' 6" 5' 8"	4' 4" 6' 0"	4' 0" 6' 7"	3' 9" 7' 5"
5 1/2	5' 5" 5' 8"	5' 4" 5' 8"	5' 3" 5' 9"	5' 2" 5' 11"	5' 0" 6' 1"	4' 10" 6' 4"	4' 8" 6' 9"	4' 4" 7' 6"	4' 0" 8' 8"
6	5' 10" 6' 2"	5' 9" 6' 3"	5' 9" 6' 4"	5' 7" 6' 6"	5' 5" 6' 8"	5' 3" 7' 0"	5' 0" 7' 6"	4' 8" 8' 5"	4' 4" 10' 0"

6 1/2	6' 4" 6' 8"	6' 3" 6' 9"	6' 2" 6' 11"	6' 0" 7' 1"	5' 10" 7' 4"	5' 7" 7' 9"	5' 4" 8' 3"	4' 11" 9' 6"	4' 6" 11' 5"
7	6' 10" 7' 3"	6' 9" 7' 4"	6' 7" 7' 5"	6' 5" 7' 8"	6' 3" 7' 11"	6' 0" 8' 5"	5' 8" 9' 1"	5' 3" 10' 7"	4' 9" 13' 1"
8	7' 9" 8' 3"	7' 8" 8' 5"	7' 6" 8' 7"	7' 4" 8' 10"	7' 1" 9' 3"	6' 8" 9' 11"	6' 4" 10' 11"	5' 9" 13' 1"	5' 3" 17' 2"
9	8' 8" 9' 4"	8' 6" 9' 6"	8' 4" 9' 9"	8' 1" 10' 1"	7' 10" 10' 8"	7' 5" 11' 6"	6' 11" 12' 11"	6' 3" 16' 0"	5' 7" 22' 7"
10	9' 7" 10' 5"	9' 5" 10' 8"	9' 3" 10' 11"	8' 11" 11' 5"	8' 7" 12' 1"	8' 0" 13' 3"	7' 6" 15' 0"	6' 9" 19' 6"	6' 0" 30' 4"
12	11' 5" 12' 8"	11' 2" 12' 11"	10' 11" 13' 4"	10' 6" 14' 1"	9' 11" 15' 1"	9' 3" 17' 0"	8' 7" 20' 1"	7' 7" 29' 0"	6' 8" 62' 0"
14	13' 2" 14' 11"	12' 11" 15' 4"	12' 6" 15' 11"	11' 11" 16' 11"	11' 3" 18' 5"	10' 5" 21' 4"	9' 6" 26' 6"	8' 4" 44' 6"	7' 2" INF
16	15' 0" 17' 2"	14' 7" 17' 9"	14' 1" 18' 7"	13' 5" 19' 11"	12' 7" 22' 1"	11' 6" 26' 4"	10' 5" 34' 9"	9' 0" 74' 4"	7' 8" INF
18	16' 8" 19' 6"	16' 3" 20' 3"	15' 7" 21' 4"	14' 9" 23' 1"	13' 9" 26' 1"	12' 6" 32' 3"	11' 2" 45' 10"	9' 7" INF	8' 2" INF
20	18' 5" 21' 11"	17' 10" 22' 10"	17' 1" 24' 2"	16' 1" 26' 6"	14' 11" 30' 6"	13' 5" 39' 4"	11' 11" 61' 8"	10' 1" INF	8' 6" INF
25	22' 7" 28' 0"	21' 8" 29' 7"	20' 7" 31' 10"	19' 1" 36' 1"	17' 6" 43' 11"	15' 6" 65' 0"	13' 7" 162' 4"	11' 2" INF	9' 3" INF
50	41' 1" 63' 9"	38' 2" 72' 4"	34' 11" 88' 1"	30' 11" 130' 8"	26' 10" 368' 4"	22' 4" INF	18' 6" INF	14' 5" INF	11' 5" INF

For circle of confusion = .0005 use depth data two columns left of chosen F-Stop.

75mm

ALL FORMATS DEPTH OF FIELD TABLE — CIRCLE OF CONFUSION=0.0010 inches

	f/1.4	f/2	f/2.8	f/4	f/5.6	f/8	f/11	f/16	f/22
Hyper. Dist.	519' 0"	363' 3"	259' 6"	181' 8"	129' 9"	90' 10"	66' 1"	45' 5"	33' 0"
FOCUS (feet)	NEAR FAR	NEAR FAR	NEAR FAR	NEAR FAR	NEAR FAR	NEAR FAR	NEAR FAR	NEAR FAR	NEAR FAR
2	2' 0" 2' 0"	2' 0" 2' 0"	2' 0" 2' 0"	2' 0" 2' 0"	2' 0" 2' 0"	2' 0" 2' 0"	1' 11" 2' 1"	1' 11" 2' 1"	1' 11" 2' 1"
2 1/2	2' 6" 2' 6"	2' 6" 2' 6"	2' 6" 2' 6"	2' 6" 2' 6"	2' 5" 2' 7"	2' 5" 2' 7"	2' 5" 2' 7"	2' 5" 2' 8"	2' 4" 2' 8"
3	3' 0" 3' 0"	3' 0" 3' 0"	3' 0" 3' 0"	2' 11" 3' 1"	2' 11" 3' 1"	2' 11" 3' 1"	2' 11" 3' 2"	2' 10" 3' 2"	2' 9" 3' 3"
3 1/2	3' 6" 3' 6"	3' 6" 3' 6"	3' 5" 3' 7"	3' 5" 3' 7"	3' 5" 3' 7"	3' 5" 3' 8"	3' 4" 3' 8"	3' 3" 3' 9"	3' 2" 3' 11"
4	4' 0" 4' 0"	4' 0" 4' 1"	3' 11" 4' 1"	3' 11" 4' 1"	3' 11" 4' 1"	3' 10" 4' 2"	3' 9" 4' 3"	3' 8" 4' 4"	3' 7" 4' 6"
4 1/2	4' 6" 4' 6"	4' 5" 4' 7"	4' 5" 4' 7"	4' 5" 4' 7"	4' 4" 4' 8"	4' 4" 4' 9"	4' 3" 4' 10"	4' 1" 5' 0"	4' 0" 5' 2"
5	4' 11" 5' 1"	4' 11" 5' 1"	4' 11" 5' 1"	4' 10" 5' 2"	4' 10" 5' 2"	4' 9" 5' 3"	4' 8" 5' 5"	4' 6" 5' 7"	4' 4" 5' 10"
5 1/2	5' 5" 5' 7"	5' 5" 5' 7"	5' 5" 5' 7"	5' 4" 5' 8"	5' 3" 5' 9"	5' 2" 5' 10"	5' 1" 6' 0"	4' 11" 6' 3"	4' 9" 6' 6"
6	5' 11" 6' 1"	5' 11" 6' 1"	5' 10" 6' 2"	5' 10" 6' 2"	5' 9" 6' 3"	5' 8" 6' 5"	5' 6" 6' 7"	5' 4" 6' 10"	5' 1" 7' 3"

6 1/2	6' 5" 6' 7"	6' 5" 6' 7"	6' 4" 6' 8"	6' 3" 6' 9"	6' 2" 6' 10"	6' 1" 7' 0"	5' 11" 7' 2"	5' 9" 7' 6"	5' 6" 8' 0"
7	6' 11" 7' 1"	6' 10" 7' 2"	6' 10" 7' 2"	6' 9" 7' 3"	6' 8" 7' 5"	6' 6" 7' 7"	6' 4" 7' 10"	6' 1" 8' 3"	5' 10" 8' 10"
8	7' 11" 8' 1"	7' 10" 8' 2"	7' 9" 8' 3"	7' 8" 8' 4"	7' 7" 8' 6"	7' 4" 8' 9"	7' 2" 9' 1"	6' 10" 9' 8"	6' 6" 10' 5"
9	8' 10" 9' 2"	8' 9" 9' 3"	8' 8" 9' 4"	8' 7" 9' 5"	8' 5" 9' 8"	8' 3" 10' 0"	7' 11" 10' 5"	7' 7" 11' 2"	7' 1" 12' 3"
10	9' 10" 10' 2"	9' 9" 10' 3"	9' 8" 10' 5"	9' 6" 10' 7"	9' 4" 10' 10"	9' 0" 11' 2"	8' 9" 11' 9"	8' 3" 12' 9"	7' 9" 14' 2"
12	11' 9" 12' 3"	11' 7" 12' 5"	11' 6" 12' 7"	11' 3" 12' 10"	11' 0" 13' 2"	10' 7" 13' 9"	10' 2" 14' 7"	9' 6" 16' 2"	8' 10" 18' 8"
14	13' 8" 14' 5"	13' 6" 14' 7"	13' 4" 14' 9"	13' 0" 15' 2"	12' 8" 15' 8"	12' 2" 16' 6"	11' 7" 17' 8"	10' 9" 20' 1"	9' 11" 24' 0"
16	15' 6" 16' 6"	15' 4" 16' 9"	15' 1" 17' 0"	14' 9" 17' 6"	14' 3" 18' 3"	13' 8" 19' 4"	12' 11" 21' 0"	11' 11" 24' 6"	10' 10" 30' 7"
18	17' 5" 18' 8"	17' 2" 18' 11"	16' 10" 19' 4"	16' 5" 19' 11"	15' 10" 20' 10"	15' 1" 22' 4"	14' 2" 24' 7"	12' 11" 29' 7"	11' 8" 38' 11"
20	19' 3" 20' 9"	19' 0" 21' 2"	18' 7" 21' 8"	18' 0" 22' 5"	17' 4" 23' 7"	16' 5" 25' 7"	15' 5" 28' 6"	13' 11" 35' 5"	12' 6" 49' 9"
25	23' 10" 26' 3"	23' 5" 26' 10"	22' 10" 27' 8"	22' 0" 28' 11"	21' 0" 30' 11"	19' 8" 34' 4"	18' 2" 40' 0"	16' 2" 55' 0"	14' 3" 99' 10"
50	45' 8" 55' 4"	44' 0" 57' 11"	41' 11" 61' 10"	39' 3" 68' 10"	36' 2" 81' 1"	32' 4" 110' 7"	28' 6" 202' 8"	23' 10" INF	19' 11" INF

For circle of confusion = .0005 use depth data two columns left of chosen F-Stop.

85mm — ALL FORMATS DEPTH OF FIELD TABLE — CIRCLE OF CONFUSION=0.0010 inches

	f/1.4	f/2	f/2.8	f/4	f/5.6	f/8	f/11	f/16	f/22
Hyper. Dist.	666' 7"	466' 7"	333' 4"	233' 4"	166' 8"	116' 8"	84' 10"	58' 4"	42' 5"
FOCUS (feet)	NEAR FAR	NEAR FAR	NEAR FAR	NEAR FAR	NEAR FAR	NEAR FAR	NEAR FAR	NEAR FAR	NEAR FAR
2	2' 0" 2' 0"	2' 0" 2' 0"	2' 0" 2' 0"	2' 0" 2' 0"	2' 0" 2' 0"	2' 0" 2' 0"	2' 0" 2' 0"	1' 11" 2' 1"	1' 11" 2' 1"
2 1/2	2' 6" 2' 6"	2' 6" 2' 6"	2' 6" 2' 6"	2' 6" 2' 6"	2' 6" 2' 6"	2' 5" 2' 7"	2' 5" 2' 7"	2' 5" 2' 7"	2' 5" 2' 8"
3	3' 0" 3' 0"	3' 0" 3' 0"	3' 0" 3' 0"	3' 0" 3' 0"	2' 11" 3' 1"	2' 11" 3' 1"	2' 11" 3' 1"	2' 10" 3' 2"	2' 10" 3' 2"
3 1/2	3' 6" 3' 6"	3' 6" 3' 6"	3' 6" 3' 6"	3' 5" 3' 7"	3' 5" 3' 7"	3' 5" 3' 7"	3' 4" 3' 8"	3' 4" 3' 8"	3' 3" 3' 9"
4	4' 0" 4' 0"	4' 0" 4' 0"	3' 11" 4' 1"	3' 11" 4' 1"	3' 11" 4' 1"	3' 11" 4' 2"	3' 10" 4' 2"	3' 9" 4' 3"	3' 8" 4' 5"
4 1/2	4' 6" 4' 6"	4' 6" 4' 6"	4' 5" 4' 7"	4' 5" 4' 7"	4' 5" 4' 7"	4' 4" 4' 8"	4' 3" 4' 9"	4' 2" 4' 10"	4' 1" 5' 0"
5	5' 0" 5' 0"	4' 11" 5' 1"	4' 11" 5' 1"	4' 11" 5' 1"	4' 10" 5' 2"	4' 10" 5' 3"	4' 9" 5' 4"	4' 8" 5' 5"	4' 6" 5' 8"
5 1/2	5' 5" 5' 7"	5' 5" 5' 7"	5' 5" 5' 7"	5' 5" 5' 8"	5' 4" 5' 8"	5' 3" 5' 9"	5' 2" 5' 10"	5' 1" 6' 0"	4' 11" 6' 3"
6	5' 11" 6' 1"	5' 11" 6' 1"	5' 11" 6' 1"	5' 10" 6' 2"	5' 10" 6' 3"	5' 9" 6' 4"	5' 7" 6' 5"	5' 6" 6' 8"	5' 3" 6' 11"

6 1/2	6' 5" 6' 7"	6' 5" 6' 7"	6' 5" 6' 7"	6' 4" 6' 8"	6' 3" 6' 9"	6' 2" 6' 10"	6' 1" 7' 0"	5' 10" 7' 3"	5' 8" 7' 7"
7	6' 11" 7' 1"	6' 11" 7' 1"	6' 10" 7' 2"	6' 10" 7' 2"	6' 9" 7' 4"	6' 7" 7' 5"	6' 6" 7' 7"	6' 3" 7' 11"	6' 1" 8' 4"
8	7' 11" 8' 1"	7' 10" 8' 2"	7' 10" 8' 2"	7' 9" 8' 3"	7' 8" 8' 5"	7' 6" 8' 7"	7' 4" 8' 10"	7' 1" 9' 3"	6' 9" 9' 9"
9	8' 11" 9' 1"	8' 10" 9' 2"	8' 9" 9' 3"	8' 8" 9' 4"	8' 7" 9' 6"	8' 4" 9' 9"	8' 2" 10' 0"	7' 10" 10' 7"	7' 6" 11' 4"
10	9' 10" 10' 2"	9' 10" 10' 3"	9' 9" 10' 4"	9' 7" 10' 5"	9' 5" 10' 7"	9' 3" 10' 11"	9' 0" 11' 4"	8' 7" 12' 0"	8' 2" 13' 0"
12	11' 10" 12' 3"	11' 8" 12' 4"	11' 7" 12' 5"	11' 5" 12' 8"	11' 3" 12' 11"	10' 11" 13' 4"	10' 7" 13' 11"	10' 0" 15' 0"	9' 5" 16' 7"
14	13' 9" 14' 4"	13' 7" 14' 5"	13' 5" 14' 7"	13' 3" 14' 10"	12' 11" 15' 3"	12' 6" 15' 10"	12' 1" 16' 8"	11' 4" 18' 4"	10' 7" 20' 8"
16	15' 8" 16' 5"	15' 6" 16' 7"	15' 3" 16' 10"	15' 0" 17' 2"	14' 7" 17' 8"	14' 1" 18' 6"	13' 6" 19' 8"	12' 7" 21' 11"	11' 8" 25' 5"
18	17' 6" 18' 6"	17' 4" 18' 9"	17' 1" 19' 0"	16' 9" 19' 6"	16' 3" 20' 2"	15' 8" 21' 3"	14' 11" 22' 9"	13' 10" 25' 10"	12' 8" 30' 11"
20	19' 5" 20' 7"	19' 2" 20' 11"	18' 11" 21' 3"	18' 5" 21' 10"	17' 11" 22' 8"	17' 1" 24' 1"	16' 3" 26' 1"	14' 11" 30' 3"	13' 8" 37' 5"
25	24' 1" 26' 0"	23' 9" 26' 5"	23' 3" 27' 0"	22' 7" 28' 0"	21' 9" 29' 4"	20' 8" 31' 9"	19' 4" 35' 3"	17' 7" 43' 5"	15' 10" 59' 11"
50	46' 6" 54' 0"	45' 2" 56' 0"	43' 6" 58' 9"	41' 3" 63' 6"	38' 6" 71' 3"	35' 1" 87' 2"	31' 6" 120' 9"	27' 0" 338' 11"	23' 0" INF

For circle of confusion = .0005 use depth data two columns left of chosen F-Stop.

100mm — ALL FORMATS DEPTH OF FIELD TABLE — CIRCLE OF CONFUSION=0.0010 inches

	f/1.4	f/2	f/2.8	f/4	f/5.6	f/8	f/11	f/16	f/22
Hyper. Dist.	INF	645' 10"	461' 4"	322' 11"	230' 8"	161' 6"	117' 5"	80' 9"	58' 9"
FOCUS (feet)	NEAR FAR	NEAR FAR	NEAR FAR	NEAR FAR	NEAR FAR	NEAR FAR	NEAR FAR	NEAR FAR	NEAR FAR
2	2' 0" 2' 0"	2' 0" 2' 0"	2' 0" 2' 0"	2' 0" 2' 0"	2' 0" 2' 0"	2' 0" 2' 0"	2' 0" 2' 0"	2' 0" 2' 1"	1' 11" 2' 1"
2 ½	2' 6" 2' 6"	2' 6" 2' 6"	2' 6" 2' 6"	2' 6" 2' 6"	2' 6" 2' 6"	2' 6" 2' 6"	2' 5" 2' 7"	2' 5" 2' 7"	2' 5" 2' 7"
3	3' 0" 3' 0"	3' 0" 3' 0"	3' 0" 3' 0"	3' 0" 3' 0"	3' 0" 3' 0"	2' 11" 3' 1"	2' 11" 3' 1"	2' 11" 3' 1"	2' 10" 3' 2"
3 ½	3' 6" 3' 6"	3' 6" 3' 6"	3' 6" 3' 6"	3' 6" 3' 6"	3' 5" 3' 7"	3' 5" 3' 7"	3' 5" 3' 7"	3' 4" 3' 8"	3' 4" 3' 8"
4	4' 0" 4' 0"	4' 0" 4' 0"	4' 0" 4' 0"	3' 11" 4' 1"	3' 11" 4' 1"	3' 11" 4' 1"	3' 11" 4' 2"	3' 10" 4' 2"	3' 9" 4' 3"
4 ½	4' 6" 4' 6"	4' 6" 4' 6"	4' 6" 4' 6"	4' 5" 4' 7"	4' 5" 4' 7"	4' 5" 4' 7"	4' 4" 4' 8"	4' 3" 4' 9"	4' 2" 4' 10"
5	5' 0" 5' 0"	5' 0" 5' 0"	4' 11" 5' 1"	4' 11" 5' 1"	4' 11" 5' 1"	4' 10" 5' 2"	4' 10" 5' 2"	4' 9" 5' 4"	4' 8" 5' 5"
5 ½	5' 6" 5' 6"	5' 5" 5' 7"	5' 5" 5' 7"	5' 5" 5' 7"	5' 5" 5' 8"	5' 4" 5' 8"	5' 3" 5' 9"	5' 2" 5' 11"	5' 1" 6' 0"
6	6' 0" 6' 0"	5' 11" 6' 1"	5' 11" 6' 1"	5' 11" 6' 1"	5' 10" 6' 2"	5' 10" 6' 3"	5' 9" 6' 4"	5' 7" 6' 5"	5' 6" 6' 8"

6 1/2	6' 5" 6' 7"	6' 5" 6' 7"	6' 5" 6' 7"	6' 5" 6' 8"	6' 4" 6' 8"	6' 3" 6' 9"	6' 2" 6' 10"	6' 0" 7' 0"	5' 11" 7' 3"
7	6' 11" 7' 1"	6' 11" 7' 1"	6' 11" 7' 1"	6' 10" 7' 2"	6' 10" 7' 3"	6' 9" 7' 4"	6' 7" 7' 5"	6' 6" 7' 8"	6' 3" 7' 11"
8	7' 11" 8' 1"	7' 11" 8' 1"	7' 10" 8' 2"	7' 10" 8' 2"	7' 9" 8' 3"	7' 8" 8' 5"	7' 6" 8' 7"	7' 4" 8' 10"	7' 1" 9' 2"
9	8' 11" 9' 1"	8' 11" 9' 1"	8' 10" 9' 2"	8' 9" 9' 3"	8' 8" 9' 4"	8' 6" 9' 6"	8' 5" 9' 9"	8' 2" 10' 1"	7' 10" 10' 7"
10	9' 11" 10' 1"	9' 10" 10' 2"	9' 10" 10' 3"	9' 9" 10' 4"	9' 7" 10' 5"	9' 5" 10' 8"	9' 3" 10' 11"	8' 11" 11' 4"	8' 7" 12' 0"
12	11' 10" 12' 2"	11' 9" 12' 3"	11' 8" 12' 4"	11' 7" 12' 5"	11' 5" 12' 8"	11' 2" 12' 11"	10' 11" 13' 4"	10' 6" 14' 0"	10' 0" 15' 0"
14	13' 10" 14' 3"	13' 9" 14' 4"	13' 7" 14' 5"	13' 5" 14' 7"	13' 3" 14' 11"	12' 11" 15' 4"	12' 6" 15' 10"	12' 0" 16' 10"	11' 4" 18' 3"
16	15' 9" 16' 3"	15' 7" 16' 5"	15' 6" 16' 7"	15' 3" 16' 10"	15' 0" 17' 2"	14' 7" 17' 9"	14' 1" 18' 6"	13' 5" 19' 10"	12' 8" 21' 10"
18	17' 8" 18' 4"	17' 6" 18' 6"	17' 4" 18' 9"	17' 1" 19' 1"	16' 9" 19' 6"	16' 3" 20' 3"	15' 8" 21' 2"	14' 9" 23' 1"	13' 10" 25' 9"
20	19' 7" 20' 5"	19' 5" 20' 8"	19' 2" 20' 11"	18' 10" 21' 4"	18' 5" 21' 10"	17' 10" 22' 9"	17' 2" 24' 0"	16' 1" 26' 5"	15' 0" 30' 1"
25	24' 4" 25' 8"	24' 1" 26' 0"	23' 9" 26' 5"	23' 3" 27' 1"	22' 7" 28' 0"	21' 8" 29' 6"	20' 8" 31' 8"	19' 2" 36' 0"	17' 7" 43' 1"
50	47' 5" 52' 10"	46' 5" 54' 2"	45' 2" 56' 0"	43' 4" 59' 1"	41' 2" 63' 9"	38' 3" 72' 3"	35' 2" 86' 8"	30' 11" 130' 0"	27' 1" 324' 9"

For circle of confusion = .0005 use depth data two columns left of chosen F-Stop.

105mm

ALL FORMATS DEPTH OF FIELD TABLE **CIRCLE OF CONFUSION=0.0010 inches**

	f/1.4	f/2	f/2.8	f/4	f/5.6	f/8	f/11	f/16	f/22
Hyper. Dist.	INF	712' 0"	508' 7"	356' 0"	254' 4"	178' 0"	129' 6"	89' 0"	64' 9"
FOCUS (feet)	NEAR FAR	NEAR FAR	NEAR FAR	NEAR FAR	NEAR FAR	NEAR FAR	NEAR FAR	NEAR FAR	NEAR FAR
5	5' 0" 5' 0"	5' 0" 5' 0"	4' 11" 5' 1"	4' 11" 5' 1"	4' 11" 5' 1"	4' 10" 5' 2"	4' 10" 5' 2"	4' 9" 5' 3"	4' 8" 5' 5"
5 ½	5' 6" 5' 6"	5' 6" 5' 6"	5' 5" 5' 7"	5' 5" 5' 7"	5' 5" 5' 7"	5' 4" 5' 8"	5' 3" 5' 9"	5' 2" 5' 10"	5' 1" 6' 0"
6	6' 0" 6' 0"	5' 11" 6' 1"	5' 11" 6' 1"	5' 11" 6' 1"	5' 10" 6' 2"	5' 10" 6' 2"	5' 9" 6' 3"	5' 8" 6' 5"	5' 6" 6' 7"
6 ½	6' 6" 6' 6"	6' 5" 6' 7"	6' 5" 6' 7"	6' 5" 6' 7"	6' 4" 6' 8"	6' 3" 6' 9"	6' 2" 6' 10"	6' 1" 7' 0"	5' 11" 7' 2"
7	6' 11" 7' 1"	6' 11" 7' 1"	6' 11" 7' 1"	6' 10" 7' 2"	6' 10" 7' 2"	6' 9" 7' 3"	6' 8" 7' 5"	6' 6" 7' 7"	6' 4" 7' 10"
8	7' 11" 8' 1"	7' 11" 8' 1"	7' 11" 8' 1"	7' 10" 8' 2"	7' 9" 8' 3"	7' 8" 8' 4"	7' 7" 8' 6"	7' 4" 8' 9"	7' 2" 9' 1"
9	8' 11" 9' 1"	8' 11" 9' 1"	8' 10" 9' 2"	8' 9" 9' 3"	8' 8" 9' 4"	8' 7" 9' 6"	8' 5" 9' 8"	8' 2" 10' 0"	7' 11" 10' 5"
10	9' 11" 10' 1"	9' 10" 10' 2"	9' 10" 10' 2"	9' 9" 10' 3"	9' 8" 10' 5"	9' 6" 10' 7"	9' 4" 10' 10"	9' 0" 11' 3"	8' 8" 11' 9"
12	11' 10" 12' 2"	11' 10" 12' 2"	11' 9" 12' 3"	11' 7" 12' 5"	11' 6" 12' 7"	11' 3" 12' 10"	11' 0" 13' 2"	10' 7" 13' 10"	10' 2" 14' 8"

14	13' 10" 14' 2"	13' 9" 14' 3"	13' 8" 14' 5"	13' 6" 14' 7"	13' 3" 14' 10"	13' 0" 15' 2"	12' 8" 15' 8"	12' 2" 16' 6"	11' 7" 17' 9"
16	15' 9" 16' 3"	15' 8" 16' 4"	15' 6" 16' 6"	15' 4" 16' 9"	15' 1" 17' 1"	14' 8" 17' 7"	14' 3" 18' 2"	13' 7" 19' 5"	12' 11" 21' 1"
18	17' 8" 18' 4"	17' 7" 18' 5"	17' 5" 18' 8"	17' 2" 18' 11"	16' 10" 19' 4"	16' 5" 20' 0"	15' 10" 20' 10"	15' 0" 22' 5"	14' 2" 24' 9"
20	19' 7" 20' 5"	19' 6" 20' 7"	19' 3" 20' 10"	18' 11" 21' 2"	18' 7" 21' 8"	18' 0" 22' 6"	17' 4" 23' 7"	16' 5" 25' 8"	15' 4" 28' 9"
25	24' 5" 25' 7"	24' 2" 25' 11"	23' 10" 26' 3"	23' 5" 26' 10"	22' 9" 27' 8"	22' 0" 29' 0"	21' 0" 30' 11"	19' 7" 34' 7"	18' 1" 40' 5"
50	47' 8" 52' 7"	46' 9" 53' 9"	45' 7" 55' 5"	43' 11" 58' 1"	41' 10" 62' 2"	39' 1" 69' 4"	36' 2" 81' 1"	32' 1" 113' 1"	28' 4" 214' 8"
75	69' 10" 80' 11"	67' 11" 83' 9"	65' 5" 87' 11"	62' 0" 94' 11"	58' 0" 106' 2"	52' 10" 129' 2"	47' 7" 177' 2"	40' 9" 465' 3"	34' 10" INF
100	91' 1" 110' 10"	87' 9" 116' 3"	83' 7" 124' 4"	78' 2" 138' 10"	71' 10" 164' 5"	64' 1" 227' 2"	56' 6" 434' 4"	47' 2" INF	39' 5" INF
125	111' 4" 142' 5"	106' 5" 151' 6"	100' 5" 165' 7"	92' 7" 192' 4"	83' 11" 245' 2"	73' 6" 417' 1"	63' 8" INF	52' 1" INF	42' 9" INF
150	130' 9" 175' 11"	123' 11" 189' 11"	115' 11" 212' 6"	105' 7" 258' 9"	94' 5" 364' 6"	81' 6" 941' 9"	69' 7" INF	55' 11" INF	45' 3" INF
175	149' 4" 211' 3"	140' 6" 231' 11"	130' 3" 266' 6"	117' 5" 343' 6"	103' 9" 558' 9"	88' 4" INF	74' 6" INF	59' 1" INF	47' 4" INF
200	167' 2" 248' 10"	156' 2" 277' 11"	143' 7" 329' 3"	128' 2" 455' 5"	112' 0" 930' 9"	94' 3" INF	78' 8" INF	61' 8" INF	49' 0" INF

For circle of confusion = .0005 use depth data two columns left of chosen F-Stop.

135mm — ALL FORMATS DEPTH OF FIELD TABLE — CIRCLE OF CONFUSION=0.0010 inches

	f/1.4	f/2	f/2.8	f/4	f/5.6	f/8	f/11	f/16	f/22
Hyper. DIST.	INF	INF	INF	588' 6"	420' 4"	294' 3"	214' 0"	147' 2"	107' 0"
FOCUS (FEET)	NEAR FAR	NEAR FAR	NEAR FAR	NEAR FAR	NEAR FAR	NEAR FAR	NEAR FAR	NEAR FAR	NEAR FAR
5	5' 0" 5' 0"	5' 0" 5' 0"	5' 0" 5' 0"	5' 0" 5' 0"	4' 11" 5' 1"	4' 11" 5' 1"	4' 11" 5' 1"	4' 10" 5' 2"	4' 10" 5' 3"
5 1/2	5' 6" 5' 6"	5' 6" 5' 6"	5' 6" 5' 6"	5' 5" 5' 7"	5' 5" 5' 7"	5' 5" 5' 7"	5' 4" 5' 8"	5' 4" 5' 8"	5' 3" 5' 9"
6	6' 0" 6' 0"	6' 0" 6' 0"	6' 0" 6' 0"	5' 11" 6' 1"	5' 11" 6' 1"	5' 11" 6' 1"	5' 10" 6' 2"	5' 9" 6' 3"	5' 8" 6' 4"
6 1/2	6' 6" 6' 6"	6' 6" 6' 6"	6' 5" 6' 7"	6' 5" 6' 7"	6' 5" 6' 7"	6' 4" 6' 8"	6' 4" 6' 8"	6' 3" 6' 9"	6' 2" 6' 11"
7	7' 0" 7' 0"	7' 0" 7' 0"	6' 11" 7' 1"	6' 11" 7' 1"	6' 11" 7' 1"	6' 10" 7' 2"	6' 10" 7' 3"	6' 8" 7' 4"	6' 7" 7' 5"
8	8' 0" 8' 0"	7' 11" 8' 1"	7' 11" 8' 1"	7' 11" 8' 1"	7' 10" 8' 2"	7' 10" 8' 3"	7' 9" 8' 4"	7' 7" 8' 5"	7' 6" 8' 7"
9	8' 11" 9' 1"	8' 11" 9' 1"	8' 11" 9' 1"	8' 10" 9' 2"	8' 10" 9' 2"	8' 9" 9' 3"	8' 8" 9' 4"	8' 6" 9' 7"	8' 4" 9' 9"
10	9' 11" 10' 1"	9' 11" 10' 1"	9' 11" 10' 1"	9' 10" 10' 2"	9' 9" 10' 3"	9' 8" 10' 4"	9' 7" 10' 6"	9' 5" 10' 8"	9' 2" 11' 0"
12	11' 11" 12' 1"	11' 11" 12' 1"	11' 10" 12' 2"	11' 9" 12' 3"	11' 8" 12' 4"	11' 7" 12' 6"	11' 5" 12' 8"	11' 2" 13' 0"	10' 10" 13' 5"

14	13' 11" 14' 1"	13' 10" 14' 2"	13' 9" 14' 3"	13' 8" 14' 4"	13' 7" 14' 6"	13' 5" 14' 8"	13' 2" 14' 11"	12' 10" 15' 5"	12' 5" 16' 0"
16	15' 10" 16' 2"	15' 9" 16' 3"	15' 9" 16' 4"	15' 7" 16' 5"	15' 5" 16' 7"	15' 2" 16' 11"	14' 11" 17' 3"	14' 6" 17' 11"	14' 0" 18' 9"
18	17' 10" 18' 2"	17' 9" 18' 3"	17' 8" 18' 5"	17' 6" 18' 7"	17' 3" 18' 9"	17' 0" 19' 2"	16' 8" 19' 7"	16' 1" 20' 5"	15' 6" 21' 6"
20	19' 9" 20' 3"	19' 8" 20' 4"	19' 7" 20' 6"	19' 4" 20' 8"	19' 1" 21' 0"	18' 9" 21' 5"	18' 4" 22' 0"	17' 8" 23' 1"	16' 11" 24' 6"
25	24' 8" 25' 4"	24' 6" 25' 6"	24' 3" 25' 9"	24' 0" 26' 1"	23' 7" 26' 7"	23' 1" 27' 3"	22' 5" 28' 3"	21' 5" 30' 0"	20' 4" 32' 5"
50	48' 7" 51' 6"	48' 0" 52' 2"	47' 3" 53' 2"	46' 1" 54' 7"	44' 9" 56' 8"	42' 10" 60' 2"	40' 7" 65' 1"	37' 5" 75' 5"	34' 2" 93' 2"
75	71' 10" 78' 6"	70' 6" 80' 1"	68' 11" 82' 4"	66' 7" 85' 11"	63' 8" 91' 2"	59' 10" 100' 5"	55' 7" 115' 1"	49' 9" 152' 1"	44' 2" 247' 4"
100	94' 5" 106' 4"	92' 2" 109' 3"	89' 5" 113' 5"	85' 6" 120' 4"	80' 10" 131' 0"	74' 9" 151' 2"	68' 3" 187' 0"	59' 8" 309' 3"	51' 10" INF
125	116' 5" 135' 0"	113' 0" 139' 10"	108' 10" 146' 9"	103' 2" 158' 7"	96' 5" 177' 8"	87' 10" 216' 9"	79' 0" 299' 1"	67' 8" 814' 9"	57' 9" INF
150	137' 9" 164' 8"	133' 1" 171' 10"	127' 4" 182' 5"	119' 7" 201' 1"	110' 8" 232' 10"	99' 5" 305' 0"	88' 4" 498' 1"	74' 5" INF	62' 7" INF
175	158' 6" 195' 3"	152' 5" 205' 6"	144' 11" 220' 10"	135' 0" 248' 10"	123' 8" 299' 3"	109' 10" 430' 2"	96' 5" 949' 4"	80' 0" INF	66' 6" INF
200	178' 9" 226' 11"	171' 0" 240' 10"	161' 8" 262' 3"	149' 4" 302' 7"	135' 7" 380' 9"	119' 2" 621' 5"	103' 6" INF	84' 11" INF	69' 10" INF

For circle of confusion = .0005 use depth data two columns left of chosen F-Stop.

150mm ALL FORMATS DEPTH OF FIELD TABLE CIRCLE OF CONFUSION=0.0010 inches

	f/1.4	f/2	f/2.8	f/4	f/5.6	f/8	f/11	f/16	f/22
Hyper. Dist.	INF	INF	726' 7"	519' 0"	363' 3"	264' 2"	181' 8"	132' 1"	90' 10"
FOCUS (feet)	NEAR FAR	NEAR FAR	NEAR FAR	NEAR FAR	NEAR FAR	NEAR FAR	NEAR FAR	NEAR FAR	NEAR FAR
5	5' 0" 5' 0"	5' 0" 5' 0"	5' 0" 5' 0"	4' 11" 5' 1"	4' 11" 5' 1"	4' 11" 5' 1"	4' 11" 5' 2"	4' 10" 5' 2"	4' 9" 5' 3"
5 1/2	5' 6" 5' 6"	5' 6" 5' 6"	5' 6" 5' 6"	5' 5" 5' 7"	5' 5" 5' 7"	5' 5" 5' 7"	5' 4" 5' 8"	5' 4" 5' 9"	5' 3" 5' 10"
6	6' 0" 6' 0"	6' 0" 6' 0"	5' 11" 6' 1"	5' 11" 6' 1"	5' 11" 6' 1"	5' 11" 6' 2"	5' 10" 6' 2"	5' 9" 6' 3"	5' 8" 6' 5"
6 1/2	6' 6" 6' 6"	6' 6" 6' 6"	6' 5" 6' 7"	6' 5" 6' 7"	6' 5" 6' 7"	6' 4" 6' 8"	6' 4" 6' 9"	6' 3" 6' 10"	6' 1" 7' 0"
7	7' 0" 7' 0"	6' 11" 7' 1"	6' 11" 7' 1"	6' 11" 7' 1"	6' 11" 7' 2"	6' 10" 7' 2"	6' 9" 7' 3"	6' 8" 7' 4"	6' 6" 7' 6"
8	8' 0" 8' 0"	7' 11" 8' 1"	7' 11" 8' 1"	7' 11" 8' 1"	7' 10" 8' 2"	7' 9" 8' 3"	7' 8" 8' 4"	7' 7" 8' 6"	7' 5" 8' 9"
9	8' 11" 9' 1"	8' 11" 9' 1"	8' 11" 9' 1"	8' 10" 9' 2"	8' 10" 9' 3"	8' 9" 9' 4"	8' 7" 9' 5"	8' 5" 9' 7"	8' 3" 9' 11"
10	9' 11" 10' 1"	9' 11" 10' 1"	9' 10" 10' 2"	9' 10" 10' 2"	9' 9" 10' 3"	9' 8" 10' 4"	9' 6" 10' 7"	9' 4" 10' 9"	9' 1" 11' 2"
12	11' 11" 12' 1"	11' 10" 12' 2"	11' 10" 12' 2"	11' 9" 12' 3"	11' 8" 12' 5"	11' 6" 12' 7"	11' 3" 12' 10"	11' 0" 13' 2"	10' 8" 13' 9"

14	13' 10" 14' 2"	13' 10" 14' 2"	13' 9" 14' 3"	13' 8" 14' 4"	13' 6" 14' 6"	13' 4" 14' 9"	13' 0" 15' 1"	12' 8" 15' 7"	12' 2" 16' 5"
16	15' 10" 16' 2"	15' 9" 16' 3"	15' 8" 16' 4"	15' 6" 16' 6"	15' 4" 16' 9"	15' 1" 17' 0"	14' 9" 17' 6"	14' 4" 18' 2"	13' 8" 19' 4"
18	17' 9" 18' 3"	17' 8" 18' 4"	17' 7" 18' 5"	17' 5" 18' 8"	17' 2" 18' 11"	16' 11" 19' 3"	16' 5" 19' 11"	15' 11" 20' 9"	15' 1" 22' 4"
20	19' 9" 20' 3"	19' 8" 20' 5"	19' 6" 20' 7"	19' 3" 20' 9"	19' 0" 21' 2"	18' 7" 21' 7"	18' 1" 22' 5"	17' 5" 23' 6"	16' 6" 25' 6"
25	24' 7" 25' 5"	24' 5" 25' 7"	24' 2" 25' 10"	23' 10" 26' 3"	23' 5" 26' 10"	22' 11" 27' 7"	22' 0" 28' 11"	21' 1" 30' 8"	19' 8" 34' 3"
50	48' 4" 51' 9"	47' 9" 52' 6"	46' 10" 53' 8"	45' 8" 55' 3"	44' 0" 57' 11"	42' 1" 61' 6"	39' 3" 68' 9"	36' 4" 80' 0"	32' 4" 109' 11"
75	71' 4" 79' 1"	70' 0" 80' 10"	68' 0" 83' 7"	65' 7" 87' 7"	62' 3" 94' 4"	58' 6" 104' 5"	53' 2" 127' 2"	47' 11" 172' 0"	41' 2" 417' 7"
100	93' 7" 107' 4"	91' 3" 110' 7"	87' 11" 115' 10"	83' 11" 123' 9"	78' 6" 137' 9"	72' 8" 160' 5"	64' 7" 221' 2"	57' 0" 405' 3"	47' 9" INF
125	115' 2" 136' 9"	111' 7" 142' 0"	106' 9" 150' 10"	100' 10" 164' 5"	93' 1" 190' 2"	85' 0" 236' 5"	74' 2" 397' 5"	64' 4" INF	52' 9" INF
150	136' 0" 167' 2"	131' 1" 175' 3"	124' 5" 188' 10"	116' 5" 210' 8"	106' 3" 254' 11"	95' 10" 345' 6"	82' 3" 847' 11"	70' 4" INF	56' 8" INF
175	156' 3" 198' 11"	149' 10" 210' 4"	141' 1" 230' 4"	131' 0" 263' 8"	118' 3" 336' 9"	105' 5" 515' 6"	89' 3" INF	75' 5" INF	59' 11" INF
200	175' 10" 231' 10"	167' 9" 247' 7"	156' 11" 275' 8"	144' 6" 324' 11"	129' 1" 443' 8"	113' 11" 816' 9"	95' 4" INF	79' 8" INF	62' 7" INF

For circle of confusion = .0005 use depth data two columns left of chosen F-Stop.

200mm

ALL FORMATS DEPTH OF FIELD TABLE — CIRCLE OF CONFUSION=0.0010 inches

	f/1.4	f/2	f/2.8	f/4	f/5.6	f/8	f/11	f/16	f/22
Hyper. Dist.	INF	INF	INF	INF	645' 10"	469' 8"	322' 11"	234' 10"	161' 6"
FOCUS (feet)	NEAR FAR	NEAR FAR	NEAR FAR	NEAR FAR	NEAR FAR	NEAR FAR	NEAR FAR	NEAR FAR	NEAR FAR
5	5' 0" 5' 0"	5' 0" 5' 0"	5' 0" 5' 0"	5' 0" 5' 0"	5' 0" 5' 0"	4' 11" 5' 1"	4' 11" 5' 1"	4' 11" 5' 1"	4' 10" 5' 2"
5 1/2	5' 6" 5' 6"	5' 6" 5' 6"	5' 6" 5' 6"	5' 6" 5' 6"	5' 6" 5' 6"	5' 5" 5' 7"	5' 5" 5' 7"	5' 5" 5' 7"	5' 4" 5' 8"
6	6' 0" 6' 0"	6' 0" 6' 0"	6' 0" 6' 0"	6' 0" 6' 0"	5' 11" 6' 1"	5' 11" 6' 1"	5' 11" 6' 1"	5' 10" 6' 2"	5' 10" 6' 2"
6 1/2	6' 6" 6' 6"	6' 6" 6' 6"	6' 6" 6' 6"	6' 6" 6' 6"	6' 5" 6' 7"	6' 5" 6' 7"	6' 5" 6' 7"	6' 4" 6' 8"	6' 3" 6' 9"
7	7' 0" 7' 0"	7' 0" 7' 0"	7' 0" 7' 0"	6' 11" 7' 1"	6' 11" 7' 1"	6' 11" 7' 1"	6' 10" 7' 2"	6' 10" 7' 2"	6' 9" 7' 3"
8	8' 0" 8' 0"	8' 0" 8' 0"	7' 11" 8' 1"	7' 11" 8' 1"	7' 11" 8' 1"	7' 11" 8' 2"	7' 10" 8' 2"	7' 9" 8' 3"	7' 8" 8' 5"
9	9' 0" 9' 0"	9' 0" 9' 0"	8' 11" 9' 1"	8' 11" 9' 1"	8' 11" 9' 1"	8' 10" 9' 2"	8' 9" 9' 3"	8' 8" 9' 4"	8' 7" 9' 6"
10	10' 0" 10' 0"	9' 11" 10' 1"	9' 11" 10' 1"	9' 11" 10' 1"	9' 10" 10' 2"	9' 10" 10' 2"	9' 9" 10' 4"	9' 7" 10' 5"	9' 5" 10' 7"
12	11' 11" 12' 1"	11' 11" 12' 1"	11' 11" 12' 1"	11' 10" 12' 2"	11' 10" 12' 3"	11' 9" 12' 4"	11' 7" 12' 5"	11' 5" 12' 7"	11' 3" 12' 11"

14	13' 11" 14' 1"	13' 11" 14' 1"	13' 10" 14' 2"	13' 10" 14' 2"	13' 9" 14' 4"	13' 7" 14' 5"	13' 5" 14' 7"	13' 3" 14' 10"	12' 11" 15' 3"
16	15' 11" 16' 1"	15' 10" 16' 2"	15' 10" 16' 2"	15' 9" 16' 3"	15' 8" 16' 5"	15' 6" 16' 6"	15' 3" 16' 10"	15' 0" 17' 1"	14' 7" 17' 8"
18	17' 11" 18' 1"	17' 10" 18' 2"	17' 9" 18' 3"	17' 8" 18' 4"	17' 6" 18' 6"	17' 4" 18' 8"	17' 1" 19' 0"	16' 9" 19' 5"	16' 3" 20' 2"
20	19' 10" 20' 2"	19' 10" 20' 3"	19' 8" 20' 4"	19' 7" 20' 5"	19' 5" 20' 7"	19' 3" 20' 10"	18' 10" 21' 3"	18' 6" 21' 10"	17' 10" 22' 9"
25	24' 9" 25' 3"	24' 8" 25' 4"	24' 6" 25' 6"	24' 4" 25' 8"	24' 1" 26' 0"	23' 9" 26' 4"	23' 3" 27' 0"	22' 8" 27' 11"	21' 9" 29' 5"
50	49' 1" 51' 0"	48' 8" 51' 4"	48' 2" 52' 0"	47' 6" 52' 10"	46' 5" 54' 2"	45' 3" 55' 10"	43' 4" 59' 0"	41' 4" 63' 4"	38' 4" 72' 0"
75	72' 11" 77' 3"	72' 1" 78' 2"	70' 11" 79' 7"	69' 5" 81' 7"	67' 3" 84' 9"	64' 9" 89' 1"	61' 0" 97' 5"	57' 0" 109' 9"	51' 4" 139' 0"
100	96' 4" 104' 0"	94' 11" 105' 8"	92' 10" 108' 4"	90' 3" 112' 1"	86' 8" 118' 2"	82' 7" 126' 10"	76' 6" 144' 5"	70' 3" 173' 4"	61' 11" 259' 11"
125	119' 3" 131' 4"	117' 1" 134' 0"	114' 0" 138' 4"	110' 2" 144' 6"	104' 10" 154' 10"	98' 10" 170' 0"	90' 3" 203' 3"	81' 9" 265' 8"	70' 7" 543' 9"
150	141' 10" 159' 2"	138' 9" 163' 3"	134' 5" 169' 7"	129' 1" 179' 0"	121' 10" 195' 1"	113' 10" 219' 11"	102' 7" 279' 1"	91' 8" 412' 0"	77' 11" INF
175	163' 11" 187' 8"	159' 11" 193' 3"	154' 2" 202' 4"	147' 2" 215' 9"	137' 10" 239' 9"	127' 8" 278' 4"	113' 8" 380' 4"	100' 5" 679' 3"	84' 2" INF
200	185' 8" 216' 9"	180' 6" 224' 3"	173' 3" 236' 6"	164' 6" 255' 1"	152' 10" 289' 4"	140' 5" 347' 6"	123' 8" 522' 8"	108' 2" 1322' 11"	89' 6" INF

For circle of confusion = .0005 use depth data two columns left of chosen F-Stop.

300mm

ALL FORMATS DEPTH OF FIELD TABLE — CIRCLE OF CONFUSION=0.0010 inches

	f/2	f/2.8	f/4	f/5.6	f/8	f/11	f/16	f/22	f/32
Hyper. Dist.	INF	INF	INF	INF	INF	INF	INF	INF	363' 3"
FOCUS (feet)	NEAR FAR	NEAR FAR	NEAR FAR	NEAR FAR	NEAR FAR	NEAR FAR	NEAR FAR	NEAR FAR	NEAR FAR
10	10' 0" 10' 0"	10' 0" 10' 0"	10' 0" 10' 0"	9' 11" 10' 1"	9' 11" 10' 1"	9' 11" 10' 1"	9' 11" 10' 2"	9' 10" 10' 2"	9' 9" 10' 3"
12	12' 0" 12' 0"	12' 0" 12' 0"	11' 11" 12' 1"	11' 11" 12' 1"	11' 11" 12' 1"	11' 11" 12' 2"	11' 10" 12' 2"	11' 9" 12' 3"	11' 8" 12' 5"
14	14' 0" 14' 0"	13' 11" 14' 1"	13' 11" 14' 1"	13' 11" 14' 1"	13' 11" 14' 2"	13' 10" 14' 2"	13' 9" 14' 3"	13' 8" 14' 4"	13' 6" 14' 6"
16	16' 0" 16' 0"	15' 11" 16' 1"	15' 11" 16' 1"	15' 11" 16' 1"	15' 10" 16' 2"	15' 9" 16' 3"	15' 8" 16' 4"	15' 7" 16' 6"	15' 4" 16' 8"
18	17' 11" 18' 1"	17' 11" 18' 1"	17' 11" 18' 1"	17' 10" 18' 2"	17' 9" 18' 3"	17' 9" 18' 4"	17' 7" 18' 5"	17' 5" 18' 7"	17' 2" 18' 11"
20	19' 11" 20' 1"	19' 11" 20' 1"	19' 10" 20' 2"	19' 10" 20' 2"	19' 9" 20' 3"	19' 8" 20' 4"	19' 6" 20' 6"	19' 4" 20' 9"	19' 0" 21' 1"
25	24' 11" 25' 1"	24' 10" 25' 2"	24' 10" 25' 2"	24' 9" 25' 4"	24' 7" 25' 5"	24' 5" 25' 7"	24' 2" 25' 10"	23' 11" 26' 2"	23' 5" 26' 9"
50	49' 7" 50' 5"	49' 5" 50' 7"	49' 2" 50' 10"	48' 10" 51' 3"	48' 4" 51' 9"	47' 9" 52' 5"	46' 10" 53' 7"	45' 9" 55' 1"	44' 1" 57' 10"
75	74' 1" 76' 0"	73' 8" 76' 4"	73' 2" 77' 0"	72' 5" 77' 9"	71' 4" 79' 0"	70' 1" 80' 8"	68' 1" 83' 6"	65' 9" 87' 3"	62' 4" 94' 2"

100	98' 4" 101' 9"	97' 8" 102' 5"	96' 8" 103' 6"	95' 5" 105' 0"	93' 7" 107' 4"	91' 5" 110' 4"	88' 0" 115' 9"	84' 3" 123' 1"	78' 7" 137' 6"
125	122' 5" 127' 9"	121' 4" 128' 10"	119' 11" 130' 7"	117' 11" 132' 11"	115' 2" 136' 8"	111' 10" 141' 7"	106' 9" 150' 9"	101' 3" 163' 4"	93' 2" 189' 9"
150	146' 3" 153' 11"	144' 10" 155' 7"	142' 8" 158' 1"	139' 11" 161' 7"	136' 1" 167' 2"	131' 6" 174' 7"	124' 6" 188' 8"	117' 0" 208' 11"	106' 4" 254' 4"
175	169' 11" 180' 5"	168' 0" 182' 8"	165' 1" 186' 2"	161' 6" 191' 0"	156' 3" 198' 10"	150' 3" 209' 6"	141' 2" 230' 1"	131' 8" 260' 11"	118' 4" 335' 11"
200	193' 5" 207' 1"	190' 10" 210' 1"	187' 2" 214' 8"	182' 6" 221' 2"	175' 11" 231' 9"	168' 4" 246' 5"	157' 0" 275' 5"	145' 3" 320' 10"	129' 3" 442' 4"
250	239' 9" 261' 2"	235' 10" 265' 11"	230' 3" 273' 5"	223' 3" 284' 1"	213' 5" 301' 8"	202' 4" 327' 1"	186' 2" 380' 4"	169' 11" 472' 10"	148' 4" 794' 10"
300	285' 4" 316' 3"	279' 10" 323' 3"	272' 0" 334' 5"	262' 3" 350' 6"	248' 10" 377' 9"	233' 10" 418' 4"	212' 6" 509' 10"	191' 7" 691' 1"	164' 7" 1695' 10"
350	330' 2" 372' 4"	322' 10" 382' 1"	312' 6" 397' 9"	299' 7" 420' 9"	282' 3" 460' 8"	263' 1" 522' 7"	236' 5" 673' 7"" 1"	210' 9" 030' 11"	178' 6" INF
400	374' 4" 429' 6"	364' 11" 442' 6"	351' 9" 463' 8"	335' 6" 495' 2"	313' 10" 551' 5"	290' 4" 642' 8"	258' 2" 887' 3"" 1"	227' 11" 633' 6"	190' 7" INF

For circle of confusion = .0005 use depth data two columns left of chosen F-Stop.

400mm — ALL FORMATS DEPTH OF FIELD TABLE — CIRCLE OF CONFUSION=0.0010 inches

	f/2	f/2.8	f/4	f/5.6	f/8	f/11	f/16	f/22	f/32
Hyper. Dist.	INF	INF	INF	INF	INF	INF	INF	INF	INF
FOCUS (feet)	NEAR FAR	NEAR FAR	NEAR FAR	NEAR FAR	NEAR FAR	NEAR FAR	NEAR FAR	NEAR FAR	NEAR FAR
10	10' 0" 10' 0"	10' 0" 10' 0"	10' 0" 10' 0"	10' 0" 10' 0"	10' 0" 10' 0"	9' 11" 10' 1"	9' 11" 10' 1"	9' 11" 10' 1"	9' 10" 10' 2"
12	12' 0" 12' 0"	12' 0" 12' 0"	12' 0" 12' 0"	12' 0" 12' 0"	11' 11" 12' 1"	11' 11" 12' 1"	11' 11" 12' 1"	11' 10" 12' 2"	11' 10" 12' 2"
14	14' 0" 14' 0"	14' 0" 14' 0"	14' 0" 14' 0"	13' 11" 14' 1"	13' 11" 14' 1"	13' 11" 14' 1"	13' 10" 14' 2"	13' 10" 14' 2"	13' 9" 14' 3"
16	16' 0" 16' 0"	16' 0" 16' 0"	15' 11" 16' 1"	15' 11" 16' 1"	15' 11" 16' 1"	15' 11" 16' 2"	15' 10" 16' 2"	15' 9" 16' 3"	15' 8" 16' 4"
18	18' 0" 18' 0"	18' 0" 18' 0"	17' 11" 18' 1"	17' 11" 18' 1"	17' 11" 18' 1"	17' 10" 18' 2"	17' 9" 18' 3"	17' 8" 18' 4"	17' 7" 18' 6"
20	20' 0" 20' 0"	19' 11" 20' 1"	19' 11" 20' 1"	19' 11" 20' 1"	19' 10" 20' 2"	19' 10" 20' 2"	19' 9" 20' 4"	19' 7" 20' 5"	19' 5" 20' 7"
25	24' 11" 25' 1"	24' 11" 25' 1"	24' 11" 25' 1"	24' 10" 25' 2"	24' 9" 25' 3"	24' 8" 25' 4"	24' 7" 25' 6"	24' 5" 25' 8"	24' 1" 25' 11"
50	49' 9" 50' 3"	49' 8" 50' 4"	49' 6" 50' 6"	49' 4" 50' 8"	49' 1" 51' 0"	48' 9" 51' 4"	48' 2" 52' 0"	47' 6" 52' 9"	46' 6" 54' 1"
75	74' 6" 75' 6"	74' 3" 75' 9"	73' 11" 76' 1"	73' 6" 76' 6"	72' 11" 77' 2"	72' 2" 78' 1"	70' 11" 79' 6"	69' 7" 81' 5"	67' 4" 84' 8"

100	99' 1" 101' 0"	98' 8" 101' 4"	98' 2" 101' 11"	97' 5" 102' 9"	96' 4" 104' 0"	95' 0" 105' 7"	92' 11" 108' 3"	90' 6" 111' 9"	86' 9" 118' 0"
125	123' 6" 126' 6"	122' 11" 127' 2"	122' 1" 128' 1"	120' 11" 129' 4"	119' 3" 131' 3"	117' 3" 133' 10"	114' 1" 138' 3"	110' 5" 143' 11"	104' 11" 154' 7"
150	147' 10" 152' 2"	147' 0" 153' 1"	145' 10" 154' 5"	144' 2" 156' 4"	141' 10" 159' 2"	139' 0" 162' 11"	134' 6" 169' 6"	129' 6" 178' 2"	121' 11" 194' 10"
175	172' 1" 178' 0"	171' 0" 179' 3"	169' 4" 181' 1"	167' 2" 183' 8"	164' 0" 187' 7"	160' 2" 192' 10"	154' 3" 202' 2"	147' 8" 214' 8"	137' 11" 239' 5"
200	196' 3" 203' 11"	194' 9" 205' 6"	192' 7" 208' 0"	189' 9" 211' 5"	185' 9" 216' 8"	180' 10" 223' 8"	173' 4" 236' 4"	165' 1" 253' 8"	152' 11" 288' 10"
250	244' 1" 256' 2"	241' 10" 258' 9"	238' 6" 262' 8"	234' 3" 268' 1"	228' 1" 276' 8"	220' 9" 288' 2"	209' 8" 309' 7"	197' 8" 340' 0"	180' 6" 406' 7"
300	291' 7" 308' 11"	288' 4" 312' 8"	283' 7" 318' 5"	277' 6" 326' 5"	268' 11" 339' 3"	258' 10" 356' 9"	243' 8" 390' 3"	227' 8" 439' 10"	205' 2" 558' 1"
350	338' 7" 362' 3"	334' 3" 367' 4"	327' 10" 375' 4"	319' 9" 386' 6"	308' 5" 404' 7"	295' 3" 429' 9"	275' 7" 479' 5"	255' 3" 556' 7"	227' 3" 760' 8"
400	385' 2" 416' 1"	379' 6" 422' 10"	371' 4" 433' 5"	361' 0" 448' 5"	346' 6" 473' 0"	330' 0" 507' 9"	305' 8" 578' 7"	280' 10" 694' 11"	247' 4" 1045' 3"

For circle of confusion = .0005 use depth data two columns left of chosen F-Stop.

8mm FIELD OF VIEW

SETUPS (Approximate Distance)

SETUPS	Full Aperture	Academy 1.33:1	Academy 1.66:1	Academy 1.85:1	Anamorphic 2.40:1	Super 35 1.85:1	Super 35 2.40:1	VistaVision	VistaVision 1.85:1	VistaVision 2.40:1	65mm
Ext Close Up	0' 4"	0' 4"	0' 5"	0' 6"	NA	0' 6"	0' 7"	0' 3"	0' 4"	0' 5"	NA
Close Up	0' 6"	0' 7"	0' 8"	0' 9"	NA	0' 9"	0' 11"	0' 4"	0' 5"	0' 7"	NA
Medium Shot	0' 11"	1' 1"	1' 4"	1' 5"	NA	1' 4"	1' 9"	0' 8"	0' 10"	1' 1"	NA
Full Figure	2' 7"	3' 0"	3' 7"	4' 0"	NA	3' 8"	4' 10"	1' 11"	2' 4"	3' 1"	NA
Angle of View	V 98.8° H 114.5°	V 87.4° H 105.3°	V 76.5° H 105.3°	V 70.6° H 105.3°		V 78.1° H 112.6°	V 64.0° H 112.6°	V 115.1° H 134.0°	V 113.8° H 134.0°	V 89.2° H 134.0°	
2	4' 8" 6' 3"	4' 0" 5' 6"	3' 4" 5' 6"	3' 0" 5' 6"	NA NA	3' 3" 6' 0"	2' 6" 6' 0"	6' 3" 9' 5"	5' 1" 9' 5"	3' 11" 9' 5"	NA NA
2 1/2	5' 10" 7' 9"	5' 0" 6' 10"	4' 2" 6' 10"	3' 9" 6' 10"	NA NA	4' 1" 7' 6"	3' 2" 7' 6"	7' 9" 11' 9"	6' 4" 11' 9"	4' 11" 11' 9"	NA NA
3	7' 0" 9' 4"	6' 0" 8' 3"	5' 0" 8' 3"	4' 5" 8' 3"	NA NA	4' 10" 9' 0"	3' 9" 9' 0"	9' 4" 14' 2"	7' 8" 14' 2"	5' 11" 14' 2"	NA NA
3 1/2	8' 2" 10' 11"	7' 0" 9' 7"	5' 10" 9' 7"	5' 2" 9' 7"	NA NA	5' 8" 10' 6"	4' 5" 10' 6"	10' 11" 16' 6"	8' 11" 16' 6"	6' 11" 16' 6"	NA NA
4	9' 4" 12' 6"	8' 0" 11' 0"	6' 8" 11' 0"	5' 11" 11' 0"	NA NA	6' 6" 12' 0"	5' 0" 12' 0"	12' 6" 18' 10"	10' 2" 18' 10"	7' 11" 18' 10"	NA NA
4 1/2	10' 6" 14' 0"	9' 0" 12' 4"	7' 5" 12' 4"	6' 8" 12' 4"	NA NA	7' 4" 13' 6"	5' 8" 13' 6"	14' 0" 21' 3"	11' 6" 21' 3"	8' 10" 21' 3"	NA NA
5	11' 8" 15' 7"	10' 0" 13' 9"	8' 3" 13' 9"	7' 5" 13' 9"	NA NA	8' 1" 15' 0"	6' 3" 15' 0"	15' 7" 23' 7"	12' 9" 23' 7"	9' 10" 23' 7"	NA NA
5 1/2	12' 10" 17' 2"	11' 0" 15' 1"	9' 1" 15' 1"	8' 2" 15' 1"	NA NA	8' 11" 16' 6"	6' 11" 16' 6"	17' 2" 25' 11"	14' 0" 25' 11"	10' 10" 25' 11"	NA NA
6	14' 0" 18' 8"	12' 0" 16' 6"	9' 11" 16' 6"	8' 11" 16' 6"	NA NA	9' 9" 18' 0"	7' 6" 18' 0"	18' 8" 28' 3"	15' 4" 28' 3"	11' 10" 28' 3"	NA NA

6 ½	15' 2" 20' 3"	13' 0" 17' 10"	10' 9" 17' 10"	9' 8" 17' 10"	NA NA	10' 7" 19' 6"	8' 2" 19' 6"	20" 3" 30' 8"	16' 7" 30' 8"	12' 10" 30' 8"	NA NA
7	16' 4" 21' 10"	14' 0" 19' 3"	11' 7" 19' 3"	10' 5" 19' 3"	NA NA	11' 4" 21' 0"	8' 9" 21' 0"	21' 10" 33' 0"	17' 10" 33' 0"	13' 10" 33' 0"	NA NA
8	18' 8" 24' 11"	16' 0" 22' 0"	13' 3" 22' 0"	11' 11" 22' 0"	NA NA	13' 0" 24' 0"	10' 0" 24' 0"	24' 11" 37' 9"	20' 5" 37' 9"	15' 9" 37' 9"	NA NA
9	21' 0" 28' 0"	18' 0" 24' 9"	14' 11" 24' 9"	13' 4" 24' 9"	NA NA	14' 7" 27' 0"	11' 3" 27' 0"	28' 0" 42' 5"	22' 11" 42' 5"	17' 9" 42' 5"	NA NA
10	23' 4" 31' 2"	20' 0" 27' 6"	16' 7" 27' 6"	14' 10" 27' 6"	NA NA	16' 3" 30' 0"	12' 6" 30' 0"	31' 2" 47' 2"	25' 6" 47' 2"	19' 9" 47' 2"	NA NA
12	28' 0" 37' 5"	24' 0" 33' 0"	19' 11" 33' 0"	17' 10" 33' 0"	NA NA	19' 6" 36' 0"	15' 0" 36' 0"	37' 5" 56' 7"	30' 7" 56' 7"	23' 8" 56' 7"	NA NA
14	32' 8" 43' 7"	28' 1" 38' 6"	23' 2" 38' 6"	20' 10" 38' 6"	NA NA	22' 9" 42' 0"	17' 6" 42' 0"	43' 7" 66' 0"	35' 8" 66' 0"	27' 7" 66' 0"	NA NA
16	37' 4" 49' 10"	32' 1" 44' 0"	26' 6" 44' 0"	23' 9" 44' 0"	NA NA	26' 0" 48' 0"	20' 0" 48' 0"	49' 10" 75' 5"	40' 10" 75' 5"	31' 7" 75' 5"	NA NA
18	42' 0" 56' 1"	36' 1" 49' 6"	29' 10" 49' 6"	26' 9" 49' 6"	NA NA	29' 2" 54' 0"	22' 6" 54' 0"	56' 1" 84' 10"	45' 11" 84' 10"	35' 6" 84' 10"	NA NA
20	46' 8" 62' 4"	40' 1" 55' 0"	33' 2" 55' 0"	29' 9" 55' 0"	NA NA	32' 5" 60' 0"	25' 0" 60' 0"	62' 4" 94' 4"	51' 0" 94' 4"	39' 5" 94' 4"	NA NA
25	58' 4" 77' 10"	50' 1" 68' 9"	41' 5" 68' 9"	37' 2" 68' 9"	NA NA	40' 7" 75' 0"	31' 3" 75' 0"	77' 10" 117' 10"	63' 9" 117' 10"	49' 4" 117' 10"	NA NA
50	116' 8" 155' 9"	100' 2" 137' 6"	82' 10" 137' 6"	74' 4" 137' 6"	NA NA	81' 1" 150' 0"	62' 7" 150' 0"	155' 9" 235' 9"	127' 6" 235' 9"	98' 7" 235' 9"	NA NA

9.8mm FIELD OF VIEW

SETUPS (Approximate Distance)											
Ext Close Up Close Up Medium Shot Full Figure	0' 5" 0' 7" 1' 2" 3' 2"	0' 6" 0' 9" 1' 4" 3' 8"	0' 7" 0' 10" 1' 7" 4' 5"	0' 7" 1' 0" 1' 9" 4' 11"	NA NA NA NA	0' 7" 0' 11" 1' 8" 4' 6"	0' 9" 1' 2" 2' 1" 5' 11"	NA NA NA NA	NA NA NA NA	NA NA NA NA	NA NA NA NA
Angle of View	V 87.2° H 103.6°	V 75.9° H 93.8°	V 65.6° H 93.8°	V 60.1° H 93.8°		V 67.0° H 101.5°	V 54.1° H 101.5°				
	Full Aperture	Academy 1.33:1	Academy 1.66:1	Academy 1.85:1	Anamorphic 2.40:1	Super 35 1.85:1	Super 35 2.40:1	VistaVision	VistaVision 1.85:1	VistaVision 2.40:1	65mm
2	3' 10" 5' 1"	3' 3" 4' 6"	2' 8" 4' 6"	2' 5" 4' 6"	NA NA	2' 8" 4' 11"	2' 1" 4' 11"	NA NA	NA NA	NA NA	NA NA
2 ½	4' 9" 6' 4"	4' 1" 5' 7"	3' 5" 5' 7"	3' 0" 5' 7"	NA NA	3' 4" 6' 1"	2' 7" 6' 1"	NA NA	NA NA	NA NA	NA NA
3	5' 9" 7' 8"	4' 11" 6' 9"	4' 1" 6' 9"	3' 8" 6' 9"	NA NA	4' 0" 7' 4"	3' 1" 7' 4"	NA NA	NA NA	NA NA	NA NA
3 ½	6' 8" 8' 11"	5' 9" 7' 10"	4' 9" 7' 10"	4' 3" 7' 10"	NA NA	4' 8" 8' 7"	3' 7" 8' 7"	NA NA	NA NA	NA NA	NA NA
4	7' 7" 10' 2"	6' 7" 9' 0"	5' 5" 9' 0"	4' 10" 9' 0"	NA NA	5' 4" 9' 10"	4' 1" 9' 10"	NA NA	NA NA	NA NA	NA NA
4 ½	8' 7" 11' 5"	7' 4" 10' 1"	6' 1" 10' 1"	5' 6" 10' 1"	NA NA	6' 0" 11' 0"	4' 7" 11' 0"	NA NA	NA NA	NA NA	NA NA
5	9' 6" 12' 9"	8' 2" 11' 3"	6' 9" 11' 3"	6' 1" 11' 3"	NA NA	6' 7" 12' 3"	5' 1" 12' 3"	NA NA	NA NA	NA NA	NA NA
5 ½	10' 6" 14' 0"	9' 0" 12' 4"	7' 5" 12' 4"	6' 8" 12' 4"	NA NA	7' 3" 13' 6"	5' 7" 13' 6"	NA NA	NA NA	NA NA	NA NA
6	11' 5" 15' 3"	9' 10" 13' 6"	8' 1" 13' 6"	7' 3" 13' 6"	NA NA	7' 11" 14' 8"	6' 2" 14' 8"	NA NA	NA NA	NA NA	NA NA

6 1/2	12' 5" 16' 6"	10' 8" 14' 7"	8' 10" 14' 7"	7' 11" 14' 7"	NA NA	8' 7" 15' 11"	6' 8" 15' 11"	NA NA	NA NA	NA NA	NA NA
7	13' 4" 17' 10"	11' 5" 15' 9"	9' 6" 15' 9"	8' 6" 15' 9"	NA NA	9' 3" 17' 2"	7' 2" 17' 2"	NA NA	NA NA	NA NA	NA NA
8	15' 3" 20' 4"	13' 1" 17' 11"	10' 10" 17' 11"	9' 8" 17' 11"	NA NA	10' 7" 19' 7"	8' 2" 19' 7"	NA NA	NA NA	NA NA	NA NA
9	17' 2" 22' 11"	14' 9" 20' 2"	12' 2" 20' 2"	10' 11" 20' 2"	NA NA	11' 11" 22' 1"	9' 2" 22' 1"	NA NA	NA NA	NA NA	NA NA
10	19' 1" 25' 5"	16' 4" 22' 5"	13' 6" 22' 5"	12' 2" 22' 5"	NA NA	13' 3" 24' 6"	10' 3" 24' 6"	NA NA	NA NA	NA NA	NA NA
12	22' 10" 30' 6"	19' 8" 26' 11"	16' 3" 26' 11"	14' 7" 26' 11"	NA NA	15' 11" 29' 5"	12' 3" 29' 5"	NA NA	NA NA	NA NA	NA NA
14	26' 8" 35' 7"	22' 11" 31' 5"	18' 11" 31' 5"	17' 0" 31' 5"	NA NA	18' 7" 34' 3"	14' 4" 34' 3"	NA NA	NA NA	NA NA	NA NA
16	30' 6" 40' 8"	26' 2" 35' 11"	21' 8" 35' 11"	19' 5" 35' 11"	NA NA	21' 2" 39' 2"	16' 4" 39' 2"	NA NA	NA NA	NA NA	NA NA
18	34' 3" 45' 9"	29' 5" 40' 5"	24' 4" 40' 5"	21' 10" 40' 5"	NA NA	23' 10" 44' 1"	18' 5" 44' 1"	NA NA	NA NA	NA NA	NA NA
20	38' 1" 50' 10"	32' 9" 44' 11"	27' 1" 44' 11"	24' 3" 44' 11"	NA NA	26' 6" 49' 0"	20' 5" 49' 0"	NA NA	NA NA	NA NA	NA NA
25	47' 8" 63' 7"	40' 11" 56' 1"	33' 10" 56' 1"	30' 4" 56' 1"	NA NA	33' 1" 61' 3"	25' 6" 61' 3"	NA NA	NA NA	NA NA	NA NA
50	95' 3" 127' 2"	81' 9" 112' 3"	67' 8" 112' 3"	60' 8" 112' 3"	NA NA	66' 3" 122' 6"	51' 1" 122' 6"	NA NA	NA NA	NA NA	NA NA

10mm FIELD OF VIEW

SETUPS (Approximate Distance)											
Ext Close Up **Close Up** **Medium Shot** **Full Figure**	0' 5" 0' 7" 1' 2" 3' 3"	0' 6" 0' 9" 1' 4" 3' 9"	0' 7" 0' 11" 1' 8" 4' 6"	0' 8" 1' 0" 1' 10" 5' 1"	NA NA NA NA	0' 7" 0' 11" 1' 8" 4' 7"	0' 9" 1' 2" 2' 2" 6' 0"	NA NA NA NA	NA NA NA NA	NA NA NA NA	NA NA NA NA
Angle of View	V 86.1° H 102.4°	V 74.8° H 97.7°	V 64.5° H 92.7°	V 59.1° H 92.1°		V 66.0° H 100.4°	V 53.2° H 100.4°				
	Full Aperture	**Academy 1.33:1**	**Academy 1.66:1**	**Academy 1.85:1**	**Anamorphic 2.40:1**	**Super 35 1.85:1**	**Super 35 2.40:1**	**VistaVision**	**VistaVision 1.85:1**	**VistaVision 2.40:1**	**65mm**
2	3' 9" 5' 0"	3' 2" 4' 5"	2' 8" 4' 5"	2' 5" 4' 5"	NA NA	2' 7" 4' 10"	2' 0" 4' 10"	NA NA	NA NA	NA NA	NA NA
2 1/2	4' 8" 6' 3"	4' 0" 5' 6"	3' 4" 5' 6"	3' 0" 5' 6"	NA NA	3' 3" 6' 0"	2' 6" 6' 0"	NA NA	NA NA	NA NA	NA NA
3	5' 7" 7' 6"	4' 10" 6' 7"	4' 0" 6' 7"	3' 7" 6' 7"	NA NA	3' 11" 7' 2"	3' 0" 7' 2"	NA NA	NA NA	NA NA	NA NA
3 1/2	6' 6" 8' 9"	5' 7" 7' 8"	4' 8" 7' 8"	4' 2" 7' 8"	NA NA	4' 7" 8' 5"	3' 6" 8' 5"	NA NA	NA NA	NA NA	NA NA
4	7' 6" 10' 0"	6' 5" 8' 10"	5' 4" 8' 10"	4' 9" 8' 10"	NA NA	5' 2" 9' 7"	4' 0" 9' 7"	NA NA	NA NA	NA NA	NA NA
4 1/2	8' 5" 11' 3"	7' 3" 9' 11"	6' 0" 9' 11"	5' 4" 9' 11"	NA NA	5' 10" 10' 10"	4' 6" 10' 10"	NA NA	NA NA	NA NA	NA NA
5	9' 4" 12' 6"	8' 0" 11' 0"	6' 8" 11' 0"	5' 11" 11' 0"	NA NA	6' 6" 12' 0"	5' 0" 12' 0"	NA NA	NA NA	NA NA	NA NA
5 1/2	10' 3" 13' 8"	8' 10" 12' 1"	7' 4" 12' 1"	6' 6" 12' 1"	NA NA	7' 2" 13' 2"	5' 6" 13' 2"	NA NA	NA NA	NA NA	NA NA
6	11' 2" 14' 11"	9' 7" 13' 2"	7' 11" 13' 2"	7' 2" 13' 2"	NA NA	7' 9" 14' 5"	6' 0" 14' 5"	NA NA	NA NA	NA NA	NA NA

6½	12' 2" 16' 2"	10' 5" 14' 4"	8' 7" 14' 4"	7' 9" 14' 4"	NA NA	8' 5" 15' 7"	6' 6" 15' 7"	NA NA	NA NA	NA NA	NA NA
7	13' 1" 17' 5"	11' 3" 15' 5"	9' 3" 15' 5"	8' 4" 15' 5"	NA NA	9' 1" 16' 10"	7' 0" 16' 10"	NA NA	NA NA	NA NA	NA NA
8	14' 11" 19' 11"	12' 10" 17' 7"	10' 7" 17' 7"	9' 6" 17' 7"	NA NA	10' 5" 19' 2"	8' 0" 19' 2"	NA NA	NA NA	NA NA	NA NA
9	16' 10" 22' 5"	14' 5" 19' 10"	11' 11" 19' 10"	10' 8" 19' 10"	NA NA	11' 8" 21' 7"	9' 0" 21' 7"	NA NA	NA NA	NA NA	NA NA
10	18' 8" 24' 11"	16' 0" 22' 0"	13' 3" 22' 0"	11' 11" 22' 0"	NA NA	13' 0" 24' 0"	10' 0" 24' 0"	NA NA	NA NA	NA NA	NA NA
12	22' 5" 29' 11"	19' 3" 26' 5"	15' 11" 26' 5"	14' 3" 26' 5"	NA NA	15' 7" 28' 10"	12' 0" 28' 10"	NA NA	NA NA	NA NA	NA NA
14	26' 2" 34' 11"	22' 5" 30' 10"	18' 7" 30' 10"	16' 8" 30' 10"	NA NA	18' 2" 33' 7"	14' 0" 33' 7"	NA NA	NA NA	NA NA	NA NA
16	29' 10" 39' 10"	25' 8" 35' 2"	21' 3" 35' 2"	19' 0" 35' 2"	NA NA	20' 9" 38' 5"	16' 0" 38' 5"	NA NA	NA NA	NA NA	NA NA
18	33' 7" 44' 10"	28' 10" 39' 7"	23' 10" 39' 7"	21' 5" 39' 7"	NA NA	23' 4" 43' 2"	18' 0" 43' 2"	NA NA	NA NA	NA NA	NA NA
20	37' 4" 49' 10"	32' 1" 44' 0"	26' 6" 44' 0"	23' 9" 44' 0"	NA NA	26' 0" 48' 0"	20' 0" 48' 0"	NA NA	NA NA	NA NA	NA NA
25	46' 8" 62' 4"	40' 1" 55' 0"	33' 2" 55' 0"	29' 9" 55' 0"	NA NA	32' 5" 60' 0"	25' 0" 60' 0"	NA NA	NA NA	NA NA	NA NA
50	93' 4" 124' 7"	80' 2" 110' 0"	66' 4" 110' 0"	59' 5" 110' 0"	NA NA	64' 11" 120' 0"	50' 0" 120' 0"	NA NA	NA NA	NA NA	NA NA

12mm FIELD OF VIEW

SETUPS (Approximate Distance)	Full Aperture	Academy 1.33:1	Academy 1.66:1	Academy 1.85:1	Anamorphic 2.40:1	Super 35 1.85:1	Super 35 2.40:1	VistaVision	VistaVision 1.85:1	VistaVision 2.40:1	65mm
Ext Close Up Close Up Medium Shot Full Figure	0' 6" 0' 9" 1' 5" 3' 10"	0' 7" 0' 10" 1' 7" 4' 6"	0' 8" 1' 1" 2' 0" 5' 5"	0' 9" 1' 2" 2' 2" 6' 1"	NA NA NA NA	0' 8" 1' 1" 2' 0" 5' 7"	0' 11" 1' 5" 2' 7" 7' 2"	NA NA NA NA	NA NA NA NA	NA NA NA NA	NA NA NA NA
Angle of View	V 75.8° H 92.1°	V 65.0° H 82.2°	V 55.5° H 82.2°	V 50.5° H 82.2°		V 56.8° H 90.0°	V 45.3° H 90.0°				
2	3' 1" 4' 2"	2' 8" 3' 8"	2' 3" 3' 8"	2' 0" 3' 8"	NA NA	2' 2" 4' 0"	1' 8" 4' 0"	NA NA	NA NA	NA NA	NA NA
2 ½	3' 11" 5' 2"	3' 4" 4' 7"	2' 9" 4' 7"	2' 6" 4' 7"	NA NA	2' 8" 5' 0"	2' 1" 5' 0"	NA NA	NA NA	NA NA	NA NA
3	4' 8" 6' 3"	4' 0" 5' 6"	3' 4" 5' 6"	3' 0" 5' 6"	NA NA	3' 3" 6' 0"	2' 6" 6' 0"	NA NA	NA NA	NA NA	NA NA
3 ½	5' 5" 7' 3"	4' 8" 6' 5"	3' 10" 6' 5"	3' 6" 6' 5"	NA NA	3' 9" 7' 0"	2' 11" 7' 0"	NA NA	NA NA	NA NA	NA NA
4	6' 3" 8' 4"	5' 4" 7' 4"	4' 5" 7' 4"	4' 0" 7' 4"	NA NA	4' 4" 8' 0"	3' 4" 8' 0"	NA NA	NA NA	NA NA	NA NA
4 ½	7' 0" 9' 4"	6' 0" 8' 3"	5' 0" 8' 3"	4' 5" 8' 3"	NA NA	4' 10" 9' 0"	3' 9" 9' 0"	NA NA	NA NA	NA NA	NA NA
5	7' 9" 10' 5"	6' 8" 9' 2"	5' 6" 9' 2"	4' 11" 9' 2"	NA NA	5' 5" 10' 0"	4' 2" 10' 0"	NA NA	NA NA	NA NA	NA NA
5 ½	8' 7" 11' 5"	7' 4" 10' 1"	6' 1" 10' 1"	5' 5" 10' 1"	NA NA	5' 11" 11' 0"	4' 7" 11' 0"	NA NA	NA NA	NA NA	NA NA
6	9' 4" 12' 6"	8' 0" 11' 0"	6' 8" 11' 0"	5' 11" 11' 0"	NA NA	6' 6" 12' 0"	5' 0" 12' 0"	NA NA	NA NA	NA NA	NA NA

6 ½	10' 1" 13' 6"	8' 8" 11' 11"	7' 2" 11' 11"	6' 5" 11' 11"	NA NA	7' 0" 13' 0"	5' 5" 13' 0"	NA NA	NA NA	NA NA	NA NA
7	10' 11" 14' 6"	9' 4" 12' 10"	7' 9" 12' 10"	6' 11" 12' 10"	NA NA	7' 7" 14' 0"	5' 10" 14' 0"	NA NA	NA NA	NA NA	NA NA
8	12' 5" 16' 7"	10' 8" 14' 8"	8' 10" 14' 8"	7' 11" 14' 8"	NA NA	8' 8" 16' 0"	6' 8" 16' 0"	NA NA	NA NA	NA NA	NA NA
9	14' 0" 18' 8"	12' 0" 16' 6"	9' 11" 16' 6"	8' 11" 16' 6"	NA NA	9' 9" 18' 0"	7' 6" 18' 0"	NA NA	NA NA	NA NA	NA NA
10	15' 7" 20' 9"	13' 4" 18' 4"	11' 1" 18' 4"	9' 11" 18' 4"	NA NA	10' 10" 20' 0"	8' 4" 20' 0"	NA NA	NA NA	NA NA	NA NA
12	18' 8" 24' 11"	16' 0" 22' 0"	13' 3" 22' 0"	11' 11" 22' 0"	NA NA	13' 0" 24' 0"	10' 0" 24' 0"	NA NA	NA NA	NA NA	NA NA
14	21' 9" 29' 1"	18' 8" 25' 8"	15' 6" 25' 8"	13' 10" 25' 8"	NA NA	15' 2" 28' 0"	11' 8" 28' 0"	NA NA	NA NA	NA NA	NA NA
16	24' 11" 33' 3"	21' 4" 29' 4"	17' 8" 29' 4"	15' 10" 29' 4"	NA NA	17' 4" 32' 0"	13' 4" 32' 0"	NA NA	NA NA	NA NA	NA NA
18	28' 0" 37' 5"	24' 0" 33' 0"	19' 11" 33' 0"	17' 10" 33' 0"	NA NA	19' 6" 36' 0"	15' 0" 36' 0"	NA NA	NA NA	NA NA	NA NA
20	31' 1" 41' 6"	26' 9" 36' 8"	22' 1" 36' 8"	19' 10" 36' 8"	NA NA	21' 8" 40' 0"	16' 8" 40' 0"	NA NA	NA NA	NA NA	NA NA
25	38' 11" 51' 11"	33' 5" 45' 10"	27' 7" 45' 10"	24' 9" 45' 10"	NA NA	27' 0" 50' 0"	20' 10" 50' 0"	NA NA	NA NA	NA NA	NA NA
50	77' 9" 103' 10"	66' 9" 91' 8"	55' 3" 91' 8"	49' 6" 91' 8"	NA NA	54' 1" 100' 0"	41' 8" 100' 0"	NA NA	NA NA	NA NA	NA NA

14mm FIELD OF VIEW

SETUPS (Approximate Distance)											
Ext Close Up Close Up Medium Shot Full Figure	0' 7" 0' 10" 1' 7" 4' 6"	0' 8" 1' 0" 1' 11" 5' 3"	0' 10" 1' 3" 2' 3" 6' 4"	0' 11" 1' 4" 2' 7" 7' 1"	NA NA NA NA	0' 10" 1' 3" 2' 4" 6' 6"	1' 1" 1' 8" 3' 0" 8' 5"	0' 5" 0' 8" 1' 3" 3' 4"	0' 6" 0' 10" 1' 6" 4' 1"	0' 8" 1' 0" 1' 1" 5' 4"	NA NA NA NA
Angle of View	V 67.4° H 83.3°	V 57.3° H 73.6°	V 48.5° H 73.6°	V 44.1° H 73.6°		V 49.7° H 81.2°	V 39.3° H 81.2°	V 83.9° H 106.8°	V 72.1° H 106.8°	V 58.8° H 106.8°	
	Full Aperture	**Academy 1.33:1**	**Academy 1.66:1**	**Academy 1.85:1**	**Anamorphic 2.40:1**	**Super 35 1.85:1**	**Super 35 2.40:1**	**VistaVision**	**VistaVision 1.85:1**	**VistaVision 2.40:1**	**65mm**
2	2' 8" 3' 7"	2' 3" 3' 2"	1' 11" 3' 2"	1' 8" 3' 2"	NA NA	1' 10" 3' 5"	1' 5" 3' 5"	3' 7" 5' 5"	2' 11" 5' 5"	2' 3" 5' 5"	NA NA
2 ½	3' 4" 4' 5"	2' 10" 3' 11"	2' 4" 3' 11"	2' 1" 3' 11"	NA NA	2' 4" 4' 3"	1' 9" 4' 3"	4' 5" 6' 9"	3' 8" 6' 9"	2' 10" 6' 9"	NA NA
3	4' 0" 5' 4"	3' 5" 4' 9"	2' 10" 4' 9"	2' 7" 4' 9"	NA NA	2' 9" 5' 2"	2' 2" 5' 2"	5' 4" 8' 1"	4' 4" 8' 1"	3' 5" 8' 1"	NA NA
3 ½	4' 8" 6' 3"	4' 0" 5' 6"	3' 4" 5' 6"	3' 0" 5' 6"	NA NA	3' 3" 6' 0"	2' 6" 6' 0"	6' 3" 9' 5"	5' 1" 9' 5"	3' 11" 9' 5"	NA NA
4	5' 4" 7' 1"	4' 7" 6' 3"	3' 9" 6' 3"	3' 5" 6' 3"	NA NA	3' 9" 6' 10"	2' 10" 6' 10"	7' 1" 10' 9"	5' 10" 10' 9"	4' 6" 10' 9"	NA NA
4 ½	6' 0" 8' 0"	5' 2" 7' 1"	4' 3" 7' 1"	3' 10" 7' 1"	NA NA	4' 2" 7' 9"	3' 3" 7' 9"	8' 0" 12' 1"	6' 7" 12' 1"	5' 1" 12' 1"	NA NA
5	6' 8" 8' 11"	5' 9" 7' 10"	4' 9" 7' 10"	4' 3" 7' 10"	NA NA	4' 8" 8' 7"	3' 7" 8' 7"	8' 11" 13' 6"	7' 3" 13' 6"	5' 8" 8' 7"	NA NA
5 ½	7' 4" 9' 9"	6' 4" 8' 8"	5' 3" 8' 8"	4' 8" 8' 8"	NA NA	5' 1" 9' 5"	3' 11" 9' 5"	9' 9" 14' 10"	8' 0" 14' 10"	6' 2" 14' 10"	NA NA
6	8' 0" 10' 8"	6' 10" 9' 5"	5' 8" 9' 5"	5' 1" 9' 5"	NA NA	5' 7" 10' 3"	4' 3" 10' 3"	10' 8" 16' 2'	8' 9" 16' 2"	6' 9" 16' 2"	NA NA

6 1/2	8' 8" 11' 7"	7' 5" 10' 3"	6' 2" 10' 3"	5' 6" 10' 3"	NA NA	6' 0" 11' 2"	4' 8" 11' 2"	11' 7" 17' 6"	9' 6" 17' 6"	7' 4" 17' 6"	NA NA
7	9' 4" 12' 6"	8' 0" 11' 0"	6' 8" 11' 0"	5' 11" 11' 0"	NA NA	6' 6" 12' 0"	5' 0" 12' 0"	12' 6" 18' 10"	10' 2" 18' 10"	7' 11" 18' 10"	NA NA
8	10' 8" 14' 3"	9' 2" 12' 7"	7' 7" 12' 7"	6' 10" 12' 7"	NA NA	7' 5" 13' 9"	5' 9" 13' 9"	14' 3" 21' 7"	11' 8" 21' 7"	9' 0" 21' 7"	NA NA
9	12' 0" 16' 0"	10' 4" 14' 2"	8' 6" 14' 2"	7' 8" 14' 2"	NA NA	8' 4" 15' 5"	6' 5" 15' 5"	16' 0" 24' 3"	13' 1" 24' 3"	10' 2" 24' 3"	NA NA
10	13' 4" 17' 10"	11' 5" 15' 9"	9' 6" 15' 9"	8' 6" 15' 9"	NA NA	9' 3" 17' 2"	7' 2" 17' 2"	17' 10" 26' 11"	14' 7" 26' 11"	11' 3" 26' 11"	NA NA
12	16' 0" 21' 4"	13' 9" 18' 10"	11' 4" 18' 10"	10' 2" 18' 10"	NA NA	11' 2" 20' 7"	8' 7" 20' 7"	21' 4" 32' 4"	17' 6" 32' 4"	13' 6" 32' 4"	NA NA
14	18' 8" 24' 11"	16' 0" 22' 0"	13' 3" 22' 0"	11' 11" 22' 0"	NA NA	13' 0" 24' 0"	10' 0" 24' 0"	24' 11" 37' 9"	20' 5" 37' 9"	15' 9" 37' 9"	NA NA
16	21' 4" 28' 6"	18' 4" 25' 2"	15' 2" 25' 2"	13' 7" 25' 2"	NA NA	14' 10" 27' 5"	11' 5" 27' 5"	28' 6" 43' 1"	23' 4" 43' 1"	18' 0" 43' 1"	NA NA
18	24' 0" 32' 0"	20' 7" 28' 3"	17' 1" 28' 3"	15' 3" 28' 3"	NA NA	16' 8" 30' 10"	12' 10" 30' 10"	32' 0" 48' 6"	26' 3" 48' 6"	20' 3" 48' 6"	NA NA
20	26' 8" 35' 7"	22' 11" 31' 5"	18' 11" 31' 5"	17' 0" 31' 5"	NA NA	18' 7" 34' 3"	14' 4" 34' 3"	35' 7" 53' 11"	29' 2" 53' 11"	22' 6" 53' 11"	NA NA
25	33' 4" 44' 6"	28' 7" 39' 3"	23' 8" 39' 3"	21' 3" 39' 3"	NA NA	23' 2" 42' 10"	17' 10" 42' 10"	44' 6" 67' 4"	36' 5" 67' 4"	28' 2" 67' 4"	NA NA
50	66' 8" 89' 0"	57' 3" 78' 7"	47' 4" 78' 7"	42' 5" 78' 7"	NA NA	46' 4" 85' 9"	35' 9" 85' 9"	89' 0" 134' 9"	72' 10" 134' 9"	56' 4" 134' 9"	NA NA

16mm FIELD OF VIEW

SETUPS (Approximate Distance)	Full Aperture	Academy 1.33:1	Academy 1.66:1	Academy 1.85:1	Anamorphic 2.40:1	Super 35 1.85:1	Super 35 2.40:1	VistaVision	VistaVision 1.85:1	VistaVision 2.40:1	65mm
Ext Close Up Close Up Medium Shot Full Figure	0' 8" 1' 0" 1' 10" 5' 2"	0' 9" 1' 2" 2' 2" 6' 0"	0' 11" 1' 5" 2' 7" 7' 3"	1' 0" 1' 7" 2' 11" 8' 1"	NA NA NA NA	0' 11" 1' 5" 2' 8" 7' 5"	1' 2" 1' 10" 3' 6" 9' 7"	NA NA NA NA	NA NA NA NA	NA NA NA NA	NA NA NA NA
Angle of View	V 60.5° H 75.8°	V 51.1° H 66.4°	V 43.1° H 66.4°	V 39.0° H 66.4°		V 44.2° H 73.7°	V 34.7° H 73.7°				
2	2' 4" 3' 1"	2' 0" 2' 9"	1' 8" 2' 9"	1' 6" 2' 9"	NA NA	1' 7" 3' 0"	1' 3" 3' 0"	NA NA	NA NA	NA NA	NA NA
2 ½	2' 11" 3' 11"	2' 6" 3' 5"	2' 1" 3' 5"	1' 10" 3' 5"	NA NA	2' 0" 3' 9"	1' 7" 3' 9"	NA NA	NA NA	NA NA	NA NA
3	3' 6" 4' 8"	3' 0" 4' 1"	2' 6" 4' 1"	2' 3" 4' 1"	NA NA	2' 5" 4' 6"	1' 11" 4' 6"	NA NA	NA NA	NA NA	NA NA
3 ½	4' 1" 5' 5"	3' 6" 4' 10"	2' 11" 4' 10"	2' 7" 4' 10"	NA NA	2' 10" 5' 3"	2' 2" 5' 3"	NA NA	NA NA	NA NA	NA NA
4	4' 8" 6' 3"	4' 0" 5' 6"	3' 4" 5' 6"	3' 0" 5' 6"	NA NA	3' 3" 6' 0"	2' 6" 6' 0"	NA NA	NA NA	NA NA	NA NA
4 ½	5' 3" 7' 0"	4' 6" 6' 2"	3' 9" 6' 2"	3' 4" 6' 2"	NA NA	3' 8" 6' 9"	2' 10" 6' 9"	NA NA	NA NA	NA NA	NA NA
5	5' 10" 7' 9"	5' 0" 6' 10"	4' 2" 6' 10"	3' 9" 6' 10"	NA NA	4' 1" 7' 6"	3' 2" 7' 6"	NA NA	NA NA	NA NA	NA NA
5 ½	6' 5" 8' 7"	5' 6" 7' 7"	4' 7" 7' 7"	4' 1" 7' 7"	NA NA	4' 6" 8' 3"	3' 5" 8' 3"	NA NA	NA NA	NA NA	NA NA
6	7' 0" 9' 4"	6' 0" 8' 3"	5' 0" 8' 3"	4' 5" 8' 3"	NA NA	4' 10" 9' 0"	3' 9" 9' 0"	NA NA	NA NA	NA NA	NA NA

6 ½	7' 7" 10' 1"	6' 6" 8' 11"	5' 5" 8' 11"	4' 10" 8' 11"	NA NA	5' 3" 9' 9"	4' 1" 9' 9"	NA NA	NA NA	NA NA	NA NA
7	8' 2" 10' 11"	7' 0" 9' 7"	5' 10" 9' 7"	5' 2" 9' 7"	NA NA	5' 8" 10' 6"	4' 5" 10' 6"	NA NA	NA NA	NA NA	NA NA
8	9' 4" 12' 6"	8' 0" 11' 0"	6' 8" 11' 0"	5' 11" 11' 0"	NA NA	6' 6" 12' 0"	5' 0" 12' 0"	NA NA	NA NA	NA NA	NA NA
9	10' 6" 14' 0"	9' 0" 12' 4"	7' 5" 12' 4"	6' 8" 12' 4"	NA NA	7' 4" 13' 6"	5' 8" 13' 6"	NA NA	NA NA	NA NA	NA NA
10	11' 8" 15' 7"	10' 0" 13' 9"	8' 3" 13' 9"	7' 5" 13' 9"	NA NA	8' 1" 15' 0"	6' 3" 15' 0"	NA NA	NA NA	NA NA	NA NA
12	14' 0" 18' 8"	12' 0" 16' 6"	9' 11" 16' 6"	8' 11" 16' 6"	NA NA	9' 9" 18' 0"	7' 6" 18' 0"	NA NA	NA NA	NA NA	NA NA
14	16' 4" 21' 10"	14' 0" 19' 3"	11' 7" 19' 3"	10' 5" 19' 3"	NA NA	11' 4" 21' 0"	8' 9" 21' 0"	NA NA	NA NA	NA NA	NA NA
16	18' 8" 24' 11"	16' 0" 22' 0"	13' 3" 22' 0"	11' 11" 22' 0"	NA NA	13' 0" 24' 0"	10' 0" 24' 0"	NA NA	NA NA	NA NA	NA NA
18	21' 0" 28' 0"	18' 0" 24' 9"	14' 11" 24' 9"	13' 4" 24' 9"	NA NA	14' 7" 27' 0"	11' 3" 27' 0"	NA NA	NA NA	NA NA	NA NA
20	23' 4" 31' 2"	20' 0" 27' 6"	16' 7" 27' 6"	14' 10" 27' 6"	NA NA	16' 3" 30' 0"	12' 6" 30' 0"	NA NA	NA NA	NA NA	NA NA
25	29' 2" 38' 11"	25' 1" 34' 4"	20' 9" 34' 4"	18' 7" 34' 4"	NA NA	20' 3" 37' 6"	15' 8" 37' 6"	NA NA	NA NA	NA NA	NA NA
50	58' 4" 77' 10"	50' 1" 68' 9"	41' 5" 68' 9"	37' 2" 68' 9"	NA NA	40' 7" 75' 0"	31' 3" 75' 0"	NA NA	NA NA	NA NA	NA NA

SETUPS (Approximate Distance)

18mm FIELD OF VIEW

	Full Aperture	Academy 1.33:1	Academy 1.66:1	Academy 1.85:1	Anamorphic 2.40:1	Super 35 1.85:1	Super 35 2.40:1	VistaVision	VistaVision 1.85:1	VistaVision 2.40:1	65mm
Ext Close Up	0' 9"	0' 10"	1' 0"	1' 2"	0' 9"	1' 0"	1' 4"	0' 7"	0' 8"	0' 10"	NA
Close Up	1' 1"	1' 4"	1' 7"	1' 9"	1' 2"	1' 7"	2' 1"	0' 10"	1' 0"	1' 4"	NA
Medium Shot	2' 1"	2' 5"	2' 11"	3' 3"	2' 1"	3' 0"	3' 11"	1' 7"	1' 11"	2' 6"	NA
Full Figure	5' 9"	6' 9"	8' 2"	9' 1"	5' 10"	8' 4"	10' 10"	4' 4"	5' 4"	6' 10"	NA
Angle of View	V 54.8° H 69.3°	V 46.0° H 60.4°	V 38.6° H 60.4°	V 34.9° H 60.4°	V 52.6° H 99.6°	V 39.7° H 67.4°	V 31.1° H 67.4°	V 69.9° H 92.7°	V 59.1° H 92.7°	V 47.3° H 92.7°	
2	2' 1" 2' 9"	1' 9" 2' 5"	1' 6" 2' 5"	1' 4" 2' 5"	2' 1" 4' 11"	1' 5" 2' 8"	1' 1" 2' 8"	2' 9" 4' 2"	2' 3" 4' 2"	1' 9" 4' 2"	NA NA
2 1/2	2' 7" 3' 6"	2' 3" 3' 1"	1' 10" 3' 1"	1' 8" 3' 1"	2' 7" 6' 1"	1' 10" 3' 4"	1' 5" 3' 4"	3' 6" 5' 3"	2' 10" 5' 3"	2' 2" 5' 3"	NA NA
3	3' 1" 4' 2"	2' 8" 3' 8"	2' 3" 3' 8"	2' 0" 3' 8"	3' 1" 7' 4"	2' 2" 4' 0"	1' 8" 4' 0"	4' 2" 6' 3"	3' 5" 6' 3"	2' 8" 6' 3"	NA NA
3 1/2	3' 8" 4' 10"	3' 1" 4' 3"	2' 7" 4' 3"	2' 4" 4' 3"	3' 7" 8' 7"	2' 6" 4' 8"	1' 11" 4' 8"	4' 10" 7' 4"	4' 0" 7' 4"	3' 1" 7' 4"	NA NA
4	4' 2" 5' 6"	3' 7" 4' 11"	2' 11" 4' 11"	2' 8" 4' 11"	4' 2" 9' 9"	2' 11" 5' 4"	2' 3" 5' 4"	5' 6" 8' 5"	4' 6" 8' 5"	3' 6" 8' 5"	NA NA
4 1/2	4' 8" 6' 3"	4' 0" 5' 6"	3' 4" 5' 6"	3' 0" 5' 6"	4' 8" 11' 0"	3' 3" 6' 0"	2' 6" 6' 0"	6' 3" 9' 5"	5' 1" 9' 5"	3' 11" 9' 5"	NA NA
5	5' 2" 6' 11"	4' 5" 6' 1"	3' 8" 6' 1"	3' 4" 6' 1"	5' 2" 12' 3"	3' 7" 6' 8"	2' 9" 6' 8"	6' 11" 10' 6"	5' 8" 10' 6"	4' 5" 10' 6"	NA NA
5 1/2	5' 8" 7' 7"	4' 11" 6' 9"	4' 1" 6' 9"	3' 8" 6' 9"	5' 8" 13' 5"	4' 0" 7' 4"	3' 1" 7' 4"	7' 7" 11' 6"	6' 3" 11' 6"	4' 10" 11' 6"	NA NA
6	6' 3" 8' 4"	5' 4" 7' 4"	4' 5" 7' 4"	4' 0" 7' 4"	6' 2" 14' 8"	4' 4" 8' 0"	3' 4" 8' 0"	8' 4" 12' 7"	6' 10" 12' 7"	5' 3" 12' 7"	NA NA

6½	6' 9" 9' 0"	5' 9" 7' 11"	4' 9" 7' 11"	4' 4" 7' 11"	6' 9" 15' 11"	4' 8" 8' 8"	3' 7" 8' 8"	9' 0" 13' 7"	7' 4" 13' 7"	5' 8" 13' 7"	NA NA
7	7' 3" 9' 8"	6' 3" 8' 7"	5' 2" 8' 7"	4' 7" 8' 7"	7' 3" 17' 1"	5' 1" 9' 4"	3' 11" 9' 4"	9' 8" 14' 8"	7' 11" 14' 8"	6' 2" 14' 8"	NA NA
8	8' 4" 11' 1"	7' 1" 9' 9"	5' 11" 9' 9"	5' 3" 9' 9"	8' 3" 19' 7"	5' 9" 10' 8"	4' 5" 10' 8"	11' 1" 16' 9"	9' 1" 16' 9"	7' 0" 16' 9"	NA NA
9	9' 4" 12' 6"	8' 0" 11' 0"	6' 8" 11' 0"	5' 11" 11' 0"	9' 4" 22' 0"	6' 6" 12' 0"	5' 0" 12' 0"	12' 6" 18' 10"	10' 2" 18' 10"	7' 11" 18' 10"	NA NA
10	10' 4" 13' 10"	8' 11" 12' 3"	7' 4" 12' 3"	6' 7" 12' 3"	10' 4" 24' 5"	7' 3" 13' 4"	5' 7" 13' 4"	13' 10" 20' 11"	11' 4" 20' 11"	8' 9" 20' 11"	NA NA
12	12' 5" 16' 7"	10' 8" 14' 8"	8' 10" 14' 8"	7' 11" 14' 8"	12' 5" 29' 4"	8' 8" 16' 0"	6' 8" 16' 0"	16' 7" 25' 2"	13' 7" 25' 2"	10' 6" 25' 2"	NA NA
14	14' 6" 19' 5"	12' 6" 17' 1"	10' 4" 17' 1"	9' 3" 17' 1"	14' 6" 34' 3"	10' 1" 18' 8"	7' 9" 18' 8"	19' 5" 29' 4"	15' 10" 29' 4"	12' 3" 29' 4"	NA NA
16	16' 7" 22' 2"	14' 3" 19' 7"	11' 9" 19' 7"	10' 7" 19' 7"	16' 6" 39' 1"	11' 6" 21' 4"	8' 11" 21' 4"	22' 2" 33' 6"	18' 2" 33' 6"	14' 0" 33' 6"	NA NA
18	18' 8" 24' 11"	16' 0" 22' 0"	13' 3" 22' 0"	11' 11" 22' 0"	18' 7" 44' 0"	13' 0" 24' 0"	10' 0" 24' 0"	24' 11" 37' 9"	20' 5" 37' 9"	15' 9" 37' 9"	NA NA
20	20' 9" 27' 8"	17' 10" 24' 5"	14' 9" 24' 5"	13' 2" 24' 5"	20' 8" 48' 11"	14' 5" 26' 8"	11' 1" 26' 8"	27' 8" 41' 11"	22' 8" 41' 11"	17' 6" 41' 11"	NA NA
25	25' 11" 34' 7"	22' 3" 30' 7"	18' 5" 30' 7"	16' 6" 30' 7"	25' 10" 61' 1"	18' 0" 33' 4"	13' 11" 33' 4"	34' 7" 52' 5"	28' 4" 52' 5"	21' 11" 52' 5"	NA NA
50	51' 10" 69' 3"	44' 6" 61' 1"	36' 10" 61' 1"	33' 0" 61' 1"	51' 8" 122' 2"	36' 1" 66' 8"	27' 10" 66' 8"	69' 3" 104' 9"	56' 8" 104' 9"	43' 10" 104' 9"	NA NA

20mm FIELD OF VIEW

SETUPS (Approximate Distance)											
Ext Close Up Close Up Medium Shot Full Figure	0' 10" 1' 3" 2' 4" 6' 5"	0' 11" 1' 5" 2' 8" 7' 6"	1' 2" 1' 9" 3' 3" 9' 1"	1' 3" 2' 0" 3' 8" 10' 1"	NA NA NA NA	1' 2" 1' 10" 3' 4" 9' 3"	1' 6" 2' 4" 4' 4" 12' 0"	0' 7" 0' 11" 1' 9" 4' 10"	0' 9" 1' 2" 2' 1" 5' 11"	0' 11" 1' 6" 2' 9" 7' 7"	NA NA NA NA
Angle of View	V 50.0° H 63.8°	V 41.8° H 55.3°	V 35.0° H 55.3°	V 31.6° H 55.3°		V 36.0° H 61.9°	V 28.1° H 61.9°	V 64.4° H 86.6°	V 54.0° H 86.6°	V 43.0° H 86.6°	
	Full Aperture	**Academy 1.33:1**	**Academy 1.66:1**	**Academy 1.85:1**	**Anamorphic 2.40:1**	**Super 35 1.85:1**	**Super 35 2.40:1**	**VistaVision**	**VistaVision 1.85:1**	**VistaVision 2.40:1**	**65mm**
2	1' 10" 2' 6"	1' 7" 2' 2"	1' 4" 2' 2"	1' 2" 2' 2"	NA NA	1' 4" 2' 5"	1' 0" 2' 5"	2' 6" 3' 9"	2' 0" 3' 9"	1' 7" 3' 9"	NA NA
2 ½	2' 4" 3' 1"	2' 0" 2' 9"	1' 8" 2' 9"	1' 6" 2' 9"	NA NA	1' 7" 3' 0"	1' 3" 3' 0"	3' 1" 4' 9"	2' 7" 4" 9"	2' 0" 4' 9"	NA NA
3	2' 10" 3' 9"	2' 5" 3' 4"	2' 0" 3' 4"	1' 9" 3' 4"	NA NA	1' 11" 3' 7"	1' 6" 3' 7"	3' 9" 5' 8"	3' 1" 5' 8"	2' 4" 5' 8"	NA NA
3 ½	3' 3" 4' 4"	2' 10" 3' 10"	2' 4" 3' 10"	2' 1" 3' 10"	NA NA	2' 3" 4' 2"	1' 9" 4' 2"	4' 4" 6' 7"	3' 7" 6' 7"	2' 9" 6' 7"	NA NA
4	3' 9" 5' 0"	3' 2" 4' 5"	2' 8" 4' 5"	2' 5" 4' 5"	NA NA	2' 7" 4' 10"	2' 0" 4' 10"	5' 0" 7' 7"	4' 1" 7' 7"	3' 2" 7' 7"	NA NA
4 ½	4' 2" 5' 7"	3' 7" 4' 11"	3' 0" 4' 11"	2' 8" 4' 11"	NA NA	2' 11" 5' 5"	2' 3" 5' 5"	5' 7" 8' 6"	4' 7" 8' 6"	3' 7" 8' 6"	NA NA
5	4' 8" 6' 3"	4' 0" 5' 6"	3' 4" 5' 6"	3' 0" 5' 6"	NA NA	3' 3" 6' 0"	2' 6" 6' 0"	6' 3" 9' 5"	5' 1" 9' 5"	3' 11 9' 5"	NA NA
5 ½	5' 2" 6' 10"	4' 5" 6' 1"	3' 8" 6' 1"	3' 3" 6' 1"	NA NA	3' 7" 6' 7"	2' 9" 6' 7"	6' 10" 10' 4"	5' 7" 10' 4"	4' 4" 10' 4"	NA NA
6	5' 7" 7' 6"	4' 10" 6' 7"	4' 0" 6' 7"	3' 7" 6' 7"	NA NA	3' 11" 7' 2"	3' 0" 7' 2"	7' 6" 11' 4"	6' 1" 11' 4"	4' 9" 11' 4"	NA NA

6½	6' 1" 8' 1"	5' 3" 7' 2"	4' 4" 7' 2"	3' 10" 7' 2"	NA NA	4' 3" 7' 10"	3' 3" 7' 10"	8' 1" 12' 3"	6' 8" 12' 3"	5' 2" 12' 3"	NA NA
7	6' 6" 8' 9"	5' 7" 7' 8"	4' 8" 7' 8"	4' 2" 7' 8"	NA NA	4' 7" 8' 5"	3' 6" 8' 5"	8' 9" 13' 2"	7' 2" 13' 2"	5' 6" 13' 2"	NA NA
8	7' 6" 10' 0"	6' 5" 8' 10"	5' 4" 8' 10"	4' 9" 8' 10"	NA NA	5' 2" 9' 7"	4' 0" 9' 7"	10' 0" 15' 1"	8' 2" 15' 1"	6' 4" 15' 1"	NA NA
9	8' 5" 11' 3"	7' 3" 9' 11"	6' 0" 9' 11"	5' 4" 9' 11"	NA NA	5' 10" 10' 10"	4' 6" 10' 10"	11' 3" 17' 0"	9' 2" 17' 0"	7' 1" 17' 0"	NA NA
10	9' 4" 12' 6"	8' 0" 11' 0"	6' 8" 11' 0"	5' 11" 11' 0"	NA NA	6' 6" 12' 0"	5' 0" 12' 0"	12' 6" 18' 10"	10' 2" 18' 10"	7' 11" 18' 10"	NA NA
12	11' 2" 14' 11"	9' 7" 13' 2"	7' 11" 13' 2"	7' 2" 13' 2"	NA NA	7' 9" 14' 5"	6' 0" 14' 5"	14' 11" 22' 8"	12' 3" 22' 8"	9' 6" 22' 8"	NA NA
14	13' 1" 17' 5"	11' 3" 15' 5"	9' 3" 15' 5"	8' 4" 15' 5"	NA NA	9' 1" 16' 10"	7' 0" 16' 10"	17' 5" 26' 5"	14' 3" 26' 5"	11' 0" 26' 5"	NA NA
16	14' 11" 19' 11"	12' 10" 17' 7"	10' 7" 17' 7"	9' 6" 17' 7"	NA NA	10' 5" 19' 2"	8' 0" 19' 2"	19' 11" 30' 2"	16' 4" 30' 2"	12' 7" 30' 2"	NA NA
18	16' 10" 22' 5"	14' 5" 19' 10"	11' 11" 19' 10"	10' 8" 19' 10"	NA NA	11' 8" 21' 7"	9' 0" 21' 7"	22' 5" 33' 11"	18' 4" 33' 11"	14' 2" 33' 11"	NA NA
20	18' 8" 24' 11"	16' 0" 22' 0"	13' 3" 22' 0"	11' 11" 22' 0"	NA NA	13' 0" 24' 0"	10' 0" 24' 0"	24' 11" 37' 9"	20' 5" 37' 9"	15' 9" 37' 9"	NA NA
25	23' 4" 31' 2"	20' 0" 27' 6"	16' 7" 27' 6"	14' 10" 27' 6"	NA NA	16' 3" 30' 0"	12' 6" 30' 0"	31' 2" 47' 2"	25' 6" 47' 2"	19' 9" 47' 2"	NA NA
50	46' 8" 62' 4"	40' 1" 55' 0"	33' 2" 55' 0"	29' 9" 55' 0"	NA NA	32' 5" 60' 0"	25' 0" 60' 0"	62' 4" 94' 4"	51' 0" 94' 4"	39' 5" 94' 4"	NA NA

SETUPS (Approximate Distance)	**24mm FIELD OF VIEW**										
Ext Close Up **Close Up** **Medium Shot** **Full Figure**	1' 0" 1' 6" 2' 9" 7' 9"	1' 1" 1' 9" 3' 3" 9' 0"	1' 4" 2' 1" 3' 11" 10' 10"	1' 6" 2' 4" 4' 4" 12' 1"	1' 0" 1' 6" 2' 10" 7' 9"	1' 5" 2' 2" 4' 0" 11' 1"	1' 10" 2' 10" 5' 2" 14' 5"	0' 9" 1' 1" 2' 1" 5' 9"	0' 11" 1' 4" 2' 7" 7' 1"	1' 2" 1' 9" 3' 4" 9' 2"	0' 9" 1' 3" 2' 3" 6' 3"
Angle of View	V 42.5° H 54.8°	V 35.3° H 47.2°	V 29.5° H 47.2°	V 26.6° H 47.2°	V 40.7° H 83.2°	V 30.3° H 53.1°	V 23.6° H 53.1°	V 55.3° H 76.3°	V 46.0° H 76.3°	V 36.4° H 76.3°	V 49.4° H 90.7°
	Full Aperture	**Academy 1.33:1**	**Academy 1.66:1**	**Academy 1.85:1**	**Anamorphic 2.40:1**	**Super 35 1.85:1**	**Super 35 2.40:1**	**VistaVision**	**VistaVision 1.85:1**	**VistaVision 2.40:1**	**65mm**
2	1' 7" 2' 1"	1' 4" 1' 10"	1' 1" 1' 10"	1' 0" 1' 10"	1' 7" 3' 8"	1' 1" 2' 0"	0' 10" 2' 0"	2' 1" 3' 2"	1' 8" 3' 2"	1' 4" 3' 2"	1' 11" 4' 5"
2 ½	1' 11" 2' 7"	1' 8" 2' 3"	1' 5" 2' 3"	1' 3" 2' 3"	1' 11" 4' 7"	1' 4" 2' 6"	1' 1" 2' 6"	2' 7" 3' 11"	2' 1" 3' 11"	1' 8" 3' 11"	2' 5" 5' 6"
3	2' 4" 3' 1"	2' 0" 2' 9"	1' 8" 2' 9"	1' 6" 2' 9"	2' 4" 5' 6"	1' 7" 3' 0"	1' 3" 3' 0"	3' 1" 4' 9"	2' 7" 4' 9"	2' 0" 4' 9"	2' 11" 6' 7"
3 ½	2' 9" 3' 8"	2' 4" 3' 2"	1' 11" 3' 2"	1' 9" 3' 2"	2' 9" 6' 5"	1' 11" 3' 6"	1' 6" 3' 6"	3' 8" 5' 6"	3' 0" 5' 6"	2' 4" 5' 6"	3' 4" 7' 8"
4	3' 1" 4' 2"	2' 8" 3' 8"	2' 3" 3' 8"	2' 0" 3' 8"	3' 1" 7' 4"	2' 2" 4' 0"	1' 8" 4' 0"	4' 2" 6' 3"	3' 5" 6' 3"	2' 8" 6' 3"	3' 10" 8' 9"
4 ½	3' 6" 4' 8"	3' 0" 4' 1"	2' 6" 4' 1"	2' 3" 4' 1"	3' 6" 8' 3"	2' 5" 4' 6"	1' 11" 4' 6"	4' 8" 7' 1"	3' 10" 7' 1"	2' 11" 7' 1"	4' 4" 9' 10"
5	3' 11" 5' 2"	3' 4" 4' 7"	2' 9" 4' 7"	2' 6" 4' 7"	3' 10" 9' 2"	2' 8" 5' 0"	2' 1" 5' 0"	5' 2" 7' 10"	4' 3" 7' 10"	3' 3" 7' 10"	4' 10" 11' 0"
5 ½	4' 3" 5' 9"	3' 8" 5' 0"	3' 0" 5' 0"	2' 9" 5' 0"	4' 3" 10' 1"	3' 0" 5' 6"	2' 4" 5' 6"	5' 9" 8' 8"	4' 8" 8' 8"	3' 7" 8' 8"	5' 3" 12' 1"
6	4' 8" 6' 3"	4' 0" 5' 6"	3' 4" 5' 6"	3' 0" 5' 6"	4' 8" 11' 0"	3' 3" 6' 0"	2' 6" 6' 0"	6' 3" 9' 5"	5' 1" 9' 5"	3' 11" 9' 5"	5' 9" 13' 2"

6½	5' 1" 6' 9"	4' 4" 5' 11"	3' 7" 5' 11"	3' 3" 5' 11"	5' 0" 11' 11"	3' 6" 6' 6"	2' 9" 6' 6"	6' 9" 10' 3"	5' 6" 10' 3"	4' 3" 10' 3"	6' 3" 14' 3"
7	5' 5" 7' 3"	4' 8" 6' 5"	3' 10" 6' 5"	3' 6" 6' 5"	5' 5" 12' 10"	3' 9" 7' 0"	2' 11" 7' 0"	7' 3" 11' 0"	5' 11" 11' 0"	4' 7" 11' 0"	6' 9" 15' 4"
8	6' 3" 8' 4"	5' 4" 7' 4"	4' 5" 7' 4"	4' 0" 7' 4"	6' 2" 14' 8"	4' 4" 8' 0"	3' 4" 8' 0"	8' 4" 12' 7"	6' 10" 12' 7"	5' 3" 12' 7"	7' 8" 17' 7"
9	7' 0" 9' 4"	6' 0" 8' 3"	5' 0" 8' 3"	4' 5" 8' 3"	7' 0" 16' 6"	4' 10" 9' 0"	3' 9" 9' 0"	9' 4" 14' 2"	7' 8" 14' 2"	5' 11" 14' 2"	8' 8" 19' 9"
10	7' 9" 10' 5"	6' 8" 9' 2"	5' 6" 9' 2"	4' 11" 9' 2"	7' 9" 18' 4"	5' 5" 10' 0"	4' 2" 10' 0"	10' 5" 15' 9"	8' 6" 15" 9"	6' 7" 15' 9"	9' 7" 21' 11"
12	9' 4" 12' 6"	8' 0" 11' 0"	6' 8" 11' 0"	5' 11" 11' 0"	9' 4" 22' 0"	6' 6" 12' 0"	5' 0" 12' 0"	12' 6" 18' 10"	10' 2" 18' 10"	7' 11" 18' 10"	11' 6" 26' 4"
14	10' 11" 14' 6"	9' 4" 12' 10"	7' 9" 12' 10"	6' 11" 12' 10"	10' 10" 25' 8"	7' 7" 14' 0"	5' 10" 14' 0"	14' 6" 22' 0"	11' 11" 22' 0"	9' 2" 22' 0"	13' 5" 30' 8"
16	12' 5" 16' 7"	10' 8" 14' 8"	8' 10" 14' 8"	7' 11" 14' 8"	12' 5" 29' 4"	8' 8" 16' 0"	6' 8" 16' 0"	16' 7" 25' 2"	13' 7" 25' 2"	10' 6" 25' 2"	15' 4" 35' 1"
18	14' 0" 18' 8"	12' 0" 16' 6"	9' 11" 16' 6"	8' 11" 16' 6"	13' 11" 33' 0"	9' 9" 18' 0"	7' 6" 18' 0"	18' 8" 28' 3"	15' 4" 28' 3"	11' 10" 28' 3"	17' 3" 39' 6"
20	15' 7" 20' 9"	13' 4" 18' 4"	11' 1" 18' 4"	9' 11" 18' 4"	15' 6" 36' 8"	10' 10" 20' 0"	8' 4" 20' 0"	20' 9" 31' 5"	17' 0" 31' 5"	13' 2" 31' 5"	19' 2" 43' 10"
25	19' 5" 25' 11"	16' 8" 22' 11"	13' 10" 22' 11"	12' 5" 22' 11"	19' 4" 45' 10"	13' 6" 25' 0"	10' 5" 25' 0"	25' 11" 39' 3"	21' 3" 39' 3"	16' 5" 39' 3"	24' 0" 54' 10"
50	38' 11" 51' 11"	33' 5" 45' 10"	27' 7" 45' 10"	24' 9" 45' 10"	38' 9" 91' 8"	27' 0" 50' 0"	20' 10" 50' 0"	51' 11" 78' 7"	42' 6" 78' 7"	32' 10" 78' 7"	47' 11" 109' 8"

25mm FIELD OF VIEW

SETUPS (Approximate Distance)											
Ext Close Up **Close Up** **Medium Shot** **Full Figure**	1' 0" 1' 7" 2' 11" 8' 0"	1' 2" 1' 10" 3' 5" 9' 4"	1' 5" 2' 2" 4' 1" 11' 4"	1' 7" 2' 5" 4' 7" 12' 7"	1' 0" 1' 7" 2' 11" 8' 1"	1' 5" 2' 3" 4' 2" 11' 7"	1' 10" 2' 11" 5' 5" 15' 0"	0' 9" 1' 2" 2' 2" 6' 0"	0' 11" 1' 5" 2' 8" 7' 4"	1' 2" 1' 10" 3' 5" 9' 6"	0' 10" 1' 3" 2' 4" 6' 6"
Angle of View	V 40.9° H 52.9°	V 34.0° H 45.5°	V 28.3° H 45.5°	V 25.5° H 45.5°	V 39.2° H 80.9°	V 29.1° H 51.3°	V 22.6° H 53.1°	V 53.4° H 74.1°	V 44.4° H 74.1°	V 35.0° H 74.1°	V 49.4° H 92.9°
	Full Aperture	**Academy 1.33:1**	**Academy 1.66:1**	**Academy 1.85:1**	**Anamorphic 2.40:1**	**Super 35 1.85:1**	**Super 35 2.40:1**	**VistaVision**	**VistaVision 1.85:1**	**VistaVision 2.40:1**	**65mm**
2	1' 6" 2' 0"	1' 3" 1' 9"	1' 1" 1' 9"	0' 11" 1' 9"	1' 6" 3' 6"	1' 0" 1' 11"	0' 10" 1' 11"	2' 0" 3' 0"	1' 8" 3' 0"	1' 3" 3' 0"	1' 10" 4' 3"
2 ½	1' 10" 2' 6"	1' 7" 2' 2"	1' 4" 2' 2"	1' 2" 2' 2"	1' 10" 4' 5"	1' 4" 2' 5"	1' 0" 2' 5"	2' 6" 3' 9"	2' 0" 3' 9"	1' 7" 3' 9"	2' 4" 5' 3"
3	2' 3" 3' 0"	1' 11" 2' 8"	1' 7" 2' 8"	1' 5" 2' 8"	2' 3" 5' 3"	1' 7" 2' 11"	1' 2" 2' 11"	3' 0" 4' 6"	2' 5" 4' 6"	1' 11" 4' 6"	2' 9" 6' 4"
3 ½	2' 7" 3' 6"	2' 3" 3' 1"	1' 10" 3' 1"	1' 8" 3' 1"	2' 7" 6' 2"	1' 10" 3' 4"	1' 5" 3' 4"	3' 6" 5' 3"	2' 10" 5' 3"	2' 2" 5' 3"	3' 3" 7' 4"
4	3' 0" 4' 0"	2' 7" 3' 6"	2' 1" 3' 6"	1' 11" 3' 6"	3' 0" 7' 0"	2' 1" 3' 10"	1' 7" 3' 10"	4' 0" 6' 0"	3' 3" 6' 0"	2' 6" 6' 0"	3' 8" 8' 5"
4 ½	3' 4" 4' 6"	2' 11" 4' 0"	2' 5" 4' 0"	2' 2" 4' 0"	3' 4" 7' 11"	2' 4" 4' 4"	1' 10" 4' 4"	4' 6" 6' 9"	3' 8" 6' 9"	2' 10" 6' 9"	4' 2" 9' 6"
5	3' 9" 5' 0"	3' 2" 4' 5"	2' 8" 4' 5"	2' 5" 4' 5"	3' 9" 8' 10"	2' 7" 4' 10"	2' 0" 4' 10"	5' 0" 7' 7"	4' 1" 7' 7"	3' 2" 7' 7"	4' 7" 10' 6"
5 ½	4' 1" 5' 6"	3' 6" 4' 10"	2' 11" 4' 10"	2' 7" 4' 10"	4' 1" 9' 8"	2' 10" 5' 3"	2' 2" 5' 3"	5' 6" 8' 4"	4' 6" 8' 4"	3' 6" 8' 4"	5' 1" 11' 7"
6	4' 6" 6' 0"	3' 10" 5' 3"	3' 2" 5' 3"	2' 10" 5' 3"	4' 6" 10' 7"	3' 1" 5' 9"	2' 5" 5' 9"	6' 0" 9' 1"	4' 11" 9' 1"	3' 9" 9' 1"	5' 6" 12' 8"

6 ½	4' 10" 6' 6"	4' 2" 5' 9"	3' 5" 5' 9"	3' 1" 5' 9"	4' 10" 11' 5"	3' 4" 6' 3"	2' 7" 6' 3"	6' 6" 9' 10"	5' 4" 9' 10"	4' 1" 9' 10"	6' 0" 13' 8"
7	5' 3" 7' 0"	4' 6" 6' 2"	3' 9" 6' 2"	3' 4" 6' 2"	5' 2" 12' 4"	3' 8" 6' 9"	2' 10" 6' 9"	7' 0" 10' 7"	5' 9" 10' 7"	4' 5" 10' 7"	6' 5" 14' 9"
8	6' 0" 8' 0"	5' 2" 7' 0"	4' 3" 7' 0"	3' 10" 7' 0"	5' 11" 14' 1"	4' 2" 7' 8"	3' 2" 7' 8"	8' 0" 12' 1"	6' 6" 12' 1"	5' 1" 12' 1"	7' 4" 16' 10"
9	6' 9" 9' 0"	5' 9" 7' 11"	4' 9" 7' 11"	4' 3" 7' 11"	6' 8" 15' 10"	4' 8" 8' 8"	3' 7" 8' 8"	9' 0" 13' 7"	7' 4" 13' 7"	5' 8" 13' 7"	8' 3" 18' 11"
10	7' 6" 10' 0"	6' 5" 8' 10"	5' 4" 8' 10"	4' 9" 8' 10"	7' 5" 17' 7"	5' 2" 9' 7"	4' 0" 9' 7"	10' 0" 15' 1"	8' 2" 15' 1"	6' 4" 15' 1"	9' 2" 21' 1"
12	9' 0" 12' 0"	7' 8" 10' 7"	6' 4" 10' 7"	5' 8" 10' 7"	8' 11" 21' 1"	6' 3" 11' 6"	4' 10" 11' 6"	12' 0" 18' 1"	9' 9" 18' 1"	7' 7" 18' 1"	11' 1" 25' 3"
14	10' 5" 13' 11"	9' 0" 12' 4"	7' 5" 12' 4"	6' 8" 12' 4"	10' 5" 24' 8"	7' 3" 13' 5"	5' 7" 13' 5"	13' 11" 21' 1"	11' 5" 21' 1"	8' 10" 21' 1"	12' 11" 29' 6"
16	11' 11" 15' 11"	10' 3" 14' 1"	8' 6" 14' 1"	7' 7" 14' 1"	11' 11" 28' 2"	8' 4" 15' 4"	6' 5" 15' 4"	15' 11" 24' 2"	13' 1" 24' 2"	10' 1" 24' 2"	14' 9" 33' 8"
18	13' 5" 17' 11"	11' 6" 15' 10"	9' 7" 15' 10"	8' 7" 15' 10"	13' 5" 31' 8"	9' 4" 17' 3"	7' 2" 17' 3"	17' 11" 27' 2"	14' 8" 27' 2"	11' 4" 27' 2"	16' 7" 37' 11"
20	14' 11" 19' 11"	12' 10" 17' 7"	10' 7" 17' 7"	9' 6" 17' 7"	14' 10" 35' 2"	10' 5" 19' 2"	8' 0" 19' 2"	19' 11" 30' 2"	16' 4" 30' 2"	12' 7" 30' 2"	18' 5" 42' 1"
25	18' 8" 24' 11"	16' 0" 22' 0"	13' 3" 22' 0"	11' 11" 22' 0"	18' 7" 44' 0"	13' 0" 24' 0"	10' 0" 24' 0"	24' 11" 37' 9"	20' 5" 37' 9"	15' 9" 37' 9"	23' 0" 52' 8"
50	37' 4" 49' 10"	32' 1" 44' 0"	26' 6" 44' 0"	23' 9" 44' 0"	37' 2" 88' 0"	26' 0" 48' 0"	20' 0" 48' 0"	49' 10" 75' 5"	40' 10" 75' 5"	31' 7" 75' 5"	46' 0" 105' 3"

28mm FIELD OF VIEW

SETUPS (Approximate Distance)											
Ext Close Up Close Up Medium Shot Full Figure	1' 1" 1' 9" 3' 3" 9' 0"	1' 4" 2' 0" 3' 9" 10' 6"	1' 7" 2' 6" 4' 7" 12' 8"	1' 9" 2' 9" 5' 1" 14' 2"	1' 2" 1' 9" 3' 3" 9' 0"	1' 7" 2' 6" 4' 8" 12' 11"	2' 1" 3' 3" 6' 1" 16' 9"	0' 10" 1' 4" 2' 5" 6' 9"	1' 0" 1' 7" 3' 0" 8' 3"	1' 4" 2' 1" 3' 10" 10' 8"	0' 11" 1' 5" 2' 8" 7' 4"
Angle of View	V 36.9° H 47.9°	V 30.5° H 41.0°	V 25.4° H 41.0°	V 22.9° H 41.0°	V 35.2° H 74.5°	V 26.1° H 46.4°	V 20.3° H 46.4°	V 48.4° H 67.9°	V 40.0° H 67.9°	V 31.5° H 67.9°	
	Full Aperture	**Academy 1.33:1**	**Academy 1.66:1**	**Academy 1.85:1**	**Anamorphic 2.40:1**	**Super 35 1.85:1**	**Super 35 2.40:1**	**VistaVision**	**VistaVision 1.85:1**	**VistaVision 2.40:1**	**65mm**
2	1' 4" 1' 9"	1' 2" 1' 7"	0' 11" 1' 7"	0' 10" 1' 7"	1' 4" 3' 2"	0' 11" 1' 9"	0' 9" 1' 9"	1' 9" 2' 8"	1' 5" 2' 8"	1' 2" 2' 8"	NA NA
2 ½	1' 8" 2' 3"	1' 5" 2' 0"	1' 2" 2' 0"	1' 1" 2' 0"	1' 8" 3' 11"	1' 2" 2' 2"	0' 11" 2' 2"	2' 3" 3' 4"	1' 10" 3' 4"	1' 5" 3' 4"	NA NA
3	2' 0" 2' 8"	1' 9" 2' 4"	1' 5" 2' 4"	1' 3" 2' 4"	2' 0" 4' 9"	1' 5" 2' 7"	1' 1" 2' 7"	2' 8" 4' 0"	2' 2" 4' 0"	1' 8" 4' 0"	NA NA
3 ½	2' 4" 3' 1"	2' 0" 2' 9"	1' 8" 2' 9"	1' 6" 2' 9"	2' 4" 5' 6"	1' 7" 3' 0"	1' 3" 3' 0"	3' 1" 4' 9"	2' 7" 4' 9"	2' 0" 4' 9"	NA NA
4	2' 8" 3' 7"	2' 3" 3' 2"	1' 11" 3' 2"	1' 8" 3' 2"	2' 8" 6' 3"	1' 10" 3' 5"	1' 5" 3' 5"	3' 7" 5' 5"	2' 11" 5' 5"	2' 3" 5' 5"	NA NA
4 ½	3' 0" 4' 0"	2' 7" 3' 6"	2' 2" 3' 6"	1' 11" 3' 6"	3' 0" 7' 1"	2' 1" 3' 10"	1' 7" 3' 10"	4' 0" 6' 1"	3' 3" 6' 1"	2' 6" 6' 1"	NA NA
5	3' 4" 4' 5"	2' 10" 3' 11"	2' 4" 3' 11"	2' 1" 3' 11"	3' 4" 7' 10"	2' 4" 4' 3"	1' 9" 4' 3"	4' 5" 6' 9"	3' 8" 6' 9"	2' 10" 6' 9"	NA NA
5 ½	3' 8" 4' 11"	3' 2" 4' 4"	2' 7" 4' 4"	2' 4" 4' 4"	3' 8" 8' 8"	2' 7" 4' 9"	2' 0" 4' 9"	4' 11" 7' 5"	4' 0" 7' 5"	3' 1" 7' 5"	NA NA
6	4' 0" 5' 4"	3' 5" 4' 9"	2' 10" 4' 9"	2' 7" 4' 9"	4' 0" 9' 5"	2' 9" 5' 2"	2' 2" 5' 2"	5' 4" 8' 1"	4' 4" 8' 1"	3' 5" 8' 1"	NA NA

6 1/2	4' 4" 5' 9"	3' 9" 5' 1"	3' 1" 5' 1"	2' 9" 5' 1"	4' 4" 10' 3"	3' 0" 5' 7"	2' 4" 5' 7"	5' 9" 8' 9"	4' 9" 8' 9"	3' 8" 8' 9"	NA NA
7	4' 8" 6' 3"	4' 0" 5' 6"	3' 4" 5' 6"	3' 0" 5' 6"	4' 8" 11' 0"	3' 3" 6' 0"	2' 6" 6' 0"	6' 3" 9' 5"	5' 1" 9' 5"	3' 11" 9' 5"	NA NA
8	5' 4" 7' 1"	4' 7" 6' 3"	3' 9" 6' 3"	3' 5" 6' 3"	5' 4" 12' 7"	3' 9" 6' 10"	2' 10" 6' 10"	7' 1" 10' 9"	5' 10" 10' 9"	4' 6" 10' 9"	NA NA
9	6' 0" 8' 0"	5' 2" 7' 1"	4' 3" 7' 1"	3' 10" 7' 1"	6' 0" 14' 2"	4' 2" 7' 9"	3' 3" 7' 9"	8' 0" 12' 1"	6' 7" 12' 1"	5' 1" 12' 1"	NA NA
10	6' 8" 8' 11"	5' 9" 7' 10"	4' 9" 7' 10"	4' 3" 7' 10"	6' 8" 15' 9"	4' 8" 8' 7"	3' 7" 8' 7"	8' 11" 13' 6"	7' 3" 13' 6"	5' 8" 13' 6"	NA NA
12	8' 0" 10' 8"	6' 10" 9' 5"	5' 8" 9' 5"	5' 1" 9' 5"	8' 0" 18' 10"	5' 7" 10' 3"	4' 3" 10' 3"	10' 8" 16' 2"	8' 9" 16' 2"	6' 9" 16' 2"	NA NA
14	9' 4" 12' 6"	8' 0" 11' 0"	6' 8" 11' 0"	5' 11" 11' 0"	9' 4" 22' 0"	6' 6" 12' 0"	5' 0" 12' 0"	12' 6" 18' 10"	10' 2" 18' 10"	7' 11" 18' 10"	NA NA
16	10' 8" 14' 3"	9' 2" 12' 7"	7' 7" 12' 7"	6' 10" 12' 7"	10' 7" 25' 2"	7' 5" 13' 9"	5' 9" 13' 9"	14' 3" 21' 7"	11' 8" 21' 7"	9' 0" 21' 7"	NA NA
18	12' 0" 16' 0"	10' 4" 14' 2"	8' 6" 14' 2"	7' 8" 14' 2"	11' 11" 28' 3"	8' 4" 15' 5"	6' 5" 15' 5"	16' 0" 24' 3"	13' 1" 24' 3"	10' 2" 24' 3"	NA NA
20	13' 4" 17' 10"	11' 5" 15' 9"	9' 6" 15' 9"	8' 6" 15' 9"	13' 3" 31' 5"	9' 3" 17' 2"	7' 2" 17' 2"	17' 10" 26' 11"	14' 7" 26' 11"	11' 3" 26' 11"	NA
25	16' 8" 22' 3"	14' 4" 19' 8"	11' 10" 19' 8"	10' 7" 19' 8"	16' 7" 39' 3"	11' 7" 21' 5"	8' 11" 21' 5"	22' 3" 33' 8"	18' 3" 33' 8"	14' 1" 33' 8"	NA NA
50	33' 4" 44' 6"	28' 7" 39' 3"	23' 8" 39' 3"	21' 3" 39' 3"	33' 2" 78' 7"	23' 2" 42' 10"	17' 10" 42' 10"	44' 6" 67' 4"	36' 5" 67' 4"	28' 2" 67' 4"	NA NA

32mm FIELD OF VIEW

SETUPS (Approximate Distance)											
Ext Close Up Close Up Medium Shot Full Figure	1' 3" 2' 0" 3' 9" 10' 3"	1' 6" 2' 4" 4' 4" 12' 0"	1' 10" 2' 10" 5' 3" 14' 6"	2' 0" 3' 2" 5' 10" 16' 2"	1' 3" 2' 0" 3' 9" 10' 4"	1' 10" 2' 11" 5' 4" 14' 10"	2' 5" 3' 9" 6' 11" 19' 2"	1' 0" 1' 6" 2' 9" 7' 8"	1' 2" 1' 10" 3' 5" 9' 5"	1' 6" 2' 4" 4' 5" 12' 2"	1' 1" 1' 7" 3' 0" 8' 4"
Angle of View	V 32.5° H 42.5°	V 26.9° H 36.3°	V 22.3° H 36.3°	V 20.1° H 36.3°	V 31.1° H 67.3°	V 22.9° H 41.1°	V 17.8° H 41.1°		V 35.4° H 61.0°	V 27.7° H 61.0°	
	Full Aperture	**Academy 1.33:1**	**Academy 1.66:1**	**Academy 1.85:1**	**Anamorphic 2.40:1**	**Super 35 1.85:1**	**Super 35 2.40:1**	**VistaVision**	**VistaVision 1.85:1**	**VistaVision 2.40:1**	**65mm**
2	1' 2" 1' 7"	1' 0" 1' 4"	0' 10" 1' 4"	0' 9" 1' 4"	1' 2" 2' 9"	0' 10" 1' 6"	0' 8" 1' 6"	NA NA	1' 3" 2' 4"	1' 0" 2' 4"	NA NA
2 1/2	1' 6" 1' 11"	1' 3" 1' 9"	1' 0" 1' 9"	0' 11" 1' 9"	1' 5" 3' 5"	1' 0" 1' 11"	0' 9" 1' 11"	NA NA	1' 7" 2' 11"	1' 3" 2' 11"	NA NA
3	1' 9" 2' 4"	1' 6" 2' 1"	1' 3" 2' 1"	1' 1" 2' 1"	1' 9" 4' 1"	1' 3" 2' 3"	0' 11" 2' 3"	NA NA	1' 11" 3' 6"	1' 6" 3' 6"	NA NA
3 1/2	2' 1" 2' 9"	1' 9" 2' 5"	1' 5" 2' 5"	1' 4" 2' 5"	2' 0" 4' 10"	1' 5" 2' 8"	1' 1" 2' 8"	NA NA	2' 3" 4' 2"	1' 9" 4' 2"	NA NA
4	2' 4" 3' 1"	2' 0" 2' 9"	1' 8" 2' 9"	1' 6" 2' 9"	2' 4" 5' 6"	1' 7" 3' 0"	1' 3" 3' 0"	NA NA	2' 7" 4' 9"	2' 0" 4' 9"	NA NA
4 1/2	2' 8" 3' 6"	2' 3" 3' 1"	1' 10" 3' 1"	1' 8" 3' 1"	2' 7" 6' 2"	1' 10" 3' 5"	1' 5" 3' 5"	NA NA	2' 10" 5' 4"	2' 3" 5' 4"	NA NA
5	2' 11" 3' 11"	2' 6" 3' 5"	2' 1" 3' 5"	1' 10" 3' 5"	2' 11" 6' 10"	2' 0" 3' 9"	1' 7" 3' 9"	NA NA	3' 2" 5' 11"	2' 6" 5' 11"	NA NA
5 1/2	3' 3" 4' 3"	2' 9" 3' 9"	2' 3" 3' 9"	2' 1" 3' 9"	3' 2" 7' 7"	2' 3" 4' 2"	1' 9" 4' 2"	NA NA	3' 6" 6' 6"	2' 9" 6' 6"	NA NA
6	3' 6" 4' 8"	3' 0" 4' 1"	2' 6" 4' 1"	2' 3" 4' 1"	3' 6" 8' 3"	2' 5" 4' 6"	1' 11" 4' 6"	NA NA	3' 10" 7' 1"	2' 11" 7' 1"	NA NA

6½	3' 10" 5' 1"	3' 3" 4' 6"	2' 8" 4' 6"	2' 5" 4' 6"	3' 9" 8' 11"	2' 8" 4' 11"	2' 0" 4' 11"	NA NA	4' 2" 7' 8"	3' 2" 7' 8"	NA NA
7	4' 1" 5' 5"	3' 6" 4' 10"	2' 11" 4' 10"	2' 7" 4' 10"	4' 1" 9' 7"	2' 10" 5' 3"	2' 2" 5' 3"	NA NA	4' 6" 8' 3"	3' 5" 8' 3"	NA NA
8	4' 8" 6' 3"	4' 0" 5' 6"	3' 4" 5' 6"	3' 0" 5' 6"	4' 8" 11' 0"	3' 3" 6' 0"	2' 6" 6' 0"	NA NA	5' 1" 9' 5"	3' 11" 9' 5"	NA NA
9	5' 3" 7' 0"	4' 6" 6' 2"	3' 9" 6' 2"	3' 4" 6' 2"	5' 3" 12' 4"	3' 8" 6' 9"	2' 10" 6' 9"	NA NA	5' 9" 10' 7"	4' 5" 10' 7"	NA NA
10	5' 10" 7' 9"	5' 0" 6' 10"	4' 2" 6' 10"	3' 9" 6' 10"	5' 10" 13' 9"	4' 1" 7' 6"	3' 2" 7' 6"	NA NA	6' 4" 11' 9"	4' 11" 11' 9"	NA NA
12	7' 0" 9' 4"	6' 0" 8' 3"	5' 0" 8' 3"	4' 5" 8' 3"	7' 0" 16' 6"	4' 10" 9' 0"	3' 9" 9' 0"	NA NA	7' 8" 14' 2"	5' 11" 14' 2"	NA NA
14	8' 2" 10' 11"	7' 0" 9' 7"	5' 10" 9' 7"	5' 2" 9' 7"	8' 2" 19' 3"	5' 8" 10' 6"	4' 5" 10' 6"	NA NA	8' 11" 16' 6"	6' 11" 16' 6"	NA NA
16	9' 4" 12' 6"	8' 0" 11' 0"	6' 8" 11' 0"	5' 11" 11' 0"	9' 4" 22' 0"	6' 6" 12' 0"	5' 0" 12' 0"	NA NA	10' 2" 18' 10"	7' 11" 18' 10"	NA NA
18	10' 6" 14' 0"	9' 0" 12' 4"	7' 5" 12' 4"	6' 8" 12' 4"	10' 6" 24' 9"	7' 4" 13' 6"	5' 8" 13' 6"	NA NA	11' 6" 21' 3"	8' 10" 21' 3"	NA NA
20	11' 8" 15' 7"	10' 0" 13' 9"	8' 3" 13' 9"	7' 5" 13' 9"	11' 7" 27' 6"	8' 1" 15' 0"	6' 3" 15' 0"	NA NA	12' 9" 23' 7"	9' 10" 23' 7"	NA NA
25	14' 7" 19' 6"	12' 6" 17' 2"	10' 4" 17' 2"	9' 3" 17' 2"	14' 6" 34' 4"	10' 2" 18' 9"	7' 10" 18' 9"	NA NA	15' 11" 29' 6"	12' 4" 29' 6"	NA NA
50	29' 2" 38' 11"	25' 1" 34' 4"	20' 9" 34' 4"	18' 7" 34' 4"	29' 1" 68' 9"	20' 3" 37' 6"	15' 8" 37' 6"	NA NA	31' 10" 58' 11"	24' 8" 58' 11"	NA NA

35mm FIELD OF VIEW

SETUPS (Approximate Distance)											
Ext Close Up **Close Up** **Medium Shot** **Full Figure**	1' 5" 2' 2" 4' 1" 11' 3"	1' 8" 2' 7" 4' 9" 13' 1"	2' 0" 3' 1" 5' 9" 15' 10"	2' 2" 3' 5" 6' 5" 17' 8"	1' 5" 2' 2" 4' 1" 11' 4"	2' 0" 3' 2" 5' 10" 16' 2"	2' 7" 4' 1" 7' 7" 21' 0"	1' 1" 1' 8" 3' 1" 8' 5"	1' 3" 2' 0" 3' 9" 10' 4"	1' 8" 2' 7" 4' 10" 13' 4"	1' 2" 1' 9" 3' 4" 9' 2"
Angle of View	V 29.9° H 39.2°	V 24.6° H 33.3°	V 20.4° H 33.3°	V 18.4° H 33.3°	V 28.5° H 62.7°	V 21.0° H 37.9°	V 16.3° H 37.9°	V 39.6° H 56.6°	V 32.5° H 56.6°	V 25.4° H 56.6°	V 36.4° H 73.9°
	Full Aperture	**Academy 1.33:1**	**Academy 1.66:1**	**Academy 1.85:1**	**Anamorphic 2.40:1**	**Super 35 1.85:1**	**Super 35 2.40:1**	**VistaVision**	**VistaVision 1.85:1**	**VistaVision 2.40:1**	**65mm**
2	1' 1" 1' 5"	0' 11" 1' 3"	0' 9" 1' 3"	0' 8" 1' 3"	1' 1" 2' 6"	0' 9" 1' 4"	0' 7" 1' 4"	1' 5" 2' 2"	1' 2" 2' 2"	0' 11" 2' 2"	1' 4" 3' 0"
2 ½	1' 4" 1' 9"	1' 2" 1' 7"	0' 11" 1' 7"	0' 10" 1' 7"	1' 4" 3' 2"	0' 11" 1' 9"	0' 9" 1' 9"	1' 9" 2' 8"	1' 5" 2' 8"	1' 2" 2' 8"	1' 8" 3' 9"
3	1' 7" 2' 2"	1' 4" 1' 11"	1' 2" 1' 11"	1' 0" 1' 11"	1' 7" 3' 9"	1' 1" 2' 1"	0' 10" 2' 1"	2' 2" 3' 3"	1' 9" 3' 3"	1' 4" 3' 3"	2' 0" 4' 6"
3 ½	1' 10" 2' 6"	1' 7" 2' 2"	1' 4" 2' 2"	1' 2" 2' 2"	1' 10" 4' 5"	1' 4" 2' 5"	1' 0" 2' 5"	2' 6" 3' 9"	2' 0" 3' 9"	1' 7" 3' 9"	2' 4" 5' 3"
4	2' 2" 2' 10"	1' 10" 2' 6"	1' 6" 2' 6"	1' 4" 2' 6"	2' 1" 5' 0"	1' 6" 2' 9"	1' 2" 2' 9"	2' 10" 4' 4"	2' 4" 4' 4"	1' 10" 4' 4"	2' 8" 6' 0"
4 ½	2' 5" 3' 2"	2' 1" 2' 10"	1' 8" 2' 10"	1' 6" 2' 10"	2' 5" 5' 8"	1' 8" 3' 1"	1' 3" 3' 1"	3' 2" 4' 10"	2' 7" 4' 10"	2' 0" 4' 10"	3' 0" 6' 9"
5	2' 8" 3' 7"	2' 3" 3' 2"	1' 11" 3' 2"	1' 8" 3' 2"	2' 8" 6' 3"	1' 10" 3' 5"	1' 5" 3' 5"	3' 7" 5' 5"	2' 11" 5' 5"	2' 3" 5' 5"	3' 3" 7' 6"
5 ½	2' 11" 3' 11"	2' 6" 3' 5"	2' 1" 3' 5"	1' 10" 3' 5"	2' 11" 6' 11"	2' 0" 3' 9"	1' 7" 3' 9"	3' 11" 5' 11"	3' 2" 5' 11"	2' 6" 5' 11"	3' 7" 8' 3"
6	3' 2" 4' 3"	2' 9" 3' 9"	2' 3" 3' 9"	2' 0" 3' 9"	3' 2" 7' 6"	2' 3" 4' 1"	1' 9" 4' 1"	4' 3" 6' 6"	3' 6" 6' 6"	2' 8" 6' 6"	3' 11" 9' 0"

6½	3' 6" 4' 8"	3' 0" 4' 1"	2' 6" 4' 1"	2' 2" 4' 1"	3' 5" 8' 2"	2' 5" 4' 5"	1' 10" 4' 5"	4' 8" 7' 0"	3' 9" 7' 0"	2' 11" 7' 0"	4' 3" 9' 9"
7	3' 9" 5' 0"	3' 2" 4' 5"	2' 8" 4' 5"	2' 5" 4' 5"	3' 9" 8' 10"	2' 7" 4' 10"	2' 0" 4' 10"	5' 0" 7' 7"	4' 1" 7' 7"	3' 2" 7' 7"	4' 7" 10' 6"
8	4' 3" 5' 8"	3' 8" 5' 0"	3' 0" 5' 0"	2' 9" 5' 0"	4' 3" 10' 1"	3' 0" 5' 6"	2' 3" 5' 6"	5' 8" 8' 7"	4' 8" 8' 7"	3' 7" 8' 7"	5' 3" 12' 0"
9	4' 10" 6' 5"	4' 1" 5' 8"	3' 5" 5' 8"	3' 1" 5' 8"	4' 9" 11' 4"	3' 4" 6' 2"	2' 7" 6' 2"	6' 5" 9' 8"	5' 3" 9' 8"	4' 1" 9' 8"	5' 11" 13' 6"
10	5' 4" 7' 1"	4' 7" 6' 3"	3' 9" 6' 3"	3' 5" 6' 3"	5' 4" 12' 7"	3' 9" 6' 10"	2' 10" 6' 10"	7' 1" 10' 9"	5' 10" 10' 9"	4' 6" 10' 9"	6' 7" 15' 0"
12	6' 5" 8' 7"	5' 6" 7' 6"	4' 7" 7' 6"	4' 1" 7' 6"	6' 4" 15' 1"	4' 5" 8' 3"	3' 5" 8' 3"	8' 7" 12' 11"	7' 0" 12' 11"	5' 5" 12' 11"	7' 11" 18' 1"
14	7' 6" 10' 0"	6' 5" 8' 10"	5' 4" 8' 10"	4' 9" 8' 10"	7' 5" 17' 7"	5' 2" 9' 7"	4' 0" 9' 7"	10' 0" 15' 1"	8' 2" 15' 1"	6' 4" 15' 1"	9' 2" 21' 1"
16	8' 6" 11' 5"	7' 4" 10' 1"	6' 1" 10' 1"	5' 5" 10' 1"	8' 6" 20' 1"	5' 11" 11' 0"	4' 7" 11' 0"	11' 5" 17' 3"	9' 4" 17' 3"	7' 3" 17' 3"	10' 6" 24' 1"
18	9' 7" 12' 10"	8' 3" 11' 4"	6' 10" 11' 4"	6' 1" 11' 4"	9' 7" 22' 7"	6' 8" 12' 4"	5' 2" 12' 4"	12' 10" 19' 5"	10' 6" 19' 5"	8' 1" 19' 5"	11' 10" 27' 1"
20	10' 8" 14' 3"	9' 2" 12' 7"	7' 7" 12' 7"	6' 10" 12' 7"	10' 7" 25' 2"	7' 5" 13' 9"	5' 9" 13' 9"	14' 3" 21' 7"	11' 8" 21' 7"	9' 0" 21' 7"	13' 2" 30' 1"
25	13' 4" 17' 10"	11' 5" 15' 9"	9' 6" 15' 9"	8' 6" 15' 9"	13' 3" 31' 5"	9' 3" 17' 2"	7' 2" 17' 2"	17' 10" 26' 11"	14' 7" 26' 11"	11' 3" 26' 11"	16' 5" 37' 7"
50	26' 8" 35' 7"	22' 11" 31' 5"	18' 11" 31' 5"	17' 0" 31' 5"	26' 7" 62' 10"	18' 7" 34' 3"	14' 4" 34' 3"	35' 7" 53' 11"	29' 2" 53' 11"	22' 6" 53' 11"	32' 10" 75' 2"

SETUPS (Approximate Distance) — 40mm FIELD OF VIEW

Ext Close Up Close Up Medium Shot Full Figure	1' 7" 2' 6" 4' 8" 12' 10"	1' 10" 2' 11" 5' 5" 15' 0"	2' 3" 3' 6" 6' 6" 18' 1"	2' 6" 3' 11" 7' 3" 20' 2"	1' 7" 2' 6" 4' 8" 12' 11"	2' 4" 3' 7" 6' 8" 18' 6"	3' 0" 4' 8" 8' 8" 24' 0"	1' 2" 1' 10" 3' 6" 9' 8"	1' 6" 2' 3" 4' 3" 11' 9"	1' 11" 3' 0" 5' 6" 15' 3"	1' 4" 2' 0" 3' 9" 10' 5"
Angle of View	V 26.3° H 34.6°	V 21.6° H 29.4°	V 17.9° H 29.4°	V 16.1° H 29.4°	V 25.1° H 56.1°	V 18.4° H 33.4°	V 14.3° H 33.4°	V 34.9° H 50.5°	V 28.6° H 50.5°	V 22.3° H 50.5°	V 30.9° H 62.5°
	Full Aperture	**Academy 1.33:1**	**Academy 1.66:1**	**Academy 1.85:1**	**Anamorphic 2.40:1**	**Super 35 1.85:1**	**Super 35 2.40:1**	**VistaVision**	**VistaVision 1.85:1**	**VistaVision 2.40:1**	**65mm**
2	0' 11" 1' 3"	0' 10" 1' 1"	0' 8" 1' 1"	0' 7" 1' 1"	0' 11" 2' 2"	0' 8" 1' 2"	0' 6" 1' 2"	1' 3" 1' 11"	1' 0" 1' 11"	0' 9" 1' 11"	1' 2" 2' 8"
2 1/2	1' 2" 1' 7"	1' 0" 1' 4"	0' 10" 1' 4"	0' 9" 1' 4"	1' 2" 2' 9"	0' 10" 1' 6"	0' 8" 1' 6"	1' 7" 2' 4"	1' 3" 2' 4"	1' 0" 2' 4"	1' 5" 3' 3"
3	1' 5" 1' 10"	1' 2" 1' 8"	1' 0" 1' 8"	0' 11" 1' 8"	1' 5" 3' 4"	1' 0" 1' 10"	0' 9" 1' 10"	1' 10" 2' 10"	1' 6" 2' 10"	1' 2" 2' 10"	1' 9" 3' 11"
3 1/2	1' 8" 2' 2"	1' 5" 1' 11"	1' 2" 1' 11"	1' 0" 1' 11"	1' 8" 3' 10"	1' 2" 2' 1"	0' 11" 2' 1"	2' 2" 3' 4"	1' 9" 3' 4"	1' 5" 3' 4"	2' 0" 4' 7"
4	1' 10" 2' 6"	1' 7" 2' 2"	1' 4" 2' 2"	1' 2" 2' 2"	1' 10" 4' 5"	1' 4" 2' 5"	1' 0" 2' 5"	2' 6" 3' 9"	2' 0" 3' 9"	1' 7" 3' 9"	2' 4" 5' 3"
4 1/2	2' 1" 2' 10"	1' 10" 2' 6"	1' 6" 2' 6"	1' 4" 2' 6"	2' 1" 4' 11"	1' 6" 2' 8"	1' 2" 2' 8"	2' 10" 4' 3"	2' 4" 4' 3"	1' 9" 4' 3"	2' 7" 5' 11"
5	2' 4" 3' 1"	2' 0" 2' 9"	1' 8" 2' 9"	1' 6" 2' 9"	2' 4" 5' 6"	1' 7" 3' 0"	1' 3" 3' 0"	3' 1" 4' 9"	2' 7" 4' 9"	2' 0" 4' 9"	2' 11" 6' 7"
5 1/2	2' 7" 3' 5"	2' 2" 3' 0"	1' 10" 3' 0"	1' 8" 3' 0"	2' 7" 6' 1"	1' 9" 3' 4"	1' 5" 3' 4"	3' 5" 5' 2"	2' 10" 5' 2"	2' 2" 5' 2"	3' 2" 7' 3"
6	2' 10" 3' 9"	2' 5" 3' 4"	2' 0" 3' 4"	1' 9" 3' 4"	2' 9" 6' 7"	1' 11" 3' 7"	1' 6" 3' 7"	3' 9" 5' 8"	3' 1" 5' 8"	2' 4" 5' 8"	3' 5" 7' 11"

6½	3' 0" 4' 1"	2' 7" 3' 7"	2' 2" 3' 7"	1' 11" 3' 7"	3' 0" 7' 2"	2' 1" 3' 11"	1' 8" 3' 11"	4' 1" 6' 2"	3' 4" 6' 2"	2' 7" 6' 2"	3' 9" 8' 7"
7	3' 3" 4' 4"	2' 10" 3' 10"	2' 4" 3' 10"	2' 1" 3' 10"	3' 3" 7' 8"	2' 3" 4' 2"	1' 9" 4' 2"	4' 4" 6' 7"	3' 7" 6' 7"	2' 9" 6' 7"	4' 0" 9' 3"
8	3' 9" 5' 0"	3' 2" 4' 5"	2' 8" 4' 5"	2' 5" 4' 5"	3' 9" 8' 10"	2' 7" 4' 10"	2' 0" 4' 10"	5' 0" 7' 7"	4' 1" 7' 7"	3' 2" 7' 7"	4' 7" 10' 6"
9	4' 2" 5' 7"	3' 7" 4' 11"	3' 0" 4' 11"	2' 8" 4' 11"	4' 2" 9' 11"	2' 11" 5' 5"	2' 3" 5' 5"	5' 7" 8' 6"	4' 7" 8' 6"	3' 7" 8' 6"	5' 2" 11' 10"
10	4' 8" 6' 3"	4' 0" 5' 6"	3' 4" 5' 6"	3' 0" 5' 6"	4' 8" 11' 0"	3' 3" 6' 0"	2' 6" 6' 0"	6' 3" 9' 5"	5' 1" 9' 5"	3' 11" 9' 5"	5' 9" 13' 2"
12	5' 7" 7' 6"	4' 10" 6' 7"	4' 0" 6' 7"	3' 7" 6' 7"	5' 7" 13' 2"	3' 11" 7' 2"	3' 0" 7' 2"	7' 6" 11' 4"	6' 1" 11' 4"	4' 9" 11' 4"	6' 11" 15' 9"
14	6' 6" 8' 9"	5' 7" 7' 8"	4' 8" 7' 8"	4' 2" 7' 8"	6' 6" 15' 5"	4' 7" 8' 5"	3' 6" 8' 5"	8' 9" 13' 2"	7' 2" 13' 2"	5' 6" 13' 2"	8' 1" 18' 5"
16	7' 6" 10' 0"	6' 5" 8' 10"	5' 4" 8' 10"	4' 9" 8' 10"	7' 5" 17' 7"	5' 2" 9' 7"	4' 0" 9' 7"	10' 0" 15' 1"	8' 2" 15' 1"	6' 4" 15' 1"	9' 2" 21' 1"
18	8' 5" 11' 3"	7' 3" 9' 11"	6' 0" 9' 11"	5' 4" 9' 11"	8' 4" 19' 10"	5' 10" 10' 10"	4' 6" 10' 10"	11' 3" 17' 0"	9' 2" 17' 0"	7' 1" 17' 0"	10' 4" 23' 8"
20	9' 4" 12' 6"	8' 0" 11' 0"	6' 8" 11' 0"	5' 11" 11' 0"	9' 4" 22' 0"	6' 6" 12' 0"	5' 0" 12' 0"	12' 6" 18' 10"	10' 2" 18' 10"	7' 11" 18' 10"	11' 6" 26' 4"
25	11' 8" 15' 7"	10' 0" 13' 9"	8' 3" 13' 9"	7' 5" 13' 9"	11' 7" 27' 6"	8' 1" 15' 0"	6' 3" 15' 0"	15' 7" 23' 7"	12' 9" 23' 7"	9' 10" 23' 7"	14' 5" 32' 11"
50	23' 4" 31' 2"	20' 0" 27' 6"	16' 7" 27' 6"	14' 10" 27' 6"	23' 3" 55' 0"	16' 3" 30' 0"	12' 6" 30' 0"	31' 2" 47' 2"	25' 6" 47' 2"	19' 9" 47' 2"	28' 9" 65' 9"

50mm FIELD OF VIEW

SETUPS (Approximate Distance)											
Ext Close Up Close Up Medium Shot Full Figure	2' 0" 3' 1" 5' 10" 16' 1"	2' 4" 3' 8" 6' 9" 18' 9"	2' 10" 4' 5" 8' 2" 22' 8"	3' 2" 4' 11" 9' 1" 25' 3"	2' 0" 3' 2" 5' 10" 16' 2"	2' 11" 4' 6" 8' 4" 23' 1"	3' 9" 5' 10" 10' 10" 30' 0"	1' 6" 2' 4" 4' 4" 12' 0"	1' 10" 2' 10" 5' 4" 14' 9"	2' 5" 3' 8" 6' 10" 19' 0"	1' 8" 2' 6" 4' 8" 13' 0"
Angle of View	V 21.1° H 28.0°	V 17.4° H 23.7°	V 14.4° H 23.7°	V 12.9° H 23.7°	V 20.2° H 46.2°	V 14.8° H 27.0°	V 11.4° H 27.0°	V 28.3° H 41.3°	V 23.1° H 41.3°	V 17.9° H 41.3°	V 24.9° H 51.8°
	Full Aperture	**Academy 1.33:1**	**Academy 1.66:1**	**Academy 1.85:1**	**Anamorphic 2.40:1**	**Super 35 1.85:1**	**Super 35 2.40:1**	**VistaVision**	**VistaVision 1.85:1**	**VistaVision 2.40:1**	**65mm**
2	0' 9" 1' 0"	0' 8" 0' 11"	0' 6" 0' 11"	0' 6" 0' 11"	0' 9" 1' 9"	0' 6" 1' 0"	0' 5" 1' 0"	1' 0" 1' 6"	0' 10" 1' 6"	0' 8" 1' 6"	0' 11" 2' 1"
2 1/2	0' 11" 1' 3"	0' 10" 1' 1"	0' 8" 1' 1"	0' 7" 1' 1"	0' 11" 2' 2"	0' 8" 1' 2"	0' 6" 1' 2"	1' 3" 1' 11"	1' 0" 1' 11"	0" 9" 1' 11"	1' 2" 2' 8"
3	1' 1" 1' 6"	1' 0" 1' 4"	0' 10" 1' 4"	0' 9" 1' 4"	1' 1" 2' 8"	0' 9" 1' 5"	0' 7" 1' 5"	1' 6" 2' 3"	1' 3" 2' 3"	0' 11" 2' 3"	1' 5" 3' 2"
3 1/2	1' 4" 1' 9"	1' 1" 1' 6"	0' 11" 1' 6"	0' 10" 1' 6"	1' 4" 3' 1"	0' 11" 1' 8"	0' 8" 1' 8"	1' 9" 2' 8"	1' 5" 2' 8"	1' 1" 2' 8"	1' 7" 3' 8"
4	1' 6" 2' 0"	1' 3" 1' 9"	1' 1" 1' 9"	0' 11" 1' 9"	1' 6" 3' 6"	1' 0" 1' 11"	0' 10" 1' 11"	2' 0" 3' 0"	1' 8" 3' 0"	1' 3" 3' 0"	1' 10" 4' 3"
4 1/2	1' 8" 2' 3"	1' 5" 2' 0"	1' 2" 2' 0"	1' 1" 2' 0"	1' 8" 4' 0"	1' 2" 2' 2"	0' 11" 2' 2"	2' 3" 3' 5"	1' 10" 3' 5"	1' 5" 3' 5"	2' 1" 4' 9"
5	1' 10" 2' 6"	1' 7" 2' 2"	1' 4" 2' 2"	1' 2" 2' 2"	1' 10" 4' 5"	1' 4" 2' 5"	1' 0" 2' 5"	2' 6" 3' 9"	2' 0" 3' 9"	1' 7" 3' 9"	2' 4" 5' 3"
5 1/2	2' 1" 2' 9"	1' 9" 2' 5"	1' 6" 2' 5"	1' 4" 2' 5"	2' 1" 4' 10"	1' 5" 2' 8"	1' 1" 2' 8"	2' 9" 4' 2"	2' 3" 4' 2"	1' 9" 4' 2"	2' 6" 5' 9"
6	2' 3" 3' 0"	1' 11" 2' 8"	1' 7" 2' 8"	1' 5" 2' 8"	2' 3" 5' 3"	1' 7" 2' 11"	1' 2" 2' 11"	3' 0" 4' 6"	2' 5" 4' 6"	1' 11" 4' 6"	2' 9" 6' 4"

6½	2' 5" 3' 3"	2' 1" 2' 10"	1' 9" 2' 10"	1' 7" 2' 10"	2' 5" 5' 9"	1' 8" 3' 1"	1' 4" 3' 1"	3' 3" 4' 11"	2' 8" 4' 11"	2' 1" 4' 11"	3' 0" 6' 10"
7	2' 7" 3' 6"	2' 3" 3' 1"	1' 10" 3' 1"	1' 8" 3' 1"	2' 7" 6' 2"	1' 10" 3' 4"	1' 5" 3' 4"	3' 6" 5' 3"	2' 10" 5' 3"	2' 2" 5' 3"	3' 3" 7' 4"
8	3' 0" 4' 0"	2' 7" 3' 6"	2' 1" 3' 6"	1' 11" 3' 6"	3' 0" 7' 0"	2' 1" 3' 10"	1' 7" 3' 10"	4' 0" 6' 0"	3' 3" 6' 0"	2' 6" 6' 0"	3' 8" 8' 5"
9	3' 4" 4' 6"	2' 11" 4' 0"	2' 5" 4' 0"	2' 2" 4' 0"	3' 4" 7' 11"	2' 4" 4' 4"	1' 10" 4' 4"	4' 6" 6' 9"	3' 8" 6' 9"	2' 10" 6' 9"	4' 2" 9' 6"
10	3' 9" 5' 0"	3' 2" 4' 5"	2' 8" 4' 5"	2' 5" 4' 5"	3' 9" 8' 10"	2' 7" 4' 10"	2' 0" 4' 10"	5' 0" 7' 7"	4' 1" 7' 7"	3' 2" 7' 7"	4' 7" 10' 6"
12	4' 6" 6' 0"	3' 10" 5' 3"	3' 2" 5' 3"	2' 10" 5' 3"	4' 6" 10' 7"	3' 1" 5' 9"	2' 5" 5' 9"	6' 0" 9' 1"	4' 11" 9' 1"	3' 9" 9' 1"	5' 6" 12' 8"
14	5' 3" 7' 0"	4' 6" 6' 2"	3' 9" 6' 2"	3' 4" 6' 2"	5' 2" 12' 4"	3' 8" 6' 9"	2' 10" 6' 9"	7' 0" 10' 7"	5' 9" 10' 7"	4' 5" 10' 7"	6' 5" 14' 9"
16	6' 0" 8' 0"	5' 2" 7' 0"	4' 3" 7' 0"	3' 10" 7' 0"	5' 11" 14' 1"	4' 2" 7' 8"	3' 2" 7' 8"	8' 0" 12' 1"	6' 6" 12' 1"	5'1" 12' 1"	7' 4" 16' 10"
18	6' 9" 9' 0"	5' 9" 7' 11"	4' 9" 7' 11"	4' 3" 7' 11"	6' 8" 15' 10"	4' 8" 8' 8"	3' 7" 8' 8"	9' 0" 13' 7"	7' 4" 13' 7"	5' 8" 13' 7"	8' 3" 18' 11"
20	7' 6" 10' 0"	6' 5" 8' 10"	5' 4" 8' 10"	4' 9" 8' 10"	7' 5" 17' 7"	5' 2" 9' 7"	4' 0" 9' 7"	10' 0" 15' 1"	8' 2" 15' 1"	6' 4" 15' 1"	9' 2" 21' 1"
25	9' 4" 12' 6"	8' 0" 11' 0"	6' 8" 11' 0"	5' 11" 11' 0"	9' 4" 22' 0"	6' 6" 12' 0"	5' 0" 12' 0"	12' 6" 18' 10"	10' 2" 18' 10"	7' 11" 18' 10"	11' 6" 26' 4"
50	18' 8" 24' 11"	16' 0" 22' 0"	13' 3" 22' 0"	11' 11" 22' 0"	18' 7" 44' 0"	13' 0" 24' 0"	10' 0" 24' 0"	24' 11" 37' 9"	20' 5" 37' 9"	15' 9" 37' 9"	23' 0" 52' 8"

SETUPS (Approximate Distance)	**75mm FIELD OF VIEW**										
Ext Close Up Close Up Medium Shot Full Figure	3' 0" 4' 8" 8' 8" 24' 1"	3' 6" 5' 6" 10' 2" 28' 1"	4' 3" 6' 7" 12' 3" 33' 11"	4' 9" 7' 4" 13' 8" 37' 10"	3' 0" 4' 8" 8' 9" 24' 2"	4' 4" 6' 9" 12' 6" 34' 8"	5' 7" 8' 9" 16' 3" 45' 0"	2' 3" 3' 6" 6' 6" 18' 1"	2' 9" 4' 3" 8' 0" 22' 1"	3' 7" 5' 7" 10' 4" 28' 6"	2' 5" 3' 10" 7' 1" 19' 7"
Angle of View	V 14.2° H 18.8°	V 11.6° H 15.9°	V 9.6° H 15.9°	V 8.6° H 15.9°	V 13.5° H 31.7°	V 9.9° H 18.2°	V 7.6° H 18.2°	V 19.1° H 28.2°	V 15.5° H 28.2°	V 12.0° H 28.2°	V 16.8° H 35.9°
	Full Aperture	**Academy 1.33:1**	**Academy 1.66:1**	**Academy 1.85:1**	**Anamorphic 2.40:1**	**Super 35 1.85:1**	**Super 35 2.40:1**	**VistaVision**	**VistaVision 1.85:1**	**VistaVision 2.40:1**	**65mm**
2	0' 6" 0' 8"	0' 5" 0' 7"	0' 4" 0' 7"	0' 4" 0' 7"	0' 6" 1' 2"	0' 4" 0' 8"	0' 3" 0' 8"	0' 8" 1' 0"	0' 7" 1' 0"	0' 5" 1' 0"	0' 7" 1' 5"
2 1/2	0' 7" 0' 10"	0' 6" 0' 9"	0' 5" 0' 9"	0' 5" 0' 9"	0' 7" 1' 6"	0' 5" 0' 10"	0' 4" 0' 10"	0' 10" 1' 3"	0' 8" 1' 3"	0' 6" 1' 3"	0' 9" 1' 9"
3	0' 9" 1' 0"	0' 8" 0' 11"	0' 6" 0' 11"	0' 6" 0' 11"	0' 9" 1' 9"	0' 6" 1' 0"	0' 5" 1' 0"	1' 0" 1' 6"	0' 10" 1' 6"	0' 8" 1' 6"	0' 11" 2' 1"
3 1/2	0' 10" 1' 2"	0' 9" 1' 0"	0' 7" 1' 0"	0' 7" 1' 0"	0' 10" 2' 1"	0' 7" 1' 1"	0' 6" 1' 1"	1' 2" 1' 9"	0' 11" 1' 9"	0' 9" 1' 9"	1' 1" 2' 5"
4	1' 0" 1' 4"	0' 10" 1' 2"	0' 8" 1' 2"	0' 8" 1' 2"	1' 0" 2' 4"	0' 8" 1' 3"	0' 6" 1' 3"	1' 4" 2' 0"	1' 1" 2' 0"	0' 10" 2' 0"	1' 3" 2' 10"
4 1/2	1' 1" 1' 6"	1' 0" 1' 4"	0' 10" 1' 4"	0' 9" 1' 4"	1' 1" 2' 8"	0' 9" 1' 5"	0' 7" 1' 5"	1' 6" 2' 3"	1' 3" 2' 3"	0' 11" 2' 3"	1' 5" 3' 2"
5	1' 3" 1' 8"	1' 1" 1' 6"	0' 11" 1' 6"	0' 10" 1' 6"	1' 3" 2' 11"	0' 10" 1' 7"	0' 8" 1' 7"	1' 8" 2' 6"	1' 4" 2' 6"	1' 1" 2' 6"	1' 6" 3' 6"
5 1/2	1' 4" 1' 10"	1' 2" 1' 7"	1' 0" 1' 7"	0' 10" 1' 7"	1' 4" 3' 3"	0' 11" 1' 9"	0' 9" 1' 9"	1' 10" 2' 9"	1' 6" 2' 9"	1' 2" 2' 9"	1' 8" 3' 10"
6	1' 6" 2' 0"	1' 3" 1' 9"	1' 1" 1' 9"	0' 11" 1' 9"	1' 6" 3' 6"	1' 0" 1' 11"	0' 10" 1' 11"	2' 0" 3' 0"	1' 8" 3' 0"	1' 3" 3' 0"	1' 10" 4' 3"

6½	1' 7" 2' 2"	1' 5" 1' 11"	1' 2" 1' 11"	1' 0" 1' 11"	1' 7" 3' 10"	1' 1" 2' 1"	0' 10" 2' 1"	2' 2" 3' 3"	1' 9" 3' 3"	1' 4" 3' 3"	2' 0" 4' 7"
7	1' 9" 2' 4"	1' 6" 2' 1"	1' 3" 2' 1"	1' 1" 2' 1"	1' 9" 4' 1"	1' 3" 2' 3"	0' 11" 2' 3"	2' 4" 3' 6"	1' 11" 3' 6"	1' 6" 3' 6"	2' 2" 4' 11"
8	2' 0" 2' 8"	1' 9" 2' 4"	1' 5" 2' 4"	1' 3" 2' 4"	2' 0" 4' 8"	1' 5" 2' 7"	1' 1" 2' 7"	2' 8" 4' 0"	2' 2" 4' 0"	1' 8" 4' 0"	2' 5" 5' 7"
9	2' 3" 3' 0"	1' 11" 2' 8"	1' 7" 2' 8"	1' 5" 2' 8"	2' 3" 5' 3"	1' 7" 2' 11"	1' 2" 2' 11"	3' 0" 4' 6"	2' 5" 4' 6"	1' 11" 4' 6"	2' 9" 6' 4"
10	2' 6" 3' 4"	2' 2" 2' 11"	1' 9" 2' 11"	1' 7" 2' 11"	2' 6" 5' 10"	1' 9" 3' 2"	1' 4" 3' 2"	3' 4" 5' 0"	2' 9" 5' 0"	2' 1" 5' 0"	3' 1" 7' 0"
12	3' 0" 4' 0"	2' 7" 3' 6"	2' 1" 3' 6"	1' 11" 3' 6"	3' 0" 7' 0"	2' 1" 3' 10"	1' 7" 3' 10"	4' 0" 6' 0"	3' 3" 6' 0"	2' 6" 6' 0"	3' 8" 8' 5"
14	3' 6" 4' 8"	3' 0" 4' 1"	2' 6" 4' 1"	2' 3" 4' 1"	3' 6" 8' 3"	2' 5" 4' 6"	1' 10" 4' 6"	4' 8" 7' 0"	3' 10" 7' 0"	2' 11" 7' 0"	4' 4" 9' 10"
16	4' 0" 5' 4"	3' 5" 4' 8"	2' 10" 4' 8"	2' 6" 4' 8"	4' 0" 9' 5"	2' 9" 5' 1"	2' 2" 5' 1"	5' 4" 8' 1"	4' 4" 8' 1"	3' 4" 8' 1"	4' 11" 11' 3"
18	4' 6" 6' 0"	3' 10" 5' 3"	3' 2" 5' 3"	2' 10" 5' 3"	4' 6" 10' 7"	3' 1" 5' 9"	2' 5" 5' 9"	6' 0" 9' 1"	4' 11" 9' 1"	3' 9" 9' 1"	5' 6" 12' 8"
20	5' 0" 6' 8"	4' 3" 5' 10"	3' 6" 5' 10"	3' 2" 5' 10"	4' 11" 11' 9"	3' 6" 6' 5"	2' 8" 6' 5"	6' 8" 10' 1"	5' 5" 10' 1"	4' 2" 10' 1"	6' 2" 14' 0"
25	6' 3" 8' 4"	5' 4" 7' 4"	4' 5" 7' 4"	4' 0" 7' 4"	6' 2" 14' 8"	4' 4" 8' 0"	3' 4" 8' 0"	8' 4" 12' 7"	6' 10" 12' 7"	5' 3" 12' 7"	7' 8" 17' 7"
50	12' 5" 16' 7"	10' 8" 14' 8"	8' 10" 14' 8"	7' 11" 14' 8"	12' 5" 29' 4"	8' 8" 16' 0"	6' 8" 16' 0"	16' 7" 25' 2"	13' 7" 25' 2"	10' 6" 25' 2"	15' 4" 35' 1"

85mm FIELD OF VIEW

SETUPS (Approximate Distance)											
Ext Close Up **Close Up** **Medium Shot** **Full Figure**	3' 5" 5' 4" 9' 10" 27' 4"	4' 0" 6' 2" 11' 6" 31' 10"	4' 10" 7' 6" 13' 11" 38' 6"	5' 4" 8' 4" 15' 6" 42' 11"	3' 5" 5' 4" 9' 11" 27' 5"	4' 11" 7' 8" 14' 2" 39' 4"	6' 4" 9' 11" 18' 5" 51' 0"	2' 7" 4' 0" 7' 5" 20' 6"	3' 2" 4' 10" 9' 0" 25' 0"	4' 0" 6' 3" 11' 8" 32' 4"	2' 9" 4' 4" 8' 0" 22' 2"
Angle of View	V 12.5° H 16.7°	V 10.3° H 14.1°	V 8.5° H 14.1°	V 7.6° H 14.1°	V 11.9° H 28.1°	V 8.7° H 16.1°	V 6.7° H 16.1°	V 16.8° H 25.0°	V 13.7° H 25.0°	V 10.6° H 25.0°	
	Full Aperture	**Academy 1.33:1**	**Academy 1.66:1**	**Academy 1.85:1**	**Anamorphic 2.40:1**	**Super 35 1.85:1**	**Super 35 2.40:1**	**VistaVision**	**VistaVision 1.85:1**	**VistaVision 2.40:1**	**65mm**
2	0' 5" 0' 7"	0' 5" 0' 6"	0' 4" 0' 6"	0' 3" 0' 6"	0' 5" 1' 0"	0' 4" 0' 7"	0' 3" 0' 7"	0' 7" 0' 11"	0' 6" 0' 11"	0' 4" 0' 11"	NA NA
2 1/2	0' 7" 0' 9"	0' 6" 0' 8"	0' 5" 0' 8"	0' 4" 0' 8"	0' 7" 1' 4"	0' 5" 0' 8"	0' 4" 0' 8"	0' 9" 1' 1"	0' 7" 1' 1"	0' 6" 1' 1"	NA NA
3	0' 8" 0' 11"	0' 7" 0' 9"	0' 6" 0' 9"	0' 5" 0' 9"	0' 8" 1' 7"	0' 5" 0' 10"	0' 4" 0' 10"	0' 11" 1' 4"	0' 9" 1' 4"	0' 7" 1' 4"	NA NA
3 1/2	0' 9" 1' 0"	0' 8" 0' 11"	0' 7" 0' 11"	0' 6" 0' 11"	0' 9" 1' 10"	0' 6" 1' 0"	0' 5" 1' 0"	1' 0" 1' 7"	0' 10" 1' 7"	0' 8" 1' 7"	NA NA
4	0' 11" 1' 2"	0' 9" 1' 0"	0' 7" 1' 0"	0' 7" 1' 0"	0' 10" 2' 1"	0' 7" 1' 2"	0' 6" 1' 2"	1' 2" 1' 9"	1' 0" 1' 9"	0' 9" 1' 9"	NA NA
4 1/2	1' 0" 1' 4"	0' 10" 1' 2"	0' 8" 1' 2"	0' 8" 1' 2"	1' 0" 2' 4"	0' 8" 1' 3"	0' 6" 1' 3"	1' 4" 2' 0"	1' 1" 2' 0"	0' 10" 2' 0"	NA NA
5	1' 1" 1' 6"	0' 11" 1' 4"	0' 9" 1' 4"	0' 8" 1' 4"	1' 1" 2' 7"	0' 9" 1' 5"	0' 7" 1' 5"	1' 6" 2' 3"	1' 2" 2' 3"	0' 11" 2' 3"	NA NA
5 1/2	1' 2" 1' 7"	1' 0" 1' 5"	0' 10" 1' 5"	0' 9" 1' 5"	1' 2" 2' 10"	0' 10" 1' 7"	0' 8" 1' 7"	1' 7" 2' 5"	1' 4" 2' 5"	1' 0" 2' 5"	NA NA
6	1' 4" 1' 9"	1' 2" 1' 7"	0' 11" 1' 7"	0' 10" 1' 7"	1' 4" 3' 1"	0' 11" 1' 8"	0' 8" 1' 8"	1' 9" 2' 8"	1' 5" 2' 8"	1' 1" 2' 8"	NA NA

6 ½	1' 5" 1' 11"	1' 3" 1' 8"	1' 0" 1' 8"	0' 11" 1' 8"	1' 5" 3' 4"	1' 0" 1' 10"	0' 9" 1' 10"	1' 11" 2' 11"	1' 7" 2' 11"	1' 2" 2' 11"	NA NA
7	1' 6" 2' 1"	1' 4" 1' 10"	1' 1" 1' 10"	1' 0" 1' 10"	1' 6" 3' 7"	1' 1" 2' 0"	0' 10" 2' 0"	2' 1" 3' 1"	1' 8" 3' 1"	1' 4" 3' 1"	NA NA
8	1' 9" 2' 4"	1' 6" 2' 1"	1' 3" 2' 1"	1' 1" 2' 1"	1' 9" 4' 2"	1' 3" 2' 3"	0' 11" 2' 3"	2' 4" 3' 7"	1' 11" 3' 7"	1' 6" 3' 7"	NA NA
9	2' 0" 2' 8"	1' 8" 2' 4"	1' 5" 2' 4"	1' 3" 2' 4"	2' 0" 4' 8"	1' 4" 2' 6"	1' 1" 2' 6"	2' 8" 4' 0"	2' 2" 4' 0"	1' 8" 4' 0"	NA NA
10	2' 2" 2' 11"	1' 11" 2' 7"	1' 7" 2' 7"	1' 5" 2' 7"	2' 2" 5' 2"	1' 6" 2' 10"	1' 2" 2' 10"	2' 11" 4' 5"	2' 5" 4' 5"	1' 10" 4' 5"	NA NA
12	2' 8" 3' 6"	2' 3" 3' 1"	1' 10" 3' 1"	1' 8" 3' 1"	2' 7" 6' 3"	1' 10" 3' 5"	1' 5" 3' 5"	3' 6" 5' 4"	2' 11" 5' 4"	2' 3" 5' 4"	NA NA
14	3' 1" 4' 1"	2' 8" 3' 7"	2' 2" 3' 7"	1' 11" 3' 7"	3' 1" 7' 3"	2' 2" 3' 11"	1' 8" 3' 11"	4' 1" 6' 3"	3' 4" 6' 3"	2' 7" 6' 3"	NA NA
16	3' 6" 4' 8"	3' 0" 4' 2"	2' 6" 4' 2"	2' 3" 4' 2"	3' 6" 8' 3"	2' 5" 4' 6"	1' 11" 4' 6"	4' 8" 7' 1"	3' 10" 7' 1"	3' 0" 7' 1"	NA NA
18	3' 11" 5' 3"	3' 5" 4' 8"	2' 10" 4' 8"	2' 6" 4' 8"	3' 11" 9' 4"	2' 9" 5' 1"	2' 1" 5' 1"	5' 3" 8' 0"	4' 4" 8' 0"	3' 4" 8' 0"	NA NA
20	4' 5" 5' 10"	3' 9" 5' 2"	3' 1" 5' 2"	2' 10" 5' 2"	4' 4" 10' 4"	3' 1" 5' 8"	2' 4" 5' 8"	5' 10" 8' 11"	4' 10" 8' 11"	3' 9" 8' 11"	NA NA
25	5' 6" 7' 4"	4' 9" 6' 6"	3' 11" 6' 6"	3' 6" 6' 6"	5' 6" 12' 11"	3' 10" 7' 1"	2' 11" 7' 1"	7' 4" 11' 1"	6' 0" 11' 1"	4' 8" 11' 1"	NA NA
50	11' 0" 14' 8"	9' 5" 12' 11"	7' 10" 12' 11"	7' 0" 12' 11"	10' 11" 25' 11"	7' 8" 14' 1"	5' 11" 14' 1"	14' 8" 22' 2"	12' 0" 22' 2"	9' 3" 22' 2"	NA NA

100mm FIELD OF VIEW

SETUPS (Approximate Distance)											
Ext Close Up Close Up Medium Shot Full Figure	4' 0" 6' 3" 11' 7" 32' 2"	4' 8" 7' 3" 13' 6" 37' 5"	5' 8" 8' 10" 16' 4" 45' 3"	6' 4" 9' 10" 18' 3" 50' 6"	4' 0" 6' 3" 11' 8" 32' 3"	5' 9" 9' 0" 16' 8" 46' 3"	7' 6" 11' 8" 21' 8" 59' 11"	3' 0" 4' 8" 8' 8" 24' 1"	3' 8" 5' 9" 10' 7" 29' 5"	4' 9" 7' 5" 13' 9" 38' 0"	3' 3" 5' 1" 9' 5" 26' 1"
Angle of View	V 10.7° H 14.2°	V 8.7° H 12.0°	V 7.2° H 12.0°	V 6.5° H 12.0°	V 10.2° H 24.1°	V 7.4° H 13.7°	V 5.7° H 13.7°	V 14.3° H 21.4°	V 11.6° H 21.4°	V 9.0° H 21.4°	V 12.6° H 27.3°
	Full Aperture	Academy 1.33:1	Academy 1.66:1	Academy 1.85:1	Anamorphic 2.40:1	Super 35 1.85:1	Super 35 2.40:1	VistaVision	VistaVision 1.85:1	VistaVision 2.40:1	65mm
2	0' 4" 0' 6"	0' 4" 0' 5"	0' 3" 0' 5"	0' 3" 0' 5"	0' 4" 0' 11"	0' 3" 0' 6"	0' 2" 0' 6"	0' 6" 0' 9"	0' 5" 0' 9"	0' 4" 0' 9"	0' 6" 1' 1"
2 ½	0' 6" 0' 7"	0' 5" 0' 7"	0' 4" 0' 7"	0' 4" 0' 7"	0' 6" 1' 1"	0' 4" 0' 7"	0' 3" 0' 7"	0' 7" 0' 11"	0' 6" 0' 11"	0' 5" 0' 11"	0' 7" 1' 4"
3	0' 7" 0' 9"	0' 6" 0' 8"	0' 5" 0' 8"	0' 4" 0' 8"	0' 7" 1' 4"	0' 5" 0' 9"	0' 4" 0' 9"	0' 9" 1' 2"	0' 7" 1' 2"	0' 6" 1' 2"	0' 8" 1' 7"
3 ½	0' 8" 0' 10"	0' 7" 0' 9"	0' 6" 0' 9"	0' 5" 0' 9"	0' 8" 1' 6"	0' 5" 0' 10"	0' 4" 0' 10"	0' 10" 1' 4"	0' 9" 1' 4"	0' 7" 1' 4"	0' 10" 1' 10"
4	0' 9" 1' 0"	0' 8" 0' 11"	0' 6" 0' 11"	0' 6" 0' 11"	0' 9" 1' 9"	0' 6" 1' 0"	0' 5" 1' 0"	1' 0" 1' 6"	0' 10" 1' 6"	0' 8" 1' 6"	0' 11" 2' 1"
4 ½	0' 10" 1' 1"	0' 9" 1' 0"	0' 7" 1' 0"	0' 6" 1' 0"	0' 10" 2' 0"	0' 7" 1' 1"	0' 5" 1' 1"	1' 1" 1' 8"	0' 11" 1' 8"	0' 9" 1' 8"	1' 0" 2' 4"
5	0' 11" 1' 3"	0' 10" 1' 1"	0' 8" 1' 1"	0' 7" 1' 1"	0' 11" 2' 2"	0' 8" 1' 2"	0' 6" 1' 2"	1' 3" 1' 11"	1' 0" 1' 11"	0' 9" 1' 11"	1' 2" 2' 8"
5 ½	1' 0" 1' 4"	0' 11" 1' 3"	0' 9" 1' 3"	0' 8" 1' 3"	1' 0" 2' 5"	0' 9" 1' 4"	0' 7" 1' 4"	1' 4" 2' 1"	1' 1" 2' 1"	0' 10" 2' 1"	1' 3" 2' 11"
6	1' 1" 1' 6"	1' 0" 1' 4"	0' 10" 1' 4"	0' 9" 1' 4"	1' 1" 2' 8"	0' 9" 1' 5"	0' 7" 1' 5"	1' 6" 2' 3"	1' 3" 2' 3"	0' 11" 2' 3"	1' 5" 3' 2"

6 ½	1' 3" 1' 7"	1' 1" 1' 5"	0' 10" 1' 5"	0' 9" 1' 5"	1' 3" 2' 10"	0' 10" 1' 7"	0' 8" 1' 7"	1' 7" 2' 5"	1' 4" 2' 5"	1' 0" 2' 5"	1' 6" 3' 5"
7	1' 4" 1' 9"	1' 1" 1' 6"	0' 11" 1' 6"	0' 10" 1' 6"	1' 4" 3' 1"	0' 11" 1' 8"	0' 8" 1' 8"	1' 9" 2' 8"	1' 5" 2' 8"	1' 1" 2' 8"	1' 7" 3' 8"
8	1' 6" 2' 0"	1' 3" 1' 9"	1' 1" 1' 9"	0' 11" 1' 9"	1' 6" 3' 6"	1' 0" 1' 11"	0' 10" 1' 11"	2' 0" 3' 0"	1' 8" 3' 0"	1' 3" 3' 0"	1' 10" 4' 3"
9	1' 8" 2' 3"	1' 5" 2' 0"	1' 2" 2' 0"	1' 1" 2' 0"	1' 8" 4' 0"	1' 2" 2' 2"	0' 11" 2' 2"	2' 3" 3' 5"	1' 10" 3' 5"	1' 5" 3' 5"	2' 1" 4' 9"
10	1' 10" 2' 6"	1' 7" 2' 2"	1' 4" 2' 2"	1' 2" 2' 2"	1' 10" 4' 5"	1' 4" 2' 5"	1' 0" 2' 5"	2' 6" 3' 9"	2' 0" 3' 9"	1' 7" 3' 9"	2' 4" 5' 3"
12	2' 3" 3' 0"	1' 11" 2' 8"	1' 7" 2' 8"	1' 5" 2' 8"	2' 3" 5' 3"	1' 7" 2' 11"	1' 2" 2' 11"	3' 0" 4' 6"	2' 5" 4' 6"	1' 11" 4' 6"	2' 9" 6' 4"
14	2' 7" 3' 6"	2' 3" 3' 1"	1' 10" 3' 1"	1' 8" 3' 1"	2' 7" 6' 2"	1' 10" 3' 4"	1' 5" 3' 4"	3' 6" 5' 3"	2' 10" 5' 3"	2' 2" 5' 3"	3' 3" 7' 4"
16	3' 0" 4' 0"	2' 7" 3' 6"	2' 1" 3' 6"	1' 11" 3' 6"	3' 0" 7' 0"	2' 1" 3' 10"	1' 7" 3' 10"	4' 0" 6' 0	3' 3" 6' 0"	2' 6" 6' 0"	3' 8" 8' 5"
18	3' 4" 4' 6"	2' 11" 4' 0"	2' 5" 4' 0"	2' 2" 4' 0"	3' 4" 7' 11"	2' 4" 4' 4"	1' 10" 4' 4"	4' 6" 6' 9"	3' 8" 6' 9"	2' 10" 6' 9"	4' 2" 9' 6"
20	3' 9" 5' 0"	3' 2" 4' 5"	2' 8" 4' 5"	2' 5" 4' 5"	3' 9" 8' 10	2' 7" 4' 10"	2' 0" 4' 10"	5' 0" 7' 7"	4' 1" 7' 7"	3' 2" 7' 7"	4' 7" 10' 6"
25	4' 8" 6' 3"	4' 0" 5' 6"	3' 4" 5' 6"	3' 0" 5' 6"	4' 8" 11' 0"	3' 3" 6' 0"	2' 6" 6' 0"	6' 3" 9' 5"	5' 1" 9' 5"	3' 11" 9' 5"	5' 9" 13' 2"
50	9' 4" 12' 6"	8' 0" 11' 0"	6' 8" 11' 0"	5' 11" 11' 0"	9' 4" 22' 0"	6' 6" 12' 0"	5' 0" 12' 0"	12' 6" 18' 10"	10' 2" 18' 10"	7' 11" 18' 10"	11' 6" 26' 4"

105mm FIELD OF VIEW

SETUPS (Approximate Distance)											
Ext Close Up Close Up Medium Shot Full Figure	4' 3" 6' 7" 12' 2" 33' 9"	4' 11" 7' 8" 14' 2" 39' 4"	5' 11" 9' 3" 17' 2" 47' 6"	6' 7" 10' 4" 19' 2" 53' 0"	4' 3" 6' 7" 12' 3" 33' 11"	6' 1" 9' 5" 17' 6" 48' 6"	7' 10" 12' 3" 22' 9" 62' 11"	3' 2" 4' 11" 9' 2" 25' 3"	3' 10" 6' 0" 11' 2" 30' 11"	5' 0" 7' 9" 14' 5" 39' 11"	3' 3" 5' 1" 9' 5" 26' 1"
Angle of View	V 10.2° H 13.5°	V 8.3° H 11.4°	V 6.9° H 11.4°	V 6.2° H 11.4°		V 7.1° H 13.0°	V 5.5° H 13.0°	V 13.7° H 20.4°	V 11.1° H 20.4°	V 8.6° H 20.4°	
	Full Aperture	**Academy 1.33:1**	**Academy 1.66:1**	**Academy 1.85:1**	**Anamorphic 2.40:1**	**Super 35 1.85:1**	**Super 35 2.40:1**	**VistaVision**	**VistaVision 1.85:1**	**VistaVision 2.40:1**	**65mm**
5	0' 11" 1' 2"	0' 9" 1' 1"	0' 8" 1' 1"	0' 7" 1' 1"	NA NA	0' 7" 1' 2"	0' 6" 1' 2"	1' 2" 1' 10"	1' 0" 1' 10"	0' 9" 1' 10"	NA NA
5 ½	1' 0 1' 4"	0' 10" 1' 2"	0' 8" 1' 2"	0' 7" 1' 2"	NA NA	0' 8" 1' 3"	0' 6" 1' 3"	1' 4" 2' 0"	1' 1" 2' 0"	0' 10" 2' 0"	NA NA
6	1' 1" 1' 5"	0' 11" 1' 3"	0' 9" 1' 3"	0' 8" 1' 3"	NA NA	0' 9" 1' 4"	0' 7" 1' 4"	1' 5" 2' 2"	1' 2" 2' 2"	0' 11" 2' 2"	NA NA
6 ½	1' 2" 1' 7"	1' 0" 1' 4"	0' 10" 1' 4"	0' 9" 1' 4"	NA NA	0' 10" 1' 6"	0' 7" 1' 6"	1' 7" 2' 4"	1' 3" 2' 4"	1' 0" 2' 4"	NA NA
7	1' 3" 1' 8"	1' 1" 1' 6"	0' 11" 1' 6"	0' 10" 1' 6"	NA NA	0' 10" 1' 7"	0' 8" 1' 7"	1' 8" 2' 6"	1' 4" 2' 6"	1' 1" 2' 6"	NA NA
8	1' 5" 1' 11"	1' 3" 1' 8"	1' 0" 1' 8"	0' 11" 1' 8"	NA NA	1' 0" 1' 10"	0' 9" 1' 10"	1' 11" 2' 10"	1' 7" 2' 10"	1' 2" 2' 10"	NA NA
9	1' 7" 2' 2"	1' 4" 1' 11"	1' 2" 1' 11"	1' 0" 1' 11"	NA NA	1' 1" 2' 1"	0' 10" 2' 1"	2' 2" 3' 3"	1' 9" 3' 3"	1' 4" 3' 3"	NA NA
10	1' 9" 2' 4"	1' 6" 2' 1"	1' 3" 2' 1"	1' 2" 2' 1"	NA NA	1' 3" 2' 3"	0' 11" 2' 3"	2' 4" 3' 7"	1' 11" 3' 7"	1' 6" 3' 7"	NA NA
12	2' 2" 2' 10"	1' 10" 2' 6"	1' 6" 2' 6"	1' 4" 2' 6"	NA NA	1' 6" 2' 9"	1' 2" 2' 9"	2' 10" 4' 4"	2' 4" 4' 4"	1' 10" 4' 4"	NA NA

14	2' 6" 3' 4"	2' 2" 2' 11"	1' 9" 2' 11"	1' 7" 2' 11"	NA NA	1' 9" 3' 2"	1' 4" 3' 2"	3' 4" 5' 0"	2' 9" 5' 0"	2' 1" 5' 0"	NA NA
16	2' 10" 3' 10"	2' 5" 3' 4"	2' 0" 3' 4"	1' 10" 3' 4"	NA NA	2' 0" 3' 8"	1' 6" 3' 8"	3' 10" 5' 9"	3' 1" 5' 9"	2' 5" 5' 9"	NA NA
18	3' 2" 4' 3"	2' 9" 3' 9"	2' 3" 3' 9"	2' 0" 3' 9"	NA NA	2' 3" 4' 1"	1' 9" 4' 1"	4' 3" 6' 6"	3' 6" 6' 6"	2' 8" 6' 6"	NA NA
20	3' 7" 4' 9"	3' 1" 4' 2"	2' 6" 4' 2"	2' 3" 4' 2"	NA NA	2' 6" 4' 7"	1' 11" 4' 7"	4' 9" 7' 2"	3' 11" 7' 2"	3' 0" 7' 2"	NA NA
25	4' 5" 5' 11"	3' 10" 5' 3"	3' 2" 5' 3"	2' 10" 5' 3"	NA NA	3' 1" 5' 9"	2' 5" 5' 9"	5' 11" 9' 0"	4' 10" 9' 0"	3' 9" 9' 0"	NA NA
50	8' 11" 11' 10"	7' 8" 10' 6"	6' 4" 10' 6"	5' 8" 10' 6"	NA NA	6' 2" 11' 5"	4' 9" 11' 5"	11' 10" 18' 0"	9' 9" 18' 0"	7' 6" 18' 0"	NA NA
75	13' 4" 17' 10"	11' 5" 15' 9"	9' 6" 15' 9"	8' 6" 15' 9"	NA NA	9' 3" 17' 2"	7' 2" 17' 2"	17' 10" 26' 11"	14' 7" 26' 11"	11' 3" 26' 11"	NA NA
100	17' 9" 23' 9"	15' 3" 20' 11"	12' 8" 20' 11"	11' 4" 20' 11"	NA NA	12' 4" 22' 10"	9' 6" 22' 10"	23' 9" 35' 11"	19' 5" 35' 11"	15' 0" 35' 11"	NA NA
125	22' 3" 29' 8"	19' 1" 26' 2"	15' 9" 26' 2"	14' 2" 26' 2"	NA NA	15' 5" 28' 7"	11' 11" 28' 7"	29' 8" 44' 11"	24' 3" 44' 11"	18' 9" 44' 11"	NA NA
150	26' 8" 35' 7"	22' 11" 31' 5"	18' 11" 31' 5"	17' 0" 31' 5"	NA NA	18' 7" 34' 3"	14' 4" 34' 3"	35' 7" 53' 11"	29' 2" 53' 11"	22' 6" 53' 11"	NA NA
175	31' 1" 41' 6"	26' 9" 36' 8"	22' 1" 36' 8"	19' 10" 36' 8"	NA NA	21' 8" 40' 0"	16' 8" 40' 0"	41' 6" 62' 10"	34' 0" 62' 10"	26' 3" 62' 10"	NA NA
200	35' 7" 47' 6"	30' 6" 41' 11"	25' 3" 41' 11"	22' 8" 41' 11"	NA NA	24' 9" 45' 9"	19' 1" 45' 9"	47' 6" 71' 10"	38' 10" 71' 10"	30' 1" 71' 10"	NA NA

SETUPS (Approximate Distance)	**135mm FIELD OF VIEW**										
Ext Close Up **Close Up** **Medium Shot** **Full Figure**	5' 5" 8' 5" 15' 8" 43' 5"	6' 4" 9' 10" 18' 3" 50' 6"	7' 8" 11' 11" 22' 1" 61' 1"	8' 6" 13' 3" 24' 7" 68' 2"	5' 5" 8' 6" 15' 9" 43' 7"	7' 10" 12' 2" 22' 6" 62' 5"	10' 1" 15' 9" 29' 3" 80' 11"	4' 1" 6' 4" 11' 9" 32' 6"	5' 0" 7' 9" 14' 4" 39' 9"	6' 5" 10' 0" 18' 7" 51' 4"	4' 5" 6' 10" 12' 9" 35' 2"
Angle of View	V 7.9° H 10.5°	V 6.5° H 8.9°	V 5.4° H 8.9°	V 4.8° H 8.9°	V 7.5° H 17.9°	V 5.5° H 10.2°	V 4.2° H 10.2°	V 10.7° H 15.9°	V 8.6° H 15.9°	V 6.7° H 15.9°	
	Full Aperture	**Academy 1.33:1**	**Academy 1.66:1**	**Academy 1.85:1**	**Anamorphic 2.40:1**	**Super 35 1.85:1**	**Super 35 2.40:1**	**VistaVision**	**VistaVision 1.85:1**	**VistaVision 2.40:1**	**65mm**
5	0' 8" 0' 11"	0' 7" 0' 10"	0' 6" 0' 10"	0' 5" 0' 10"	0' 8" 1' 8"	0' 6" 0' 11"	0' 4" 0' 11"	0' 11" 1' 5"	0' 9" 1' 5"	0' 7" 1' 5"	NA NA
5 ½	0' 9" 1' 0"	0' 8" 0' 11"	0' 6" 0' 11"	0' 6" 0' 11"	0' 9" 1' 10"	0' 6" 1' 0"	0' 5" 1' 0"	1' 0" 1' 6"	0' 10" 1' 6"	0' 8" 1' 6"	NA NA
6	0' 10" 1' 1"	0' 9" 1' 0"	0' 7" 1' 0"	0' 6" 1' 0"	0' 10" 1' 11"	0' 7" 1' 1"	0' 5" 1' 1"	1' 1" 1' 8"	0' 11" 1' 8"	0' 8" 1' 8"	NA NA
6 ½	0' 11" 1' 2"	0' 9" 1' 1"	0' 8" 1' 1"	0' 7" 1' 1"	0' 11" 2' 1"	0' 7" 1' 2"	0' 6" 1' 2"	1' 2" 1' 10"	1' 0" 1' 10"	0' 9" 1' 10"	NA NA
7	1' 0" 1' 4"	0' 10" 1' 2"	0' 8" 1' 2"	0' 7" 1' 2"	1' 0" 2' 3"	0' 8" 1' 3"	0' 6" 1' 3"	1' 4" 1' 11"	1' 1" 1' 11"	0' 10" 1' 11"	NA NA
8	1' 1" 1' 6"	0' 11" 1' 4"	0' 9" 1' 4"	0' 8" 1' 4"	1' 1" 2' 7"	0' 9" 1' 5"	0' 7" 1' 5"	1' 6" 2' 3"	1' 3" 2' 3"	0' 11" 2' 3"	NA NA
9	1' 3" 1' 8"	1' 1" 1' 6"	0' 11" 1' 6"	0' 10" 1' 6"	1' 3" 2' 11"	0' 10" 1' 7"	0' 8" 1' 7"	1' 8" 2' 6"	1' 4" 2' 6"	1' 1" 2' 6"	NA NA
10	1' 5" 1' 10"	1' 2" 1' 8"	1' 0" 1' 8"	0' 11" 1' 8"	1' 5" 3' 3"	1' 0" 1' 9"	0' 9" 1' 9"	1' 10" 2' 10"	1' 6" 2' 10"	1' 2" 2' 10"	NA NA
12	1' 8" 2' 3"	1' 5" 1' 11"	1' 2" 1' 11"	1' 1" 1' 11"	1' 8" 3' 11"	1' 2" 2' 2"	0' 11" 2' 2"	2' 3" 3' 4"	1' 10" 3' 4"	1' 5" 3' 4"	NA NA

14	1' 11" 2' 7"	1' 8" 2' 3"	1' 4" 2' 3"	1' 3" 2' 3"	1' 11" 4' 7"	1' 4" 2' 6"	1' 0" 2' 6"	2' 7" 3' 11"	2' 1" 3' 11"	1' 8" 3' 11"	NA NA
16	2' 3" 2' 11"	1' 11" 2' 7"	1' 7" 2' 7"	1' 5" 2' 7"	2' 2" 5' 3"	1' 6" 2' 10"	1' 2" 2' 10"	2' 11" 4' 6"	2' 5" 4' 6"	1' 10" 4' 6"	NA NA
18	2' 6" 3' 4"	2' 2" 2' 11"	1' 9" 2' 11"	1' 7" 2' 11"	2' 6" 5' 10"	1' 9" 3' 2"	1' 4" 3' 2"	3' 4" 5' 0"	2' 9" 5' 0"	2' 1" 5' 0"	NA NA
20	2' 9" 3' 8"	2' 4" 3' 3"	2' 0" 3' 3"	1' 9" 3' 3"	2' 9" 6' 6"	1' 11" 3' 7"	1' 6" 3' 7"	3' 8" 5' 7"	3' 0" 5' 7"	2' 4" 5' 7"	NA NA
25	3' 5" 4' 7"	3' 0" 4' 1"	2' 5" 4' 1"	2' 2" 4' 1"	3' 5" 8' 2"	2' 5" 4' 5"	1' 10" 4' 5"	4' 7" 7' 0"	3' 9" 7' 0"	2' 11" 7' 0"	NA NA
50	6' 11" 9' 3"	5' 11" 8' 2"	4' 11" 8' 2"	4' 5" 8' 2"	6' 11" 16' 4"	4' 10" 8' 11"	3' 8" 8' 11"	9' 3" 14' 0"	7' 7" 14' 0"	5' 10" 14' 0"	NA NA
75	10' 4" 13' 10"	8' 11" 12' 3"	7' 4" 12' 3"	6' 7" 12' 3"	10' 4" 24' 5"	7' 3" 13' 4"	5' 7" 13' 4"	13' 10" 20' 11"	11' 4" 20' 11"	8' 9" 20' 11"	NA NA
100	13' 10" 18' 5"	11' 10" 16' 4"	9' 10" 16' 4"	8' 10" 16' 4"	13' 9" 32' 7"	9' 7" 17' 9"	7' 5" 17' 9"	18' 5" 27' 11"	15' 1" 27' 11"	11' 8" 27' 11"	NA NA
125	17' 3" 23' 1"	14' 10" 20' 4"	12' 3" 20' 4"	11' 0" 20' 4"	17' 3" 40' 9"	12' 0" 22' 3"	9' 3" 22' 3"	23' 1" 34' 11"	18' 11" 34' 11"	14' 7" 34' 11"	NA NA
150	20' 9" 27' 8"	17' 10" 24' 5"	14' 9" 24' 5"	13' 2" 24' 5"	20' 8" 48' 11"	14' 5" 26' 8"	11' 1" 26' 8"	27' 8" 41' 11"	22' 8" 41' 11"	17' 6" 41' 11"	NA NA
175	24' 2" 32' 4"	20' 9" 28' 6"	17' 2" 28' 6"	15' 5" 28' 6"	24' 1" 57' 0"	16' 10" 31' 1"	13' 0" 31' 1"	32' 4" 48' 11"	26' 5" 48' 11"	20' 5" 48' 11"	NA NA
200	27' 8" 36' 11"	23' 9" 32' 7"	19' 8" 32' 7"	17' 7" 32' 7"	27' 7" 65' 2"	19' 3" 35' 7"	14' 10" 35' 7"	36' 11" 55' 11"	30' 3" 55' 11"	23' 4" 55' 11"	NA NA

150mm FIELD OF VIEW

SETUPS (Approximate Distance)											
Ext Close Up Close Up Medium Shot Full Figure	6' 0" 9' 4" 17' 5" 48' 2"	7' 0" 10' 11" 20' 3" 56' 2"	8' 6" 13' 2" 24' 6" 67' 11"	9' 6" 14' 9" 27' 4" 75' 9"	6' 1" 9' 5" 17' 6" 48' 5"	8' 8" 13' 6" 25' 0" 69' 4"	11' 3" 17' 6" 32' 6" 89' 11"	4' 6" 7' 0" 13' 1" 36' 1"	5' 6" 8' 7" 15' 11" 44' 2"	7' 2" 11' 1" 20' 7" 57' 1"	4' 11" 7' 7" 14' 1" 39' 1"
Angle of View	V 7.1° H 9.5°	V 5.8° H 8.0°	V 4.8° H 8.0°	V 4.3° H 8.0°	V 6.8° H 16.2°	V 5.0° H 9.1°	V 3.8° H 9.1°	V 9.6° H 14.3°	V 7.8° H 14.3°	V 6.0° H 14.3°	V 8.4° H 18.4°
	Full Aperture	**Academy 1.33:1**	**Academy 1.66:1**	**Academy 1.85:1**	**Anamorphic 2.40:1**	**Super 35 1.85:1**	**Super 35 2.40:1**	**VistaVision**	**VistaVision 1.85:1**	**VistaVision 2.40:1**	**65mm**
5	0' 7" 0' 10"	0' 6" 0' 9"	0' 5" 0' 9"	0' 5" 0' 9"	0' 7" 1' 6"	0' 5" 0' 10"	0' 4" 0' 10"	0' 10" 1' 3"	0' 8" 1' 3"	0' 6" 1' 3"	0' 9" 1' 9"
5 ½	0' 8" 0' 11"	0' 7" 0' 10"	0' 6" 0' 10"	0' 5" 0' 10"	0' 8" 1' 7"	0' 6" 0' 11"	0' 4" 0' 11"	0' 11" 1' 5"	0' 9" 1' 5"	0' 7" 1' 5"	0' 10" 1' 11"
6	0' 9" 1' 0"	0' 8" 0' 11"	0' 6" 0' 11"	0' 6" 0' 11"	0' 9" 1' 9"	0' 6" 1' 0"	0' 5" 1' 0"	1' 0" 1' 6"	0' 10" 1' 6"	0' 8" 1' 6"	0' 11" 2' 1"
6 ½	0' 10" 1' 1"	0' 8" 0' 11"	0' 7" 0' 11"	0' 6" 0' 11"	0' 10" 1' 11"	0' 7" 1' 0"	0' 5" 1' 0"	1' 1" 1' 8"	0' 11" 1' 8"	0' 8" 1' 8"	1' 0" 2' 3"
7	0' 10" 1' 2"	0' 9" 1' 0"	0' 7" 1' 0"	0' 7" 1' 0"	0' 10" 2' 1"	0' 7" 1' 1"	0' 6" 1' 1"	1' 2" 1' 9"	0' 11" 1' 9"	0' 9" 1' 9"	1' 1" 2' 5"
8	1' 0" 1' 4"	0' 10" 1' 2"	0' 8" 1' 2"	0' 8" 1' 2"	1' 0" 2' 4"	0' 8" 1' 3"	0' 6" 1' 3"	1' 4" 2' 0"	1' 1" 2' 0"	0' 10" 2' 0"	1' 3" 2' 10"
9	1' 1" 1' 6"	1' 0" 1' 4"	0' 10" 1' 4"	0' 9" 1' 4"	1' 1" 2' 8"	0' 9" 1' 5"	0' 7" 1' 5"	1' 6" 2' 3"	1' 3" 2' 3"	0' 11" 2' 3"	1' 5" 3' 2"
10	1' 3" 1' 8"	1' 1" 1' 6"	0' 11" 1' 6"	0' 10" 1' 6"	1' 3" 2' 11"	0' 10" 1' 7"	0' 8" 1' 7"	1' 8" 2' 6"	1' 4" 2' 6"	1' 1" 2' 6"	1' 6" 3' 6"
12	1' 6" 2' 0"	1' 3" 1' 9"	1' 1" 1' 9"	0' 11" 1' 9"	1' 6" 3' 6"	1' 0" 1' 11"	0' 10" 1' 11"	2' 0" 3' 0"	1' 8" 3' 0"	1' 3" 3' 0"	1' 10" 4' 3"

14	1' 9" 2' 4"	1' 6" 2' 1"	1' 3" 2' 1"	1' 1" 2' 1"	1' 9" 4' 1"	1' 3" 2' 3"	0' 11" 2' 3"	2' 4" 3' 6"	1' 11" 3' 6"	1' 6" 3' 6"	2' 2" 4' 11"
16	2' 0" 2' 8"	1' 9" 2' 4"	1' 5" 2' 4"	1' 3" 2' 4"	2' 0" 4' 8"	1' 5" 2' 7"	1' 1" 2' 7"	2' 8" 4' 0"	2' 2" 4' 0"	1' 8" 4' 0"	2' 5" 5' 7"
18	2' 3" 3' 0"	1' 11" 2' 8"	1' 7" 2' 8"	1' 5" 2' 8"	2' 3" 5' 3"	1' 7" 2' 11"	1' 2" 2' 11"	3' 0" 4' 6"	2' 5" 4' 6"	1' 11" 4' 6"	2' 9" 6' 4"
20	2' 6" 3' 4"	2' 2" 2' 11"	1' 9" 2' 11"	1' 7" 2' 11"	2' 6" 5' 10"	1' 9" 3' 2"	1' 4" 3' 2"	3' 4" 5' 0"	2' 9" 5' 0"	2' 1" 5' 0"	3' 1" 7' 0"
25	3' 1" 4' 2"	2' 8" 3' 8"	2' 3" 3' 8"	2' 0" 3' 8"	3' 1" 7' 4"	2' 2" 4' 0"	1' 8" 4' 0"	4' 2" 6' 3"	3' 5" 6' 3"	2' 8" 6' 3"	3' 10" 8' 9"
50	6' 3" 8' 4"	5' 4" 7' 4"	4' 5" 7' 4"	4' 0" 7' 4"	6' 2" 14' 8"	4' 4" 8' 0"	3' 4" 8' 0"	8' 4" 12' 7"	6' 10" 12' 7"	5' 3" 12' 7"	7' 8" 17' 7"
75	9' 4" 12' 6"	8' 0" 11' 0"	6' 8" 11' 0"	5' 11" 11' 0"	9' 4" 22' 0"	6' 6" 12' 0"	5' 0" 12' 0"	12' 6" 18' 10"	10' 2" 18' 10"	7' 11" 18' 10"	11' 6" 26' 4"
100	12' 5" 16' 7"	10' 8" 14' 8"	8' 10" 14' 8"	7' 11" 14' 8"	12' 5" 29' 4"	8' 8" 16' 0"	6' 8" 16' 0"	16' 7" 25' 2"	13' 7" 25' 2"	10' 6" 25' 2"	15' 4" 35' 1"
125	15' 7" 20' 9"	13' 4" 18' 4"	11' 1" 18' 4"	9' 11" 18' 4"	15' 6" 36' 8"	10' 10" 20' 0"	8' 4" 20' 0"	20' 9" 31' 5"	17' 0" 31' 5"	13' 2" 31' 5"	19' 2" 43' 10"
150	18' 8" 24' 11"	16' 0" 22' 0"	13' 3" 22' 0"	11' 11" 22' 0"	18' 7" 44' 0"	13' 0" 24' 0"	10' 0" 24' 0"	24' 11" 37' 9"	20' 5" 37' 9"	15' 9" 37' 9"	23' 0" 52' 8"
175	21' 9" 29' 1"	18' 8" 25' 8"	15' 6" 25' 8"	13' 10" 25' 8"	21' 8" 51' 4"	15' 2" 28' 0"	11' 8" 28' 0"	29' 1" 44' 0"	23' 10" 44' 0"	18' 5" 44' 0"	26' 10" 61' 5"
200	24' 11" 33' 3"	21' 4" 29' 4"	17' 8" 29' 4"	15' 10" 29' 4"	24' 9" 58' 8"	17' 4" 32' 0"	13' 4" 32' 0"	33' 3" 50' 4"	27' 2" 50' 4"	21' 0" 50' 4"	30' 8" 70' 2"

200mm FIELD OF VIEW

SETUPS (Approximate Distance)											
Ext Close Up **Close Up** **Medium Shot** **Full Figure**	8' 0" 12' 6" 23' 3" 64' 3"	9' 4" 14' 7" 27' 0" 74' 10"	11' 4" 17' 7" 32' 8" 90' 6"	12' 7" 19' 8" 36' 5" 100' 11"	8' 1" 12' 7" 23' 4" 64' 6"	11' 7" 18' 0" 33' 5" 92' 5"	15' 0" 23' 4" 43' 4" 119' 11"	6' 0" 9' 4" 17' 5" 48' 2"	7' 4" 11' 5" 21' 3" 58' 10"	9' 6" 14' 10" 27' 6" 76' 1"	6' 6" 10' 2" 18' 10" 52' 2"
Angle of View	V 5.3° H 7.1°	V 4.4° H 6.0°	V 3.6° H 6.0°	V 3.2° H 6.0°	V 5.1° H 12.2°	V 3.7° H 6.9°	V 2.9° H 6.9°	V 7.2° H 10.8°	V 5.8° H 10.8°	V 4.5° H 10.8°	V 6.6° H 15.0°
	Full Aperture	**Academy 1.33:1**	**Academy 1.66:1**	**Academy 1.85:1**	**Anamorphic 2.40:1**	**Super 35 1.85:1**	**Super 35 2.40:1**	**VistaVision**	**VistaVision 1.85:1**	**VistaVision 2.40:1**	**65mm**
5	0' 6" 0' 7"	0' 5" 0' 7"	0' 4" 0' 7"	0' 4" 0' 7"	0' 6" 1' 1"	0' 4" 0' 7"	0' 3" 0' 7"	0' 7" 0' 11"	0' 6" 0' 11"	0' 5" 0' 11"	0' 7" 1' 4"
5 ½	0' 6" 0' 8"	0' 5" 0' 7"	0' 4" 0' 7"	0' 4" 0' 7"	0' 6" 1' 3"	0' 4" 0' 8"	0' 3" 0' 8"	0' 8" 1' 0"	0' 7" 1' 0"	0' 5" 1' 0"	0' 8" 1' 5"
6	0' 7" 0' 9"	0' 6" 0' 8"	0' 5" 0' 8"	0' 4" 0' 8"	0' 7" 1' 4"	0' 5" 0' 9"	0' 4" 0' 9"	0' 9" 1' 2"	0' 7" 1' 2"	0' 6" 1' 2"	0' 8" 1' 7"
6 ½	0' 7" 0' 10"	0' 6" 0' 9"	0' 5" 0' 9"	0' 5" 0' 9"	0' 7" 1' 5"	0' 5" 0' 9"	0' 4" 0' 9"	0' 10" 1' 3"	0' 8" 1' 3"	0' 6" 1' 3"	0' 9" 1' 9"
7	0' 8" 0' 10"	0' 7" 0' 9"	0' 6" 0' 9"	0' 5" 0' 9"	0' 8" 1' 6"	0' 5" 0' 10"	0' 4" 0' 10"	0' 10" 1' 4"	0' 9" 1' 4"	0' 7" 1' 4"	0' 10" 1' 10"
8	0' 9" 1' 0"	0' 8" 0' 11"	0' 6" 0' 11"	0' 6" 0' 11"	0' 9" 1' 9"	0' 6" 1' 0"	0' 5" 1' 0"	1' 0" 1' 6"	0' 10" 1' 6"	0' 8" 1' 6"	0' 11" 2' 1"
9	0' 10" 1' 1"	0' 9" 1' 0"	0' 7" 1' 0"	0' 6" 1' 0"	0' 10" 2' 0"	0' 7" 1' 1"	0' 5" 1' 1"	1' 1" 1' 8"	0' 11" 1' 8"	0' 9" 1' 8"	1' 0" 2' 4"
10	0' 11" 1' 3"	0' 10" 1' 1"	0' 8" 1' 1"	0' 7" 1' 1"	0' 11" 2' 2"	0' 8" 1' 2"	0' 6" 1' 2"	1' 3" 1' 11"	1' 0" 1' 11"	0' 9" 1' 11"	1' 2" 2' 8"
12	1' 1" 1' 6"	1' 0" 1' 4"	0' 10" 1' 4"	0' 9" 1' 4"	1' 1" 2' 8"	0' 9" 1' 5"	0' 7" 1' 5"	1' 6" 2' 3"	1' 3" 2' 3"	0' 11" 2' 3"	1' 5" 3' 2"

14	1' 4" 1' 9"	1' 1" 1' 6"	0' 11" 1' 6"	0' 10" 1' 6"	1' 4" 3' 1"	0' 11" 1' 8"	0' 8" 1' 8"	1' 9" 2' 8"	1' 5" 2' 8"	1' 1" 2' 8"	1' 7" 3' 8"
16	1' 6" 2' 0"	1' 3" 1' 9"	1' 1" 1' 9"	0' 11" 1' 9"	1' 6" 3' 6"	1' 0" 1' 11"	0' 10" 1' 11"	2' 0" 3' 0"	1' 8" 3' 0"	1' 3" 3' 0"	1' 10" 4' 3"
18	1' 8" 2' 3"	1' 5" 2' 0"	1' 2" 2' 0"	1' 1" 2' 0"	1' 8" 4' 0"	1' 2" 2' 2"	0' 11" 2' 2"	2' 3" 3' 5"	1' 10" 3' 5"	1' 5" 3' 5"	2' 1" 4' 9"
20	1' 10" 2' 6"	1' 7" 2' 2"	1' 4" 2' 2"	1' 2" 2' 2"	1' 10" 4' 5"	1' 4" 2' 5"	1' 0" 2' 5"	2' 6" 3' 9"	2' 0" 3' 9"	1' 7" 3' 9"	2' 4" 5' 3"
25	2' 4" 3' 1"	2' 0" 2' 9"	1' 8" 2' 9"	1' 6" 2' 9"	2' 4" 5' 6"	1' 7" 3' 0"	1' 3" 3' 0"	3' 1" 4' 9"	2' 7" 4' 9"	2' 0" 4' 9"	2' 11" 6' 7"
50	4' 8" 6' 3"	4' 0" 5' 6"	3' 4" 5' 6"	3' 0" 5' 6"	4' 8" 11' 0"	3' 3" 6' 0"	2' 6" 6' 0"	6' 3" 9' 5"	5' 1" 9' 5"	3' 11" 9' 5"	5' 9" 13' 2"
75	7' 0" 9' 4"	6' 0" 8' 3"	5' 0" 8' 3"	4' 5" 8' 3"	7' 0" 16' 6"	4' 10" 9' 0"	3' 9" 9' 0"	9' 4" 14' 2"	7' 8" 14' 2"	5' 11" 14' 2"	8' 8" 19' 9"
100	9' 4" 12' 6"	8' 0" 11' 0"	6' 8" 11' 0"	5' 11" 11' 0"	9' 4" 22' 0"	6' 6" 12' 0"	5' 0" 12' 0"	12' 6" 18' 10"	10' 2" 18' 10"	7' 11" 18' 10"	11' 6" 26' 4"
125	11' 8" 15' 7"	10' 0" 13' 9"	8' 3" 13' 9"	7' 5" 13' 9"	11' 7" 27' 6"	8' 1" 15' 0"	6' 3" 15' 0"	15' 7" 23' 7"	12' 9" 23' 7"	9' 10" 23' 7"	14' 5" 32' 11"
150	14' 0" 18' 8"	12' 0" 16' 6"	9' 11" 16' 6"	8' 11" 16' 6"	13' 11" 33' 0"	9' 9" 18' 0"	7' 6" 18' 0"	18' 8" 28' 3"	15' 4" 28' 3"	11' 10" 28' 3"	17' 3" 39' 6"
175	16' 4" 21' 10"	14' 0" 19' 3"	11' 7" 19' 3"	10' 5" 19' 3"	16' 3" 38' 6"	11' 4" 21' 0"	8' 9" 21' 0"	21' 10" 33' 0"	17' 10" 33' 0"	13' 10" 33' 0"	20' 2" 46' 1"
200	18' 8" 24' 11"	16' 0" 22' 0"	13' 3" 22' 0"	11' 11" 22' 0"	18' 7" 44' 0"	13' 0" 24' 0"	10' 0" 24' 0"	24' 11" 37' 9"	20' 5" 37' 9"	15' 9" 37' 9"	23' 0" 52' 8"

300mm FIELD OF VIEW

SETUPS (Approximate Distance)

Ext Close Up **Close Up** **Medium Shot** **Full Figure**	12' 1" 18' 9" 34' 10" 96' 5"	14' 0" 21' 10" 40' 7" 112' 4"	17' 0" 26' 5" 49' 0" 135' 9"	18' 11" 29' 5" 54' 8" 151' 5"	12' 1" 18' 10" 35' 0" 96' 10"	17' 4" 27' 0" 50' 1" 138' 8"	22' 6" 35' 0" 64' 11" 179' 10"	9' 0" 14' 1" 26' 1" 72' 3"	11' 0" 17' 2" 31' 10" 88' 3"	14' 3" 22' 2" 41' 3" 114' 1"	9' 9" 15' 3" 28' 3" 78' 3"
Angle of View	V 3.6° H 4.8°	V 2.9° H 4.0°	V 2.4° H 4.0°	V 2.2° H 4.0°	V 3.4° H 8.1°	V 2.5° H 4.6°	V 1.9° H 4.6°	V 4.8° H 7.2°	V 3.9° H 7.2°	V 3.0° H 7.2°	V 4.2° H 9.3°
	Full Aperture	**Academy 1.33:1**	**Academy 1.66:1**	**Academy 1.85:1**	**Anamorphic 2.40:1**	**Super 35 1.85:1**	**Super 35 2.40:1**	**VistaVision**	**VistaVision 1.85:1**	**VistaVision 2.40:1**	**65mm**
5	0' 4" 0' 5"	0' 3" 0' 4"	0' 3" 0' 4"	0' 2" 0' 4"	0' 4" 0' 9"	0' 3" 0' 5"	0' 2" 0' 5"	0' 5" 0' 8"	0' 4" 0' 8"	0' 3" 0' 8"	0' 5" 0' 11"
5 ½	0' 4" 0' 5"	0' 4" 0' 5"	0' 3" 0' 5"	0' 3" 0' 5"	0' 4" 0' 10"	0' 3" 0' 5"	0' 2" 0' 5"	0' 5" 0' 8"	0' 4" 0' 8"	0' 3" 0' 8"	0' 5" 1' 0"
6	0' 4" 0' 6"	0' 4" 0' 5"	0' 3" 0' 5"	0' 3" 0' 5"	0' 4" 0' 11"	0' 3" 0' 6"	0' 2" 0' 6"	0' 6" 0' 9"	0' 5" 0' 9"	0' 4" 0' 9"	0' 6" 1' 1"
6 ½	0' 5" 0' 6"	0' 4" 0' 6"	0' 3" 0' 6"	0' 3" 0' 6"	0' 5" 0' 11"	0' 3" 0' 6"	0' 3" 0' 6"	0' 6" 0' 10"	0' 5" 0' 10"	0' 4" 0' 10"	0' 6" 1' 2"
7	0' 5" 0' 7"	0' 4" 0' 6"	0' 4" 0' 6"	0' 3" 0' 6"	0' 5" 1' 0"	0' 4" 0' 7"	0' 3" 0' 7"	0' 7" 0' 11"	0' 6" 0' 11"	0' 4" 0' 11"	0' 6" 1' 3"
8	0' 6" 0' 8"	0' 5" 0' 7"	0' 4" 0' 7"	0' 4" 0' 7"	0' 6" 1' 2"	0' 4" 0' 8"	0' 3" 0' 8"	0' 8" 1' 0"	0' 7" 1' 0"	0' 5" 1' 0"	0' 7" 1' 5"
9	0' 7" 0' 9"	0' 6" 0' 8"	0' 5" 0' 8"	0' 4" 0' 8"	0' 7" 1' 4"	0' 5" 0' 9"	0' 4" 0' 9"	0' 9" 1' 2"	0' 7" 1' 2"	0' 6" 1' 2"	0' 8" 1' 7"
10	0' 7" 0' 10"	0' 6" 0' 9"	0' 5" 0' 9"	0' 5" 0' 9"	0' 7" 1' 6"	0' 5" 0' 10"	0' 4" 0' 10"	0' 10" 1' 3"	0' 8" 1' 3"	0' 6" 1' 3"	0' 9" 1' 9"
12	0' 9" 1' 0"	0' 8" 0' 11"	0' 6" 0' 11"	0' 6" 0' 11"	0' 9" 1' 9"	0' 6" 1' 0"	0' 5" 1' 0"	1' 0" 1' 6"	0' 10" 1' 6"	0' 8" 1' 6"	0' 11" 2' 1"

14	0' 10" 1' 2"	0' 9" 1' 0"	0' 7" 1' 0"	0' 7" 1' 0"	0' 10" 2' 1"	0' 7" 1' 1"	0' 6" 1' 1"	1' 2" 1' 9"	0' 11" 1' 9"	0' 9" 1' 9"	1' 1" 2' 5"
16	1' 0" 1' 4"	0' 10" 1' 2"	0' 8" 1' 2"	0' 8" 1' 2"	1' 0" 2' 4"	0' 8" 1' 3"	0' 6" 1' 3"	1' 4" 2' 0"	1' 1" 2' 0"	0' 10" 2' 0"	1' 3" 2' 10"
18	1' 1" 1' 6"	1' 0" 1' 4"	0' 10" 1' 4"	0' 9" 1' 4"	1' 1" 2' 8"	0' 9" 1' 5"	0' 7" 1' 5"	1' 6" 2' 3"	1' 3" 2' 3"	0' 11" 2' 3"	1' 5" 3' 2"
20	1' 3" 1' 8"	1' 1" 1' 6"	0' 11" 1' 6"	0' 10" 1' 6"	1' 3" 2' 11"	0' 10" 1' 7"	0' 8" 1' 7"	1' 8" 2' 6"	1' 4" 2' 6"	1' 1" 2' 6"	1' 6" 3' 6"
25	1' 7" 2' 1"	1' 4" 1' 10"	1' 1" 1' 10"	1' 0" 1' 10"	1' 7" 3' 8"	1' 1" 2' 0"	0' 10" 2' 0"	2' 1" 3' 2"	1' 8" 3' 2"	1' 4" 3' 2"	1' 11" 4' 5"
50	3' 1" 4' 2"	2' 8" 3' 8"	2' 3" 3' 8"	2' 0" 3' 8"	3' 1" 7' 4"	2' 2" 4' 0"	1' 8" 4' 0"	4' 2" 6' 3"	3' 5" 6' 3"	2' 8" 6' 3"	3' 10" 8' 9"
75	4' 8" 6' 3"	4' 0" 5' 6"	3' 4" 5' 6"	3' 0" 5' 6"	4' 8" 11' 0"	3' 3" 6' 0"	2' 6" 6' 0"	6' 3" 9' 5"	5' 1" 9' 5"	3' 11" 9' 5"	5' 9" 13' 2"
100	6' 3" 8' 4"	5' 4" 7' 4"	4' 5" 7' 4"	4' 0" 7' 4"	6' 2" 14' 8"	4' 4" 8' 0"	3' 4" 8' 0"	8' 4" 12' 7"	6' 10" 12' 7"	5' 3" 12' 7"	7' 8" 17' 7"
125	7' 9" 10' 5"	6' 8" 9' 2"	5' 6" 9' 2"	4' 11" 9' 2"	7' 9" 18' 4"	5' 5" 10' 0"	4' 2" 10' 0"	10' 5" 15' 9"	8' 6" 15' 9"	6' 7" 15' 9"	9' 7" 21' 11"
150	9' 4" 12' 6"	8' 0" 11' 0"	6' 8" 11' 0"	5' 11" 11' 0"	9' 4" 22' 0"	6' 6" 12' 0"	5' 0" 12' 0"	12' 6" 18' 10"	10' 2" 18' 10"	7' 11" 18' 10"	11' 6" 26' 4"
175	10' 11" 14' 6"	9' 4" 12' 10"	7' 9" 12' 10"	6' 11" 12' 10"	10' 10" 25' 8"	7' 7" 14' 0"	5' 10" 14' 0"	14' 6" 22' 0"	11' 11" 22' 0"	9' 2" 22' 0"	13' 5" 30' 8"
200	12' 5" 16' 7"	10' 8" 14' 8"	8' 10" 14' 8"	7' 11" 14' 8"	12' 5" 29' 4"	8' 8" 16' 0"	6' 8" 16' 0"	16' 7" 25' 2"	13' 7" 25' 2"	10' 6" 25' 2"	15' 4" 35' 1"

400mm FIELD OF VIEW

SETUPS (Approximate Distance)											
Ext Close Up **Close Up** **Medium Shot** **Full Figure**	16' 1" 25' 0" 46' 5" 128' 7"	18' 9" 29' 1" 54' 1" 149' 9"	22' 8" 35' 2" 65' 4" 181' 0"	25' 3" 39' 3" 72' 11" 201' 11"	16' 2" 25' 1" 46' 7" 129' 1"	23' 1" 35' 11" 66' 9" 184' 11"	30' 0" 46' 8" 86' 7" 239' 10"	12' 0" 18' 9" 34' 9" 96' 4"	14' 9" 22' 11" 42' 6" 117' 8"	19' 0" 29' 7" 54' 11" 152' 2"	13' 0" 20' 3" 37' 8" 104' 3"
Angle of View	V 2.7° H 3.6°	V 2.2° H 3.0°	V 1.8° H 3.0°	V 1.6° H 3.0°	V 2.5° H 6.1°	V 1.9° H 3.4°	V 1.4° H 3.4°	V 3.6° H 5.4°	V 2.9° H 5.4°	V 2.3° H 5.4°	V 3.2° H 6.9°
	Full Aperture	**Academy 1.33:1**	**Academy 1.66:1**	**Academy 1.85:1**	**Anamorphic 2.40:1**	**Super 35 1.85:1**	**Super 35 2.40:1**	**VistaVision**	**VistaVision 1.85:1**	**VistaVision 2.40:1**	**65mm**
5	0' 3" 0' 4"	0' 2" 0' 3"	0' 2" 0' 3"	0' 2" 0' 3"	0' 3" 0' 7"	0' 2" 0' 4"	0' 2" 0' 4"	0' 4" 0' 6"	0' 3" 0' 6"	0' 2" 0' 6"	0' 3" 0' 8"
5 1/2	0' 3" 0' 4"	0' 3" 0' 4"	0' 2" 0' 4"	0' 2" 0' 4"	0' 3" 0' 7"	0' 2" 0' 4"	0' 2" 0' 4"	0' 4" 0' 6"	0' 3" 0' 6"	0' 3" 0' 6"	0' 4" 0' 9"
6	0' 3" 0' 4"	0' 3" 0' 4"	0' 2" 0' 4"	0' 2" 0' 4"	0' 3" 0' 8"	0' 2" 0' 4"	0' 2" 0' 4"	0' 4" 0' 7"	0' 4" 0' 7"	0' 3" 0' 7"	0' 4" 0' 9"
6 1/2	0' 4" 0' 5"	0' 3" 0' 4"	0' 3" 0' 4"	0' 2" 0' 4"	0' 4" 0' 9"	0' 3" 0' 5"	0' 2" 0' 5"	0' 5" 0' 7"	0' 4" 0' 7"	0' 3" 0' 7"	0' 4" 0' 10"
7	0' 4" 0' 5"	0' 3" 0' 5"	0' 3" 0' 5"	0' 2" 0' 5"	0' 4" 0' 9"	0' 3" 0' 5"	0' 2" 0' 5"	0' 5" 0' 8"	0' 4" 0' 8"	0' 3" 0' 8"	0' 5" 0' 11"
8	0' 4" 0' 6"	0' 4" 0' 5"	0' 3" 0' 5"	0' 3" 0' 5"	0' 4" 0' 11"	0' 3" 0' 6"	0' 2" 0' 6"	0' 6" 0' 9"	0' 5" 0' 9"	0' 4" 0' 9"	0' 6" 1' 1"
9	0' 5" 0' 7"	0' 4" 0' 6"	0' 4" 0' 6"	0' 3" 0' 6"	0' 5" 1' 0"	0' 4" 0' 6"	0' 3" 0' 6"	0' 7" 0' 10"	0' 6" 0' 10"	0' 4" 0' 10"	0' 6" 1' 2"
10	0' 6" 0' 7"	0' 5" 0' 7"	0' 4" 0' 7"	0' 4" 0' 7"	0' 6" 1' 1"	0' 4" 0' 7"	0' 3" 0' 7"	0' 7" 0' 11"	0' 6" 0' 11"	0' 5" 0' 11"	0' 7" 1' 4"
12	0' 7" 0' 9"	0' 6" 0' 8"	0' 5" 0' 8"	0' 4" 0' 8"	0' 7" 1' 4"	0' 5" 0' 9"	0' 4" 0' 9"	0' 9" 1' 2"	0' 7" 1' 2"	0' 6" 1' 2"	0' 8" 1' 7"

14	0' 8" 0' 10"	0' 7" 0' 9"	0' 6" 0' 9"	0' 5" 0' 9"	0' 8" 1' 6"	0' 5" 0' 10"	0' 4" 0' 10"	0' 10" 1' 4"	0' 9" 1' 4"	0' 7" 1' 4"	0' 10" 1' 10"
16	0' 9" 1' 0"	0' 8" 0' 11"	0' 6" 0' 11"	0' 6" 0' 11"	0' 9" 1' 9"	0' 6" 1' 0"	0' 5" 1' 0"	1' 0" 1' 6"	0' 10" 1' 6"	0' 8" 1' 6"	0' 11" 2' 1"
18	0' 10" 1' 1"	0' 9" 1' 0"	0' 7" 1' 0"	0' 6" 1' 0"	0' 10" 2' 0"	0' 7" 1' 1"	0' 5" 1' 1"	1' 1" 1' 8"	0' 11" 1' 8"	0' 9" 1' 8"	1' 0" 2' 4"
20	0' 11" 1' 3"	0' 10" 1' 1"	0' 8" 1' 1"	0' 7" 1' 1"	0' 11" 2' 2"	0' 8" 1' 2"	0' 6" 1' 2"	1' 3" 1' 11"	1' 0" 1' 11"	0' 9" 1' 11"	1' 2" 2' 8"
25	1' 2" 1' 7"	1' 0" 1' 4"	0' 10" 1' 4"	0' 9" 1' 4"	1' 2" 2' 9"	0' 10" 1' 6"	0' 8" 1' 6"	1' 7" 2' 4"	1' 3" 2' 4"	1' 0" 2' 4"	1' 5" 3' 3"
50	2' 4" 3' 1"	2' 0" 2' 9"	1' 8" 2' 9"	1' 6" 2' 9"	2' 4" 5' 6"	1' 7" 3' 0"	1' 3" 3' 0"	3' 1" 4' 9"	2' 7" 4' 9"	2' 0" 4' 9"	2' 11" 6' 7"
75	3' 6" 4' 8"	3' 0" 4' 1"	2' 6" 4' 1"	2' 3" 4' 1"	3' 6" 8' 3"	2' 5" 4' 6"	1' 11" 4' 6"	4' 8" 7' 1"	3' 10" 7' 1"	2' 11" 7' 1"	4' 4" 9' 10"
100	4' 8" 6' 3"	4' 0" 5' 6"	3' 4" 5' 6"	3' 0" 5' 6"	4' 8" 11' 0"	3' 3" 6' 0"	2' 6" 6' 0"	6' 3" 9' 5"	5' 1" 9' 5"	3' 11" 9' 5"	5' 9" 13' 2"
125	5' 10" 7' 9"	5' 0" 6' 10"	4' 2" 6' 10"	3' 9" 6' 10"	5' 10" 13' 9"	4' 1" 7' 6"	3' 2" 7' 6"	7' 9" 11' 9"	6' 4" 11' 9"	4' 11" 11' 9"	7' 2" 16' 5"
150	7' 0" 9' 4"	6' 0" 8' 3"	5' 0" 8' 3"	4' 5" 8' 3"	7' 0" 16' 6"	4' 10" 9' 0"	3' 9" 9' 0"	9' 4" 14' 2"	7' 8" 14' 2"	5' 11" 14' 2"	8' 8" 19' 9"
175	8' 2" 10' 11"	7' 0" 9' 7"	5' 10" 9' 7"	5' 2" 9' 7"	8' 2" 19' 3"	5' 8" 10' 6"	4' 5" 10' 6"	10' 11" 16' 6"	8' 11" 16' 6"	6' 11" 16' 6"	10' 1" 23' 0"
200	9' 4" 12' 6"	8' 0" 11' 0"	6' 8" 11' 0"	5' 11" 11' 0"	9' 4" 22' 0"	6' 6" 12' 0"	5' 0" 12' 0"	12' 6" 18' 10"	10' 2" 18' 10"	7' 11" 18' 10"	11' 6" 26' 4"

16mm/SUPER 16 FIELD OF VIEW

LENS SIZE		5.9mm	8mm	10mm	12mm	16mm	25mm	37.5mm	50mm	85mm	100mm	150mm	200mm	300mm	400mm
FORMAT		16mm	16mm	16mm	16mm	16mm	16mm	16mm	16mm	16mm	16mm	16mm	16mm	16mm	16mm
		Super16	Super16	Super16	Super16	Super16	Super16	Super16	Super16	Super16	Super16	Super16	Super16	Super16	Super16
SETUPS (Approximate Distance)	Ext Cls Up	0' 7"	0' 10"	1' 0"	1' 2"	1' 7"	2' 6"	3' 9"	5' 0"	8' 6"	10' 0"	15' 0"	20' 0"	30' 0"	40' 0"
		0' 8"	0' 11"	1' 2"	1' 5"	1' 11"	2' 11"	4' 5"	5' 11"	10' 0"	11' 9"	17' 8"	23' 6"	35' 4"	47' 1"
	Close Up	0' 11"	1' 3"	1" 7"	1' 10"	2' 6"	3' 11"	5' 10"	7' 9"	13' 3"	15' 7"	23' 4"	31' 2"	46' 9"	62' 3"
		1' 1"	1' 6"	1' 10"	2' 2"	2' 11"	4' 7"	6' 10"	9' 2"	15' 7"	18' 4"	27' 5"	36' 7"	54' 11"	73' 2"
	Med Shot	1' 8"	2' 4"	2' 11"	3' 6"	4' 8"	7' 3"	10' 10"	14' 5"	24' 7"	28' 11"	43' 4"	57' 10"	86' 9"	115' 8"
		2' 0"	2' 9"	3' 5"	4' 11"	5' 5"	8' 6"	12' 9"	17' 0"	28' 11"	34' 0"	51' 0"	68' 0"	101' 11"	135' 11"
	Full Figure	4' 9"	6'5"	8' 0"	9' 7"	12' 10"	20' 0"	30' 0"	40' 0"	68' 1"	80' 1"	120' 1"	160' 2"	240' 3"	320' 4"
		5' 7"	7' 6"	9' 5"	11' 4"	15' 1"	23' 6"	35' 4"	47' 1"	80' 0"	94' 1"	141' 2"	188' 3"	282' 4"	376' 5"
ANGLE OF VIEW		V 63.2°	V 48.8°	V 39.9°	V 33.7°	V 25.6°	V 16.5°	V 11.1°	V 8.3°	V 4.9°	V 4.2°	V 2.8°	V 2.1°	V 1.4°	V 1.0°
		H 78.6°	H 62.2°	H 51.5°	H 43.8°	H 33.6°	H 21.9°	H 14.7°	H 11.0°	H 6.5°	H 5.5°	H 3.7°	H 2.8°	H 1.8°	H 1.4°
		V 56.8°	V 43.5°	V 35.4°	V 29.8°	V 22.5°	V 14.5°	V 9.7°	V 7.3°	V 4.3°	V 3.7°	V 2.4°	V 1.8°	V 1.2°	V 0.9°
		H 89.8°	H 72.6°	H 60.9°	H 52.2°	H 40.4°	H 26.5°	H 17.8°	H 13.4°	H 7.9°	H 6.7°	H 4.5°	H 3.4°	H 2.2°	H 1.7°
FOCUS (feet) 2		2' 6" 3' 6"	1' 10" 2' 7"	1' 6" 2' 1"	1'3" 1' 9"	0' 11" 1' 3"	0' 7" 0' 10"	0' 5" 0' 7"	0' 4" 0' 5"	0' 2" 0' 3"	0' 2" 0' 2"	0' 1" 0' 2"	NA NA	NA NA	NA NA
		2' 2" 4' 0"	1' 7" 2' 11"	1' 3" 2' 4"	1'1" 2' 0"	0' 10" 1' 6"	0' 6" 0' 11"	0' 4" 0' 8"	0' 3" 0' 6"	0' 2" 0' 3"	0' 2" 0' 3"	0' 1" 0' 2"	NA NA	NA NA	NA NA
2 ½		3' 2" 4' 4"	2' 4" 3' 2"	1' 10" 2' 7"	1' 7" 2' 2"	1' 2" 1' 7"	0' 9" 1' 0"	0' 6" 0' 8"	0' 4" 0' 6"	0' 3" 0' 4"	0' 2" 0' 3"	0' 1" 0' 2"	0' 1" 0' 2"	NA NA	NA NA
		2' 8" 5' 0"	2' 0" 3' 8"	1' 7" 2' 11"	1' 4" 2' 5"	1' 0" 1' 10"	0' 8" 1' 2"	0' 5" 0' 9"	0' 4" 0' 7"	0' 2" 0' 4"	0' 2" 0' 4"	0' 1" 0' 2"	0' 1" 0' 2"	NA NA	NA NA

3	3' 10" 5' 3" 3' 3" 6' 0"	2' 10" 3' 10" 2' 5" 3' 8"	2' 3" 3' 1" 1' 11" 3' 6"	1' 10" 2' 7" 1' 7" 2' 11"	1' 5" 1' 11" 1' 2" 2' 2"	0' 11" 1' 3" 0' 9" 1' 5"	0' 7" 0' 10" 0' 6" 0' 11"	0' 5" 0' 7" 0' 5" 0' 8"	0' 3" 0' 4" 0' 3" 0' 5"	0' 3" 0' 4" 0' 2" 0' 4"	0' 2" 0' 2" 0' 2" 0' 3"	0' 1" 0' 2" 0' 1" 0' 2"	NA NA NA NA	NA NA NA NA
3 ½	4' 5" 6' 1" 3' 9" 7' 0"	3' 3" 4" 6" 2' 9" 5' 2"	2' 7" 3' 7" 2' 3" 4' 1"	2' 2" 3' 0" 1' 10" 3' 5"	1' 8" 2' 3" 1' 5" 2' 7"	1' 11" 1' 5" 0' 11" 1' 8"	0' 8" 0' 11" 0' 7" 1' 1"	0' 6" 0' 9" 0' 5" 0' 10"	0' 4" 0' 5" 0' 3" 0' 6"	0' 3" 0' 4" 0' 3" 0' 5"	0' 2" 0' 3" 0' 2" 0' 3"	0' 2" 0' 2" 0' 1" 0' 2"	NA NA 0' 1" 0' 2"	NA NA NA NA
4	5' 1" 6' 11" 4' 4" 8' 0"	3' 9" 5' 2" 3' 2" 5' 11"	3' 0" 4' 1" 2' 7" 4' 8"	2' 6" 3' 5" 2' 2" 3' 11"	1' 10" 2' 7" 1' 7" 2' 11"	1' 2" 1' 8" 1' 0" 1' 11"	0' 10" 1' 1" 0' 8" 1' 3"	0' 7" 0' 10" 0' 6" 0' 11"	0' 4" 0' 6" 0' 4" 0' 7"	0' 4" 0' 5" 0' 3" 0' 6"	0' 2" 0' 3" 0' 2" 0' 4"	0' 2" 0' 2" 0' 2" 0' 3"	0' 1" 0' 2" 0' 1" 0' 2"	NA NA NA NA
4 ½	5' 9" 7' 10" 4' 10" 9' 0"	4' 3" 5' 9" 3' 7" 6' 7"	3' 4" 4' 7" 2' 10" 5' 4"	2' 10" 3' 10" 2' 5" 4' 5"	2' 1" 2' 11" 1' 10" 3' 4"	1' 4" 1' 10" 1' 2" 2' 1"	0' 11" 1' 3" 0' 9" 1' 5"	0' 8" 0' 11" 0' 7" 1' 1"	0' 5" 0' 7" 0' 4" 0' 7"	0' 4" 0' 6" 0' 3" 0' 6"	0' 3" 0' 4" 0' 2" 0' 4"	0' 2" 0' 3" 0' 2" 0' 3"	0' 1" 0' 2" 0' 1" 0' 2"	NA NA 0' 1" 0' 2"
5	6' 4" 8' 8" 5' 5" 10' 0"	4' 8" 6' 5" 4' 0" 7' 4"	3' 9" 5' 2" 3' 2" 5' 11"	3' 1" 4' 3" 2' 8" 4' 11"	2' 4" 3' 2" 2' 0" 3' 8"	1' 6" 2' 1" 1' 3" 2' 4"	1' 0" 1' 4" 0' 10" 1' 7"	0' 9" 1' 0" 0' 8" 1' 2"	0' 5" 0' 7" 0' 5" 0' 8"	0' 4" 0' 6" 0' 4" 0' 7"	0' 3" 0' 4" 0' 3" 0' 5"	0' 2" 0' 3" 0' 2" 0' 4"	0' 1" 0' 2" 0' 1" 0' 2"	0' 1" 0' 2" 0' 1" 0' 2"
5 ½	7' 0" 9' 7" 5' 11" 11' 0"	5' 2" 7' 1" 4' 5" 8' 1"	4' 1" 5' 8" 3' 6" 6' 6"	3' 5" 4' 8" 2' 11" 5' 5"	2' 7" 3' 6" 2' 2" 4' 1"	1' 8" 2' 3" 1' 5" 2' 7"	1' 1" 1' 6" 0' 11" 1' 9"	0' 10" 1' 2" 0' 8" 1' 4"	0' 6" 0' 8" 0' 5" 0' 9"	0' 5" 0' 7" 0' 4" 0' 8"	0' 3" 0' 5" 0' 3" 0' 5"	0' 2" 0' 3" 0' 2" 0' 4"	0' 2" 0' 2" 0' 1" 0' 3"	0' 1" 0' 2" 0' 1" 0' 2"
6	7' 7" 10' 5" 6' 6" 12' 0"	5' 7" 7' 8" 4' 9" 8' 10"	4' 6" 6' 2" 3' 10" 7' 1"	3' 9" 5' 2" 3' 2" 5' 11"	2' 10" 3' 10" 2' 5" 4' 5"	1' 10" 2' 6" 1' 6" 2' 10"	1' 2" 1' 8" 1' 0" 1' 11"	0' 11" 1' 3" 0' 9" 1' 5"	0' 6" 0' 9" 0' 5" 0' 10"	0' 5" 0' 7" 0' 5" 0' 8"	0' 4" 0' 5" 0' 3" 0' 6"	0' 3" 0' 4" 0' 2" 0' 4"	0' 2" 0' 2" 0' 2" 0' 3"	0' 1" 0' 2" 0' 1" 0' 2"
6 ½	8' 3" 11' 4" 7' 0" 12' 11"	6' 1" 8' 4" 5' 2" 9' 7"	4' 10" 6' 8" 4' 2" 7' 8"	4' 11" 5' 7" 3' 5" 6' 4"	3' 1" 4' 2" 2' 7" 4' 9"	1' 11" 2' 8" 1' 8" 3' 1"	1' 4" 1' 9" 1' 1" 2' 0"	1' 0" 1' 4" 0' 10" 1' 6"	0' 7" 0' 9" 0' 6" 0' 11"	0' 6" 0' 8" 0' 5" 0' 9"	0' 4" 0' 5" 0' 3" 0' 6"	0' 3" 0' 4" 0' 2" 0' 5"	0' 2" 0' 3" 0' 2" 0' 3"	0' 1" 0' 2" 0' 1" 0' 2"
7	8' 11" 12' 2" 7' 7" 13' 11"	6' 7" 9' 0" 5' 7" 10' 3"	5' 3" 7' 2" 4' 6" 8' 3"	4' 4" 6' 0" 3' 9" 6' 10"	3' 3" 4' 6" 2' 9" 5' 2"	2' 1" 2' 10" 1' 9" 3' 4"	1' 5" 1' 11" 1' 2" 2' 2"	1' 1" 1' 5" 0' 11" 1' 8"	0' 7" 0' 9" 0' 6" 0' 11"	0' 6" 0' 9" 0' 5" 0' 10"	0' 4" 0' 6" 0' 4" 0' 7"	0' 3" 0' 3" 0' 3" 0' 5"	0' 2" 0' 3" 0' 2" 0' 3"	0' 2" 0' 2" 0' 1" 0' 2"

16mm/SUPER 16 — FIELD OF VIEW (continued)

LENS SIZE	FORMAT	5.9mm	8mm	10mm	12mm	16mm	25mm	37.5mm	50mm	85mm	100mm	150mm	200mm	300mm	400mm
FOCUS (feet)															
8	16mm	10' 2" 13' 11"	7' 6" 10' 3"	6' 0" 8' 3"	5' 0" 6' 10"	3' 9" 5' 2"	2' 5" 3' 3"	1' 7" 2' 2"	1' 2" 1' 8"	0' 8" 1' 0"	0' 7" 0' 10"	0' 5" 0' 7"	0' 4" 0' 5"	0' 2" 0' 3"	0' 2" 0' 2"
	Super16	8' 8" 15' 11"	6' 5" 11' 9"	5' 1" 9' 5"	4' 3" 7' 10"	3' 2" 5' 11"	2' 0" 3' 9"	1' 4" 2' 6"	1' 0" 1' 11"	0' 7" 1' 1"	0' 6" 0' 11"	0' 4" 0' 8"	0' 3" 0' 6	0' 2" 0' 4"	0' 2" 0' 3"
9	16mm	11' 5" 15' 8"	8' 5" 11' 7"	6' 9" 9' 3"	5' 7" 7' 8"	4' 3" 5' 9"	2' 8" 3' 8"	1' 10" 2' 6"	1' 4" 1' 10"	0' 10" 1' 1"	0' 8" 0' 11"	0' 5" 0' 7"	0' 4" 0' 6"	0' 3" 0' 4"	0' 2" 0' 3"
	Super16	9' 9" 17' 11"	7' 2" 13' 3"	5' 9" 10' 7"	4' 9" 8' 10"	3' 7" 6' 7"	2' 4" 4' 3"	1' 6" 2' 10"	1' 2" 2' 1"	0' 8" 1' 3"	0' 7" 1' 1"	0' 5" 0' 8"	0' 3" 0' 6"	0' 2" 0' 4"	0' 2" 0' 3"
10	16mm	12' 8" 17' 5"	9' 4" 12' 10"	7' 6" 10' 3"	6' 3" 8' 7"	4' 8" 6' 5"	3' 0" 4' 1"	2' 0" 2' 9"	1' 6" 2' 1"	0' 11" 1' 2"	0' 9" 1' 0"	0' 6" 0' 8"	0' 4" 0' 4"	0' 3" 0' 4"	0' 2" 0' 3"
	Super16	10' 10" 19' 11"	8' 0" 14' 8"	6' 5" 11' 9"	5' 4" 9' 10"	4' 0" 7' 4"	2' 7" 4' 8"	1' 8" 3' 2"	1' 3" 2' 4"	0' 9" 1' 5"	0' 8" 1' 2"	0' 5" 0' 9"	0' 4" 0' 7"	0' 3" 0' 5"	0' 2" 0' 4"
12	16mm	15' 3" 20' 10"	11' 3" 15' 5"	9' 0" 12' 4"	7' 6" 10' 3"	5' 7" 7' 8"	3' 7" 4' 11"	2' 5" 3' 3"	1' 10" 2' 6"	1' 1" 1' 5"	0' 11" 1' 3"	0' 7" 0' 10"	0' 5" 0' 7"	0' 4" 0' 5"	0' 3" 0' 4"
	Super16	13' 0" 23' 11"	9' 7" 17' 8"	7' 8" 14' 1"	6' 5" 11' 9"	4' 9" 8' 10"	3' 1" 5' 8"	2' 0" 3' 9"	1' 6" 1' 10"	0' 11" 1' 8"	0' 9" 1' 5"	0' 6" 0' 11"	0' 5" 0' 8"	0' 3" 0' 6"	0' 2" 0' 4"
14	16mm	17' 9" 24' 4"	13' 1" 17' 11"	10' 6" 14' 4"	8' 9" 12' 0"	6' 7" 9' 0"	4' 2" 5' 9"	2' 10" 3' 10"	2' 1" 2' 10"	1' 3" 1' 8"	1' 1" 1' 5"	0' 8" 0' 11"	0' 6" 0' 9"	0' 4" 0' 6"	0' 3" 0' 4"
	Super16	15' 2" 27' 11"	11' 2" 20' 7"	8' 11" 16' 6"	7' 5" 13' 9"	5' 7" 10' 3"	3' 7" 6' 7"	2' 5" 4' 5"	1' 9" 3' 4"	1' 1" 1' 11"	0' 11" 1' 8"	0' 7" 1' 1"	0' 5" 0' 10"	0' 4" 0' 7"	0' 3" 0' 5"
16	16mm	20' 4" 27' 10"	15' 0" 20' 6"	12' 0" 16' 5"	10' 0" 13' 8"	7' 6" 10' 3"	4' 10" 6' 7"	3' 2" 4' 5"	2' 5" 3' 3"	1' 5" 1' 11"	1' 2" 1' 8"	0' 10" 1' 1"	0' 7" 0' 10"	0' 5" 0' 7"	0' 4" 0' 5"
	Super16	17' 3" 31' 11"	12' 9" 23' 6"	10' 2" 18' 10"	8' 6" 15' 8"	6' 5" 11' 9"	4' 1" 7' 6"	2' 9" 5' 0"	2' 0" 3' 9"	1' 2" 2' 3"	1' 0" 1' 11"	0' 8" 1' 3"	0' 6" 0' 11"	0' 4" 0' 8"	0' 3" 0' 6"
18	16mm	22' 10" 31' 4"	16' 10" 23' 1"	13' 6" 18' 6"	11' 3" 15' 5"	8' 5" 11' 7"	5' 5" 7' 5"	3' 7" 4' 11"	2' 8" 3' 8"	1' 7" 2' 2"	1' 4" 1' 10"	0' 11" 1' 3"	0' 8" 0' 11"	0' 5" 0' 7"	0' 4" 0' 6"
	Super16	19' 5" 35' 11"	14' 4" 26' 6"	11' 6" 21' 2"	9' 7" 17' 8"	7' 2" 13' 3"	4' 7" 8' 6"	3' 1" 5' 8"	2' 4" 4' 3"	1' 4" 2' 6"	1' 2" 2' 1"	0'9" 1' 5"	0' 7" 1' 1"	0' 5" 0' 8"	0' 3" 0' 3"

20	25' 5" 34' 9" 21' 7" 39' 10"	18' 9" 25' 8" 15' 11" 29' 5"	15' 0" 20' 6" 12' 9" 23' 6"	12' 6" 17' 1" 10' 8" 19' 7"	9' 4" 12' 10" 8' 0" 14' 8"	6' 0" 8' 3" 5' 1" 9' 5"	4' 0" 5' 6" 3' 5" 6' 3"	3' 0" 4' 1" 2' 7" 4' 8"	1' 9" 2' 5" 1' 6" 2' 9"	1' 6" 2' 1" 1' 3" 2' 4"	1' 0" 1' 4" 0' 10" 1' 7"	0' 9" 1' 0" 0' 8" 1' 2"	0' 6" 0' 8" 0' 5" 0' 9"	0' 4" 0' 6" 0' 4" 0' 7"
25	31' 9" 43' 6" 27' 0" 49' 10"	23' 5" 32' 1" 19' 11" 36' 9"	18' 9" 25' 8" 15' 11" 29' 5"	15' 7" 21' 5" 13' 3" 24' 6"	11' 8" 16' 0" 10' 0" 18' 5"	7' 6" 10' 3" 6' 5" 11' 9"	5' 0" 6' 10" 4' 3" 7' 10"	3' 9" 5' 2" 3' 2" 5' 11"	2' 2" 3' 0" 1' 11" 3' 6"	1' 10" 2' 7" 1' 7" 2' 11"	1' 3" 1' 9" 1' 1" 2' 0"	0' 11" 1' 3" 0' 10" 1' 6"	0' 7" 0' 10" 0' 6" 1' 0"	0' 6" 0' 8" 0' 5" 0' 9"
50	63' 6" 87' 0" 54' 0" 99' 8"	46' 10" 64' 2" 39' 10" 73' 6"	37' 6" 51' 4" 31' 11" 58' 10"	31' 3" 42' 9" 26' 7" 49' 0"	23' 5" 32' 1" 19' 11" 36' 9"	12' 9" 20' 6" 12' 9" 23' 6"	10' 0" 13' 8" 8' 6" 15' 8"	7' 6" 10' 3" 6' 5" 11' 9"	4' 5" 6' 0" 3' 9" 6' 11"	3' 9" 5' 2" 3' 2" 5' 11"	2' 6" 3' 5" 2' 2" 3' 11"	1' 10" 2' 7" 1' 7" 2' 11"	1' 3" 1' 9" 1' 1" 2' 0"	0' 11" 1' 3" 0' 10" 1' 6"
75	95' 3" 130' 5" 81' 1" 149' 6"	70' 3" 96' 2" 59' 9" 110' 3"	56' 2" 77' 0" 47' 10" 88' 2"	46' 10" 64' 2" 39' 10" 73' 6"	35' 1" 48' 1" 29' 11" 55' 2"	22' 6" 30' 9" 19' 2" 35' 3"	15' 0" 20' 6" 12' 9" 23' 6"	11' 3" 15' 5" 9' 7" 17' 8"	6' 7" 9' 1" 5' 8" 10' 5"	5' 7" 7' 8" 4' 9" 8' 10"	3' 9" 5' 2" 3' 2" 5' 11"	2' 10" 3' 10" 2' 5" 4' 5"	1' 10" 2' 7" 1' 7" 2' 11"	1' 5" 1' 11" 1' 2" 2' 2"
100	127' 0" 173' 11" 108' 1" 199' 4"	93' 8" 128' 3" 79' 8" 147' 0"	74' 11" 102' 7" 63' 9" 117' 7"	62' 5" 85' 6" 53' 2" 98' 0"	46' 10" 64' 2" 39' 10" 73' 6"	30' 0" 41' 1" 25' 6" 47' 0"	20' 0" 27' 4" 17' 0" 31' 4"	15' 0" 20' 6" 12' 9" 23' 6"	8' 10" 12' 1" 7' 6" 13' 10"	7' 6" 10' 3" 6' 5" 11' 9"	5' 0" 6' 10" 4' 3" 7' 10"	3' 9" 5' 2" 3' 2" 5' 11"	2' 6" 3' 5" 2' 2" 3' 11"	1' 10" 2' 7" 1' 7" 2' 11"
125	158' 9" 217' 5" 135' 1" 249' 2"	117' 1" 160' 4" 99' 7" 183' 9"	93' 8" 128' 3" 79' 8" 147' 0"	78' 1" 106' 11" 66' 5" 122' 6"	58' 6" 80' 2" 49' 10" 91' 11"	37' 6" 51' 4" 31' 11" 58' 10"	25' 0" 34' 2" 21' 3" 39' 2"	18' 9" 25' 8" 15' 11" 29' 5"	11' 0" 12' 1" 9' 5" 17' 4"	9' 4" 12' 10" 8' 0" 14' 8"	6' 3" 8' 7" 5' 4" 9' 10"	4' 8" 6' 5" 4' 0" 7' 4"	3' 1" 4' 3" 2' 8" 4' 11"	2' 4" 3' 2" 2' 0" 3' 8"
150	190' 6" 260' 11" 162' 1" 299' 0"	140' 6" 192' 5" 119' 6" 220' 6"	112' 5" 153' 11" 95' 8" 176' 5"	93' 8" 128' 3" 79' 8" 147' 6"	70' 3" 96' 2" 59' 9" 110' 3"	44' 11" 61' 7" 38' 3" 70' 7"	30' 0" 41' 1" 25' 6" 47' 0"	22' 6" 30' 9" 19' 2" 35' 3"	13' 3" 18' 1" 11' 3" 20' 9"	11' 3" 15' 5" 9' 7" 17' 8"	7' 6" 10' 3" 6' 5" 11' 9"	5' 7" 7' 8" 4' 9" 8' 10"	3' 9" 5' 2" 3' 2" 5' 11"	2' 10" 3' 10" 2' 5" 4' 5"
175	222' 3" 304' 4" 348' 10" 189' 1"	163' 11" 224' 6" 139' 6" 257' 3"	131' 2" 179' 7" 111' 7" 205' 10"	109' 3" 149' 8" 93' 0" 171' 6"	81' 11" 112' 3" 69' 9" 128' 8"	52' 5" 71' 10" 44' 8" 82' 4"	35' 0" 47' 11" 29' 9" 54' 11"	26' 3" 35' 11" 22' 4" 41' 2"	15' 5" 21' 2" 13' 2" 24' 3"	13' 1" 17' 11" 11' 2" 20' 7"	8' 9" 12' 0" 7' 5" 13' 9"	6' 7" 9' 0" 5' 7" 10' 3"	4' 4" 6' 0" 3' 9" 6' 10"	3' 3" 4' 6" 2' 9" 5' 2"
200	254' 0" 347' 10" 216' 1" 398' 8"	187' 4" 256' 6" 159' 5" 294' 0"	149' 10" 205' 3" 127' 6" 235' 2"	124' 11" 171' 0" 106' 3" 196' 0"	93' 8" 128' 3" 79' 8" 147' 0"	59' 11" 82' 1" 51' 0" 94' 1"	40' 0" 54' 9" 34' 0" 62' 9"	30' 0" 41' 1" 25' 6" 47' 0"	17' 8" 24' 2" 15' 0" 27' 8"	15' 0" 20' 6" 12' 9" 23' 6"	10' 0" 13' 8" 8' 6" 15' 8"	7' 6" 10' 3" 6' 5" 11' 9"	5' 0" 6' 10" 4' 3" 7' 10"	3' 9" 5' 2" 3' 2" 5' 11"

SUPER 8mm/6.5mm CAMERA DEPTH-OF-FIELD, HYPERFOCAL DISTANCE, AND FIELD OF VIEW

CAMERA APERTURE: 0.224 x 0.166 inches **CIRCLE OF CONFUSION=0.0020 inches**

	f/1.4	f/2.0	f/2.8	f/4.0	f/5.6	f/8.0	f/11.0	f/16.0	f/22.0	
Hyperfocal Distance	1' 11"	1' 4"	1' 0"	0' 8"	0' 6"	0' 4	0' 3"	0' 2"	0' 1"	ANGLE OF VIEW H 47.3° / V 35.9°
FOCUS	NEAR FAR	NEAR FAR	NEAR FAR	NEAR FAR	NEAR FAR	NEAR FAR	NEAR FAR	NEAR FAR	NEAR FAR	FIELD OF VIEW
2	1' 0" INF	0' 10" INF	0' 8" INF	0' 6" INF	0' 5" INF	0' 4" INF	0' 3" INF	0' 2" INF	0' 1" INF	1' 9" x 1' 3"
4	1' 4" INF	1' 0" INF	0' 9" INF	0' 7" INF	0' 5" INF	0' 4" INF	0' 3" INF	0' 2" INF	0' 1" INF	3' 6" x 2' 7"
6	1' 6" INF	1' 1" INF	0' 10" INF	0' 7" INF	0' 5" INF	0' 4" INF	0' 3" INF	0' 2" INF	0' 1" INF	5' 3" x 3' 11"
8	1' 7" INF	1' 2" INF	0' 10" INF	0' 8" INF	0' 6" INF	0' 4" INF	0' 3" INF	0' 2" INF	0' 1" INF	7' 0" x 5' 2"
10	1' 8" INF	1' 2" INF	0' 11" INF	0' 8" INF	0' 6" INF	0' 4" INF	0' 3" INF	0' 2" INF	0' 1" INF	8' 9" x 6' 6"
12	1' 8" INF	1' 3" INF	0' 11" INF	0' 8" INF	0' 6" INF	0' 4" INF	0' 3" INF	0' 2" INF	0' 1" INF	10' 6" x 7' 9"
16	1' 9" INF	1' 3" INF	0' 11" INF	0' 8" INF	0' 6" INF	0' 4" INF	0' 3" INF	0' 2" INF	0' 1" INF	14' 0" x 10' 4"
25	1' 10" INF	1' 4" INF	0' 11" INF	0' 8" INF	0' 6" INF	0' 4" INF	0' 3" INF	0' 2" INF	0' 1" INF	21' 10" x 16' 2"

SUPER 8mm/13mm CAMERA DEPTH-OF-FIELD, HYPERFOCAL DISTANCE, AND FIELD OF VIEW

CAMERA APERTURE: 0.224 x 0.166 inches **CIRCLE OF CONFUSION=0.0020 inches**

	f/1.4	f/2.0	f/2.8	f/4.0	f/5.6	f/8.0	f/11.0	f/16.0	f/22.0	
Hyperfocal Distance	7' 10"	5' 5"	3' 11"	2' 9"	1' 11"	1' 4"	1' 0"	0' 8"	0' 6"	ANGLE OF VIEW H 27.7° / V 18.4°
FOCUS	NEAR FAR	NEAR FAR	NEAR FAR	NEAR FAR	NEAR FAR	NEAR FAR	NEAR FAR	NEAR FAR	NEAR FAR	FIELD OF VIEW
2	1' 7" 2' 8"	1' 6" 3' 1"	1' 4" 4' 0"	1' 2" 7' 1"	1' 0" INF	0' 10" INF	0' 8" INF	0' 6" INF	0' 5" INF	0' 10" x 0' 8"
4	2' 8" 8' 1"	2' 4" 14' 7"	2' 0" INF	1' 8" INF	1' 4" INF	1' 0" INF	0' 10" INF	0' 7" INF	0' 5" INF	1' 9" x 1' 3.5"
6	3' 5" 25' 5"	2' 10" INF	2' 4" INF	1' 11" INF	1' 6" INF	1' 1" INF	0' 10" INF	0' 7" INF	0' 6" INF	2' 7" x 1' 11"
8	4' 0" INF	3' 3" INF	2' 8" INF	2' 1" INF	1' 7" INF	1' 2" INF	0' 11" INF	0' 8" INF	0' 6" INF	3' 6" x 2' 7"
10	4' 5" INF	3' 6" INF	2' 10" INF	2' 2" INF	1' 8" INF	1' 2" INF	0' 11" INF	0' 8" INF	0' 6" INF	4' 4" x 3' 3"
12	4' 9" INF	3' 9" INF	2' 11" INF	2' 3" INF	1' 8" INF	1' 3" INF	0' 11" INF	0' 8" INF	0' 6" INF	5' 3" x 3' 11"
16	5' 3" INF	4' 1" INF	3' 2" INF	2' 4" INF	1' 9" INF	1' 3" INF	0' 11" INF	0' 8" INF	0' 6" INF	7' 0" x 5' 2"
25	5' 11" INF	4' 6" INF	3' 5" INF	2' 6" INF	1' 10" INF	1' 4" INF	0' 11" INF	0' 8" INF	0' 6" INF	10' 11" x 8' 1"

SUPER 8mm/38mm CAMERA DEPTH-OF-FIELD, HYPERFOCAL DISTANCE, AND FIELD OF VIEW

CAMERA APERTURE: 0.224 x 0.166 inches **CIRCLE OF CONFUSION=0.0020 inches**

	f/1.4	f/2.0	f/2.8	f/4.0	f/5.6	f/8.0	f/11.0	f/16.0	f/22.0	
Hyperfocal Distance	66' 7"	46' 8"	33' 4"	23' 4"	16' 8"	11' 8"	8' 6"	5' 10"	4' 3"	ANGLE OF VIEW H 8.5° / V 6.3°
FOCUS	NEAR FAR	NEAR FAR	NEAR FAR	NEAR FAR	NEAR FAR	NEAR FAR	NEAR FAR	NEAR FAR	NEAR FAR	FIELD OF VIEW
2	1' 11" 2' 1"	1' 11" 2' 1"	1' 11" 2' 1"	1' 10" 2' 2"	1' 10" 2' 3"	1' 9" 2' 5"	1' 8" 2' 7"	1' 6" 2' 11"	1' 5" 3' 7"	0' 4" x 0' 2.6"
4	3' 9" 4' 3"	3' 8" 4' 4"	3' 7" 4' 6"	3' 5" 4' 10"	3' 3" 5' 3"	3' 0" 6' 0"	2' 9" 7' 4"	2' 5" 11' 11"	2' 1" INF	0' 5" x 0' 5.3"
6	5' 6" 6' 7"	5' 4" 6' 10"	5' 1" 7' 3"	4' 10" 8' 0"	4' 5" 9' 3"	4' 0" 12' 1"	3' 7" 19' 7"	3' 0" INF	2' 6" INF	0' 11" x 0' 8"
8	7' 2" 9' 1"	6' 10" 9' 8"	6' 6" 10' 6"	6' 0" 12' 1"	5' 5" 15' 2"	4' 9" 24' 8"	4' 2" INF	3' 5" INF	2' 10" INF	1' 2" x 0' 11"
10	8' 9" 11' 9"	8' 3" 12' 8"	7' 9" 14' 3"	7' 0" 17' 4"	6' 3" 24' 7"	5' 5" 65' 5"	4' 7" INF	3' 9" INF	3' 0" INF	1' 6" x 1' 1"
12	10' 2" 14' 7"	9' 7" 16' 1"	8' 10" 18' 8"	7' 11" 24' 5"	7' 0" 41' 10"	5' 11" INF	5' 0" INF	3' 11" INF	3' 2" INF	1' 9" x 1' 4"
16	12' 11" 21' 0"	11' 11" 24' 3"	10' 10" 30' 7"	9' 6" 50' 2"	8' 2" INF	6' 9" INF	5' 7" INF	4' 4" INF	3' 4" INF	2' 5" x 1' 9"
25	18' 2" 39' 11"	16' 4" 53' 7"	14' 4" 98' 9"	12' 1" INF	10' 0" INF	8' 0" INF	6' 4" INF	4' 9" INF	3' 8" INF	3' 9" x 2' 9"

SUPER 8mm/50mm CAMERA DEPTH-OF-FIELD, HYPERFOCAL DISTANCE, AND FIELD OF VIEW

CAMERA APERTURE: 0.224 x 0.166 inches **CIRCLE OF CONFUSION=0.0020 inches**

	f/1.4	f/2.0	f/2.8	f/4.0	f/5.6	f/8.0	f/11.0	f/16.0	f/22.0	
Hyperfocal Distance	115' 4"	80' 9"	57' 8"	40' 4"	28' 10"	20' 2"	14' 8'	10' 1"	7' 4'	ANGLE OF VIEW H 6.5° / V 4.8°
FOCUS	NEAR FAR	NEAR FAR	NEAR FAR	NEAR FAR	NEAR FAR	NEAR FAR	NEAR FAR	NEAR FAR	NEAR FAR	FIELD OF VIEW
2	NA NA	1' 11" 2' 1"	1' 11" 2' 1"	1' 11" 2' 1"	1' 11" 2' 2"	1' 10" 2' 2"	1' 9" 2' 3"	1' 8" 2' 5"	1' 7" 2' 8"	0' 2.7" x 0' 2"
4	3' 10" 4' 2"	3' 10" 4' 2"	3' 9" 4' 3"	3' 8" 4' 5"	3' 6" 4' 7"	3' 4" 4' 11"	3' 2" 5' 5"	2' 11" 6' 5"	2' 8" 8' 5"	0'5.5" x 0' 4"
6	5' 9" 6' 4"	5' 7" 6' 6"	5' 5" 6' 8"	5' 3" 7' 0"	5' 0" 7' 6"	4' 8" 8' 5"	4' 4" 10' 0"	3' 10" 14' 3"	3' 4" 29' 4"	0' 8" x 0' 6"
8	7' 6" 8' 7"	7' 4" 8' 10"	7' 1" 9' 3"	6' 8" 9' 11"	6' 3" 11' 0"	5' 9" 13' 1"	5' 3" 17' 2"	4' 6" 35' 10"	3' 10" INF	0' 11" x 0' 8"
10	9' 3" 10' 11"	8' 11" 11' 5"	8' 7" 12' 1"	8' 0" 13' 3"	7' 5" 15' 2"	6' 9" 19' 6"	6' 0" 30' 4"	5' 1" INF	4' 3" INF	1' 2.6" x 0' 10"
12	10' 11" 13' 4"	10' 6" 14' 1"	9' 11" 15' 1"	9' 3" 17' 0"	8' 6" 20' 4"	7' 7" 29' 0"	6' 8" 62' 0"	5' 6" INF	4' 7" INF	1' 4" x 1' 0"
16	14' 1" 18' 7"	13' 5" 19' 11"	12' 7" 22' 1"	11' 6" 26' 4"	10' 4" 35' 6"	9' 0" 74' 4"	7' 8" INF	6' 3" INF	5' 1" INF	1' 10" x 1' 4"
25	20' 7" 31' 10"	19' 1" 36' 1"	17' 6" 43' 11"	15' 6" 65' 0"	13' 5" 180' 5"	11' 2" INF	9' 3" INF	7' 3" INF	5' 8" INF	2' 10" x 2' 1"

VERTICAL ANGLE VS. EFFECTIVE FOCAL LENGTH
(Focal Length In Millimeters)

TRANSMITTED OR PROJECTED IMAGE	0.189"	0.260"	0.375"	0.500"	0.158"	0.286"	0.251"	0.446"	0.594"	0.700"	0.991"	0.870"
ANGLE (DEGREES)	**TV 1/2" CCD**	**TV 2/3" CCD**	**TV 1" CCD**	**TV 1 2/3" CCD**	**SUPER -8**	**16mm**	**SUPER -16 1.85:1 AR**	**35mm 1.85:1 AR**	**35mm TV TRANS**	**35mm ANA**	**35mm VISTA**	**65mm**
0.5	550	757	1091	1445	460	832	731	1298	1729	2037	2884	2532
0.7	393	541	780	1039	328	595	522	927	1235	1455	2060	1809
1	275	378	546	728	230	416	365	649	864	1019	1442	1266
1.5	183	252	364	485	153	277	244	433	576	679	961	844
2	138	189	273	364	115	280	183	325	432	509	721	633
2.5	110	151	218	291	92	166	146	260	346	407	577	506
3	92	126	182	242	77	139	122	216	288	339	481	422
3.5	79	108	156	208	66	119	104	185	247	291	412	362
4	69	95	136	182	57	104	91	162	216	256	360	316
4.5	61	84	121	162	51	92	81	144	192	226	320	281
5	55	76	109	145	46	83	73	130	173	204	288	253
6	46	63	91	121	38	69	61	108	144	170	240	211
7	39	54	78	104	33	59	52	93	123	145	206	181
8	34	47	68	91	29	52	46	81	108	127	180	158
9	30	42	61	81	25	46	41	72	96	113	160	140
10	27	38	54	73	23	42	36	65	86	102	144	126
15	18	25	36	48	15	28	24	43	57	68	96	84
20	14	19	27	36	11	21	18	32	43	50	71	63
25	11	15	21	29	9	16	14	26	34	40	57	50
30	9	12	18	24	7	14	12	21	28	33	47	41
35	8	10	15	20	6	12	10	18	24	28	40	35
40	7	9	13	17	6	10	9	16	21	24	35	30
45	6	8	11	15	5	9	8	14	18	21	30	27
50	5	7	10	14	4	8	7	12	16	19	27	24
55	5	6	9	12	4	7	6	11	15	17	24	21
60	4	6	8	11	3	6	6	10	13	15	22	19
65	4	5	7	10	3	6	5	9	12	14	20	17
70	3	5	7	9	3	5	5	8	11	13	18	16
75	3	4	6	8	3	5	4	7	10	12	16	14
80	3	4	6	8	2	4	4	7	9	11	15	13
85	3	4	5	7	2	4	3	6	8	10	14	12
90	2	3	5	6	2	4	3	6	8	9	13	11
95	2	3	4	6	2	3	3	5	7	8	12	10
100	2	3	4	5	2	3	3	5	6	7	11	9

HORIZONTAL ANGLE VS. EFFECTIVE FOCAL LENGTH
(Focal Length In Millimeters)

TRANSMITTED OR PROJECTED IMAGE	0.252"	0.346"	0.5"	0.667"	0.209"	0.380"	0.463"	0.825"	1.676"	1.485"	1.912"
ANGLE (DEGREES)	**TV 1/2" CCD**	**TV 2/3" CCD**	**TV 1" CCD**	**TV 1 2/3" CCD**	**SUPER -8**	**16mm**	**SUPER -16 1.85:1 AR**	**35mm 1.85:1 AR**	**35mm ANA**	**35mm VISTA**	**65mm**
0.5	733	1007	1455	1941	608	1106	1348	2401	4878	4322	5565
0.7	524	719	1039	1387	435	790	963	1715	3484	3087	3975
1	367	504	728	971	304	553	674	1201	2439	2161	2782
1.5	244	336	485	647	203	369	449	800	1626	1441	1855
2	183	252	364	485	152	276	337	600	1219	1081	1391
2.5	147	201	291	388	122	221	269	480	975	864	1113
3	122	168	242	323	101	184	225	400	813	720	927
3.5	105	144	208	277	87	158	192	343	697	617	795
4	92	126	182	243	76	138	168	300	610	540	695
4.5	81	112	162	216	68	123	150	267	542	480	618
5	73	101	145	194	61	111	135	240	488	432	556
6	61	84	121	162	51	92	112	200	406	360	463
7	52	72	104	138	43	79	96	171	348	308	397
8	46	63	91	121	38	69	84	150	304	270	347
9	41	56	81	108	34	61	75	133	270	240	309
10	37	50	73	97	30	55	67	120	243	216	278
15	24	33	45	64	20	37	45	80	162	143	184
20	18	25	36	48	15	27	33	59	121	107	138
25	14	20	29	38	12	22	27	47	96	85	110
30	12	16	24	32	10	18	22	39	79	70	91
35	10	14	20	27	8	15	19	33	68	60	77
40	9	12	17	23	7	13	16	29	58	52	67
45	8	11	15	20	6	12	14	25	51	46	59
50	7	9	14	18	6	10	13	22	46	40	52
55	6	8	12	16	5	9	11	20	41	36	47
60	6	8	11	15	5	8	10	18	37	33	42
65	5	7	10	13	4	8	9	16	33	30	38
70	5	6	9	12	4	7	8	15	30	27	35
75	4	6	8	11	3	6	8	14	28	25	32
80	4	5	8	10	3	6	7	12	25	22	29
85	3	5	7	9	3	5	6	11	23	21	26
90	3	4	6	8	3	5	6	10	21	19	24
95	3	4	6	8	2	4	5	10	20	17	22
100	3	4	5	7	2	4	5	9	18	16	20

35mm — DEPTH OF FIELD and EXPOSURE FACTOR vs. MAGNIFICATION or FIELD OF VIEW

Extreme Close Up — **CIRCLE OF CONFUSION=0.001 inches**

Magnification Ratio		Field of View	DEPTH OF FIELD (Total: front + back, in inches)									Exposure Increase Factor	T-Stop Increase
Dec.	Frac.	1.85:1 AR	f/1.4	f/2	f/2.8	f/4	f/5.6	f/8	f/11	f/16	f/22		
0.100	**1/10**	4.46" x 8.25"	0.31"	0.44"	0.62"	0.88"	0.1.23"	1.76"	2.42"	3.52"	4.84"	1.21	.27
0.111	**1/9**	4.01" x 7.43"	0.25"	0.36"	0.51"	0.72"	1.01"	1.44"	1.98"	2.89"	3.97"	1.23	.30
0.125	**1/8**	3.57" x 6.6"	0.20"	0.29"	0.40"	0.58"	0.81"	1.15"	1.58"	2.30"	3.17"	1.27	1/3
0.143	**1/7**	3.12" x 5.78"	0.16"	0.22"	0.31"	0.45"	0.63"	0.89"	1.23"	1.79"	2.46"	1.31	.39
0.167	**1/6**	2.68" x 4.95"	0.12"	0.17"	0.23"	0.34"	0.47"	0.67"	0.92"	1.34"	1.84"	1.36	.45
0.200	**1/5**	2.23" x 4.12"	0.08"	0.12"	0.17"	0.24"	0.34"	0.48"	0.66"	0.96"	1.32"	1.44	.53
0.250	**1/4**	1.78" x 3.3"	0.06"	0.08"	0.11"	0.16"	0.22"	0.32"	0.44"	0.64"	0.88"	1.56	2/3
0.333	**1/3**	1.34" x 2.48"	0.03"	0.05"	0.07"	0.09"	0.14"	0.19"	0.26"	0.38"	0.53"	1.78	.83
0.500	**1/2**	.89" x 1.65"	0.017"	0.02"	0.03"	0.05"	0.07"	0.10"	0.13"	0.19"	0.26"	2.25	1 1/3
0.667	**2/3**	067" x 1.24"	0.010"	0.015"	0.02"	0.03"	0.04"	0.06"	0.08"	0.12"	0.17"	2.78	1.47
0.750	**3/4**	.59" x 1.10"	0.009"	0.012"	0.017"	0.03"	0.04"	0.05"	0.07"	0.10"	0.14"	3.06	1 2/3
0.875	**7/8**	.50" x .94"	0.007"	0.010"	0.014"	0.02"	0.03"	0.04"	0.05"	0.08"	0.11"	3.52	1.81
1.0	**1/1**	.45" x .83"	0.006"	0.008"	0.011"	0.016"	0.03"	0.03"	0.04"	0.06"	0.09"	4.0	2.0

16mm DEPTH OF FIELD and EXPOSURE FACTOR vs. MAGNIFICATION or FIELD OF VIEW

Extreme Close Up — CIRCLE OF CONFUSION=0.006 inches

Magnification Ratio		FOV (projected image)		DEPTH OF FIELD (Total: front + back, in inches)									Exposure Increase Factor	T-Stop Inc.
		.286" x .380"	.251" x .463"											
Dec.	Frac.	16mm	SUPER 16	f/1.4	f/2	f/2.8	f/4	f/5.6	f/8	f/11	f/16	f/22		
0.100	1/10	2.86" x 3.80"	2.51" x 4.63"	0.19"	0.26"	0.37"	0.53"	0.74"	1.06"	1.45"	2.11"	2.90"	1.21	.27
0.111	1/9	2.58" x 3.42"	2.26" x 4.17"	0.15"	0.22"	0.30"	0.43"	0.61"	0.87"	1.19"	1.73"	2.38"	1.23	.30
0.125	1/8	2.9" x3.04"	2.01" x 3.70"	0.12"	0.17"	0.24"	0.35"	0.48"	0.69"	0.95"	1.38"	1.90"	1.27	1/3
0.143	1/7	2.0" x 2.66"	1.76" x 3.24"	0.09"	0.13"	0.19"	0.27"	0.38"	0.54"	0.74"	1.07"	1.48"	1.31	.39
0.167	1/6	1.71" x 2.28"	1.50" x 2.78"	0.07"	0.10"	0.14"	0.20"	0.28"	0.40"	0.55"	0.80"	1.11"	1.36	.45
0.200	1/5	1.43" x 1.90"	1.26" x 2.32"	0.05"	0.07"	0.10"	0.14"	0.20"	0.29"	0.40"	0.58"	0.79"	1.44	.53
0.250	1/4	1.14" x 1.52"	1.00" x 1.85"	0.03"	0.05"	0.07"	0.10"	0.13"	0.19"	0.26"	0.38"	0.53"	1.53	2/3
0.333	1/3	.859" x 1.14"	.754" x 1.39"	0.02"	0.03"	0.04"	0.06"	0.08"	0.12"	0.16"	0.23"	0.32"	1.78	.83
0.500	1/2	.572" x .760"	.502" x .926"	0.010"	0.014"	0.02"	0.03"	0.04"	0.06"	0.08"	0.12"	0.16"	2.25	1 1/3
0.667	2/3	.429" x .570"	.376" x .694"	0.006"	0.009"	0.013"	0.018"	0.03"	0.04"	0.05"	0.07"	0.10"	2.78	1.47
0.750	3/4	.381" x .507"	.335" x .617"	0.005"	0.007"	0.010"	0.015"	0.02"	0.03"	0.04"	0.06"	0.08"	3.06	1 2/3
0.875	7/8	.327" x .434"	.286" x .529"	0.004"	0.006"	0.008"	0.012"	0.016"	0.02"	0.03"	0.05"	0.07"	3.52	1.81
1.0	1/1	.286" x.380"	.251" x .463"	0.003"	0.005"	0.007"	0.010"	0.013"	0.019"	0.03"	0.04"	0.05"	4.0	2.0

APERTURE COMPENSATOR FOR EXTREME CLOSE-UPS

2 INCH LENS (16mm OR 35mm CAMERAS)

EXAMPLE: A 2 inch lens photographing an object at a distance of 4 inches would require an f/8 light level to film it with the lens set at f/4.

DISTANCES IN INCHES		ACTUAL LENS APERTURE SETTINGS							
LENS DIAPHRAGM TO FILM	LENS DIAPHRAGM TO OBJECT	f/2	f/2.8	f/4	f/5.6	f/8	f/11	f/16	f/22
		EFFECTIVE f/STOP (LIGHT REQUIRED FOR ABOVE f/STOPS)							
2 ¼	18	f/2.2	f/3.2	f/4.5	f/6.3	f/9	f/12.7	f/18	f/25
2 ½	10	f/2.5	f/3.5	f/5	f/7	f/10	f/14	f/20	f/28
2 3/4	7	f/2.8	f/4	f/5.6	f/8	f/11	f/16	f/22	f/32
3	6	f/3.2	f/4.5	f/6.3	f/9	f/12.7	f/18	f/25	f/36
4	4	f/4	f/5.6	f/8	f/11	f/16	f/22	f/32	f/45
5	3 ½	f/4.5	f/6.3	f/9	f/12.7	f/18	f/25	f/36	f/50
6	3	f/6.3	f/9	f/12.7	f/18	f/25	f/36	f/50	f/72

PLUS DIOPTER LENSES FOCAL LENGTH CONVERSION TABLE

For 50mm, 75mm, 100mm and 150mm Lenses
16mm or 35mm

Example: A 75mm lens with +3 diopter lens is converted to a focal length of 61.21mm. It will be in focus at 13.11 inches when set at infinity.

Power of Supplementary Lens in Diopters	Focal Length in Meters	Focal Length in mm	Lens in Focus at This Distance When Set at Infinity: Focal Length in Inches	Actual Focal Length in mm: 50	75	100	150
				Focal Length of Lens in Combination with Diopter Lens			
+1	1	1000	39.37	47.62	69.77	90.91	130.43
+2	1/2	500	19.68	45.45	65.22	83.33	115.38
+3 (2+1)	1/3	333	13.11	43.47	61.21	76.91	103.42
+4 (3+1)	1/4	250	9.84	41.67	57.69	71.43	93.75
+5 (3+2)	1/5	200	7.87	40.00	54.55	66.66	85.71
+6 (3+3)	1/6	166.6	6.53	38.48	51.76	62.55	79.02
+7	1/7	142.8	5.62	37.05	49.20	58.85	73.21
+8	1/8	125	4.92	35.71	46.88	55.55	68.18
+9	1/9	111.1	4.37	34.47	44.76	52.61	63.79
+10	1/10	100	3.93	33.33	42.85	50.00	60.00

EXPOSURE COMPENSATION FOR EXTREME CLOSE-UP CINEMATOGRAPHY (16mm or 35mm)

This table Shows the Light Level Required for Filming Close-Ups of Objects from 1/10th to 5X Actual Size

EXAMPLE: Shooting an Object at 2X Magnification an Actual Lens Setting of f/4 Requires an f/12 Light Level

			ACTUAL LENS APERTURE SETTING													
			f/2	f/2.3	f/2.8	f/3.2	f/4	f/4.5	f/5.6	f/6.3	f/8	f/9	f/11	f/12.7	f/16	f/18
Reduction or Magni-fication	Image to Object Ratio	Exposure Factor	Light levels shown below must be employed for above lens aperture settings when using various image to object ratios shown at left.													
1/10	1:10	1.2	2.2	2.5	3.1	3.5	4.4	5	6.1	7	8.8	10	12.1	13.8	17.6	19.8
1/8	1:8	1.3	2.3	2.6	3.2	3.6	4.5	5.1	6.3	7.1	9	10.2	12.4	14	18	20
1/6	1:6	1.4	2.4	2.7	3.3	3.7	4.7	5.3	6.6	7.4	9.4	10.6	12.8	14.6	18.7	21
1/5	1:5	1.5	2.4	2.8	3.4	3.8	4.8	5.5	6.8	7.6	9.7	11	13.2	15	19.2	21.5
1/4	1:4	1.6	2.5	2.9	3.5	4	5	5.6	7	7.9	10	11.3	13.8	15.6	20	22
1/3	1:3	1.8	2.7	3.1	3.8	4.3	5.4	6	7.6	8.4	11	12.1	14.6	16.7	21.6	24
1/2	1:2	2.3	3	3.5	4.2	4.8	6	6.8	8.4	9.5	12	13.7	16.5	18.8	24	27
1	**1:1**	**4**	**4**	**4.5**	**5.6**	**6.3**	**8**	**9**	**11**	**12.7**	**16**	**18**	**22**	**25**	**32**	**36**
1 1/3X	1.33:1	5.4	4.7	5.4	6.6	7.5	9.4	10.5	13	14.7	19	21	26	29	38	42
1 1/2X	1.5:1	6.3	5	5.8	7	8	10	11.3	14	15.8	20	23	28	31	40	45
1 3/4X	1.75:1	8	5.6	6.3	8	9	11	12.7	16	18	22	25	32	36	45	48
2X	2:1	9	6	6.9	8.4	9.6	12	13.5	18	19	24	27	33	38	48	54
3X	3:1	16	8	9.1	11	12.5	16	18	22	25	32	36	44	50	64	72
4X	4:1	25	10	11	14	16	20	22	28	32	40	46	55	63	80	90
5X	5:1	36	12	13.8	16	19	24	27	34	38	48	55	66	75	96	—

EXTREME CLOSE-UP FOCUSING CHART FOR 2, 3, 4, & 6 INCH LENSES (16mm or 35mm Cameras)

(EXTENSION TUBES OR BELLOWS REQUIRED)

Distances from lens diaphragm to object and lens diaphragm to film in inches
Magnification ratio (Number of times object is enlarged on film) • Exposure factor (and number of f/stops increase required)

(Note: These values are approximate since lens focal length will vary slightly. Many lenses will deliver a better quality image if reversed in their mounts at high magnification.)

Number of f/Stops Increase	Exposure Factor	Magnification Ratio	2 INCH LENS		3 INCH LENS		4 INCH LENS		6 INCH LENS	
			Diaphragm to Object	Diaphragm to Film	Diaphragm to Object	Diaphragm to Film	Diaphragm to Object	Diaphragm to Film	Diaphragm to Object	Diaphragm to Film
2	4	1:1	4	4	6	6	8	8	12	12
3 1/6	9	2:1	3	6	4 1/2	9	6	12	9	18
4	16	3:1	2 5/8	8	4	12	5 3/8	16	8	24
4 2/3	25	4:1	2 1/2	10	3 3/4	15	5	20	7 1/2	30
5 1/6	36	5:1	2 7/16	12	3 5/8	18	4 3/4	24	7 3/8	36
5 2/3	49	6:1	2 3/8	14	3 1/2	21	4 5/8	28	7	42
6	64	7:1	2 5/16	16	3 7/16	24	4 9/16	32	6 7/8	48
6 1/3	81	8:1	2 1/4	18	3 3/8	27	4 1/2	36	6 3/4	54
6 2/3	100	9:1	2 3/16	20	3 5/16	30	4 7/16	40	6 5/8	60
7	121	10:1	2 1/8	22	3 1/4	33	4 3/8	44	6 1/2	66

LENS FOCAL LENGTH CONVERSION TABLE

(16mm or 35mm CAMERAS)

The table on the following page supplies the multiplying factor required for obtaining same size images with lenses of different focal length at different distances. Lenses being compared must be used with the same size film. Although perspective will vary with camera distance, the table will prove handy for matching image sizes with cameras having different focal length lenses. It is also useful for obtaining same size images when the camera must be set at a different distance because of space limitations and physical obstructions.

EXAMPLE: How far must a 28mm lens be positioned to obtain the same size image as a 32mm lens 15 feet from the subject? Pick out 32mm in the left column, cross the row horizontally to the 28mm column to find the number .88. Multiply .88 by 15 feet to obtain 13.2 feet.

ORIGINAL FOCAL LENGTH (MM)	NEW FOCAL LENGTH (MM)																						
	9	10	12.5	13	14.5	15	16	18	20	25	28	30	32	35	37.5	40	50	75	85	100	150	200	250
9	1.0	1.1	1.4	1.4	1.6	1.7	1.8	2.0	2.2	2.8	3.1	3.3	3.6	3.9	4.2	4.4	5.6	8.3	9.4	11.1	16.7	22.2	27.8
10	.90	1.0	1.3	1.3	1.5	1.5	1.6	1.8	2.0	2.5	2.8	3.0	3.2	3.5	3.8	4.0	5.0	7.5	8.5	10.0	15.0	20.0	25.0
12.5	.72	.80	1.0	1.0	1.2	1.2	1.3	1.4	1.6	2.0	2.2	2.4	2.6	2.8	3.0	3.2	4.0	6.0	6.8	8.0	12.0	16.0	20.0
13	.69	.77	.96	1.0	1.1	1.2	1.2	1.4	1.5	1.9	2.2	2.3	2.5	2.7	2.9	3.1	3.8	5.8	6.5	7.7	11.5	15.4	19.2
14.5	.62	.69	.86	.90	1.0	1.0	1.1	1.2	1.4	1.7	1.9	2.1	2.2	2.4	2.6	2.8	3.4	5.2	5.9	6.9	10.3	13.8	17.2
15	.60	.67	.83	.87	.97	1.0	1.1	1.2	1.3	1.7	1.9	2.0	2.1	2.3	2.5	2.7	3.3	5.0	5.7	6.7	10.0	13.3	16.7
16	.56	.63	.78	.81	.91	.94	1.0	1.1	1.3	1.6	1.8	1.9	2.0	2.2	2.3	2.5	3.1	4.7	5.3	6.3	9.4	12.5	15.6
18	.50	.56	.69	.72	.81	.83	.89	1.0	1.1	1.4	1.6	1.7	1.8	1.9	2.1	2.2	2.8	4.2	4.7	5.6	8.3	11.1	13.9
20	.45	.50	.63	.65	.73	.75	.80	.90	1.0	1.3	1.4	1.5	1.6	1.8	1.9	2.0	2.5	3.8	4.3	5.0	7.5	10.0	12.5
25	.36	.40	.50	.52	.58	.60	.64	.72	.80	1.0	1.1	1.2	1.3	1.4	1.5	1.6	2.0	3.0	3.4	4.0	6.0	8.0	10.0
28	.32	.36	.45	.46	.52	.54	.57	.64	.71	.89	1.0	1.1	1.1	1.3	1.3	1.4	1.8	2.7	3.0	3.6	5.4	7.1	8.9
30	.30	.33	.42	.43	.48	.50	.53	.60	.67	.83	.93	1.0	1.1	1.2	1.3	1.3	1.7	2.5	2.8	3.3	5.0	6.7	8.3
32	.28	.31	.39	.41	.45	.47	.50	.56	.63	.78	.88	.94	1.0	1.1	1.2	1.3	1.6	2.3	2.7	3.1	4.7	6.3	7.8
35	.26	.29	.36	.37	.41	.43	.46	.51	.57	.71	.80	.86	.91	1.0	1.1	1.1	1.4	2.1	2.4	2.9	4.3	5.7	7.1
37.5	.24	.27	.33	.35	.39	.40	.43	.48	.53	.67	.75	.80	.85	.93	1.0	1.1	1.3	2.0	2.3	2.7	4.0	5.3	6.7
40	.23	.25	.31	.33	.36	.38	.40	.45	.50	.63	.70	.75	.80	.88	.94	1.0	1.3	1.9	2.1	2.5	3.8	5.0	6.3
50	.18	.20	.25	.26	.29	.30	.32	.36	.40	.50	.56	.60	.64	.70	.75	.80	1.0	1.5	1.7	2.0	3.0	4.0	5.0
75	.12	.13	.17	.17	.19	.20	.21	.24	.27	.33	.37	.40	.43	.47	.50	.53	.67	1.0	1.1	1.3	2.0	2.7	3.3
85	.11	.12	.15	.15	.17	.18	.19	.21	.24	.29	.33	.35	.38	.41	.44	.47	.59	.88	1.0	1.2	1.8	2.4	2.9
100	.09	.10	.13	.13	.15	.15	.16	.18	.20	.25	.28	.30	.32	.35	.38	.40	.50	.75	.85	1.0	1.5	2.0	2.5
150	.06	.07	.08	.09	.10	.10	.11	.12	.13	.17	.19	.20	.21	.23	.25	.27	.33	.50	.57	.67	1.0	1.3	1.7
200	.05	.05	.06	.07	.07	.08	.08	.09	.10	.13	.14	.15	.16	.18	.19	.20	.25	.38	.43	.50	.75	1.0	1.3
250	.04	.04	.05	.05	.06	.06	.06	.07	.08	.10	.11	.12	.13	.14	.15	.16	.20	.30	.34	.40	.60	.80	1.0

PLUS DIOPTER LENSES
FOCUS CONVERSION TABLE
16mm or 35mm Camera
(MAY BE USED WITH ANY FOCAL LENGTH LENS)

NOTE: Position diopter lens in front of camera lens so that arrow (if inscribed on rim) points toward subject., or with convex (outward) curve toward subject. When two diopters are used in combination, place highest power nearest camera lens. The acutual field size photographed depends slightly on the separation between diopter and camera lens.

Power of Supplementary Lens in Diopters	Focusing Distance on Lens Mount in FEET	Actual Distance Focused on in INCHES From Diopter Lens
$+1/4$	Inf.	157 $1/2$
	25	139
	15	129 $1/2$
	10	118 $1/2$
	6	102
	4	86 $1/2$
$+1/2$	Inf.	78 $3/4$
	25	69 $1/2$
	15	64 $3/4$
	10	59 $1/4$
	6	51
	4	43 $1/4$
+1	Inf.	39 $3/8$
	25	34 $3/8$
	15	32 $3/8$
	10	29 $5/8$
	6	25 $1/2$
	4	21 $5/8$
+2	Inf.	19 $5/8$
	25	18 $1/2$
	15	17 $3/3$
	10	16 $7/8$
	6	15 $1/2$
	4	14
+3 (2+1)	Inf.	13 $1/8$
	25	12 $1/2$
	15	12 $1/4$
	10	11 $7/8$
	6	11 $1/8$
	4	10 $3/8$
+4	Inf.	9 $7/8$
+5	Inf.	7 $7/8$
+6	Inf.	6 $1/2$
+8	Inf.	5
+10	Inf.	4

<table>
<tr><th colspan="6">Selected Color Filters for B&W Cinematography
Daylight Exteriors</th></tr>
<tr><th rowspan="2">Kodak Wratten #</th><th rowspan="2">Color</th><th rowspan="2"></th><th rowspan="2">Effect/Use</th><th colspan="2">Average Exposure</th></tr>
<tr><th>Factor</th><th>T/stop Increase</th></tr>
<tr><td>3</td><td>Light Yellow</td><td rowspan="8">From 3 to 29 – renders blue skies increasingly darker and increasingly penetrates haze. Yellow & Red will not darken a misty sky.</td><td>Slight Correction</td><td>1.5</td><td>⅔</td></tr>
<tr><td>8</td><td>Yellow</td><td>Corrects color rendition to visual appearance as gray</td><td>2</td><td>1</td></tr>
<tr><td>12</td><td>Deep Yellow</td><td>Slight over correction. Useful in aerial cinematography</td><td>2.5 (Reversal Film 2)</td><td>1 ⅓ (1)</td></tr>
<tr><td>15</td><td>Deep Yellow</td><td>Greater contrast. Useful with the tele lenses and for aerial cinematography</td><td>3</td><td>1 ⅔-</td></tr>
<tr><td>21</td><td>Orange</td><td>Same but stronger than#15. Makes blue water dark</td><td>3.5 (Reversal Film 3)</td><td>1 ⅚ (1 ⅔)</td></tr>
<tr><td>23A</td><td>Light Red</td><td>Moderate over correction. Not for close ups–whitens faces</td><td>5</td><td>2 ⅓</td></tr>
<tr><td>25</td><td>Red</td><td>Very dark sky. Day-for-Night. (complete red separation). No faces!</td><td>8 (Reversal film 10)</td><td>3 (3 ⅓)</td></tr>
<tr><td>29</td><td>Deep Red</td><td>Black sky, greenery. Day-for-Night. No faces!</td><td>25 (Reversal film 40)</td><td>4 ⅔ (5 ⅓)</td></tr>
<tr><td>11</td><td>Yellowish Green</td><td colspan="2">Similar to #8 but better flesh tones and flower colors</td><td>2</td><td>1</td></tr>
<tr><td>56</td><td>Light Green</td><td colspan="2">Darkens sky, lightens foliage</td><td>4</td><td>2</td></tr>
<tr><td>58</td><td>Green</td><td colspan="2">(Complete green separation) Lightens dark foliage, darkens sky</td><td>6</td><td>2 ⅔</td></tr>
<tr><td>47</td><td>Blue</td><td colspan="2">(Complete blue separation) Accentuates haze. Darkens reds, Lightens blues</td><td>5</td><td>2 ⅓</td></tr>
<tr><td>23A + 56</td><td></td><td colspan="2">Helps flesh renditions for Day-for-Night. Darkens sky</td><td>Day-for-Night 6</td><td>2 ⅔</td></tr>
<tr><td>POLA</td><td>Gray</td><td colspan="2">Darkens sky, removes reflections.</td><td>2.5 to 4</td><td>1 ⅓ to 2</td></tr>
</table>

Color Filters for Altering B&W Contrast of Colored Subjects

Kodak Wratten #	Color of Subject				Tungsten Exposure	
	Blue	Green	Yellow	Red	Factor	T/stop Increase
3	Very Slightly Darker	Very Slightly Lighter	Very Slightly Lighter	Very Slightly Lighter	NR	NR
8	Slightly Darker	Very Slightly Lighter	Slightly Lighter	Very Slightly Lighter	1.5	⅔
12	Fairly Dark	Fairly Light	Light	Fairly Light	1.5	⅔
15	Dark	Light	Very Light	Light	2	1
21	Dark	Very Slightly Darker	Very Light	Very Light	4	2
23A	Very Dark	Dark	Slightly Lighter	Very Light	3	1 ⅔
25	Black	Very Dark	Fairly Light	Very Light	6	2 ⅔
29	Black	Black	Very Light	White	4	2
11	Fairly Dark	Light	Fairly Light	Medium Dark	3	1 ⅔
56	Fairly Dark	Fairly Light	Slightly Light	Fairly Dark	6	2 ⅔
58	Very Dark	Very Light	Light	Very Dark	8	3
47	White	Dark	Very Dark	Black	8	3
23A + 56	Very Dark	Very Dark	White	Light	NR	NR

Note: Relative to a neutral gray subject, any given filter will render its own color lighter and its complimentary color darker.

Correlated Color Temperature of Typical Light Sources

Artificial Light		
Source		**Mireds**
Match flame	1700°K	588
Candle flame	1850°K	541
Tungsten-gas filled lamps		
40-100W	2650-2900°K	317-345
200-500W	2980°K	336
1000W	2990°K	334

Daylight		
Source		**Mireds**
Sunlight		
Sunrise or sunset	2000°K	500
One hour after sunrise	3500°K	286
Early morning, late afternoon	4300°K	233
Average noon, (Wash. D.C.)	5400°K	185
Midsummer	5800°K	172
Overcast sky	6000°K	167
Average summer daylight	6500°K	154
Light summer shade	7100°K	141
Average summer shade	8000°K	125
Partly cloudy sky	8000-10000°K	125-100
Summer skylight	9500-30000°K	105-33

Sunlight should not be confused with daylight. Sunlight is the light of the sun only. Daylight is a combination of sunlight and skylight. These values are approximate since many factors affect the correlated color temperature. For consistency, 5500°K is considered to be nominal photographic daylight. The difference between 5000°K and 6000°K is only 33 mireds, the same photographic or visual difference as that between household tungsten lights and 3200°K photolamps (the approximate equivalent of ¼ Blue or ⅛ Orange lighting filters).

Kodak Conversion Filters for Color Films

Filter Color	Filter Number	Exposure Increase In Stops*	Conversion In Degrees °K	Mired Shift Value
Blue	80A	2	3200 to 5500°K	-131
	80B	1 ⅔	3400 to 5500°K	-112
	80C	1	3800 to 5500°K	-81
	80D	⅓	4200 to 5500°K	-56
Amber	85C	⅓	5500 to 3800°K	+81
	85	⅔	5500 to 3400°K	+112
	85N3	1 ⅔	5500 to 3400°K	+112
	85N6	2 ⅔	5500 to 3400°K	+112
	85N9	3 ⅔	5500 to 3400°K	+112
	85B	⅔	5500 to 3200°K	+131

*These values are approximate. For critical work, they should be checked by practical test, especially if more than one filter is used.

Kodak Light Balancing Filters

Filter Color	Filter Number	Exposure Increase In Stops*	To Obtain 3200 °K From:	To Obtain 3400 °K From:	Mired Shift Value
Bluish	82C + 82C	1 ⅓	2490°K	2610°K	-89
	82C + 82B	1 ⅓	2570°K	2700°K	-77
	82C + 82A	1	2650°K	2780°K	-65
	82C + 82	1	2720°K	2870°K	-55
	82C	⅔	2800°K	2950°K	-45
	82B	⅔	2900°K	3060°K	-32
	82A	⅓	3000°K	3180°K	-21
	82	⅓	3100°K	3290°K	-10
	No Filter Necessary		**3200 °K**	**3400 °K**	
Yellowish	81	⅓	3300°K	3510°K	+9
	81A	⅓	3400°K	3630°K	+18
	81B	⅓	3500°K	3740°K	+27
	81C	⅓	3600°K	3850°K	+35
	81D	⅔	3700°K	3970°K	+42
	81EF	⅔	3850°K	4140°K	+52

*These values are approximate. For critical work, they should be checked by practical test, especially if more than one filter is used.

Kodak Color Compensating Filters for Color Films

Peak Density	Yellow (Absorbs Blue)	Exposure Increase In Stops*	Magenta (Absorbs Green)	Exposure Increase In Stops*	Cyan (Absorbs Red)	Exposure Increase In Stops*
.05	CC-05Y	1/6	CC-05M	1/3	CC-05C	1/3
.10	CC-10Y	1/3	CC-10M	1/3	CC-10C	1/3
.20	CC-20Y	1/3	CC-20M	1/3	CC-20C	1/3
.30	CC-30Y	1/3	CC-30M	2/3	CC-30C	2/3
.40	CC-40Y	1/3	CC-40M	2/3	CC-40C	2/3
.50	CC-50Y	2/3	CC-50M	2/3	CC-50C	1
Peak Density	**Red (Absorbs Blue and Green)**	**Exposure Increase In Stops***	**Green (Absorbs Blue and Red)**	**Exposure Increase In Stops***	**Blue (Absorbs Red and Green)**	**Exposure Increase In Stops***
.05	CC-05R	1/3	CC-05G	1/3	CC-05B	1/3
.10	CC-10R	1/3	CC-10G	1/3	CC-10B	1/3
.20	CC-20R	1/3	CC-20G	1/3	CC-20B	2/3
.30	CC-30R	2/3	CC-30G	2/3	CC-30B	2/3
.40	CC-40R	2/3	CC-40G	2/3	CC-40B	1
.50	CC-50R	1	CC-50G	1	CC-50B	1 1/3

* These values are approximate. For critical work, they should be checked by practical test, especially if more than one filter is used.

Kodak Ultraviolet and Haze Cutting Filters

Kodak Wratten #	Color	Effect/Use (no exposure increase required)
1A (skylight)	Pale Pink	Absorbs ultraviolet for color film. To reduce blue outdoors in open shade under clear blue sky.
2A	Pale Yellow	Absorbs ultraviolet below 405nm. Reduces haze in black-and-white film.
2B	Pale Yellow	Absorbs ultraviolet below 390nm. More effective than 2A in haze reduction.
2C	Pale Yellow	Absorbs ultraviolet below 385nm. Less effective than 2B in haze reduction.
2E	Pale Yellow	Absorbs ultaviolet below 415nm. Similar to 2B, but absorbs more violet.
HF-3	Light Yellow	Haze cutting filter for aerial photography.
HF-4	Very Light Yellow	Haze cutting filter. Always used in combination with HF-3 filter. For color balancing of different sky conditions and altitudes.
HF-5	Very Light Yellow	Haze cutting filter. Always used in combination with HF-3 filter. For color balancing of different sky conditions and altitudes.

ND Filter Selector Chart

Stop for correct exposure					1.4	2	2.8	4	5.6	8	11	16	22	32	45	64	90	128	180	256
	Stops	Factor	% Trans	ND Filter																
↑	1/3	1.25	80	.10	1.3	1.8	2.5	3.5	5	7	10	14	20	28	40					
	2/3	1.5	63	.20	1.1	1.6	2.2	3.2	4.5	6.3	9	12.7	18	25	35					
1/3 Stops Steps	1	2	50	.30	1	1.4	2	2.8	4	5.6	8	11	16	22	32	45				
	1 1/3	2.5	40	.40	.9	1.3	1.8	2.5	3.5	5	7	10	14	20	28	40				
	1 2/3	3	32	.50	.8	1.1	1.6	2.2	3.2	4.5	6.3	9	12.7	18	25	35				
↓	2	4	25	.60	.7	1	1.4	2	2.8	4	5.6	8	11	16	22	32	45			
↑	3	8	12.5	.90		.7	1	1.4	2	2.8	4	5.6	8	11	16	22	32	45		
one stop steps	4	16	6.25	1.2			.7	1	1.4	2	2.8	4	5.6	8	11	16	22	32	45	
	5	32	3	1.5				.7	1	1.4	2	2.8	4	5.6	8	11	16	22	32	45
	6	64	1.6	1.8					.7	1	1.4	2	2.8	4	5.6	8	11	16	22	32
	7	128	0.8	2.1						.7	1	1.4	2	2.8	4	5.6	8	11	16	22
↓	8	256	0.4	2.4							.7	1	1.4	2	2.8	4	5.6	8	11	16

The columns to the left of the "ND Filter" show the filter factor both numerically and in the lens stops and the percent transmission of each. Up to 0.6ND, increments are in ⅓ stop steps. From 0.6ND to 2.4ND the increments are in full stops. Densities may be added: (0.6ND plus 0.9ND equals 1.5ND). If correct exposure indicates a very small stop beyond the calibration of the lens AND/OR: If it is desired to open the lens to a wide aperture to throw the background out of focus: Select the desired lens stop in the column under indicated stop, and use the corresponding ND Filter from the left shaded column. (For B&W photography, account for the factor of any color filter also.)

Filter Compensator

Lens stop no filter	Filter Factors													
	1.25	1.5	2	2.5	3	4	5	6	8	10	12	16	20	25
22	20	18	16	14	12.7	11	10	9	8	7	6.3	5.6	5	4.5
20	18	16	14	12.7	11	10	9	8	7	6.3	5.6	5	4.5	4
18	16	14	12.7	11	10	9	8	7	6.3	5.6	5	4.5	4	3.5
16	14	12.7	11	10	9	8	7	6.3	5.6	5	4.5	4	3.5	3.2
14	12.7	11	10	9	8	7	6.3	5.6	5	4.5	4	3.5	3.2	2.8
12.7	11	10	9	8	7	6.3	5.6	5	4.5	4	3.5	3.2	2.8	2.5
11	10	9	8	7	6.3	5.6	5	4.5	4	3.5	3.2	2.8	2.5	2.2
10	9	8	7	6.3	5.6	5	4.5	4	3.5	3.2	2.8	2.5	2.2	2
9	8	7	6.3	5.6	5	4.5	4	3.5	3.2	2.8	2.5	2.2	2	1.8
8	7	6.3	5.6	5	4.5	4	3.5	3.2	2.8	2.5	2.2	2	1.8	1.6
7	6.3	5.6	5	4.5	4	3.5	3.2	2.8	2.5	2.2	2	1.8	1.6	1.4
6.3	5.6	5	4.5	4	3.5	3.2	2.8	2.5	2.2	2	1.8	1.6	1.4	1.3
5.6	5	4.5	4	3.5	3.2	2.8	2.5	2.2	2	1.8	1.6	1.4	1.3	1.1
5	4.5	4	3.5	3.2	2.8	2.5	2.2	2	1.8	1.6	1.4	1.3	1.1	1
4.5	4	3.5	3.2	2.8	2.5	2.2	2	1.8	1.6	1.4	1.3	1.1	1	.9
4	3.5	3.2	2.8	2.5	2.2	2	1.8	1.6	1.4	1.3	1.1	1	.9	.8
3.5	3.2	2.8	2.5	2.2	2	1.8	1.6	1.4	1.3	1.1	1	.9	.8	.7
3.2	2.8	2.5	2.2	2	1.8	1.6	1.4	1.3	1.1	1	.9	.8	.7	
2.8	2.5	2.2	2	1.8	1.6	1.4	1.3	1.1	1	.9	.8	.7		
2.5	2.2	2	1.8	1.6	1.4	1.3	1.1	1	.9	.8	.7			
2.2	2	1.8	1.6	1.4	1.3	1.1	1	.9	.8	.7				
2	1.8	1.6	1.4	1.3	1.1	1	.9	.8	.7					
1.8	1.6	1.4	1.3	1.1	1	.9	.8	.7						
1.6	1.4	1.3	1.1	1	.9	.8	.7							
1.4	1.3	1.1	1	.9	.8	.7								
1.3	1.1	1	.9	.8	.7									
1.1	1	.9	.8	.7										
1	.9	.8	.7											
.9	.8	.7												

COLOR FILTER SELECTION CHART FOR UNDERWATER PHOTOGRAPHY

Filter Density/Depth-Distance

Depth (feet)	Subject Distance from Camera (feet)	Total Distance from Surface to Subject to Camera (feet)	C.C. Filter Density		
			CC-Y (yellow)	CC-M (magenta)	CC-R (red)
Surface to 5	0–10	0–15	none to .05	none to .05	none to .05
	10–20	10–25	.10	.10–.20	.10
	20–40	20–45	.10–.20	.10–.30	.10–.20
	40–	40–	.30–.40*	.30–.40*	.30–.40*
5–15	0–10	5-25	.05–.10	.10–.20	.05–.10
	10–20	15-35	.10–.20	.10–.30	.10–.20
	20–40	25-55	.20–.30	.20–.40*	.20–.30
	40–	45–	.30–.40*	.20–.40*	.30–.40*
15–30	0–10	15–40	.10–.20	.20–.30	.10–.20
	10–20	25–50	.20–.30	.20–.40*	.20–.30
	20–40	35–70	.20–.40	.20–.40*	.20–.40*
	40–	55–	.30–.40*	.20–.40*	.30–.40*
30–50	0–10	30–60	.20–.30	.20–.40*	.20–.30
	10–20	40–70	.20–.30	.20–.40*	.20–.30
	20–40	50–90	.30–.40*	.20–.40*	.30–.40*
50	0–10	50–60	.30	.30–.40*	.30
	10-	60-	.30–.40*	.30–.40*	.30–.40*

*Use only when absolutely certain of high enough light level.

Comparison of Filter System Names

Wratten	Mired	European	Mired	Hasselblad	Mired	Fuji	Mired	Nikon
80A	-131	KB 15	-150	CB	-150	LBB-12	-120	
80B	-112	KB 12	-120	CB	-120			B12
80C	-81	KB 12	-90	CB	-90	LBB-8	-80	B8
80D	-56	KB 6	-60	CB	-60	LBB-6	-60	
82	-10					LBB-1	-10	
82A	-21	KB 1.5	-15	CB	-15	LBB-2	-20	B2
82B	-32	KB 3	-30	CB	-30	LBB-3	-30	
82C	-45	KB 6	-60	CB	-60	LBB-4	-40	
81	+9					LBA-1	+10	
81A	+18	KR 1.5	+15	CR	+15	LBA-2	+20	A2
81B	+27					LBA-3	+30	
81C	+35	KR 3	+30	CR	+30			
81D	+42					LBA-4	+40	
81EF	+52	KR6	+60	CR	+60	LBA-6	+60	
85	+112	KR 12	+120	CR	+120			A12
85B	+131	KR15	+150	CR	+150	LBA-12	+120	
85C	+81	KR 9	+90	CR	+90	LBA-8	+80	

MOST COMMON FILTER SIZES FOR MOTION PICTURES

40.5mm	2" x 2"
48mm	3" x 3"
Series 9 (82.55mm)	4" x 4"
4.5" round	4" x 5.650" (Panavision)
138mm	6" x 6" 6.6" x 6.6"

TYPICAL COMMERCIAL/INDUSTRIAL LIGHT SOURCE CHARACTERISTICS

Description	Correlated Color Temperature (°Kelvin)	Color Rendering Index	Efficacy (Lumens/Watt)
Fluorescent Types			
Daylight	6500°K	79	60
Design White	5200°K	82	50
Cool White	4300°K	67	70
Deluxe Cool White	4100°K	86	50
Natural White	3700°K	81	45
White	3500°K	62	70
Warm White	3050°K	55	70
Deluxe Warm White	2950°K	73	45
Incandescent	2700°K	90	35
***Mercury Vapor* Types**			
Clear Mercury	5900°K	17	50
White Deluxe	4000°K	45	55
Warm Deluxe	3500°K	62	70
***Metal Halide* Additive Types**			
Muti-arc ™; Metal Vapor ™	5900°K	65	80-115
Metalarc C ™	3800°K	70	80-115
High Pressure Sodium			
Lucalox ™	2100°K	25	80-140
Lumalox ™			

CHARACTERISTICS OF PHOTOGRAPHIC LIGHT SOURCES

Description	Correlated Color Temperature (at rated voltage)	Mired Value	Efficacy Lumens/Watt
Incandescent			
Standard and tungsten/ halogen	3200°K	312	26
CP gas filled	3350°K	299	32
Photoflood	3400°K	294	34
Daylight blue photoflood	4800°K	208	
Carbon arc (225A Brute)			
White Flame, Y-1 filter	5100°K	196	24
White Flame, no filter	5800°K	172	
Yellow flame YF 101 filter	3350°K	299	
***Xenon, high pressure DC short arc**	6000°K	167	35-50
***Metal halide additive AC Arc**			
HMI	5600°K	179	80-102
CID	5600°K	179	80
CSI	4200°K	238	85

*** Need filtering for color photography**

Filters for Daylight Correction

Neutral Density and Combinations (for Windows)

Neutral Density	N.D. Value	Stops Loss
Rosco #3415	.15	½
Lee #29B	.15	½
GAM #1514	.15	½
Formatt #298	.15	½
Rosco #3402	.30	1
Lee #209	.30	1
GAM #1515	.30	1
Formatt #209	.30	1
Rosco #3403	.60	2
Lee #210	.60	2
GAM #1516	.60	1.7
Formatt #210	.60	2
Rosco #3404	.90	3
Lee #211	.90	3
GAM #1517	.90	2½
Formatt #211	.90	3
Lee # 299	1.20	4
GAM #1518	1.20	2.7
Formatt #299	1.20	4

Combinations	Mired Shift Value	Effect On: 5500°K (182 Mireds)	6000°K (167 Mireds)
Lee #207 Full CTO + .3ND	+159	2930°K	3070°K
Lee #208 Full CTO + .6ND	+159	2930°K	3070°K
Rosco #3405 Roscosun 85N.3	+131	3200°K	3360°K
Rosco #3406 Roscosun 85N.6	+131	3200°K	3360°K
GAM #1556 Full CTO + .3ND	+96	3540°K	4040°K
GAM #1557 Full CTO + .6ND	+89	3650°K	4150°K
GAM #1558 Full CTO + .9ND	+13	5100°K	5600°K
Formatt #207 Full CTO + .3ND	+159	2930°K	3070°K
Formatt #208 Full CTO + .6ND	+159	2930°K	3070°K
Acrylic Panels			
Lee #A204 Full CTO*	+159	2930°K	3070°K
Roscolex #85 3761**	+131	3200°K	3360°K
Lee #A205 Half CTO	+109	3440°K	3629°K
Roscolex #3751 ½ CTO	+ 81	3800°K	4030°K
Lee #A207 Full CTO + .3ND	+159	2930°K	3070°K
Lee #A208 Full CTO + .6ND	+159	2930°K	3070°K

Lee #A209 .3 ND
Roscolex #3762 .3 ND
Lee #A210 .6 ND
Roscolex #3763 .3 ND
Lee #A211 .9 ND
Roscolex #3764 .9 ND

Notes:
* Lee Acrylic Panels are available 5 x 8 feet (152 x 244 cm)
** Rosco Acrylic Panels are available in either 4 x 8 feet (122 x 244 cm) or 5 x 8 feet (152 x 244 cm)

Lighting Filters for Color Temperature Adjustment

This Table, listing the most commonly used filters for adjusting color temperature, are presented along with their primary characteristics and the effect that they have on light sources at 2900°K and 3200°K, along with the Mired Shift value for each.

Increase Color Temperature (Blue)	Mired Shift Value	Effect On: 3200°K (312 Mired)	2900°K (345 Mired)
Lee #200 Double C.T. Blue	-274	26,000°K	14,000°K
Rosco #3220 Double C.T. Blue	-274	26,000°K	14,000°K
GAM #1520 Extra C.T. Blue	-190	8150°K	7850°K
Formatt #200 Double C.T. Blue	-274	26,000°K	14,000°K
Lee #201 Full C.T. Blue	-137	5700°K	4800°K
Rosco #3202 Full Blue	-131	5500°K	4670°K
GAM #1523 Full C.T. Blue	-141	5500°K	5200°K
Formatt #201 Full C.T. Blure	-137	5700°K	4910°K
Lee #281 Three Quarter C.T. Blue	-112	5000°K	4290°K
Rosco #3203 Three Quarter Blue	-100	4720°K	4080°K
GAM #1526 Three Quarter C.T. Blue	-108	4750°K	4450°K
Formatt #281 Three Quarter C.T. Blue	-112	5000°K	4290°K
Lee #202 Half C.T. Blue	- 78	4270°K	3750°K
Rosco #3204 Half Blue	- 68	4100°K	3610°K
GAM #1529 Half C.T. Blue	-75	4100°K	3800°K
Formatt #202 Half C.T. Blue	-78	4270°K	3750°K
Rosco #3206 Third Blue	- 49	3800°K	3380°K
Lee #203 Quarter C.T. Blue	- 35	3610°K	3230°K
Rosco #3208 Quarter Blue	- 30	3550°K	3180°K
GAM #1532 Quarter C.T. Blue	-38	3600°K	3300°K
GAM #1534 Sixth C.T. Blue	-28	3520°K	3220°K
Lee #218 Eighth C.T. Blue	- 18	3400°K	3060°K
Rosco #3216 Eighth Blue	- 12	3330°K	3000°K
GAM #1535 Eighth Blue	- 20	3400°K	3100°K
Formatt #218 Eighth C.T. Blue	-18	3400°K	3060°K

Lighting Filters for Color Temperature Adjustment

This Table, listing the most commonly used filters for adjusting color temperature, are presented along with their primary characteristics and the effect that they have on light sources at 5500°K and 6000°K, along with the Mired Shift value for each.

Decrease Color Temperature(Amber)	Mired Shift Value	Effect On: 5500°K (182 Mireds)	6000°K (167 Mireds)
Rosco #3407 Roscosun CTO	+167	2865°K	3000°K
Rosco #3441 Full Straw (CTS)	+167	2865°K	3000°K
Rosco #3420 Double CTO	+334	2900°K	3400°K
GAM #1540 Extra CTO	+240	2290°K +30G	2690°K +30G
Lee #204 Full C.T. Orange	+159	2930°K	3070°K
Lee #441 Full Straw	+160	2925°K	3060°K
Formatt #204 Full C.T. Orange	+159	2930°K	3070°K
Formatt #441 Full C.T. Straw	+160	3061°K	2925°K
GAM #1543 Full CTO	+146	2990°K	3390°K
Rosco #3401 Roscosun 85	+131	3200°K	3360°K
Rosco #3411 Three-Quarters CTO	+131	3200°K	3360°K
Lee #285 Three-Quarters C.T. Orange	+124	3270°K	3440°K
GAM #1546 Three-Quarters CTO	+125	3200°K	3600°K
Formatt #285 Three-Quarters C.T. Orange	+124	3436°K	3268°K
Lee #205 Half C.T. Orange	+109	3440°K	3620°K
GAM #1549 Half CTO	+ 79	3800°K	4200°K
Formatt #205 Half C.T. Orange	+109	3440°K	3629°K
Rosco #3408 Roscosun ½ CTO	+ 81	3800°K	4030°K
Rosco #3442 Half Straw (½ CTS)	+ 81	3800°K	4030°K
Lee #442 Half Straw	+ 81	3800°K	4030°K
Formatt #442 Half C.T. Straw	+ 81	3800°K	4030°K
Lee #206 Quarter C.T. Orange	+ 64	4060°K	4330°K
GAM #1552 Quarter CTO	+ 40	4480°K	4880°K
Formatt #206 Quarter C.T. Orange	+ 64	4060°K	4330°K
Rosco #3409 Roscosun ¼ CTO	+ 42	4460°K	4800°K
Rosco #3443 Quarter Straw (¼ CTS)	+ 42	4460°K	4800°K
Lee #443 Quarter C.T. Straw	+ 42	4460°K	4780°K
Formatt #443 Quarter C.T. Straw	+ 42	4460°K	4800°K
Lee #223 Eighth C.T. Orange	+ 26	4810°K	5180°K
Formatt #223 Eighth C.T. Orange	+ 26	4680°K	5180°K
GAM #1555 Eighth CTO	+ 20	4950°K	5350°K
Rosco #3410 Roscosun ⅛ CTO	+ 20	4950°K	5350°K
Rosco #3444 Eighth Straw (⅛ CTS)	+ 20	4950°K	5350°K
Lee #444 Eighth C.T. Straw	+ 20	4950°K	5350°K
Formatt #444 Eighth C.T. Straw	+20	4950°K	5350°K
Rosco #3414 UV Filter	+ 8	5260°K	5710°K
Lee UV	+ 2	5430°K	5920°K

Decrease Color Temperature(Red-Amber)	Mired Shift Value	Effect On: 5500°K (182 Mireds)	6000°K (167 Mireds)
Lee #236 HMI (To Tungsten)	+134	3160°K	3320°K
Rosco #3106 Tough MTY	+131	3200°K	3360°K
Lee #237 CID (To Tungsten)	+131	3200°K	3360°K
Rosco 3102 Tough MT2	+110	3425°K	3790°K
Lee #238 CSI (To Tungsten)	+ 49	4330°K	4630°K

Filters for Arc Discharge and Fluorescent Lamps

Green/Magenta Adjusting Filters for Arc Discharge and Fluorescent (May be Used with Blue/Amber Color Temperature Filters)

Green Filters (Decrease Red/Blue (Magenta))	CC Equivalent
Rosco #3304 Tough Plusgreen	CC30G
Lee #244 Plus Green	CC30G
GAM #1585 Plus Green	CC15G
Formatt #244 Plus Green	CC30G
Rosco #3315 Tough ½ Plusgreen	CC15G
Lee #245 Half Plus Green	CC15G
GAM #1587 Half Plus Green	CC10G
Formatt #245 Half Plus Green	CC15G
Rosco # 3316 Tough ¼ Plusgreen	CC075G
Lee #246 Quarter Plus Green	CC075G
GAM #1588 Quarter Plus Green	CC05G
Formatt #246 Quarter Plus Green	CC075G
Lee #278 Eighth Plus Green	CC035G
Rosco #3317 ⅛ Plusgreen	CC035G
GAM #1589 Eighth Plus Green	CC05G
Formatt #278 Eighth Plus Green	CC035G
Lee #241 Fluorescent 5700° K	CC30G + 80A
Formatt #241 Fluorescent 5700° K	
Lee #242 Fluorescent 4300° K	CC30G + 80C
Formatt #242 Fluorescent 4300° K	
Lee #243 Fluorescent 3600° K	CC30G + 82B
Formatt #243 Fluorescent 3600° K	
Formatt #219 Fluorescent Green	
Magenta Filters (Decrease Green)	
GAM #1578 Extra Minus Green	CC90M
Rosco #3308 Tough Minusgreen	CC30M
Lee # 247 Minus Green	CC30M
GAM #1580 Minus Green	CC55M
Formatt #247 Minus Green	CC30M
GAM #1581 Three Quarter Minus Green	CC45M
Rosco #3313 Tough ½ Minusgreen	CC15M
Lee #248 Half Minus Green	CC15M
GAM #1582 Half Minus Green	CC25M
Formatt #248 Half Minus Green	CC15M
Rosco #3314 Tough ¼ Minusgreen	CC075M
Lee #249 Quarter Minus Green	CC075M
GAM #1583 Quarter Minus Green	CC15M
Formatt #249 Quarter Minus Green	CC075M
Rosco #3318 Tough ⅛ Minusgreen	CC035M
Lee #279 Eighth Minus Green	CC035M
GAM #1584 Eighth Minus Green	CC10M
Formatt #279 Eighth Minus Green	CC035M
Rosco #3310 Fluorofilter	CC30M + 85B
GAM #1590 Fluorofilter CW	CC30M +85

Color Correction for Carbon Arcs

LEE	
Arc Correction (Carbon-Regular)	
212 LC.T. Yellow (Y1)	Reduces color temperature of low carbon arcs to 3200°K
213 White Flame Green	Corrects white flame carbon arcs by absorbing ultra violet.
Arc Correction (Carbon-Color Balanced)	
230 Super Correction LC. T. Yellow	Converts yellow carbon arc (of low color temperature) to tungsten.
232 Super Correction W.F. Green to Tungsten	Converts white flame arc to 3200°K, for use with tunsten film.
ROSCO	
3107 Tough Y1	Pale straw filter for use on white flame arcs to absorb UV and provide daylight balance.
3106 Tough MTY	A single filter for correcting white flame arcs to 3200°K tungsten.
3102 Tough MT2	When used with Y1 converts white flame arcs to 3200°K tungsten.
3134 Tough MT54	A pale straw, gentle warming filter for arcs and HMI.
3114 Tough UV Filter	A slightly warm filter that absorbs 90% of UV output below 390 nm. Eliminates fluorescing of dyes and pigments caused by arcs.
GAM Color Cinefilters	
1560 Y-1 LGT Yellow 1565 MTY 1570 MT2 1575 ⅓ MT2	**SAME EFFECTS AS ABOVE**
FORMATT	
Arc Correction (Carbon-Regular)	
212 LC.T. Yellow (Y1)	Reduces color temperature of low carbon arcs to 3200°K
213 White Flame Green	Corrects white flame carbon arcs by absorbing ultra violet.
Arc Correction (Carbon-Color Balanced)	
230 Super Correction LC. T. Yellow	Converts yellow carbon arc (of low color temperature) to tungsten.
232 Super Correction W.F. Green to Tungsten	Converts white flame arc to 3200°K, for use with tungsten film.
Arc Correction (Compact Source)	
236 HMI (To Tungsten)	Converts HMI to 3200°K, use with tungsten film
237 CID (To Tungsten)	Converts CID to 3200°K, use with tungsten film
238 CSI (To Tungsten)	Converts CSI to 3200°K, use with tungsten film
Ultra Violet Absorbtion	
226 UV	Transmission of less than 50% at 410nms

CalColor

Calibrated Color by Rosco is a series of color effects lighting filters designed specifically to the spectral sensitivity of color film. The series includes the primary colors Blue, Green and Red, along with the secondary colors Yellow, Magenta and Cyan and the intermediary colors Pink and Lavender. Each color is designed in four densities: 15, 30, 60 and 90, corresponding to the familiar ½, 1, 2 and 3 stop calibrations.

4215	15 Blue (½ stop)
4230	30 Blue (1 stop)
4260	60 Blue (2 stop)
4290	90 Blue (3 stop)
4307	07 Cyan (¼ stop)
4315	15 Cyan (½ stop)
4330	30 Cyan (1 stop)
4360	60 Cyan (2 stop)
4390	90 Cyan (3 stop)
4415	15 Green (½ stop)
4430	30 Green (1 stop)
4460	60 Green (2 stop)
4490	90 Green (3 stop)
4515	15 Yellow (½ stop)
4530	30 Yellow (1 stop)
4560	60 Yellow (2 stop)
4590	90 Yellow (3 stop)
4615	15 Red (½ stop)
4630	30 Red (1 stop)
4660	60 Red (2 stop)
4690	90 Red (3 stop)
4715	15 Magenta (½ stop)
4730	30 Magenta (1 stop)
4760	60 Magenta (2 stop)
4790	90 Magenta (3 stop)
4815	15 Pink (½ stop)
4830	30 Pink (1 stop)
4860	60 Pink (2 stop)
4890	90 Pink (3 stop)
4915	15 Lavender (½ stop)
4930	30 Lavender (1 stop)
4960	60 Lavender (2 stop)
4990	90 Lavender (3 stop)

Tiffen Decamired Filters

	Filter	Mired Shift	Exposure Increase
Blue	B1.5	-15	⅓
	B3	-30	⅔
	B6	-60	1
	B12	-120	1½
Red	R1.5	+15	⅓
	R3	+30	½
	R6	+60	⅔
	R12	+120	1⅓

* These values are approximate. For critical work, they should be checked by practical test, especially if more than one filter is used.

Examples of Mired Shift Value (Filter) Effects

Initial Source		Filter Mired Shift	Filtered Source		° Kelvin Changes
°K	Mireds		Mireds	°K	
10,000	100	+112	212	4720	5280
6,000	167	+112	279	3600	2400
5,000	200	+112	312	3200	1800
2,600	385	-21	364	2750	150
2,900	345	-21	324	3090	190
3,200	312	-21	291	3440	240

Mired Values of Color Temperatures from 2000°K – 10,000°K

°K	+0	100	200	300	400	500	600	700	800	900
2000	500	476	455	435	417	400	385	370	357	345
3000	333	323	312	303	294	286	278	270	263	256
4000	250	244	238	233	227	222	217	213	208	204
5000	200	196	192	189	185	182	179	175	172	169
6000	167	164	161	159	156	154	152	149	147	145
7000	143	140	139	137	135	133	132	130	128	126
8000	125	123	122	120	119	118	116	115	114	112
9000	111	110	109	108	106	105	104	103	102	101
10,000	100									

HMI LAMPS — Summary of Electrical and Physical Characteristics

Lamp Power Rating (Watts)	**200**	**575**	**1200**	**2500**	**4000**	**6000**	**12000**	**18000**
Minimum Open Circuit A.C. Voltage to the lamp for Ignition (Volts)	198	198	198	209	360	220	380	380
Lamp Operating Voltage (Volts)	80	95	100	115	200	135	160	225
Lamp Operating Current (Amperes)	3.1	7.0	13.8	25.6	24.0	55	65.0	88
Luminous Flux (Light output in Lumens)	16,000	49,000	110,000	240,000	410,000	630,000	1,008,000	1,700,000
Luminous Efficacy (Lumens/Watt)	80	85	92	96	102	105	84	94.4
Average Life (Hours)	300	750	750	500	500	350	300	300
Burning Position	Horizontal 15°	Any	Any	Horizontal 15°	Horizontal 15°	Horizontal 15°	Horizontal 15°	Horizontal 15°

Characteristics of Typical Photographic Light Sources

Type	Range (Watts)	Temperature (°Kelvin)	Efficacy (lm/Watt)	Luminance (cd/cm^2)	Current	Life (Hours)
HMI	125–18,000	6000 °K	70-96	3000-30,000	AC	150–1,000
Tungsten-Halogen	5–24,000	3000-3400 °K	Max. 37	200–5,000	AC/DC	15–2,000
Xenon-Short Arc	10,000 max.	6000 °K	15–20	20,000-500,000	DC	500–2000
Lo-Pressure Xenon	1100–15,000	5400 °K	18-50	Not Available	DC	200
Lo-Pressure Xenon	10K–50K	5400 °K	18-50	Not Available	AC	100–200
Fluorescent	35–50	various	45-80	0.3-2	AC	10,000

National Carbons for Studio Lighting						
Fixture Type	**Carbon No.**	**Positive Description**	**Carbon No.**	**Negative Description**	**Arc D.C. Electrical Amperes**	**Rating Volts**
Duarc 40	1	8mm x 12 in. CC MP Studio	8	7mm x 9 in. CC MP Studio	40	36
M.R. 90	2	13.6mm x 22 in. H.I. Studio	9	7/16 in. x 8 ½ in. CC MP Studio	120	58
M.R. 170	3	16mm x 20 in. H.I. Studio	10	½ in. x 8 ¼ in. CC MP Studio	150	68
M.R. Brute 4691 4611	4	16mm x 22 in. Super H.I. Studio Positive-White Flame	11	17/32 in. x 9 in. Special CC	225	73
	5	16mm x 22 in. Super H.I. Studio Positive-Yellow Flame				
M.R. Titan	6	16mm x 25 in. Ultrex HIWF Studio	12	11/16 in. x 9 in. CC MP Studio	350	79
	7	16mm x 25 in. HIYF Special Studio			300	73

Stanley Cortez, ASC and Mole-Richardson founder Peter Mole with MR 225 amp Brute Arc type 450.

Color Balancing for Existing Non-Photographic Lighting

Common Fluorescent and AC Discharge Commercial Lighting	Using existing fluorescent lighting unfiltered								Filtering fluorescent lights to match photo lamps			
	Camera filters (Kodak or equivalent)				Photo lamp filters to match Fluorescent Lamps (Rosco, Lee, Gam or Formatt)				Camera filter: none (Tungsten negative Or reversal)		Camera filter: Tungsten Negative: #85 Daylight film: none	
	3200°K film (Tungsten)	S.I.*	5500°K film (Daylight)	S.I.*	3200°K	L.L.*	5500°K	L.L.*	To match 3200°K	L.L.*	To match 5500°K	L.L.*
Cool white	CC10M +#85	1⅓	CC20M	⅓	Full blue CTB +Plusgreen +Quarter Blue +¼ Plusgreen	3	Plusgreen +Third blue	1	Fluorofilter +½ Minusgreen	1	Minusgreen	⅔
Cool white deluxe	CC10R +#85C	⅔	#82C	⅔	Half blue +¼ Plusgreen +Eighth Blue	1⅓	MT54 +Eighth Blue +UV Filter	1	Sun ½ CTO +¼ Minusgreen +Quarter Blue	1⅓	Quarter blue +¼ Minusgreen +Eighth Blue	1
Warm white	CC30M +#81EF	1⅓	CC50B +CC15M	1⅔	Half Blue +Plusgreen +Quarter blue	2	Plusgreen +½ Plusgreen +Sun ⅛ CTO	1	Minusgreen +¼ Minusgreen +Sun ¼ CTO	1½	Half blue +Minusgreen +Eighth blue	2
Warm white deluxe	CC10M +#81	⅔	#80B +CC05G	2	¼ Plusgreen +Quarter blue +UV Filter	⅔	Sun ½ CTO +UV Filter	⅓	¼ Minusgreen	⅓	Full blue CTB +½ Minusgreen	2⅓
Mercury vapor	CC50M + #85	1⅓	CC50M + #81A	1	½ to Full CTO + 2x to 3x Minusgreen	3⅔ to 2⅓	Full CTB + 2x to 3x Plusgreen	3 to 2⅓	NR		NR	
Sodium vapor	CC30 to 50M +#80A	2 ⅔	CC30M + #80A	2 ⅔	¾ CTO + 101 Yellow	1⅓	1½ to 2x Full CTO + 101 Yellow	2½ to 1⅔	NR		NR	

Check with color temperature meter. *S. I. = Stop Increase *L.L. = Light Loss in stops

COLOR BALANCING TO MATCH DAYLIGHT OR AMBIENT LIGHT ON LOCATION INTERIORS

EMULSION BALANCE	EXPOSURE BALANCE	CAMERA FILTER	PHOTOGRAPHIC LIGHTS/FILTERS	PRACTICAL Existing LIGHTS/FILTERS	Window Filters
BALANCING INTERIOR TO DAYLIGHT FROM WINDOWS					
3200°K	Daylight	85Neg 85B Rev.	**3200°K Tungsten/** Full Blue CTB or Dichroic	**Household Tungsten/** Full Blue + ¼ CTB	ND as required
			White flame Arc/Y-1	See pp 773 for Fluorescent, Mercury and Sodium Vapor Lamps	
			HMI, CID/Y-1		
			5500°K Kino Flo GE Cinema55/None		
Daylight	Daylight	None	Use same filters as above		
BALANCING COLOR OF AMBIENT LIGHTING TO 3200°K					
3200°K	3200°K	None	**3200°K Tungsten/** None	**Household Tungsten/** ¼ CTB	Full or ¾ CTO or Sun 85 plus ND as required
			3200°K HMI/ None		
			3200°K Kino Flo, GE Cinema32/None	See pp 773 for Fluorescent, Mercury and Sodium Vapor Lamps	
			Yellow Flame Arc/YF 101		
			HMI, CID, White Flame Arc/ Y-1+MT2* or MTY or ¾ CTO		
Daylight	3200°K	80A	Use same filters as above		

Exact conversion requires both source and filter to be precise. Artificial daylight sources vary greatly in their ability to replicate photographic daylight (5500°K). White-Flame Carbon Arcs and Xenon lamps are very stable and excellent continuous-spectrum photographic daylight sources. HMI and CID sources are problematic. There can be variations in green output and they tend to lose one degree of Kelvin per hour of lamp life. The consistency in manufacturing of these globes is a factor that requires checking. Even so-called "full-spectrum color-correct" fluorescents will have excess green when they overheat. 3200°K Tungsten-Halogen photographic globes are very stable and have excellent color rendering when operated at 117–120V throughout their life. Filtering systems vary by manufacturer. They must be checked by a color-temperature meter for accuracy.

Color Balancing for Existing Fluorescent Lighting

Typical Fluorescent Lights	Using existing fluorescent lighting unfiltered: Camera filters (Kodak or equivalent) 3200°K film	S.I.*	Camera filters 5500°K film	S.I.*	Photo lamp filters (Rosco, Lee, GAM or Formatt) 3200°K	L.L.*	Photo lamp filters 5500°K	L.L.*	Filtering fluorescent lights to match photo lights: Camera filter: none (Tungsten negative Or reversal) To match 3200°K	L.L.*	Camera filter: Tungsten Negative: #85 Daylight film: none To match 5500°K	L.L.*
Durotest Optima 50	+#85	2/3	#82A +CC05M	2/3	Full blue (CTB) +Sun 1/4 (CTO)	2	1/4 Plusgreen	1/3	Sun 1/2 (CTO)	1/2	1/4 Minusgreen +1/4 blue	1
Durotest Optima 32	#81 +CC05M	2/3	#80C +#82A	1 1/3	1/4 blue +UV Filter	1/2	Sun 1/2 (CTO) +Sun 1/4 (CTO)	1	1/4 Minusgreen +Sun 1/4 (CTO)	2/3	Half blue +1/4 blue	1 1/2
General Electric Chroma 50	CC05M +#81 +#85	1 1/3	CC10M +#82A	2/3	Full blue (CTB) +1/4 Plusgreen +Sun 1/8 (CTO)	2	1/4 Plusgreen	1/3	Sun 1/2(CTO) +1/4 Minusgreen	1	Minusgreen +1/4 blue	1 1/3
General Electric SPX-35	CC40R +#81A	1	CC15M +CC30B	1	Half blue Plusgreen +1/3 blue	2	Plusgreen + 1/2 Plusgreen	2/3	1/2 Minusgreen +Sun 1/4 (CTO) + 1/4 Minusgreen +Sun 1/4 (CTO)	1 1/2	Half blue + 1/2 Minusgreen + 1/4 Minusgreen	1 2/3

Check with color temperature meter. S.I.* = Stop Increase L. L.* = Light Loss in Stops

Sunpath Computer Software

One of the most difficult parts of cinematography is scouting specific locations for a film that actually will be shot at another time of the year. A valuable tool used by many cinematographers is Sunpath computer software. Cinematographers using Sunpath can accurately predict the sun's position at virtually any location at any time of the year. This ensures that a production company can forecast on the actual day of photography how much available light will be "available." The software also plots out the location of the sun at each hour of the day, enabling you to predict when or if the sun will be obscured by landscape features or buildings. Sunpath contains a comprehensive, worldwide database of over 39,000 locations. The database includes coordinates, time zone, daylight saving's time and magnetic declination information for each location. The filmmaker simply selects the location and date range. Sunpath will display the sun's information on the screen and in a detailed printed report. The report contains a daily summary of sunrise, sunset, day length, estimated "magic hour" times, and the sun's position in 15-minute intervals with shadow-length information and a graphical plot of the sun's path during the day. Filmmakers take the printed report to locations, leaving the computer behind.

The size of the sun as seen from earth is 0° 32' 35" or about ½°. The sun moves 15° every hour; 1° every four minutes

In the northern hemisphere, the longest day is June 21, the shortest is December 22. The reverse is true in the south.

Cities with the approx. Latitudes.
The first are cities in the US followed by Cities outside the US.
The format is City, State/Country

USA

City	Latitude	City	Latitude
Anchorage, AK	61°N	Boston, MA	42°N
Los Angeles, CA	34°N	Detroit, MI	42°N
San Francisco, CA	38°N	Atlantic City, NJ	39°N
Denver, CO	40°N	Las Vegas, NV	36°N
Washington, DC	39°N	New York, NY	41°N
Miami, FL	26°N	Portland, OR	46°N
Orlando, FL	29°N	Philadelphia, PA	40°N
Atlanta, GA	34°N	Sioux Falls, SD	44°N
Honolulu, HI	21°N	Memphis, TN	35°N
Des Moines, IA	42°N	Dallas, TX	33°N
Boise, ID	44°N	Houston, TX	30°N
Chicago, IL	42°N	Seattle, WA	48°N
New Orleans, LA	30°N	Jackson, WY	44°N

Outside USA			
Algiers, Algeria	37°N	New Delhi, India	29°N
Buenos Aires, Argentina	35°S	Jakarta, Indonesia	6°S
Melbourne, Australia	38°S	Dublin, Ireland	53°N
Sydney, Australia	34°S	Jerusalem, Israel	32°N
Vienna, Austria	48°N	Rome, Italy	42°N
Nassau, Bahamas	25°N	Venice, Italy	45°N
Brasilia, Brazil	16°S	Kingston, Jamaica	18°N
Rio De Janeiro, Brazil	23°S	Tokyo, Japan	36°N
Sofia, Bulgaria	43°N	Amman, Jordan	32°N
Rangoon, Burma	17°N	Nairobi, Kenya	1°S
Phnom Penh, Cambodia	12°N	Acapulco, Mexico	17°N
Montreal, Canada	46°N	Mexico City, Mexico	19°N
Toronto, Canada	44°N	Amsterdam, Netherlands	52°N
Vancouver, Canada	49°N	Auckland, New Zealand	37°S
Santiago, Chile	34°S	Wellington, New Zealand	41°S
Beijing, China	40°N	Islamabad, Pakistan	34°N
Hong Kong, China	22°N	Manila, Philippines	15°N
Shanghai, China	31°N	Warsaw, Poland	52°N
Bogota, Colombia	5°N	Lisbon, Portugal	39°N
Prague, Czech Republic	50°N	Moscow, Russia	56°N
Copenhagen, Denmark	56°N	Vladivostok, Russia	43°N
Cairo, Egypt	30°N	Riyadh, Saudi Arabia	25°N
Helsinki, Finland	60°N	Singapore City, Singapore	1°N
Nice, France	44°N	Cape Town, South Africa	34°S
Paris, France	49°N	Johannesburg, South Africa	26°S
Berlin, Germany	53°N	Seoul, South Korea	38°N
Munich, Germany	48°N	Madrid, Spain	40°N
Athens, Greece	38°N	Stockholm, Sweden	59°N
Budapest, Hungary	48°N	Geneva, Switzerland	46°N
Reykjavik, Iceland	64°N	Bangkok, Thailand	14°N
Bombay, India	19°N	Edinburgh, United Kingdom	56°N
Calcutta, India	23°N	London, United Kingdom	52°N

Maximum Height of the Sun

Latitude	Jan	Feb	March	April	May	June	July	Aug	Sept	Oct	Nov	Dec
65°N	4°	12°	23°	35°	44°	48°	46°	39°	28°	16°	6°	2°
60°N	9°	17°	28°	40°	49°	53°	51°	44°	33°	21°	11°	7°
55°N	14°	22°	33°	45°	54°	58°	56°	49°	38°	26°	16°	12°
50°N	19°	27°	38°	50°	59°	63°	61°	54°	43°	31°	21°	17°
45°N	24°	32°	43°	55°	64°	68°	66°	59°	48°	36°	26°	22°
40°N	29°	37°	48°	60°	69°	73°	71°	64°	53°	41°	31°	27°
35°N	34°	42°	53°	65°	74°	78°	76°	69°	58°	46°	36°	32°
30°N	39°	47°	58°	70°	79°	83°	81°	74°	63°	51°	41°	37°
25°N	44°	52°	63°	75°	84°	88°	86°	79°	68°	56°	46°	42°
20°N	49°	57°	68°	80°	89°	87°	88°	84°	73°	61°	51°	47°
15°N	54°	62°	73°	85°	86°	82°	83°	89°	78°	66°	56°	52°
10°N	59°	67°	78°	90°	81°	77°	78°	86°	83°	71°	61°	57°
5°N	61°	72°	83°	85°	76°	72°	73°	81°	88°	76°	66°	60°
0°	69°	77°	87°	80°	71°	67°	68°	76°	87°	81°	71°	67°
5°S	74°	82°	87°	75°	66°	62°	63°	71°	82°	86°	76°	72°
10°S	79°	87°	82°	70°	61°	57°	58°	66°	77°	89°	81°	77°
15°S	84°	88°	77°	65°	56°	52°	53°	61°	72°	84°	86°	82°
20°S	88°	83°	72°	60°	51°	47°	48°	56°	67°	79°	89°	87°

Maximum Height of the Sun

Latitude	Jan	Feb	March	April	May	June	July	Aug	Sept	Oct	Nov	Dec
25°S	86°	78°	67°	55°	46°	42°	43°	51°	62°	74°	84°	88°
30°S	81°	73°	62°	50°	41°	37°	38°	46°	57°	69°	79°	83°
35°S	76°	68°	57°	45°	36°	32°	33°	41°	52°	64°	74°	78°
40°S	71°	63°	52°	40°	31°	27°	28°	36°	47°	59°	69°	73°
45°S	66°	58°	47°	35°	26°	22°	24°	31°	42°	54°	64°	68°
50°S	61°	53°	42°	30°	21°	17°	19°	26°	37°	49°	59°	63°
55°S	56°	48°	37°	25°	16°	12°	14°	21°	32°	44°	54°	58°
60°S	51°	43°	32°	20°	11°	7°	9°	16°	27°	39°	49°	53°

Hours of Daylight

Latitude	Jan	Feb	March	April	May	June	July	Aug	Sept	Oct	Nov	Dec
65°N	5.0	8.5	11.8	15.3	18.8	21.9	20.0	16.5	13.0	9.6	6.2	3.6
60°N	6.7	9.2	11.8	14.6	17.2	18.8	18.0	15.6	12.8	10.1	7.5	5.9
55°N	7.8	9.7	11.9	14.2	16.2	17.4	16.8	14.9	12.7	10.5	8.4	7.2
50°N	8.5	10.1	11.9	13.8	15.5	16.4	15.9	14.5	12.6	10.8	9.0	8.1
45°N	9.2	10.4	11.9	13.5	14.9	15.6	15.3	14.0	12.5	11.0	9.5	8.8
40°N	9.7	10.7	12.0	13.3	14.4	15.0	14.7	13.7	12.4	11.2	10.0	9.4
35°N	10.1	10.9	12.0	13.1	14.0	14.5	14.3	13.5	12.4	11.3	10.3	9.8

Hours of Daylight

Latitude	Jan	Feb	March	April	May	June	July	Aug	Sept	Oct	Nov	Dec
30°N	10.4	11.1	12.0	12.9	13.7	14.1	13.9	13.2	12.3	11.4	10.6	10.2
25°N	10.8	11.3	12.0	12.8	13.4	13.7	13.5	13.0	12.3	11.6	10.9	10.6
20°N	11.1	11.5	12.0	12.6	13.1	13.3	13.2	12.8	12.3	11.7	11.2	11.0
15°N	11.3	11.7	12.1	12.5	12.8	13.0	12.9	12.6	12.2	11.8	11.4	11.3
10°N	11.6	12.8	12.1	12.4	12.6	12.7	12.6	12.5	12.2	11.9	11.6	11.5
5°N	11.9	12.0	12.1	12.2	12.4	12.4	12.4	12.3	12.1	12.0	11.9	11.8
0°	12.0	12.0	12.1	12.0	12.0	12.0	12.0	12.0	12.1	12.0	12.0	12.0
5°S	12.4	12.3	12.1	12.0	11.9	11.8	11.9	12.0	12.1	12.2	12.4	12.4
10°S	13.7	12.4	12.2	11.9	11.7	11.6	11.6	11.8	12.0	12.3	12.6	12.7
15°S	12.9	12.6	12.2	11.8	11.4	11.3	11.3	11.6	12.0	12.4	12.8	13.0
20°S	13.2	12.8	12.2	11.6	11.2	10.9	11.0	11.4	12.0	12.6	13.1	13.3
25°S	13.5	12.9	12.2	11.5	10.9	10.6	10.7	11.3	12.0	12.7	13.4	13.7
30°S	13.9	13.1	12.3	11.3	10.6	10.2	10.4	11.1	11.9	12.8	13.7	14.1
35°S	14.3	13.4	12.3	11.2	10.3	9.8	10.0	10.8	11.9	13.0	14.0	14.5
40°S	14.7	13.6	12.3	11.0	9.9	9.3	9.6	10.6	11.9	13.2	14.4	15.0
45°S	15.2	13.9	12.4	10.8	9.5	8.8	9.1	10.3	11.8	13.4	14.8	15.6
50°S	15.9	14.3	12.5	10.5	9.0	8.1	8.5	9.9	11.8	13.6	15.4	16.4
55°S	16.7	14.7	12.5	10.2	8.3	7.2	7.7	9.5	11.7	13.9	16.1	17.3
60°S	18.0	15.3	12.6	9.8	7.4	5.9	6.6	8.9	11.6	14.3	17.1	18.8

Calculations were made for the 15th of each month using sunPATH

Sunrise / Sunset at Sea Level (Azimuth Bearings from True North)

Latitude	Jan Sunrise/Sunset	Feb Sunrise/Sunset	March Sunrise/Sunset	April Sunrise/Sunset	May Sunrise/Sunset	June Sunrise/Sunset
65°N	145°/215°	119°/241°	93°/268°	64°/297°	37°/324°	14°/346°
60°N	134°/226°	115°/246°	92°/268°	68°/292°	47°/313°	35°/325°
55°N	127°/233°	111°/249°	92°/268°	71°/289°	54°/306°	45°/315°
50°N	123°/237°	109°/251°	92°/268°	73°/287°	58°/302°	51°/309°
45°N	120°/240°	107°/253°	92°/268°	75°/285°	62°/298°	55°/305°
40°N	117°/243°	106°/254°	92°/268°	76°/284°	64°/296°	58°/302°
35°N	115°/245°	105°/255°	92°/268°	77°/283°	66°/294°	60°/300°
30°N	114°/246°	104°/256°	92°/268°	78°/282°	68°/293°	62°/298°
25°N	113°/247°	104°/257°	92°/268°	79°/281°	69°/292°	64°/296°
20°N	112°/248°	103°/257°	92°/268°	79°/281°	70°/291°	65°/295°
15°N	112°/248°	103°/257°	92°/268°	80°/281°	70°/290°	66°/294°
10°N	111°/249°	103°/257°	92°/268°	80°/280°	71°/289°	66°/294°
5°N	111°/249°	103°/258°	92°/268°	80°/280°	71°/289°	67°/294°
0°	111°/249°	103°/258°	92°/268°	80°/280°	71°/289°	67°/293°
5°S	111°/249°	103°/257°	92°/268°	80°/280°	71°/289°	67°/293°

Sunrise / Sunset at Sea Level (Azimuth Bearings from True North)

Latitude	Jan Sunrise/Sunset	Feb Sunrise/Sunset	March Sunrise/Sunset	April Sunrise/Sunset	May Sunrise/Sunset	June Sunrise/Sunset
10°S	112°/248°	103°/257°	92°/268°	80°/280°	71°/289°	66°/294°
15°S	112°/248°	103°/257°	92°/268°	80°/280°	71°/289°	66°/294°
20°S	113°/247°	104°/256°	93°/268°	80°/280°	70°/290°	65°/295°
25°S	114°/246°	104°/256°	93°/268°	80°/281°	69°/291°	65°/295°
30°S	115°/245°	105°/255°	93°/267°	79°/281°	69°/292°	63°/297°
35°S	117°/243°	106°/254°	93°/267°	79°/282°	67°/293°	62°/298°
40°S	119°/241°	107°/253°	93°/267°	78°/282°	66°/294°	60°/300°
45°S	122°/239°	109°/251°	94°/267°	77°/283°	64°/297°	57°/303°
50°S	125°/235°	111°/249°	94°/266°	75°/285°	61°/299°	53°/307°
55°S	131°/230°	114°/246°	95°/266°	74°/287°	57°/303°	48°/312°
60°S	138°/222°	118°/243°	95°/265°	71°/289°	51°/309°	40°/320°

Sunrise / Sunset at Sea Level (Azimuth Bearings from True North)

Latitude	July Sunrise/Sunset	Aug Sunrise/Sunset	Sept Sunrise/Sunset	Oct Sunrise/Sunset	Nov Sunrise/Sunset	Dec Sunrise/Sunset
65°N	26°/333°	53°/306°	81°/278°	109°/250°	137°/223°	155°/205°
60°N	41°/319°	60°/300°	83°/277°	106°/253°	128°/232°	140°/220°
55°N	49°/311°	64°/296°	84°/276°	104°/256°	122°/237°	!32°/228°
50°N	54°/306°	67°/293°	84°/275°	103°/257°	119°/241°	127°/233°
45°N	58°/302°	69°/291°	85°/275°	101°/258°	116°/244°	123°/237°
40°N	61°/299°	71°/289°	85°/274°	101°/259°	114°/246°	120°/240°
35°N	63°/297°	72°/288°	86°/274°	100°/260°	112°/248°	118°/242°
30°N	64°/295°	73°/287°	86°/274°	99°/260°	111°/249°	117°/243°
25°N	66°/294°	74°/286°	86°/273°	99°/261°	110°/250°	115°/245°
20°N	67°/293°	75°/285°	86°/273°	99°/261°	109°/250°	115°/245°
15°N	67°/292°	75°/285°	87°/273°	99°/261°	109°/251°	114°/246°
10°N	68°/292°	76°/284°	87°/273°	99°/261°	109°/251°	114°/246°
5°N	68°/292°	76°/284°	87°/273°	98°/261°	108°/251°	113°/247°
0°	68°/291°	76°/284°	87°/273°	99°/261°	108°/251°	113°/247°
5°S	68°/291°	76°/284°	87°/273°	99°/261°	109°/251°	113°/247°

Sunrise / Sunset at Sea Level (Azimuth Bearings from True North)

Latitude	July Sunrise/Sunset	Aug Sunrise/Sunset	Sept Sunrise/Sunset	Oct Sunrise/Sunset	Nov Sunrise/Sunset	Dec Sunrise/Sunset
10°S	68°/292°	76°/284°	87°/273°	99°/261°	109°/251°	114°/246°15°S
15°S	68°/292°	76°/284°	87°/273°	99°/261°	109°/250°	114°/246°
20°S	67°/293°	75°/284°	87°/273°	99°/260°	110°/250°	115°/245°
25°S	67°/293°	75°/285°	87°/273°	100°/260°	111°/249°	116°/244°
30°S	65°/294°	74°/286°	87°/273°	100°/259°	112°/248°	118°/242°
35°S	64°/296°	73°/286°	87°/273°	101°/259°	113°/246°	119°/240°
40°S	62°/298°	72°/287°	87°/273°	102°/258°	115°/244°	122°/238°
45°S	60°/300°	71°/289°	87°/273°	103°/257°	118°/242°	125°/235°
50°S	57°/303°	69°/291°	87°/273°	105°/255°	121°/239°	129°/231°
55°S	52°/308°	67°/293°	86°/273°	107°/253°	125°/234°	135°/225°
60°S	45°/315°	63°/297°	86°/274°	109°/250°	132°/228°	145°/215°

Calculations were made for the 15th of each month using sunPATH

EASTMAN KODAK — Color Negative Films

Color Negative	Balance	Emulsion Type 35mm/16mm	Edge	EI			
				T	filter	D	filter
Kodak Vision2 50D	D	5201/7201	EK	12	80A	50	–
Kodak Vision2 100T	T	5212/7212	EM	100	–	64	85
Kodak Vision2 200T	T	5217/7217	EL	200	–	125	85
Kodak Vision2 500T	T	5218/7218	EH	500	–	320	85
Kodak Vision2 Expression 500T	T	5229/7229	EB	500	–	320	85
Kodak Vision2 250D	D	5205/7205	EQ	64	80A	250	–
Kodak Vision 500T	T	5279/7279	KU	500	–	320	85
Kodak Vision2 HD	T	5299/7299	EI	500	–	320	85

All stocks also available in 65mm.
All print stocks are 70mm. All camera stocks are 65mm

EASTMAN KODAK — Color Reversal Films

Color Reversal	Balance	Emulsion Type 35mm\16mm	Edge	EI			
				T	filter	D	filter
Kodak Ektachrome 100D	D	5285/7285	EA	25	80A	100	–

EASTMAN KODAK — Color Reversal Films

Color Reversal	Balance	Emulsion Type 8mm ONLY	Edge	EI			
				T	filter	D	filter
Kodak Ektachrome 64T	T	7280	KCD	64	–	40	85

EASTMAN KODAK — Black-and-White Negative Films

B&W Negative	Emulsion Type 35mm/16mm	Edge	EI T	EI D
Eastman Double-X	5222/7222	E	200	250
Eastman Plus-X	5231/7231	H	64	80

EASTMAN KODAK — Black-and-White Reversal Films

B&W Reversal	Emulsion Type 16mm	Edge	EI T	EI D
Kodak Tri-X Reversal	7266 (16mm only)	ED	160	200
	*in manually operated & automatic Super 8 cameras		160	160
	*for negative processing in motion picture negative developer		100	125
Kodak Plus-X Reversal	7265 (16mm only)	EC	80	100
	*in manually operated Super 8 cameras		80	100
	*in automatic Super 8 cameras		80	64
	*for negative processing in motion picture negative developer		20	25

EASTMAN KODAK — Super 8 Films

Color Negative and Reversal		T	D
Kodak Vision2 (7217)	200T	200	125 (with an 85 filter)
Kodak Vision2 (7218)	500T	500	320 (with an 85 filter)
Kodak Ektachrome (7280)	64T	64	40 (with an 85 filter)
Black and White Reversal		**T**	**D**
Tri-X Reversal (7266)		160	200
Plus-X Reversal (7265)		80	100

EASTMAN KODAK — Laboratory Films

Color Print Film	**Emulsion Type 35mm/16mm**
Kodak Vision Color Teleprint Film	2395/3395
Kodak Vision Premier Color Print Film	2393 (35mm & 70mm only)
Kodak Vision Color Print Film	2383/3383
Black and White Print Film	**Emulsion Type 35mm/16mm**
Eastman Fine Grain Release Positive Film	5302/7302
Kodak Black and White Print Film	2302/3302
Black and White Reversal Print Film	7367 (16mm only)
Color Intermediate Films	**Emulsion Type 35mm/16mm**
Kodak Vision Color Intermediate Film	2242/5242/7242/3242
Kodak Vision Color Internegative II Film	2272/5272/7272/3272
Black and White Intermediate Films	**Emulsion Type 35mm/16mm**
Kodak Vision Fine Grain Duplicating Positive Film	2366/5366/7366/3366/2365
Kodak Vision Fine Grain Duplicating Panchromatic Negative Film	2234/5234/7234/3234
Kodak Vision High Contrast Panchromatic Film	2369/3369/5369
Kodak Vision High Contrast Positive Film II	5363/7363
Kodak Vision Panchromatic Separation Film	2238 (35mm and 65mm only)
Sound Film	**Emulsion Type 35mm/16mm**
Kodak Panchromatic Sound Recording Film	2374/3374
Eastman EXR Sound Recording Film	2378/3378
Direct Motion Picture Film (B&W reversal duping film for B&W or color negatives and positives)	**Emulsion Type 35mm/16mm**
Kodak Vision Direct MP Film	Estar Base 2360/5360

FUJI Film — Color Negative Films

Color Negative	Balance	Emulsion Type 35mm/16mm	Edge	ASA\ISO T	filter	D	filter
ETERNA 500	T	8573/8673	FN73	500	–	320	85
REALA 500D	D	8592/8692	FN92	125	80A	500	–
ETERNA 400	T	8583/8683	FN83	400	–	250	85
ETERNA 250	T	8553/8653	FN53	250	–	160	85
ETERNA 250D	D	8563/8663	FN63	64	80A	250	–
ETERNA VIVID 160	T	8543/8643	FN43	160	–	100	85
F-125	T	8532/8632	N32	125	–	80	85
F-64D	D	8522/8622	N22	16	80A	64	–

FUJI Film — Laboratory Films

Color print film	Emulsion Type 35mm/16mm
Fujicolor positive film ETERNA	3510/3610 (not available in U.S.) 3513DI/3613DI 3521XD (35mm, higher contrast film, available in U.S. only)
Black-and-White Print Film	**Emulsion Type 35mm**
Panchromatic High-Con, fine grain positive film	71371
Color Intermediate Films	**Emulsion Type 35mm**
Fujicolor intermediate film	8502 (acetate base) 4502 (estar base)
ETERNA RDI (for digital intermediates)	8511 (acetate base) 4511 (estar base)
ETERNA CI	8503 (acetate base) 4503 (estar base)

FILM WEIGHT IN CANS

16mm	35mm
100 ft. = 3 ¼ oz. (200 grams) 400 ft. = 1 lb. (500 grams)	400 ft. = 2 lbs. 3 oz. (1 Kg.) 1000 ft. = 5 lbs. 8 oz. (2.5 Kg.)
65mm	
1000 ft. = 10 lbs. (4.54 Kg.)	

COMPARISON OF FILM SPEEDS

EI/ASA/ BSI/JSA	Weston	General Electric	DIN	GOST	SCHEINER
3	2.5	4	6	2.8	16°
4	3	4.5	7	3.6	17°
5	4	6	8	4.5	18°
6	5	8	9	5.8	19°
8	6	10	10	7.2	20°
10	8	12	11	9	21°
12	10	16	12	11	22°
16	12	20	13	14	23°
20	16	24	14	18	24°
25	20	32	15	23	25°
32	24	40	16	29	26°
40	32	48	17	36	27°
50	40	64	18	45	28°
64	50	80	19	58	29°
80	64	100	20	72	30°
100	80	125	21	90	31°
125	100	150	22	112	32°
160	125	200	23	144	33°
200	160	250	24	180	34°
250	200	300	25	225	35°
320	250	400	26	288	36°
400	320	500	27	360	37°
500	400	600	28	450	38°
640	500	800	29	576	39°
800	650	900	30	720	40°
1000	800	1000	31	900	41°
1250	1000	NA	32	1125	42°
1600	1250	NA	33	1440	43°
2000	1600	NA	34	1800	44°
2500	2000	NA	35	2250	45°
3200	2500	NA	36	2880	46°

For practical purposes EI/ASA/BSA/JSA are the same. The DIN system is calculated Log 10. In the past DIN speeds were written with the speed number followed by /10. (example: 2/10) The Scheiner system is obsolete. It was distinguished by ° following the number. Today ° is used with DIN speeds. The Weston and General Electric systems are also obsolete. The GOST system was used in Russia.

Incident Key Light/T-Stop
(Foot Candles)

EI/ASA	2000	1600	1250	1000	800	640	500	400	320
T-stop 1.4	1.25	1.5	2	2.5	3	4	5	6	8
1.6	1.5	2	2.5	3	4	5	6	8	10
1.8	2	2.5	3	4	5	6	8	10	12
2	2.5	3	4	5	6	8	10	12	16
2.2	3	4	5	6	8	10	12	16	20
2.5	4	5	6	8	10	12	16	20	25
2.8	5	6	8	10	12	16	20	25	32
3.2	6	8	10	12	16	20	25	32	40
3.5	8	10	12	16	20	25	32	40	50
4	10	12	16	20	25	32	40	50	64
4.5	12	16	20	25	32	40	50	64	80
5	16	20	25	32	40	50	64	80	100
5.6	20	25	32	40	50	64	80	100	125
6.3	25	32	40	50	64	80	100	125	160
7	32	40	50	64	80	100	125	160	200
8	40	50	64	80	100	125	160	200	250
9	50	64	80	100	125	160	200	250	320
10	64	80	100	125	160	200	250	320	400
11	80	100	125	160	200	250	320	400	500
12.7	100	125	160	200	250	320	400	500	650
14	125	160	200	250	320	400	500	650	800
16	160	200	250	320	400	500	650	800	1000
18	200	250	320	400	500	650	800	1000	1290
20	250	320	400	500	650	800	1000	1290	1625
22	320	400	500	650	800	1000	1290	1625	2050

Most cinematography is at 24 frames per second. The table is calculated for foot candles incident light on a fully lighted subject at 1⁄50 second exposure (172.8°precisely, but 170° to 180° varies from this by less than a printer point for normally processed color negative). For photography at 1⁄60 second (30 frames per second, 180° shutter; or 24 frames per second, 144° shutter), use one-third wider lens stop or one column to the right (one ASA step lower) on the incident light table.

Incident Key Light/T-Stop
(Foot Candles)

EI/ASA	250	200	160	125	100	80	64	50	40
T-stop 1.4	10	12	16	20	25	32	40	50	64
1.6	12	16	20	25	32	40	50	64	80
1.8	16	20	25	32	40	50	64	80	100
2	20	25	32	40	50	64	80	100	125
2.2	25	32	40	50	64	80	100	125	160
2.5	32	40	50	64	80	100	125	160	200
2.8	40	50	64	80	100	125	160	200	250
3.2	50	64	80	100	125	160	200	250	320
3.5	64	80	100	125	160	200	250	320	400
4	80	100	125	160	200	250	320	400	500
4.5	100	125	160	200	250	320	400	500	650
5	125	160	200	250	320	400	500	650	800
5.6	160	200	250	320	400	500	650	800	1000
6.3	200	250	320	400	500	650	800	1000	1290
7	250	320	400	500	650	800	1000	1290	1625
8	320	400	500	650	800	1000	1290	1625	2050
9	400	500	650	800	1000	1290	1625	2050	2580
10	500	650	800	1000	1290	1625	2050	2580	3250
11	650	800	1000	1290	1625	2050	2580	3250	4100
12.7	800	1000	1290	1625	2050	2580	3250	4100	5160
14	1000	1290	1625	2050	2580	3250	4100	5160	6500
16	1290	1625	2050	2580	3250	4100	5160	6500	8200
18	1625	2050	2580	3250	4100	5160	6500	8200	10000
20	2050	2580	3250	4100	5160	6500	8200	10000	
22	2580	3250	4100	5160	6500	8200	10000		

COMPARISON OF LIGHT VALUES

1 Footcandle = 10.764 Lux

1 Lux = .0929 Footcandles

1 Foot Lambert = 3.426 candelas per square meter

1 Candela per square meter = .292 Foot Lamberts

Incident Key Light/T-Stop
(Foot Candles)

EI/ASA	32	25	20	16	12	10	8	6
T-stop 1.4	80	100	125	160	200	250	320	400
1.6	100	125	160	200	250	320	400	500
1.8	125	160	200	250	320	400	500	650
2	160	200	250	320	400	500	650	800
2.2	200	250	320	400	500	650	800	1000
2.5	250	320	400	500	650	800	1000	1290
2.8	320	400	500	650	800	1000	1290	1625
3.2	400	500	650	800	1000	1290	1625	2050
3.5	500	650	800	1000	1290	1625	2050	2580
4	650	800	1000	1290	1625	2050	2580	3250
4.5	800	1000	1290	1625	2050	2580	3250	4100
5	1000	1290	1625	2050	2580	3250	4100	5160
5.6	1290	1625	2050	2580	3250	4100	5160	6500
6.3	1625	2050	2580	3250	4100	5160	6500	8200
7	2050	2580	3250	4100	5160	6500	8200	10,000
8	2580	3250	4100	5160	6500	8200	10,000	
9	3250	4100	5160	6500	8200	10,000		
10	4100	5160	6500	8200	10,000			
11	5160	6500	8200	10,000				
12.7	6500	8200	10,000					
14	8200	10,000						
16	10,000							
18								
20								
22								

1 Foot Lambert = .31831 Candelas per square foot
1 Foot Lambert = .0010764 Lamberts
1 Foot Lambert = 1 Lumen per square foot
1 Lumen = .07958 Candle Power (spherical)
1 Lumen = .00015 Watts

EI/ASA Exposure Index Reduction Table

(Figures are rounded to nearest exposure index Example: ASA 200 with factor of 4 is reduced to ASA 50.)

	Filter or Other Factor										
ASA	**1.5**	**2**	**2.5**	**3**	**4**	**5**	**8**	**12**	**16**	**24**	**32**
1000	640	500	400	320	250	200	125	80	64	40	32
800	500	400	320	250	200	160	100	64	50	32	25
640	400	320	250	200	160	125	80	50	40	25	20
500	320	250	200	160	125	100	64	40	32	20	16
400	250	200	160	125	100	80	50	32	25	16	12
320	200	160	125	100	80	64	40	24	20	12	10
250	160	125	100	80	64	50	32	20	16	10	8
200	125	100	80	64	50	40	25	16	12	8	6
160	100	80	64	50	40	32	20	12	10	6	5
125	80	64	50	40	32	25	16	10	8	5	4
100	64	50	40	32	25	20	12	8	6	4	3
80	50	40	32	25	20	16	10	6	5	3	2.5
64	40	32	24	20	16	12	8	5	4	2.5	2
50	32	25	20	16	12	10	6	4	3	2	1.6
40	25	20	16	12	10	8	5	3	2.5	1.6	1.2
32	20	16	12	10	8	6	4	2.5	2	1.2	1
25	16	12	10	8	6	5	3	2	1.6	1	
20	12	10	8	6	5	4	2.5	1.6	1.2		
16	10	8	6	5	4	3	2	1.2	1		
12	8	6	5	4	3	2.5	1.6	1			
10	6	5	4	3	2.5	2	1.2				
8	5	4	3	2.5	2	1.6	1				

T-Stop Compensation for Camera Speed
(constant shutter)

fps	**6**	7.5	9.5	**12**	15	19	**24**	30	38	**48**
ft/min	**22.5**	28	36	**45**	56	71	**90**	112	142	**180**
	2.8	2.5	2.2	**2**	1.8	1.6	**1.4**	1.3	1.1	**1**
	3.2	2.8	2.5	2.2	2	1.8	1.6	1.4	1.3	1.1
	3.5	3.2	2.8	2.5	2.2	2	1.8	1.6	1.4	1.3
	4	3.5	3.2	**2.8**	2.5	2.2	**2**	1.8	1.6	**1.4**
	4.5	4	3.5	3.2	2.8	2.5	2.2	2	1.8	1.6
	5	4.5	4	3.5	3.2	2.8	2.5	2.2	2	1.8
	5.6	5	4.5	**4**	3.5	3.2	**2.8**	2.5	2.2	**2**
	6.3	5.6	5	4.5	4	3.5	3.2	2.8	2.5	2.2
	7	6.3	5.6	5	4.5	4	3.5	3.2	2.8	2.5
	8	7	6.3	**5.6**	5	4.5	**4**	3.5	3.2	**2.8**
	9	8	7	6.3	5.6	5	4.5	4	3.5	3.2
	10	9	8	7	6.3	5.6	5	4.5	4	3.5
	11	10	9	**8**	7	6.3	**5.6**	5	4.5	**4**
	12.7	11	10	9	8	7	6.3	5.6	5	4.5
	14	12.7	11	10	9	8	7	6.3	5.6	5
	16	14	12.7	**11**	10	9	**8**	7	6.3	**5.6**
	18	16	14	12.7	11	10	9	8	7	6.3
	20	18	16	14	12.7	11	10	9	8	7
	22	20	18	**16**	14	12.7	**11**	10	9	**8**
	25	22	20	18	16	14	12.7	11	10	9
	28	25	22	20	18	16	14	12.7	11	10
	32	28	25	**22**	20	18	**16**	14	12.7	**11**
	35	32	28	25	22	20	18	16	14	12.7
	40	35	32	28	25	22	20	18	16	14
	45	40	35	**32**	28	25	**22**	20	18	**16**

T-Stop Compensation for Camera Speed — continued
(constant shutter)

fps	60	76	**96**	120	150	**192**	240	300	**384**	484
ft/min	225	285	**360**	450	562	**720**	900	1125	**1440**	1815
	.9	.8	**.7**							
	1	.9	.8	.7						
	1.1	1	.9	.8	.7					
	1.3	1.1	**1**	.9	.8	**.7**				
	1.4	1.3	1.1	1	.9	.8	.7			
	1.6	1.4	1.3	1.1	1	.9	.8	.7		
	1.8	1.6	**1.4**	1.3	1.1	**1**	.9	.8	**.7**	
	2	1.8	1.6	1.4	1.3	1.1	1	.9	.8	.7
	2.2	2	1.8	1.6	1.4	1.3	1.1	1	.9	.8
	2.5	2.2	**2**	1.8	1.6	**1.4**	1.3	1.1	**1**	.9
	2.8	2.5	2.2	2	1.8	1.6	1.4	1.3	1.1	1
	3.2	2.8	2.5	2.2	2	1.8	1.6	1.4	1.3	1.1
	3.5	3.2	**2.8**	2.5	2.2	**2**	1.8	1.6	**1.4**	1.3
	4	3.5	3.2	2.8	2.5	2.2	2	1.8	1.6	1.4
	4.5	4	3.5	3.2	2.8	2.5	2.2	2	1.8	1.6
	5	4.5	**4**	3.5	3.2	**2.8**	2.5	2.2	**2**	1.8
	5.6	5	4.5	4	3.5	3.2	2.8	2.5	2.2	2
	6.3	5.6	5	4.5	4	3.5	3.2	2.8	2.5	2.2
	7	6.3	**5.6**	5	4.5	**4**	3.5	3.2	**2.8**	2.5
	8	7	6.3	5.6	5	4.5	4	3.5	3.2	2.8
	9	8	7	6.3	5.6	5	4.5	4	3.5	3.2
	10	9	**8**	7	6.3	**5.6**	5	4.5	**4**	3.5
	11	10	9	8	7	6.3	5.6	5	4.5	4
	12.7	11	10	9	8	7	6.3	5.6	5	4.5
	14	12.7	**11**	10	9	**8**	7	6.3	**5.6**	5

Shutter Angle / f.p.s. / T-stop change

(for 24 or 30 f.p.s. projection)

f.p.s.	**24**	22	20	**19**	18	16	**15**	14	**12**	**9.5**	**7.6**	**6.**	**4.8(5)**	**3.8(4)**	**3**	**2.4**
f.p.s.	**30**	27	25	**24**	22	20	**19**	17	**15**	**12**	**9.5**	**7.6**	**6.**	**5(4.8)**	**4(3.8)**	**3**
Exposure change in T-stops	0			**1/3**			**2/3**		**1**	**1 1/3**	**1 2/3**	**2**	**2 1/3**	**2 2/3**	**3**	**3 1/3**
Maximum Shutter	235°	215°	196°	**188°**	176°	157°	**147°**	137°	**118°**	**93°**	**74°**	**59°**	**47°**	**37°**	**29°**	**24°**
	200	183°	167°	**158°**	150°	133°	**125°**	117°	**100°**	**79°**	**63°**	**50°**	**40°**	**32°**	**25°**	**20°**
	180	165°	150°	**143°**	135°	120°	**113°**	105°	**90°**	**71°**	**57°**	**45°**	**36°**	**29°**	**23°**	**18°**
	170	156°	142°	**135°**	128°	113°	**106°**	99°	**85°**	**67°**	**54°**	**43°**	**34°**	**27°**	**21°**	**17°**
	150	138°	125°	**119°**	113°	100°	**94°**	88°	**75°**	**59°**	**48°**	**38°**	**30°**	**24°**	**19°**	**15°**
	140	128°	117°	**111°**	105°	93°	**88°**	82°	**70°**	**55°**	**44°**	**35°**	**28°**	**22°**	**18°**	**14°**
	135	124°	113°	**107°**	101°	90°	**84°**	79°	**68°**	**53°**	**43°**	**34°**	**27°**	**21°**	**17°**	**14°**

If it is desired to slow the camera without varying the lens stop but maintain constant exposure:

If it is desired to reduce exposure without varying the lens stop:

If it is desired to reduce the exposure time per frame without reducing exposure:

This table gives shutter angles in one-third T-stop exposure intervals (bold columns) as well as for some camera speeds in less than one-third stop intervals.

SHUTTER ANGLE COMPENSATOR FOR CONSTANT EXPOSURE

(Below 24 F.P.S.)

Choose any shutter angle in left column,
then read across to find reduced angle at lower speeds.
(These are exact shutter angles for perfectly constant exposure.
In practice it may be necessary to use the nearest calibrated angle.)

(Constant Lens Aperture)

FRAMES PER SECOND							
24	22	20	18	16	14	12	8
235°	215°	196°	176°	153°	134°	118°	77°
200°	183°	167°	150°	133°	117°	100°	67°
180°	165°	150°	135°	120°	105°	90°	60°
175°	160°	146°	131°	117°	102°	88°	58°
170°	156°	142°	128°	113°	99°	85°	57°
165°	151°	138°	124°	110°	96°	83°	55°
160°	147°	133°	120°	107°	93°	80°	53°
145°	133°	121°	109°	97°	85°	73°	48°
130°	119°	108°	98°	87°	76°	65°	43°
115°	105°	96°	86°	77°	67°	58°	38°
100°	92°	83°	75°	67°	58°	50°	33°
90°	83°	75°	68°	60°	53°	45°	30°
80°	73°	67°	60°	53°	47°	40°	27°
75°	69°	63°	56°	50°	44°	38°	25°
65°	60°	54°	49°	43°	38°	33°	22°
60°	55°	50°	45°	40°	35°	30°	20°
50°	46°	42°	38°	33°	29°	25°	17°
45°	41°	38°	34°	30°	26°	23°	15°

CAMERA SPEED EXPOSURE COMPENSATOR

Exposure Increase and Decrease
Above And Below Normal 24 F.P.S.

ABOVE NORMAL SPEED

Frames Per Second	Factor	Stops Increase (open up)
24	0	0
30	1.25	⅓
38	1.5	⅔
48	2	1
60	2.5	1 ⅓
76	3	1 ⅔
96	4	2
120	5	2 ⅓
150	6	2 ⅔
192	8	3
240	10	3 ⅓
300	12	3 ⅔
384	16	4
484	20	4 ⅓

BELOW NORMAL SPEED

Frames Per Second	Factor	Stops Decrease (close down)
24	0	0
19	1.25	⅓
15	1.5	⅔
12	2	1
9 1/2	2.5	1 ⅓
7 1/2	3	1 ⅔
6	4	2
3	8	3

REDUCED SHUTTER ANGLE EXPOSURE COMPENSATOR

(May be used at any constant camera speed)

Max. shutter exposure time at 24 F.P.S.		Max.	A ⅓ stop exposure is required for each column of reduced shutter angles.								
1/37	(.0272)	235°	188°	147°	118°	93°	74°	59°	47°	37°	29°
1/42	(.0236)	204°	162°	128°	102°	81°	64°	51°	40°	32°	25°
1/43	(.0231)	200°	158°	125°	100°	79°	63°	50°	40°	32°	25°
1/44	(.0226)	195°	155°	123°	97°	77°	61°	49°	39°	31°	24°
1/48	(.0208)	180°	143°	113°	90°	71°	57°	45°	36°	28°	22°
1/49	(.0203)	175°	139°	110°	87°	69°	55°	44°	35°	28°	22°
1/50	(.0200)	173°	137°	109°	86°	68°	54°	43°	34°	27°	22°
1/51	(.0197)	170°	135°	106°	85°	67°	54°	43°	34°	27°	21°
1/52	(.0190)	165°	131°	104°	82°	65°	52°	41°	33°	26°	21°
1/54	(.0185)	160°	127°	101°	80°	63°	50°	40°	32°	25°	20°
1/60	(.0167)	144°	114°	91°	72°	57°	45°	36°	29°	23°	18°
1/66	(.0150)	130°	103°	82°	65°	52°	41°	32°	26°	20°	16°
1/72	(.0139)	120°	95°	76°	60°	48°	38°	30°	24°	19°	15°

(These are exact shutter angles relating to ⅓ stop exposure intervals. In practice it may be necessary to use the nearest calibrated angle.) The maximum shutter angles listed are from actual cameras in use.

Exposure at Various Speeds and Shutter Openings

Shutter Angle	Frames per Second									
	2	4	6	8	10	12	14	16	18	20
280°	2/5	1/5	1/7	1/10	1/13	1/15	1/18	1/21	1/23	1/26
235°	1/3	1/6	1/9	1/12	1/15	1/18	1/21	1/25	1/27	1/31
200°	2/7	1/7	1/11	1/14	1/18	1/22	1/25	1/29	1/32	1/36
180°	1/4	1/8	1/12	1/16	1/20	1/24	1/28	1/32	1/36	1/40
175°	1/4	1/8	1/12	1/16	1/20	1/25	1/29	1/33	1/37	1/41
170°	2/9	1/9	1/13	1/17	1/21	1/26	1/30	1/34	1/38	1/42
160°	2/9	1/9	1/13	1/18	1/22	1/27	1/32	1/36	1/40	1/45
150°	1/5	1/10	1/14	1/19	1/24	1/29	1/33	1/38	1/42	1/48
140°	1/5	1/11	1/15	1/21	1/25	1/31	1/36	1/41	1/45	1/51
135°	1/5	1/11	1/16	1/21	1/26	1/32	1/37	1/43	1/47	1/53
120°	1/6	1/12	1/18	1/24	1/30	1/36	1/42	1/48	1/54	1/60
100°	1/7	1/15	1/21	1/29	1/36	1/43	1/51	1/58	1/65	1/72
90°	1/8	1/16	1/24	1/32	1/40	1/48	1/56	1/64	1/72	1/80
80°	1/9	1/18	1/27	1/36	1/45	1/54	1/63	1/72	1/81	1/90
75°	1/10	1/19	1/28	1/38	1/48	1/57	1/66	1/77	1/84	1/96
60°	1/12	1/24	1/36	1/48	1/60	1/72	1/84	1/96	1/111	1/120
45°	1/16	1/32	1/48	1/64	1/80	1/96	1/112	1/128	1/144	1/160
22.5°	1/32	1/64	1/96	1/128	1/160	1/192	1/224	1/256	1/288	1/320
10°	1/72	1/144	1/216	1/288	1/360	1/432	1/504	1/576	1/648	1/720
5°	1/144	1/288	1/432	1/576	1/720	1/864	1/1008	1/1152	1/1296	1/1440

Exposure at Various Speeds and Shutter Openings — continued

Shutter Angle	Frames per Second									
	22	24	32	40	48	64	72	96	120	128
280°	1/28	1/31	1/41	1/52	1/62	1/82	1/93	1/123	1/154	1/165
235°	1/34	1/37	1/49	1/62	1/77	1/98	1/110	1/147	1/184	1/196
200°	1/38	1/43	1/58	1/72	1/86	1/115	1/130	1/173	1/216	1/230
180°	1/44	1/48	1/64	1/80	1/96	1/128	1/144	1/192	1/240	1/256
175°	1/45	1/49	1/66	1/82	1/99	1/132	1/148	1/197	1/247	1/263
170°	1/47	1/51	1/68	1/84	1/102	1/136	1/152	1/204	1/254	1/271
160°	1/50	1/54	1/72	1/90	1/108	1/144	1/162	1/216	1/270	1/288
150°	1/53	1/58	1/77	1/96	1/115	1/154	1/173	1/230	1/288	1/307
140°	1/56	1/62	1/82	1/102	1/123	1/164	1/185	1/247	1/309	1/329
135°	1/58	1/64	1/85	1/106	1/128	1/171	1/192	1/260	1/320	1/341
120°	1/66	1/72	1/96	1/120	1/144	1/192	1/216	1/288	1/360	1/384
100°	1/76	1/86	1/115	1/144	1/173	1/230	1/259	1/346	1/432	1/461
90°	1/88	1/96	1/128	1/160	1/192	1/256	1/288	1/384	1/480	1/512
80°	1/99	1/108	1/144	1/180	1/216	1/288	1/324	1/432	1/540	1/576
75°	1/106	1/115	1/154	1/192	1/230	1/307	1/346	1/461	1/576	1/614
60°	1/132	1/144	1/192	1/240	1/288	1/384	1/432	1/576	1/720	1/768
45°	1/176	1/192	1/256	1/320	1/384	1/512	1/576	1/768	1/960	1/1024
22.5°	1/352	1/384	1/512	1/640	1/768	1/1024	1/1152	1/1536	1/1920	1/2048
10°	1/792	1/864	1/1152	1/1440	1/1728	1/2304	1/2592	1/3456	1/4320	1/4608
5°	1/1584	1/1728	1/2304	1/2880	1/3456	1/4608	1/5184	1/6912	1/8640	1/9216

Super 8mm Footage Table

Running Times and Film Lengths for Common Projection Speeds

Super 8 (72 frames per foot)					
Projection speed in frames per second		**18**		**24**	
Running time and film length		**Feet**	**+ Frames**	**Feet**	**+ Frames**
Seconds	1	0	18	0	24
	2	0	36	0	48
	3	0	54	1	0
	4	1	0	1	24
	5	1	18	1	48
	6	1	36	2	0
	7	1	54	2	24
	8	2	0	2	48
	9	2	18	3	0
	10	2	36	3	24
	20	5	0	6	48
	30	7	36	10	0
	40	10	0	13	24
	50	12	36	16	48
Minutes	1	15	0	20	0
	2	30	0	40	0
	3	45	0	60	0
	4	60	0	80	0
	5	75	0	100	0
	6	90	0	120	0
	7	105	0	140	0
	8	120	0	160	0
	9	135	0	180	0
	10	150	0	200	0
	15	225	0	300	0
	20	300	0	400	0
	30	450	0	600	0

Super 8mm Footage/Time Table
Typical Running Times

Super 8 (72 frames per foot)				
Projection speed in frames per second	18		24	
Inches per second	3.0		4.0	
Film length and screen time	Minutes	Seconds	Minutes	Seconds
Feet 50	3	20	2	30
100	6	40	5	0
150	10	0	7	30
200	13	20	10	0
300	20	0	15	0
400	26	40	20	0
500	33	20	25	0
600	40	0	30	0
700	46	40	35	0
800	53	20	40	0
900	60	0	45	0
1000	66	40	50	0
1100	73	20	55	0
1200	80	0	60	0
2000	133	20	100	0
3000	200	0	150	0
4000	266	40	200	0
5000	333	20	250	0
6000	400	0	300	0
7000	466	40	350	0
8000	533	20	400	0
9000	600	0	450	0
10,000	666	40	500	0

16mm FOOTAGE TABLE — 24 F.P.S.

24 F.P.S. Sound Speed (1 foot = 40 frames)

Seconds						Minutes			
SECONDS	FEET	FRAMES	SECONDS	FEET	FRAMES	MINUTES	FEET	MINUTES	FEET
1		24	31	18	24	1	36	31	1116
2	1	8	32	19	8	2	72	32	1152
3	1	32	33	19	32	3	108	33	1188
4	2	16	34	20	16	4	144	34	1224
5	3		35	21		5	180	35	1260
6	3	24	36	21	24	6	216	36	1296
7	4	8	37	22	8	7	252	37	1332
8	4	32	38	22	32	8	288	38	1368
9	5	16	39	23	16	9	324	39	1404
10	6	10	40	24		10	360	40	1440
11	6	24	41	24	24	11	396	41	1476
12	7	8	42	25	8	12	432	42	1512
13	7	32	43	25	32	13	468	43	1548
14	8	16	44	26	16	14	504	44	1584
15	9		45	27		15	540	45	1620
16	9	24	46	27	24	16	576	46	1656
17	10	8	47	28	8	17	612	47	1692
18	10	32	48	28	32	18	648	48	1728
19	11	16	49	29	16	19	684	49	1764
20	12		50	30		20	720	50	1800
21	12	24	51	30	24	21	756	51	1836
22	13	8	52	31	8	22	792	52	1872
23	13	32	53	31	32	23	828	53	1908
24	14	16	54	32	16	24	864	54	1944
25	15		55	33		25	900	55	1980
26	15	24	56	33	24	26	936	56	2016
27	16	8	57	34	8	27	972	57	2052
28	16	32	58	34	32	28	1008	58	2088
29	17	16	59	35	16	29	1044	59	2124
30	18		60	36		30	1080	60	2160

16mm FOOTAGE TABLE — 25 F.P.S.

25 F.P.S. European Television Film Sound Speed (1 foot = 40 frames)

Seconds						Minutes					
SECONDS	FEET	FRAMES	SECONDS	FEET	FRAMES	MINUTES	FEET	FRAMES	MINUTES	FEET	FRAMES
1		25	31	19	15	1	37	20	31	1162	20
2	1	10	32	20		2	75		32	1200	
3	1	35	33	20	25	3	112	20	33	1237	20
4	2	20	34	21	10	4	150		34	1275	
5	3	5	35	21	35	5	187	20	35	1312	20
6	3	30	36	22	20	6	225		36	1350	
7	4	15	37	23	5	7	262	20	37	1387	20
8	5		38	23	30	8	300		38	1425	
9	5	25	39	24	15	9	337	20	39	1462	20
10	6	10	40	25		10	375		40	1500	
11	6	35	41	25	25	11	412	20	41	1537	20
12	7	20	42	26	10	12	450		42	1575	
13	8	5	43	26	35	13	487	20	43	1612	20
14	8	30	44	27	20	14	525		44	1650	
15	9	15	45	28	5	15	562	20	45	1687	20
16	10		46	28	30	16	600		46	1725	
17	10	25	47	29	15	17	637	20	47	1762	20
18	11	10	48	30		18	675		48	1800	
19	11	35	49	30	25	19	712	20	49	1837	20
20	12	20	50	31	10	20	750		50	1875	
21	13	5	51	31	35	21	787	20	51	1912	20
22	13	30	52	32	20	22	825		52	1950	
23	14	15	53	33	5	23	862	20	53	1987	20
24	15		54	33	30	24	900		54	2025	
25	15	25	55	34	15	25	937	20	55	2062	20
26	16	10	56	35		26	975		56	2100	
27	16	35	57	35	25	27	1012	20	57	2137	20
28	17	20	58	36	10	28	1050		58	2175	
29	18	5	59	36	35	29	1087	20	59	2212	20
30	18	30	60	37	20	30	1125		60	2250	

16mm FOOTAGE TABLE 29.97 F.P.S.

29.97 F.P.S. U.S. Television Film Sound Speed (1 foot = 40 frames)

Seconds						Minutes					
SECONDS	FEET	FRAMES	SECONDS	FEET	FRAMES	MINUTES	FEET	FRAMES	MINUTES	FEET	FRAMES
1	0	30	31	23	9	1	44	38	31	1393	24
2	1	20	32	23	39	2	89	36	32	1438	22
3	2	10	33	24	29	3	134	35	33	1483	21
4	3	0	34	25	19	4	179	33	34	1528	19
5	3	30	35	26	9	5	224	31	35	1573	17
6	4	20	36	26	39	6	269	29	36	1618	15
7	5	10	37	27	29	7	314	27	37	1663	13
8	6	0	38	28	9	8	359	26	38	1708	12
9	6	30	39	29	39	9	404	24	39	1753	10
10	7	20	40	29	39	10	449	22	40	1798	8
11	8	10	41	30	29	11	494	20	41	1843	6
12	9	0	42	31	19	12	539	18	42	1888	4
13	9	30	43	32	9	13	584	17	43	1933	3
14	10	20	44	32	39	14	629	15	44	1978	1
15	11	10	45	33	29	15	674	13	45	2022	39
16	12	0	46	34	19	16	719	11	46	2067	37
17	12	29	47	35	9	17	764	9	47	2112	35
18	13	19	48	35	39	18	809	8	48	2157	34
19	14	9	49	36	29	19	854	6	49	2202	32
20	14	39	50	37	19	20	899	4	50	2247	30
21	15	29	51	38	8	21	944	2	51	2292	28
22	16	19	52	38	38	22	989	0	52	2337	26
23	17	9	53	39	28	23	1033	39	53	2382	25
24	17	39	54	40	18	24	1078	37	54	2427	23
25	18	29	55	41	8	25	1123	35	55	2472	21
26	19	19	56	41	38	26	1168	33	56	2517	19
27	20	9	57	42	28	27	1213	31	57	2562	17
28	20	39	58	43	18	28	1258	30	58	2607	16
29	21	29	59	44	8	29	1303	28	59	2652	14
30	22	19	60	44	38	30	1338	26	60	2697	12

35mm FOOTAGE TABLE — 24 F.P.S.

24 F.P.S. Sound Speed (1 foot = 16 frames)

Seconds						Minutes			
SECONDS	FEET	FRAMES	SECONDS	FEET	FRAMES	MINUTES	FEET	MINUTES	FEET
1	1	8	31	46	8	1	90	31	2790
2	3		32	48		2	180	32	2880
3	4	8	33	49	8	3	270	33	2970
4	6		34	51		4	360	34	3060
5	7	8	35	52	8	5	450	35	3150
6	9		36	54		6	540	36	3240
7	10	8	37	55	8	7	630	37	3330
8	12		38	57		8	720	38	3420
9	13	8	39	58	8	9	810	39	3510
10	15		40	60		10	900	40	3600
11	16	8	41	61	8	11	990	41	3690
12	18		42	63		12	1080	42	3780
13	19	8	43	64	8	13	1170	43	3870
14	21		44	66		14	1260	44	3960
15	22	8	45	67	8	15	1350	45	4050
16	24		46	69		16	1440	46	4140
17	25	8	47	70	8	17	1530	47	4230
18	27		48	72		18	1620	48	4320
19	28	8	49	73	8	19	1710	49	4410
20	30		50	75		20	1800	50	4500
21	31	8	51	76	8	21	1890	51	4590
22	33		52	78		22	1980	52	4680
23	34	8	53	79	8	23	2070	53	4770
24	36		54	81		24	2160	54	4860
25	37	8	55	82	8	25	2250	55	4950
26	39		56	84		26	2340	56	5040
27	40	8	57	85	8	27	2430	57	5130
28	42		58	87		28	2520	58	5220
29	43	8	59	88	8	29	2610	59	5310
30	45		60	90		30	2700	60	5400

35mm FOOTAGE TABLE — 25 F.P.S.

25 F.P.S. European Television Film Sound Speed (1 foot = 16 frames)

Seconds						Minutes					
SECONDS	FEET	FRAMES	SECONDS	FEET	FRAMES	MINUTES	FEET	FRAMES	MINUTES	FEET	FRAMES
1	1	9	31	48	7	1	93	12	31	2906	4
2	3	2	32	50		2	187	8	32	3000	
3	4	11	33	51	9	3	281	4	33	3093	12
4	6	4	34	53	2	4	375		34	3187	8
5	7	13	35	54	11	5	468	12	35	3281	4
6	9	6	36	56	4	6	562	8	36	3375	
7	10	15	37	57	13	7	656	4	37	3468	12
8	12	8	38	59	6	8	750		38	3562	8
9	14	1	39	60	15	9	843	12	39	3656	4
10	15	10	40	62	8	10	937	8	40	3750	
11	17	3	41	64	1	11	1031	4	41	3843	12
12	18	12	42	65	10	12	1125		42	3937	8
13	20	5	43	67	3	13	1218	12	43	4031	4
14	21	14	44	68	12	14	1312	8	44	4125	
15	23	7	45	70	5	15	1406	4	45	4218	12
16	25		46	71	14	16	1500		46	4312	8
17	26	9	47	73	7	17	1593	12	47	4406	4
18	28	2	48	75		18	1687	8	48	4500	
19	29	11	49	76	9	19	1781	4	49	4593	12
20	31	4	50	78	2	20	1875		50	4687	8
21	32	13	51	79	11	21	1968	12	51	4781	4
22	34	6	52	81	4	22	2062	8	52	4875	
23	35	15	53	82	13	23	2156	4	53	4968	12
24	37	8	54	84	6	24	2250		54	5062	8
25	39	1	55	85	15	25	2343	12	55	5156	4
26	40	10	56	87	8	26	2437	8	56	5250	
27	42	3	57	89	1	27	2531	4	57	5343	12
28	43	12	58	90	10	28	2625		58	5437	8
29	45	5	59	92	3	29	2718	12	59	5531	4
30	46	14	60	93	12	30	2812	8	60	5625	

35mm FOOTAGE TABLE — 29.97 F.P.S.

29.97 F.P.S. U.S. Television Film Sound Speed (1 foot = 16 frames)

Seconds						Minutes					
SECONDS	FEET	FRAMES	SECONDS	FEET	FRAMES	MINUTES	FEET	FRAMES	MINUTES	FEET	FRAMES
1	1	14	31	58	1	1	112	6	31	3484	0
2	3	12	32	59	15	2	224	12	32	3596	6
3	5	10	33	61	13	3	337	3	33	3708	13
4	7	8	34	63	11	4	449	9	34	3821	3
5	9	6	35	65	9	5	561	15	35	3933	9
6	11	4	36	67	7	6	674	5	36	4045	15
7	13	2	37	69	5	7	786	11	37	4158	5
8	15	0	38	71	3	8	899	2	38	4270	12
9	16	14	39	73	1	9	1011	8	39	4383	2
10	18	12	40	74	15	310	1123	14	40	4495	8
11	20	10	41	76	13	11	1236	4	41	4607	14
12	22	8	42	78	11	12	1348	10	42	4720	4
13	24	6	43	80	9	13	1461	1	43	4832	11
14	26	4	44	82	7	14	1573	7	44	4945	1
15	28	2	45	84	5	15	1685	13	45	5057	7
16	30	0	46	86	3	16	1798	3	46	5169	13
17	31	13	47	88	1	17	1910	9	47	5282	3
18	33	11	48	89	15	18	2023	0	48	5394	10
19	35	9	49	91	13	19	2135	6	49	5507	0
20	37	7	50	93	11	20	2247	12	50	5619	6
21	39	5	51	95	8	21	2360	2	51	5731	12
22	41	3	52	97	6	22	2472	8	52	5844	2
23	43	1	53	99	4	23	2584	15	53	5956	9
24	44	15	54	101	2	24	2697	5	54	6068	15
25	46	13	55	103	0	25	2809	11	55	6181	5
26	48	11	56	104	14	26	2922	1	56	6293	11
27	50	9	57	106	12	27	3034	7	57	6406	1
28	52	7	58	108	10	28	3146	14	58	6518	8
29	54	5	59	110	8	29	3259	4	59	6630	14
30	56	3	60	112	6	30	3371	10	60	6743	4

65/70mm FOOTAGE TABLE 24 F.P.S.

24 F.P.S. SOUND SPEED (1 foot = 12.8 frames)

Seconds						Minutes					
SECONDS	FEET	FRAMES	SECONDS	FEET	FRAMES	MINUTES	FEET	FRAMES	MINUTES	FEET	FRAMES
1	1	11.2	31	58	1.6	1	112	6.4	31	3487	6.4
2	3	9.6	32	60	0	2	225	0	32	3600	0
3	5	8.0	33	61	11.2	3	337	6.4	33	3712	6.4
4	7	6.4	34	63	9.6	4	450	0	34	3825	0
5	9	4.8	35	65	8.0	5	562	6.4	35	3937	6.4
6	11	3.2	36	67	6.4	6	675	0	36	4050	0
7	13	1.6	37	69	4.8	7	787	6.4	37	4162	6.4
8	15	0	38	71	3.2	8	900	0	38	4275	0
9	16	11.2	39	73	1.6	9	1012	6.4	39	4387	6.4
10	18	9.6	40	75	0	10	1125	0	40	4500	0
11	20	8.0	41	76	11.2	11	1237	6.4	41	4612	6.4
12	22	6.4	42	78	9.6	12	1350	0	42	4725	0
13	24	4.8	43	80	8.0	13	1462	6.4	43	4837	6.4
14	26	3.2	44	82	6.4	14	1575	0	44	4950	0
15	28	1.6	45	84	4.8	15	1687	6.4	45	5062	6.4
16	30	0	46	86	3.2	16	1800	0	46	5175	0
17	31	11.2	47	88	1.6	17	1912	6.4	47	5287	6.4
18	33	9.6	48	90	0	18	2025	0	48	5400	0
19	35	8.0	49	91	11.2	19	2137	6.4	49	5512	6.4
20	37	6.4	50	93	9.6	20	2250	0	50	5625	0
21	39	4.8	51	95	8.0	21	2362	6.4	51	5737	6.4
22	41	3.2	52	97	6.4	22	2475	0	52	5850	0
23	43	1.6	53	99	4.8	23	2587	6.4	53	5962	6.4
24	45	0	54	101	3.2	24	2700	0	54	6075	0
25	46	11.2	55	103	1.6	25	2812	6.4	55	6187	6.4
26	48	9.6	56	105	0	26	2925	0	56	6300	0
27	50	8.0	57	106	11.2	27	3037	6.4	57	6412	6.4
28	52	6.4	58	108	9.6	28	3150	0	58	6525	0
29	54	4.8	59	110	8.0	29	3262	6.4	59	6637	6.4
30	56	3.2	60	112	6.4	30	3375	0	60	6750	0

16mm Film
FOOTAGE OBTAINED AT VARIOUS CAMERA SPEEDS

Sec	FRAMES PER SECOND 1	2	4	8	12	16	20	22	24	32	48	64	96	120	128
5	1/8	1/4	1/2	1	1 1/2	2	2 1/2	2 3/4	**3**	4	6	8	12	15	16
10	1/4	1/2	1	2	3	4	5	5 1/2	**6**	8	12	16	24	30	32
15	3/8	3/4	1 1/2	3	4 1/2	6	7 1/2	8 1/4	**9**	12	18	24	36	45	48
20	1/2	1	2	4	6	8	10	11	**12**	16	24	32	48	60	64
30	3/4	1 1/2	3	6	9	12	15	16 1/2	**18**	24	36	48	72	90	96
60	1 1/2	3	6	12	18	24	30	33	**36**	48	72	96	144	180	192

1 Foot = 40 Frames	1/2 Foot = 20 Frames
4/5 Foot = 32 Frames	2/5 Foot = 16 Frames
3/5 Foot = 24 Frames	1/5 Foot = 8 Frames

35mm FILM FOOTAGE + FRAMES OBTAINED AT VARIOUS CAMERA SPEEDS

(1 Ft = 16 frames)

Frames Per Sec	1	2	4	8	12	16	20	22	24	32	48	64	96	120	128
Sec															
5	0'+5	0+10	1+4	2+8	3+12	5+0	6+4	6+14	**7+8**	10+0	15+0	20+0	30+0	37+8	40+0
10	0+10	1+4	2+8	5+0	7+8	10+0	12+8	13+4	**15+0**	20+0	30+0	40+0	60+0	75+0	80+0
15	0+15	1+14	3+12	7+8	11+4	15+0	18+12	20+10	**22+8**	30+0	45+0	60+0	90+0	112+8	120+0
20	1+4	2+8	5+0	10+0	15+0	20+0	25+0	27+8	**30+0**	40+0	60+0	80+0	120+0	150+0	160+0
30	1+14	3+12	7+8	15+0	22+8	30+0	37+8	41+4	**45+0**	60+0	90+0	120+0	180+0	225+0	240+0
60	3+12	7+8	15+0	30+0	45+0	60+0	75+0	82+8	**90+0**	120+0	180+0	240+0	360+0	450+0	480+0

65mm FILM FOOTAGE OBTAINED AT VARIOUS CAMERA SPEEDS

(1 Ft = 12-4/5 frames

Frames Per Sec	1	2	4	8	12	16	20	22	24	32	48	64	96	120	128
Sec															
5	0'+5fr.	0+10	1+7	3+2	4+9	6+3	7+10	8+8	**9+5**	12+6	18+10	25+0	37+6	46+12	50+0
10	0+10	1+7	3+2	6+3	9+5	12+6	15+8	17+2	**18+10**	25+0	37+6	50+0	75+0	94+2	100+0
15	1+2	2+4	4+9	9+5	14+1	18+10	23+6	25+10	**28+4**	37+6	56+3	75+0	112+6	141+7	150+0
20	1+7	3+2	6+3	12+6	18+10	25+0	31+3	34+5	**37+6**	50+0	75+0	100+0	150+0	187+4	200+0
30	2+4	4+9	9+5	18+10	28+4	37+6	46+11	51+7	**56+3**	75+0	112+6	150+0	225+0	281+2	300+0
60	4+9	9+5	18+10	37+6	56+3	75+0	93+10	103+2	**112+6**	150+0	225+0	300+0	450+0	562+4	600+0

1 Foot = 12 4/5 Frames   5/8 Foot = 8 Frames   1/16 Foot = 4 Frames   3/4 Foot = 10 Frames   1/2 Foot = 6 2/5 Frames   1/8 Foot = 1 3/5 Frames

16mm Frame Totalizer

Showing Amount of Frames in Various Footage Totals of **16mm** Film

1⁄20 foot = 2 frames	3⁄10 foot = 12 frames	7⁄10 foot = 28 frames
1⁄10 foot = 4 frames	3⁄8 foot = 15 frames	3⁄4 foot = 30 frames
1⁄8 foot = 5 frames	2⁄5 foot = 16 frames	4⁄5 foot = 32 frames
1⁄5 foot = 8 frames	1⁄2 foot = 20 frames	9⁄10 foot = 36 frames
1⁄4 foot = 10 frames	3⁄5 foot = 24 frames	1 foot = 40 frames

Feet	Frames	Feet	Frames	Feet	Frames	Feet	Frames	Feet	Frames
1 =	40	21 =	840	41 =	1640	61 =	2440	81 =	3240
2 =	80	22 =	880	42 =	1680	62 =	2480	82 =	3280
3 =	120	23 =	920	43 =	1720	63 =	2520	83 =	3320
4 =	160	24 =	960	44 =	1760	64 =	2560	84 =	3360
5 =	200	25 =	1000	45 =	1800	65 =	2600	85 =	3400
6 =	240	26 =	1040	46 =	1840	66 =	2640	86 =	3440
7 =	280	27 =	1080	47 =	1880	67 =	2680	87 =	3480
8 =	320	28 =	1120	48 =	1920	68 =	2720	88 =	3520
9 =	360	29 =	1160	49 =	1960	69 =	2760	89 =	3560
10 =	400	30 =	1200	50 =	2000	70 =	2800	90 =	3600
11 =	440	31 =	1240	51 =	2040	71 =	2840	91 =	3640
12 =	480	32 =	1280	52 =	2080	72 =	2880	92 =	3680
13 =	520	33 =	1320	53 =	2120	73 =	2920	93 =	3720
14 =	560	34 =	1360	54 =	2160	74 =	2960	94 =	3760
15 =	600	35 =	1400	55 =	2200	75 =	3000	95 =	3800
16 =	640	36 =	1440	56 =	2240	76 =	3040	96 =	3840
17 =	680	37 =	1480	57 =	2280	77 =	3080	97 =	3880
18 =	720	38 =	1520	58 =	2320	78 =	3120	98 =	3920
19 =	760	39 =	1560	59 =	2360	79 =	3160	99 =	3960
20 =	800	40 =	1600	60 =	2400	80 =	3200	100 =	4000

35mm Frame Totalizer

Showing Amount of Frames in Various Footage Totals of **35mm** Film

1/8 foot = 2 frames	5/8 foot = 10 frames
1/4 foot = 4 frames	3/4 foot = 12 frames
3/8 foot = 6 frames	7/8 foot = 14 frames
1/2 foot = 8 frames	1 foot = 16 frames

Feet	Frames	Feet	Frames	Feet	Frames	Feet	Frames	Feet	Frames
1 =	16	23 =	368	45 =	720	67 =	1072	89 =	1424
2 =	32	24 =	368	46 =	736	68 =	1088	90 =	1440
3 =	48	25 =	400	47 =	752	69 =	1104	91 =	1456
4 =	64	26 =	416	48 =	768	70 =	1120	92 =	1472
5 =	80	27 =	432	49 =	784	71 =	1136	93 =	1488
6 =	96	28 =	448	50 =	800	72 =	1152	94 =	1504
7 =	112	29 =	464	51 =	816	73 =	1168	95 =	1520
8 =	128	30 =	480	52 =	832	74 =	1184	96 =	1536
9 =	144	31 =	496	53 =	848	75 =	1200	97 =	1552
10 =	160	32 =	512	54 =	864	76 =	1216	98 =	1568
11 =	176	33 =	528	55 =	880	77 =	1232	99 =	1584
12 =	192	34 =	544	56 =	896	78 =	1248	100 =	1600
13 =	208	35 =	560	57 =	912	79 =	1264	200 =	3200
14 =	224	36 =	576	58 =	928	80 =	1280	300 =	4800
15 =	240	37 =	592	59 =	944	81 =	1296	400 =	6400
16 =	256	38 =	608	60 =	960	82 =	1312	500 =	8000
17 =	272	39 =	624	61 =	976	83 =	1328	600 =	9600
18 =	288	40 =	640	62 =	992	84 =	1344	700 =	11200
19 =	304	41 =	656	63 =	1008	85 =	1360	800 =	12800
20 =	320	42 =	672	64 =	1024	86 =	1376	900 =	14400
21 =	336	43 =	688	65 =	1040	87 =	1392	1000 =	16000
22 =	352	44 =	704	66 =	1056	88 =	1408	2000 =	32000

35mm CAMERA RECOMMENDED PANNING SPEEDS AT VARIOUS FRAME RATES

Approximately 180° shutter – for static scenes

For 90° Sweep With Various Camera Speeds and Different Focal Length Lenses
EXAMPLE: 24 f.p.s. with 50mm Lens Should Take 23 Seconds to Pan 90° Sweep

CAMERA SPEED FRAMES PER/SEC.	FOCAL LENGTH OF LENS IN MM										
	18 to 20	25 to 28	35	40	50	75	85	100	150	180	300
	PANNING SPEED										
	Unshaded Numbers: Seconds										Shaded Numbers: Minutes
8	27	45	55	60	1.5	2.0	2.5	3.0	4.0	5.0	7.0
12	18	30	36	42	54	70	1.5	2.0	2.5	3.5	5.0
16	13	23	27	32	41	55	70	1.5	2.0	2.5	3.5
20	11	18	22	25	27	43	60	70	1.5	2.0	3.0
24	9	15	18	21	23	36	50	60	80	1.5	2.5
32	7	11	14	16	20	27	38	45	60	75	2.0
48	4.5	7.5	9	11	13	18	25	30	40	55	75
60	3.5	6	7	8	11	14	20	24	32	40	60
75	3	5	6	7	9	12	17	19	26	35	50
90	2.4	4	5	6	7	10	14	16	21	29	40
120	1.8	3	4	4	5	7	10	12	16	22	30
150	1.4	2.4	3	3.5	4	6	8	10	13	17	25

35mm CAMERA RECOMMENDED PANNING SPEEDS IN DEGREES PER SECOND

Approximately 180° shutter – for static scenes

For Various Camera Speeds and Different Focal Length Lenses
Example: 24 f.p.s. with 50mm Lens Should Be Panned 3.6° Per Second or 36° in 10 Seconds, etc.

Lens Focal Length: mm	24 f.p.s.	60 f.p.s.	80 f.p.s.	100 f.p.s.	120 f.p.s.
17	9.9°	25.0°	33.3°	41.6°	49.9°
25	7.0°	17.5°	23.3°	29.1°	34.9°
28	6.3°	15.7°	20.9°	26.1°	31.3°
32	5.5°	13.7°	28.2°	22.9°	27.4°
35	5.0°	12.7°	26.9°	21.1°	25.4°
50	3.6°	8.7°	11.7°	14.6°	17.5°
75	2.4°	6.0°	8.0°	9.9°	12.0°
85	1.7°	4.3°	5.8°	7.2°	8.7°
100	1.5°	3.9°	5.2°	6.4°	7.7°
125	1.3°	3.3°	4.3°	5.4°	6.5°
150	1.1°	2.8°	3.7°	4.6°	5.5°
180	0.95°	2.4°	3.2°	4.0°	4.7°
300	0.58°	1.5°	1.9°	2.4°	2.9°
500	0.36°	0.64°	0.9°	1.07°	1.3°

35mm CAMERA RECOMMENDED PANNING SPEEDS

180° Shutter & Various Degrees of Sweep – For Static Scenes

EXAMPLE: 60° Pan with 75mm Lens Should Take 24 Seconds

PANNING ANGLE IN DEGREES	FOCAL LENGTH OF LENS IN MM											
	18 to 20	25 to 28	35	40	50	75	85	100	150	180	300	500
	PANNING SPEED											
	Unshaded Numbers: SECONDS									Shaded Numbers: MINUTES		
30°	3	5	6	7	9	12	18	20	27	32	50	80
60°	6	10	12	14	18	24	36	40	55	60	95	2.5
90°	9	15	18	21	23	36	50	60	80	90	2.5	4.0
120°	12	20	24	28	36	48	65	80	100	2.0	3.5	5.0
150°	15	25	30	35	41	60	86	100	2.0	2.5	4.0	6.5
180°	18	30	36	42	56	72	100	2.0	2.5	3.0	5.0	8.0

Camera Speed To Auto

	Shutter Openings								
175°	161°	146°	131°	117°	102°	88°	73°	58°	44°
24	22	20	18	16	14	12	10	8	6
	Pictures Per Second								
ACTUAL AUTO SPEED PER HOUR	Desired Onscreen Effective Speed								
6	7	8	9	10	11	12	15	18	24
8	9	10	12	14	15	16	20	24	32
10	11	12	15	17	18	20	25	30	40
12	13	15	18	21	22	24	30	36	48
15	16	18	22	25	27	30	37	45	60
20	22	25	30	35	37	40	50	60	80
25	28	31	37	43	47	50	62	75	100
30	34	37	45	52	56	60	75	90	120
35	39	43	52	59	65	70	87	105	140
40	45	50	60	70	75	80	100	120	160
45	51	56	72	79	85	90	113	135	180
50	56	62	75	87	94	100	125	150	200
55	62	69	82	96	103	110	137	165	220
60	67	75	90	105	112	120	150	180	240

Example: An auto traveling 30mph can be made to appear as if it is traveling 60mph, by using a shutter speed of 12 fps with an 88° shutter opening.

TIME-LAPSE CHART

ONE FRAME EXPOSURE INTERVALS	LENGTH OF SCENE IN SECONDS AT 24 FPS							
	5	10	15	20	25	30	45	60
SECONDS	TIME OF ACTION (HOURS AND MINUTES)							
2	0:04	0:08	0:12	0:16	0:20	0:24	0:36	0:48
3	0:06	0:12	0:18	0:24	0:30	0:36	0:54	1:12
4	0:08	0:16	0:24	0:32	0:40	0:48	1:12	1:36
5	0:10	0:20	0:30	0:40	0:50	1:00	1:30	2:00
6	0:12	0:24	0:36	0:48	1:00	1:12	1:48	2:24
7	0:14	0:28	0:42	0:56	1:10	1:24	2:06	2:48
8	0:16	0:32	0:48	1:04	1:20	1:36	2:24	3:12
9	0:18	0:36	0:54	1:12	1:30	1:48	2:42	3:36
10	0:20	0:40	1:00	1:20	1:40	2:00	3:00	4:00
12	0:24	0:48	1:12	1:36	2:00	2:24	3:36	4:48
14	0:28	0:56	1:24	1:52	2:20	2:48	4:12	5:36
16	0:32	1:04	1:36	2:08	2:40	3:12	4:48	6:24
18	0:36	1:12	1:48	2:24	3:00	3:36	5:24	7:12
20	0:40	1:20	2:00	2:40	3:20	4:00	6:00	8:00
25	0:50	1:40	2:30	3:20	4:10	5:00	7:30	10:00
30	1:00	2:00	3:00	4:00	5:00	6:00	9:00	12:00
35	1:10	2:20	3:30	4:40	5:50	7:00	10:30	14:00
40	1:20	2:40	4:00	5:20	6:40	8:00	12:00	16:00
45	1:30	3:00	4:30	6:00	7:30	9:00	13:30	18:00
50	1:40	3:20	5:00	6:40	8:20	10:00	15:00	20:00
55	1:50	3:40	5:30	7:20	9:10	11:00	16:30	22:00
MINUTES								
1	2:00	4:00	6:00	8:00	10:00	12:00	18:00	24:00
1.5	3:00	6:00	9:00	12:00	15:00	18:00	27:00	36:00
2	4:00	8:00	12:00	16:00	20:00	24:00	36:00	48:00
2.5	5:00	10:00	15:00	20:00	25:00	30:00	45:00	60:00
3	6:00	12:00	18:00	24:00	30:00	36:00	54:00	72:00
3.5	7:00	14:00	21:00	28:00	35:00	42:00	63:00	84:00
4	8:00	16:00	24:00	32:00	40:00	48:00	72:00	96:00
5	10:00	20:00	30:00	40:00	50:00	60:00	90:00	120:00
6	12:00	24:00	36:00	48:00	60:00	72:00	108:00	144:00
7	14:00	28:00	42:00	56:00	70:00	84:00	126:00	168:00
8	16:00	32:00	48:00	64:00	80:00	96:00	144:00	192:00
9	18:00	36:00	54:00	72:00	90:00	108:00	162:00	216:00
10	20:00	40:00	60:00	80:00	100:00	120:00	180:00	240:00
12	24:00	48:00	72:00	96:00	120:00	144:00	216:00	288:00
14	28:00	56:00	84:00	112:00	140:00	168:00	252:00	336:00
16	32:00	64:00	96:00	128:00	160:00	192:00	288:00	384:00
18	36:00	72:00	108:00	144:00	180:00	216:00	324:00	432:00
20	40:00	80:00	120:00	160:00	200:00	240:00	360:00	480:00
22	44:00	88:00	132:00	176:00	220:00	264:00	396:00	528:00
25	50:00	100:00	150:00	200:00	250:00	300:00	450:00	600:00
30	60:00	120:00	180:00	240:00	300:00	360:00	540:00	720:00
35	70:00	140:00	210:00	280:00	350:00	420:00	630:00	840:00
40	80:00	160:00	240:00	320:00	400:00	480:00	720:00	960:00
45	90:00	180:00	270:00	360:00	450:00	540:00	810:00	1080:00
50	100:00	200:00	300:00	400:00	500:00	600:00	900:00	1200:00
55	110:00	220:00	330:00	440:00	550:00	660:00	990:00	1320:00
HOURS								
1	120:00	240:00	360:00	480:00	600:00	720:00	1080:00	1440:00
1.5	180:00	360:00	540:00	720:00	900:00	1080:00	1620:00	2160:00
2	240:00	480:00	720:00	960:00	1200:00	1440:00	2160:00	2880:00
2.5	300:00	600:00	900:00	1200:00	1500:00	1800:00	2700:00	3600:00
3	360:00	720:00	1080:00	1440:00	1800:00	2160:00	3240:00	4320:00

Example: 20 second scene over four hours equals one exposure every 30 seconds.

Miniatures: Camera speed, model speed, exposure factors vs. miniature scale

Scale: inches per foot	3	2	1 1/2	1	3/4	3/8	1/4	1/8
fraction of full size	1/4	1/6	1/8	1/12	1/16	1/32	1/48	1/96
Frames per second	48	59	68	84	96	136	166	235
Exposure factor	2x	2.5x	2.8x	3.5x	4x	5.7x	6.9x	9.8x
Exposure increase, lens T-stops	1	1 1/3	1 1/2	1 3/4	2	2 1/2	2 3/4	3 1/3
Portrayed Speed miles per hour	**Model Speed-Feet per second** (Expalnation and formula on page 263)							
60	44	36	31.1	25.4	22	15.6	12.7	9
40	29.3	24	20.7	16.9	14.7	10.4	8.5	6
30	22	18	15.6	12.7	11	7.8	6.4	4.5
20	14.7	12	10.4	8.5	7.3	5.2	4.2	3
10	7.3	6	5.2	4.2	3.7	2.6	2.1	1.5
5	3.7	3	2.6	2.1	1.8	1.3	1.1	.7

PROJECTION CHART FOR PROCESS BACKGROUNDS

SIZE OF PICTURE OBTAINED WITH VARIOUS LENSES/ DISTANCE FROM LENS TO SCREEN

Lens Size inches	20 FEET	25 FEET	30 FEET	40 FEET	50 FEET	60 FEET	70 FEET	80 FEET	90 FEET	100 FEET	110 FEET	120 FEET	130 FEET	140 FEET	150 FEET	160 FEET	170 FEET	180 FEET
	SIZE OF PICTURE														Based on Projection Aperture .906 x .679			
3	W 6' 0"	7' 6"	9' 1"	12' 1"	15' 0"	18' 1"	21' 1"	24' 2"	27' 2"	30' 1"	33' 1"	36' 3"	39' 2"	42' 3"	45' 2"	48' 4"	52' 2"	56' 6"
	H 4' 5"	5' 7"	6' 8"	9' 0"	11' 4"	13' 6"	15' 8"	18' 1"	20' 3"	22' 7"	24' 8"	27' 2"	29' 5"	31' 8"	33' 8"	35' 9"	38' 3"	42' 2"
4	W 4' 5"	5' 8"	6' 8"	9' 0"	11' 3"	13' 6"	15' 7"	18' 1"	20' 2"	22' 6"	24' 7"	27' 3"	29' 4"	31' 6"	33' 9"	36' 3"	38' 6"	40' 8"
	H 3' 4"	4' 4"	5' 1"	6' 8"	8' 5"	10' 1"	11' 9"	13' 6"	15' 1"	16' 9"	18' 7"	20' 4"	22' 1"	23' 7"	25' 4"	27' 1"	28' 6"	41' 0"
4 ½	W 4' 1"	5' 1"	6' 0"	8' 1"	10' 1"	12' 1"	14' 1"	16' 2"	18' 1"	20' 1"	22' 0"	24' 1"	26' 2"	23' 8'	30' 3"	32' 2"	34' 3"	36' 0"
	H 3' 1"	3' 9"	4' 5"	6' 1"	7' 7"	9' 2"	10' 7"	12' 2"	13' 6"	15' 2"	16' 7"	18' 3"	19' 7"	21' 1"	22' 5"	24' 0"	25' 7"	27' 2"
5	W 3' 6"	4' 6"	5' 4"	7' 3"	9' 1"	10' 9"	12' 7"	14' 5"	16' 3"	18' 3"	19' 7"	21' 3"	23' 4"	25' 5"	27' 2"	28' 6"	30' 6"	32' 5"
	H 2' 7"	3' 5"	4' 1"	5' 5"	6' 8"	8' 2"	9' 5"	10' 8"	12' 1"	13' 4"	14' 8"	16' 4"	17' 5"	19' 1"	20' 2"	21' 8"	23' 4"	24' 4"
5 ½	W 3' 3"	4' 2"	4' 9"	6' 7"	8' 2"	9' 9"	11' 5"	13' 2"	14' 7"	16' 4"	18' 2"	19' 6"	21' 4"	23' 2"	24' 6"	26' 3"	27' 8"	29' 8"
	H 2' 6"	3' 2"	3' 7"	5' 1"	6' 1"	7' 5"	8' 4"	9' 9"	11' 2"	12' 3"	13' 7"	14' 9"	16' 2"	17' 2'	18' 6"	19' 8"	20' 6"	22' 4"
6	W 3' 0"	3' 8"	4' 5"	6' 1"	7' 5"	9' 1"	10' 4"	12' 2"	13' 4"	15' 2"	16' 6"	18' 2"	19' 4"	21' 1"	22' 6"	24' 2"	25' 6"	27' 1"
	H 2' 3"	2' 9"	3' 4"	4' 7"	5' 6"	6' 8"	7' 8"	9' 1"	10' 2"	11' 4"	12' 5"	13' 4"	14' 8"	15' 9"	16' 8"	18' 2"	19' 3"	20' 4"
6 ½	W 2' 8"	3' 6"	4' 3"	5' 6"	6' 9"	8' 4"	10' 1"	11' 2"	12' 6"	13' 9"	15' 4"	16' 6"	18' 2"	19' 4"	20' 6"	22' 4"	23' 6"	25' 2"
	H 2' 1"	2' 7"	3' 3"	4' 2"	5' 3"	6' 2"	7' 6"	8' 2"	9' 5"	10' 4"	11' 4"	12' 6"	13' 6"	14' 6"	15' 8"	16' 4"	17' 8"	18' 8"
7	W 2' 6"	3' 3"	3' 9"	5' 2"	6' 4"	7' 1"	9' 1"	10' 2"	11' 5"	12' 9"	14' 3"	15' 5"	16' 8"	18' 4"	19' 6"	20' 6"	21' 8"	23' 2"
	H 1' 9"	2' 5"	2' 9"	3' 9"	4' 9"	5' 4"	6' 8"	7' 6"	8' 8"	9' 7"	10' 7"	11' 6"	12' 8"	13' 2'	14' 6"	15' 4"	16' 4"	17' 4"
8	W	2' 9"	3' 4"	4' 5"	5' 6"	6' 8"	7' 9"	9' 1"	10' 1"	11' 2"	12' 3"	13' 5"	14' 6'	15' 8"	16' 8"	18' 1"	19' 2"	20' 3"
	H	2' 2"	2' 6"	3' 4"	4' 3"	5' 1"	5' 9"	6' 8"	7' 7"	8' 4"	9' 4"	10' 2"	11' 2"	11' 7"	12' 8"	13' 5"	14' 2"	15' 2"
9	W		3' 3"	4' 1"	5' 0"	6' 0"	7' 0"	8' 1"	9' 1"	10' 1"	11' 2"	12' 1"	13' 1"	14' 2"	15' 2"	16' 1"	17' 2"	18' 0"
	H		3' 0"	3' 1"	3' 9"	4' 5"	5' 3"	6' 1"	6' 8"	7' 6"	8' 3"	9' 1"	9' 9"	10' 6"	11' 4"	12' 0"	12' 8"	13' 6"

Open Face and Softlights

Lighting Charts

The values in these charts are generic. They may vary by ± 5% depending on the condition and design of luminaire.

	Size	Watts	Feet	FC	Beam	Feet	FC	Beam	Feet	FC	Beam
Softlights	6.25"	600	**4'**	150	5.0'	**8'**	38	10.0'	**12'**	17	15.3'
	8.0"	650	**4'**	200	5.6'	**8'**	50	11.2'	**12'**	20	16.8'
	8" x 17"	2000	**4'**	540	5.3' x 5.3'	**8'**	70	17.4' x 15.5'	**12'**	25	29.0' x 25.8'
	18"	4000	**4'**	1030	5.6'	**8'**	270	11.2'	**12'**	125	16.8'
	6.25"	600	**6'**	67	7.6'	**10'**	24	12.7'	**20'**		
	8.0"	650	**6'**	90	8.4'	**10'**	30	14.0'	**20'**		
	8" x 17"	2000	**6'**	150	11.6' x 10.3'	**10'**	40	23.2' x 20.7'	**20'**		
	18"	4000	**6'**			**10'**			**20'**	45	28'

	Watts	Feet	FC FL	Beam Size	FC SP	Beam Size	Feet	FC FL	Beam Size	FC SP	Beam Size	Feet	FC FL	Beam Size	FC SP	Beam Size
Open Face	600	**4'**	940	3.5'	3020	1.6	**8'**	215	7.9'	785	3.3'	**12'**	95	12.3'	345	5.0'
	650	**4'**	640	4.4' x 5.6'	4800	1.3' x 1.3'	**8'**	135	8.8' x 11.2'	1200	2.6' x 2.6'	**12'**	60	13.2' x 16.8'	540	4.0' x 4.0'
	1000	**4'**	1000	3.2' x 4.2'	7330	1.2' x 1.1'	**8'**	250	7.0' x 9.8'	1900	2.4' x 2.3'	**12'**				
	2000	**4'**					**8'**					**12'**				
	600	**6'**	400	5.7'	1380	2.5'	**10'**	135	10.2'	500	4.2'	**20'**	35	5.0	125	8.4'
	650	**6'**	265	6.6' x 8.4'	2160	2.0' x 1.3'	**10'**	85	11.2' x 14.0'	780	3.3' x 3.3'	**20'**	20	4' x 4'	195	6.6' x 6.6'
	1000	**6'**	450	5.2' x 7.4'	3350	1.8' x 1.7'	**10'**	160	8.8' x 12.5'	1220	3.0' x 2.9'	**20'**	40	22.0' x 28.0'	305	6.0' x 5.9'
	2000	**6'**					**10'**	330	9.8' x 12.5'	2500	3.2' x 3.2'	**20'**	85	19.5' x 25.0'	625	6.4' x 6.4'

Tungsten Fresnels

	Watts	Lens	Field Angle	Feet	FC FL	Beam Size	FC SP	Beam Size	Feet	FC FL	Beam Size	FC SP	Beam Size	Feet	FC FL	Beam Size	FC SP	Beam Size
Fresnel 120 V	250	2"	22° to 57°	**10'**	28	8.1'	57	2.4'	**20'**					**30'**				
	300	3"	12° to 58°	**10'**	45	8.8'	248	1.5'	**20'**					**30'**				
	650	4.5"	17° to 70°	**10'**	78	11.3'	660	1.4'	**20'**	18	22.7'	180	3.0'	**30'**				
	1000	4.5"	21° to 70°	**10'**	140	11.2'	980	2.0'	**20'**	35	22.4'	250	4.0'	**30'**	15	33.6'	110	6.0'
	1000	6"	15° to 58°	**10'**	130	10.5'	600	2.5'	**20'**	30	21.1'	165	5.1'	**30'**	15	31.7'	70	7.8'
	2000	6"	27° to 55°	**10'**	400	8.5'	1500	2.8'	**20'**	100	16.9'	375	5.3'	**30'**	45	25.2'	165	7.9'
	2000	8"	15° to 65°	**10'**	490	8.8'	3920	1.6'	**20'**	130	17.4'	1000	3.4'	**30'**	55	26.1'	445	5.1'
	2000	10"	20° to 55°	**10'**	440	13.3'	3920	1.6'	**20'**	110	26.5'	1000	3.4'	**30'**	49	39.8'	445	5.1'
	5000	10"	17° to 61°	**10'**	950	9.3'	5800	1.9'	**20'**	240	18.3'	1470	3.7'	**30'**	110	27.5'	655	5.5'
	5000	14"	18° to 70°	**10'**	875	13.0'	5812	1.5'	**20'**	219	26.0'	1453	3.0'	**30'**	97	39.0'	646	4.4'
	10000	14"	15° to 63°	**10'**	1600	10.0'	12100	1.6'	**20'**	420	20.0'	3200	3.3'	**30'**	185	30.0'	1430	4.9'
	10000	20"	17° to 43°	**10'**	2440	10.5'	21200	2.1'	**20'**	610	20.3'	5300	4.1'	**30'**	271	30.5'	2358	6.2'
	12000	17"	13° to 54°	**10'**					**20'**	813	20.4'	3875	4.6'	**30'**	361	30.6'	1722	6.8'
	12000	20"	17° to 43°	**10'**	2440	10.5'	21200	2.1'	**20'**	610	20.3'	5300	4.1'	**30'**	271	30.5'	2356	6.2'
	10000	25"	21.8° to 66.5°	**10'**	3400	9.5'	22000	1.5'	**20'**	850	19.0'	5500	3.0'	**30'**	378	28.5'	2444	4.5'
	12000	25"	21.8° to 66.5°	**10'**	3800	9.5'	23600	1.5'	**20'**	950	19.0'	5900	3.0'	**30'**	422	28.5'	2622	4.5'
Fresnel 240 V	20000	25"	21.8° to 66.5°	**10'**	4275	9.9'	21900	2.1'	**20'**	1070	19.8'	6975	4.3'	**30'**	474	29.7'	3100	6.4'
	24000	25"	21.8° to 66.5°	**10'**	11700	9.9'	47700	2.1'	**20'**	2925	19.8'	11925	4.3'	**30'**	1300	29.7'	5300	6.4'

Tungsten Fresnels

	Watts	Lens	Field Angle	Feet	FC FL	Beam Size	FC SP	Beam Size	Feet	FC FL	Beam Size	FC SP	Beam Size	Feet	FC FL	Beam Size	FC SP	Beam Size
Fresnel 120 V	250	2"	22° to 57°	**40'**					**50'**					**100'**				
	300	3"	12° to 58°	**40'**					**50'**					**100'**				
	650	4.5"	17° to 70°	**40'**					**50'**					**100'**				
	1000	4.5"	21° to 70°	**40'**					**50'**					**100'**				
	1000	6"	15° to 58°	**40'**					**50'**					**100'**				
	2000	6"	27° to 55°	**40'**	20	33.6'	95	10.5'	**50'**					**100'**				
	2000	8"	15° to 65°	**40'**	30	34.8'	250	6.8'	**50'**					**100'**				
	2000	10"	20° to 55°	**40'**	28	53.0'	250	6.8'	**50'**					**100'**				
	5000	10"	17° to 61°	**40'**	60	36.6'	370	7.3'	**50'**	40	45.8'	235	9.2'	**100'**				
	5000	14"	18° to 70°	**40'**	55	52.0'	363	5.9'	**50'**	35	65.0'	233	7.4'	**100'**				
	10000	14"	15° to 63°	**40'**	105	40.0'	805	6.5'	**50'**	70	50.0'	515	8.2'	**100'**				
	10000	20"	17° to 43°	**40'**	153	40.8'	1325	8.2'	**50'**	98	50.8'	848	10.3'	**100'**	24	101.5'	212	20.5'
	12000	17"	13° to 54°	**40'**	203	40.8'	969	9.1'	**50'**	130	51.0'	620	11.4'	**100'**				
	12000	20"	17° to 43°	**40'**	153	40.6'	1325	8.2'	**50'**	98	50.8'	848	10.3'	**100'**	24	101.5'	212	20.5'
	10000	25"	21.8° to 66.5°	**40'**	212	38.0'	1375	6.0'	**50'**	136	47.5'	880	7.5'	**100'**	34	95.0'	220	15.0'
	12000	25"	21.8° to 66.5°	**40'**	238	38.0'	1475	6.0'	**50'**	152	47.5'	944	7.5'	**100'**	38	95.0'	236	15.0'
Fresnel 240 V	20000	25"	21.8° to 66.5°	**40'**	265	39.6'	1745	8.5'	**50'**	170	49.5'	1115	10.7'	**100'**	43	99.0'	280	21.3'
	24000	25"	21.8° to 66.5°	**40'**	731	39.6'	2981	8.5'	**50'**	468	49.5'	1908	10.7'	**100'**	117	99.0'	477	21.3'

HMI Fresnels

HMI Fresnel

Watts	Lens	Field Angle	Feet	FC FL	Beam Size	FC SP	Beam Size	Feet	FC FL	Beam Size	FC SP	Beam Size	Feet	FC FL	Beam Size	FC SP	Beam Size
575	6"	15° to 58°	**10'**	160	8.4'	2160	1.2'	**25'**	25	21.1'	345	3.0'	**40'**				
1200	8"	11° to 46°	**10'**	645	6.9'	7100	1.0'	**25'**	105	17.2'	1130	2.5'	**40'**	40	27.5'	445	4.0'
2500	10"	17° to 61°	**10'**	1600	11.6'	16400	1.0'	**25'**	256	29.0'	2624	2.5'	**40'**	100	46.4'	1025	4.0'
6000	14"	14° to 64°	**10'**	2700	11.5'	40500	.9'	**25'**	432	28.8'	6480	2.3'	**40'**	169	46.1'	2531	3.7'
12000	25"	17° to 74°	**10'**	4050	10.9'	59980	1.3'	**25'**	650	27.2'	12096	3.2'	**40'**	255	43.5'	4725	5.1'
18000	25"	17° to 74°	**10'**	6800	11.2'	83400	1.5'	**25'**	1095	28.0'	15265	3.7'	**40'**	428	44.8'	5963	5.9'
575	6"	15° to 58°	**15'**	70	12.6'	960	1.8'	**30'**	18	25.2'	240	3.6'	**50'**				
1200	8"	11° to 46°	**15'**	285	10.3'	3150	1.5'	**30'**	70	20.6'	785	3.0'	**50'**	25	34.4'	280	5.0'
2500	10"	17° to 61°	**15'**	711	17.4'	7288	1.5'	**30'**	177	34.8'	1822	3.0'	**50'**	64	58.0'	656	5.0'
6000	14"	14° to 64°	**15'**	1200	17.3'	18000	1.4'	**30'**	300	34.6'	4500	2.8'	**50'**	108	57.7'	1620	4.7'
12000	25"	17° to 74°	**15'**	1800	16.3'	30350	1.9'	**30'**	450	32.6'	8400	3.8'	**50'**	162	54.3'	3025	6.3'
18000	25"	17° to 74°	**15'**	3040	16.8'	41975	2.2'	**30'**	760	33.6'	10600	4.4'	**50'**	275	56.0'	3816	7.3'
575	6"	15° to °58	**20'**	40	17.1'	540	2.4'										
1200	8"	11° to 46°	**20'**	160	13.7'	1770	2.0'										
2500	10"	17° to 61°	**20'**	400	23.2'	4100	2.0'										
6000	14"	14° to 64°	**20'**	675	23.1'	10125	1.9'										
12000	25"	17° to 74°	**20'**	1012	21.7'	18400	2.5'										
18000	25"	17° to 74°	**20'**	1710	22.4'	21850	2.9'										

Watts	Lens	Field Angle	Feet	FC FL	Beam	FC SP	Beam
12000	25"	17° to 74°	**100'**	40	108.7'	756	12.7'
18000	25"	17° to 74°	**100'**	68	112.0'	954	14.7'
12000	25"	17° to 74°	**150'**	18	163.0'	335	19.0'
18000	25"	17° to 74°	**150'**	30	168.0'	424	22.0'
12000	25"	17° to 74°	**200'**	10	217.3'	190	25.3'
18000	25"	17° to 74°	**200'**	17	224.0'	239	29.3'

HMI and Quartz Beam Projectors

	Watts	Lens	Feet	FC FL	Beam Size	FC SP	Beam Size	Feet	FC FL	Beam Size	FC SP	Beam Size	Feet	FC FL	Beam Size	FC SP	Beam Size
HMI Beam Projector	1200	18"	**25'**	720	5.0'	5760	1.5'	**125'**	29	26.0'	230	1.5'	**225'**	9	47.0'	71	1.5'
	2500	24"	**25'**	2016	6.0'	17280	2.0'	**125'**	806	31.0'	691	2.0'	**225'**	25	56.0'	213	2.0'
	4000	24"	**25'**	2016	6.0'	23673	2.0'	**125'**	806	31.0'	947	2.0'	**225'**	25	56.0'	292	2.0'
	12000	36"	**25'**	6912	7.4'	89120	N/A	**125'**	278	32.0'	2784	N/A	**225'**	85	66.7'	853	N/A
	1200	18"	**75'**	80	15.0'	640	1.5'	**175'**	15	36.0'	118	1.5'	**300'**	5	63.0'	40	1.5'
	2500	24"	**75'**	224	18.0'	1920	2.0'	**175'**	41	43.0'	353	2.0'	**300'**	14	75.0'	120	2.0'
	4000	24"	**75'**	224	18.0'	2630	2.0'	**175'**	41	43.0'	843	2.0'	**300'**	14	75.0'	300	2.0'
	12000	36"	**75'**	788	22.2'	7680	N/A	**175'**					**300'**	48	89.0'	480	N/A
Quartz Beam Projector	2000	18"	**25'**	576	5.0'	5472	1.5'	**125'**	23	26.0'	219	1.5'	**225'**	7	47.0'	68	1.5'
	5000	24"	**25'**	1152	6.0'	4032	2.0'	**125'**	46	30.0'	161	10.0'	**225'**	14	55.0'	50	1.9'
	10000	24"	**25'**	1120	10.74'	4800	3.25'	**125'**	45	53.7'	192	16.25'	**225'**	14	96.6'	59	29.25'
	20000	36"	**25'**	3600	7.4'	13880	N/A	**125'**	144	37.0'	547	N/A	**225'**	44	66.7'	168	N/A
	2000	18"	**75'**	64	15.0'	608	1.5'	**175'**	12	36.0'	112	1.5'	**300'**	4	63.0'	38	1.5'
	5000	24"	**75'**	128	18.0'	448	6.0'	**175'**	24	42.0'	82	15.0'	**300'**	8	73.0'	28	25.0'
	10000	24"	**75'**	124	32.23'	533	9.75'	**175'**	23	75.2'	96	22.75'	**300'**	6	128.9'	33	39.0'
	20000	36"	**75'**	400	22.2'	1520	N/A	**175'**					**300'**	18	103.8'	70	N/A

HMI PAR

	Lens	Feet	FC	Beam	Lens	Feet	FC	Beam	Lens	Feet	FC	Beam	Lens	Feet	FC	Beam
575 W HMI PAR 7amps Max	NONE	**20'**	3216	2.4'	NONE	**40'**	804	4.8'	NONE	**75'**	229	9.1'	NONE	**150'**	57	18.3'
	VNS	**20'**	1103	4.1'	VNS	**40'**	275	8.1'	VNS	**75'**	78	15.2'	VNS	**150'**	20	30.4'
	NS	**20'**	613	5.2,	NS	**40'**	153	10.5'	NS	**75'**	44	19.7'	NS	**150'**	11	39.4'
	W	**20'**	245	16.7'	W	**40'**	61	33.5'	W	**75'**	17	62.9'	W	**150'**	4	125.8'
	XW	**20'**	92	28.6'	XW	**40'**	23	57.1'	XW	**75'**	7	107.0'	XW	**150'**	2	214.0'
	NONE	**30'**	1429	3.7'	NONE	**50'**	515	6.1'	NONE	**100'**	129	12.2'	NONE	**200'**	32	24.5'
	VNS	**30'**	490	6.1'	VNS	**50'**	176	10.1'	VNS	**100'**	44	20.3'	VNS	**200'**	11	40.5'
	NS	**30'**	272	7.8'	NS	**50'**	98	13.1'	NS	**100'**	25	26.3'	NS	**200'**	6	52.7'
	W	**30'**	109	25.2'	W	**50'**	39	42.0'	W	**100'**	9.8	83.9'	W	**200'**	3	168.0'
	XW	**30'**	41	42.8'	XW	**50'**	15	71.4'	XW	**100'**	4	143.0'	XW	**200'**	1	285.0'
1200 W HMI PAR 15.6 amps Max	NONE	**20'**	4000	2.1'	NONE	**40'**	1000	4.2'	NONE	**75'**	284	7.9'	NONE	**150'**	71	15.8'
	VNS	**20'**	2200	3.3'	VNS	**40'**	550	6.6'	VNS	**75'**	156	12.4'	VNS	**150'**	39	24.8'
	NS	**20'**	1000	6.5'	NS	**40'**	250	13.0'	NS	**75'**	71	24.4'	NS	**150'**	18	48.8'
	W	**20'**	300	17.2'	W	**40'**	75	34.4'	W	**75'**	21	64.5'	W	**150'**	5	129.0'
	XW	**20'**	100	26.4'	XW	**40'**	25	52.8'	XW	**75'**	7	99.0'	XW	**150'**	2	198.0'
	NONE	**30'**	1777	3.2'	NONE	**50'**	640	5.3'	NONE	**100'**	160	10.5'	NONE	**200'**		
	VNS	**30'**	978	5.0'	VNS	**50'**	352	8.3'	VNS	**100'**	88	16.5'	VNS	**200'**		
	NS	**30'**	444	9.8'	NS	**50'**	160	16.3'	NS	**100'**	40	32.5'	NS	**200'**		
	W	**30'**	133	25.8'	W	**50'**	48	43.0'	W	**100'**	12	86.0'	W	**200'**		
	XW	**30'**	44	39.6'	XW	**50'**	16	66.0'	XW	**100'**	4	132.0'	XW	**200'**		

HMI PAR

	Lens	Feet	FC	Beam	Lens	Feet	FC	Beam	Lens	Feet	FC	Beam	Lens	Feet	FC	Beam
2500 W HMI PAR 25.6 amps Max	NONE	**20'**	11025	2.6'	NONE	**40'**	2755	5.2'	NONE	**75'**	784	9.8'	NONE	**150'**	195	19.5'
	VNS	**20'**	5960	6.9'	VNS	**40'**	1490	13.9'	VNS	**75'**	425	26.0'	VNS	**150'**	105	52.0'
	NS	**20'**	2025	11.3'	NS	**40'**	505	22.7'	NS	**75'**	145	42.5'	NS	**150'**	35	85.0'
	W	**20'**	1015	21.7'	W	**40'**	255	43.5'	W	**75'**	70	81.5'	W	**150'**	20	163.0'
	XW	**20'**	450	24.5'	XW	**40'**	115	49.1'	XW	**75'**	30	92.0'	XW	**150'**		
	NONE	**30'**	4900	3.9'	NONE	**50'**	1765	6.5'	NONE	**100'**	440	13.0'	NONE	**200'**	110	26.0'
	VNS	**30'**	2650	10.4'	VNS	**50'**	955	17.3'	VNS	**100'**	240	34.7'	VNS	**200'**	60	69.3'
	NS	**30'**	900	17.0'	NS	**50'**	325	28.3'	NS	**100'**	80	56.7'	NS	**200'**	20	113.3'
	W	**30'**	450	32.6'	W	**50'**	160	54.3'	W	**100'**	40	108.7'	W	**200'**		
	XW	**30'**	200	36.8'	XW	**50'**	70	61.3'	XW	**100'**	18	122.7'	XW	**200'**		
4000 W HMI PAR 24 amps Max	NONE	**20'**	19800	2.7'	NONE	**40'**	4950	5.3'	NONE	**75'**	1410	10.0'	NONE	**150'**	350	20.0'
	VNS	**20'**	7650	3.9'	VNS	**40'**	1910	7.7'	VNS	**75'**	545	14.5'	VNS	**150'**	135	29.0'
	NS	**20'**	2250	8.7'	NS	**40'**	560	17.3'	NS	**75'**	160	32.5'	NS	**150'**	40	65.0'
	W	**20'**	1240	15.7'	W	**40'**	310	31.5'	W	**75'**	90	59.0'	W	**150'**	22	118.0'
	XW	**20'**	675	19.5'	XW	**40'**	169	39.1'	XW	**75'**	50	73.3'	XW	**150'**		
	NONE	**30'**	8800	4.0'	NONE	**50'**	3170	6.7'	NONE	**100'**	790	13.3'	NONE	**200'**	200	26.7'
	VNS	**30'**	3400	5.8'	VNS	**50'**	1225	9.7'	VNS	**100'**	305	19.3'	VNS	**200'**	80	38.7'
	NS	**30'**	1000	13.0'	NS	**50'**	360	21.7'	NS	**100'**	90	43.3'	NS	**200'**	20	86.7'
	W	**30'**	550	23.6'	W	**50'**	200	39.3'	W	**100'**	50	78.7'	W	**200'**		
	XW	**30'**	300	29.3'	XW	**50'**	110	48.8'	XW	**100'**	30	97.7'	XW	**200'**		

HMI PAR

	Lens	Feet	FC	Beam	Lens	Feet	FC	Beam	Lens	Feet	FC	Beam	Lens	Feet	FC	Beam
6000 W HMI PAR 65 amps Max	NONE	**20'**	25200	2.9'	NONE	**40'**	6300	5.7'	NONE	**75'**	1792	10.7'	NONE	**150'**	448	21.5'
	VNS	**20'**	8100	5.3'	VNS	**40'**	2025	10.6'	VNS	**75'**	576	20.0'	VNS	**150'**	144	40.0'
	NS	**20'**	4950	10.0'	NS	**40'**	1238	20.0'	NS	**75'**	352	37.5'	NS	**150'**	88	75.0'
	W	**20'**	2475	19.6'	W	**40'**	619	39.2'	W	**75'**	176	73.5'	W	**150'**	44	147.0'
	XW	**20'**	900	22.7'	XW	**40'**	225	45.3'	XW	**75'**	64	85.0'	XW	**150'**	16	170.0'
	NONE	**30'**	11200	4.3'	NONE	**50'**	4032	7.2'	NONE	**100'**	1008	14.3'	NONE	**200'**	252	28.7'
	VNS	**30'**	3600	8.0'	VNS	**50'**	1296	13.3'	VNS	**100'**	324	26.4'	VNS	**200'**	81	53.3'
	NS	**30'**	2200	15.0'	NS	**50'**	792	25.0'	NS	**100'**	198	50.0'	NS	**200'**	50	100.0'
	W	**30'**	1100	29.4'	W	**50'**	396	49.0'	W	**100'**	99	98.0'	W	**200'**	25	196.0'
	XW	**30'**	400	34.0'	XW	**50'**	144	56.7'	XW	**100'**	36	113.3'	XW	**200'**	9	226.7'
12000 W HMI PAR 78 amps Max	NONE	**20'**			NONE	**40'**	10718	6.9'	NONE	**75'**	3048	13.0'	NONE	**150'**	762	25.8'
	VNS	**20'**			VNS	**40'**	6450	8.0'	VNS	**75'**	1830	15.0'	VNS	**150'**	458	30.0'
	NS	**20'**			NS	**40'**	2290	9.4'	NS	**75'**	650	17.7'	NS	**150'**	163	35.4'
	W	**20'**			W	**40'**	1182	27.5'	W	**75'**	336	51.6'	W	**150'**	84	103.2'
	XW	**20'**			XW	**40'**	717	32.8'	XW	**75'**	204	61.5'	XW	**150'**	51	123.0'
	NONE	**30'**	19055	5.2'	NONE	**50'**	6860	8.6'	NONE	**100'**	1715	17.2'	NONE	**200'**	430	34.4'
	VNS	**30'**	11460	6.0'	VNS	**50'**	4125	10.0'	VNS	**100'**	1031	20.0'	VNS	**200'**	260	40.0'
	NS	**30'**	4070	7.0'	NS	**50'**	1465	12.0'	NS	**100'**	366	23.6'	NS	**200'**	92	47.21'
	W	**30'**	2100	20.6'	W	**50'**	456	34.4'	W	**100'**	189	68.8'	W	**200'**	47	137.6'
	XW	**30'**	1275	24.6'	XW	**50'**	460	41.0'	XW	**100'**	118	82.0'	XW	**200'**	30	164.0'

HMI PAR

	Lens	Feet	FC	Beam	Lens	Feet	FC	Beam	Lens	Feet	FC	Beam	Lens	Feet	FC	Beam
12000 W HMI PAR 78amps Max(focusable)	SPOT	**20'**			NONE	**40'**	4106	7.3'	NONE	**75'**	1168	13.7	NONE	**150'**	292	27.5'
	FLOOD	**20'**			VNS	**40'**	1181	21.4'	VNS	**75'**	336	40.1'	VNS	**150'**	84	80.3'
	SPOT	**30'**	7300	5.5'	NS	**50'**	2628	9.1'	NS	**100'**	657	18.3'	NS	**200'**	164	36.6'
	FLOOD	**30'**	2100	16.0'	W	**50'**	756	26.7'	W	**100'**	189	56.6'	W	**200'**	47	107.1'
18000 W HMI PAR 78amps Max(focusable)	SPOT	**20'**			XW	**40'**	5338	7.3'	XW	**75'**	1518	13.7'	XW	**150'**	380	27.5'
	FLOOD	**20'**			NONE	**40'**	1535	21.4'	NONE	**75'**	437	40.1'	NONE	**150'**	109	80.3'
	SPOT	**30'**	9490	5.5'	VNS	**50'**	3416	9.1'	VNS	**100'**	845	18.3'	VNS	**200'**	213	36.6'
	FLOOD	**30'**	2730	16.0'	NS	**50'**	983	26.7'	NS	**100'**	246	56.6'	NS	**200'**	61	107.1'

225A Brute Arc

	Lens	Feet	FC	Beam	Feet	FC	Beam	Feet	FC	Beam	Feet	FC	Beam
Using White Flame or Yellow Flame Carbons without Filters	SPOT	**10'**	62,300	1.0'	**30'**	9000	2.8'	**75'**	1440	6.9'	**175'**	265	16.1'
	FLOOD	**10'**	10,000	5.5'	**30'**	1190	15.8'	**75'**	190	39.0'	**175'**	35	92.0'
	SPOT	**15'**	34,200	1.4'	**40'**	5060	3.7'	**100'**	810	9.2'	**200'**	200	18.4'
	FLOOD	**15'**	4750	7.9'	**40'**	670	21.0'	**100'**	110	53.0'	**200'**	30	105.0'
	SPOT	**20'**	19,500	1.8'	**50'**	3240	4.6'	**125'**	520	11.5'			
	FLOOD	**20'**	2650	10.5'	**50'**	430	26.0'	**125'**	70	66.0'			
	SPOT	**25'**	12,950	2.3'	**60'**	2250	5.5'	**150'**	360	13.8'			
	FLOOD	**25'**	1700	13.1'	**60'**	300	32.0'	**150'**	50	79.0'			

*Filter Light Losses: White Flame Carbon 10% with Y-1, 40% with MT-2 plus Y-1, Yellow Flame Carbon 15% with YF-101.

Courtesy of Mole-Richardson

PAR 64 Fixtures

1000 W PAR 64 Single 1000 W Globe

Color Temp	Lens	Feet	FC	Beam	Color Temp	Lens	Feet	FC	Beam	Color Temp	Lens	Feet	FC	Beam
3200	VNS	**5'**	5040	2.1' x 1.2'	3200	VNS	**15'**	560	6.4' x 3.7'	3200	VNS	**30'**	200	10.7' X 16.2'
3200	NS	**5'**	3600	2.6' x 1.4'	3200	NS	**15'**	400	7.7' x 4.2'	3200	NS	**30'**	145	12.8' x 7'
3200	MF	**5'**	1350	5.2' x 2.2'	3200	MF	**15'**	150	15.5' x 6.5'	3200	MF	**30'**	55	25.8' x 10.8'
3200	WF	**5'**	470	8.7' x 4.6'	3200	WF	**15'**	52	26' x 13.7'	3200	WF	**30'**	20	43.3' x 22.8'
DAYLIGHT	NS	**5'**	2700	2.5' x 1.3'	DAYLIGHT	NS	**15'**	300	7.5' x 3.9'	DAYLIGHT	NS	**30'**	110	12.5' x 6.5'
DAYLIGHT	MF	**5'**	900	5' x 2.2'	DAYLIGHT	MF	**15'**	100	15' x 6.5'	DAYLIGHT	MF	**30'**	35	25.6' x 10.8'
3200	VNS	**10'**	1260	4.3' x 2.5'	3200	VNS	**20'**	315	8.5' x 4.9'	3200	VNS	**40'**	150	16' x 9.2'
3200	NS	**10'**	900	5.1' x 2.8'	3200	NS	**20'**	225	10.3' x 5.6'	3200	NS	**40'**	65	19.2' x 10.5'
3200	MF	**10'**	340	10.3' x 4.3'	3200	MF	**20'**	85	20.7' x 8.7'	3200	MF	**40'**	25	38.7' x 16.3'
3200	WF	**10'**	120	17.3' x 9.1'	3200	WF	**20'**	30	34.7' x 18.3'	3200	WF	**40'**		
DAYLIGHT	NS	**10'**	675	5' x 2.6'	DAYLIGHT	NS	**20'**	170	10' x 5.2'	DAYLIGHT	NS	**40'**	50	18.8' x 9.8'
DAYLIGHT	MF	**10'**	225	10' x 4.3'	DAYLIGHT	MF	**20'**	55	20' x 8.7'	DAYLIGHT	MF	**40'**	15	37.5' x 16.2'

PAR 64 Fixtures

6000 W PAR 64 Six 1000 W Globe

Color Temp	Lens	Feet	FC	Beam	Color Temp	Lens	Feet	FC	Beam	Color Temp	Lens	Feet	FC	Beam
3200	VNS	**20'**	6300	4.7' x 2.8'	3200	MF	**40'**	505	20.7' x 9.2'	DAYLIGHT	NS	**75'**	225	19.8' x 11'
3200	NS	**20'**	5220	5.3' x 3.3'	3200	WF	**40'**	175	36' x 18.7'	DAYLIGHT	MF	**75'**	95	37.5' x 17.3'
3200	MF	**20'**	2025	10.3' x 4.6'	DAYLIGHT	NS	**40'**	900	10.5' x 5.9'	3200	VNS	**100'**	250	23.3' x 14'
3200	WF	**20'**	700	18' x 9.3'	DAYLIGHT	MF	**40'**	340	20' x 9.2'	3200	NS	**100'**	210	26.7' x 16.7'
DAYLIGHT	NS	**20'**	3600	5.3' x 2.9'	3200	VNS	**50'**	1010	11.7' x 7'	3200	MF	**100'**	80	51.7' x 23'
DAYLIGHT	MF	**20'**	1350	10' x 4.6'	3200	NS	**50'**	835	13.3' x 8.3'	3200	WF	**100'**	30	90' x 46.7'
3200	VNS	**30'**	2800	7' x 4.2'	3200	MF	**50'**	325	25.8' x 11.5'	DAYLIGHT	NS	**100'**	145	26.3' x 14.7'
3200	NS	**30'**	2320	8' x 5'	3200	WF	**50'**	110	45' x 23.3'	DAYLIGHT	MF	**100'**	55	50' x 23'
3200	MF	**30'**	900	15.5' x 6.9'	DAYLIGHT	NS	**50'**	575	13.2' x 7.3'	3200	VNS	**150'**	110	35' x 21'
3200	WF	**30'**	310	27' x 14'	DAYLIGHT	MF	**50'**	215	25' x 11.5'	3200	NS	**150'**	90	40' x 25'
DAYLIGHT	NS	**30'**	1600	7.9' x 4.4'	3200	VNS	**75'**	450	17.5' x 10.5'	3200	MF	**150'**	35	77.5' x 34.5'
DAYLIGHT	MF	**30'**	600	15' x 6.9'	3200	NS	**75'**	370	20' x 12.5'	3200	WF	**150'**		
3200	VNS	**40'**	1575	9.3' x 5.6'	3200	MF	**75'**	145	38.8' x 17.3'	DAYLIGHT	NS	**150'**	65	39.5' x 22'
3200	NS	**40'**	1305	10.7' x 6.7'	3200	WF	**75'**	50	67.5' x 35'	DAYLIGHT	MF	**150'**	25	75' x 34.5'

PAR 64 Fixtures

9000 W PAR 64 Nine 1000 W Globe

Color Temp	Lens	Feet	FC	Beam	Color Temp	Lens	Feet	FC	Beam	Color Temp	Lens	Feet	FC	Beam
3200	VNS	**20'**	10000	4.7' x 3'	3200	MF	**40'**	760	20.7' x 9.5'	DAYLIGHT	NS	**75'**	370	19.8' x 11.5'
3200	NS	**20'**	8100	5.3' x 3.4'	3200	WF	**40'**	255	36' x 18.8'	DAYLIGHT	MF	**75'**	130	37.5' x 17.8'
3200	MF	**20'**	3040	10.3' x 4.7'	DAYLIGHT	NS	**40'**	1295	10.5' x 6.1'	3200	VNS	**100'**	405	23.3' x 15'
3200	WF	**20'**	1010	18' x 9.4'	DAYLIGHT	MF	**40'**	450	20' x 9.5'	3200	NS	**100'**	325	26.7' x 17'
DAYLIGHT	NS	**20'**	5175	5.3' x 3.1'	3200	VNS	**50'**	1620	11.7' x 7.5'	3200	MF	**100'**	120	51.7' x 23.7'
DAYLIGHT	MF	**20'**	1800	10' x 4.7'	3200	NS	**50'**	1300	13.3' x 8.5'	3200	WF	**100'**	40	90' x 47'
3200	VNS	**30'**	4500	7' x 4.5'	3200	MF	**50'**	485	25.8' x 11.8'	DAYLIGHT	NS	**100'**	210	26.3' x 15.3'
3200	NS	**30'**	3600	8' x 5.1'	3200	WF	**50'**	160	45' x 23.5'	DAYLIGHT	MF	**100'**	70	50' x 23.7'
3200	MF	**30'**	1350	15.5' x 7.1'	DAYLIGHT	NS	**50'**	830	13.2' x 7.7'	3200	VNS	**150'**	180	35' x 22.5'
3200	WF	**30'**	450	27' x 14.1'	DAYLIGHT	MF	**50'**	290	25' x 11.8'	3200	NS	**150'**	145	40' x 25.5'
DAYLIGHT	NS	**30'**	2300	7.9' x 4.6'	3200	VNS	**75'**	720	17.5' x 11.3'	3200	MF	**150'**	55	77.5' x 35.5'
DAYLIGHT	MF	**30'**	800	15' x 7.1'	3200	NS	**75'**	575	20' x 12.8'	3200	WF	**150'**	20	135' x 70.5'
3200	VNS	**40'**	2530	9.3' x 6'	3200	MF	**75'**	215	38.8' x 17.8'	DAYLIGHT	NS	**150'**	90	39.5' x 23'
3200	NS	**40'**	2025	10.7' x 6.8'	3200	WF	**75'**	70	67.5' x 35.3'	DAYLIGHT	MF	**150'**	30	75' x 35.5'

12000 W PAR 64 Twelve 1000 W Globe

Color Temp	Lens	Feet	FC	Beam	Color Temp	Lens	Feet	FC	Beam	Color Temp	Lens	Feet	FC	Beam
3200	VNS	**20'**	13300	4.7' x 3.1'	3200	MF	**40'**	1010	20.7' x 10'	DAYLIGHT	NS	**75'**	492	19.8' x 13.2'
3200	NS	**20'**	10773	5.3' x 3.5'	3200	WF	**40'**	340	36' x 19.5'	DAYLIGHT	MF	**75'**	172	37.5' x 18.8'
3200	MF	**20'**	4044	10.3' x 5'	DAYLIGHT	NS	**40'**	1795	10.5' x 17.1'	3200	VNS	**100'**	538	23.3' x 15.3'
3200	WF	**20'**	1343	18' x 9.7'	DAYLIGHT	MF	**40'**	598	20' x 10'	3200	NS	**100'**	432	26.7' x 17.7'
DAYLIGHT	NS	**20'**	6882	5.3' x 3.5'	3200	VNS	**50'**	2120	11.7' x 7.7'	3200	MF	**100'**	160	51.7' x 25'
DAYLIGHT	MF	**20'**	2394	10' x 5'	3200	NS	**50'**	1729	13.3' x 8.8'	3200	WF	**100'**	53	90' x 48.7'
3200	VNS	**30'**	5985	7' x 4.6'	3200	MF	**50'**	645	25.8' x 12.5'	DAYLIGHT	NS	**100'**	280	26.3' x 17.7'
3200	NS	**30'**	4788	8' x 5.3'	3200	WF	**50'**	212	45' x 24.3'	DAYLIGHT	MF	**100'**	93	50' x 25'
3200	MF	**30'**	1795	15.5' x 7.5'	DAYLIGHT	NS	**50'**	1104	13.2' x 8.8'	3200	VNS	**150'**	240	35' x 23'
3200	WF	**30'**	598	27' x 14.6'	DAYLIGHT	MF	**50'**	386	25' x 12.5'	3200	NS	**150'**	193	40' x 26.5'
DAYLIGHT	NS	**30'**	3059	7.9' x 5.3'	3200	VNS	**75'**	957	17.5' x 11.5'	3200	MF	**150'**	73	77.5' x 37.5'
DAYLIGHT	MF	**30'**	1064	15' x 7.5'	3200	NS	**75'**	765	20' x 13.2'	3200	WF	**150'**	27	
3200	VNS	**40'**	3364	9.3' x 6.1'	3200	MF	**75'**	285	38.8' x 18.8'	DAYLIGHT	NS	**150'**	120	39.5' x 26.5'
3200	NS	**40'**	2693	10.7' x 7.1'	3200	WF	**75'**	93	67.5' x 36.5'	DAYLIGHT	MF	**150'**	40	75' x 37.5'

PAR 64 Fixtures

24000 W PAR 64 Twenty Four 1000 W Globe

Color Temp	Lens	Feet	FC	Beam	Color Temp	Lens	Feet	FC	Beam	Color Temp	Lens	Feet	FC	Beam
3200	VNS	**20'**	16400	4.9' x 3.1'	3200	MF	**40'**	1155	21.5' x 10'	DAYLIGHT	NS	**75'**	599	21' x 13.2'
3200	NS	**20'**	13000	5.6' x 3.5'	3200	WF	**40'**	365	37.1' x 19.5'	DAYLIGHT	MF	**75'**	212	40.3' x 18.5'
3200	MF	**20'**	4620	10.7' x 5'	DAYLIGHT	NS	**40'**	2098	11.2' x 17.1'	3200	VNS	**100'**	660	24.3' x 15.3'
3200	WF	**20'**	1460	18.5' x 9.7'	DAYLIGHT	MF	**40'**	734	21.5' x 10'	3200	NS	**100'**	520	28' x 13.7'
DAYLIGHT	NS	**20'**	8332	5.6' x 3.5'	3200	VNS	**50'**	2630	12.2' x 7.7'	3200	MF	**100'**	185	53.7' x 25'
DAYLIGHT	MF	**20'**	2934	10.7' x 5'	3200	NS	**50'**	2090	14' x 8.8'	3200	WF	**100'**	58	92.7' x 48.7'
3200	VNS	**30'**	7300	7' x 4.6'	3200	MF	**50'**	740	26.8' x 12.5'	DAYLIGHT	NS	**100'**	340	28' x 17.7'
3200	NS	**30'**	5800	8.4' x 5.3'	3200	WF	**50'**	235	46.3' x 24.3'	DAYLIGHT	MF	**100'**	114	53.7' x 25'
3200	MF	**30'**	2055	16.1' x 17.5'	DAYLIGHT	NS	**50'**	1345	14' x 18.8'	3200	VNS	**150'**	290	36.5' x 23'
3200	WF	**30'**	650	27.8' x 14.6'	DAYLIGHT	MF	**50'**	473	26.8' x 12.5'	3200	NS	**150'**	232	42' x 26.5'
DAYLIGHT	NS	**30'**	3726	18.4' x 15.3'	3200	VNS	**75'**	1170	18.3' x 11.5'	3200	MF	**150'**	82	80.5' x 37.5'
DAYLIGHT	MF	**30'**	1304	16.1' x 17.5'	3200	NS	**75'**	930	21' x 13.2'	3200	WF	**150'**	26	139' x 73'
3200	VNS	**40'**	4100	9.7' x 6.1'	3200	MF	**75'**	330	40.3' x 18.8'	DAYLIGHT	NS	**150'**	146	42' x 26.5'
3200	NS	**40'**	3260	11.2' x 7.1'	3200	WF	**75'**	105	69.5' x 36.5'	DAYLIGHT	MF	**150'**	49	80.5' x 37.5'

PAR 64 Fixtures

36000 W PAR 64 Thirty-Six 1000 W Globe

Color Temp	Lens	Feet	FC	Beam	Color Temp	Lens	Feet	FC	Beam	Color Temp	Lens	Feet	FC	Beam
3200	VNS	**20'**	26650	5.1' x 3.3'	3200	MF	**40'**	1877	22' x 10.6'	DAYLIGHT	NS	**75'**	973	21.6' x 13.8'
3200	NS	**20'**	21125	6' x 4'	3200	WF	**40'**	593	37.8' x 20.2'	DAYLIGHT	MF	**75'**	344	41' x 19.3'
3200	MF	**20'**	7508	11.2' x 5.6'	DAYLIGHT	NS	**40'**	3410	11.7' x 7.6'	3200	VNS	**100'**	1072	74.7' x 15.8'
3200	WF	**20'**	2373	19.1' x 10.3'	DAYLIGHT	MF	**40'**	1192	22' x 10.6'	3200	NS	**100'**	845	28.8' x 18.3'
DAYLIGHT	NS	**20'**	13540	6' x 4'	3200	VNS	**50'**	4274	12.6' x 8'	3200	MF	**100'**	300	54.2' x 25.6'
DAYLIGHT	MF	**20'**	4767	11.2' x 5.6'	3200	NS	**50'**	3396	14.6' x 9.3'	3200	WF	**100'**	94	93.2' x 49.2'
3200	VNS	**30'**	11862	7.6' x 4.8'	3200	MF	**50'**	1202	27.4' x 13'	DAYLIGHT	NS	**100'**	552	28.8' x 18.3'
3200	NS	**30'**	9425	8.8' x 5.9'	3200	WF	**50'**	382	46.9' x 24.9'	DAYLIGHT	MF	**100'**	185	54.2' x 25.6'
3200	MF	**30'**	3340	16.7' x 8.2'	DAYLIGHT	NS	**50'**	2186	14.6' x 9.3'	3200	VNS	**150'**	471	37' x 23.8'
3200	WF	**30'**	1056	28.4' x 15.1'	DAYLIGHT	MF	**50'**	768	27.8' x 13'	3200	NS	**150'**	377	42.6' x 27.6'
DAYLIGHT	NS	**30'**	6054	8.8' x 5.9'	3200	VNS	**75'**	1901	18.6' x 12'	3200	MF	**150'**	133	81' x 38'
DAYLIGHT	MF	**30'**	2120	16.7' x 8.2'	3200	NS	**75'**	1511	21.6' x 13.8'	3200	WF	**150'**	42	139.7' x 73.8'
3200	VNS	**40'**	6662	10' x 6.5'	3200	MF	**75'**	536	41' x 19.3'	DAYLIGHT	NS	**150'**	273	42.6' x 27.2'
3200	NS	**40'**	5298	11.7' x 7.6'	3200	WF	**75'**	170	70.1' x 37'	DAYLIGHT	MF	**150'**	80	81' x 38'

ILLUMINATION DATA FOR SOURCE FOUR ELLIPSOIDAL SPOTLIGHTS				
Lens Angle	**Candle Power**	**Field Lumens**	**Beam Lumens**	
5°	**1,370,000**	**9,770**	**8,530**	**Globe for all lamps: HpL 750/115 750 watts 115 volts Initial Lumens: 21, 900 3250°K**
10°	**838,000**	**12,300**	**8,770**	
19°	**288,000**	**9,960**	**7,120**	
26°	**159,000**	**12,400**	**8,250**	
36°	**82,000**	**12,300**	**8,030**	
50°	**34,900**	**12,400**	**8,220**	

For illumination in foot candles or LUX divide candle power by distance squared. **Example:** 34,900 ÷ 10^2 feet = 349fc.

To find field diameter, multiply distance by multiplying factor in chart below. **Example:** 10 feet x .95 = 9.5 foot diameter.

To find beam diameter, multiply distance by multiplying factor in chart below. **Example:** 10 feet x .60 = 60 foot beam diameter.

MULTIPLYING FACTORS AS SUPPLIED BY MANUFACTURER

Lens Angle	Field Diameter	Beam Diameter	CONVERSIONS
5°	.12	.11	For feet to meter, multiply by .305 Meters to feet multiply by 3.28 For footcandles to Lux multiply by 10.764 Lux to footcandles multiply by .0929
10°	.19	.16	
19°	.31	.27	
26°	.45	.33	
36°	.63	.45	
50°	.95	.60	

Kino Flo Fixtures

Lamp	Globe	2'	4'	6'	8'	10'	12'	14'	16'	18'	20'
2' X 1	F20/T12	82	23	10	6	4	3				
2' X 2	F20/T12	141	41	19	11	7	5				
2' X 4	F20/T12	292	82	37	22	15	11				
4' X 1	F40/T12	101	35	17	10	7	5				
4' X 2	F40/T12	233	82	40	23	16	11				
4' X 4	F40/T12	432	140	70	41	28	20				
4' X 8	F40/T12		285	140	85	58	42			21	18
4' X 10	F40/T12		350	180	110	75	60				
6' X 1	F72/T12	130	49	26	16	11	8				
6' X 2	F72/T12		100	50	30	21	16				
6' X 16	F72/T12		550	306	200	137	100			53	46

Lamps are identified by length of globe then number of globes in the fixture as 4 foot 4 lamp or 4'X4'. The globes are KinoFlo TruMatch lamps. The units listed are the most common used. There are other units and globes available

Kino Flo Fixtures

Lamp	Globe	2'	4'	6'	8'	10'	12'	14'	16'	18'	20'
ParaBeam 400	KF29	1050	367	186	112	77	54	40.3	31.3	25.5	21
ParaBeam 400	Studioline 32	1490	531	265	155	108	76	56	43.8	35	29.4
ParaBeam 200	KF29	525	184	93	56	39	27	20	15.6	13	11
ParaBeam 200	Studioline 32	745	266	133	77	54	38	28	22	18	14.7
Diva-Lite 400		540	153	75	45	30	25				
Diva-Lite 200		360	95	45	27	15	10				

Lamp	Globe	1'	2'	3'	4'	5'	6'	8'
Kamio		112	45	27	17		5	2.6
12V Single	15" lamp	95	30	14	8			
12V Single	24" lamp	112	45	27	17			
12V Single	48" lamp	165	75	40	25			
Mini-Flo	9" lamp	70	21	10	6			
Mini-Flo	12" lamp	82	27	13	7.2			
Lamp	**Globe**	**2"**	**4"**	**6"**	**8"**	**10"**	**12"**	
Micro-Flo	100mm lamp	130	50	25	15	10	7	
Micro-Flo	150mm lamp	146	60	30	17	13	9	

Note: The General Electric Studioline 32 globes while more efficient tend to have a green spike. This is not a problem in video, but needs correction for film.

SoftSun 5400°K

Fixture		Beam Angle		Distance (data in Footcandles)							
		Vert	Horiz	5'	10'	25'	50'	75'	100'	150'	200'
3.3 KW	Spot	15°	120°	5,500	2,200	88	22	10	4.5	N/A	N/A
3.3 KW	Flood	53°	120°	1,080	275	44	11	5	2.2	N/A	N/A
10 KW	Spot	14°	108°	20,000	5,600	940	244	107	58	N/A	N/A
10 KW	Flood	28°	108°	8,000	2,580	455	122	55	32	N/A	N/A
15 KW		80° Circular Beam		2,800	680	123	30	13	7	N/A	N/A
25 KW		30° Circular Beam		N/A	8,000	1,280	320	142	80	N/A	N/A
25 KW Linear		13°	100°	N/A	N/A	1,800	450	200	109	N/A	N/A
25 KW Linear	Flood	36°	100°	N/A	N/A	590	150	66	44	N/A	N/A
50 KW	Spot	11°	100°	N/A	N/A	3,800	1,040	472	267	116	68
50 KW	Flood	35°	100°	N/A	N/A	1,680	420	186	105	46	25
100 KW	Spot	16°	100°	N/A	N/A	8,330	2,400	1,111	630	278	151
100 KW	Flood	35°	100°	N/A	N/A	3,830	1,147	526	297	131	62

Courtesy of Lighting Strikes!

Further Reference

3-D

Spottiswood, Raymond, *Theory of Stereoscopic Transmission,* Berkeley, CA; University of California Press, 1953.

Aerial Cinematography

Wagtendonk, W.J., *Principles of Helicopter Flight,* Aviation Supplies & Academics, Newcastle, WA, 1996.

Crane, Dale, *Dictionary of Aeronatical Terms,* Aviation Supplies & Academics, Newcastle, WA, 1997.

Spence, Charles, *Aeronautical Information Manual and Federal Aviation Regulations,* McGraw-Hill, New York, NY, 2000.

Padfield, R., *Learning to Fly Helicopters,* McGraw-Hill, New York, NY, 1992.

Industry-Wide Labor-Management Safety Bulletins at: http://www.csatf.org/bulletintro.shtml

Arctic Cinematography

Eastman Kodak Publication: Photography Under Artic Conditions.

Fisher, Bob, "*Cliffhanger's* Effects were a Mountainous Task," *American Cinematographer,* Vol. 74, No. 6, pp. 66-74, 1993.

Miles, Hugh, "Filming in Extreme Climactic Conditions" *BKSTS Journal Image Technology,* February 1988.

Moritsugu, Louise, "Crew's Peak Performance Enhanced Alive," *American Cinematographer,* Vol. 74, No. 6, pp. 78-84, 1993.

Biographies and Interviews

Almendros, ASC, Nestor, *A Man With a Camera,* New York, Farrar, Straus, Giroux, 1984.

Bitzer, ASC, Billy, *Billy Bitzer—His Story: The Autobioagraphy of D.W. Griffith's Master Cameraman,* New York, Farrar, Straus, Giroux, 1973.

Brown, ASC, Karl, with Brownlow, Kevin, *Adventures With D.W. Griffith,* New York, Farrar, Straus, Giroux, 1973.

Cardiff, BSC, Jack, *Magic Hour,* London, Faber and Faber, 1996.

Challis, BSC, Christopher, *Are They Really So Awful?: A Cameraman's Chronicle,* Paul & Co. Publishing Consortium, 1995.

Clarke, ASC, Charles G., *Highlights and Shadows: The Memoirs of a Hollywood Cameraman,* Metuchen, NJ; Scarecrow Press, 1989.

Eyman, Scott, *Five American Cinematographers: Interviews with Karl Struss, Joseph Ruttenberg, James Wong Howe, Linwood Dunn and William H. Clothier,* Metuchen, NJ; Scarecrow Press, 1987.

Higham, Charles, *Hollywood Cameramen: Sources of Light,* Indiana University Press, 1970.

Kalmus, Herbert T. and Eleanor King, *Mr. Technicolor,* Abescon, NJ; Magic Image Filmbooks, 1993.

Lassally, BSC, Walter, *Itinerant Cameraman,* London, Murray, 1987.

Laszlo, ASC, Andrew, *Every Frame a Rembrandt: Art and Practice of Cinematography,* Boston, MA; Focal Press, 2000.

Laszlo, ASC, Andrew, *It's A Wrap!,* Hollywood, CA; ASC Press, 2004.

LoBrutto, Vincent, *Principal Photography: Interviews with Feature Film Cinematographers,* Westport, CT; Praeger, 1999.

Maltin, Leonard, *The Art of the Cinematographer: A Survey and Interviews with Five Masters,* New York, Dover Publications, 1978.

McCandless, Barbara, *New York to Hollywood: The Photography of Karl Struss, ASC,* Albuquerque, NM; University of New Mexico, 1995.

Miller, ASC, Virgil E., *Splinters From Hollywood Tripods: Memoirs of a Cameraman,* New York, Exposition Press, 1964.

Rainsberger, Todd, *James Wong Howe Cinematographer,* San Diego, CA; A.S. Barnes, 1981.

Rogers, Pauline B., *More Contemporary Cinematographers on Their Art,* Boston, MA; Focal Press, 2000.

Schaefer, Dennis and Salvato, Larry, *Masters of Light: Conversations with Contemporary Cinematographers,* Berkeley, CA; University of California Press, 1985.

Sterling, Anna Kate, *Cinematographers on the Art and Craft of Cinematography,* Metuchen, NJ; Scarecrow Press, 1987.

Walker, ASC, Joseph, *The Light On Her Face,* Hollywood, CA; ASC Press, 1984.

Young, BSC, Freddie, *Seventy Light Years: An Autobiography as told to Peter Busby,* London, Faber and Faber, 1999.

Camera

Adams, Ansel, *The Camera,* New York, Morgan and Morgan, Inc., 1975.

Fauer, ASC, Jon, *Arricam Book*, Hollywood, CA; ASC Press, 2002.

Fauer, ASC, Jon, *Arriflex 16 SR Book*, Boston, MA; Focal Press, 1999.

Fauer, ASC, Jon, *Arriflex 16 SR3 the Book*, Arriflex Corp., 1996.

Fauer, ASC, Jon, *Arriflex 35 Book*, Boston, MA; Focal Press, 1999.

Fauer, ASC, Jon, *Arriflex 435 Book*, Arriflex Corp., 2000.

Samuelson, David W., *Panaflex Users' Manual*, Boston, MA; Focal Press, 1990

Camera Manufacturers

Aaton, +33 47642 9550, www.aaton.com

ARRI, (818) 841-7070, www.arri.com

Fries Engineering, (818) 252-7700, www.frieseng.com

Ikonoskop AB, +46 8673 6288, info@ikonoskop.com

Panavision, (818) 316-1000, www.panavision.com

Photo-Sonics, (818) 842-2141, www.photosonics.com

Pro8mm, (818) 848-5522, www.pro8mm.com

Camera Supports

A + C Ltd., +44 (0) 208-427 5168, www.powerpod.co.uk

Aerocrane, (818) 785-5681, www.aerocrane.com

Akela: Shotmaker, (818) 623-1700, www.shotmaker.com

Aquapod, (818) 999-1411

Chapman/Leonard Studio Equipment, (888) 883-6559, www.chapman-leonard.com

Egripment B.V., +31 (0)2944-253.988, Egripment USA, (818) 787-4295, www.egripment.com

Fx-Motion, +32 (0)24.12.10.12, www.fx-motion.com

Grip Factory Munich (GFM), +49 (0)89 31901 29-0, www.g-f-m.net

Hot Gears, (818) 780-2708, www.hotgears.com

Hydroflex, (310) 301-8187, www.hydroflex.com

Isaia & Company, (818) 752-3104, www.isaia.com

J.L. Fisher, Inc., (818) 846-8366, www.jlfisher.com

Jimmy Fisher Co., (818) 769-2631

Libra, (310) 966-9089

Louma, +33 (0)1 48 13 25 60, www.loumasystems.biz

Megamount, +44 (0)1 932 592 348, www.mega3.tv

Movie Tech A.G., +49 0 89-43 68 913, Movie Tech L.P., (678) 417-6352, www.movietech.de

Nettman Systems International, (818) 623-1661, www.camerasystems.com

Orion Technocrane, +49 171-710-1834, www.technocrane.de

Pace Technologies, (818) 759-7322, www.pacetech.com

Panavision Remote Systems, (818) 316-1080, www.panavision.com

Panther, +49 89 61 39 00 01, www.panther-gmbh.de

Spacecam, (818) 889-6060, www.spacecam.com

Strada, (541) 549-4229, www.stradacranes.com

Straight Shoot'r, (818) 340-9376, www.straightshootr.com

Technovision, (818) 782-9051, www.technovision-global.com

Wescam, (818) 785-9282, www.wescam.com

Cinematography

Brown, Blain, *Cinematography*, Boston, MA; Focal Press, 2002.

Campbell, Russell, *Photographic Theory for the Motion Picture Cameraman,* London, Tantivy Press, 1970.

Campbell, Russell, *Practical Motion Picture Photography,* London, Tantivy Press, 1970.

Carlson, Verne and Sylvia, *Professional Cameraman's Handbook 4th ed.,* Boston, MA; Focal Press, 1994.

Clarke, ASC, Charles G., *Professional Cinematography,* Hollywood, CA; ASC Press, 2002.

Cornwell-Clyne, Major Adrian, *Color Cinematography, 3rd Edition*, Chapman Hall LTD 1951.

Malkiewicz, Kris J., *Cinematography: A Guide for Film Makers and Film Teachers,* New York, Van Nostrand Reinhold, 1973.

Mascelli, ASC, Joseph V., *The 5 C's of Cinematography,* Beverly Hills, CA, Silman-James Press, 1998 (c1965).

Wilson, Anton, *Anton Wilson's Cinema Workshop,* Hollywood, CA; ASC Press, 1983, 1994.

Color

Albers, J., *Interaction of Color*, New Haven and London; Yale University Press, 1963.

Eastman Kodak Publication H-12, *An Introduction to Color,* Rochester, 1972.

Eastman Kodak Publication E-74, *Color As Seen and Photographed,* Rochester, 1972.

Eastman Kodak Publication H-188, *Exploring the Color Image,* Rochester.

Evans, R. M., *An Introduction to Color,* New York, NY; John Wiley & Sons, 1948.

Evans, R. M., *Eye, Film, and Camera Color Photography,* New York, NY; John Wiley & Sons, 1959.

Evans, R. M., *The Perception of Color,* New York, NY; John Wiley & Sons, 1974.

Friedman, J. S., *History of Color Photography,* Boston, MA; American Photographic Publishing Company, 1944.

Hardy, A. C., *Handbook of Colorimetry,* MIT, Cambridge, MA; Technology Press, 1936.

Hunt, R. W. G., *The Reproduction of Colour,* Surrey, UK, Fountain Press, 1995.

Itten, J., *The Art of Color,* New York, Van Nostrand Reinhold, 1973.

National Bureau of Standards Circular 553, *The ISCC-NBS Method of Designating Colors and A Dictionary of Color Names,* Washington D. C., 1955.

Optical Society of America, *The Science of Color,* New York, NY; Thomas Y. Crowell Company, 1953.

Society of Motion Picture and Teclevision Engineers, *Elements of Color in Professional Motion Pictures,* New York, NY, 1957.

Wall, E. J.,History of Three-Color Photography, New York and London, Boston, MA; American Photographic Publishing Company, 1925.

Film

Adams, Ansel, *The Negative,* New York, Little Brown, 1989.

Adams, Ansel, *The Print,* New York, Little Brown,1989.

Eastman Kodak Publication H-1: Eastman Professional Motion Picture Films.

Eastman Kodak Publication H-23: The Book of Film Care.

Eastman Kodak Publication H-188: Exploring the Color Image.

Eastman Kodak Publication N-17: Infrared Films.

Eastman Kodak Publication: ISO vs EI Speed Ratings.

Eastman Kodak Publication: Ultraviolet and Fluorescence Photography.

Hayball, Laurie White, *Advanced Infrared Photography Handbook,* Amherst Media, 2001.

Hayball, Laurie White, *Infrared Photography Handbook,* Amherst Media, 1997.

Film Design

Affron, Charles and Affron, Mirella Jona, *Sets in Motion*, Rutgers University Press, 1995.

Carrick, Edward, *Designing for Films*, The Studio LTD and the Studio Publications Inc, 1941, 1947.

Carter, Paul, *Backstage Handbook - 3rd Edition*, Broadway Press, 1994.

Cruickshank, Dan, *Sir Banister Fletcher's A History of Architecture* (tweintieth edition), New York, NY, Architectural Press, 1996.

Edwards, Betty, *Drawing on the Right Side of the Brain* (revised edition), Jeremy P. Tarcher, 1989.

de Vries, Jan Vredeman, *Perspective,* Dover Publications, 1968.

Heisner, Beverly, *Studios*, McFarland and Co., 1990.

Katz, Stephen D., *Shot by Shot - Visualizing from Concept to Screen*, Boston, MA; Focal Press, 1991, pp. 337-356.

Preston, Ward, *What an Art Director Does*, Silman-James Press, 1994.

Raoul, Bill, *Stock Scenery Construction Handbook,* 2nd Addtion Broadway Press, 1999.

St John Marner, Terrance, *Film Design*, The Tantivy Press, 1974.

Film History

The American Film Institute Catalog: Feature Films 1911–1920, Berkeley and Los Angeles, University of California Press, 1989.

The American Film Institute Catalog: Feature Films 1931–1940, Berkeley and Los Angeles, University of California Press, 1993.

The American Film Institute Catalog: Feature Films 1921–1930, Berkeley and Los Angeles, University of California Press, 1997.

The American Film Institute Catalog: Feature Films 1961–1970, Berkeley and Los Angeles, University of California Press, 1997.

The American Film Institute Catalog: Within Our Gates: Ethnicity in American Feature Films 1911–1960, Berkeley and Los Angeles, University of California Press, 1989.

The American Film Institute Catalog: Feature Films 1941–1950, Berkeley and Los Angeles, University of California Press, 1999.

Belton, John, *Widescreen Cinema,* Cambridge, MA; Harvard University Press, 1992.

Brownlow, Kevin, *Hollywood the Pioneers*, New York, NY; Alfred A. Knopf, 1979.

Brownlow, Kevin, *The Parade's Gone By,* New York, Knopf, 1968.

Coe, Brian, *The History of Movie Photography,* New York, Zoetrope, 1982.

Fielding, Raymond, *A Technological History of Motion Pictures and Television,* University of California Press, 1967.

Finler, Joel W., *The Hollywood Story,* New York, Crown, 1988.

Ryan, R.T., *A History of Motion Picture Color Technology,* London, Focal Press, 1977.

MacGowan, Kenneth, *Behind the Screen: the History and Techniques of the Motion Picture,* New York, Delacorte Press, 1965.

Rotha, Paul and Griffith, Richard, *The Film Till Now: A Survey of World Cinema,* London, Spring Books, 1967. (New York, Funk & Wagnalls, 1951.)

Schatz, Thomas, *The Genius of the System: Hollywood Filmmaking in the Studio Era,* New York, Pantheon, 1988.

Turner, George E., *The Cinema of Adventure, Romance and Terror,* Hollywood, CA; ASC Press, 1989.

Film Processing

ACVL Handbook, Association of Cinema and Video Laboratories.

Case, Dominic, *Motion Picture Film Processing,* London, Butterworth and Co. Ltd. (Focal Press), 1985.

Eastman Kodak publications: H-1, H-2, H-7, H-17, H-21, H-23, H-24.07, H-26, H-36, H-37, H-37A, H-44, H-61, H-61A, H-61B, H-61C, H-61D, H-61E, H-61F, H-807 and H-822.

Happe, L. Bernard, *Your Film and the Lab,* London, Focal Press, 1974.

Kisner, W.I., *Control Techniques in Film Processing,* New York, SMPTE, 1960.

Ryan, R.T., *Principles of Color Sensitometry,* New York, SMPTE, 1974.

Filters

Eastman Kodak Publication B-3: Filters.

Harrison, H.K., *Mystery of Filters-II,* Porterville, CA; Harrison & Harrison, 1981.

Hirschfeld, ASC, Gerald, *Image Control,* Boston, MA; Focal Press, 1993.

Hypia, Jorma, *The Complete Tiffen Filter Manual,* AmPhoto, New York, 1981.

Smith, Robb, Tiffen Practical Filter Manual.

Tiffen Manufacturing Corporation Publication T179: Tiffen Photar Filter Glass

Journals, Magazines and Associations

ANSI Standards, American National Standards Institute, www.ansi.org.

American Cinematographer, ASC Holding Corp.,www.cinematographer.com.

BKSTS Journal, “Image Technology,” British Kinematograph, Sound and Television Society, www.bksts.com.

SMPTE Journal, Society Of Motion Picture and Television Engineers, www.smpte.org.

Lenses

Angenieux, P., “Variable focal length objectives,” U.S. Patent No. 2,847,907, 1958.

Bergstein, L., “General theory of optically compensated varifocal systems,” *JOSA* Vol. 48, No. 9, pp. 154-171, 1958.

Cook, G.H.,"Recent developments in television optics," Royal Television Society Journal, pp. 158-167, 1973.

Cox, Arthur, *Photographic Optics, A Modern Approach to the Technique of Definition* (expanded edition), London, Focal Press, 1971.

Kingslake, R. “The development of the zoom lens,” *SMPTE* Vol. 69, pp. 534-544, 1960.

Mann, A., Ed., “Zoom lenses,” *SPIE Milestone Series* Vol. MS 85, 1993.

Neil, I.A. and Betensky, E.I, "High performence, wide angle, macro focus, zoom lens for 35mm cinematography," *SPIE* Vol. 3482, pp. 213-228, Kona, Hawaii, U.S.A., 1998.

Neil, I.A., "First order principles of zoom optics explained via macro focus conditions of fixed focal length lenses," *SPIE* Vol. 2539, San Diego, California, U.S.A., 1995.

Neil, I.A., "Liquid optics create high performance zoom lens," *Laser Focus World,* Vol. 31, No. 11, 1995.

Neil, I.A., "Uses of special glasses in visual objective lenses, *SPIE* Vol. 766, pp. 69-74, Los Angeles, California, U.S. A., 1987.

Zuegge, H. and Moellr, B., "A complete set of cinematographic zoom lenses and their fundamental design considerations," *Proceedings of the 22nd Optical Symposium,* pp. 13-16, Tokyo, Japan, 1997.

Lighting

Adams, Ansel, *Artificial Light Photography,* New York, Morgan and Morgan, Inc., 1956.

Alton, John, *Painting With Light,* Berkeley and Los Angeles, University of California Press, 1995.

Bergery, Benjamin, *Reflections - 21 Cinematographers at Work*, Hollywood, CA; ASC Press, 2002.

Box, Harry, *Set Lighting Technician's Handbook,* Boston, MA, Focal Press, 2003.

Malkiewicz, Kris J., *Film Lighting: Talk with Hollywood's Cinematographers and Gaffers,* New York, Prentice Hall Press, 1999.

Millerson, Gerald, *The Technique of Lighting for Television and Film,* Boston, Focal Press, 1991.

Miscellaneous

Arnheim, Rudolf, *Art and Visual Perception,* Berkley, CA, University of California Press, 1974.

Darby, William, *Masters of Lens and Light: A Checklist of Major Cinematographers and Their Feature Films,* Metuchen, NJ, Scarecrow Press, 1991.

Houghton, Buck, *What a Producer Does*, Silman-James Press, 1991.

Kehoe, Vincent J. R., *The Technique of the Professional Makeup Artist,* Boston, MA, Focal Press, 1995.

Kepes, Gyorgy, *Language of Vision,* New York, MA, Dover Publications, 1995.

Moholy-Nagy, L., *Vision in Motion,* Wisconsin; Cuneo Press, 1997.

Nilsen, Vladimir, *The Cinema as a Graphic Art,* New York; Garland Pub., 1985.

Waner, John, *Hollywood's Conversion of All Production to Color Using*

Eastman Color Professional Motion Picture Films, Newcastle, ME; Tobey Publishing, 2000.

Photography

Evans, R.M., W.T. Hanson Jr., and W.L. Brewer, *Principles of Color Photography,* New York, John Wiley & Sons Inc., 1953.

Mees, C.E.K., The Theory of the Photographic Process, New York, Macmillan, 1977.

Thomas Jr., Woodlief, *SPSE Handbook of Photographic Science and Engineering,* New York, John Wiley & Sons, 1973.

Woodbury, Walter E., *The Encyclopaedic Dictionary of Photography,* New York, The Scovill and Adams Company, 1898.

Traveling Matte Composites

Composite Components Corp. (323) 257-1163,
www.digitalgreenscreen.com

Curious Software (gFx roto)
UK: Tel: +44 (0)20 7428 0288   Fax: +44 (0)20 7428 5811
US: Tel: +1 505 988 7243, Fax: +1 505 988 1654
Email: info@curious-software.com
Web: www.curious-software.com

Dazian Theatrical Fabrics: East Coast (877) 232-9426 or East Coast Design Studio (212) 206-3515, West Coast (877) 432-9426 or West Coast Design Studio (818) 841-6500.

Flo Co (818) 780-0039 or (661) 269-2065, www.flo-co.com

Keylight (650) 326-2656, www.thefoundry.com

Kino Flo (818) 767-6528, www.kinoflo.com

Pinnacle Systems, (Commotion, Primatte) www.pinnaclesys.com

Primatte: Phototron USA, Inc. (530) 677 9980, www.primatte.com
or www.phototron.com

Red*D*Mix [Ray McMillan, Flo Co Distributor] (416) 879-3761
email: mcmillan20@cogeco.ca

RFX (compositing software and hardware) (323) 962-7400, www.rfx.com

The Science and Technology Council of the Motion Picture Acadamy
(310) 247 3000, www.oscars.org/council/index.html

Stewart Filmscreen Corp. (310) 784-5300, www.stewartfilm.com

Ultimatte Corp. (818) 993-8007, www.ultimatte.com

Underwater Cinematography

Mertens, Lawrence, *In Water Photography: Theory and Practice,* Wiley Interscience, New York, John Wiley & Sons, 1970.

Ryan, R.T., *Underwater Photographic Applications – Introduction,* SMPTE Journal, Vol. 82, No. 12, December 1973.

Industry-Wide Labor-Management Safety Bulletins at:
http://www.csatf.org/bulletintro.shtml

Visual Effects

Abbott, ASC, L.B., *Special Effects with Wire, Tape and Rubber Bands,* Hollywood, CA; ASC Press, 1984.

Bulleid, H.A.V. (Henry Anthony Vaughan), *Special Effects in Cinematography,* London, Fountain Press, 1960.

Clark, Frank P., *Special Effects in Motion Pictures Some Methods for Producing Mechanical Effects,* New York, SMPTE, 1966.

Dunn, ASC, Linwood, and Turner, George E., *ASC Treasury of Visual Effects,* Hollywood, CA; ASC Press,1983.

Fielding, Raymond, *The Technique of Special Effects Cinematography,* Boston, MA; Focal Press, 1985.

Glover, Thomas J., *Pocket Ref,* Littleton, CO, Sequoia Publishing, 1997.

Harryhausen, Ray, *Ray Harryhausen: An Animated Life,* New York, NY, Billboards Books, 2004.

Rogers, Pauline B., *The Art of Visual Effects: Interviews on the Tools of the Trade,* Boston, MA; Focal Press, 1999.

The Nautical Almanac (commercial edition), Arcata, CA, Paradise Cay Publications (yearly).

Vaz, Matt Cotta and Barron, Craig, *The Invisible Art: The Legends of Movie Matte Painting,* SanFrancisco, CA; Chronicle Books, 2002.

Index

Page numbers followed by an "f" refer to a figure or illustration

B

M

X

Y

Z

Printed in the United States
200138BV00009B/67-282/A

9 780935 578324